1992 Children's Writer's & Illustrator's Market

1992
Children's Writer's & Illustrator's Market

Edited by
Lisa Carpenter
Assisted by
Roseann Shaughnessy

Writer's
Digest
Books

Cincinnati, Ohio

Distributed in Canada by McGraw-Hill Ryerson, 300 Water St., Whitby, Ontario M1P 2Z5. Also distributed in Australia by Kirby Books, Private Bag No. 19, P.O. Alexandria NSW/2015 and in New Zealand by David Bateman, P.O. Box 100-242, N. Shore Mail Centre, Auckland 10

Managing Editor, Market Books Department: Constance J. Achabal; Assistant Managing Editor: Glenda Tennant Neff.

Children's Writer's & Illustrator's Market.

International Standard Serial Number 0897-9790
International Standard Book Number 0-89879-487-0

Portrait Artist: Leslie Sowers Slaughter

Contents

From the Editor

The fact you are reading these words proves you are serious about your craft. As you probably know, writing and illustrating for children are not easy tasks. Like any other trade, true professionals must possess, and then continually develop, the necessary skills in order to be successful.

What you might not know is the skills necessary for making it in the field consist of more than creative abilities in writing and/or illustrating. Unless you know *where* and *how* to market your work, you'll never have it published. This is where *Children's Writer's & Illustrator's Market* comes into the picture.

What you will learn

A wealth of information about marketing your material resides within these pages. In Elaine Alphin's article, A Writer's Guide to the Juvenile Market: Ten Steps to That First Sale (starting on page 6), writers will learn what steps to take toward making that first sale. One highlight of this article is that Alphin supplies samples of a query letter and a cover letter for those not sure about how to approach an editor with a manuscript.

Illustrators will learn the basics of compiling a strong portfolio by reading Portfolio Power for Children's Illustrators: Putting It All Together, starting on page 16. Accompanying the article are portfolio pieces illustrator Claire Ewart used to successfully break into the field.

Both writers *and* illustrators will benefit from the business section, starting on page 24. Ample information about manuscript formats, agents, copyrights, contracts, business records and taxes can be found here. At the end of the section you'll find a list of books and publications that will be of interest to children's writers and illustrators.

Introductions at the beginning of each section of listings will give you an idea of what's going on in that particular part of the industry. You'll learn by reading these introductions whether the boom in children's books is going to continue, especially taking in account the recession; why magazine editors are more willing to take a chance on new material; why audiovisual products are now significantly present in the industry; the trend of performing interactive plays for children; and much, much more.

Finally, you'll learn something from each of the 614 listings (of which 226 are new) in this book, whether it's what type of material to submit, how to enter a contest or who to contact to attend a workshop or join an organization. Editors' helpful tips included in the listings will further increase your knowledge about how to market work to particular publishers.

Experts share what they've learned

The close-up interviews not only serve as sources of inspiration for hopeful writers and illustrators, but also provide solid advice to those who read them. This year, some very talented people have graciously given of their time to share what they know with readers of *Children's Writer's & Illustrator's Market*. Writer/editor James Cross Giblin discusses his methods of writing nonfiction and the problems with a lot of manuscripts he sees. Lois Lowry describes how the letters she gets from her readers influence her ideas on what to write about. Illustrator/writer Felicia Bond shares the method of her madness in creating a picture book. Poet Jack Prelutsky explains how subject ideas can be as close as the corner grocery store. Tim Davin, art director of *Chickadee/Owl* magazines, provides insight on what an artist's work should show. Illustrator Anni Matsick dwells on the importance of multiculturalism and the essentials of starting your own illustration business. *Venture*'s Deborah Christensen indicates religious publications don't have to consist of all "sugar and spice," and are willing to tackle controversial issues. Kathryn Schultz Miller of ArtReach Touring Theatre tells playwrights most plays for children should *not* be extravagant productions. Finally, *Boodle*'s Mavis Catalfio advises young writers and illustrators on submitting material to her publication.

What I hope to learn

As editor of *Children's Writer's & Illustrator's Market*, I receive many phone calls and letters from readers with questions, comments and complaints about anything from the industry as a whole to policies of individual publishers. I welcome this feedback and consider it valuable because it helps me better serve your needs and results in, hopefully, a better book each year. If publishers in this book are not living up to the information they've given us for their listings, I want to know. If you're unsure about the services of agents, details concerning rights or anything else, feel free to write me regarding your questions. I may not know the answers, but I'll do my best to seek them out.

I'm thrilled to know I have been able to help writers and illustrators make their dreams become reality, and I cherish all the success stories that have been shared with me. For those of you who have found success using previous editions, congratulations! I hope this edition brings you continued sales of your work. And for those of you just getting started in writing or illustrating for children, I assure you this book is a wise investment and will serve as a valuable tool as you research markets.

Now it's time to get to work. Roll up your sleeves and start climbing the ladder to success. At this moment, you are holding the first step of that ladder in your hands.

How to Use Children's Writer's & Illustrator's Market

Take a few minutes to familiarize yourself with the format of this hypothetical listing before browsing through the book. Each component of the listing is numbered for your convenience and corresponds to an explanation following this sample. Note this sample listing is for a book publisher. Listing formats in other sections vary. "Ms" or "mss" refers to "manuscript" or "manuscripts" respectively.

Be sure to *always* include a self-addressed, stamped envelope (SASE) with submissions. If you are a foreigner marketing to a listing within the United States, or a United States citizen marketing work abroad, send a self-addressed envelope (SAE) and the appropriate number of International Reply Coupons (IRCs).

Throughout many listings you will find four categories of children's writing/ illustrating; they are defined as: "picture books," written/illustrated for preschool-8 year olds; "young readers" for 5-8 year olds; "middle readers" for 9-11 year olds; and "young adults" for those 12 and older. These age breakdowns may vary slightly from publisher to publisher.

> **(1) INSPIRATION PRESS,** imprint of the National Worship Society. **(2)** 222 Anywhere Ave., Mercer WY 99999. (123)555-4567. FAX: (123)555-7890. **(3)** Book publisher. **(4)** Editor: Wilma Carter. **(5)** Publishes 10-12 picture books/year; 1-2 young readers/year; 3-5 middle readers/year; 1-2 young adult titles/year. **(6)** 25% of books by first-time authors; 10% of books from agented authors. **(7)** "We publish stories with spiritual themes."
> **Fiction: (8)** Picture books, young readers: animal, religion. Middle readers, young adults: problem novels, religion. **(9)** Does not want to see fantasy or secular material. **(10)** Average word length: picture books—750; young readers—2,000; middle readers—20,000; young adults—50,000. **(11)** Recently published *Jesus Loves Me*, by Irma Brown (ages 3-5, picture book); *Joshua's Story*, by John Smith (ages 5-8, young reader).
> **Nonfiction: (12)** Picture books, young readers, middle readers: activity books, biography, history, religion. **(13)** Does not want to see secular material. **(14)** Average word length: picture books—1,000; young readers—2,000; middle readers—12,000. **(15)** Recently published *The Story of Moses*, by Jack Blair (ages 9-11, middle reader); *The Journey of Jesus*, by Anita Silver (ages 4-6, picture book).
> **How to Contact/Writers: (16)** Fiction: Submit complete ms. Nonfiction: Query. **(17)** Reports on queries in 6 weeks; on mss in 1 month. **(18)** Publishes a book 1 year after acceptance. **(19)** Will consider simultaneous submissions, electronic submissions via disk or modem and previously published work.
> **Illustration: (20)** Average number of illustrations used for fiction and nonfiction: picture books—30; young readers—15; middle readers—10; young adults—1. **(21)** Will review ms/illustration packages. Will review artwork for future assignments. Contact Claudia Young, art director. **(22)** Uses color artwork only. **(23)** "Most of our artists work with watercolors."

How to Contact/Illustrators: (24) Ms/illustration packages: Submit ms with 2 pieces of final art. Illustrations only: Query with samples. **(25)** Reports in 3 weeks. **(26)** Original artwork returned at job's completion.

Photography: (27) Photographers should contact Cecil Brown, photo editor. **(28)** Uses photos "which directly or indirectly convey spiritual messages." **(29)** Model/property releases and captions required. **(30)** Interested in stock photos. **(31)** Publishes photo essays and photo concept books. **(32)** Uses b&w prints and 35mm transparencies. **(33)** To contact, provide résumé and promotional literature to be kept on file.

Terms: (34) Pays authors royalty of 5-10% based on retail price. **(35)** Offers advances. **(36)** Pays illustrators by the project (range: $2,000-4,000). **(37)** Photographers paid per photo (range: $50-100). **(38)** Sends galleys to authors; dummies to illustrators. **(39)** Book catalog available for 9 × 12 SAE and 5 first class stamps. Ms and art guidelines available for SASE.

Tips: (40) "Be familiar with the types of books we publish."

(1)(2) The full name, mailing address and phone number of the book or magazine publishing company, organization, workshop or contest. A phone number in a listing does not mean the market accepts phone queries. Make a phone query only when your story's timeliness would be lost by following the standard procedures. As a rule, don't call unless you have been invited to do so.
(3) The type of business.
(4) Title and name of contact person. Always try to address your submission to a specific person. It is a good idea to call the market prior to sending material to confirm the contact person is still with the company.
(5) Breakdown of the type and number of books published annually. Use this breakdown to choose a company most receptive to your type of work.
(6) The percentage of books by first-time authors indicates how open a market is to new authors. Also included is the percentage of authors represented by agents. If the publisher subsidy publishes, it will be noted here. Within the book, subsidy publishers are marked with a solid block (■).
(7) A general description of the types of subject matter this market deals with.
(8) The specific fictional material desired by the market.
(9) Types of fictional material the market is not interested in.
(10) Length specifications for fiction for each age group. If your manuscript is longer or shorter by a large margin, submit to a more appropriate market.
(11) Examples of fiction recently published by this market.
(12) Specific nonfiction material desired.
(13) Types of nonfiction material the market is not interested in.
(14) Length specifications for nonfiction for each age group.
(15) Examples of nonfiction recently published by this market.
(16) Details on how writers should submit material.
(17) Reporting times indicate how soon a market will respond to your query or manuscript, but times listed are approximate. Wait four weeks beyond the stated reporting time before checking on the status of your submission.
(18) If your manuscript is accepted, this information gives you the approximate time it will take for it to be published.
(19) Details about whether the market accepts simultaneous submissions, electronic submissions via disk or modem or previously published work. If sending

a simultaneous submission, state in your cover letter your manuscript is being considered elsewhere.

(20) The average number of illustrations required per type of book gives the illustrator an idea of how much work a project might entail.

(21) This information informs the illustrator if the market reviews manuscript/illustration packages. Also included is whether an illustrator's work can be reviewed for future assignments and the person who should be contacted.

(22) Indications about whether the market uses color art only or primarily black and white.

(23) Specific information regarding preferences in the medium/style/size of artwork.

(24) Details on submitting manuscript/illustration packages and illustrations only.

(25) The approximate amount of time it will take to receive a response regarding illustrations.

(26) Information about whether original artwork is returned to the illustrator.

(27) Contact person for freelance photographers.

(28) Subject matter desired for photographs.

(29) Information about whether model/property releases or photo captions are required.

(30) Whether the market is interested in reviewing stock photography.

(31) Whether the market publishes photo essays or photo concept books.

(32) Types of photographs the market uses.

(33) Submission information for photographs.

(34) Payment information for authors.

(35) Information on whether advances are offered.

(36) Payment information for illustrators.

(37) Payment information for photographers.

(38) Terms about whether galleys are sent to authors and dummies are sent to illustrators for review prior to publication.

(39) If catalogs or submission guidelines are available, it will be noted here.

(40) Helpful suggestions for writers and illustrators.

Key to Symbols

* *Symbol indicating listing is new in this edition*
■ *Symbol indicating a market subsidy publishes manuscripts*
‡ *Symbol indicating a contest is for students*

A Writer's Guide to the Juvenile Market: Ten Steps to That First Sale

by Elaine Marie Alphin

Unsolicited manuscripts from first-time authors pour into publishers' mail-rooms. Some juvenile publishers receive 9,000 book manuscripts per year—that's 750 a month, or nearly 40 books submitted by hopeful authors every working day. That publisher will buy at most 300 manuscripts in a year, fewer than one a day. In the face of such odds, do you stand a chance of ever selling your book?

The answer is a resounding YES. Children's publishing is hitting an all-time high. Publishers are hungry for well-written, high quality books, and editors are eager to develop new authors. You may have the drive and enthusiasm to write a children's book, but you still need more. Knowing how to make your manuscript stand out can definitely work to your advantage. By following a few simple steps, your manuscript could spend less time in the slush pile and more time in an editor's hands. Consider these ten steps to put you on the right track toward that first sale.

1. Write the best story possible.

The first step to selling your book is producing a good story. The key to your best writing is in careful planning. I recommend a loose-leaf planning notebook divided into sections for plot outline, chapter summaries, character development, research on settings, title ideas and general brainstorming.

Character and plot questionnaires are useful in this planning notebook. As you answer questions about your characters, their goals, and their obstacles, those characters become real people and the plot races toward its resolution. I use worksheets and checklists from Ploeger's Services. (Write for a free catalog at this address: Suite 224, 751 Laurel Street, San Carlos CA 94070). They can be revised to suit your personal requirements or to help you generate your own lists of questions. Whatever your system, it's best to do *something* to plan your book before you start writing.

When you take the time to plan your manuscript, you ensure strong characters who are involved in a logical plot with real conflict, real goals, and a well-paced series of ups and downs. This will hook the editor who reads your manuscript and keep her turning the pages.

Elaine Marie Alphin *has proven her steps to getting published are effective. Her first novel,* The Ghost Cadet *(for ages 8-12), was published by Henry Holt in 1991. In addition, Henry Holt has accepted and is currently preparing for publication her second novel,* The Proving Ground *(for ages 10-14). Alphin's articles and stories have appeared in numerous national children's magazines. In 1990, she received the Society of Children's Book Writer's Magazine Merit Award in the fiction category for her story, "A Song in the Dark."*

2. Seek feedback on your writing.

Get independent, unbiased criticism on your manuscript. Don't ask for opinions from your best friend, your mother or your spouse. Because these people love you and want to assure you that your manuscript is wonderful, it's hard for them to be objective. The best feedback is unbiased, constructive criticism from people whose only interest is making your book the best it can be.

Join a writer's group. Ideally, the group should consist of 8-10 people who meet once a month to exchange manuscripts. Members should read these manuscripts carefully and critically in order to offer constructive comments for improving manuscripts.

Listen to this feedback—you are all professionals wanting to produce your best work. When your fellow writers tell you your characters aren't believable, or suggest ways of developing your theme more effectively, they're doing you a big favor. So pay attention to this feedback—but don't make changes blindly. Your writer's group can help pinpoint problems, but it's up to you to decide solutions. In the end, this is *your* book. After you get thoughtful criticism from your fellow writers, you must make your own call as to which comments to use and which to discard in rewriting your manuscript.

3. Prepare your manuscript for submission.

You now have a well-written book which you are eager to send to a publisher. First, produce a clean, polished copy of the manuscript on white, 25 lb. bond paper. The typing should be black, clear, sharp and error-free. Never, not even for the shortest picture book, think about submitting a handwritten manuscript. Editors equate handwriting with eyestrain. At best, a handwritten submission will boomerang immediately with a form rejection in the return envelope. At worst, editors will have a good laugh at the ignorant amateur's expense before rejecting the book. No handwritten manuscript will be seriously considered. Margins on each page should be approximately one inch on top and bottom and either side. (This allows editors room for their own notations.) The first pages of chapters should start one third to one half of the way down the page with the chapter number and chapter title (if one is used) centered. The top left corner of each page should be clearly labeled with your surname and the key words of your title. The page number should appear on each page at the top right corner.

Invest in a personal computer or word processor with a 10-pitch letter quality printer. For those of you who weren't weaned on computers in grade school, I realize they can be intimidating. Personally, I was convinced I could never write on a computer, but my husband insisted on buying one anyway. I made up my mind to prove my writing was incompatible with high tech. I dove into the manuals, determined to become hopelessly bogged down and unable to generate a single creative thought. To my surprise, I instead realized the potential my new computer offered for polishing, revising and printing a perfect manuscript.

By choosing user-friendly software, you'll be able to type as though the computer were an ordinary typewriter. Learning a few commands will enable you to insert, delete and move blocks of text. Formatting capabilities of the software will allow a printed final manuscript with every page looking identical—no sentences running off the right margin and no paragraphs trailing off the bottom. The final printout of your manuscript will be well worth the initial investment put forth for the computer and software.

Your title page should include the title, your name, address, Social Security number, phone number, and an approximate word count (**see Figure 1**). *Do not* register the copyright for your manuscript, and *do not* include the copyright symbol on your title page. This is my recommendation. Use of the copyright symbol has become controversial. Many editors are offended by the implication that authors suspect them of stealing their words. Remember—*ideas cannot be copyrighted*. Let's say you send your manuscript about blade skating to a publisher and it's rejected. Then later on, that publisher puts out a book on the same topic. Unless the published book contains the same words that you used, and in the same order, your manuscript was not stolen.

If you feel it is necessary to protect your work, one way is to mail yourself a copy of the work via certified mail. This will prove the work was written and in your possession by a certain date. However, the act of writing your manuscript provides a de facto copyright under current copyright law. In other words, your words are protected as soon as they are written. So you really are protected in case some unscrupulous reader should try to plagiarize your work. If you do register your own copyright, tell the publisher. They will register the copyright when they publish your book and the process is different with a work which has been previously copyrighted.

Place the manuscript in a padded envelope or a mailing box. If you're submitting a picture book, you can use a 9 × 12 unpadded envelope. Always include a return envelope, large enough for your entire manuscript, with sufficient postage. Hopefully it won't be needed, but its presence tells the editor you are a professional.

Do not send your manuscript by certified mail. If you do, someone in the publisher's office will have to sign for it. That person may view this task as a waste of time, tedious and annoying. The last thing you want to do is annoy someone in the publisher's office. However, you want to be certain your manuscript is received. The best way to assure arrival of your submission without irritating the publisher is to send the manuscript by UPS.

4. Research the markets.

Now your manuscript is ready to send to a publisher. Which one?

Choosing the correct publisher for your manuscript is every bit as important as writing the best possible story. Many form rejection letters are sent because the manuscript was totally unsuitable for that publisher in the first place.

If your manuscript is 50-2,000 words, first decide whether it should be submitted to a magazine or a book publisher. Your picture book or short chapter book may really be a short story, and therefore better suited to a magazine. If your story contains a clear series of visual images that build to a climax, then it should be submitted as a picture book. But a simple plot with only one or two visual scenes is a short story.

The main reference sources are annual market guides, publishers' catalogs, and bookstore and library shelves. Peruse the newest releases and try to locate a publisher who tends to publish books that address the same concerns and audience that you're interested in, but who hasn't just published a book that is too much like yours. Be aware, though, that while bookstores, libraries and publishers' catalogs reveal what's been published in the past, they do not necessarily indicate what will be published in the future.

Also, watch for new developments in publishers' needs. If you are a member

Elaine Marie Alphin   About 7,000 words
1507 Dana Avenue
Cincinnati, OH 45207
SSN: 123-45-6789
513-555-3021

A BEAR FOR MIGUEL

by

Elaine Marie Alphin

Figure 1: Sample title page.

of the Society of Children's Book Writers (SCBW), read the Publisher's Corner listings in the *Bulletin* (SCBW's bimonthly newsletter) to learn what editors currently want to see. *Children's Book Insider*, a monthly newsletter for children's writers and illustrators, also contains timely market listings with publishers' updated needs. Good additional sources are the Markets sections of *Writer's Digest* and *The Writer*, although they are not oriented solely to juvenile publishers.

5. Write a dynamite cover letter.

Once you have matched your manuscript to a suitable publisher, your next step is to write an irresistible cover letter. This is your personal introduction to the editor, so you must make a good first impression. Let's take a look at my sample cover letter (**see Figure 2**):

- **Salutation:** Direct your letter to the proper editor. I called the publisher and asked who was in charge of chapter books and the correct spelling of her name. Though annual directories such as *Children's Writer's & Illustrator's Market* contain the names of editors, turnover in this industry is rampant. Therefore, it's a good idea to call and confirm the name of the contact person.

- **Paragraphs 1 & 2:** In the letter explain what age group the book is aimed for and why. Then, in a couple of sentences, whet the editor's appetite by telling her what the story is about. Here, my main character was nine years old and was dealing with a problem that helped her see her family as part of a larger world.

- **Paragraph 3:** Tell the editor what special marketing bonuses the manuscript has (in this case, the timeliness of the problems in El Salvador). Explain why you are particularly well suited to write this book (my family is from El Salvador).

- **Paragraph 4:** If you are a member of SCBW or any other relevant professional organization, say so. SCBW is a respected professional organization and being a member tells the editor you consider yourself a professional. Mention any writing awards you have received and cite any magazine credentials as a published author, heading the list with your best credits, or course. If you have not previously been published, don't make excuses to the editor. Instead, don't mention publishing credits at all.

- **Paragraph 5:** Finally, assure the editor you are willing to revise as required. Many editors worry authors will be reluctant to do this. Your willingness to work with them will calm their fears, and therefore work to your advantage.

Some publishers prefer to receive a query instead of the complete manuscript. This is particularly true with nonfiction books. As in the cover letter, you must make your best first impression (**see Figure 3**).

As stated before, address the letter to a particular editor. Then use a hook to grab that editor's attention. Explain why your book idea is suited to the age group and why you are the person to write it. Give an idea of the book's length.

As with a cover letter, discuss marketing bonuses, your credentials, and your willingness to revise.

6. Play the waiting game.

Wait patiently and keep busy. Get out your planning notebook and start working on a new book.

If you haven't heard from the publisher after a reasonable amount of time (three months), write a letter inquiring about the status of your manuscript

1507 Dana Avenue
Cincinnati, OH 45207
March 5, 1992

Sycamore Publishing
Attn: Althea Smith
10 Main Street
Cincinnati, OH 45202

Dear Ms. Smith:

Please find enclosed my chapter book, A BEAR FOR MIGUEL, for your consideration. This manuscript is aimed at 6 to 9 year olds.

A BEAR FOR MIGUEL is the story of Maria, a 9 year old girl living in a village in El Salvador. Her family has already had to make sacrifices because of the constant turmoil between the government forces and the guerrillas, and Maria's market holiday with her father becomes a time for her to make a difficult choice between her own wishes and the needs of her family.

My background is Hispanic; my father emigrated from El Salvador as a teenager, and most of our family still lives there. This story reflects the day-to-day life of many of the people of El Salvador. With the United States located so near Central America and the troubles in El Salvador a regular part of our evening news, this story is particularly timely and should be readily marketable in our Hispanic communities.

I am a member of the Society of Children's Book Writers and the recipient of their 1989 Magazine Merit Award for fiction. My articles and stories regularly appear in such magazines as Cricket, Highlights, Child Life, Children's Digest, Story Friends, Alive! for Young Teens, Junior Trails, On the Line, Bread for Children, Journey, TeenQuest, Young and Alive, Primary Treasure, The Friend, Wonder Time, Quest and Houston City Magazine.

Thank you for your attention and for your consideration of A BEAR FOR MIGUEL. Should you be interested in publishing this manuscript, I would look forward to working with you and your editorial staff on revision as required. Should you wish to return the manuscript to me, I enclose a SASE for your convenience.

Sincerely,

Elaine Marie Alphin

Elaine Marie Alphin

Figure 2: A cover letter *that Elaine Alphin sent to an editor (the names and addresses* have been changed to insure privacy).

1507 Dana Avenue
Cincinnati, OH 45207
March 5, 1992

Pioneer Publishing Company
Attn: Dirk Russell
2105 Fagle Parkway
Nashville TN 37221

Dear Mr. Russell:

A complaining old woman climbs the branches of a sycamore tree,
searching for her lost children. Suddenly, the fruit of the tree is filled
with eyes which stare at her accusingly. Terrified, the old woman must
shriek for her friends to come and save her.

Kenya is the setting for this 900 word picture book, THE CHILDREN OF
THE SYCAMORE TREE. Small children should enjoy this tale of an old
woman who wishes for children because she has none of her own. When
she magically gets children from the sycamore tree, however, she fails
to appreciate them, and the children return to the tree to await a mother
who will love them for themselves. Youngsters should delight in sharing
the folktale's message with their parents.

THE CHILDREN OF THE SYCAMORE TREE is a retelling of a Masai folktale. My husband spends one to three months in Africa each year and,
during my opportunities to travel there with him, I have come to appreciate the tribal folktales.

I am a member of the Society of Children's Book Writers and the recipi-
ent of their 1989 Magazine Merit Award for fiction. My articles and sto-
ries regularly appear in such magazines as Cricket, Highlights, Child
Life, Children's Digest, Story Friends, Alive! for Young Teens, Junior
Trails, On the Line, Bread for Children, Journey, TeenQuest, Young and
Alive, Primary Treasure, The Friend, Wonder Time, Quest and Houston
City Magazine.

May I submit THE CHILDREN OF THE SYCAMORE TREE for your consideration? Should you be interested in publishing this manuscript, I
would look forward to working with you and your editorial staff on revision as required.

Thank you very much for your attention. I look forward to hearing from
you, and I enclose a SASE for your convenience.

Sincerely,

Elaine Marie Alphin

Elaine Marie Alphin

**Figure 3: A sample of one of Elaine Alphin's query letters (the names and addresses
have been changed to insure privacy).**

and enclose a letter-size SASE. If there's still no response, call and ask if your manuscript was received and whether it is under consideration.

Whether it's your first book or your fifteenth, the waiting period is difficult. Considering the long response times, there's a terrible temptation to send your manuscript to several publishers at once. However, many publishers frown on simultaneous submissions. Some editors who invest their time and effort in considering your manuscript feel they deserve the courtesy of being the only ones reading it.

SCBW recommends that if there is no response in three months, the author should write the publisher to withdraw the manuscript and then send it elsewhere. Personally, I think you have to play it by ear. If you have gotten to know an editor over the years, even through letters of rejection, you may want to let that editor keep the manuscript longer than three months. You should, however, follow up with a letter and SASE, to make sure your manuscript is being read and has not been lost.

Giving the editor more time is a risk, because the manuscript could still be rejected after a nine- or ten-month wait. You could have tried three different publishers in that time. On the other hand, the risk can pay off. I sold three different manuscripts after they sat on editors' desks for over a year each.

7. Negotiate the contract.

Finally the news you've been waiting for comes—the publisher wants your book! Now what do you do about the contract?

There's no reason you can't negotiate a contract yourself, without an agent. You do need an advisor—either a lawyer or someone who deals with contracts on a regular basis. Also essential is a copy of Richard Balkin's book, *A Writer's Guide to Contract Negotiations* (Writer's Digest Books). This book will help you become familiar with clauses that are standard and not negotiable, as well as clauses that can be changed.

Don't be afraid to ask questions or request changes. Use Balkin's book as a guideline—and be willing to compromise. For instance, if the publisher offers you 8% royalties on wholesale price, and you ask for 10% on retail price, you should be pleased if they come back with 8% on retail price, or with an increased advance offer.

Expect the negotiation to take time. Your editor may negotiate in writing (by mail or by fax) or over the phone. Verbal offers from reputable publishers are equally as valid as written offers. You should respond in writing or by phone, whichever way the publisher chooses.

The editor will explain the contract offer. Take detailed notes and thank the editor, but don't commit to anything yet. Tell the editor you'll consult your advisor and get back to her. After talking to your advisor and re-reading the sample contract in Balkin's book, make notes on changes you want and things you need explained. Wait a day, then call or write the editor back and work through your list of questions and changes. Some questions the editor will be able to answer immediately. Others will have to be checked on.

The ball is now in their court. When the editor calls (or writes) back, note what is offered in response to your negotiation points. Again thank the editor, but do not commit yourself to the contract yet. As you did before, consult your advisor.

This process will go on for several days (even longer if it's all done in writing).

When both sides finally reach an agreement on terms, the publisher's legal department will send you the contract. Read it carefully! If the typist makes an innocent error but you sign it anyway, you could be in trouble. Watch out for clauses not in line with what was previously agreed upon. Be sure to talk with the editor about any contradictions between the oral agreement and the written contract.

Pay particular attention to the split in subsidiary rights sales, option clauses (which obligate you to automatically show the publisher your next book), and clauses altering your royalties arrangements if sales drop below a certain floor. Remember—the lawyers who prepared this contract made it safe and advantageous for the publisher. It's your responsibility to make it safe and advantageous for yourself. If you ask for reasonable contract changes and are willing to compromise, you will end up with a mutually beneficial contract that satisfies both you and your publisher.

8. Be willing to revise.

Though the publisher likes your book, the editor will ask you to make revisions. Writers resist revisions because of all the hard work that goes into their manuscripts. They love each and every word, and any revision seems insulting.

Actually, revision isn't an insult at all. When an editor makes suggestions, ask yourself if they will sharpen your book's focus or clarify a character. If you can improve your manuscript by revising, then it's in your best interest to do so. Occasionally an editor will make a revision based on personal bias. Then the writer should calmly explain why he disagrees. Just make sure that, despite the changes, the basic message of your book stays the same.

Some writers don't like revision because the idea of re-typing the manuscript or paying for a professional typist doesn't exactly thrill them. Here's where your computer pays off. You will be able to respond quickly to revision requests because you will easily be able to add or delete text and print out a new copy to send to your editor.

So keep an open mind about revision. And remember, it's not necessary to follow every sugestion blindly. You may feel there is a better way to make the change than what the editor suggests. If you make a revision that works well, the editor will be satisfied.

9. Respond promptly to copy editor comments and to the galleys.

The revisions are done and the end is in sight. But you have two final tasks. First, evaluate the copy editor's feedback on your book. The copy editor can do a lot of good for you, in the sense of checking spelling, correcting grammar and noticing errors in consistency (in case you said someone was age 15 on page 20 and then said he was age 14 on page 150).

But the copy editor can overdo it by concentrating only on small details— like whether you used the word "look" three times in five pages. You may have repeated "look" deliberately, but the copy editor only saw the repetition, not the effect. Work through the copy editor's notes, okay the ones which are acceptable corrections, and say no to the ones you disagree with. You will have to justify every no, but if you disagree, say so. An over-zealous copy editor can change the language and flavor of your book.

Second, check the galleys, which show what your book is actually going to look like. Check for errors and misspellings. If you don't check carefully, you could wind up with errors in the final version. Don't be blinded by how beautiful it looks! Fortunately, three or four other people at the publisher are also checking the galleys, as is your copy editor. Among all of you, most of the errors should be spotted.

10. Start selling your next book.

Your first bound book will soon be in your hands. Before you celebrate, however, mention to your editor you have another manuscript in progress. If the editor is pleased with the development of your first book, she will eagerly ask to read your new manuscript.

So go back to your planning notebook, get your critique group's feedback, prepare a clean copy of your new manuscript, write a cover letter telling the editor this is the manuscript you discussed—and be ready to sign your second contract by the time your first book hits the stores!

Portfolio Power for Children's Illustrators: Putting It All Together

by Lisa Carpenter

Currently, the field of children's publishing is welcoming competent new artists, more so than new writers. To take advantage of this vigorous demand, you will have to develop your self-promotion and organizational skills and showcase your artistic talent. Editors and art directors will be glad to open doors for you, but you'll have to supply them with the key—a well-organized, professional-looking portfolio.

Variety vs. specialty

In the past, the general rule was to display one style per portfolio, especially when it pertained to adult illustrations. The logic behind featuring just one style was art directors would be better able to categorize you. Associating an artist with one unique way of painting or drawing was supposedly less confusing for an art director because overwhelming him with a variety of styles would make him unable to associate you with one. Thus, by showing a variety, you were less likely to land assignments.

The above logic sounds sensible. But it's not true, at least for children's illustration (not to mention less and less these days for adult illustration). In this field, versatility is what increases your chances of getting work. Showing only one style may be beneficial if you know the art director has one particular job in mind. Chances are, though, if you get in to see an art director, you will be trying to open yourself up to any jobs available now or in the future. In this case, your portfolio needs to reflect all the styles you are interested in. Be sure all your samples emphasize your strengths. Don't include any type of work which you're not enthusiastic about doing because it could result in assignments you don't want. Of course, if you feel there's only one style you're good at, don't force yourself to show diversity. It's better to earn a good reputation with one specialty than to damage your credibility drawing in styles you're weak at.

What to show in your artwork

Your portfolio is a display of not only your artistic talent, but your ability to illustrate a book for children. Children's publishers are not interested in seeing the bowl of fruit or bouquet of roses you painted last summer, even if they're masterpieces; they only want to see pieces that will appeal to children and demonstrate your skills in figure drawing, character, setting and narrative. One method of making yourself more marketable through your portfolio is to show a wide range of subject matter dealing with various people, animals and moods.

Lisa Carpenter is editor of Children's Writer's & Illustrator's Market.

Concentrate especially on showing action and interaction. Children's editors and art directors are interested in how you make characters relate to each other, so show your people engaging in various activities. Portraits and landscapes/townscapes are also acceptable samples to show. In addition, the ability to realistically depict various age levels and ethnic races will be advantageous to your career.

Keep in mind good illustrations are supposed to communicate, so make sure each sample you choose stands on its own. The person looking at your artwork is expecting to see your strongest work and will assume what you're presenting is your best. It is said a chain is only as strong as its weakest link—don't allow any weak links in your portfolio. If you feature nine good pieces and one mediocre piece in your portfolio, chances are the latter one is the one an editor or art director will notice.

What to include in your portfolio

When compiling your portfolio, it is best to include a total of 10-15 samples. Be sensitive of the art director's time limitations. He's busy, so don't approach him with your life's work. Attempting to show more than 15 samples could actually hamper your chances of getting an assignment. Large quantities of work are more likely to be skimmed through, meaning less attention will be paid to each piece.

If you have any published material you feel is superior, it is to your advantage to include the tearsheets. Not only will this give the art director an opportunity to view how your work looks printed, but it will also indicate you have carried out a job successfully in the agreed manner.

It is advisable that you not use original artwork, but rather color photocopies. Even if you are showing the work in person and feel it is adequately protected while in your possession, be aware that some publishers do not see illustrators personally. Instead, they ask them to drop off their portfolios for a day or two. Unfortunately, there's the possibility the publisher could misplace it. If you're really adamant about showing original artwork at your personal appointments, then consider compiling photocopies for a separate portfolio that can be used for drop-offs only.

Make the sizes of your artwork consistent with standard sizes used in children's books and magazines. The majority of children's books range in size from 7×4 inches (for paperbacks) to 12×9 inches (for the largest hardback picture books). Though there are exceptions, only a few children's books are produced in a larger format. It is important for an art director to see that you can indeed work within stated size specifications.

If you specialize in black and white only, there's no reason to include color art. But even if you are strongest in a color medium, it is still essential to include some black and white artwork in your first portfolio. Opportunities in color illustration are usually not available to newcomers in the field because they have not yet proven themselves. Editors at large publishing houses may be wary of assigning rookies costly full-color picture books for first assignments, but may be willing to take a chance on them supplying black and white illustrations for middle grade novels. Many small presses with smaller budgets use primarily black and white artwork even in their picture books and early chapter books.

Since there's a good chance your initial assignments (whether with a commercial publisher or a small press) will involve black and white artwork, it is imperative to demonstrate your capabilities in this area by showing strong black and white samples.

When compiling your first portfolio, don't use all full-color art. Demonstrate your skills using limited color. Include at least one example of art using black and other colors. Also, if you know how to do color separations, use one of your limited color pieces and prepare a separation. Demonstrating your ability to prepare color preseparations could make you an art director's first choice for work in the future.

One way to break into doing full-color artwork is to start out doing jacket illustrations. Books for older children may feature only one illustration—the cover. Being willing to take on assignments for jacket illustrations will not only allow you to view your printed color work, but it might also enable you to score some points with the publisher—at least enough to qualify you for bigger projects. If jacket illustration seems like a good option, prepare a sample book jacket (from your own story or another well-known one). Be sure any characters included fit into the appropriate age levels. (Remember—jackets for young adult novels will require older characters.)

Storyboards

So that you can demonstrate your ability to carry a story with your art, consider using a storyboard (where the whole story is laid out on one page in black and white rough miniature sketches). Storyboard sketches are the same as thumbnail sketches, though for a portfolio storyboard sketches should be a little more sophisticated and not quite as rough as the average thumbnail sketches. As was suggested for jackets, when creating a storyboard for your portfolio, use either your own story or another one that's well-known (such as a classic fairy tale). Storyboards are effective aids for demonstrating your sense of continuity. They're good to use because in one page an art director can see how you handle double page spreads (one illustration which takes up two pages in a book) and sequences (two separate illustrations involving the same characters which appear one after the other in a book). It is important to make sure your storyboard conforms with the typical format of a picture book. Most picture books are 32 pages, and five or six of the 32 pages will consist of the copyright page, title page, etc. Make sure you account for all the pages on your storyboard, including the ones that have nothing to do with the actual story. Also, pay attention to the way you incorporate your text with the sketches. In order to prove your ability to transfer storyboard sketches into finished art, be sure to accompany your storyboard with one or two pieces of finished full-color art.

Dummies

An excellent dummy could very well be the highlight of your portfolio. Like a storyboard, including a dummy in your portfolio also shows your skills at pacing, drawing in sequence, maintaining a character and visualizing an entire book. The dummy offers a bigger medium for presenting your story and incorporating text. In addition, it is the preferred means to demonstrate how your story will look in color. Samples for a dummy should be as close to actual size of a standard picture book as possible. Like the storyboard, be particular about the 32-page format and allow for front and back matter. Creating a dummy is the best way to indicate to the art director/editor what your vision for a story is and how you see things. Though it is an option, you may also want to design your own jacket cover for your dummy. As with storyboards, accompany your finished dummy with one or two pieces of finished artwork.

Arranging your portfolio pieces

There is no one perfect way to arrange portfolio pieces. Various systems exist (as well as no system at all), and artists must determine the arrangement best for them.

In *The Ultimate Portfolio* by Martha Metzdorf (North Light Books, 1991), Metzdorf claims building a portfolio is like building a fence. The three or four pieces you feel are your best work should be considered "posts" that hold the portfolio together, while the other pieces serve as "rails" that link your strongest pieces together and give an idea of the full range of your work. The advantage to using this system is your strong pieces are spread out through your portfolio. If you have a strong piece in the middle, perhaps—if you're presenting the portfolio—you can find a story or reason to pause and go into a little more detail about the particular artwork. This allows you to slow down the pace at which your work is being reviewed, and possibly result in your strong work receiving more attention.

No matter what your system is, it is absolutely essential to show your best sample first. If it's superior, it will set the tone of the portfolio and validate the rest of it in the art director's mind. In her book, Metzdorf explains she feels it's equally mandatory to close the portfolio with a smashing piece because the final impression is just as important as the first. Also, Metzdorf informs that with bound portfolios, some art directors like to thumb through the portfolio from back to front, thus justifying the need for a strong back piece.

Some artists prefer to group artwork of the same style, theme or medium together for a greater impact. For example, if an artist feels he is strong painting animals, he may opt to show all his animal pieces first, and then move on to drawings of children. Another common way of grouping is by medium. If an illustrator strives to do color work, she may show all of her full-color work first before showing her black and white samples.

Freshness in presentation is vital, and some artists find scrambling pieces between appointments makes presenting the portfolio less monotonous for them. Scrambling samples for this reason may be effective in adding spark to each presentation, but keep in mind the necessity to start off with your strongest work.

If you meet with an art director, don't show up with scrambled samples. Make sure they are arranged in some professional form, the backs clearly labeled with your name, address and telephone number. It is wise to invest in a portfolio case, though it's not necessary to have one that's top-of-the-line. Most art and business supply stores sell them.

Where to present your portfolio

Research where to market your work. Seek out publishers and magazines that have needs consistent with your style and interests. Artists serious about breaking into the field of children's illustration should attempt at some time to present their portfolios via personal appointments with art directors. Though there are publishers spread out all through the country, for the most part New York City is the home of most large publishers. If you're interested in submitting work to a publisher located far from where you live, then it would make sense to just mail samples. But if you are really serious about the profession, it's essential to make a trip to New York City to show your work in person. Many illustrators can tell you from experience that one trip visiting publishers in New York City can net greater results than many years of mailing submissions. After all, showing up in person is a much more assertive means of trying to get your artwork noticed; samples that are mailed are much easier for an art director to disregard. Those considering making the trip are advised to make arrangements for appointments and portfolio drop-offs several weeks in advance. Then, shortly before going to New York City, call to confirm these appointments. Each day while you're there, call to confirm your appointments for the following day. Also be aware that New York is a big city, so buy a map and familiarize yourself with the city before making appointments. Try to schedule each day's appointments within the same geographic area. Finally, timing can make or break your trip. Don't make the trip right before or during any major conventions, such as the annual American Booksellers Association Convention (which starts the first weekend in June), American Library Association meetings or the Bologna Children's Book Fair.

For more information about submitting to specific book publishers, send a SASE to the Children's Books Council (Suite 404, 568 Broadway, New York NY 10012) requesting the guide for illustrators. This pamphlet furnishes valuable information about arranging appointments, including what specific publishers would like to see, what they would like left with them and their special interests. Artists who are unable to visit publishers personally will also benefit from this pamphlet because it includes arrangements for illustrators who live outside a publisher's immediate geographic area.

Following up

Once the appointment is over, be sure to leave samples of your work for the art director's files, whether it be a full-color flier with two or three examples of your work or a couple of illustrated postcards. Ideally, you will leave samples of both color and black and white work. If there were any particular pieces the art director liked in which you didn't have copies available, be sure to make and send copies as soon as you get back home (plus, a thank you note to the art director for his time would also be a nice gesture). Once or twice a year make it a point to send more samples (in the form of postcards or fliers) for the files. Believe it or not, art directors do refer to their files periodically, and it's not uncommon for an illustrator to be called for an assignment a couple of years after making initial contact.

Once you have presented your portfolio, be persistent by staying in touch. By doing this, you can be assured that someday your time for breaking into the field of children's illustration will come!

ample Portfolio: Claire Ewart

fter 10 years of submitting
aterial through the mail and re-
iving no better than a personal
jection letter, Claire Ewart de-
ded a trip to New York City was
 order. In 1989 she travelled
ere to visit publishers person-
ly. The trip was a success. Her
st picture book, *Time Train*
vritten by Paul Fleischman),
me out in September 1991. Her
cond picture book, *Sister Yessa's*
ory (written by Karen Green-
eld), will be released in August
992. Both are published by
arperCollins. These pieces were
art of her portfolio.

Ewart considers this watercolor and colored pencil Egyptian scene her strongest piece. While a student at the Rhode Island School of Design, she lived briefly in Egypt and believes her experiences wandering about Cairo and the Egyptian countryside deeply influenced her work.

Ewart's travels aren't limited to Egypt. As a result of visiting Indonesia twice, she created this piece. Ewart says she showed it to art directors to indicate her interest in illustrating folktales.

Visiting Bali in Indonesia made it possible for Ewart to create this painting, entitled "When the Gamelan Plays." She feels this art was instrumental in emphasizing her strengths.

This piece effectively demonstrates Ewart's artistic range. Shades of the Southwest are exhibited in this art. She painted this picture after visiting the Arizona Sonora Desert Museum in Tucson.

She used this piece to express her interest in drawing nature, animals, the environment and primitive cultures. The zebras and rhino depicted here helped Ewart land the assignment for Time Train.

Ewart included this illustration to show variety and demonstrate her abilities working with mainstream subject matter.

In her portfolio, Ewart included storyboards with accompanying pieces of final art. To the right is a sample of one of her original storyboards and below it is the final art she included with the storyboard. Though Ewart claims her original storyboards helped her, she is quick to admit several editors criticized them because they deviated from the standard 32-page picture book format. Also, Ewart says she should have paid more attention to text placement. Today she is more careful about sticking to proper formats.

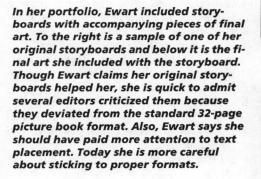

Though she feels she is not strong working with black and white, Ewart felt it necessary to include black and white samples. This Egyptian boy and his sheep was rendered in pen and ink. Ewart once used the drawing for her personal Christmas cards.

The Business of Children's Writing & Illustrating

by Lisa Carpenter

Even though creative talent is a vital key to success, knowing about the business of children's publishing is also essential. This section is designed to expose you to the business techniques needed to successfully market your work. In case you have no idea what to do after finishing your creation, the following will provide some insight on what comes next.

Researching markets

There are two basic elements to submitting your work successfully: good research and persistence. Read through the listings in this book and familiarize yourself with the publications that interest you. Then study the specific needs and the required submission procedures of each publisher or publication. Editors hate to receive inappropriate submissions because handling them wastes precious time. By randomly sending out manuscripts without knowledge of the needs of whom you're sending them to, you risk irritating the editors. Because editors may remember your name and associate it with inappropriate submissions, this practice actually hurts you more than it helps you.

If you're interested in submitting to a particular magazine, write to request a sample copy. For a book publisher, obtain a book catalog or a couple of books produced by that publisher. By doing this, you can better acquaint yourself with that market's writing and illustration styles and formats.

Most of the book publishers and magazines listed offer some sort of writer's/artist's guidelines. It is recommended you read these guidelines before submitting.

Formats for submission

Throughout these listings you will read editors' requests for a query letter, cover letter, book proposal, complete manuscript or resume as all or part of the initial contact procedure. Any correspondence or submissions should be directed to a specific person. Turnover at publishing companies and magazines is rampant. Therefore, it is a good idea to call the publisher to confirm a contact name before sending anything. There is no need to disturb the contact person by asking to speak with her; merely ask the receptionist or secretary if the person still works there and if she still handles the same manuscripts/artwork.

Query letters. A query letter should be no more than a one-page, well written, concise piece to arouse an editor's interest in your manuscript. Queries are usually required from writers submitting nonfiction material to a publisher. In the query letter you want to convince the editor that your idea is perfect for his readership and that you're the writer qualified to do the job. Include any previous writing experience in your letter plus published samples to prove your credentials, especially any samples that relate to the subject matter about which you're querying.

Many query letters start with a lead similar to the lead that would be used in the actual manuscript. Next, you want to briefly outline the work and include facts, anecdotes, interviews or any other pertinent information that give the editor a feel for the manuscript's premise. Your goal is to entice him to want to know more. End your letter with a straight-forward request to write (or submit) the work, and include information on its approximate length, date it could be completed and the availability of accompanying photos or artwork.

More and more, queries are being used for fiction manuscripts because slush piles at some publishing houses have become virtually uncontrollable. Most initial slush pile reading is performed by editorial assistants and junior editors. However, as the number of submissions continues to skyrocket, several publishers have stopped accepting slush. Though these publishers no longer accept unsolicited submissions, they are still open to queries. For a fiction query you want to explain the story's plot, main characters, conflict and resolution. Just as in nonfiction queries, you want to make the editor eager to see more. See Elaine Alphin's sample query letter on page 12 of this book. Or, for more information on writing good queries, consult *How to Write Irresistible Query Letters*, by Lisa Collier Cool (Writer's Digest Books).

Cover letters. Many editors prefer to review a complete manuscript, especially for fiction. In such a case, the cover letter will serve to introduce you and establish your credentials as a writer plus give the editor an overview of the manuscript. (See Elaine Alphin's sample cover letter on page 11 of this book.) If you're sending the manuscript after a "go-ahead" from the editor, the cover letter should serve as a reminder of this commitment.

For an illustrator, the cover letter will also serve as your introduction to the art director and establish your credentials as a professional artist. Be sure to explain what services you can provide as well as what type of follow-up contact you plan to make, if any. If you are sending samples of your work, indicate whether they should be returned or filed. Never send original artwork! If you wish to have the samples returned, include a self-addressed, stamped envelope (SASE) with your submission packet. Cover letters, like the query, should be no longer than one page.

Resumes. Often writers and illustrators are asked to submit a resume with their cover letter and writing/art samples. Resumes can be created in a variety of formats ranging from a single page listing information to color brochures featuring your art. Keep the resume brief, and focus on your artistic achievements, not your whole life. On your resume you want to include your clients and the work you did for them. Also include your educational background and any awards you've won.

Book proposals. Throughout the listings in the Book Publishers section you will find references to submission of a synopsis, outline and sample chapters. Depending on an editor's preference, some or all of these components, as well as inclusion of a cover letter, comprise a book proposal.

A synopsis summarizes the book. Such a summary includes the basic plot of the book (including the ending), is easy to read and flows well.

An outline can also be used to set up fiction, but is more effective as a tool for nonfiction. The outline covers your book chapter by chapter and provides highlights of each. If you are developing an outline for fiction you will want to include major characters, plots and subplots, and length of the book. An outline can run 3 to 30 pages depending on the complexity of your manuscript.

Sample chapters give a more comprehensive idea of your writing skill. Some editors may request the first two or three chapters to see how your material is set up; others may request a beginning, middle and ending chapter to get a better feel for the entire plot. Be sure to determine what the editor needs to see before investing time in writing sample chapters.

Many picture book editors require an outline or synopsis, sample chapters and a variation of roughs or finished illustrations from the author/illustrator. Listings specifying an interest in picture books will detail what type of artwork should accompany manuscripts. If you want to know more about putting together a book proposal, read *How to Write a Book Proposal*, by Michael Larsen (Writer's Digest Books).

Manuscript formats. If an editor specifies that you should submit a complete manuscript for review, here is some format information to guide you. In the upper left corner of your title page, type your legal name (not pseudonym), address, phone number and Social Security number (publishers must have this to file payment records with the government). In the upper right corner you should type the approximate word length. All material in the upper corners should be typed single-spaced, not double. Then type the title (centered) almost halfway down the page with the word "by" two spaces under that and your name or pseudonym two spaces under "by." (See Elaine Alphin's sample title page on page 9.)

The first page should include the title (centered) one-third of the way down. Two spaces under that type "by" and your name or pseudonym. To begin the body of your manuscript, drop down two double spaces and indent five spaces for each new paragraph. There should be 1¼ inch margins around all sides of a full typewritten page. (Manuscripts with wider margins are easier to edit. Also, a page that isn't cramped with a lot of words is more readable and appealing to an editor.) Be sure to set your typewriter on double-space for the manuscript body. From page 2 to the end of your manuscript just include your last name followed by a comma and the title (or key words of the title) in the upper left corner. The page number should go in the top right corner. Drop down two double spaces to begin the body of the page and follow this format throughout the manuscript. If you're submitting a novel, type each chapter title one-third of the way down the page.

When typing text of a picture book, it is not necessary to include page breaks or worry about supplying art. Editors prefer to find the illustrators for picture books. Most of the time, a writer and an illustrator who work on the same book don't know and never meet each other. In this kind of an arrangement, the editor acts as a go-between in case either the writer or illustrator has any problems with text or artwork.

If you are an illustrator who has written your own book, create a dummy or storyboard containing both art and text. Then submit it along with sample pieces of final art (color photocopies—no originals). For a step-by-step guide on creating a good dummy, refer to Frieda Gates' book, *How to Write, Illustrate, and Design Children's Books* (Lloyd-Simone Publishing Company).

For more information on manuscript formats read *Manuscript Submission*, by Scott Edelstein (Writer's Digest Books).

To get an approximate word count for your manuscript, first count the number of characters and spaces in an average line, next count the number of lines on a representative page and multiply these two factors to get your average number of characters per page. Finally, count the number of pages in your manuscript, multiply by the characters per page, then divide by 6 (the average number of characters in a word). You will have your approximate word count.

Mailing and recording submissions

Your primary concern in packaging material is to ensure that it arrives undamaged.

If your manuscript is fewer than six pages it is safe to simply fold it in thirds and send it out in a #10 (business-size) envelope. For a self-addressed, stamped envelope (SASE) you can then fold another #10 envelope in thirds or insert a #9 (reply) envelope which fits in a #10 neatly without any folding at all. Some editors appreciate receiving a manuscript folded in half into a 6x9 envelope. For larger manuscripts you will want to use a 9x12 envelope both for mailing the submission out and as a SASE for its return. The SASE envelope can be folded in half. Book manuscripts will require a sturdy box such as a typing paper or envelope box for mailing. Include a self-addressed mailing label and return postage so it can also double as your SASE.

Artwork requires a bit more packaging care to guarantee that it arrives in presentable form. Sandwich illustrations between heavy cardboard that is slightly larger than the work and tape it closed. You will want to write your name and address on each piece in case the inside material becomes separated from the outer envelope upon receipt. For the outer wrapping you can use either a manila envelope, foam-padded envelope, a mailer with plastic air bubbles as a liner or brown wrapping paper. Bind non-joined edges with reinforced mailing tape and clearly write your address.

You will want to mail material first-class to ensure quick delivery. Also, first-class mail is forwarded for one year if the addressee has moved (which does happen with some magazine and book publishers), and can be returned if undeliverable.

If you are concerned about your material safely reaching its destination, consider other mailing options, such as UPS. If material needs to reach your editor or art director quickly, you can elect to use overnight delivery services

Occasionally throughout this book you will see the term International Reply Coupon (IRC). Keep in mind foreign markets cannot use U.S. postage when returning a manuscript to you, which therefore renders moot any SASE you may have sent. When mailing a submission to another country (Canada too), include IRCs in lieu of U.S. postage. The U.S. Post Office can help you determine, based on your package's weight, the correct number of IRCs to include to ensure its return.

If it is not necessary for an editor to return your work, such as with photocopies of manuscripts or art, don't include return postage. This saves you the cost of extra postage. Instead, track the status of your submissions by enclosing a postage-paid reply postcard (which requires less postage) with options for the editor to check, such as "yes, I am interested" or "no, the material is not appropriate for my needs at this time."

Some writers or illustrators simply set a deadline date. If nothing is heard from the editor or art director by this date, the manuscript or artwork is automatically withdrawn from consideration. Because many publishing houses are overstocked with manuscripts, a minimum deadline should be no less than 3 months.

If you opt for simultaneous submissions, be sure to inform the editor your work is being considered elsewhere. Though it's not set in stone, it is a professional courtesy that is encouraged throughout the field. Most editors are reluctant to receive simultaneous submissions, but understand the frustration experienced by hopeful authors who have to wait many months for a response. In some cases, an editor may actually be more inclined to read your manuscript sooner because he knows it's being considered elsewhere. The Society of Children's Book Writers warns against simultaneous submissions, the feeling being eventually they will cause publishers to quit accepting unsolicited material altogether. Also, since manuscripts that are simultaneously submitted are not specifically tailored to any one publisher, SCBW feels the act will result in less than serious consideration of work received. The official recommendation of the SCBW is to submit to one publisher at a time, but wait only three months (note you will do so in your cover letter). If no response is received, then send a note withdrawing your manuscript from consideration. SCBW considers multiple submissions acceptable if you have a manuscript dealing with a timely issue.

One thing you should never do is use a publisher's fax number to send queries, manuscripts or illustration samples. Only use a fax number after acquiring proper authorization. Don't disrupt the publisher's pace of doing internal business by sending a long manuscript via fax.

Many times writers and illustrators devote their attention to submitting material to editors or art directors, then fail to follow up on overdue responses because they feel the situation is out of their hands. By tracking those submissions still under consideration and then following up, you may be able to refresh a buyer's memory who temporarily forgot about your submission, or revise a troublesome point to make your work more enticing to him. At the very least you will receive a definite "no," thereby freeing you to send your material to another market.

It is especially important to keep track of submissions when you are submitting simultaneously. This way if you get an offer on that manuscript, you will be able to notify the other publishers to withdraw your work from consideration.

When recording your submissions be sure to include the date they were sent, the business and contact name, and any enclosures that were inserted such as samples of writing, artwork or photography. Keep copies of the article or manuscript as well as related correspondence for easier follow up. When you sell rights to a manuscript or artwork you can "close" your file by noting the date the material was accepted, what rights were purchased, the publication date and payment.

Agents

Many children's writers and illustrators, especially those who are just beginning, are confused about whether to utilize the services of an agent. The decision about obtaining an agent's services is strictly one that each writer or illustrator must decide for himself. There are some who are confident enough with their own negotiation skills and feel acquiring an agent is not in their best interest. Still, others scare easily at the slightest mention of business and are not willing to sacrifice valuable writing or illustrating time for the time it takes to market their work. Before you put any thought into whether to contact an agent, read on to become familiar with what an agent can — and cannot — do.

There is enough demand for children's material that breaking into children's publishing without an agent is easier than breaking in with adult titles. In fact, many agents avoid working with children's books because traditionally low advances and trickling royalty payments over long periods of time make children's books less lucrative to deal with. Acquiring an agent to market short stories is next to impossible — there just isn't enough of a financial incentive for an agent to be interested.

One benefit of having an agent, though, is it may expedite the process of getting your work looked at, especially with publishers who don't accept unagented submissions. If an agent has a good reputation and submits your manuscript to an editor, that manuscript may actually bypass the first-read stage (which is done by editorial assistants and junior editors) and end up on that editor's desk sooner.

Illustrators who live elsewhere often seek representatives based in New York City when they want their work shown to New York City publishers.

When agreeing to have a reputable agent represent you, keep in mind he should be familiar with the needs of the current market and evaluate your manuscript/artwork accordingly. He should also be able to determine the quality of your piece and whether it is salable. Upon selling your manuscript, your agent should be able to negotiate a favorable contract. Also, sometimes royalty statements can be confusing; your agent should be able to clear up any questions you have about monetary payments. One advantage to having an agent be the "go-between" is his acting as the bad guy during the negotiations. This allows you, as an individual, to preserve your good faith with the publisher.

Keep in mind, though, that however reputable the agent is, he has limitations. An agent's representation does not guarantee sale of your work. It just means he sees potential in your writing or art. Though an agent may offer criticism or advice on how to improve your book, he cannot make you a better writer or give you fame.

Agents typically charge a 15 percent commission from the sale of your writing or art material. Such fees will be taken from your advance and royalty earnings. If your agent sells foreign rights to your work, he will deduct 20 percent because he will most likely be dealing with an overseas agent with whom he must split the fee.

Some agents offer reading services. If you are a new writer, you will probably be charged a fee of less than $75. Many times, if an agent agrees to represent you, the fee will be reimbursed (though not always). If you take advantage of an agency's critique service, you will probably pay a range of $25-200 depending on the length of the manuscript. The purpose of a critique service is not to polish the manuscript, but to offer advice based on the agent's knowledge of what sells in juvenile publishing. Prior to engaging in a reading or critique service, you should find out up front what results to expect. Watch out for agencies that derive most of their income from reading and critique services.

Unfortunately, there are "quacks" in this business who are more interested in earning their money from services than from selling books. Other standard fees incurred from an agent include miscellaneous expenses such as photocopying, phone bills, postage or messenger services. Before signing a contract with an agent, be sure you know exactly what the terms are, such as what rate of commission is charged and what expenses you will be expected to pay.

Be advised that not every agent is open to representing a writer or artist who doesn't have some sort of track record. Your manuscript or artwork, and query or cover letters, must be attractive and professional looking. Your first impression must be that of an organized, articulate person.

Feel free to investigate an agent before contacting him. Determine how familiar—and successful—he is with selling to children's publishers. For a detailed directory of literary agents and art/photo reps refer to *Guide to Literary Agents and Art/Photo Reps* (Writer's Digest Books).

Negotiating contracts and royalties

Negotiation is a two-way street on which, hopefully, both the author/artist and editor/art director will feel mutual satisfaction prior to signing a contract.

Book publishers pay authors and artists in royalties, or rather, a percentage of either the wholesale or retail price of each book sold. Usually with large publishing houses, before the book is published, the author or artist receives an advance issued against future royalties. Half of the advance amount is issued upon signing the book contract. The other half is issued when the book is finished. For illustrations, one-third of the advance should be collected upon signing the contract; one-third upon delivery of sketches; and one-third upon delivery of finished art. After your book has sold enough copies to earn back your advance, you will start to get royalty checks. Some publishers hold a reserve against returns. In other words, a percentage of royalties is held back in case books are returned. If you have such a reserve clause in your contract, make sure to be informed of the exact percentage of total sales that will be withheld and the time period the publisher will hold this money. You should be reimbursed this amount after a reasonable time period, such as a year. Royalty percentages vary with each publisher, but there are standard ranges.

For picture books, the writer and illustrator (if two people) should each be able to get $2,000-5,000 advances. Royalties range from 6-10% and are usually split equally between the writer and illustrator. A writer who also does the illustrations usually gets a higher advance ($4,000-7,000) and the full royalty.

Writers of chapter books or middle grade novels should expect royalties of 5-10% and an advance of $3,000-6,000. Illustrators who do 10-15 black and white illustrations and a color cover for these books should get a $3,000-5,000 advance and 2-5% royalties.

Authors of young adult novels can expect a $3,500-6,000 advance with royalty rates of 2-5%. Usually, an artist is paid one flat fee to do one color illustration for the cover.

For all types of books, royalty rates for hardcover books should be higher than percentage rates for paperbacks.

One way to determine a fair advance is to multiply the print run by the cover price and then multiply that figure with the royalty percentage. If you feel the advance is too low, ask for higher royalties.

Price structures for magazines are based on a per-word rate or range for a specific length of article.

Artists have a few more variables to contend with prior to contracting their services. Payment for illustrations can be set by such factors as whether the piece will be rendered in black and white or four-color, how many illustrations are to be purchased and the artist's prior experience. Determine an hourly rate by using the annual salary of a staff artist doing similar work in an economically similar geographic area (try to find an artist willing to share this information), then dividing that salary by 52 (the number of weeks in a year) and again by 40 (the number of hours in a work week). You will want to add your overhead expenses such as rent, utilities, art supplies, etc. to this answer by multiplying your hourly rate by 2.5. Research, again, may have to come into play to be sure your rate is competitive within the marketplace.

Once you make a sale you will probably sign a contract. A contract is an agreement between two or more parties that specifies the fee to be paid, services to be rendered, deadlines, rights purchased and, for artists, return (or not) of original artwork. Most publishers have a standard contract they offer to writers and illustrators. The specifics (such as royalty rates, advances, delivery dates, etc.) are typed in after negotiations. Though it is okay to conduct negotiations over the telephone, be sure to secure a tangible written contract once both parties have agreed on terms. Do not depend on oral stipulations; written contracts protect both parties from misunderstandings and faulty memories. Look out for clauses that may not be in your best interest, such as "work-for-hire." When you do work for hire, you give up all rights to your creations. There are several reputable children's magazines that buy all rights only, and many writers and illustrators believe it is worth the concession in order to break into the field. However, once you've entered the field of book publishing, it's in your best interest to try to keep the rights to your work.

Be sure you know whether or not your contract contains an option clause. This clause requires the author to give the publisher a first look at his next work before marketing it to other publishers. Though it is editorial etiquette to give the publisher the first chance at publishing your next work, be wary of statements in the contract which could trap you. Don't allow the publisher to consider the next project for more than 30 days and be specific about what type of work should actually be considered "next work" (i.e., if the book under contract is a young adult novel, specify that the publisher will only receive an exclusive look at the next young adult novel).

If there are clauses that appear vague or confusing, get some legal advice. The time and money invested in counseling up front could protect you from more serious problems down the road. If you have an agent, he will review any contract.

Rights for the writer and illustrator

A copyright is a form of protection provided to creators of original works, published or unpublished. The Copyright Act of 1976 (which went into effect January 1, 1978) states that work is protected as soon as it's created.

So that the United States may have copyright relations with 80 other countries, in March 1989 Congress voted to amend our copyright law and ratify the

Berne Convention, the major international copyright convention. Because of this, most works created after March 1989 that are protected by United States copyright are also protected under the laws of most other countries.

The international recognition of copyright protection provided in the Berne Convention prevents foreign piracy of works copyrighted in the U.S. and allows prosecution of foreign copyright infringers in foreign courts. (Principal countries that haven't yet adopted the convention are China and the Soviet Union.)

From the second works are created, they are protected by the copyright law. However, in order to proceed with an infringement lawsuit, the work must be registered. A person who infringes upon a registered copyright is subject to greater liabilities, even when no damages or profits are made as a result of the infringement. Some feel a copyright notice should be included on all work, registered or not. Others feel it is not necessary and a copyright notice will only confuse publishers about whether the material is registered (acquiring rights to previously registered material is a more complicated process). Most publishers are reputable and will not steal your work; therefore, including a copyright notice on unregistered work is not necessary. However, if you don't feel your work is safe without it, it is your right to include it. Including a copyright notice — © (your name, year of work) — should ensure your work against plagiarism.

Registration is a legal formality intended to make your copyright public record. As stated above, registration of work is necessary to file any infringement suits. Also, registration can help you win more money in a court case. By registering work within three months of publication or before an infringement occurs, you are eligible to collect statutory damages and attorney's fees. If you register later than three months after publication, you will qualify only for actual damages and profits.

Keep in mind that ideas and concepts are not copyrightable, but rather the expression of those ideas and concepts. A character type or basic plot outline is not subject to a copyright infringement lawsuit. Also, titles, names, short phrases or slogans, and lists of contents are not subject to copyright protection, though titles and names may be protected through the Trademark Office.

In general, copyright protection ensures you, the writer or illustrator, have the power to decide how the work is used and that you receive payment for each use. Not only does a copyright protect you, it essentially encourages you to create new works by guaranteeing you the power to sell rights to their use in the marketplace. As the copyright holder you can print, reprint or copy your work; sell or distribute copies of your work; or prepare derivative works such as plays, collages or recordings. The Copyright Law is designed to protect a writer's or illustrator's work (copyrighted on or after January 1, 1978) for his lifetime plus 50 years. If you collaborate with someone else on a written or artistic project, the copyright will last for the lifetime of the last survivor plus 50 years. A writer's heirs may hold a copyright for an additional 50 years. After that, the work becomes public domain. In addition, works created anonymously or under a pseudonym are protected for 100 years, or 75 years after publication, whichever is shorter. Incidentally, this latter rule is also true of work-for-hire agreements. Under work-for-hire you relinquish your copyright to your "employer." Try to avoid agreeing to such terms.

For work published before January 1, 1978, the copyright protection is valid for 28 years with an option to renew the last year of the first term. For most copyrights, the law has extended renewal terms from 28 to 47 years, so these works can now be protected for up to 75 years.

For members of the Society of Children's Book Writers, in-depth information about copyrights and the law is available. Send a self-addressed, stamped envelope to the Society of Children's Book Writers (P.O. Box 66296, Mar Vista Station, Los Angeles CA 90066) and request their brochure, "Copyright Facts for Writers."

For more information about the proper procedure to register works, contact the Register of Copyrights, Copyright Office, Library of Congress, Washington D.C. 20559. The forms available are **TX** for writing (books, articles, etc.); **VA** for pictures (photographs, illustrations); and **PA** for plays and music. To learn more about how to go about using the copyright forms, request a copy of Circular I on Copyright Basics. All of these forms are free. Send the completed registration form along with the stated fee and a copy of the work to the Copyright Office. You can register a group of articles or illustrations if:

- the group is assembled in order, such as in a notebook;
- the works bear a single title, such as "Works by (your name)";
- they are the work of one writer or artist;
- the material is the subject of a single claim to copyright.

It is the publisher's responsibility to register your book for copyright. If you have previously registered the same material, you must inform your editor and supply the previous copyright information. Otherwise, the publisher cannot register the book in its published form.

The copyright law specifies that writers generally sell one-time rights to their work unless they and the buyer agree otherwise in writing. Be forewarned that many editors aren't aware of this. Many publications will want more exclusive rights from you than just one-time usage of your work; some will even require you to sell all rights to your work. Be sure that you are monetarily compensated for the additional rights you give up to your material. It is always to your benefit to retain as much control as possible over your work. Writers who only give up limited rights to their work can then sell reprint rights to other publications, foreign rights to international publications, or even movie rights, should the opportunity arise. Likewise, artists can sell their illustrations to other book and magazine markets as well as to paper-product companies who may use an image on a calendar or greeting card. In some cases, illustrators are now selling original artwork after it has been published. There are now galleries throughout the United States that display the works of children's illustrators.

You can see that exercising more control over ownership of your work gives you a greater marketing edge for resale. If you do have to give up all rights to a work, think about the price you are being offered to determine whether it will compensate you for the loss of other sales.

Rights acquired through sale of a book manuscript are explained in each publisher's contract. Take the time to read through relevant clauses to be sure you understand what each contract is specifying prior to signing. Make sure your contract contains a clause allowing all rights to revert back to you in the event the publisher goes out of business. The rights you will most often be selling to publishers and periodicals in the marketplace are:

- One-time rights—The buyer has no guarantee that he is the first to use a piece. One-time permission to run a written or illustrated work is acquired, then the rights revert back to the creator.

● First rights—The creator offers rights to use the work for the first time in any medium. All other rights remain with the creator. When material is excerpted from a soon-to-be-published book for use in a newspaper or periodical, first serial rights are also purchased.

● First North American serial rights—This is similar to first rights, except that publishers who distribute both in the U.S. and Canada will stipulate these rights to ensure that a publication in the other country won't come out with simultaneous usage of the same work.

● Second serial (reprint) rights—In this case newspapers and magazines are granted the right to reproduce a work that already has appeared in another publication. These rights also are purchased by a newspaper or magazine editor who wants to publish part of a book after the book has been published (such as an excerpt from a just-published biography). The proceeds from reprint rights are often split 50/50 between the author and his publishing company.

● Simultaneous rights—Use of such rights occurs among magazines with circulations that don't overlap, such as many religious publications. Many spiritual stories or illustrations are appropriate for a variety of denominational publications. Be sure you submit to a publication that allows simultaneous submissions, and be sure to state in your cover letter to the editor that the submission is being considered elsewhere (to a non-competing market).

● All rights—Rights such as these are purchased by publishers who pay premium usage fees, have an exclusive format, or have other book or magazine interests from which the purchased work can generate more "mileage" for their interests. (Some magazines that purchase all rights to artwork use the same work again several years later.) When the writer or illustrator sells all rights to a market he no longer has any say in who acquires rights to use his piece. Synonymous with purchase of all rights is the term "work-for-hire." Under such an agreement the creator of a work gives away all rights—and his copyright—to the company buying his work. Try to avoid such agreements; they're not in your best interest. If a market is insistent upon acquiring all rights to your work, see if you can negotiate for the rights to revert back to you after a reasonable period of time. It can't hurt to ask. If they're agreeable to such a proposal, be sure you get it in writing.

● Foreign serial rights—Be sure before you market to foreign publications that you have only sold North American—not worldwide—serial rights to previous markets. If not, you are free to market to publications you think may be interested in using material that has appeared in a U.S. or North American-based periodical.

● Syndication rights—This is a division of serial rights. For example, if a syndicate prints portions of a book in installments in its newspapers, it would be syndicating second serial rights. The syndicate would receive a commission and leave the remainder to be split between the author and publisher.

● Subsidiary rights—These are rights, other than book rights, and should be specified in a book contract. Subsidiary rights include serial rights, dramatic rights, book club rights or translation rights. The contract should specify what percentage of profits from sales of these rights go to the author and publisher.

● Dramatic, television and motion picture rights—During the specified time

the interested party tries to sell the story to a producer or director. Many times options are renewed because the selling process can be lengthy.
• Display rights—Watch out for these. They're also known as "Electronic Publishing Rights" or "Data, Storage and Retrieval." Usually listed under subsidiary rights, they're not clear. They refer to many means of publication not yet invented. If a display rights clause is listed in your contract, try to negotiate its elimination. Otherwise, demand the clause be restricted to things designed to be read only. By doing this, you maintain your rights to use your work for things such as games and interactive software.

Business records

It is imperative to keep accurate business records in order to determine if you are making a profit as a writer or illustrator. You will definitely want to keep a separate bank account and ledger apart from your personal finances. Also, if writing or illustrating is secondary to another freelance career, maintain separate business records from that career.

If you're just starting your career, you will most likely be accumulating some business expenses prior to showing any profit. To substantiate your income and expenses to the IRS be sure to keep all invoices, cash receipts, sales slips, bank statements, cancelled checks plus receipts related to travel expenses and entertaining clients. For entertainment expenditures you also will want to record the date, place and purpose of the business meeting as well as gas mileage. Be sure to file all receipts in chronological order; if you maintain a separate file for each month of the year it will provide for easier retrieval of records at year's end. Keeping receipts is important for all purchases, big and small. Don't take the small purchases for granted. Enough of them can result in a rather substantial monetary figure.

When setting up a single-entry bookkeeping system you will want to record income and expenses separately. It may prove easier to use some of the subheads that appear on Schedule C (the form used for recording income from a business) of the 1040 tax form. This way you can transfer information more easily onto the tax form when filing your return. In your ledger you will want to include a description of each transaction—date, source of income (or debts from business purchases), description of what was purchased or sold; whether pay was by cash, check or credit card, and the amount of the transaction.

You don't have to wait until January 1 to start keeping records, either. The moment you first make a business-related purchase or sell an article, book manuscript or illustrations you will need to begin tracking your profits and losses. If you keep records from January 1 to December 31 you are using a calendar-year accounting method. Any other accounting period is known as a fiscal year. You also can choose between two types of accounting methods—the cash method and the accrual method. The cash method is used more often: You record income when it is received and expenses when they are disbursed. Under the accrual method you report income at the time you earn it rather than when it is actually received. Similarly, expenses are recorded at the time they are incurred rather than when you actually pay them. If you choose this method you will need to keep separate records for "accounts receivable" and "accounts payable."

Taxes

To successfully (and legally) compete in the business of writing or illustrating you must have knowledge of what income you should report and deductions you can claim. Before you can do this however, you must prove to the IRS that you are in business to make a profit, that your writing or illustrations are not merely a hobby. Under the Tax Reform Act of 1986 it was determined that you should show a profit for three years out of a five-year period to attain professional status. What does the IRS look for as proof of your professionalism? Keeping accurate financial records (see previous section on business records), maintaining a business bank account separate from your personal account, the time you devote to your profession and whether it is your main or secondary source of income, and your history of profits and losses. The amount of training you have invested in your field is also a contributing factor to your professional status, as well as your expertise in the field.

If your business is unincorporated, you will fill out tax information on Schedule C of Form 1040. If you're unsure of what deductions you can take, request the appropriate IRS publication containing this information. Under the Tax Reform Act, only 80 percent (formerly it was 100 percent) of business meals, entertainment and related tips and parking charges are deductible. Other deductibles allowed on Schedule C include: capital expenditures (such as a computer), car expenses for business-related trips, professional courses and seminars, depreciation of office equipment, dues and publications and miscellaneous expenses, such as postage used for business needs, etc.

If you're working out of a home office, a portion of your mortgage (or rent), related utilities, property taxes, repair costs and depreciation can be deducted as business expenses. To qualify though, your office must be used only for business activities. It can't double as a family room during nonbusiness hours. To determine what portion of business deductions can be taken, simply divide the square footage of your business area into the total square footage of your house. You will want to keep a log of what business activities, and sales and business transactions occur each day; the IRS may want to see records to substantiate your home office deductions. For more information on home office deductions, consult Publication 587 (Business Use of Your Home) from the IRS.

The method of paying taxes on income not subject to withholding is your "estimated tax." If you expect to owe more than $500 at year's end and if the total amount of income tax that will be withheld during the year will be less than 90% of the tax shown on the previous year's return, you will generally make estimated tax payments. Estimated tax payments are made in four equal installments due on April 15, June 15, September 15 and January 15. For more information, request Publication 505, Self-Employment Tax.

Depending on your net income you may be liable for a Social Security tax. This is a tax designed for those who don't have Social Security withheld from their paychecks. You're liable if your net income is $400 or more per year. Net income is the difference between your income and allowable business deductions. Request Schedule SE, Computation of Social Security Self-Employment Tax, if you qualify.

If completing your income tax return proves to be a complex affair, call the IRS for assistance. In addition to walk-in centers, the IRS has various publications to instruct you in various facets of preparing a tax return.

Insurance

As a self-employed professional you need to be aware of what health and business insurance coverage is available to you. Unless you're a Canadian who is covered by national health insurance or a fulltime freelancer covered by your spouse's policy, health insurance will no doubt be one of your biggest expenses. Under the terms of the Consolidated Omnibus Budget Reconciliation Act (COBRA) of 1985, if you leave a job with health benefits, you are entitled to continue that coverage for at least 18 months at the insurer's cost plus a small administration charge. Eventually, though, you will have to search for your own health plan. Also be mindful of the fact you may also need disability and life insurance.

Disability insurance is offered through many private insurance companies and state governments, and pays a monthly fee that covers living and business expenses during periods of long-term recuperation from a health problem. The amount of money paid monthly is based on the writer's or artist's annual earnings.

Before contacting any insurance representative, talk to other writers or illustrators to find out about insurance companies they could recommend. If you belong to a writer's or artist's organization, be sure to contact them to determine if any insurance coverage for professionals is offered to members. Such group coverage may prove less expensive and yield more comprehensive coverage than an individual policy.

Building business—and creative—skills

Now that you have an idea of what it takes to set up your freelance writing or illustrating practice, you may want to consult further publications to read in depth about business, writing or illustrating specialties you don't feel quite as comfortable with. Many of the publications recommended here incorporate business-oriented material with information about how to write or illustrate more creatively and skillfully.

Books of interest

The Artist's Friendly Legal Guide. Conner, Floyd; Karlen, Peter; Perwin, Jean; Spatt, David M. North Light Books, 1991.
The Children's Picture Book: How to Write It, How to Sell It. Roberts, Ellen E.M. Writer's Digest Books, 1984.
Getting Started as a Freelance Illustrator or Designer. Fleischman, Michael. North Light Books.
Guide to Writing for Children. Yolen, Jane. The Writer, 1989.
How to Sell Your Photographs & Illustrations. Gordon, Elliott & Barbara. North Light Books.
How to Write, Illustrate, and Design Children's Books. Gates, Frieda. Lloyd-Simone Publishing Company, 1986.
How to Write a Children's Book & Get It Published. Seuling, Barbara. Charles Scribner's Sons, 1991.

How to Write and Illustrate Children's Books. Bicknell, Treld Pelkey; Trotman, Felicity, eds. North Light Books, 1988.
Illustrating Children's Books. Hands, Nancy S. Prentice Hall Press, 1986.
Success Kits for Artists and Illustrators. Crawford, Tad. North Light Books.
The Writer's Essential Desk Reference. Neff, Glenda, ed. Writer's Digest Books, 1991.
A Writer's Guide to a Children's Book Contract. Flower, Mary. Fern Hill Books, 1988.
Writing Books for Children. Yolen, Jane. The Writer, Inc., 1983.
Writing Books for Young People. Giblin, James Cross. The Writer, Inc., 1990.
Writing for Children & Teenagers. Wyndham, Lee & Madison, Arnold. Writer's Digest Books, 1988.
Writing with Pictures: How to Write and Illustrate Children's Books. Shulevitz, Uri. Watson-Guptill Publications, 1985.

Publications of interest
Byline. Preston, Marcia, ed. P.O. Box 130596, Edmond OK 73013.
Book Links. American Library Association. 50 E. Huron St. Chicago IL 60611.
Children's Book Insider. Backes, Laura, ed. 254 E. Mombasha Road, Monroe NY 10950.
The Five Owls. 2004 Sheridan Ave. S., Minneapolis MN 55405.
The Horn Book Magazine. Silvey, Anita, ed. The Horn Book, Inc., 14 Beacon St., Boston MA 02108.
The Lion and the Unicorn: A Critical Journal of Children's Literature. The Johns Hopkins University Press—Journals Publishing Division, Suite 275, 701 W. 40th St., Baltimore MD 21211-2190.
Once Upon a Time . . . . Baird, Audrey, ed. 553 Winston Court, St. Paul MN 55118.
Society of Children's Book Writers Bulletin. Mooser, Stephen; Oliver, Lin, eds. Society of Children's Book Writers, Box 296, Mar Vista Station, Los Angeles CA 90066.

Important Market Listing Information

● *Listings are based on questionnaires, phone calls and updated copy. They are not advertisements nor are markets reported here necessarily endorsed by the editor of this book.*
● *Information in the listings comes directly from the company and is as accurate as possible, but situations change and needs fluctuate between the publication of this directory and the time you use it.*
● **Children's Writer's & Illustrator's Market** *reserves the right to exclude any listing that does not meet its requirements.*

Book Publishers

Enthusiasm for the promising future of children's books reached an all-time high in 1990. After all, the rate of growth for children's books was higher that year than for any other type of books. Statistics supplied by the American Association of Publishers show in 1990 juvenile hardcover sales were up 19.1% from 1989; paperback sales increased 20.7%. Comparing these increases to the increases in adult books (5.5% hardcover; 6.9% paperback) is another indicator of the phenomenal growth of children's books. Over the last 10 years, new book titles for children have increased from 2,500 per year to 4,500 per year.

The question now, though, is will the boom last? Hard times have hit everywhere because of the 1991 Persian Gulf War, the recession, and federal budget cuts. Like everything else, the children's book industry has been affected—it's just a question of how much. Experts in the field assure a strong demand for children's books in the future. However, a "leveling off" is foreseen.

Library and school sales down, retail sales up

Unfortunately, the primary markets for hardcover books, libraries and schools, have been victims of federal budget cuts. There is less money to buy books. Also, librarians are having to dip into their book money to purchase other educational supplements such as videotapes and computer software. James Giblin, former children's publisher at Clarion (and close-up celebrity— see page 62) thinks in this instance, a delayed recession is likely. He explains that last year's books were bought on budgets approved before the recession. So 1992 is when publishers will start feeling the effects.

On the brighter side, retail sales of children's books are up. Part of this is attributed to the increase in the number of children's booksellers—particularly children's-only booksellers. There are approximately 450 children's bookstores in the country today, compared with about 50 ten years ago. Chain and independent adult bookstores are also stocking kids' books at record rates.

Unlike libraries and schools which depend on outside funding, retail outlets get their revenues directly from the individual consumer. One group of major consumers is baby boom parents who are now raising young children. Since today's parents are more likely to have more education than in the past, their concern for their children's literacy and education has resulted in skyrocketing retail sales—even in a recession. (Keep in mind that even in the days of the Depression, book sales remained strong.)

Considering the fact children's books are showing up on national bestseller lists, it's fair to say they are actually competing with adult titles. Margaret Frith, president of The Putnam & Grosset Book Group, said in *Publishers Weekly*, "When eight books for children appear on the *New York Times* bestseller list in one week, you've got to know that something is in the air."

Publishers are quite aware of what's going on in the retail market. Unfortunately, the increased competition with adult titles may adversely affect opportunities for unpublished children's writers. To assure sales, children's publishers are luring established big-name children's writers and illustrators with exorbitant sums of money. Of course, because of this, there's less money to develop new authors. Also, the demands for children's books in recent years has resulted in overpublishing. Some feel the increased quantity of titles has caused the overall quality of children's books to deteriorate. Maria Modugno, editor-in-chief of children's books at Little, Brown & Co. told *Publishers Weekly,* "Lots of books out there have been published only in response to the boom, and that can't continue indefinitely." Apparently, booksellers are not standing for it. They're being much more selective with the overwhelming amount of titles offered on frontlists—so much that they don't always buy all the frontlist titles. Publishers can survive this by resting on the laurels of their backlists. (Children's titles are far less ephemeral than adult titles.) But for aspiring writers and illustrators, it's going to be a case of "Survival of the Fittest." The bottom line is this: The market for freelance work in the children's book industry is healthy, but only for quality work that fits into appropriate categories.

Whole Language is here!

Remember Dick, Jane and Spot? To the delight of people in the educational field, these superficial characters, long used to teach young children to read, are in grave danger of becoming extinct. Actually, it was the late Theodor Geisel (better known as Dr. Seuss) who originally waged war against Dick and Jane decades ago. His 1957 book, *The Cat in the Hat* is credited with revolutionizing children's reading habits. "That is what I am proudest of, that I had something to do with getting rid of Dick and Jane," he said in 1982. Now Whole Language curriculums, where trade books are used instead of textbooks to teach in the classroom, are currently being implemented nationwide. Teachers are opting to buy trade books from booksellers rather than textbooks. In fact, 30% of all children's-only bookstore sales are to teachers. And it is teachers who can be credited with popularizing titles such as *The True Story of the Three Little Pigs* and *Chicka Chicka Boom Boom.*

Nonfiction books have greatly benefited from the Whole Language movement. Unlike in the past, historical nonfiction no longer contains invented dialogue or fictionalized accounts of events. They have proven to be valuable tools for the classroom. But history and literature are not the only subjects being taught with trade books. Science can also be taught. Over 50% of the pop-up books published by Intervisual Communications, Inc. are nonfiction. ICI publishes a Young Science series which better illustrates difficult concepts (such as outer space). Nature and environmental issues are other subjects children are interested in. Also, fictionalized nonfiction (teaching facts within a fictional setting), such as the *Magic Schoolbus* series by Joanna Cole, is an effective resource for teaching science.

In light of the current literature-based curriculums, writers need to become familiar with how to go about composing a book appropriate for the classroom. Children are not patient with boring text (that's why trade books are supposed to be more effective than textbooks), so make sure to write with an upbeat and interesting tone. Humor is a nice touch, as are little-known anecdotes and pieces of trivia.

Multiculturalism

There's a need to create awareness of other cultures among children. Like everybody else, minority children like to see themselves in books, and they might not view themselves as important if they don't. In the last few years, there has been a great demand for books with ethnic themes. Minority groups want to be represented, while non-minorities seek books to teach their kids about other races and religions. In the September 9, 1991 issue of *Newsweek*, Malcolm Jones Jr. writes in an article examining multicultural children's literature: "No one wants to fire the traditional heroes and heroines of children's literature. It's just that, well, there've been complaints. From Birmingham, Alabama (where the schools are 80% black) to California (where nonwhites will be in the majority around the year 2000), the largely lily-white world of children's books has been found lacking. The traditional fare, critics say, doesn't begin to reflect the complicated, diverse world that children live in." In his article, Jones gladly says the most recent trend in children's literature is multiculturalism. He goes on to write, "Whatever it's called, the phenomenon is plain: we aren't in Kansas anymore." Ample opportunity exists for writers and illustrators interested in ethnic themes. Illustrators able to draw and paint ethnic children are especially in demand, and are practically guaranteed a spot in the field. Multicultural characters should be the main protagonists for entire books, and tokenism should be avoided. Though there is a huge demand for these books, multicultural titles make up only about 10% of what's published for children.

Other categories with needs

Needs vary in the marketplace. Though there seems to be enough main-stream fiction, some specialized categories are open to expansion. For example, religious publishers of all faiths are actively developing children's lines. Creative, imaginative Christian books (especially picture books and juvenile fiction) are emerging. A few years ago most Jewish children's books were poorly produced. Today, high-quality children's books with Jewish themes are now available from both major trade houses and Jewish publishers.

Seasonal and holiday books are especially popular among children. In fact, booksellers have had trouble acquiring sufficient quantities of seasonal books from publishers because of the high demand. Christmas books, most with secular plots, seem to be the choice among holiday-loving kids. Though there are many in print, there always seems to be room for one more.

Appropriate material for special needs children, such as those with Down's Syndrome, is desperately needed. Barnes & Noble now includes a "Children with Special Needs" section in 700 of its 800 stores. Steve Riggio, the executive vice president and chief operating officer of Barnes & Noble, launched the project, which was inspired by his own difficulties at obtaining material for his disabled child. He and his staff were only able to find a little more than four dozen titles, most published by independent presses. Riggio says the greatest need is for books parents can read to their children.

Who's reading?

The birth rate still remains high and picture books are continuing to sell well. Offspring of the current baby boom are starting to grow up, and early chapter books are coming into prominence because these children are starting to read. Middle readers will be next in line. Some experts predict that as the children of the baby boom reach pre-teen age, young adult titles, now suffering, will once again be in demand. However, others are not so sure. There are questions about what a young adult book is and what a young adult section should consist of. Pre-teens and teenagers are thought to be more sophisticated today than in the past; they don't want books that look childish. Many bypass YA titles altogether and turn to adult titles for recreational reading. To combat this, suggestions have been made to publish YA books with "adult" covers and market them near the adult sections. Time will tell on the YA issue.

Subsidy publishing

Some writers who are really determined to get their work into print, but who receive rejections from all the royalty publishers, look to subsidy publishers as an option. Subsidy publishers ask writers to pay all or part of the costs of producing a book. You will notice some of the listings in this section give percentages of subsidy-published material. Such listings are marked with a solid block (■).

Aspiring writers should strongly consider working only with publishers who pay. They will be active in marketing your work because they profit only through these efforts. Subsidy publishers make their money from writers who pay to have their books published; so be prepared to do your own marketing and promotion. In fact, some operations are more interested in the contents of your wallet than the contents of your book. Though there are reputable subsidy publishers, those considering such services should take a "buyer beware" attitude. Any contracts offered by these houses should be carefully inspected by a lawyer or someone qualified to analyze these types of documents.

If you're interested in publishing your book just to share it with friends and relatives, self publishing is a viable option. In self publishing, an author oversees all of the details of book production. A local printer may be able to help you, or you may want to arrange some type of desk-top computer publishing.

Don't write to order

"Write what you know," or "Write about something that interests you," is the most common advice offered by established authors. Writing about a subject just because there's a demand for it doesn't warrant all the time spent putting it together unless you are truly and sincerely excited about the topic. Otherwise, don't expect your readers to get excited about (or for that matter, finish reading) the material. The same thing goes for illustrators. Creating artwork for children is more challenging than one might think. It's important to draw and paint with the children in mind—not adults. Be sure you are able to show children interacting with each other. Don't underestimate the intelligence of children—they're quick to pick up on substandard material.

And finally, don't treat writing for children as a starter course into the world of "real writing." Creating a children's book is *not* a quick and easy project. Actually, aspects of the craft make writing for this audience more difficult. Writing for children *is* real writing, and what follows in this section are listings of *real* markets—one of which might someday make your dreams of being published a reality.

ADDISON-WESLEY PUBLISHING CO., Trade Dept., Route 128, Reading MA 01867. (617)944-3700. Book publisher. Estab. 1942. Associate Editor: John Bell. Publishes 6 middle reader titles/year. 33% of books by first-time authors.
Nonfiction: Middle readers: science, hobbies, nature/environment. "All of our children's books are science activity books."
How to Contact/Writers: Nonfiction: Query. Reports on queries/mss in 6 weeks. Publishes a book 2 years after acceptance. Will consider simultaneous submissions.
Illustration: Number of illustrations used for fiction and nonfiction: middle readers—90 full page. Editorial will review ms/illustration packages. Prefers "4-color representational art for covers and b&w for interior."
How to Contact/Illustrators: Ms/illustration packages: "Query first." Illustrations only: Send "résumé and tearsheets." Original artwork returned at job's completion.
Terms: Pays authors in royalties based on retail price. Pays for illustrators: by the project. Sends galleys to authors; dummies to illustrators. Book catalog for 7 × 10 SASE.
Tips: The writer and/or illustrator have the best chance of selling "science activity books *only*. Increasing competition in our field (science projects) means finding more focused and more imaginative books."

ADVOCACY PRESS, div. of The Girls Club of Santa Barbara, Box 236, Santa Barbara CA 93102. (805)962-2728. FAX: (805)963-3580. Book publisher. Editorial Contact: Kathy Araujo. Publishes 3-5 picture books/year; 2-4 young reader titles/year. 25% of books by first-time authors.
Fiction: Picture books and young readers: gender equity, concepts in self-esteem; young adults: gender equity, life planning. "We are only allowed to publish books that are relevant to Equity (equal opportunity) issues. Two series: self-esteem concept stories and little known women in history "role models." Recently published titles include *Mother Nature Nursery Rhymes*, (birth-6 years, fiction/rhymes); *Mimi Takes Charge* and *Mimi Makes a Splash*, by Agnes Rosensteihl (ages 3-8, fiction/graphic picture book series).
How to Contact/Writers: Fiction/nonfiction: Submit outline/synopsis and sample chapters. Reports on queries/mss in 2 weeks. Will consider simultaneous submissions. Send for editorial policy.
Illustration: Number of illustrations used for fiction/nonfiction: picture books—30; middle readers—200; young adults—200. Editorial will review ms/illustration packages. Contact Penny Paine, marketing director. Will review artwork for future assignments.
How to Contact/Illustrators: Ms/illustration packages: Query first. Illustrations only: query with samples. Reports in 1 month.
Terms: Illustrators paid by the project. Sends galleys to authors; dummies to illustrators. Book catalog/manuscript guidelines available for #10 SASE.

✱ *The asterisk before a listing indicates the listing is new in this edition.*

■**AEGINA PRESS/UNIVERSITY EDITIONS, INC.**, 59 Oak Lane, Spring Valley, Huntington WV 25704. (304)429-7204. Book publisher. Estab. 1983. Managing Editor: Ira Herman. Publishes 3 picture books/year; 4 young reader titles/year; 4 middle reader titles/year; 6 young adult titles/year. 40% of books by first-time authors; 5% of books from agented writers; "over 50% of books are subsidy published."

Fiction: Picture books, young readers, middle readers, young adults: "Will consider most categories." Average word length: picture books—1,000; young readers—2,000; middle readers—10,000; young adults—20,000. Recently published *The Hallelujah Corncobs*, by Linda George (young reader, religious story); *Bunny Butz Sings the Blues*, by Sha Gaff (young reader, humor); *Secret Doors and Treasure*, by Robert Newbury (young adult, adventure).

Nonfiction: "Will consider all types of manuscripts, especially those usable in classrooms." Recently published *The First Families of West Virginia*, by Grace Wavra (middle readers, introductory text on archeology).

How to Contact/Writers: Fiction/nonfiction: Submit complete ms. Reports on queries in 1 week; on mss in 1 month. Publishes a book 5-6 months after acceptance. Will consider simultaneous submissions.

Illustration: Number of illustrations used for fiction: picture books—15-20; young readers—10; middle readers—5-6. Editorial will review ms/illustration packages. Primarily uses b&w artwork only.

How to Contact/Illustrators: Ms/illustration packages: query first. Illustrations only: query with samples. "We generally use our own artists. We will consider outside art. Artists should send photocopies or non-returnable samples." Reports on art samples in 1 month. Original artwork returned at job's completion.

Terms: Pays authors in royalties of 10-15% based on retail price. Pays freelance artists per project. Payment "negotiated individually for each book." Sends galleys to authors. Book catalog available for $2 and SAE and 4 first-class stamps; manuscript guidelines for #10 envelope and 1 first-class stamp.

Tips: "Focus your subject and plotline. For younger readers, stress visual imagery and fantasy characterizations. A cover letter should accompany the manuscript, which states the approximate length (not necessary for poetry). A brief synopsis of the manuscript and a listing of the author's publishing credits (if any) should also be included. Queries, sample chapters, synopses and completed manuscripts are welcome." For the future, "we plan to stress stories for middle readers and older children. Will consider all types, however."

*****AFRICAN AMERICAN IMAGES**, 9204 Commercial, Chicago IL 60617. (312)375-9682. FAX: (312)375-9349. Book publisher. Editor: Jawanza Kunjufu. Publishes 2 picture books/year; 1 young reader title/year; 1 middle reader title/year; 1 young adult title/year. 90% of books by first-time authors.

Fiction/Nonfiction: All levels: black culture.

How to Contact/Writers: Fiction/nonfiction: Submit complete ms. Reports on queries in 1 week; on mss in 3 weeks. Publishes a book 9 months after acceptance. Will consider simultaneous submissions.

Illustration: Number of illustrations used for fiction/nonfiction: picture books—20; young readers—15; middle readers—12; young adults—7. Editorial will review ms/illustration packages.

How to Contact/Illustrators: Ms/illustration packages: Send 3 chapters of ms with 1 piece of final art. Illustrations only: Send tearsheets. Reports on art samples in 2 weeks. Original artwork returned at job's completion.

Terms: Buys ms outright. Illustrator paid by the project. Book catalog, manuscript/artist's guidelines free on request.

ALADDIN BOOKS/COLLIER BOOKS FOR YOUNG READERS, Paperback imprints of Macmillan Children's Book Group, 24th floor, 866 Third Avenue, New York NY 10022. (212)702-9043. Book publisher. Estab. 1986. Editor-in-Chief: Whitney Malone. Publishes 30 picture books/year; 5 young reader titles/year; 15 middle reader titles/year; 8 young adult titles/year; 10 novelty titles/year. 5% of books by first-time authors; 40% of books from agented writers.
Fiction: Young readers: easy-to-read. Middle readers: contemporary, fantasy, romance, science fiction, sports, spy/mystery/adventure. Young adults: contemporary, fantasy, romance, science fiction, sports, spy/mystery/adventure.
Nonfiction: Middle readers, young adults: sports, self-help.
How to Contact/Writers: Fiction/nonfiction: Query; submit outline/synopsis and sample chapters. Reports on queries in 2-6 weeks; on mss in 3-4 months. Publishes a book 1-2 years after acceptance. Will consider simultaneous submissions. Book catalog and ms guidelines available for SASE.
Illustration: Editorial will review illustration package submitted by artists. Seek cover artists for paperback fiction for middle grades and young adults. No original picture books.
How to Contact/Illustrators: Illustrations only: submit résumé/tearsheets. Reports on art samples only if interested. Original artwork returned at job's completion. Pay for illustrators: by the project.
Tips: "We are currently concentrating on reprinting successful titles originally published by the hardcover imprints of the Macmillan Children's Book Group. However, we do occasionally publish original material. We will be publishing fewer young adult titles (Collier imprint) and will be concentrating on several genres for this age group: science fiction, fantasy and mysteries. The bulk of our purchases will be novelty projects: lift-the-flaps, musical books, books with an interactive component etc. Other purchases of original material are the exception, rather than the rule. We prefer that longer manuscripts be preceded by a query letter and two or three sample chapters. We do not generally consider picture book manuscripts. Please do not submit more than two short (under 15 typed pages) or one longer manuscript at one time. If you wish to confirm that your manuscript has arrived safely, please include a self-addressed stamped postcard, or send the manuscript via registered mail." Regarding illustrations: "Remember that what appeals to adults may not necessarily appeal to children." (See also Atheneum Publishers, Bradbury Press, Four Winds Press, Margaret K. McElderry Books.)

ALYSON PUBLICATIONS, INC., 40 Plympton Street, Boston MA 02118. (617)542-5679. Book publisher. Editorial Contact: Sasha Alyson. Publishes 5 (projected) picture books/year; 3 (projected) young adult titles/year. "Alyson Wonderland is a new line of kids' books. We are looking for diverse depictions of family life for children of gay and lesbian parents."
Fiction: All levels: Books aimed at the children of lesbian and gay parents. "Our YA books should deal with issues faced by kids growing up gay or lesbian." Recently published *Families*, by Michael Willhoite; *How Would You Feel If Your Dad Was Gay?*, by Ann Heron and Meredith Maran, illustrated by Kris Kovick.

Market conditions are constantly changing! If you're still using this book and it is 1993 or later, buy the newest edition of Children's Writer's & Illustrator's Market *at your favorite bookstore or order directly from Writer's Digest Books.*

How to Contact/Writers: Submit outline/synopsis and sample chapters (young adults); submit complete manuscript (picture books/young readers). Reports on queries in 3 weeks; reports on mss in 3-4 weeks.

Illustration: Send "representative art that can be *kept on file*. Good quality photocopies are OK."

Terms: Prefer to discuss terms with the authors and artists. "We *do* offer advances." Book catalog and/or manuscript guidelines free on request.

Tips: "We only publish kids' books aimed at the children of gay or lesbian parents."

AMERICAN BIBLE SOCIETY, 1865 Broadway, New York NY 10023. (212)408-1235. FAX: (212)408-1512. Book publisher. Estab. 1816. Manager of Scripture Resource Development: Charles Houser. Publishes 2 picture books/year; 4 young reader titles/year; 4 young adult titles/year. Publishes books with spiritual/religious themes based on the Bible.

Nonfiction: Picture books, young readers, middle readers, young adults: religion. Recently published *Be the Best You Can Be: Achieving your Potential Through God's Word*, (young adult, Bible passages used to address youth issues).

How to Contact/Writers: "All manuscripts developed in-house; unsolicited mss rejected."

Illustration: Number of illustrations used for nonfiction: picture book—5-10; young reader—5-60; middle reader—1-5 (cover); young adult—1-5 (cover). Editorial will review artwork for possible future assignments. "Would be more interested in artwork for teens which is influenced by the visual 'vocabulary' of videos."

How to Contact/Illustrators: Ms/illustration packages: "Query first." Illustrations only: Query with samples; arrange a personal interview to show portfolio; send "ré-

Kimanne Uhler was commissioned for this project by the American Bible Society because "she seemed particularly gifted at portraying young people from a variety of cultural and ethnic backgrounds," says Manager of Scripture Resource Development Charles Houser. "With this project," he says, "we were looking for illustrations that would show young people engaged in activities typical of their age groups and which would have a strong contemporary feel." Uhler was paid $5,500 for the entire project, which included a full-color cover and six black and white illustrations.

© American Bible Society 1991

sumés, tearsheets and promotional literature to keep; slides will be returned promptly." Reports back in 6 weeks. Factors used to determine payment ms/illustration package include "Nature and scope of project; complexity of illustration and continuity of work; number of illustrations." Pay for illustrators: Pays $200-30,000; based on fair market value. Sends two complimentary copies of pubilshed work to illustrators. Book catalog free on request.

Photography: Photographers should contact Charles Houser. Looking for "Nature, scenic, interracial, intergenerational people shots." Model/property releases required. Uses any size b&w prints; 35mm, 2¼×2¼ and 4×5 transparencies. To contact, photographers should query with samples; arrange a personal interview to show portfolio; provide résumé, promotional literature or tearsheets.

Terms: Photographers paid by the project (range: $800-5,000); per photo (range $150-1,500).

■ARCADE PUBLISHING, Subsidiary of Little Brown & Co., 141 Fifth Ave., New York NY 10010. (212)475-2633. Book publisher. President and Publisher: Richard Seaver. Publishes 8-12 picture books/year; 3-5 young reader titles/year; 5-8 middle reader titles/year. 50% of books from agented writers. 25% of books by first-time authors.

Fiction: Young readers, middle readers. Recently published *I Am the Ocean*, by Suzanna Marshak (ages 4-8, picture book).

Nonfiction: Will consider general nonfiction—"all ages." Recently published *Water's Way*, by Lisa Westberg Peters, illustrated by Ted Rand (ages 4-7, picture book).

How to Contact/Writers: Fiction: Submit complete ms. Nonfiction: Query. Reports on queries in 2 months. Publishes ms 18 months after acceptance. Will consider simultaneous submissions.

Illustration: Number of illustrations used for fiction: picture books—30; young readers—12; middle readers 8-12. Number of illustrations used for nonfiction: picture books—30; young readers—25; middle readers—25. Will review ms/illustration packages.

How to Contact/Illustrators: "*No* original art—send slides or color photocopies." Illustrations only: Send tearsheets and slides. Reports on ms/art samples in 3 weeks. Original artwork returned at job's completion.

Terms: Pays authors in variable royalties; or buys ms outright for $400-$3,000; "also flat fees per b&w books and jackets." Offers average advance of $2,500. Sends galleys to authors; book catalog for 8×10 SASE; manuscript guidelines for SASE.

ARCHWAY/MINSTREL BOOKS, Pocket Books, 1230 Avenue of the Americas, New York NY 10020. (212)698-7000. Book publisher. Editorial contact: Patricia McDonald. Publishes originals and reprints. Minstrel Books (ages 7-11) and Archway Paperbacks (ages 12-16).

Fiction: Middle readers: adventure, animal, funny/scary school stories. Young adults: contemporary, suspense/thrillers.

Nonfiction: Middle readers: animal, sports. Young adults: sports.

How to Contact/Writers: Fiction: Query, submit outline/synopsis and sample chapters.

Terms: Pays authors in royalties.

 The solid block before a listing indicates the market subsidy publishes manuscripts.

ATHENEUM PUBLISHERS, Macmillan Children's Book Group, 866 Third Ave., New York NY 10022. (212)702-2000. Book Publisher. Editorial Director: Jonathan Lanman. Editorial Contacts: Gail Paris, Marcia Marshall. Publishes 15-20 picture books/year; 4-5 young reader titles/year; 20-25 middle reader titles/year; 10-15 young adult titles/year. 20% of books by first-time authors; 50% of books from agented writers.

Fiction: Picture books: animal, contemporary, fantasy. Young readers: contemporary, fantasy. Middle readers: animal, contemporary, fantasy. Young adults: contemporary, fantasy.

Nonfiction: Picture books: animal, biography, education, history. Young readers: animal, biography, education, history. Middle readers: animal, biography, education, history. Young adults: animal, biography, education, history.

How to Contact/Writers: Fiction/nonfiction: Query; will consider complete picture book manuscript; submit outline/synopsis and sample chapters for longer works. Reports on queries 6-8 weeks; on mss 3 months. Publishes a book 18-24 months after acceptance. Will consider simultaneous submissions from previously unpublished authors; "we request that the author let us know it is a simultaneous submission."

Illustration: Editorial will review ms/illustration packages.

How to Contact/Illustrators: Ms/illustration packages: query first, 3 chapters of ms with 1 piece of final art. Illustrations only: résumé, tear sheets. Reports on art samples only if interested. Original artwork returned at job's completion.

Terms: Pays authors in royalties of 8-12½% based on retail price. Illustrators paid royalty or flat fee depending on the project. Sends galleys to authors; proofs to illustrators. Book catalog available for 9 × 12 SAE and 5 first-class stamps; manuscript guidelines for #10 SAE and 1 first-class stamp. (See also Aladdin Books/Collier Books for Young Adults, Bradbury Press, Four Winds Press, Margaret K. McElderry Books).

*THE AUTHOR'S CONNECTION PRESS, imprint of T.A.C. Press, 1 N.W. Alto Ave., P.O. Box 40, Waldo FL 32694-0040. (904)468-2939. FAX: (904)375-2552. Book publisher. Contact: Susan Phizer. Publishes 9 picture books/year; 2-3 young readers/year; 2 middle readers/year; 1-3 young adult titles/year. 60% of books by first-time authors; 2% of books from agented authors.

Fiction: Picture books: animal, health-related. Young readers: adventure, anthology, animal, contemporary, fantasy, folktales, health-related, history. Middle readers: adventure, anthology, animal, contemporary, fantasy, folktales, health-related, history, poetry, science-fiction, suspense/mystery. Young adults: adventure, anthology, contemporary, fantasy, folktales, health-related, history, science fiction, suspense/mystery. No romance, religion. Average word length: picture books — 150-300.

Nonfiction: Picture books: activity books, animal, biography, careers, health, history, hobbies, nature/environment. Young readers: activity books, animal, careers, health, history, hobbies. Middle readers: animal, careers, health, history, hobbies. Young adults: animal, careers, history, hobbies.

How to Contact/Writers: Fiction/nonfiction: Query. Reports on queries in 2 weeks; reports on mss in 1-3 months. Publishes a book 3-12 months after acceptance.

Illustration: Average number of illustrations used for fiction: picture books — 15-25.

How to Contact/Illustrators: Ms/illustration packages: Query. Illustrations only: Query with samples. Reports in 2 months. Original artwork returned at job's completion.

Terms: Pays authors royalty, outright purchase. Pays illustrators by the project or royalty. Sends galleys to authors; dummies to illustrators. Book catalog available for #10 SAE and 2 first class stamps; ms and art guidelines available for SASE.

AVON BOOKS/BOOKS FOR YOUNG READERS (AVON FLARE AND AVON CAM-ELOT), div. of The Hearst Corporation, 1350 Ave. of the Americas, New York NY 10019. (212)261-6817. Book publisher. Editorial Director: Ellen Krieger. Editorial Contact: Gwen Montgomery. Editorial Assistant: Lisa Norment. Publishes 25-30 middle reader titles/year; 20-25 young adult titles/year. 10% of books by first-time authors; 20% of books from agented writers.

Fiction: Middle readers: contemporary, problem novels, sports, spy/mystery/adventure, comedy. Young adults: contemporary, problem novels, romance. Average length: middle readers—100-150 pages; young adults—150-250 pages. Avon does not publish preschool picture books.

Nonfiction: Middle readers: hobbies, music/dance, sports. Young adults: music/dance, "growing up." Average length: middle readers—100-150 pages; young adults—150-250 pages.

How to Contact/Writers: Fiction: Submit complete ms. Nonfiction: Submit outline/synopsis and sample chapters. Reports on queries in 2 weeks; on mss in 1-2 months. Publishes book 18-24 months after acceptance. Will consider simultaneous submissions.

Illustration: Number of illustrations used for fiction: middle readers 6-8. Number of illustrations used for nonfiction: middle readers 8-10; young adults 6-8. Very rarely will review ms/illustration packages.

How to Contact/Illustrators: "Send samples we can keep. Need line art and cover art."

Terms: Pays authors in royalties of 6% based on retail price. Average advance payment is "very open." Sends galleys to authors; sometimes sends dummies to illustrators. Book catalog available for 9 × 12 SAE and 4 first-class stamps; manuscript guidelines for #10 SASE.

Tips: "We have two Young Readers imprints, Avon Camelot books for the middle grades, and Avon Flare for young adults. Our list is weighted more to individual titles than to series, with the emphasis in our paperback originals on high quality recreational reading—a fresh and original writing style; identifiable, three dimensional characters; a strong, well-paced story that pulls readers in and keeps them interested." Writers: "Make sure that you really know what a company's list looks like before you submit work. Is your work in line with what they usually do? Is your work appropriate for the age group that this company publishes for? Keep aware of what's in your bookstore (but not what's in there for too long!)" Illustrators: "Submit work to art directors and people who are in charge of illustration at publishers. This is usually not handled entirely by the editorial department."

*BACK TO THE BIBLE, P.O. Box 82808, Lincoln NE 68501. (402)474-4567. Book publisher. Editor: Marcia Claesson.

Fiction: Young Adults/Teens: "Must show how a relationship with Christ can make a difference in the lives of present-day teens." Average word length: 20,000-40,000.

Nonfiction: Young Adults/Teens: Must have biblical emphasis and deal with practical issues for Christian teens. Does not want to see biographies. Average word length: 20,000-40,000.

How to Contact/Writers: Query by mail. Reports on queries in 2 weeks; mss 6-8 weeks. Publishes ms 6-12 months after acceptance.

"Picture books" are geared toward the preschool—8 year old group; "Young readers" to 5-8 year olds; "Middle readers" to 9-11 year olds; and "Young adults" to those 12 and up.

Illustration: Buys 3 illustrations/year. Preferred theme or style: realistic and/or mood-capturing illustrations; size—no smaller than 8 × 10. Will review illustration packages. Works on assignment only.
How to Contact/Illustrators: Send résumé and samples. Reports in 2 weeks.
Terms: Buys all rights. Pays 10% royalty on total sales. No upfront fee.

*BANTAM DOUBLEDAY DELL, 666 Fifth Ave., New York NY 10103. (212)765-6500. Book publisher. "Because of the large number of materials we receive, it is our policy to consider only those manuscripts submitted by literary agents. *All unsolicited manuscripts are returned to the sender.*"
Illustration: Will review artwork for future assignments (Bantam books only; Dell not reviewing material at this time). Uses artwork for full color books, jacket illustration and paperback book cover illustration. Current projects include a series of young adult hardcover books. Publishes 12-15 books/month. Looking for artists whose work displays ethnic and cultural diversity.
How to Contact/Illustrators: Ms/illustration packages: Submit through agent only. Illustrations only: write or telephone to arrange drop-off of portfolio (appointments not possible). Portfolio drop-off is usually the third week of every month—illustrators should call just to confirm. Samples can be sent to Marva Martin, Art Director."

BARRONS EDUCATIONAL SERIES, 250 Wireless Blvd., Hauppauge NY 11788. (516)434-3311. FAX: (516)434-3723. Book publisher. Estab. 1945. Acquisitions Editor (picture books): Grace Freedson. Editorial contact (young/middle readers, young adult titles): Grace Freedson. Publishes 20 picture books/year; 20 young reader titles/year; 20 middle reader titles/year; 10 young adult titles/year. 25% of books by first-time authors; 25% of books from agented writers.
Fiction: Picture books/young readers: adventure, animal, contemporary, easy-to-read, health-related, nature/environment, sports, suspense/mystery. Recently published *Get Ready, Get Set, Read*, (beginning reader series).
Nonfiction: Picture books/young readers: activity book, animal, careers, health, history, nature/environment. Middle readers: nature/environment.
How to Contact/Writers: Fiction: Query. Nonfiction: Submit outline/synopsis and sample chapters. Reports on queries in 3-8 weeks; on mss in 3-6 months. Publishes a book 1 year after acceptance. Will consider simultaneous submissions.
Illustration: Number of illustrations used for fiction/nonfiction: picture books—16. Editorial will review ms/illustration packages.
How to Contact/Illustrators: Ms/illustration packages: Query first; 3 chapters of ms with 1 piece of final art, remainder roughs. Illustrations only: Tearsheets or slides plus résumé. Reports in 3-8 weeks.
Terms: Pays authors in royalties based on retail price. Illustrators paid by the project based on retail price. Sends galleys to authors; dummies to illustrators. Book catalog, manuscript/artist's guidelines free on request.
Tips: Writers: "We are predominately on the lookout for preschool storybooks and concept books. No YA fiction/romance." Illustrators: "We are happy to receive a sample illustration to keep on file for future consideration. Periodic notes reminding us of their work is acceptable." Children's book themes "are becoming much more contemporary and relevant to a child's day-to-day activities."

BEACON PRESS, 25 Beacon St., Boston MA 02108. (617)742-2110. Book publisher. Publishes 2 picture books/year; Editorial Contact: Miriam Levinson. Publishes 2 young reader titles/year; 2 middle reader titles/year.
Fiction: Young reader: contemporary, easy-to-read. Middle reader: contemporary. Other: "Multicultural stories." Average word length: picture books—2,500; middle readers—7,000.

Nonfiction: Young reader: biography, "handicaps." No nonfiction titles yet.

How to Contact/Writers: Fiction/nonfiction: Query, submit outline/synopsis and sample chapters. Reports on queries/mss in 2 months. Publishes a book 1 year after acceptance. Will consider simultaneous submissions.

Illustration: Number of illustrations used for fiction: picture books—30; young reader—10; middle reader—10. Editorial will review ms/illustration packages. Design and Production Manager, Lori Foley, will review illustrator's work for possible future assignments.

How to Contact/Illustrators: Illustrations only: Query with samples. Provide résumé, promotional literature or tearsheets to kept on file. Reports in 1 month. Original art work returned at job's completion.

Terms: Pays authors in royalties based on wholesale price. Offers average advance payment of $2,000. Pay for illustrators: by the project. Sends galleys to authors; dummies to illustrators. Book catalog, manuscript/artist's guidelines free on request.

Tips: "Submit only books with comtemporary multicultural or multiracial themes. No animal protagonists. We want relatively upbeat, positive stories that deal honestly with the concerns of children today and celebrate the growing multicultural flavor of America and the diversity of the world's people."

BEHRMAN HOUSE INC., 235 Watchung Ave., West Orange NJ 07052. (201)669-0447. FAX: (201)669-9769. Book publisher. Project Editor: Adam Siegel. Publishes 3 young reader titles/year; 3 middle reader titles/year; 3 young adult titles/year. 12% of books by first-time authors; 2% of books from agented writers. Publishes books on all aspects of Judaism: history, cultural, textbooks, holidays.

Fiction: Picture books, young readers, middle readers, young adults: history and religion.

Nonfiction: All levels: history, religion, Jewish educational textbooks. Average word length: young reader—1,200; middle reader—2,000; young adult—4,000. Published *A Child's Bible*, by Seymour Rossel (ages 9-10, Bible stories and activity book); *My Jewish World*, by Robert Thumb (ages 8-9, a kid's view of Jewish life).

How to Contact/Writers: Fiction/nonfiction: Submit outline/synopsis and sample chapters. . Reports on mss/queries in 2 months. Publishes a book 2½ years after acceptance. Will consider simultaneous submissions.

Illustration: Number of illustrations used for nonfiction: young reader—40; middle reader—35; young adult—30. Editorial will review ms/illustration packages. Will review artwork for future assignments. Contact Adam Siegel, project editor.

How to Contact/Illustrators: Ms/illustration packages: "Query first." Illustrations only: Query with samples; send unsolicited art samples by mail. Reports in 2 months.

Photography: Photographers should contact Adam Siegel. Uses photos of famililes involved in Jewish activities. Uses color and b&w prints. To contact, photographers should query with samples. Send unsolicited photos by mail. Submit portfolio for review.

Terms: Pays authors in royalties of 3-8% based on retail price or buys ms outright for $1,000-5,000. Offers average advance payment of $500. Pay for illustrators: by the project; $500-5,000. Sends galleys to authors; dummies to illustrators. Book catalog free on request.

Tips: Looking for "religious school texts."

Always include a self-addressed stamped envelope (SASE) or International Reply Coupon (IRC) with submissions.

*BLUE HERON PUBLISHING, INC., 24450 NW Hansen Rd., Hillsboro OR 97124. (503)621-3911. Book publisher. Publisher: Dennis Stovall. Publishes 3-4 young adult titles/year. Wants "novels reflecting American minority experience by minority authors (especially young writers); reprints of YA classics; and books (nonfiction) for school use. Especially interested in the previously described from Northwest authors."
Fiction: Middle readers: adventure, animal, contemporary, folktales, history, nature/environment, suspense/mystery. Young Adults: adventure, anthology, animal, contemporary, fantasy, folktales, history, nature/environment, science fiction, suspense/mystery. "Not interested in books with ethnic protagonist when author is not of that ethnic group." Average word length: young adult—60,000. Recently published *Death Walk*, by Walt Money (YA, adventure novel); *Morning Glory Afternoon,* by Irene Bennett Brown (YA, historical adventure/romance); and *Angry Waters*, by Walt Morey (YA, adventure).
Nonfiction: Middle readers and young adults: history, nature/environment, writing/publishing.
How to Contact/Writers: Nonfiction: Query. Reports on queries in 4-6 weeks; reports on mss in 6 weeks. Publishes a book 18 months after acceptance. Will consider simultaneous submissions, electronic submissions via disk or modem, and previously published work.
Illustration: Will review ms/illustration packages. Will review artwork for future assignments. Contact Linny Stovall, publisher.
How to Contact/Illustrators: Ms/illustration packages: Query. Illustrations only: Query with samples.
Terms: Pays author royalty of 5-8% on retail price. Pays illustrators by the project (range: $100-600). Sends galleys to authors; dummies to illustrators. Book catalog available for 6×9 SAE and 52¢ postage. Ms guidelines available.

*BLUESTOCKING PRESS, P.O. Box 1014-cwil, Placerville CA 95667. (916)621-1123. Book publisher. Owner: Jane A. Williams. Publishes 1 middle reader book/year; 1 young adult title/year. Wants "books with a theme of self-reliance, nonfiction preferred. Biographies that support this theme; free-market; free enterprise books; entrepreneurship for kids."
Nonfiction: Young readers, middle readers and young adults: biography, careers, history, economics and free market. "No conventional school books." Recently published *Whatever Happened to Penny Candy?* by Richard Maybury (ages 11-18+, free market economics).
How to Contact/Writers: Nonfiction: Query. Reports on queries in 3 weeks; reports on mss in 3 months. Publishes a book 1-1.5 years after acceptance. Will consider simultaneous submissions. Include SASE or appropriate return postage.
Illustration: Average number of illustrations used for fiction and nonfiction: young readers, middle readers, and young adult—10. Will review artwork for future assignments. Contact: Jane A. Williams. Uses primarily b&w artwork only.
How to Contact/Illustrators: Ms/illustration packages: Query. Illustrations only: Query with samples (will not be returned); provide tearsheets to be kept on file. Reports in 1 month. Return of originals negotiable.
Terms: Pays authors royalty of 10% on wholesale price. Pays illustrators by the project. Sends galleys to authors; dummies to illustrators.
Tips: "Review lots of excellent books of the type you want to write/illustrate—make sure your work is competitive." Interested in "historical nonfiction with general appeal and museum store possibilities. Alternative and home schooling are opening new markets."

*BOLD PRODUCTIONS, P.O. Box 152281, Arlington TX 76015. (817)468-9924. Book publisher. Publisher: Mary Bold. Publishes 1-2 young readers and middle readers/year. 80% of books by first-time authors. "All books are 'resource' books and nonfiction.

Nonfiction: Young readers and middle readers: activity books. Recently published *Art Concepts for Children*, by Carol Small (6th grade and up, paperback art instruction); *Travel-Ogs*, by Ann Brown and Mary Bold (3rd grade and up, activity book); and *Handmade Christmas Gifts that are Actually Usable*, by Ann Brown (3rd grade, activity craft book).
How to Contact/Writers: Nonfiction: Query with SASE. Reports on queries in 2-4 weeks; reports on ms in 1-4 months. Will consider simultaneous submissions and electronic submissions via disk.
Illustration: "We do not buy any freelance illustration."
Terms: Pays authors by royalty based on retail price. Offers advances; negotiable. Book catalog available for #10 SASE. Ms guidelines available.
Tips: "Polish and persist. Keep polishing your submissions as you go, and persist with your best work. Don't expect to sell immediately! Many fine writers have searched months, even years, for a publishing 'home.' Learn how to make a market survey and how to write a book proposal; in effect, learn how to look at your manuscript the way an editor will. Approach us first with an article for one of our newsletters; our booklist is limited, with just 1 to 5 titles published each year. But we publish many newsletters on family issues and activities. Send a SASE for a sample and writer's guidelines. We do not answer requests/queries without a SASE."

*BOYDS MILLS PRESS, Highlights Foundation, 910 Church St., Honesdale PA 18431. (717)253-1080. Book publisher. Manuscript Coordinator: Juanita Galuska. Publisher: Kent Brown, Jr. Publishes 25-30 picture books/year; 2 young readers/year; 2-4 middle readers/year; 2 young adult titles/year. Boyds Mills Press is made up of three imprints: Wordsong publishes poetry books; Caroline House publishes artful picture books; Bell Books publishes educational board books for schools and libraries. In nonfiction, science and environmental issues are covered. "We are just now coming out with a series on rivers."
Fiction/Nonfiction: Publishes all categories except romance and textbooks. Recently published *The Violin Man*, by Maureen Brett Hooper (ages 8-12, fiction); *Amazon*, by Peter Laurie (ages 8-12, nonfiction/travel); *Mirror Magic*, by Seymour Simon (ages 7-10, science).
How to Contact/Writers: Fiction: Submit complete manuscript (for picture books and middle readers) or submit outline/synopsis and 3 sample chapters. Nonfiction: Query. Reports on manuscripts in 1 month. Ms publishes 1-2 years after acceptance.
Illustration: Will review ms/illustration packages. Will review artwork for future assignments. Contact Juanita Galuska, manuscript coordinator or Kent Brown, publisher.
How to Contact/Illustrators: Ms/illustration packages: Query; submit complete ms. Illustrations only: query with samples; send unsolicited art samples by mail (no originals); submit portfolio for review; arrange a personal interview to show portfolio; provide promotional literature or tearsheets to be kept on file. Originals returned at job's completion.
Terms: Authors paid by royalty. Offers advances. Illustrators paid by the project and by royalty. Catalog available for 9 × 12 SASE. Ms and art guidelines available for SASE.

BRADBURY PRESS, imprint of Macmillan Publishing Company, 866 Third Ave., New York NY 10022. (212)702-9809. Book publisher. Editorial Director: Barbara Lalicki. Publishes 15-20 picture books/year; 5 young reader titles/year; 5 middle reader titles/year; 3 young adult titles/year. 25% of books by first-time authors; 75% of books from previously published or agented writers.
Fiction: Picture books: animal, contemporary, history. Young readers: animal, contemporary, easy-to-read, history. Middle readers: contemporary, fantasy, history, science fiction, spy/mystery/adventure. Young adults: science fiction, spy/mystery/adventure.

Average length: picture books—32 pages; young readers—48 pages; middle readers—112 pages; young adults—140 pages.

Nonfiction: Picture books: animal, history, music/dance, nature/environment. Young readers: animal, biography, education, history, hobbies, music/dance, nature/environment, sports. Middle readers: animal, biography, education, history, hobbies, music/dance, nature/environment, sports. Average length: picture books—32-48 pages; young and middle readers—48-64 pages.

How to Contact/Writers: Fiction: Query. Nonfiction: Submit outline/synopsis and sample chapters. Reports on queries in 2-3 weeks; on mss in 6-8 weeks. Publishes a book 18 months after acceptance.

Illustration: Number of illustrations used for fiction and nonfiction: picture books—30; young readers—1; middle readers—1; young adults—1. Art Director, Julie Quan will review illustrator's work for future assignments.

How to Contact/Illustrators: Submit ms with color photocopies of art. Illustrations only: Portfolio drop off last Thursday of every month. Reports on art samples only if interested. Original artwork returned at job's completion.

Terms: Pays author in royalties based on retail price. Average advance: "Percentage of estimated sales." Sends galleys to authors; dummies to illustrators. Book catalog available for 8×10 SAE and 4 first-class stamps; manuscript and/or artist's guidelines for business-size SAE and 1 first-class stamp.

Tips: Looks for "a strong story, nothing gimmicky, no pop-ups." Trends include "nonfiction for pre-schoolers."

BRIGHT RING PUBLISHING, 1900 N. Shore Dr., Box 5768, Bellingham WA 98227-5768. (206)734-1601. Estab. 1985. Editor: MaryAnn Kohl. Publishes 1 young reader title/year. 50% of books by first-time authors. Uses only recipe format—"but no cookbooks unless woven into another subject like art, music, science."

Nonfiction: Picture books/young reader/middle reader: activity books involving art ideas, hobbies, music/dance and nature/environment. Average word length: "about 125 ideas/book." Recently published *Good Earth Art* by Kohl, illustrated by Cindy Gaines (picture book, young reader, middle reader—art ideas). "We are moving into only recipe-style resource books in any variety of subject areas—useful with children 2-12. 'Whole language' is the buzz word in early education—so books to meet the new demands of that subject will be needed."

How to Contact/Writers: Nonfiction: submit complete ms. Reports in 1-6 weeks. Publishes a book 1 year after acceptance. Will consider simultaneous submissions.

Illustration: Editorial will review ms/illustration packages. Prefers to review "black line (drawings) for text."

How to Contact/Illustrators: Ms/illustration packages: "Query first." Illustrations only: query with samples; send tearsheets and "sample of ideas I request after query." Reports in 6-8 weeks. Original artwork returned at job's completion.

Terms: Pays authors in royalties of 5-10% based on wholesale or retail price. Pays illustrators $500-1,000. Also offers "free books and discounts for future books." Book catalog, ms/artist's guidelines for business-size SAE and 25¢ postage.

Tips: Illustrators: "Build your portfolio by taking a few jobs at lower pay—then grow. Bright Ring Publishing is not looking for picture books, juvenile fiction, or poetry at this time. We are, however, highly interested in creative activity and resource books for children to use independently or for teachers and parents to use with children. Must work for pre-school through age twelve."

Refer to the Business of Children's Writing & Illustrating for up-to-date marketing, tax and legal information.

*CANDLEWICK PRESS, 2067 Massachusettes Ave., Cambridge MA 02140. (617)661-3330. Book publisher. Assistant Editor: Jane Snyder. Publishes 80 picture books, 4 young readers, 6 middle readers, and 2 young adult titles/year. 5-50% of books by first-time authors.
Fiction: Picture books: animal, contemporary, fantasy, folktales, history. Young readers, middle readers and young adult/teens: adventure, anthology, animal, contemporary, fantasy, folktales, history, poetry.
Nonfiction: Picture books, young readers and middle readers: animal, biography, history, hobbies, music/dance, nature/environment. Young adults: animal, biography, history, music/dance.
How to Contact/Writers: Fiction: Query or submit complete ms. Nonfiction: Query or submit outline/synopsis and sample chapters. Reports in 3 weeks on queries; reports in 1 month on mss. Publishes a book 12-18 months after acceptance. Will consider simultaneous submissions.
Illustration: Will review ms/illustration packages. Will review artwork for future assignments. Contact: The Editors. Uses color artwork only.
How to Contact/Illustrators: Ms/illustration packages: submit text with photocopies of artwork. Illustrations only: Send unsolicited art samples by mail; provide tearsheets to be kept on file. Reports only if interested.
Terms: Pays authors royalty of 5-10% based on retail price. Offers advances. Pays illustrators royalty of 5-10% based on retail price. Sends galleys to author. Book catalog available for 9×12 SAE and $1.67 postage; ms guidelines available for SASE.

*CAPSTONE PRESS INC., P.O. Box 669, N. Mankato MN 56001. (507)387-7978. Book publisher. Publisher: Jean Eick. Publishes 25-30 picture books/year; 25-30 young reader titles/year; 10 middle reader titles/year. 15% of books by first-time authors; 1% of from agented authors.
Fiction: Picture books, young readers and middle readers: animal, contemporary easy-to-read, fantasy, history, science fiction, sports, spy/mystery/adventure. Middle readers: problem novels, romance. Recently published *A Kids Guide to Living on the Moon*, by Taylor (grade 5, middle reader); *Revolutionary War Soldier*, by Sanford & Green (grade 5, historical fiction); *Definitely from Out of Town*, by Seth Jarvis (grade 5, middle reader).
Nonfiction: Picture books, young readers and middle readers: animal, biography, education, history, hobbies, music/dance, nature/environment, sports. Recently published *Hot Air Ballooning*, by Costanzo (grade 5, sports); *BMX Bikes*, by Cavstensen (grade 5, sports); *18 Wheelers*, by Maifair (grade 5, sports).
How to Contact/Writers: Fiction/nonfiction: Query. Reports in 2 weeks. Publishes book in "6 months to 1 year depending upon publishing program."
How to Contact/Illustrators: Query first. Submit résumé and photocopies of work. Reports in 2 weeks. Does not return original artwork.
Terms: Outright purchase. Offers advance of one third of purchase price. Illustrators are paid by the project. Does not send galleys to authors; dummies to illustrators.

CAROLINA WREN PRESS/LOLLIPOP POWER BOOKS, Box 277, Carrboro NC 27510. (919)560-2738. Book publisher. Carolina Wren estab. 1976; Lollipop Power estab. 1971. Regular Children's Editor: Ruth Smullin. Minority Children's Editor: Pauletta Bracy. Publishes 2 picture books/year; 1 young reader title in '89. 100% of books by first-time authors.
Fiction: Picture books: contemporary, easy-to-read, fantasy, history, problem novels, science fiction, black family, "especially interested in non-sexist, multi-racial." Average length: picture books— 30 pages.
Nonfiction: Picture books: biography, education, history, hobbies, music/dance, "children of divorce and lesbian homes and black families." Average length: picture books— 30 pages.

How to Contact/Writers: Fiction/nonfiction: Query and request guidelines. Reports on queries/ms in 3 months. Publishes a book 2-3 years after acceptance "at present."
Illustration: Number of illustrations used for fiction and nonfiction: picture books— 12. Editorial will review ms/illustration packages. Martha Lange, designer, will review artwork for future assignments.
How to Contact/Illustrators: Query first to Martha Lange. Reports on art samples only if interested. Original artwork returned at job's completion.
Terms: Pays authors in royalties of 5% of print-run based on retail price, or cash, if available. Pays illustrators in royalties of 5% "of print-run based on retail price, or cash, if available." Sends galleys to authors; dummies to illustrators. Book catalog, manuscript guidelines for business-size SASE.
Tips: "Our books aim to show children that girls and women are self-sufficient; boys and men can be emotional and nurturing; families may consist of one parent only, working parents, extended families; families may rely on daycare centers or alternative child care; all children, whatever their race, creed or color, are portrayed often and fairly in ways true to their own experience. We require that childhood be taken seriously. Children's lives can be no less complex than adults; we expect that their problems are presented honestly and completely. The validity of their feelings must be recognized, as children will benefit from reading of others coping with emotions or conflicts and finding solutions to their own problems. Current publishing priorities: strong female protagonists, especially Black, Hispanic or Native-American girls and women; friendship and solidarity among girls; children working to change values and behavior; nontraditional family situations; stories with evident concern for the world around us." Writers: "Be sure you can hold the attention of a child. Practice stories on real children and become a good writer." Beginning illustrators: "Try to get classes with someone who understands illustration professionally. We are seeking new illustrators for our files. Please send us your name and current address and we will notify you when we have a manuscript ready for illustration. Keep us notified of any address change, as it may be a while before we contact you."

CAROLRHODA BOOKS, INC., Lerner Publications, 241 First Ave. N., Minneapolis MN 55401. (612)332-3344. Book publisher. Estab. 1969. Submissions Editor: Rebecca Poole. Publishes 5 picture books/year; 2 young reader titles/year; 20 middle reader titles/year. 20% of books by first-time authors; 10% of books from agented writers.
Fiction: Picture books: general. Young readers: historical. Average word length: picture books—1,000-1,500; young readers—2,000.
Nonfiction: Young readers: history, hobbies, music/dance, nature/environment. Middle readers: animal, biography, history, music/dance, nature/environment. Average word length: young readers— 2,000; middle readers—6,000.
How to Contact/Writers: Fiction/nonfiction: Submit complete ms. Reports on queries in 3 weeks; on mss in 3 months. Publishes a book 18 months after acceptance. Will consider simultaneous submissions.
Illustration: Number of illustrations used for fiction: picture books—15-20; young readers—20. Number of illustrations used for nonfiction: young readers—15-20; middle readers—10-12. Editorial will review ms/illustration packages.
How to Contact/Illustrators: Ms/illustration packages: At least one sample illustration (in form of photocopy, slide, duplicate photo) with full ms. Illustrations only: résumé/slides. Reports on art samples only if interested.
Terms: Buys ms outright for variable amount. Factors used to determine final payment: color vs. black-and-white, number of illustrations, quality of work. Sends galleys to authors; dummies to illustrators. Book catalog available for 9×12 SAE and 2 first-class stamps; manuscript guidelines for letter-size SAE and 1 first-class stamp.
Tips: Writers: "Research the publishing company to be sure it is in the market for the type of book you're interested in writing. Familiarize yourself with the company's list.

We specialize in beginning readers, photo essays, and books published in series. We do very few single-title picture books, and no novels. For more detailed information about our publishing program, consult our catalog. We do not publish any of the following: textbooks, workbooks, songbooks, puzzles, plays and religious material. In general, we suggest that you steer clear of alphabet books; preachy stories with a moral to convey; stories featuring anthropomorphic protagonists ('Amanda the Amoeba,' 'Frankie the Fire Engine,' 'Tonie the Tornado'); and stories that revolve around trite, hackneyed plots: Johnny moves to a new neighborhood and is miserable because he can't make any new friends; Steve and Jane find a sick bird with a broken wing, and they nurse it back to health; lonely protagonist is rejected by his peers — usually because he's 'different' from them in some way — until he saves the day by rescuing them from some terrible calamity; and so on. You should also avoid racial and sexual stereotypes in your writing, as well as sexist language." (See also Lerner Publications.)

*CASCADE PASS INC., Suite 235, 10734 Jefferson Blvd., Culver City CA 90230. (213)202-1468. Book publisher. President: David Katz. Publishes 2 middle readers/year; 2 young readers/year. 20% of books by first-time authors.
Fiction: Picture books, young readers and middle readers: contemporary, health-related, nature/environment, religion, dance, music, art, self-esteem. Average word length: picture books — 1,000; young readers — 500. Recently published *Reading Rap Book*, by David Katz (ages 5-8, music/poetry oriented); *You Can Be a Woman Engineer* (ages 8-14; science careers).
Nonfiction: Middle readers: careers, health, music/dance, religion.
How to Contact/Writers: Fiction/nonfiction: Query. Reports in 4 weeks. Publishes book 1 year after acceptance. Will consider simultaneous submissions.
Illustration: Average number of illustrations used for fiction: picture books — 10; young readers — 10; middle readers — 10. Average number of illustrations used for nonfiction: picture books — 5. Will review ms/illustration packages. Will review artwork for future assignments. Contact David Katz, president.
How to Contact/Illustrators: Ms/illustration packages: Query. Illustrations only: provide resume, business card, promotional literature or tearsheets to be kept on file. Reports only if interested.
Terms: Pays authors royalty of 5-10% based on wholesale price. Pays illustrators royalty of 3-7% based on wholesale price. Sends galleys to authors. Guidelines not available.
Tips: Looking for "creative, message-oriented material relating to self esteem, feminist or multicultural themes."

*CHARIOT BOOKS, a division of David C. Cook Publishing Co., 20 Lincoln Ave., Elgin IL 60120. (708)741-2400. Book publisher. Managing Editor: Jule Smith. Publishes 20-30 picture books/year; 6-8 young readers/year; 10-15 middle readers/year; 4-6 young adult titles/year. 10% of books by first-time authors; 5% of books from agented authors. "All books have overt Christian values, but there is no primary theme."
Fiction: Picture books: animal, contemporary, folktales, nature/environment, religion. Young readers: adventure, animal, contemporary, folktales, history, nature/environment, religion, sports, suspense/mystery. Middle reader: adventure, contemporary, history, problem novels, religion, sports, suspense/mystery. Young adults: adventure, contemporary, history, problem novels, religion, romance, sports, suspense/mystery. Does not want to see poetry, fantasy — science fiction. Average word length: picture books — 1,000; young readers — 1,200-1,500; middle readers — 6,000-20,000; young adult — 25,000. Recently published *Danger for Old Ruff*, by Vesta Seek (young reader, animal story); *Project Cockroach*, by Elaine McEwan (middle reader, contemporary); *Elizabeth of Capernaum*, by Edith Cutting (young adult/teen, history/romance).
Nonfiction: Picture books: activity books, animal, biography, nature/environment, religion (Bible stories), devotional. Young readers: activity books, biography, nature/envi-

ronment, religion, devotional. Middle readers: activity books, biography, religion, devotional. Young adults: religion, devotional. Does not want to see textbook, children's sermons. Average word length: picture books—1,000; young readers—1,500-2,000; middle readers—10,000. Recently published *Jellyfish Can't Swim*, by Marjorie Parker (middle reader, devotional); *Read-It-Again Bible Stories*, by Suzanne Thomas (picture book/young readers, religion).
How to Contact/Writers: Fiction/nonfiction: Query. Submit outline/synopsis and 2 sample chapters. "For picture books, submit complete manuscript." Reports on queries in 2 months; reports on mss in 3 months. Publishes a book 12-18 months after acceptance. Will consider simultaneous submissions.
Illustration: Average number of illustrations used for fiction and nonfiction: picture books—15; young readers—15. Will review artwork for future assignments. Contact Dawn Lauck, book designer.
How to Contact/Illustrators: Illustrations only: Query with samples. Reports only if interested. Original artwork returned at job's completion.
Terms: Pays authors royalty, outright purchase. Offers advances. Pays illustrators by the project, royalty. Sends galleys to authors; dummies to illustrators. Ms guidelines available for SASE.

CHARLESBRIDGE, Subsidiary of Mastery Education, 85 Main St., Watertown MA 02172. (617)926-0329. Book publisher. Publishes 4 nonfiction picture books/year. Managing Editor: Elena Dworkin Wright. Publishes nature or science for prereaders.
Nonfiction: Picture books: nature/environment. Average word length: picture books—1,000-1,500. Recently published: *Will We Miss Them? Endangered Species*, by Alexandra Wright (picture book); *Icky Bug Counting Book*, by Jerry Pallotta (picture book); *At Home in the Rainforest*, by Diane Willow (picture book).
How to Contact/Writers: Nonfiction: Submit complete ms. Reports on mss in 1 month. Publishes a book 1 year after acceptance.
Illustration: Average number of illustrations used for nonfiction: picture books—30. Will review ms/illustration packages. Will review artwork for future assignments. Uses color artwork only.
How to Contact/Illustrators: Illustrations only: Query with samples; provide tearsheets to be kept on file. Reports back only if interested. Does not return original artwork at job's completion.
Terms: Pays authors in royalties or outright purchase. Pays illustrators by the project. Sends galleys to authors. Sends dummies to illustrators.

*CHICAGO REVIEW PRESS, 814 N. Franklin St., Chicago IL 60610. (312)337-0747. Book publisher. Editorial Director: Amy Teschner. Publishes 1 middle reader/year; "about 4" young adult titles/year. 50% of books by first-time authors; 10% of books from agented authors. "We publish art activity books for young children and project books in the arts and sciences for ages 10 and up (our Zigguart Series). We do not publish fiction."
Nonfiction: Young readers, middle readers and young adults: activity books. "We're interested in hands-on, educational books; anything else probably will be rejected." Average word length: young readers and young adult—175 pages. Recently published *My Own Fun: Creative Learning Activities for Home & School*, by Carolyn Buhai Haas and Anita Cross Friedman (ages 7-12, activity book); *The Art of Construction: Projects & Principles for Beginning Engineers & Architects*, by Mario Salvadori (Ziggurat Book for 10 and up, architecture, construction projects); *The Spark in the Stone: Skills & Projects from the Native American Tradition*, by Peter Goodchild (a Ziggurat Book for ages 10 and up, activities/Native American studies/survival skills). Reports on queries/mss in 6-8 weeks. Publishes a book 6 months after acceptance. Will consider simultaneous submissions and previously published work.

Illustration: Average number of illustrations used for nonfiction: middle readers—25-50; young adult—"It varies a lot—whatever number necessary for instructional purposes for projects." Contact Fran Lee, art director.

How to Contact/Illustrators: Ms/illustration packages: Submit 1-2 chapters of ms with corresponding pieces of final art. Illustrations only: provide business card, tearsheets. Reports back only if interested. Original artwork "usually" returned at job's completion.

Photography: Photographers should contact Fran Lee, art director. "We consult our files when we know what we're looking for on a book-by-book basis." Interested in stock photos. Uses b&w prints. To contact, photographers should provide business card.

Terms: Pays authors royalty of 7½-12½% based on retail price. Offers advances ("but not always") of $500-1,000. Pays illustrators by the project (range varies considerably). Photographers paid by the project (range varies considerably). Sends galleys to authors. Book catalog available for SASE; ms guidelines available for SASE.

Tips: "We're looking for project books that encourage specific interests. We see parents becoming increasingly interested in participating in their children's education, and our Ziggurat Series—project books in the arts and sciences for talented beginners, ages 10 and up." Notices trends in multicultural books, books that share a culture and books that do not condescend to children.

*CHILD GRAPHICS PRESS, P.O. Box 7771, Hilton Head Island SC 29938. (803)689-3030. Book publisher. Editorial contact for illustrations from children's books: Bea Harmon. Publishes 6-8 illustrations from picture books/year. "All prints published are from classic children's literature or recognized illustrators."

Fiction: "We will consider only illustrations from books already published and would prefer these topics: Picture books and young readers: animal, fantasy, folktales, nature/environment, sports. Middle readers: folktales, nature/environment, sports." Recently published illustrations by Michael Hague, Trina Schart Hyman and Michelle Wiggins.

Nonfiction: Picture books, young readers and middle readers: animal, nature/environment, sports. Wants previously published illustrations only.

How to Contact/Illustrators: "Art samples will be returned only if stamped envelope is provided."

Terms: Advances negotiable. Pays illustrators royalty based on wholesale price, outright purchase. Art catalog available for $1.

CHILDREN'S WRITER'S & ILLUSTRATOR'S MARKET, Publication of Writer's Digest Books, F&W Publications, 1507 Dana Ave., Cincinnati OH 45207. Contact: Lisa Carpenter. Publishes annual directory of freelance markets for children's writers and illustrators. Send b&w samples—photographs, photostats or good quality photocopies of artwork. "Since *Children's Writer's & Illustrator's Market* is published only once a year, submissions are kept on file for the next upcoming edition until selections are made. Material is then returned by SASE." Buys one-time rights. Buys 10-20 illustrations/year. "I need examples of art that have been sold to one of the listings in *CWIM*. Thumb through the book to see the type of art I'm seeking. The art must have been freelanced; it cannot have been done as staff work. Include the name of the listing that purchased the work, what the art was used for and the payment you received." Pays $50 to holder of reproduction rights and free copy of *CWIM* when published.

■CHINA BOOKS, 2929 24th St., San Francisco CA 94110. (415)282-2994. FAX: (415)282-0994. Book publisher. Independent book producer/packager. Estab. 1960. Senior Editor: Bob Schildgen. 10% of books by first-time authors; 10% of books from agented writers. Subsidy publishes 10%.

Fiction: Picture books: animal, folktales, history, nature/environment, poetry. Young readers: animal, contemporary, folktales, history, nature/environment, religion. Middle readers: animal, contemporary, fantasy, folktales, nature/environment, poetry. Does not want to see subjects "not about China or Chinese Americans."

Nonfiction: Picture books, young readers, middle readers: activity books, biography, hobbies, nature/environment, religion, sports. Average word length: young readers—2,000; middle readers—4,000. Subjects must relate to China or Chinese Americans.

How to Contact/Writers: Fiction/nonfiction: Query; submit outline/synopsis and sample chapters. Publishes a book 9 months after acceptance. Will consider simultaneous and electronic submissions via disk or modem.

Illustration: Editorial will review ms/illustration packages.

How to Contact/Illustrators: Illustrations only: Query with samples.

Photography: Looking for Chinese or Chinese American subjects. Uses color and b&w prints; 35mm and 2¼ × 2¼ transparencies. To contact, photographers should query with samples.

Terms: Pays authors in royalties of 8-10% based on retail price; buys ms outright for $100-500. Offers average advance payment of "1/3 of total royalty." Pay for illustrators: by the project $100-500; royalties of 8% based on retail price. Pays photographers by the project (range: $50-500); per photo (range: $25-100); royalty of 4-8% based on retail price. Sends galleys to authors; dummies to illustrators. Book catalog free on request; manuscript/artist's guidelines for SASE.

Tips: Looks for "something related to China or to Chinese-Americans."

CHRONICLE BOOKS, 275 Fifth St., San Francisco CA 94103. (415)777-7240. Book publisher. Editor: Victoria Rock. Editorial Assistant: Kristen Breck. Publishes 12-16 picture books/year; 4-6 young reader titles/year; 0-1 middle reader titles/year; 0-1 young adult nonfiction titles/year. 10-50% of books by first-time authors; 10-50% of books from agented writers.

Fiction: Picture books: animal, contemporary, easy-to-read, fantasy, history, folktales, nature/environment. Young readers: anthology, contemporary, easy-to-read, history, sports. Middle readers: Anthology, animal, contemporary, easy-to-read. Recently published *Ten Little Rabbits,* by Virginia Crossman and Sylvia Lang (picture book); *Mama, Do You Love Me?,* by Barbara Tousse and Barbara Lavallee (picture book).

Nonfiction: All levels: various categories. Recently published *Wildlife California* (ages 6-12, nature); *The River,* by Susan Deming (ages 3-8, nature/board book).

How to Contact/Writers: Fiction and nonfiction: Submit complete manuscript (picture books); submit outline/synopsis and sample chapters (for older readers). Reports on queries in 1 month; 2-3 months on mss. Publishes a book 1-3 years after acceptance. Will consider simultaneous submissions, as long as marked "multiple submission."

Illustration: Number of illustrations used for fiction/nonfiction: picture books—13-30. Editorial will review ms/illustration packages. "Indicate if project *must* be considered jointly, or if editor may consider text and art separately." Editor, Victoria Rock, will review illustrator's work for future assignments. Wants "unusual art. Something that will stand out on the shelves. Either bright and modern or very traditional. Fine art, not mass market."

How to Contact/Illustrators: Picture books: complete ms and samples and artist's work (not necessarily from book, but in the envisioned style.) Slides and color photocopies OK. Dummies helpful. Slides and tearsheets preferred. Photocopies okay. Résumé helpful. "If samples sent for files, generally no response—unless samples are not suited to list, in which case samples are returned. Queries and project proposals responded to in same time frame as author query/proposals."

Terms: Generally pays authors in royalties based on retail price "though we do occasionally work on a flat fee basis." Advance "varies greatly." Illustrators paid royalty based on retail price or flat fee. Sends galleys to authors; proofs to illustrators. Book catalog for 9 × 12 SAE and 8 first class stamps; manuscript guidelines for #10 SASE.

Tips: "The children's book world is becoming increasingly competitive which means that potential projects must not only be editorially and artistically solid, but they must also be *outstanding* in some way."

CLARION BOOKS, Houghton Mifflin Company, 215 Park Ave. South, New York NY 10003. (212)420-5800. Book publisher. Editor and Publisher: Dorothy Briley. Publishes 10 picture books/year; 7 young reader titles/year; 14 middle reader titles/year; 4 young adult titles/year. 10% of books by first-time authors; 15% of books from agented writers.
Fiction: Picture books: animal, contemporary, fantasy, history, problem novels. Young readers: animal, contemporary, fantasy, history, problem novels. Middle readers: animal, contemporary, fantasy, history, problem novels, sports, spy/mystery/adventure. Young adults: history, problem novels, spy/mystery/adventure. Average word length: picture books—50-1,000; young readers—1,000-2,500; middle readers—10,000-30,000; young adults—20,000—30,000.
Nonfiction: Picture books: animal. Young readers: animal, history, nature/environment. Middle readers: biography, history, nature/environment. Average word length: picture books—750-1,000; young readers—1,000-2,500; middle readers—10,000-30,000.
How to Contact/Writers: Fiction: Query on all ms over 50 pages. Nonfiction: Query. Reports on queries in 1 month; mss in 2-3 months. Publishes a book 18 months after acceptance. Will consider simultaneous submissions.
Illustration: Number of illustrations used for fiction: picture books—20; young readers—15. Number of illustrations used for nonfiction: picture books—20; young readers—40; middle readers—20-50. Editorial will review ms/illustration packages submitted by authors/artists and ms/illustration packages. Art Director, Andrew Rhodes, will review illustrator's work for possible future assignments.
How to Contact/Illustrators: Ms/illustration packages: "Query first." Illustrations only: "tearsheets, photos or photocopies of samples." Reports on art samples only if interested. Original artwork returned at job's completion.
Terms: Pays authors in royalties of 10-12½% based on retail price. Offers average advance payment of $2,500-5,000. Sends galleys to authors; dummies to illustrators. Book catalog, manuscript/artist's guidelines free on request.

*CLYDE PRESS, 373 Lincoln Pkwy., Buffalo NY 14216. (716)875-4713 and (716)834-1254. Collector: Catherine Ainsworth. Publishes 10 young readers/year; 3 middle readers/year; 10 young adult titles/year. 100% of books by first-time author.
Fiction: All levels: folktales. Recently published *Games and Lore of Young Americans*, *Jump Rope Verses Around the U.S.*, *Black & White and Said all Over—Riddles*, all three folktale titles by Catherine Ainsworth.
Nonfiction: All levels: activity books, history/anthropology, textbooks/basal readers, folktales. No sports, religion, poetry. Average word length; picture books—25; young readers—100; middle readers—50; young adult—210. Recently published *Folktales of America, Vol. 4, 1991*, by Catherine Ainsworth (young adults, folklore).
How to Contact/Writers: Fiction/nonfiction: Query. Reports on queries in 1 week.
Illustration: Contact Catherine Ainsworth, President, Clyde Press. Primarily b&w artwork only. Wants to see color.
How to Contact/Illustrators: Ms/illustration packages: Query. Submit samples. Illustrations only: Query with samples and prices. Reports in 1 week. Does not return original artwork.
Photography: Photographers should contact Catherine Ainsworth, president. Model/property releases and captions required. Interested in stock photos. To contact, photographers should query with samples.
Terms: Pays authors outright. Photographers paid by the project. Book catalog available for SASE.

Close-up

James Cross Giblin
Editor/Writer
New York City

Whether amateur or professional, all writers should have one particular goal in common: to "reach out and connect in a lasting way with the minds and hearts of their readers," says James Cross Giblin. Having been involved in children's book editing for over 30 years, he should know. By using that knowledge he's been able to boost his own writing career.

Actually, Giblin did not originally look for a niche in the children's book field. It was as an aspiring playwright that he made his way to New York City in the 50s. It wasn't long before the desire to work *and* eat motivated him to pursue a more secure profession. Stumbling into publishing, Giblin started out as a road salesman, then worked his way into writing publicity. Eventually, he landed editorial positions in children's books.

In 1967 he went to Seabury Press, which later became Clarion. It was there he spent the bulk of his career as a children's book editor. In 1989, with his writing career rolling at a nice pace, he opted for an early retirement (though he still works with Clarion as a contributing editor). But, says Giblin, "retire" is the wrong term for what he did; he just changed jobs.

He says writing for children came long after he started editing children's books. He explains it took some time to let the writing genie out of the bottle. "I was leery about making a new commitment to writing. I guess I was a little afraid of arousing those ambitions. Maybe I wondered if I'd be successful." In a way, he says, he was really putting his whole career on the line by taking up writing. Failing would not justify his "expert" status; to prove his credibility as an editor, he had to succeed. Unlike most aspiring authors, Giblin had to start at the top and stay there.

Fortunately, he did. Two factors that may have expedited his success were the recent popularity of nonfiction and the appeal of the offbeat subjects he writes about. His award-winning books detailing histories of chimney sweeps, eating utensils, windows, skyscrapers and milk are jewels for social studies teachers around the country. It also doesn't hurt that, with ethnic diversity being stressed in books today, many of his chosen subjects are naturally multicultural. Giblin's book for 1991 was *The Truth About Unicorns*. Scheduled titles for 1992 include a biography for 8-12-year-olds, *Edith Wilson: The Woman Who Ran the United States*, and a picture book biography of George Washington (not-so-obscure subjects, for a change of pace). Also, he is currently working on *Be Seated*, a book about stools, thrones and chairs.

"All of my books are adventures of discovery," he says. "They start with an idea." Giblin says the book about unicorns was the result of requests from teachers and librarians. Other ideas come to him through reading magazine and newspaper articles, or by jotting thoughts in a writing workbook. Still other ideas for books occur to him out of the blue. For *From Hand to Mouth (Or, How We Invented Knives, Forks, Spoons, and Chopsticks & the Table Manners To Go With Them)* Giblin says, "I really got that idea in the most mundane way. One evening in a restaurant I just looked at the silverware and wondered if people had always used all those utensils." *Chimney Sweeps* was inspired by a chance meeting. During a flight, he found out the man sitting next to him was not a rock star carrying a guitar in his case, but a professional chimney sweep carrying a folding broom. The professional sweep became a vital resource for the book.

When asked how he effectively measures ideas for books, he says, "the subject has to intrigue me enough to spend two years working on it. Do I care enough about this topic?" He believes it's absolutely essential for an author to be enthusiastic about the topic. Otherwise, readers won't be able to get excited. "The basic purpose of nonfiction writing is to give knowledge of something — but if it's not treated in a lively way, the young reader won't keep reading."

In nonfiction today, the visual aspect is crucial, says Giblin. One reason for this is the need to accommodate children's requirements in an ever-increasing visual environment (i.e., television, movies, etc.). "Nonfiction books today are getting the 'Tiffany' treatment once reserved only for picture books," he says. However, the illustrations and pictures should not come first; content should be the priority. Giblin says solid text is imperative, for children today are required to investigate subjects in depth.

Primary sources serve as the best tools when researching a book, he says. Sometimes, though, it takes some digging. For *Chimney Sweeps*, one of his sources was a House of Commons Committee report on the employment of child chimney sweeps in London in 1817. For the George Washington biography, Giblin found maxims that Washington wrote as a teenager. For his book on Edith Wilson, locating an out-of-print autobiography proved to be a challenge.

Secondary sources in research often have to be relied on. However, Giblin feels double-checking secondary sources should be a basic rule. He says sometimes sources can differ on even basic things. When judging secondary sources, "I have to sense somebody delved into the material; I'm always suspicious of books with generalities." Giblin's system is to rely on two solid secondary sources with the same information. For future reference, "I keep research notes on file cards in case there are questions.

"I always have an eye out for an anecdote to add spice," says Giblin. For *Be Seated*, he read in an English social history of furniture that Louis XIV had up to 1,500 upholstered stools at Versailles. He feels using anecdotes and folklore can help to bring subjects to life, especially at the beginning of a book. Kids need to be "hooked" within the first couple of pages because they're less likely than adults to stay with flat text.

About his 1990 how-to book, *Writing Books for Young People*, Giblin says, "I really wanted to share what I've learned myself. Though I didn't realize it at the time, that book was almost a summation of my editorial career." Giblin says the book is a compendium of his two halves — his roles as both an editor and a writer. "I wrote the nonfiction chapters out of my experience as a nonfiction writer. The fiction chapters were written from my experience as an editor." He's found out feedback about the book (now in its second printing) helps him decide what other how-to subjects need to be written about.

For aspiring writers, Giblin's words of wisdom are, "Try to find out who you are, what you know and what you care about. Then make the most of that through reading a lot of current books—not with an eye on imitating, but to see what's being read today. A lot of people only remember what they read as kids." He says there are hopefuls who don't really have a sense of the field and don't put enough time into structuring their craft. "Half of unsolicited submissions are picture books or stories people think are picture book material. Another third is fiction. Most manuscripts are not horrible, but most *are* mediocre. In a blanket way, the bulk of manuscripts that come in suffer from seeming like imitations. A fresh and individual voice juts out. Editors are always hoping to find that."

—Lisa Carpenter

COBBLEHILL BOOKS, affiliate of Dutton Children's Books, a division of Penguin Books USA Inc., 375 Hudson St., New York NY 10014. (212)366-2000. Book publisher. Editorial Director: Joe Ann Daly. Sr. Editor: Rosanne Lauer. Publishes 6 picture books/year; 14 young reader titles/year; 9 middle reader titles/year; 5 young adult titles/year.
Fiction: Picture books: animal, contemporary, easy-to-read, sports, spy/mystery/adventure. Young readers: animal, contemporary, easy-to-read, sports, spy/mystery/adventure. Middle readers: contemporary, problem novels, sports, spy/mystery/adventure. Young adults: spy/mystery/adventure.
Nonfiction: Picture books: animal, nature/environment, sports. Young readers: animal, nature/environment, sports. Middle readers: nature/environment.
How to Contact/Writers: Fiction/nonfiction: query. Will consider simultaneous submissions "if we are informed about them."
How to Contact/Illustrators: Illustrations only: Send samples to keep on file, no original art work. Original art work returned at job's completion.
Terms: Pays authors in royalties. Illustrators paid in a flat fee or by royalty. Book catalog for 8½×11 SAE and 2 first class stamps; manuscript guidelines for #10 SASE.

COLORMORE, INC., Box 111249, Carrollton TX 75011-1249. (316)636-9326. Book publisher. Estab. 1987. President: Susan Koch. Publishes 4-6 young reader titles/year. 25% of books by first-time authors.
Nonfiction: Picture books, young readers: history, nature/environment, travel, world cultures and geography. Average word length: 3,000. Published *Colormore Travels—Dallas, Texas—The Travel Guide for Kids*; and *Colormore Travels—San Diego, California—The Travel Guide for Kids*, by Mary Stack (young reader, travel guide/activity book).
How to Contact/Writers: Nonfiction: Submit outline/synopsis and sample chapters; submit complete ms. Reports on queries/mss in 2-4 weeks. Publishes a book 9 months after acceptance.
Illustration: Number of illustrations used for nonfiction: young readers—25. Editorial will review ms/illustration packages. Preference for "8½×11 format books, mainly black and white, coloring-type pictures and activities."
How to Contact/Illustrators: Ms/illustration packages: Send "complete ms with 1 piece of final art." Illustrations only: Send "example(s) of black line drawing suitable for coloring." Reports in 2-4 weeks. Original art work returned at job's completion.

Terms: Authors paid a 5% royalty based on invoice price. Ms/illustration packages: 5% royalty. Pay for illustrators: 5% royalty based on invoice price. Sends galleys to authors; dummies to illustrators. Ms/artist's guidelines for legal SASE.
Tips: Looking for "a regional/local travel guide with lively, interesting illustrations and activities specifically for kids."

CONCORDIA PUBLISHING HOUSE, 3558 S. Jefferson Ave., St. Louis MO 63118. (314)268-1000. Book publisher. Contact: Ruth Geisler, Family and Children's Resources Editor. "Concordia Publishing House publishes a number of quality children's books each year. Most are fiction, with some nonfiction, based on a religious subject. Reader interest ranges from picture books to young adults. All books must contain explicit Christian content." Recently published *Hear Me Read Bible Story Series*, by Mary Manz Simon (primer, limited vocabulary Bible stories); *Jennifer of the Jungle*, by Corbin Hillam (grade 2, picture book); *Some of My Best Friends Are Trees*, by Joanne Marxhausen (grade 3, picture book).
How to Contact/Writers: Fiction: Query. Submit complete manuscript (picture books); submit outline/synopsis and sample chapters (novel-length). Reports on queries in 2 weeks; 2 months on mss. Publishes a book one year after acceptance. Will consider simultaneous submissions.
Illustration: Art director, Ed Luhmann, will review illustrator's work for possible use in future assignments.
Terms: Pays authors in royalties based on retail price and outright purchase. Sends galleys to author. Manuscript guidelines for 1 first class stamp and a #10 envelope.
Tips: "Do not send finished artwork with the manuscript. If sketches will help in the presentation of the manuscript, they may be sent. If stories are taken from the Bible, they should follow the Biblical account closely. Liberties should not be taken in fantasizing Biblical stories."

*COTEAU BOOKS LTD., Thunder Creek Publishing Co-op Ltd., 401-2206 Dewdney Ave., Regina SK, S4R 1H3 Canada. (306)352-5346. Book publisher. Managing Editor: Shelley Sopher. Publishes 1 picture book/year, 9-11 books/year. 50% of books by first-time authors.
Fiction: Picture books: animal, contemporary, fantasy, spy/mystery/adventure. Average word length: picture books — 500. Recently published *Pies*, by Wilma Riley (ages 3-10).
How to Contact/Writers: Fiction: Submit complete ms. Reports on queries in 2 weeks; on mss in 3 months. Publishes a book 12-24 months after acceptance. Coteau Books publishes Canadian writers only; manuscripts from the US are returned unopened.
Illustration: Number of illustrations used for fiction: picture books — 20. Editorial will review ms/illustration packages. Managing Editor, Shelley Sopher, will review illustrator's work for possible future assignments.
How to Contact/Illustrators: Ms/illustration packages: send "roughs." Reports on art samples within 6 weeks. Original artwork returned at job's completion.
Terms: Pays authors in royalties of 5-12% based on retail price. Other method of payment: "signing bonus." Pay for illustrators: by the project (range: $500-2,000); royalty 5% maximum based on retail price. Sends galleys to authors; dummies to illustrators. Book catalog free on request with 9 × 12 SASE (IRC).

COUNCIL FOR INDIAN EDUCATION, 517 Rimrock Rd., Billings MT 59102. (406)252-7451. Book publisher. Estab. 1968. Editor: Hap Gilliland. Publishes 1 picture book/year; 1 young reader title/year; 3 middle reader titles/year; 1 young adult title/year. 75% of books by first-time authors.
Fiction: Picture books, young readers, middle readers: adventure, anthology, animal, contemporary, folktales, history, nature/environment, poetry, sports, suspense/mystery. Young adults: adventure, anthology, animal, contemporary, folktales, health-related,

nature/environment, poetry, romance, sports. All must relate to Native American life and culture, past and present. Does not want to see "sex, vulgarity or anything not related to American Indian life and culture."

Nonfiction: Picture books, young readers: animal, biography, history, hobbies, nature/environment, sports. Middle readers, young adults: animal, biography, careers, health, history, hobbies, music/dance, nature/environment, sports. All of above must be related to American Indian life and culture, past and present.

How to Contact/Writers: Fiction: Submit complete ms. Nonfiction: Submit outline/synopsis and sample chapters, or submit complete ms. Reports on queries in 2 months; mss in 3 months. "We accept 5% of the manuscripts received. Those with potential must be evaluated by all the members of our Indian Editorial Board, who make the final selection. This board makes sure the material is true to the Indian way of life and is the kind of material they want their children to read." Publishes a book 1 year after acceptance. Will consider simultaneous submissions.

Illustration: Number of illustrations used for fiction: picture books—25; young readers—12; middle readers—10; young adults—10. Number of illustrations used for nonfiction: picture books—20; young readers—10; middle readers—10; young adults—10. Editor will review ms/illustration packages. "Black-and-white artwork only."

How to Contact/Illustrators: Ms/illustration packages: "Samples sent with manuscript." Illustrations only: Query with samples. Reports on art samples in 3 months "when we report back to author on ms." Original artwork returned at job's completion "if requested."

Terms: Pays authors in royalties of 10% based on wholesale price or buys ms outright for "1½¢ per word." Additional payment for ms/illustration packages "sometimes." Factors used to determine payment for ms/illustration package include "number of illustrations used." Sends galleys to authors. Book catalog/manuscript guidelines available for SASE.

Tips: "For our publications, write about one specific tribe or group and be sure actions portrayed are culturally correct for the group and time period portrayed. What kind of material can we use? These are our preferences, in the order listed: Contemporary Indian Life—exciting stories that could happen to Indian children now. (Be sure the children act like present-day Indians, not like some other culture.) Indians of the old days—authentically portrayed. Be specific about who, where and when. How-to—Indian arts, crafts, and activities. Biography—Indians past and present. History and culture—factual material of high interest only. If you are Indian express your ideas and ideals. Folk stories and legends—high interest expressing Indian ideas. Name the specific tribe. Poetry—possibly—if it expresses real Indian ideals. Instructional material and information for teachers of Indian children."

CROCODILE BOOKS, USA, Imprint of Interlink Publishing Group, Inc., 99 Seventh Ave., Brooklyn NY 11215. (718)797-4292. Book publisher. Vice President: Ruth Moushabeck. Publishes 16 picture books/year. 25% of books by first-time authors. *No unsolicited manuscripts accepted.*

Fiction: Picture books: animal, contemporary, history, spy/mystery/adventure.

Nonfiction: Picture book: history, nature/environment.

Terms: Pays authors in royalties. Sends galleys to author; dummies to illustrator. Book catalog free on request.

CROSSWAY BOOKS, Good News Publishers, 1300 Crescent, Wheaton IL 60187. Book Publisher. Editorial assistant: Jennifer Nahrstadt. Publishes 4 middle readers/year; 1-2 young adult titles/year. 10% of books by first-time authors. 3% of books by agented authors.

Fiction: Young readers, middle readers and young adult/teens: contemporary, fantasy, problem novels, religion, science fiction, sports, adventure and suspense/mystery. Recently published *Home By Another Way*, by Nancy N. Rue; *Sadie Rose and the Champion Sharpshooter*, by Hilda Stahl; *Daisy Punkin*, by Hilda Stahl. All books must have spiritual/ religious themes.

How to Contact/Writers: Fiction/nonfiction: Query. Reports on queries in 5 months. Publishes a book up to 1 year after acceptance. Accepts simultaneous submissions.

Illustration: Assistant Jenny Shaw will review artwork for future covers.

How to Contact/Illustrators: Query with samples. Submit resume, color photocopies or slides. Reports back only if interested. Originals returned to artist at job's completion.

Photography: Contact Jenny Shaw, assistant. Query with samples.

Terms: Pays by royalty based on wholesale price. Illustrators paid by the project (negotiable). Authors see galleys for review; illustrators see dummies for review. Book catalog for $1.50 and 9 × 12 SASE. Manuscript guidelines for #10 SASE.

CROWN PUBLISHERS (CROWN BOOKS FOR CHILDREN), Imprint of Random House, Inc. 225 Park Ave. S., New York NY 10003. (212)254-1600. Book publisher. Executive Editor: Simon Boughton. Publishes 20 pictures/year; 10 middle reader titles/year. 2% of books by first-time authors; 70% of books from agented writers.

Fiction: Picture books: adventure, animal, contemporary, fantasy, folktales, health-related, history, nature/environment, sports. Young readers: adventure, anthology, animal, contemporary, fantasy, folktales, health-related, history, nature/environment, sports. Middle reader: adventure, animal, contemporary, fantasy, folktales, health-related, history, nature/environment, problem novels, romance, sports, suspense/mystery. Average word length: picture books—750; young readers—20,000; middle readers—50,000.

Nonfiction: Picture books, young readers and middle readers: activity books, animal, biography, careers, health, history, hobbies, music/dance, nature/environment, religion, sports. Average word length: picture books—750-1,000; young readers—20,000; middle readers—50,000; Recently published: *Under the Sea from A to Z*, by Anne and David Doubilet (4-8 yrs., picture book).

How to Contact/Writers: Fiction/nonfiction: Submit complete manuscript. Reports on queries in 1 month; 2-4 months on mss. Publishes book 2 years after acceptance. Will consider simultaneous submissions.

Illustration: Number of illustrations used for fiction and nonfiction: picture books—33; young readers—10; middle readers—1. Reviews ms/illustration packages. "Double-spaced, continuous manuscripts; do not supply page-by-page breaks. One or two photocopies of art are fine. *Do not send original art.* Dummies are acceptable.

How to Contact/Illustrators: Photocopies or slides with SASE; provide business card and tearsheets. Reports in ms/art samples in 2 months. Original artwork returned at job's completion. Pays author royalty. Advance "varies greatly." Illustrators paid royalty. Sends galleys to authors; proofs to illustrators. Book catalog for 9 × 12 SAE and 4 first class stamps. Manuscript guidelines for 4¼ × 9½ SASE. Artists' guidelines not available.

MAY DAVENPORT, PUBLISHERS, 26313 Purissima Rd., Los Altos Hills CA 94022. (415)948-6499. Book publisher. Estab. 1976. Independent book producer/packager. Editor: May Davenport. Publishes 1-2 picture books/year; 2-3 young adult titles/year. 99% of books by first-time authors. Seeks books with literary merit. "We are overstocked with picture book/elementary reading material."

Fiction: Young adults: adventure, fantasy, suspense/mystery. Average word length: 20,000-30,000 words. Recently published *Creeps*, by Shelly Fredman, (grades 7-12 hardcover); *I Told The Spotted Fish*, by James D. Warwick, (grades 9-12 paperback).

Nonfiction: Young adult: biography/autobiography. Recently published 3rd reprint of *Gramma Curlychief's Pawnee Indian Stories*, by War Cry Howell (grades 9-12 paperback).

How to Contact/Writers: Fiction: Query. Reports on queries in 2-3 weeks. Publishes a book 6-12 months after acceptance.

Terms: Pays authors in royalties based on retail price. Pays "by mutual agreement, no advances." Book listing, manuscript guidelines free on request with SASE.

Tips: "When the writer shows literary talent, we are interested. If the content is worth publishing and is suitable for classroom supplementary literature, we are overjoyed. We might select that kind of book. If you are a writer—write so the words will communicate your thoughts and feelings. If your characters come alive, they will live on in great literature, and classroom teachers will appreciate your talent as models of writers for the present generation, whose models are television writers."

*DAVIS PUBLICATIONS, INC., 50 Portland St., Worcester MA 01608. (508)754-7201. FAX (508)753-3834. Book publisher. Acquisitions Editor: Martha Siegel. Publishes 10 titles total/year. 30% of books by first-time authors. "We publish books for the art education market (elementary through high school), both technique-oriented and art appreciation resource books and textbooks."

Nonfiction: Picture books, young readers, middle readers, young adults: activity books about art and art-related textbooks. Recently published *A World of Images*, by Laura Chapman (junior high school, art appreciation textbook); *The Visual Experience*, by Jack Hobbes/Richard Salome (high school, art appreciation).

How to Contact/Writers: Submit outline/synopsis and 1 sample chapter. Reports on queries in 1 month; reports on mss in 2 months. Publishes a book 1 year after acceptance. Will consider simultaneous submissions and electronic submissions via disk.

Illustration: "We use a combination of photos and line drawings" (200-300 per nonfiction title). Will review ms/illustration packages. Will review artwork for future assignments. Contact Martha Siegel, acquisitions editor.

How to Contact/Illustrators: Query with samples. Reports in 1 month.

Photography: "Rarely" purchases photos from freelancers. Contact Martha Siegel, acquisitions editor. "Usually need photos of particular artists, artworks or art forms." Model/property releases and photo captions required. Publishes photo concept books. Uses 5×7 and 8×10 glossy, b&w prints and 4×5 and 8×10 transparencies.

Terms: Pays authors royalties. Pays illustrators by the project. Sends galleys to authors. Book catalog available for SASE; ms guidelines available for SASE.

Tips: "Consider your market! Do not write merely to satisfy your own interests—consider the interests and needs of your readers."

*DAWN PUBLICATIONS, 14618 Tyler Foote, Nevada City CA 95959. (916)292-3482. FAX: (916)292-4258. Book publisher. Publisher: Bob Rinzler. Nature and holistic issues.

Fiction: All levels: adventure, animal, health-related and nature/environment.

Nonfiction: All levels: animal, health, nature/environment.

How to Contact/Writers: Nonfiction: Query; submit complete ms; submit outline/synopsis and sample chapters. Reports in 2 months on queries/mss. Publishes a book 1 year after acceptance. Will consider simultaneous submissions and previously published work.

Illustration: Will review ms/illustration packages. Will review artwork for future assignments.

How to Contact/Illustrators: Ms/illustration packages: Query; submit complete package; submit chapters of manuscript. Illustrations only: Query with samples.

Terms: Pays authors royalty. Offers advance. Sends galleys to authors; dummies to illustrators. Book catalog available for 6×9 SASE.

DELACORTE PRESS AND DOUBLEDAY BOOKS FOR YOUNG READERS, Dell Publishing, 666 5th Avenue, New York NY 10103. Book publisher. Publisher: George Nicholson. Publishes 20 picture books/year; 10 young reader titles/year; 20 middle reader titles/year; 10 young adult titles/year. 10% of books by first-time authors; 70% of books from agented writers.

Fiction: Picture books: adventure, animal, contemporary, easy-to-read, fantasy, history. Young Readers: animal, contemporary, easy-to-read, fantasy, sports, suspense/mystery. Middle Readers: adventure, animal, contemporary, easy-to-read, fantasy, sports, suspense/mystery; Young Adults/Teens: adventure, anthology, contemporary, fantasy, problem novels, sports, suspense/mystery. Recently published *Wanted . . . Mud Blossom*, by Betsy Byars (grades 3-7, novel); *The River*, by Gary Paulsen (grades 7 and up, novel).

Nonfiction: "Delacorte publishes a very limited number of nonfiction titles."

How to Contact/Writers: Submit through agent only. All unsolicited manuscripts returned unopened with the following exceptions: "Unsolicited picture book mss accepted. Unsolicited manuscripts accepted for the Delacorte Press Prize for a First Young Adult Novel contest (see contest section)." Reports on queries in 6-8 weeks; reports on mss in 3 months.

Illustration: Number of illustrations used per fiction title varies considerably. Will review manuscript illustration packages.

How to Contact/Illustrators: Query first. Do not send originals. All samples will be filed and not returned "If you submit a dummy, please submit the text separately." Illustrations only: tearsheets, résumé, samples that do not need to be returned. Reports on ms/art samples only if interested. Original artwork returned at job's completion.

Terms: Pays authors royalty based on retail price or outright purchase on some art only. Pay for illustrators: royalty based on retail price. Sends galleys to authors.

*T.S. DENISON CO. INC., 9601 Newton Ave. S., Minneapolis MN 55431. Editor: Baxter Brings. 25% of books by first-time authors. Publishes teacher resource/activity books. "We mostly publish nonfiction."

Nonfiction: Picture books, young readers and middle readers: activity books, animal, biography, careers, health, history, hobbies, music/dance, nature/environment, textbooks/basal readers.. Average word length: picture books — 96 pages; middle readers — 150 pages. Recently published *Treat the Earth Gently*, by Sherrill Flora (middle reader, activity book); *Story Sparklers*, by Jean Stangl (middle reader, language arts); *Let's Meet Famous Artists*, by Harriet Kinghorn (middle reader, art biography activity).

How to Contact/Writers: Fiction/nonfiction: Query; submit complete manuscript; submit outline/synopsis and 2 sample chapters. Reports on queries/mss in 3 weeks. Publishes a book 9 months after acceptance. Will consider simultaneous submissions and electronic submissions via disk or modem.

Illustration: Average number of illustrations used for fiction: picture books, young and middle readers — 12; nonfiction: picture books, young and middle readers — 90. Will review ms/illustrations packages. Will review artwork for future assignments. Contact Baxter Brings, editor.

How to Contact/Illustrators: Illustrations only: Query with samples; send unsolicited art samples by mail; arrange a personal interview to show portfolio; provide résumé, promotional literature and tearsheets. Reports in 1 month. Original artwork not returned at job's completion.

Terms: Pays authors royalty of 4-8% based on wholesale price. Outright purchase $300-1,000. Pays illustrators by the project (range: $400 for covers; $25 for b&w). Book catalog available for 9 × 12 SAE and 3 first class stamps; ms guidelines available for SASE.

DIAL BOOKS FOR YOUNG READERS, Penguin Books USA Inc., 375 Hudson St., New York NY 10014. (212)366-2800. Editor-in-Chief: Phyllis J. Fogelman. Publishes 40-50 picture books/year; 10 young reader titles/year; 5 middle reader titles/year; 10 young adult titles/year.
Fiction: Picture books: adventure, animal, contemporary, fantasy, folktales, history, nature/environment, poetry, religion, science fiction, sports, suspense/mystery. Young readers: animal, contemporary, easy-to-read, fantasy, folktales, history, nature/environment, poetry, science fiction, sports, mystery/adventure. Middle readers, young adults: animal, contemporary, fantasy, folktales, history, health-related, nature/environment, poetry, problem novels, religion, science fiction, sports, spy/mystery/adventure. Recently published *Max's Dragon Shirt*, by Rosemary Wells (ages 4-8, picture book); *The Whale's Song*, by Dyan Sheldon (ages 4-8, picture book); and *Rats on the Roof and Other Stories*, by James Marshall.
Nonfiction: Uses very little nonfiction but will consider submissions of outstanding artistic and literary merit. Picture books: animal, biography, history, nature/environment, sports. Young readers: activity books, animal, biography, history, nature/environment, religion, sports. Middle readers: animal, biography, careers, health, history, nature/environment, religion, sports. Young adults: animal, biography, careers, health, history, hobbies, music/dance, nature/environment, religion, sports. Recently published *A Flower Grows*, by Ken Robbins (ages 4-8, picture book); *Extraordinay Eyes*, by Sandra Sinclair (middle readers).
How to Contact/Writers: Fiction: Query, submit outline/synopsis and sample chapters for longer work, submit complete ms for short material.
Illustration: Editorial will review ms/illustration packages. Prefers to use own artists for mss submitted by authors. Will review an illustrator's work for possible future assignments.
How to Contact/Illustrators: Ms/illustration packages: Query first or 1 piece of final color art and sketches. Illustrations only: Query with samples; submit portfolio for review; arrange a personal interview to show portfolio; provide tearsheets to be kept on file.
Photography: Photographers should contact Toby Sherry. Model/property releases required with submissions. Publishes photo essays. Uses b&w, glossy prints and 35mm, 2¼×2¼, 4×5 transparencies. To contact, photographers should submit portfolio for review; arrange a personal interview to show portfolio; provide tearsheets to be kept on file.
Terms: Pays authors and illustrators in royalties based on retail price. Average advance payment "varies." Manuscript guidelines for SASE.

*■DISCOVERY ENTERPRISES, LTD., 134 Middle St., Lowell MA 01852. (508)459-1720. FAX: (508)937-5779. Book publisher and independent book producer/packager. Executive Director: JoAnne Weisman. Publishes 6 middle readers books/year. 40% of books by first-time authors; subsidy publishes 10%. Publishes all nonfiction picture book biographies in 9×12 full color format—serious histories, but original. Illustrations are key to the works. Also pen & ink drawings for history series."
Fiction: Picture books, young readers and middle readers: history, nature/environment. Young adults: history.
Nonfiction: Picture books, young readers and middle readers: biography, history, nature/environment, third world countries. Young adults: biography, history, nature/environment. "No sports, religious leaders or current entertainers for biographies." Average word length: picture books 3,000; young and middle readers 3,000-4,000; young adults 4,000-5,000. Recently published *Leonard Bernstein: America's Maestro*, by Kenneth M. Deitch (10 and up, picture book biography); *Lucretia Mott: Friend of Justice*, by Kem Knapp Sawyer (8 and up, picture book biography); *W.E.B. DuBois: Crusader for Peace*, by Kathryn Cryan-Hicks (10 and up, picture book biography).

How to Contact/Writers: Fiction: Query. Nonfiction: Query. Submit outline/synopsis and 3 sample chapters. Reports on queries in 4-6 weeks; reports on mss in 6-8 weeks. Publishes a book 6 months after acceptance. Will consider simultaneous submissions and previously published work.
Illustration: Average number of illustrations used for fiction: picture books, young readers, middle readers and young adults—22. Nonfiction: picture books—22; young readers—20-30; middle readers—22; young adults—20-30. Will review ms/illustration packages. Will review artwork for future assignments. Contact: JoAnne Weisman, executive director. "No preference in medium of style, but artist must be able to do portraits, as these are biographies."
How to Contact/Illustrators: Ms/illustration packages: Submit 2-3 chapters of ms with 4-6 pieces of final art. Send samples of artwork—color copies OK with text. Illustrations only: Query with samples; provide resume, promotional literature and tearsheets to be kept on file. Reports in 4-6 weeks. Original artwork returned at job's completion "but not for 2 years."
Photography: Photographers should contact JoAnne Weisman, executive director. Uses all types of photos. Model/property releases and captions required. Interested in stock photos. Uses 35mm, 2¼ × 2¼ and 4 × 5 transparencies. To contact, photographers should query with samples; provide resume, business card, promotional literature and tearsheets to be kept on file.
Terms: Pays authors royalty of 5-10% based on wholesale price. Offers $1,000 advance. Pays illustrators by the project (range: $600-1,500) or royalty of 5-10% based on wholesale price. Photographers paid per photo (range: $25-400). Sends galleys to authors; dummies to illustrators. Book catalog available for #10 SASE.
Tips: Wants "Neat, clean artwork, presented professionally." For writers, good cover letter, outline and sample chapters necessary. "Watch for grammatical errors. I prefer separate submissions from artists and authors. Carefully research and accurately illustrate art for histories and biographies in any medium." Sees trend toward more nonfiction for use in classrooms to supplement or replace textbooks, as well as more emphasis on multi-racial books, women' history, peace, etc.

*DISTINCTIVE PUBLISHING CORP., P.O. Box 17868, Plantation FL 33318-7868. (305)975-2413. Book publisher. Independent book producer/packager. Editor: Drollene P. Brown. Publishes 1-2 books/year. 95% of books by first-time authors.
Fiction: "We will consider all submissions." Recently published *Ships of Children*, by Richard Taylor (middle-young adult, adventure).
Nonfiction: "As with fiction we will consider all submissions."
How to Contact/Writers: Nonfiction: Submit complete ms. Reports on queries in 1-2 weeks; reports on mss in 1-2 months. Publishes book 6-12 months after acceptance. Will consider simultaneous submissions and previously published work.
Illustration: Will review ms/illustration packages.
How to Contact/Illustrators: Ms/illustration packages: Submit complete package. Reports in 1 month. Original artwork is returned at job's completion.
Photography: Photographers should contact Alan Erdlee, publisher. Type of photos used depends on project. Model/property release and photo captions required. Interested in stock photos. Publishes photo concept books. Uses 4 × 6 glossy color prints, 2¼ × 2¼ transparencies. To contact, photographer should query with samples; query with resume of credits; provide resume, business card, tearsheets to be kept on file.
Terms: Pays authors royalty based on wholesale and retail price; outright purchase; "each project is different." Offers advances. Pays illustrators by the project or royalty. Photographers are paid by the project or per photo. Sends galleys to author; dummies to illustrators. Book catalog available for 9 × 12 SASE.
Tips: Best chance of selling to this market is with adventure and educational mss.

DUTTON CHILDREN'S BOOKS, Penguin USA, 375 Hudson St., New York NY 10014. (212)366-2600. Book publisher. Editor-in-Chief: Lucia Monfried. Publishes approximately 60 picture books/year; 4 young reader titles/year; 10 middle reader titles/year; 8 young adult titles/year. 15% of books by first-time authors.
Fiction: Picture books: adventure, animal, contemporary, fantasy, folktales, suspense/ mystery. Young readers: adventure, animal, contemporary, easy-to-read, fantasy, folktales, science fiction, suspense/mystery. Middle readers: adventure, animal, contemporary, fantasy, history, science fiction, spy/mystery/adventure. Young adults: animal, contemporary, fantasy, history, science fiction, suspense/mystery. Recently published *Where's Our Mama?*, by Diane Goode (picture book, ages 3-7); *The Remarkable Journey of Prince Jen*, by Lloyd Alexander (ages 10 and up, novel); and *The Seven and a Half Labors of Hercules*, by John Bendall-Brunello (ages 7-10, speedster series for reluctant readers).
Nonfiction: Picture books: animal, nature/environment. Young readers: animal, biography, nature/environment. Middle readers: animal, biography, history, nature/environment. Young adults: animal, biography, health, history, nature/environment. Recently published *Wasps at Home*, by Bianca Lavies (ages 8 and up, photo essay); *The Story of Christmas*, words from the Gospels of Matthew and Luke, illustrated by Jane Ray (all ages, picture book published in both English and Spanish).
How to Contact/Writers: Fiction/nonfiction: query. Reports on queries in 2 months; on mss in 3 months. Publishes a book 12-18 months after acceptance. Will consider simultaneous submissions.
Illustration: Number of illustrations used for fiction: picture books—14-28; easy readers—30; middle readers—15. Editorial will review ms/illustration packages. Design department will review illustrator's work for possible future assignments.
How to Contact/Illustrators: Ms/illustration packages: Query first. Illustrations only: Query with samples; send resume, tearsheets, slides—no original art please. Reports on art samples in 2 months. Original artwork returned at job's completion.
Terms: Pays authors in royalties based on retail price. Book catalog, manuscript guidelines for SAE. Pays illustrators in royalties based on retail price unless jacket illustration—then pays by flat fee. Photographers paid royalty per photo.
Tips: Writers: "We publish high-quality trade books and are interested in well-written manuscripts with fresh ideas and child appeal. Take a look at what is on the shelves of libraries and children's books stores to get a feel for the market. Avoid topics that appear quite frequently. We have a complete publishing program. Though we publish mostly picture books, we are very interested in acquiring more novels for young, middle, and young adult readers. In nonfiction, we are looking for history, general biography, science, and photo essays for all age groups." Illustrators: "We would like to see samples and portfolios from potential illustrators of picture books (full color), young novels (black and white), and jacket artists (full color)."

WM. B. EERDMANS PUBLISHING COMPANY, 255 Jefferson Avenue S.E., Grand Rapids MI 49503. (616)459-4591. Book publisher. Children's Book Editor: Amy Eerdmans. Publishes 6 picture books/year; 4 young reader titles/year; 4 middle reader titles/year.
Fiction: All levels: religion, fantasy, problem novels, parables, retold Bible stories from a Christian perspective.
Nonfiction: All levels: biography, history, nature/environment, religion.
How to Contact/Writers: Fiction/nonfiction: Query; submit complete manuscript. Reports on queries in 1-2 weeks; mss in 4 weeks.
Illustration: Reviews manuscript packages. Willem Mineur, art director, will review illustrator's work for possible future assignments.
How to Contact/Illustrators: Illustrations only: Submit résumé, slides or color photocopy. Reports on ms/art samples in 1 month. Original artwork returned at job's completion.

Terms: Pays authors in royalties of 5-10%. Pays in royalty for the author. The illustrator receives royalty or permission fee. Sends galleys for review; dummies to illustrators. Book catalog free on request; manuscript and/or artist's guidelines free on request.

ENSLOW PUBLISHERS INC., Bloy St. & Ramsey Ave., Box 777, Hillside NJ 07205. (201)964-4116. Vice President: Brian D. Enslow. Estab. 1978. Publishes 20 middle reader titles/year; 20 young adult titles/year. 30% of books by first-time authors.
Nonfiction: Young readers, middle readers, young adults: activity books, animal, biography, careers, health, history, hobbies, nature/environment, sports. Average word length: middle readers-5,000; young adult-15,000. Recently published *Louis Armstrong*, by Patricia and Fredrick McKissack (grades 2-3, biography); *Lotteries: Who Wins, Who Loses?*, by Ann E. Weiss (grades 6-12, issues book).
How to Contact/Writers: Nonfiction: Query. Reports on queries/mss in 2 weeks. Publishes a book 18 months after acceptance. Will consider simultaneous submissions.
Illustration: Number of illustrations used for nonfiction: middle readers—28; young adults—28.
How to Contact/Illustrators: Provide résumé, business card or tearsheets to be kept on file.
Terms: Pays authors in royalties of 10% based on net price. Sends galleys to authors. Book catalog/manuscript guidelines available for $2.

ESOTERICA PRESS, P.O. Box 15607, Rio Rancho NM 87174. Book publisher. "This year we will be publishing our first children's book— a Native American tale." Editorial contact person in any category: Y. Zentella.
Fiction: Picture books and young readers: Bilingual folktales and history.
Nonfiction: Picture books and young readers: biography, history, music/dance, ethnic (bilingual).
How to Contact/Writers: Fiction/nonfiction: Query; submit outline/synopsis and sample chapters; submit complete manuscript. Reports on queries in 2-4 weeks; 2-3 months on mss. Publishes a book "About 6-9 months depending on editing needed and technical problems that can arise." Will consider simultaneous submissions.
Illustration: Editorial will review illustration packages. Publisher, Yoly Zentella, will review illustrator's work for possible future assignments. "Illustrator must be aware that we will reduce/enlarge to fit our needs." Uses primarily b&w artwork only.
How to Contact/Illustrators: Query first or submit manuscript and sketches. Submit photocopies. Reports on ms/art samples in 2-3 months. Original artwork returned at job's completion. "Please include SASE. Work sent without proper SASE will *not* be returned."
Terms: Expenses paid first. Author gets 60% of profits and 10% of print run. (Additional payment for artwork.) Pay for illustrators: by the project. Sends galleys to author; dummies to illustrators. Book catalog for legal SAE and 2 first class stamps. Manuscript/artist's guidelines for legal SAE and 2 first class stamps.
Tips: Wants "Humanist themes. We are especially interested in Latino, Native-American, Black, Arab-Muslim and Asian themes." Also looking for material addressing the handicapped, speech education, special needs, etc. (bilingual Spanish/English).

FACTS ON FILE, 460 Park Ave. S., New York NY 10016. (212)683-2244. Book publisher. Editorial Contact: James Warren. Publishes 35 young adult titles/year. 5% of books by first-time authors; 25% of books from agented writers; additional titles through book packagers, co-publishers and unagented writers.
Nonfiction: Young adults: animal, biography, science, education, history, music/dance, nature/environment, religion, sports. Published *Martin Luther King, Jr. and the Freedom Movement*, by Lillie Patterson; *The CIA*, by Graham Yost; *Opening the Space Frontier*, by Diane Moser and Ray Spangenburg. (ages 10 and up).

How to Contact/Writers: Nonfiction: Submit outline/synopsis and sample chapters. Reports on queries in 4 weeks. Publishes a book 10 months after acceptance. Will consider simultaneous submissions. Sends galleys to authors. Book catalog free on request.
Tips: "Most projects have high reference value and fit into a series format."

FARRAR, STRAUS & GIROUX, 19 Union Square West, New York NY 10003. (212)741-6934. Book publisher. Children's books Editor-in-Chief: Margaret Ferguson. Estab. 1946. Publishes 21 picture books/year; 6 middle reader titles/year; 5 young adult titles/year. 5% of books by first-time authors; 5% of books from agented writers.
Fiction: "Original and well-written material for all ages." Published *Carl's Afternoon in the Park*, by Alexandra Day (ages 3 up); *Predator!*, by Bruce Brooks (ages 10 and up); *An Acceptable Time*, by Madeleine L'Engle (young adult).
How to Contact/Writers: Fiction/nonfiction: Query; submit outline/synopsis and sample chapters. Reports on queries in 6 weeks; on mss in 12 weeks. Publishes a book 18 months after acceptance. Will consider simultaneous submissions.
Illustration: Number of illustrations used for fiction: picture books—32; middle readers—10. Number of illustrations used for nonfiction: middle readers—15. Will review ms/illustration packages.
How to Contact/Illustrators: Ms/illustration packages: Ms with 1 piece of final art, remainder roughs. Illustrations only: Tearsheets. Reports on art samples only if interested. Original artwork returned at job's completion.
Terms: "We offer an advance against royalties for both authors and illustrators." Sends galleys to authors; dummies to illustrators. Book catalog available for 6½ × 9½ SAE and 56¢ postage; manuscript guidelines for 1 first-class stamp.
Tips: "Study our catalog before submitting. We will see illustrator's portfolios by appointment."

*FIESTA CITY PUBLISHERS, Box 5861, Santa Barbara CA 93150-5861. (805)733-1984. Book publisher. Editorial contact: Ann Cooke. Publishes 1 middle reader title/year; 1 young adult title/year. 25% of books by first-time authors.
Nonfiction: Young adult: music/dance, self-help. Average word length: 30,000.
How to Contact/Writers: Fiction/nonfiction: Query. Reports on queries in 2 weeks; on ms in 1 month. Publishes a book 1 year after acceptance. Will consider simultaneous submissions.
Tips: "Write clearly and simply. Do not write 'down' to young adults (or children). Looking for self-help books on current subjects."

FOUR WINDS PRESS, imprint of Macmillan Publishing Co., 866 Third Ave., New York NY 10022. (212)702-2000. Book publisher. Editor-in-Chief: Virginia Duncan. 15-20% of books by first-time authors; 80% of books from agented writers.
Fiction: Picture books: animal, contemporary, humor, fantasy. Middle readers: history, family, contemporary. Average word length: picture books—750-1,500; middle readers—10,000-30,000. "YA books are no longer being considered."

✱ *The asterisk before a listing indicates the listing is new in this edition.*

Nonfiction: Picture books: animal, nature/environment, biography, history, concepts. Middle readers: animal, biography, history, hobbies, music/dance, nature/environment, sports. Average word length: picture books—750-1,500; middle readers—10,000-30,000.

How to Contact/Writers: Fiction: Submit outline/synopsis and complete ms. Nonfiction: Query. Reports on queries/mss in 3 months. "Due to volume of submissions received, we cannot guarantee a quick response time or answer queries about manuscript status." Publishes a book 18-24 months after acceptance. "We are *not* reviewing simultaneous submissions."

Illustration: Number of illustrations used for fiction and nonfiction: picture books—24-40 full page illustrations; middle readers—15-20 mostly full page illustrations. Editorial will review ms/illustration packages.

How to Contact/Illustrators: Picture books: Submit full ms or dummy with art samples (not originals!). Illustrations only: "Illustration portfolios are reviewed every Thursday on a drop-off basis. If you cannot drop off your portfolio, you should mail tearsheets. Your portfolio should contain samples of work that best reflect your technical and creative ability to illustrate a text for children. These samples should include two or three different scenes of animals and/or children rendered in a setting. These should show your ability to handle composition, create interesting characters, and maintain consistency between scenes. Use whatever medium is best suited to your technique. Generally, still life, three dimensional artwork and abstract compositions do not translate well to children's book illustrations." Reports on ms/art samples in 6-8 weeks; art samples only if interested. Original artwork returned at job's completion.

Terms: Pays authors in royalties of 5-10% based on retail price (depends on whether artist is sharing royalties). Pay for illustrators: by the project; royalties range from 2-5%; "fees and royalties vary widely according to budget for book." Sends galleys to authors; dummies to illustrators. Manuscript and/or artist's guidelines for 1 first-class stamp and a business-size envelope. "No calls, please."

Tips: "The length of your story depends on the age of the child for whom it is intended. There are no fixed lengths. A good story is almost always the right length or can easily be made so." (See also Aladdin Books/Collier Books for Young Adults, Atheneum Publishers, Bradbury Press, Margaret K. McElderry Books.)

FREE SPIRIT PUBLISHING, Ste. 616, 400 First Ave. N., Minneapolis MN 55401. (612)338-2068. Book publisher. Publisher/President: Judy Galbraith. Publishes 2-3 middle reader titles/year; 2-3 young adult titles/year. 80% of books by first-time authors. "Our books pertain to the education and psychological well being of young people."

Nonfiction: Picture books, young readers, middle readers and young adults: health, hobbies, nature/environment, self-esteem, psychology, education. Recently published *The Kide's Guide to Social Action: How to Solve the Social Problems You Choose-And Turn Creative Thinking Into Positive Action*, by Barbara A. Lewis (ages 10 and older, resource); *Stick Up for Yourself! Every Kid's Guide to Personal Power and Positive Self-Esteem*, by Gershen Kaufman, Ph.D and Lev Raphael, Ph.D. (ages 8-12, psychology/self-help); *Writing Down the Days: 365 Creative Journaling Ideas for Young People*, by Lorraine M. Dahlstrom (ages 12 and older, education).

How to Contact/Writers: Nonfiction: Submit résumé, outline/synopsis and sample chapters. Reports on queries in 3 months. Publishes a book 12-18 months after acceptance.

Terms: Pays authors in royalties of 8-12% based on wholesale price. Offers advance payment of $500-$1,000. Sends galleys to authors. Book catalog free on request.

Tips: Does not accept unsolicited artists' or photographers' samples. Wants to see "A book that helps kids help themselves, or that helps adults help kids help themselves."

*FRIENDSHIP PRESS, National Council of Churches of Christ in the USA, Rm. 860, 475 Riverside Dr., New York NY 10469. (212)870-2585. Book publisher. Editorial Contact: Carol Ames. Publishes 1-2 picture books/year; 1 young reader title/year; 1 middle reader title/year; 1 young adult title/year. 75% of books commissioned for set themes.
Fiction: Picture books, young readers, middle readers, young adults: mission and religion. Average word length: young adults—20,000-40,000. Recently published *Pearl Makers*, by Vilma May Fuentes (grades 1-6, stories about the Philippines); *Akiand the Bannes of Names*, by Atsuko Gōda Lolling (grades 1-6, stories about Japan).
Nonfiction: Picture books, young readers, middle readers, young adults: mission and religion. Average word length: middle readers—10,000; young adults—10,000.
How to Contact/Writers: Fiction and nonfiction: Query. Reports on queries/mss in 3-6 weeks. Publishes a book 18 months after acceptance. Will consider simultaneous submissions. Ms guidelines free on request.
Illustration: Number of illustrations used for fiction and nonfiction—8. Editorial will review ms/illustration packages. Art Director, Paul Lansdale, will review an illustrator's work for future assignments.
How to Contact/Illustrators: Ms/illustration packages: send 3 chapters of ms with 1 piece of final art. Illustrations only: send résumé and tearsheets. Reports only if interested. Original artwork returned at job's completion.
Terms: Buys ms outright for $25-1200. Sends galleys to authors; dummies to illustrators. Book catalog and ms guidelines free on request.

GOLDEN BOOKS, Western Publishing Co., 850 Third Ave., New York NY 10022. (212)753-8500. Editorial Directors: Margo Lundell, Selma Lanes. Book publisher.
Fiction: Picture books: animal, easy-to-read. Young readers: easy-to-read. Middle readers: history, sports. Young adult titles: contemporary, sports.
Nonfiction: Picture books: education, history, nature/environment, sports. Young readers: animal, education, history, nature/environment, sports. Middle readers: animal, education, history, nature/environment, sports.
How to Contact/Writers: "Not accepting any solicitations for at least a year." Fiction/nonfiction: query.
Illustration: Art directors David Werner and Linda Neilson will sometimes review ms/illustration packages. Will review an illustrator's work for possible future assignments.
How to Contact/Illustrators: Ms/illustration packages: query first.
Terms: Pays authors in royalties based on retail price.

*GOSPEL LIGHT PUBLICATIONS, Imprint of Regal Books, 2300 Knoll Dr., Ventura CA 93003. (805)644-9721. Book publisher. Acquisitions Editor: Linda Holland. Publishes 1 picture book/year; 2-3 young reader titles/year; 1 young adult title/year.
Fiction: Picture books and young readers: value-oriented. Recently published *Smarty the Adventurous Fly*, by Ethel Barrett (ages 3-8, picture book); *Jasper*, by Ethel Barrett (ages 3-8, picture book).
Nonfiction: Picture books, young readers, middle readers and young adults/teens: religion.
How to Contact/Writers: Fiction/nonfiction: Submit outline/synopsis and sample chapters. Reports on queries in 4-6 weeks; reports on mss in 6-8 weeks. Publishes book 7-12 months after acceptance. Will consider simultaneous submissions.

"Picture books" are geared toward the preschool—8 year old group; "Young readers" to 5-8 year olds; "Middle readers" to 9-11 year olds; and "Young adults" to those 12 and up.

Illustration: Will review manuscript/illustration packages. Linda Holland, acquisitions editor, will review an illustrator's work for possible future assignments.
How to Contact/Illustrators: Submit 3 chapters/1 piece final art. Provide resume and photocopies of work. Reports in 6 weeks. Original artwork returned at job's completion.
Terms: Pays authors royalty based on wholesale price or outright purchase. Sends galleys to authors; dummies to illustrators. Book catalog available for 9 × 12 and 2 first class stamps; ms guidelines available for SASE.

GREENHAVEN PRESS, 10907 Technology Place, San Diego CA 92127. (619)485-7424. Book publisher. Estab. 1970. Senior Editors: Terry O'Neill and Bonnie Szumski. Publishes 40-50 young adult titles/year. 35% of books by first-time authors.
Nonfiction: Middle readers: biography, history, controversial topics, issues. Young adults: biography, history, nature/environment. Other titles "to fit our specific series." Average word length: young adults — 15,000-18,000.
How to Contact/Writers: Nonfiction: Query. Reports on queries generally in 1-2 weeks. Publishes a book 12-15 months after acceptance.
Terms/Writers: Buys ms outright for $1,500-2,500. Offers average advance payment of ⅓-½. Sends galleys to authors. Books catalog available for 9 × 12 SAE and 65¢ postage.
Tips: "Get our guidelines first before submitting anything."

*GREENWILLOW BOOKS, imprint of William Morrow & Co., 1350 Ave. of the Americas, New York NY 10019. (212)261-6500. Book publisher. Publishes 30-40 picture books/year; 10 young readers books/year; 10 middle readers books/year; 10 young adult books/year.
Fiction: Will consider all levels of fiction; various categories.
How to Contact/Writers: Fiction: Submit complete ms. Reports on queries in 3 weeks; reports on mss in 2 months. Publishes a book 18-24 months after acceptance. Will consider simultaneous submissions.
Terms: Pays authors royalty. Offers advances. Pays illustrators royalty. Sends galleys to authors. Book catalog available for 9 × 12 SASE; ms/artist's guidelines available for SASE.

*GROSSET & DUNLAP, imprint of The Putnam & Grosset Book Group/Putnam Berkley Group, 200 Madison Ave., New York NY 10016. (212)951-8700. Book publisher. Editor-in-Chief: Craig Walker. Publishes 20 picture books/year; 10 young readers/year; 12 middle readers/year; 4 young adult titles/year; 20 board books/year; 16 novelty books/year. 5% of books by first-time authors; 10% of books from agented authors. Publishes fiction and nonfiction for mass market; novelty and board books.
Fiction: Most categories will be considered. "We publish series fiction, but not original novels in the young adult category." Recently published *The Christmas Pageant*, by Jacqueline Rogers (ages 3-7, picture book).
Nonfiction: Recently published *The Big Green Book*, by Fred Pearce (ages 7-10, environmental); *All Around the World*, by Judy Donnelly (ages 4-8, book & globe).
How to Contact/Writers: Fiction/nonfiction: Query. Reports in 4 weeks on queries; 1-2 months on mss. Publishes book 1-2 years after acceptance. Will consider simultaneous submissions.
Illustrations: Average number of illustrations used for fiction: picture books — 32; middle readers — 32. Average number of illustrations used for nonfiction: picture books — 32-48; middle readers — 32. Will review ms/illustration packages. Will review artwork for future assignments. Contact Ronnie Ann Herman, art director.
How to Contact/Illustrators: Ms/illustration packages: Query. Illustrations only: Query with samples; send unsolicited art samples by mail; submit portfolio for review; provide promotional literature or tearsheets to be kept on file. Reports only if interested. Original artwork returned at job's completion.

Photography: Photographers should contact Ronnie Ann Herman, art director. Uses photos of babies and toddlers—full color. Interested in stock photos. Publishes photo concept books. Uses color prints; 35mm, 2¼×2¼, 4×5, and 8×10 transparencies. To contact, photographers should query with samples, send unsolicited photos by mail, submit portfolio, provide promotional literature or tearsheets to be kept on file.

Terms: Pays authors royalty or by outright purchase. Offers advances. Pays illustrators by the project or by royalty. Photographers paid by the project or per photo. Book catalog available for 9×12 SASE. Ms guidelines available for SASE.

Tips: Looks for "strong and original ideas and artwork for young children."

HARBINGER HOUSE, INC., 2802 North Alvenon Way, Tucson AZ 85712. (602)326-9595. Publisher: Laurel Gregory. Publishes 2 picture books/year; 2 young reader titles/year. 40% of books by first-time authors; 10% of books from agented writers.

Fiction: Picture books: "all kinds." Young readers: adventure, fantasy, history, nature/environment. Published *The Marsh King's Daughter*, by Andersen/Gentry (all ages, classic fantasy); *One Green Mesquite Tree*, by Jernigan (ages 3-5, counting rhyme); *Mystery on Mackinac Island*, (ages 8-11).

Nonfiction: Picture books: "all kinds." Young readers: animal, history, nature/environment, geography. Published *Willy Whitefeather's Outdoor Survival Handbook for Kids*, by Whitefeather (all ages, nature/environment).

How to Contact/Writers: Fiction/nonfiction: Submit outline/synopsis and sample chapters. Reports on queries in 4-5 weeks; on mss in 7-9 weeks. Publishes a book 18-24 months after acceptance. Will consider simultaneous submissions.

Illustration: Average number of illustrations used for fiction: picture books—10; young readers—8. Number of illustrations used for nonfiction: picture books—14; young readers—14. Editorial will review ms/illustration packages.

How to Contact/Illustrators: "For picture books and young readers only: Color copies of minimum of 3 pieces of art." Illustrations only: Color copies. Reports on art samples in 6 weeks.

Terms: Pays authors in royalties based on net receipts. Average advance payment $800-1,000. Pay for illustrators: "royalties based on net receipts." Sends galleys to authors; sometimes sends dummies to illustrators. Book catalog free on request.

Tips: Looks for "manuscripts with a particular, well-articulated message or purpose." Illustrators: Looks for "art of imagination and skill that has something special."

HARCOURT BRACE JOVANOVICH, Children's Books Division which includes: HBJ Children's Books, Gulliver Books, Voyager Paperbacks, Odyssey Paperbacks, Jane Yolen Books, 1250 Sixth Ave., San Diego CA 92101. (619)699-6810. Book publisher. Attention: Manuscript Submissions, Children's Books Division. Publishes 40-45 picture books/year; 15-20 middle reader titles/year; 8-12 young adult titles/year. 20% of books by first-time authors; 50% of books from agented writers.

Fiction: Picture books, young readers: animal, contemporary, fantasy, history. Middle readers, young adults: animal, contemporary, fantasy, history, problem novels, romance, science fiction, sports, spy/mystery/adventure. Average word length: picture books—"varies greatly"; middle readers—20,000-50,000; young adults—35,000-65,000.

Nonfiction: Picture books, young readers: animal, biography, history, hobbies, music/dance, nature/environment, religion, sports. Middle readers, young adults: animal, biography, education, history, hobbies, music/dance, nature/environment, religion, sports. Average word length: picture books—"varies greatly"; middle readers—20,000-50,000; young adults—35,000-65,000.

How to Contact/Writers: Fiction/nonfiction: Query; submit outline/synopsis and sample chapters; submit complete ms for picture books only. "Only HBJ Children's Books accepts unsolicited manuscripts." Reports on queries/mss in 6-8 weeks.

Illustration: Number of illustrations used for fiction and nonfiction: picture books— 25-30; middle readers—6-12; young adults—jacket. Editorial will review ms/illustration packages. Art Director of Children's Books, Michael Farmer, will review an illustrator's work for possible future assignments.
How to Contact/Illustrators: Ms/illustration packages: picture books ms—complete ms acceptable. Longer books—outline and 2-4 sample chapters. Send several samples of art; no original art. Illustrations only: Résumé, tearsheets, color photocopies, color stats all accepted. Please DO NOT send original artwork or transparencies. Include SASE for return, please. Reports on art samples in 6-10 weeks. Original artwork returned at job's completion.
Terms: Pays authors in royalties based on retail price. Pay for illustrators: by the project. Sends galleys to authors; dummies to illustrators. Book catalog available for 9×12 SASE; manuscript/artist's guidelines for business-size SASE.
Tips: "Become acquainted with HBJ's books in particular if you are interested in submitting proposals to us."

HARPERCOLLINS CHILDREN'S BOOKS, (formerly Harper & Row Junior Books Group), 10 E. 53rd St., New York NY 10022. (212)207-7044. Contact: Submissions Editor. Book publisher.
Fiction: Picture books: animal, sports. Young readers: easy-to-read, sports. Middle readers: adventure, fantasy, history, sports. Young adult titles: contemporary, history, problem novels, sports.
Nonfiction: Picture books, young readers, middle readers, young adult titles: animal, biography, history, music/dance, nature/environment, sports.
How to Contact/Writers: Fiction/nonfiction: query, submit outline/synopsis and sample chapters.
Illustration: Will review ms/illustration packages (preferable to see picture books without art); illustrator's work for possible future assignments. (No original art, please).
How to Contact/Illustrators: Ms/illustrations packages: query first.
Terms: Pays authors in royalties based on retail price.

HARVEST HOUSE PUBLISHERS, 1075 Arrowsmith, Eugene OR 97402. (503)343-0123. Book publisher. Manuscript Coordinator: LaRae Weikert. Editorial Assistant: Mary Connor. Publishes 5-6 picture books/year; 3 young reader titles/year; 3 young adult titles/year. 25% of books by first-time authors.
Fiction: Christian theme. Picture books: animal, easy-to-read. Young readers: contemporary, easy-to-read. Middle readers: contemporary, fantasy. Young adults: fantasy, problem novels, romance. Recently published *My Very Own Bible*, a Harvest House product (ages 2-6); *An All-Time Awesome Bible Search*, by Sandy Silverthorne (ages 4-12).
Nonfiction: Religion: picture books, young readers, middle readers, young adults.
How to Contact/Writers: Fiction/nonfiction: Query; submit outline/synopsis and sample chapters; submit complete ms. Publishes a book 1 year after acceptance. Will consider simultaneous submissions.
Illustration: Number of illustrations used for fiction: picture books—32. Editorial will review ms/illustration packages.
How to Contact/Illustrators: Ms/illustration packages: "3 chapters of ms with 1 piece of final art and any approximate rough sketches." Illustrations only: "résumé, tear-

Always include a self-addressed stamped envelope (SASE) or International Reply Coupon (IRC) with submissions.

sheets." Reports on art samples in 2 months. Original artwork returned at job's completion.
Terms: Pays authors in royalties of 10-15%. Average advance payment: "negotiable."
Pay for illustrators: "Sometimes paid by project." Sends galleys to authors; sometimes
sends dummies to illustrators. Book catalog, manuscript/artist's guidelines free on request.

HAYPENNY PRESS, 211 New St., West Paterson NJ 07424. Book publisher. Publishes
1-2 young adult titles/year. 50% of books by first-time authors.
Fiction: Young adults: anthology, animal, contemporary, easy-to-read, fantasy, problem
novels, science fiction, spy/mystery/adventure. Will also consider middle readers.
Nonfiction: Middle readers and young adults/teens: animal, biography, hobbies, music/
dance. Average word length: young adults—25,000.
How to Contact/Writers: Fiction and nonfiction: Query. Reports on queries in 2
weeks; 1 month on mss. Publishes a book up to 1 year after acceptance. Will consider
simultaneous submissions.
Illustrations: Reviews ms/illustration packages.
How to Contact/Illustrators: Query first with synopsis and one to three photocopies
of artwork. Reports on ms/art samples in 6 weeks. Original artwork returned at job's
completion.
Terms: Pays authors in royalties of 20-50% based on wholesale price. Sends galleys to
authors. Manuscript guidelines for 1 first class stamp and #10 SAE.
Tips: "Never talk down to your readers, whatever the age. Get your art out there in as
many ways as you can, whether you're paid for it or not. Look into charity, library,
school projects. Contact lots of publishers and get your name and samples into their
files!"

HENDRICK-LONG PUBLISHING COMPANY, P.O. Box 25123, Dallas TX 75225. Book
publisher. Contact: Joann Long, Vice President. Publishes 1 picture book/year; 4 young
reader titles/year; 4 middle reader titles/year. 20% of books by first-time authors.
Fiction: All levels: history books on Texas and the Southwest. No fantasy or poetry.
Recently published *Cowboy Stories from East Texas*, by John Lash (ages 6 and above);
The Mystery of Y'Barbo's Tunnel, by Martha Jones, illustrated by Donna Laughran
(grades 3 and above).
Nonfiction: All levels: history books on Texas and the Southwest. Recently published
Father Hidalgo: A Cry for Freedom, by D.E. Perlin, illustrated by Tim McClure (grades
K-6); *My Dear Mollie: Love Letters of a Texas Sheep Rancher*, edited by Agnesa Reeve
(grade 7 and above); *Explorers in Early Texas: 1519-1778*, by Betsy Warren (ages 9 and
above).
How to Contact/Writers: Fiction and nonfiction: Query with outline/synopsis and
sample chapter. Reports on queries in 1 month; mss in 6 weeks. Publishes a book 18
months after acceptance. No simultaneous submissions. Include SASE.
Illustration: Number of illustrations used for fiction and nonfiction: picture books-22;
middle readers-11; young readers-11. Uses primarily black & white artwork only. Editorial will review ms/illustration packages. Will review illustrator's work for possible future
assignments.
How to Contact/Illustrators: Query first. Submit résumé, promotional literature, photocopies or tearsheets—no original work sent unsolicited. Reports on ms/art samples in
1 month.
Terms: Pays authors in royalty based on selling price. Advances vary. Sends galleys to
author; dummies to illustrators. Book catalog for $1, 52¢ postage and large SAE; manuscript and artist's guidelines for 1 first class stamp and #10 SAE.

HERALD PRESS, Mennonite Publishing House, 616 Walnut Ave., Scottdale PA 15683. (412)887-8500. Estab. 1908. Publishes 1 young reader title/year; 2-3 middle reader titles/year; 1-2 young adult titles/year; no picture storybooks. Editorial Contact: S. David Garber. 20% of books by first-time authors; 10% of books from agented writers.
Fiction: Young readers: religious, social problems. Middle readers: religious, social problems. Young adults: religious, social problems.
Nonfiction: Young readers: religious, social concerns. Middle readers: religious, social concerns. Young adults: religious, social concerns.
How to Contact/Writers: Fiction/nonfiction: Submit outline/synopsis and sample chapters. Reports on queries in 3 weeks; ms in 2 months. Publishes a book in 12 months. Will consider simultaneous submissions but prefer not to.
Illustration: Will review ms/illustration packages. Jim Butti, art director, will review an illustrator's work for possible future assignments.
How to Contact/Illustrators: Illustrations only: Send tearsheets and slides.
Terms: Pays authors in royalties of 10-12% based on retail price. Pay for illustrators: by the project; $220-600. Sends galleys to authors. Book catalog for 3 first-class stamps; manuscript guidelines free on request.

HOLIDAY HOUSE INC., 425 Madison Ave., New York NY 10017. (212)688-0085. Book publisher. Editorial Contacts: Alyssa Chase and Margery Cuyler. Publishes 30 picture books/year; 7 young reader titles/year; 7 middle reader titles/year; 3 young adult titles/year. 20% of books by first-time authors; 10% from agented writers.
Fiction: Picture book: animal, sports, folk tales. Young reader: contemporary, easy-to-read, history, sports, spy/mystery/adventure. Middle reader: contemporary, fantasy, history, sports, spy/mystery/adventure. Recently published *Red Sky at Morning*, by Andrea Wyman (middle reader, novel); *Critter Sitters*, by Connie Hiser (young reader, chapter book); and *The Disappearing Bike Shop*, by Elvira Woodruff (young reader/middle reader, short novel).
Nonfiction: Picture books: biography, history, nature. Young reader: biography, history, nature/environment, sports. Middle reader: biography, history, nature/environment, sports. Recently published *African Elephants*, by Dorothy Hinshaw Patent (young reader, nature/environment); *The Wright Brothers*, by Russell Freedman (middle reader, historical).
How to Contact/Writers: Fiction/nonfiction: Submit complete ms. Reports on queries in 4-6 weeks; on mss in 8-10 weeks. Publishes a book 10 months after acceptance. Will consider simultaneous submissions.
Illustration: Editorial will review ms/illustration packages. Tere Lo Prete, art director, will review an illustrator's work for possible future assignments. Alyssa Chase will also view artists' portfolios inhouse.
How to Contact/Illustrators: Ms/illustration packages: Query first. Illustrations only: send résumé, and tearsheets. Reports within 6 weeks with SASE or only if interested (if no SASE). Original art work returned at job's completion.
Terms: Manuscript/artist's guidelines for #10 SASE.

HENRY HOLT & CO., INC., 115 W. 18th St., New York NY 10011. (212)886-9200. Book publisher. Editor-in-Chief: Brenda Bowen. Publishes 15-20 picture books/year; 40-60 young reader titles/year; 6 middle reader titles/year; 6 young adult titles/year. 5% of books by first-time authors; 40% of books from agented writers.
How to Contact/Writers: Fiction/nonfiction: Submit complete ms. Reports on queries/mss in 2 months. Publishes a book 12-18 months after acceptance. Will consider simultaneous submissions.
Illustration: Editorial will review ms/illustration packages.
How to Contact/Illustrators: Ms/illustration packages: Random samples OK. Illustrations only: Tearsheets, slides. Do *not* send originals. Reports on art samples only if

interested. If accepted, original artwork returned at job's completion.

Terms: Pays authors in royalties based on retail price. Pay for illustrators: royalties based on retail price. Sends galleys to authors; dummies to illustrators.

HOMESTEAD PUBLISHING, Box 193, Moose WY 83012. Book publisher. Editor: Carl Schreier. Publishes 8 picture books/year; 2 young reader titles/year; 2 middle reader titles/year; 2 young adult titles/year. 30% of books by first-time authors; 1% of books from agented writers.

Fiction: Average word length: young readers—1,000; middle readers—5,000; young adults—5,000.

Nonfiction: Picture books: animal, biography, history, nature/environment. Young readers: animal, nature/environment. Middle readers: animal, biography, history, nature/environment. Young adults: animal, history, nature/environment. Average word length: young readers—1,000; middle readers—5,000; young adults—5,000.

How to Contact/Writers: Fiction/nonfiction: Query; submit outline/synopsis and sample chapters. Reports on queries/mss in 4 weeks. Publishes a book 1 year after acceptance. Will consider simultaneous submissions.

Illustration: Number of illustrations used for fiction: picture books—70; young readers—50; middle readers—50; young adults—50. Number of illustrations used for nonfiction: picture books—150; young readers—50; middle readers—50; young adults—50. Editorial will review ms/illustration packages. Prefers to see "watercolor, opaque, oil" illustrations.

How to Contact/Illustrators: Ms/illustration packages: "Query first with sample writing and art style." Illustrations only: "Resumes, style samples." Reports on art samples in 1 month. Original artwork returned at job's completion.

Terms: Pays authors in royalties of 5-10% based on wholesale price. Outright purchase: "depends on project." Offers advances. Pay for illustrators: $50-10,000/project; 3-10% royalty based on wholesale price. Sends galleys to authors; dummies to illustrators.

HOUGHTON MIFFLIN CO., Children's Trade Books, 2 Park St., Boston MA 02108. (617)725-5000. Book Publisher. VP/Director: Walter Lorraine. Senior Editor: Matilda Welter; Editor: Audrey Bryant. Coordinating Editor: Laura Hornick. Averages 50-55 titles/year. Publishes hardcover originals and trade paperback reprints (some simultaneous hard/soft).

How to Contact/Writers: Fiction: Submit complete ms. Nonfiction: Submit outline/ synopsis and sample chapters. Reports on queries in 1 month; on mss in 2 months.

How to Contact/Illustrators: Review artwork/photos as part of ms package.

Terms: Pays standard royalty; offers advance. Book catalog free on request.

Tips: "The growing independent-retail book market will no doubt affect the number and kinds of books we publish in the near future. Booksellers are more informed about children's books today than ever before."

HUMANICS LIMITED, (formerly Humanics Children's House), 1482 Mecaslin St. N.W., Atlanta GA 30308. (404)874-1930. Book publisher. Editor: Robert Grayson Hall. Publishes 4 picture books/year; 4 young reader titles/year. 85% of books by first-time authors.

Fiction: Picture books: contemporary, easy-to-read, fantasy, adventure, self-image concentration. Average word length: picture books—250-350.

Nonfiction: "Educational materials, teacher supplementary texts, Author-Ph.D, M.A. level, activities, project books." Average word length: picture books—500-600. Published *Lessons From Mother Goose*, by E. Commins (grades 1-6, teacher's aid); *Teaching Terrific Twos*, by Graham and Camp (grades 1-6, teacher's aid).

How to Contact/Writers: Fiction: Submit outline/synopsis and sample chapters or submit complete ms. Nonfiction: Query; submit outline/synopsis and sample chapters

Close-up

Lois Lowry
Writer
Boston, Massachusetts

Children who read Lois Lowry's books have no problem making friends with her characters. Anastasia Krupnik is irreverent and sarcastic. Annemarie Johansen is loyal and brave. Meg Chalmers is shy and insecure. At first glance, these three young girls have next to nothing in common. However, they, in addition to all of Lowry's other characters, *do* share one thing — a creator renowned for her realistic portrayals of adolescence.

Had it not been for one editor's encouragement, though, the kids in Lowry's books may have never come to life. As a freelance writer and photographer, Lowry started out writing articles on a variety of topics for adult publications. Though the assignments she landed were primarily nonfiction, her prime interest was fiction.

In 1976, *Redbook* published one of her short stories. "When it was published, a children's book editor read it, wrote to me and asked if I would consider writing for children," she says. Lowry explains that though the story was written for adults, it was written from a child's perspective. The editor made no guarantees her company, Houghton Mifflin, would publish Lowry's first book. But the encouragement was all Lowry needed to write it anyway. It turned out Houghton Mifflin *did* publish that first book. *A Summer to Die*, (the story of Meg Chalmers, a 13-year-old facing up to her sister's imminent death) came out in 1977. Lowry says the Houghton Mifflin editor "saw what I hadn't. Once I tried it (writing for children), I could see how comfortable I was with it."

Today, her critically-acclaimed books have accumulated numerous awards and are staples on children's recommended reading lists. One piece of historical fiction in particular, 1989's *Number the Stars,* (about a 1940s Danish family's attempt to save Jewish friends from the Nazis) netted her the precious Newbery Medal.

There really are no tricks to writing for children, says Lowry. It's simply a matter of writing with the child in mind and from the child's viewpoint. One aid to doing this is to look back on one's own childhood. At the risk of sounding mystical, she says, "I can transport myself back into my own childhood anytime I want." As an example, she recalls a time when, as a little girl, she got into trouble with a teacher at school. "The teacher was wearing a blue and white dress with little figures on it. When I remember that incident, I can see that dress, but it's blurred. This is because I look at it through my eyes when I was eight years old. The eyes are filled with tears."

Though Lowry avoids fads ("You won't find any Ninja Turtles in my books."), she does write about the general interests of today's youth. Adding contemporary flavor to her novels is a little more challenging, she admits. Fortunately, her grandson is a great source of information.

Also, the letters she gets are invaluable. "The kids who write to me are very helpful. Their ideas are somewhat simplistic, but I can sift through and see what it is they're really saying underneath the goofy ideas they have." She cites one girl's letter containing several suggestions for the light-hearted Anastasia Krupnik series. "One idea was that Anastasia's father fall down the stairs and break his back. Well, obviously I'm not going to do that because it's not funny. But what she was really interested in was a parent being disenfranchised somehow — a parent losing power. In the same letter she said she wanted Anastasia to get drunk with her boyfriend," she says. Obviously, Lowry struck that one down, too. She feels, though, that this particular suggestion stemmed from the little girl's interest to read more about Anastasia's behavioral misdeeds. For Lowry, analyzing her readers' suggestions is a matter of pulling generalities out of specifics.

Anastasia Krupnik is the most well-known of all Lowry's characters. In fact, her two newest books are additions to the series — 1991's *Anastasia at This Address* and 1992's *Atta Boy Sam* (about Anastasia's kid brother).

Kids love Anastasia and find her quite real, though Lowry personally feels the character is sometimes exaggerated. It's the appeal of the Anastasia books on adults that has been a major contributor to their popularity. Lowry explains adult humor is included in those books as well. "There's stuff in those books that goes over the heads of kids, although kids can read the books without feeling they don't understand them." By including adult situations, the books are not boring for teachers and librarians when they read them out loud, she says.

Lowry feels the best questions for aspiring writers to ask are questions about writing. "It seems somewhat unfortunate to me, but it is true, that the questions mostly asked of me have to do with very pragmatic things. 'How do you get an agent?' seems to me an irrelevent type of question." She concedes, though, that given the big business of children's publishing today, she can't really blame people for asking those types of questions. However, she does caution against getting too involved in the peripheral aspects of children's writing. "Everyone is getting into it — buying how-to books, joining organizations, attending workshops and all that. None of that has anything to do with writing." Lowry is quick to add, though, that she'd probably be guilty of doing just those things if starting out today.

Finally, she points out that writing for children can't be treated as a stepping stone into the world of adult books. She notes there have been a number of established writers for adults who have been unsuccessful at writing for children, primarily due to the inability to acquire the child's viewpoint. It's imperative to include that viewpoint, she says. So therefore, when writing about a child, "I become that child."

—Lisa Carpenter

or submit complete ms. Reports on queries/mss in 6 months. Publishes a book 12-18 months after acceptance. Will consider simultaneous and electronic submissions via disk or modem.

Illustration: Number of illustrations used for fiction: picture books—16. Number of illustrations used for nonfiction: picture books—25-80. Editorial will review ms/illustration packages.

How to Contact/Illustrators: Ms/illustration packages: Preferably complete ms with 3-4 illustrations. Illustrations only: Send résumé, tearsheets. Original artwork returned at job's completion "depending on contract."

Terms: Pays authors in royalties of 3-10% based on wholesale price. Outright purchase "dependent on ms, previous work." Ideally, prefer authors to be the illustrator for the work." Sends galleys to authors; dummies to illustrators. Book catalog free on request; manuscript/artist's guidelines for regular SAE and 1 first-class stamp.

Tips: "Always send a cover letter with submissions!! I often receive stories that arrive like lost children: I have no clue as to the author's background, intentions, reason for writing, etc. I consider this thoughtless and inconsiderate and these kind of submissions go directly into the trash. Also, *please* include a SASE or stamped package if you want materials returned. We receive so many unsolicited manuscripts, it's just not an option to pay for their way back home." Writers: "Have some academic educational background. Ms should be creative, innovative, and have an approach geared toward self-image, social and intellectual development." Illustrators: "Take chances! I like abstract, thought provoking illustrations as well as simple line drawings. (Actually, we prefer the more fantastic, abstract illustrations)."

*■HUNTER HOUSE PUBLISHERS, Suite 202, 2200 Central, Alameda CA 94501. Book publisher. Independent book producer/packager. Editorial Manager: Jennifer D. Trzyna. Publishes 1 young adult title/year. 80% of books by first-time authors; 5% of books from agented writers; 50% subsidy published.

Nonfiction: Young adults: activity books, self-help. Published *Getting High in Natural Ways*, by Rocklin/Levinson (young adults, alternatives to drug use); *Raising Each Other*, by Brondino et al. (young adults, parent/teen relationships); *PMS: A Guide for Young Women* (young adults, health/menstruation).

How to Contact/Writers: Nonfiction: Query; submit outline/synopsis and sample chapters. Reports on queries in 3-4 weeks; on mss in 8-16 weeks. Publishes a book 18 months after acceptance. Will consider simultaneous submissions.

Illustration: Number of illustrations used for nonfiction: young adults—5-25. Uses primarily b&w artwork only.

How to Contact/Illustrators: Illustrators only: Query with samples. Provide résumé, promotional literature or tearsheets to be kept on file.

Terms: Pays authors in royalties "depends on individual case." Sends galleys to authors. Book catalog available for 9 × 12 SAE and 65¢ postage; manuscript guidelines for standard SAE and 1 first-class stamp.

*HYPERION BOOKS FOR CHILDREN, an operating unit of Walt Disney Publishing Group, Inc., 114 Fifth Avenue, New York NY 10011. (212)633-2419. Book publisher. Editorial Director: Andrea Cascardi. 30% of books by first-time authors; 40% of books from agented authors. Publishes various categories.

Fiction: Picture books, young readers, middle readers and young adults: adventure, anthology (short stories), animal, contemporary, fantasy, folktales, history, poetry, sci-

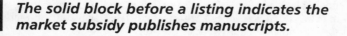

The solid block before a listing indicates the market subsidy publishes manuscripts.

ence fiction, sports, suspense/mystery. Middle readers and young adults: problem novels, romance. Recently published *Rescue Josh McGuire*, by Ben Mikaelsen (ages 10-14, adventure).

Nonfiction: All trade subjects for all levels.

How to Contact/Writers: Fiction: Submit complete ms. Nonfiction: Query. Submit outline/synopsis and 2 sample chapters. Reports on queries in 1 month; reports on mss in 3 months.

Illustration: Average number of illustrations used for fiction and nonfiction: "Picture books are fully illustrated throughout. All others depend on individual project." Will review ms/illustration packages. Will review artwork for future assignments. Contact Ellen Friedman, art director.

How to Contact/Illustrators: Ms/illustration packages: Submit complete package. Illustrations only: provide résumé, business card, promotional literature or tearsheets to be kept on file. Reports back only if interested. Original artwork returned at job's completion.

Photography: Photographers should contact Ellen Friedman, art director. Publishes photo essays and photo concept books. To contact, photographers should provide résumé, business card, promotional literature or tearsheets to be kept on file.

Terms: Pays authors royalty based on retail price. Offers advances. Pays illustrators royalty based on retail price, flat fee. Pays photographers royalty based on retail price, flat fee. Sends galleys to authors; dummies to illustrators. Book catalog available for 9 × 12 SAE and 3 first class stamps; ms guidelines available for SASE.

IDEALS PUBLISHING CORPORATION, Box 140300, Nashville TN 37214. (615)885-8270. Book publisher. Children's Book Editor: Peggy Schaefer. Publishes 50-60 picture books/year; 15-20 young reader titles/year. 5-10% of books by first-time authors; 5-10% of books from agented writers.

Fiction: Picture books: adventure, animal, contemporary, easy-to-read, fantasy, history, sports. Young readers: animal, contemporary, easy-to-read, history, sports, spy/mystery/adventure. Average word length: picture books—200-1,200; young readers—1,200-2,400. Recently published *Alfie*, by Fred Harsh (ages 4-8); *Excalibur*, by Carol Heyer (ages 5-9); *Wildebeest*, by Franz Berliner (ages 4-8).

Nonfiction: Picture books: animal, biography, history, hobbies, music/dance, nature/environment, religion, sports. Young readers: animal, biography, history, hobbies, music/dance, nature/environment, religion, sports. Average word length: picture books—200-1,000; young readers—1,000-2,400. Recently published *An Easter Celebration*, by Pamela Kennedy (ages 6-10); *A Pop-Up Book of North American Cities*, by Pat Pierce (ages 7-12).

How to Contact/Writers: Fiction/nonfiction: Submit complete ms through agent. **Will accept submissions from agented or previously published writers only.** Reports on queries/mss in 3-6 months. Publishes a book 18-24 months after acceptance.

Illustration: Number of illustrations used for fiction and nonfiction: picture books—12-18; young readers—12-18. Editorial will review ms/illustration packages. Preference: No cartoon—tight or loose, but realistic watercolors, acrylics.

How to Contact/Illustrators: Ms/illustration packages: Ms with 1 color photocopy of final art and remainder roughs. Illustrations only: Resume and tearsheets showing variety of styles. Reports on art samples only if interested. "No original artwork, please."

Terms: "All terms vary according to individual projects and authors/artists."

Tips: "Trend is placing more value on nonfiction and packaging. (i.e., We are not interested in young adult romances.)" Illustrators: "Be flexible in contract terms—and be able to show as much final artwork as possible."

INCENTIVE PUBLICATIONS, INC., 3835 Cleghorn Ave., Nashville TN 37215. (615)385-2934. Editor: Jan H. Keeling. Approximately 20% of books by first-time authors.
Nonfiction: Young reader/middle reader/young adult: education. Recently published *Small Projects for Small Hands*, by Lynn Brisson (pre K-1, arts & crafts); *I've Got Me and I'm Glad*, by Farnette, Forte and Loss (grades 4-7, self-esteem).
How to Contact/Writers: Nonfiction: Submit outline/synopsis and sample chapters. Usually reports on queries/mss in approximately 1 month. Publishes a book 18 months after acceptance. Will consider simultaneous submissions.
Terms: Pays in royalties or outright purchase. Book catalog for SAE and 90¢ postage.
Tips: Most likely to buy teacher resource material.

JALMAR PRESS, Subsidiary of B.L. Winch and Associates, 45 Hitching Post Dr., Bldg. 2, Rolling Hills Estates CA 90274. (213)547-1240. FAX: (213)547-1644. Book publisher. Estab. 1971. President: B.L. Winch. Publishing Assistant: Susan O'Hara. Publishes 3 picture books and young reader titles/year. 40% of books by first-time authors. Publishes self esteem, growth (emotional) and curriculum content books.
Fiction: All levels: health-related, nature/environment, self esteem. Recently published *Ta for Tots*, by Dr. Alvyn Freed (ages 1-4, emotional growth).
Nonfiction: All levels: activity books.
How to Contact/Writers: Fiction/nonfiction: Submit complete ms. Reports on queries in 2 weeks; on mss in 1 year (for review). Publishes a book 6 months after acceptance. Will consider simultaneous submissions.
Illustration: Editorial will review ms/illustration packages. Will review artwork for future assignments.
How to Contact/Illustrators: Ms/illustration packages: Submit complete package. Illustrations only: Send unsolicited art samples by mail. Reports in 2 weeks. Originals returned upon job's completion.
Terms: Pays authors 7-15% royalty based on a combination of wholesale and retail prices. Average advance "varies." Pay for illustrators: 7-15% royalty based on combination of wholesale and retail prices. Book catalog free on request.
Tips: Looks for a "positive self-esteem type of book that deals with feelings."

JEWISH PUBLICATION SOCIETY, Room 1339, 60 E. 42 St., New York NY 10165. (212)687-0809. Editor: Alice Belgray. Acquisitions Editor: David Adler. Book publisher.
Fiction: "All must have Jewish content." Picture books, young readers, middle readers and young adults: contemporary, folktales, history, poetry, problem novels, religion, romance, sports.
Nonfiction: "All must have Jewish theme." Picture books: biography, history, religion. Young readers, middle readers, young adults: biography, history, religion, sports.
How to Contact/Writers: Fiction/nonfiction: query, submit outline/synopsis and sample chapters. Will consider simultaneous submissions (please advise).
Illustration: Will review ms/illustration packages.
How to Contact/Illustrators: Ms/illustration packages: query first or send three chapters of ms with one piece of final art, remainder roughs. Illustrations only: query with photocopies; arrange a personal interview to show portfolio.
Terms: Pays authors in royalties based on retail price.
Tips: Writer/illustrator currently has best chance of selling picture books to this market.

Refer to the Business of Children's Writing & Illustrating
for up-to-date marketing, tax and legal information.

BOB JONES UNIVERSITY PRESS/LIGHT LINE BOOKS, 1500 Wade Hampton Blvd. Greenville SC 29614. (803)242-5100 ext. 4315. Book publisher. Contact: Mrs. Gloria Repp, Editor. Publishes 4 picture books/year; 4 young reader titles/year; 4 middle reader titles/year; 2 young adult titles/year. 50% of books by first-time authors.
Fiction: Picture books: animal, contemporary, easy-to-read. Young readers: animal, contemporary, easy-to-read, history, sports, spy/mystery/adventure. Middle readers: animal, contemporary, history, problem novels, sports, spy/mystery/adventure. Young adults/teens: contemporary, history, problem novels, sports, spy/mystery/adventure. Average word length: picture books—1,000-5,000; young readers—20,000; middle readers—30,000; young adult/teens—50,000. Recently published *Very Like A Star*, by Dawn Watkins (ages 0-6, picture book—animal); *The Treasure of Pelican Cove*, by Milly Howard (grades 2-4, adventure story); *Best of Friends*, by Susan Walley (grades 5-8, contemporary)
Nonfiction: Picture books: animal, nature/environment. Young readers: animal, biography, nature/environment. Middle readers: animal, biography, history, nature/environment. Young adults/teens: biography, history, nature/environment. Average word length: picture books—2,000; young readers—20,000; middle readers—30,000; young adult/teens—50,000. Recently published *With Daring Faith*, by Becky Davis (grades 5-8, biography); *Morning Star of the Reformation*, by Andy Thomson (grades 9-12, biography).
How to Contact/Writers: Fiction: "Send the complete manuscript for these genres: Christian biography, modern realism, historical realism, regional realism and mystery/adventure. Query with a synopsis and five sample chapters for these genres: Fantasy and science fiction (no extra-terrestrials). We do not publish these genres: Romance, poetry and drama." Nonfiction: Query, submit complete manuscript or submit outline/synopsis and sample chapters. Reports on queries in 3 weeks; mss in 2 months. Publishes book "approximately one year" after acceptance. Will consider simultaneous and electronic submissions via disk or modem.
Terms: Buys ms outright for $500-1,000. Book catalog and ms guidelines free on request.
Tips: "Write something fresh and unique to carry a theme of lasting value. We publish only books with high moral tone, preferably with strong evangelical Christian content. Stories for *Light Line* should reflect highest Christian standards of thought, feeling and action. Text should make no reference to drinking, smoking, profanity or minced oaths. Other unacceptable story elements include unrelieved suspense, sensationalism and themes advocating secular attitudes of cynicism, rebellion or materialism."

■**JORDAN ENTERPRISES PUBLISHING CO.**, 6457 Wilcox Station, Box 38002, Los Angeles CA 90038. Book publisher. Estab. 1989. Managing Editor: Patrique Quintahlen. Publishes 2 picture books/year; 1 young reader title/year; 1 middle reader title/year; 1 young adult title/year. 90% of books by first-time authors; 50% of books from agented writers; 1% subsidy published.
Fiction: Picture books: adventure, animal, fantasy, folktales, health-related, history, nature/environment, poetry, science fiction, sports, spiritual. Young readers: adventure, animal, fantasy, folktales, health-related, history, nature/environment, poetry, religion, science fiction, sports, spiritual. Middle readers: adventure, anthology, animal, fantasy, folktales, health-related, history, nature/environment, poetry, problem novels, religion, romance, science fiction, sports, spiritual. Young adult: adventure, anthology, animal, contemporary, fantasy, folktales, health-related, history, nature/environment, poetry, problem novels, religion, romance, science fiction, suspense/mystery, spiritual. "No mystery, horror, feminist or sexist." Average word length: picture books—2,000; young readers—3,000; middle readers—2,500; young adults—20,000. Recently published *The Strawberry Fox*, by Prentiss Van Daves.
Nonfiction: Picture books: activity books, animal, biography, health, history, music/dance, nature/environment, sports, spiritual. Young readers and middle readers: activity books, animal, biography, careers, health, history, music/dance, nature/environment,

religion, sports, spiritual. Young adult: activity books, animal, biography, careers, health, history, hobbies, music/dance, nature/environment, religion, sports, spiritual.
How to Contact/Writers: Fiction/nonfiction: Query; submit outline/synopsis and sample chapters. Reports on queries/mss in 4 months. Publishes a book 1 year after acceptance. Will consider simultaneous and electronic submissions via disk or modem.
Illustration: Number of illustrations used for fiction and nonfiction: picture books—25; young readers—25; middle readers—8; young adults—8. Editorial will review ms/illustration packages.
How to Contact/Illustrators: Ms/illustration packages: Query first. Illustrations only: Query with samples; provide résumé, promotional literature or tearsheets to be kept on file. Reports on art samples in 4 months. Original artwork returned at job's completion.
Photography: Photographers should contact Patrique Quintahlen. Needs photos showing nature, art, school, dances, Christmas settings. Model/property releases and photo captions required. Publishes photo essays and photo concept books. Uses 8×11 color, b&w prints; 35mm, 2¼×2¼, 4×5 transparencies. To contact, photographers should query with samples; provide résumé, promotional literature or tearsheets to be kept on file.
Terms: Pays authors in royalties of 4-8% based on retail price. Buys ms outright for $20-$200. Offers average advance payment of $500. Pay for illustrators: By the project, $60-$600 or 1 to 2% royalties for juvenile novels. Photographers paid by the project (range: $60-600); per photo (range: $10-200); by royalty of 1-2% based on retail price. Sends galleys to authors; dummies to illustrators.
Tips: Other needs are nature and children's Christmas themes. "Commercialism has brought about writers and artists who are no longer writing so much on the level of children. They are instead writing for the business. Even themes are taken from adult movies. In the future, we must write stories that inspire children to use the infinite possibilities of their own creativity and imaginations. Fantasy on the children's level is as splendid as the classics, and helps children from this perspective."

JOY STREET BOOKS, Imprint of Little, Brown and Company, 34 Beacon St., Boston MA 02108. (617)227-0730. Editor-in-Chief: Melanie Kroupa. Publishes 20-25 picture books/year; 5-10 young reader/middle reader/young adult titles/year.
Fiction/Nonfiction: All levels: various categories.
How to Contact/Writers: Fiction/nonfiction: Submit outline/synopsis and sample chapters or submit complete ms. Reports on queries in 2-4 weeks; on mss in 4-8 weeks. Publishes a book 18 months after acceptance. Will consider simultaneous submissions if informed, but prefers single submissions.
Illustration: Will review artwork for future assignments.
How to Contact/Illustrators: Illustrations only: Query with samples.
Terms: Pays authors in royalties or outright purchase. Book catalog for 8×10 SASE; ms guidelines for legal-size SASE.
Tips: Looking for "good middle grade fiction and strong nonfiction."

JUST US BOOKS, INC., Imprint of Afro-Bets Series, Suite 22-24, 301 Main St., Orange NJ 07050. (201)672-7701. FAX: (201)677-7570. Book publisher; "for selected titles" book packager. Estab. 1987. Vice President/Publisher: Cheryl Willis Hudson. Publishes 3-4 picture books/year; "projected 4" young reader/middle reader titles/year. 33% books by first-time authors. Also publishes *Harambee*, a newspaper for young readers 6 times during the school year.
Fiction: Picture books: easy-to-read, African-American themes. Young readers: contemporary, history, African-American themes. Middle reader: history, sports. Average word length: "varies" per picture book; young reader—500-2,000; middle reader—5,000. Recently published *Great Women in the Struggle*, by Toyomi Igus et al.; *Bright*

Eyes, Brown Skin, by Cheryl Hudson and Bernette Ford, illus. by George Ford (ages 6-9, picture book).

Nonfiction: Picture book: African-American themes; young reader: biography, history, African-American themes; middle reader: biography, history, African-American themes. Recently published *Book of Black Heroes from A to Z*, by Wade Hudson and Valerie Wilson Wesley (biography for young and middle readers); *Afro-Bets First Book About Africa*, by Veronica F. Ellis.

How to Contact/Writers: Fiction/nonfiction: Query or submit outline/synopsis for proposed title. Reports on queries in 4-6 weeks; on ms in 8 weeks "or as soon as possible." Publishes a book 12-18 months after acceptance. Will consider simultaneous submissions (with prior notice).

Illustration: Number of illustrations used for fiction: picture book—12-24; for nonfiction: young reader—25-30. Editorial department will review ms/illustration packages.

How to Contact/Illustrators: Ms/illustration packages: "Query first." Illustrations only: Send résumé, tearsheets, and slides. Reports in 2-3 weeks. Original artwork returned at job's completion "depending on project."

Photography: Interested in stock photos.

Terms: Pays authors a "flat fee and royalty depending on project." Royalties based on retail price. Sends galleys to author; dummies to illustrator. Book catalog for business-size SAE and 29-65¢ postage; ms/artist's guidelines for business-size SAE and 1 first class stamp.

Tips: Writers: "Keep the subject matter fresh and lively. Avoid "preachy" stories with stereotyped characters. Rely more on authentic stories with sensitive three-dimensional characters." Illustrators: "Submit 5-10 good, neat samples. Be willing to work with an art director for the type of illustration desired by a specific house and grow into larger projects."

KAR-BEN COPIES, INC., 6800 Tildenwood Lane, Rockville MD 20852. (301)984-8733. FAX: (301)881-9195. Book publisher. Estab. 1975. Editor: Madeline Wikler. Publishes 10 picture books/year; 10 young reader titles/year. 20% of books by first-time authors.

Fiction: Picture books: Jewish Holiday, Jewish storybook. Average word length: picture books—2,000. Recently published *Daddy's Chair*, by Sandy Lanton (ages 5-8); *Sophie's Name*, by Phyllis A Grode (ages 5-8); *Bible Heroes I Can Be*, by Ann Eisenberg (ages 5-8); all picture books.

Nonfiction: Picture books: religion-Jewish interest. Average word length: picture books—2,000. Recently published *Two by Two: Favorite Bible Stories*, by Harry Araten (ages 5-8); *Kids Love Israel*, by Barbara Sofer (adult, family travel guide); *Alef Is One*, by Katherine Kahn (grades K-3, a Hebrew counting book).

How to Contact/Writers: Fiction/nonfiction: Submit complete ms. Reports on queries in 3 weeks; ms in 6 weeks. Publishes a book 1 year after acceptance. Will consider simultaneous submissions. "We don't like them, but we'll look at them—as long as we *know* it's a simultaneous submission."

Illustration: Number of illustrations used for fiction: picture books—15. Number of illustrations used for nonfiction: picture books—10. Editorial will review ms/illustration packages. Prefers "4-color art to any medium that is scannable."

How to Contact/Illustrators: Ms illustration packages: Send whole ms and sample of art (no originals). Illustrations only: Tearsheets, photocopies or anything representative that does *not* need to be returned. Reports on art samples in 4 weeks.

Terms: Pays authors in royalties of 5-10% based on net sales. Offers average advance payment of $1,000. Sends galleys to authors. Book catalog free on request. Ms guidelines for #10 SAE and 1 first class stamp.

Tips: Looks for "books for young children with Jewish interest and content, modern, non-sexist, not didactic. Fiction or nonfiction with a *Jewish* theme—can be serious or humorous, life cycle, Bible story, or holiday-related."

This illustration by Shelly Haas appeared in Daddy's Chair, a book about the death of a parent, published by Kar-Ben Copies, Inc. According to Vice President Madeline Wikler, Haas was chosen to illustrate the book because her style is suitable for the somber mood of the story. This was Haas' fourth book project for Kar-Ben.

KENDALL GREEN PUBLICATIONS, imprint of Gallaudet University Press, 800 Florida Ave. NE, Washington DC 20002. (202)651-5488. Book publisher. Estab. 1980. Publishes 2-3 picture books/year; 2-3 young reader titles/year; 1-2 middle reader titles/year; 1-2 young adult titles/year. 75% of books by first-time authors. All titles deal with hearing loss or deafness.
Fiction: Picture books, young readers: contemporary. Middle readers, young adults: contemporary, problem novels, spy/mystery/adventure. Average word length: picture

books—50; young readers—1,300; middle readers—26,000; young adults—52,000. Recently published *Little Red Riding Hood Told in Signed English*, by Harry Bornstein and Karen L. Saulnier (picture book); *Matthew Pinkowski's Special Summer*, by Patrick Quinn (young adult).

Nonfiction: Picture books; young readers: sign language. Middle readers; young adults: biography, history, sign language. Average word length: picture books—50; young readers—1,300; middle readers—26,000; young adults—52,000. Recently published *My Signing Book of Opposites*, by Pamela Baker, (picture book, sign language); *Buffy's Orange Leash*, by Stephen Golder and Lise Memling (young readers, informational); *Clerc: Portrait of a Deaf Teacher as a Youth*, by Cathryn Carroll (young adults, biography).

How to Contact/Writers: Fiction/nonfiction: submit outline/synopsis and sample chapters; submit complete ms. Reports on queries/mss in 1-2 months. Publishes a book 10-18 months after acceptance. Will consider simultaneous submissions.

Illustration: Number of illustrations used for fiction: young readers—32; middle readers—1-5; young adults—1-5. Number of illustrations used for nonfiction: picture books—30-40; young readers—32; middle readers—20; young adults—5. Editorial will review ms/illustration packages.

How to Contact/Illustrators: Ms/illustration packages: Full ms with 2 finished pieces, remainder roughs. Illustrations only: Tearsheets, finished art, résumé. Reports on art samples in 1 month. Original artwork returned at job's completion.

Terms: Pays authors in royalties of 10-15% based on net price. Pay for illustrators: by the project; royalties of 5% based on net price. Send galleys to authors; sometimes sends dummies to illustrators. Manuscript guidelines free with SASE.

Tips: "All books published by Kendall Green Publications have to be related to hearing loss. This includes sign language books, books explaining hearing loss, and fiction with hard-of-hearing character(s)."

*THE KENNEBEC RIVER PRESS, INC., 36 Old Mill Rd., Falmouth ME 04105. Contact: Thea Wheelwright. "Children's books are at present a limited category in my publishing. I have a number of manuscripts in the works that I am determined will be my final contribution to the grown-up readers who like what this press produces. Once these are done, I hope to do a few children's books each year for as long as I publish."

Fiction: *Wind, Waves and Away!* is the title of a series (in progress) devoted to the adventures of a brother and sister aboard various crafts during one summer."

Nonfiction: Recent projects: *The Maine Art Series for Young Readers*. "Works on Bernard Langlair and Dahlov Ipcar are available. One on William Thon is in progress."

How to Contact/Writers: "I have no set rules for submission.

Tips: "I simply am glad to receive manuscripts (with postage provided for their return) and am always hopeful of something good."

KINGSWAY PUBLICATIONS, 1 St. Anne's Rd., Eastbourne, E. Sussex BN21 3UN England. (011-44)323-410930. Book publisher. Contact: Carolyn Owen. Publishes 1-2 young reader titles/year; 2-4 middle reader titles/year; 2-4 young adult titles/year. 25% of books by first-time authors; very few through agents. All children's books are published under the Phoenix imprint.

Fiction: Picture book: easy-to-read, with Evangelical Christian content. Middle reader: animal, contemporary, easy-to-read, fantasy, science fiction, Evangelical Christian content. Young adult: contemporary, easy-to-read, fantasy, problem novels, romance, science fiction, spy/mystery/adventure, "religious content." Average word length: picture book—700; young reader—20,000-60,000; middle reader—20,000-60,000; young adult—60,000. Recently published *The Muselings* and *The Screeps*, by Ed Wicke (middle reader, fantasy).

Nonfiction: Evangelical Christian books (medical/ethics/faith). Recently published *The Teenage Revival Kit*, by Pete Gilbert.

How to Contact/Writers: Fiction/nonfiction: Submit outline/synopsis and 1 sample chapter. Reports on queries/mss in 2 months. Publishes a book 1-2 years after acceptance. Send IRC.

Illustration: Number of illustrations used for fiction: young readers—8+; middle readers—8+; young adult—0-6. Editorial will review ms/illustration packages. "Send photocopies for safety."

KNOPF BOOKS FOR YOUNG READERS, Random House, Inc., 8th Floor, 225 Park Ave., South, New York NY 10003. (212)254-1600. Book publisher. Estab. 1915. Publisher: J. Schulman; Associate Publisher: S. Spinner. 90% of books published through agents.

Fiction: Upmarket picture books: adventure, animal, contemporary, fantasy, retellings of folktales, original stories. Young readers: adventure, animal, contemporary, nature/environment, science fiction, sports, suspense/mystery. Middle readers: adventure, animal, fantasy, nature/environment, science fiction, sports, suspense/mystery. Young adult: adventure, contemporary, fantasy, science fiction—very selective; few being published currently.

Nonfiction: Picture books, young readers and middle readers: animal, biography, nature/environment, sports.

How to Contact/Writers: Fiction/nonfiction: submit through agent only. Publishes a book in 12-18 months. Will consider simultaneous submissions.

Illustration: Will review ms/illustration packages (through agent only). Art Director will review an illustrator's work for possible future assignments.

Terms: Pays authors in royalties. Book catalog free on request.

KRUZA KALEIDOSCOPIX, INC., Box 389, Franklin MA 02038. (508)528-6211. Book publisher. Picture Books Editor: Jay Kruza. Young/middle readers editorial contact: Russ Burbank. Publishes 4 picture books/year; 2 young reader titles/year; 1 middle reader title/year. 50% of books by first-time authors.

Fiction: Picture books: animal, fantasy, history. Young readers: animal, fantasy, history. Average word length: picture books—200-500; young readers—500-2,000; middle readers—1,000-10,000.

Nonfiction: Picture books: animal, history, nature/environment. Young readers: animal, history, nature/environment, religion. Middle readers: biography, sports.

How to Contact/Writers: Fiction/nonfiction: Query; submit outline/synopsis and sample chapters; submit complete ms. Reports on queries/mss in 2-8 weeks.

Illustration: Number of illustrations used for fiction: 20-36. Art Editor, Brian Sawyer, will review an illustrator's work for possible future assignments. Prefers to see "realistic" illustrations.

How to Contact/Illustrators: Illustrations only: "Submit actual work sample photocopies in color, and photos." Reports on art samples only if interested.

Terms: Buys ms outright for $250-500. Pay for illustrators: $25-100/illustration. Manuscript/artist's guidelines available for #10 SASE.

Tips: Writers: "Rework your story several times before submitting it without grammatical or spelling mistakes. *Our company charges a $3 reading fee per manuscript* to reduce unprepared manuscripts." Illustrators: "Submit professional looking samples for file. The correct manuscript may come along." Wants ms/illustrations "that teach a moral. Smooth prose that flows like poetry is preferred. The story will be read aloud. Vocabulary and language should fit actions. Short staccato words connote fast action; avoid stories that solve problems by the 'wave of a wand' or that condone improper behavior. Jack of Beanstalk fame was a dullard, a thief and even a murderer. We seek to purchase all rights to the story and artwork. Payment may be a lump sum in cash."

*LEE & LOW BOOKS, INC., 14th Floor, 228 East 45th Street, New York NY 10017. (212)867-6155. FAX: (212)490-1846. Book publisher. Publisher: Philip Lee. Publishes 6-8 picture books/year. "The company only publishes books on multicultural subjects."
Fiction: Picture books: adventure, contemporary, history, nature/environment, sports, suspense/mystery. Young readers: adventure, anthology, contemporary, folktales, history, nature/environment, sports, suspense/mystery. Middle readers: adventure, anthology, contemporary, history, nature/environment, problem novels, sports, suspense/mystery. Does not want to see stories using animals as main characters. Average word length: picture books—1,000.
Nonfiction: Picture books, young readers, middle readers: biography and history. Average word length: picture books—1,000.
How to Contact/Writers: Nonfiction: Query; submit complete ms; submit outline/synopsis and sample chapters. Reports in 3 weeks on queries; reports in 1 month on mss. Publishes a book "18 months after illustration is accepted." Will consider simultaneous submissions.
Illustration: Will review ms/illustration packages. Will review artwork for future assignments. Contact: Philip Lee, publisher.
How to Contact/Illustrators: Ms/illustration packages: Query; submit complete package. Reports in 1 month. Return of originals negotiable.
Photography: Photographers should contact Philip Lee. Publishes photo essays and photo concept books. To contact, photographers should query with samples; query with resume of credits.
Terms: Pays authors royalty on retail price. Offers advances. Pays illustrators royalty on retail price. Photographers paid by the project. Sends galleys to author.
Tips: "Do your homework. Visit a bookstore or a library and find out what kind of children's books are being published. Should it be a picture book or story book? Is the story visual? Is the idea original? Are the characters well developed and believable? We specialize in multicultural stories. Rather than folklores, we would like to see more contemporary stories that are set in the U.S."

LERNER PUBLICATIONS CO., 241 First Ave. N., Minneapolis MN 55401. (612)332-3344. FAX: (612)332-7615. Book publisher. Editor: Jennifer Martin. Publishes 15 young reader titles/year; 25 middle reader titles/year; 30 young adult titles/year. 20% of books by first-time authors; 5% of books from agented writers. "Most books are nonfiction for children, grades 2 through 12."
Fiction: Middle readers: adventure, anthology, animal, contemporary, folktales, health-related, history, natuer/environment, religion, sports, suspense/mystery. Young adults: adventure, anthology, contemporary, folktales, health-related, history, nature/environment, poetry, problem novels, religion, sports, suspense/mystery. "Especially interested in books with ethnic characters." Recently published *The Shimmering Ghost of Riversend*, by Norma Lehr (grades 4-8, mystery).
Nonfiction: Young readers, middle readers, and young adults: activity books, animal, biography, careers, health, history, nature/environment, sports, science/math, social

* *The asterisk before a listing indicates the listing is new in this edition.*

studies, geography, social issues. Average word length: young readers—3,000; middle readers—7,000; young adults—12,000. Recently published *Discovering Christopher Columbus: How History Is Invented*, by Kathy Pelta (grades 4-6 and up, history); *Roses Red, Violets Blue: Why Flowers Have Colors*, by Sylvia A. Johnson (grades 5 and up, science); *Rickey Henderson: Record Stealer*, by Ann Bauleke (grades 4-9, sports biography).

How to Contact/Writers: Fiction: Submit outline/synopsis and sample chapters. Nonfiction: Query; submit outline/synopsis and sample chapters. Reports on queries in 1 month; on mss in 2 months. Publishes a book 12-18 months after acceptance. Will consider simultaneous submissions.

Illustration: Will review artwork for future assignments.

How to Contact/Illustrators: Query with samples to art director.

Photography: Photographers should contact Photo Research Department. Model/property releases required. Publishes photo essays. To contact, photographers should query with samples.

Terms: Sends galleys to authors. Book catalog available for 9×12 SAE and $1.90 postage; manuscript guidelines for 4×9 SAE and 1 first-class stamp.

Tips: No textbooks, poetry, workbooks, songbooks, puzzles, plays, religious material, fiction for adults, picture books or alphabet books. "Before you send your manuscript to us, you might first take a look at the kinds of books that our company publishes. We specialize in publishing high-quality educational books for children from second grade through high school. Avoid sex stereotypes (e.g., strong, aggressive, unemotional males/weak, submissive, emotional females) in your writing, as well as sexist language." (See also Carolrhoda Books, Inc.)

*LESTER PUBLISHING LIMITED, Suite 507 A, 56 The Esplanade, Toronto, Ontario M5E 1A7 Canada. (416)362-1032. Book publisher. Executive Editor: Kathy Lowinger. Publishes 5 picture books/year; 1 middle readers/year; 2 young adult titles/year. 20% of books by first-time authors; 20% of books from agented authors. "We strive for literary merit."

Fiction: Picture books: animal, contemporary, folktales, history, nature/environment, religion. Young readers: adventure, anthology, animal, contemporary, folktales, history, religion, suspense/mystery. Middle readers: adventure, animal, contemporary, folktales, history, problem novels, suspense/mystery. Young adults: adventure, contemporary, folktales, history, problem novels, religion, suspense/mystery. Average word length: picture books—500-1,500; young adult—20,000-40,000. Recently published *Redwork*, by Michael Bedard (young adult, fiction); *100 Shining Candles*, by Janet Lunn (ages 6-8, picture book); *The Huron Carol*, by Frances Tyrrell (all ages, picture book).

Nonfiction: Picture books: activity books, biography, health, history, hobbies, music/dance, nature/environment, religion, sports. Young readers, middle readers and young adults: activity books, animal, biography, health, history, hobbies, music/dance, nature/environment, religion, sports. Does not want to see textbooks.

How to Contact/Writers: Fiction: Submit complete manuscript. Nonfiction: Submit outline/synopsis and 2 sample chapters. Reports on queries/mss in 3 months. After acceptance, publication date "depends on when it is received and accepted during the year. In other words, a manuscript might come in which has a Christmas theme so it will be held until that time."

Illustration: Average number of illustrations used for fiction: picture books—32; young adults—1. Will review ms/illustration packages. Will review artwork for future assignments. Contact Kathy Lowinger, executive editor.

How to Contact/Illustrators: Ms/illustration packages: Submit complete package. Illustrations only: Query with samples. Reports in 2 months. Original artwork returned at job's completion.

Photography: Photographers should contact Kathy Lowinger. Model/property releases required.

Terms: Pays authors royalty of 5-10% based on retail price. Offers advances. Sends galleys to authors. Illustrators might see dummies "depending on project." Book catalog available for SASE.
Tips: "Read everything for children that you can get your hands on. Don't rely on your fond memories of your own reading when you were a child. Don't even begin to think that you can write successfully unless you are very well read in the field."

LIGUORI PUBLICATIONS, 1 Liguori Dr., Liguori MO 63057-9999. (314)464-2500. FAX: (314)464-8449. Book publisher. Estab. 1947. Editor-in-Chief: Rev. Paul Coury, C.S.S.R. Managing Editor: Audrey Vest. Publishes 1 middle reader title/year; 3 young adult titles/year. 10% of books by first-time authors.
Nonfiction: Young readers, middle readers, young adults: religion. Average word length: young readers—10,000; young adults—15,000.
How to Contact/Writers: Nonfiction: Query; submit outline/synopsis and sample chapters. Include Social Security number with submission. Reports on queries in 6 weeks; on mss in 6-8 weeks. Publishes a book 1 year after acceptance. Will consider electronic submissions via disk or modem.
Illustration: Number of illustrations used for nonfiction: young readers—40. Editorial will review ms/illustration packages.
How to Contact/Illustrators: Ms/illustration packages: Query first.
Terms: Pays authors in royalties of 9% based on retail price. Book catalog available for 9×12 SAE and 3 first-class stamps; manuscript guidelines for #10 SAE and 1 first-class stamp.
Tips: Ms/illustrations "must be religious and suitable to a Roman Catholic audience."

LION BOOKS, PUBLISHER, Imprint of Sayre Ross Co., Suite B, 210 Nelson, Scarsdale NY 10583. (914)725-2280. Book publisher. Editorial contact: Harriet Ross. Publishes 2 picture books/year; 5 middle reader titles/year; 10 young adult titles/year. 50-70% of books by first-time authors.
Fiction: [Historical fiction], sports. Average word length: middle reader—30,000-35,000; young adult—40,000-50,000.
Nonfiction: Biography, history, sports, black nonfiction. Average word length: young adult—50,000.
How to Contact/Writers: Fiction/nonfiction: Query, submit complete ms. Reports on queries in 1 month; on ms in 2 months.
How to Contact/Illustrators: Reports in 2 weeks.
Terms: Pays in outright purchase—$250-5,000. Average advance: $750-4,000. Illustrators paid $250-5,000. Sends galleys to author. Book catalog is free on request.

LION PUBLISHING CORPORATION, 1705 Hubbard Ave., Batavia IL 60510. (708)879-0707. Book publisher. Estab. 1971. Publishes 8-10 children's books a year. 1% of books by first-time authors.
Fiction: Open subjects. No sports or romance. Average word length: picture books and young readers—1,000; middle readers—25,000; young adults—40,000. Published *The Tale of Three Trees*, by Angela Hunt (4 and up, picture book, folktale); *Midnight Blue*, by Pauline Fisk (10-16, young adults, fantasy); *The Tale of Anabelle Hedgehog*, by Stephen Lawhead (9-14, middle readers, fantasy).
Nonfiction: Picture books, young readers: activity books, nature/environment, religion. Middle readers, young adults: biography, history, hobbies, nature/environment, religion. Average word length: picture books and young readers—1,000; middle readers and young adults—"varies." Published *Caring for Planet Earth*, by Lucas/Holland (8-12, ecological concerns); *365 Children's Prayers*, by Carol Watson (4-12, prayers).

How to Contact/Writers: Fiction: Submit complete ms. Nonfiction: Submit outline/ synopsis and 2-3 consecutive sample chapters. Reports on queries in 4 weeks; mss in 8 weeks. Publishes a book 18 months after acceptance.
Illustration: Editorial will review ms/illustration packages.
How to Contact/Illustrators: Ms/illustration packages: "Query first." Illustrations only: query with samples.
Terms: Pays authors in variable royalties based on wholesale price. Sometimes buys ms outright. Book catalog/manuscript guidelines for SAE and 2 first class stamps.
Tips: "Lion publishes Christian books for the general reader. A writer should carefully study our guidelines before submitting manuscripts or querying. We are always looking for well-written nonfiction for children. Please, no alphabet or rhyming books; no 'cutesy' illustrations; nothing overly sentimental or 'precious.' Keep the *general* market in mind, but remember that all Lion books are inherently Christian in perspective."

LITTLE, BROWN AND COMPANY, 34 Beacon St., Boston MA 02108. (617)227-0730. Book publisher. Editor-in-Chief: Maria Modugno. Senior Editor: Stephanie O. Lurie. Estab. 1837. Publishes 30% picture books/year; 10% young reader titles/year; 30% middle reader titles/year; 10% young adult titles/year. 10% of books by first-time authors; 50% of books from agented writers.
Fiction: Picture books, young readers, middle readers and young adults: various categories; no religion. Average word length: picture books—1,000; young readers—6,000; middle readers—15,000-25,000; young adults—20,000-40,000. Recently published *The Rag Coat*, by Lauren Mills (ages 3-8, picture book); *A Wish for Wings That Work*, by Berkeley Breathed (all ages, picture book); *Song of the Giraffe*, by Shannon Jacobs (ages 7-9, first chapter book); *Mama Let's Dance*, by Patricia Hermes (ages 10 and up, young adult novel).
Nonfiction: Picture books, young readers, middle readers, young adults: various categories; no religion or textbooks. Average word length: picture books—2,000; young readers—4,000-6,000; middle readers—15,000-25,000; young adults—20,000-40,000. Recently published *Careers in Television*, by Howard Blumestal (ages 10 and up, young adult); *Georgia O'Keefe*, by Robin Turner (ages 6-10, picture book).
How to Contact/Writers: Fiction: Submit complete ms. Nonfiction: Submit outline/ synopsis and 3 sample chapters. Reports on queries in 6 weeks; on mss in 6-8 weeks. Publishes a book 18 months after acceptance. Will consider simultaneous submissions.
Illustration: Number of illustrations used for fiction: picture books—32; young readers—8-10; middle readers—1-5; young adults—1. Number of illustrations used for nonfiction: picture books—32; young readers—32-48; middle readers—1; young adults—1. Editorial will review ms/illustration packages. Sue Sherman, art director, will review illustrator's work for possible future assignments.
How to Contact/Illustrators: Ms/illustration packages: complete ms with 1 piece of final art. Illustrations only: Query with samples/slides; provide résumé, promotional literature or tearsheets to be kept on file. Reports on art samples in 6-8 weeks. Original artwork returned at job's completion.
Photography: Photographers should contact Sue Sherman, art director. Model/property releases and captions required. Publishes photo essays and photo concept books. Uses 35mm transparencies. To contact, photographers should provide résumé, promotional literature or tearsheets to be kept on file.
Terms: Pays authors in royalties based on retail price. Offers average advance payment of $2,000-10,000. Photographers paid by the project, by royalty based on retail price. Sends galleys to authors; dummies to illustrators. Book catalog, manuscript/artist's guidelines free on request.
Tips: "Send something fresh and imaginative—written from the heart rather than in answer to a trend. There's an interest in books by, for, and about minorities and about other cultures. Booksellers are limiting their buys to big-name authors and illustrators.

YA fiction has to be either very literary or very commercial—no room for the mid-list book."

LODESTAR BOOKS, Affiliate of Dutton Children's Books, a division of Penguin Books, USA, Inc., 375 Hudson St., New York NY 10014. (212)366-2627. FAX: (212)366-2011. Estab. 1980. Editorial Director: Virginia Buckley. Senior Editor: Rosemary Brosnan. Publishes 5 picture books/year; 15-20 middle reader titles/year; 5 young adult titles/year (30 books a year). 5-10% of books by first-time authors; 50% through agents.
Fiction: Picture books: animal, contemporary, folktales, nature/environment. Young readers: adventure, animal, contemporary, fantasy, nature/environment. Middle reader: adventure, animal, contemporary, fantasy, folktales, nature/environment, science fiction, suspense/mystery. Young adult: adventure, contemporary, history, problem novels, science fiction. Recently published *Lyddie*, by Katherine Paterson (ages 10 and up, novel about 1840's mill worker in Lowell, Massachusetts); *Hello, Tree!*, by Joanne Ryder, illustrated by Michael Hays (ages 5-8, picture book); *Love, David*, by Dianne Case, illustrated by Dan Andreasen (ages 8-12, novel set in South Africa).
Nonfiction: Picture books: activity books, animal, history, nature/environment. Young reader: animal, history, nature/environment, sports. Middle reader: animal, biography, careers, history, music/dance, nature/environment, sports. Young adult: history, music/dance, nature/environment, sports. Recently published *Insect Zoo*, by Susan Meyers, full-color photographs by Richard Hewett (ages 8-12, describes the San Francisco Insect Zoo); *Friendship Across Arctic Waters: Alaskan Cub Scouts Visit Their Soviet Neighbors*, by Claire Rudolf Murphy, full-color photographs by Charles Mason (ages 8-12, Fourth of July visit to Provideniya in the Soviet Far East); *Kitten, Puppy, Frog, Duck* (See How They Grow series), full-color photographs by Jane Burton and others (ages 5-8, natural history for the very young).
How to Contact/Writers: Fiction: submit outline/synopsis and sample chapters or submit complete ms. Nonfiction: Query or submit outline/synopsis and sample chapters. Reports on queries in 1 month; on mss in 2-3 months. Publishes a book 1 year after acceptance. Will consider simultaneous submissions.
Illustration: Number of illustrations used for fiction: picture book—16-20; middle reader—10. Number of illustrations (photographs) used for nonfiction: 30-50. Editorial will review illustrator's work for possible future assignments.
How to Contact/Illustrators: Ms/illustration packages: Send "manuscript and copies of art (no original art, please)." Illustrations only: Query with samples; send unsolicited art samples by mail; submit portfolio for review; arrange a personal interview to show portfolio; provide promotional literature or tearsheets to be kept on file. Reports back only if interested. Original art work returned at job's completion.
Terms: Pays authors and illustrators in royalties of 5% each for picture books; 8% to author, 2% to illustrator for illustrated novel; and 10% for novel based on retail price. Sends galleys to author. Book catalog for SASE; manuscript guidelines for #10 SAE and 1 first class stamp.

LOTHROP, LEE & SHEPARD BOOKS, div. and imprint of William Morrow Co. Inc., Children's Fiction and Nonfiction, 1350 Avenue of the Americas, New York NY 10019. (212)261-6500. Editor-in-Chief: Susan Pearson. Publishes 60 total titles/year.
Fiction: All levels: various categories; no religion. Recently published *Lady Bugatti*, by Joyce Maxner, illustrated by Kevin Hawkes (picture book); *The River Dragon*, by Darcy Pattison, illustrated by Jean and Mou-sien Tseng (picture book).
Nonfiction: Recently published *The Discovery of the Americas*, by Betsy and Giulio Maestro.
How to Contact/Writers: Fiction and nonfiction: Query; "no unsolicited mss."
Illustration: Editorial will review ms/illustration packages. Will review artwork for future assignments.

How to Contact/Illustrators: Ms/illustration packages: Write for guidelines first. Illustrations only: Query with samples; submit portfolio for review.
Terms: Method of payment: "varies." Manuscript/artist's guidelines free for SASE.
Tips: Currently seeking out picture books, early chapter novels, YA novels and nonfiction. "Multicultural books of all types" are popular right now.

LUCAS/EVANS BOOKS INC., 1123 Broadway, New York NY 10010. (212)929-2583. Executive Director: Barbara Lucas. Estab. 1984. Book packager specializing in children's books, preschool through high school age. Books prepared from inception to camera-ready mechanicals for all major publishers.
Fiction/Nonfiction: Particularly interested in series ideas, especially for middle grades and beginning readers. Recently published fiction titles: *Sing for a Gentle Rain*, by Alison James (YA, fantasy (Atheneum)); *Rosie's Baby Tooth*, by Maryann MacDonald (preschool, picture book (series) Atheneum). Recently published nonfiction titles: *Breaking Barriers* (Epoch Biography Series), by Jules Archer, (Viking); *Nature's Disasters* (six-book series for Crestwood House).
How to Contact/Writers: Query.
Illustration: Portfolios reviewed (bring, do not mail, original art). Color photo copies of art welcome for our file. Art not necessary to accompany mss unless artist professionally trained.
Terms: Royalty-based contracts with advance.
Tips: Prefer experienced authors and artists but will consider unpublished work. "There seems to be an enormous demand for early chapter books, although we will continue our efforts to sell to publishers in all age groups and formats. We are interested in series since publishers look to packagers for producing time-consuming projects."

LUCENT BOOKS, Sister Company to Greenhaven Press, Box 289011, San Diego CA 92128-9009. (619)485-7424. Book publisher. Editor: Bonnie Szumski. 50% of books by first-time authors; 10% of books from agented writers.
Nonfiction: Middle readers, young adults: education, heatlh, topical history, nature/environment, sports, "any overviews of specific topics—i.e., political, social, cultural, economic, criminal, moral issues." No fiction. Average word length: 15,000-20,000. Recently published *The Persian Gulf War*, by Don Nardo (grades 6-12, history); *Photography*, by Brad Steffens (grades 5-8, history); *Rainforests*, by Lois Warburton (grades 5-8, overview).
How to Contact/Writers: Nonfiction: "Writers should query first, we do writing by assignment only. If you want to write for us, send SASE for guidelines." Reports on queries in 2 weeks. Publishes a book 6 months after acceptance.
Illustration: "We use photos, mostly." Uses primarily b&w artwork only. Will review ms/illustration packages. Will review artwork for future assignments. Preference: "7×9 format—4-color cover."
How to Contact/Illustrators: Ms/illustration packages: Query first. Illustrations only: Query with samples; provide résumé, business card, promotional literature or tearsheets to be kept on file.
Terms: "Fee negotiated upon review of manuscript." Sends galleys to authors. Manuscript guidelines free on request.
Tips: Books must be written at a 7-8 grade reading level. There's a growing market for quality nonfiction. Tentative titles: Free Speech, Tobacco, Alcohol, Discrimination, Immigration, Poverty, The Homeless in America, Space Weapons, Drug Abuse, Terrorism, MAD, Arms Race, Animal Experimentation, endangered species, AIDS, pollution, gun control, etc. The above list is presented to give writers an example of the kinds of titles we are seeking. If you are interested in writing about a specific topic, please query us by mail before you begin writing to be sure we have not assigned a particular topic to another author. The author should strive for objectivity. There obviously will be many

issues on which a position should be taken—e.g. discrimination, tobacco, alcoholism, etc. However, moralizing, self-righteous condemnations, maligning, lamenting, mocking, etc. should be avoided. Moreover, where a pro/con position is taken, contrasting viewpoints should be presented. Certain moral issues such as abortion and euthanasia, if dealt with at all, should be presented with strict objectivity."

MARGARET K. McELDERRY BOOKS, imprint of Macmillan Publishing Co., 866 Third Ave., New York NY 10022. (212)702-7855. Book publisher. Publisher: Margaret K. McElderry. Publishes 10-12 picture books/year; 2-4 young reader titles/year; 8-10 middle reader titles/year; 3-5 young adult titles/year. 33% of books by first-time authors; 33% of books from agented writers.
Fiction: All levels: various categories; no health or religion. Average word length: picture books—500; young readers—2,000; middle readers—10,000-20,000; young adults—45,000-50,000. Recently published *Matthew's Dragon*, by Susan Cooper, illustrated by Jos. A. Smith (ages 4-8, a magical story and pictures); *Toughboy and Sister*, by Kirkpatrick Hill (ages 8-12, a contemporary survival story about two Alaskan Indian children); *Killing the Kudu*, by Carolyn Meyer (ages 12 up, a compelling contemporary story about an 18-year-old paraplegic boy).
Nonfiction: All levels: various categories; no religion or textbooks. Average word length: picture books—500-1,000; young readers—1,500-3,000; middle readers—10,000-20,000; young adults—30,000-45,000. Recently published *Climbing Jacob's Ladder: Heroes of the Bible in African-America Spirituals*, selected by John Langstaff, illustrated by Ashley Bryan (all ages); *Nature History from A to Z*, by Tim Arnold (ages 10-14, basic concepts of biology); *If the Owl Calls Again*, edited by Myra Cohn Livingston (ages 10 up, collection of owl poetry, illustrations in woodcut by Antonio Frasconi).
How to Contact/Writers: Fiction/nonfiction: Submit complete ms. Reports on queries in 2-3 weeks; on mss in 8 weeks. Publishes a book 12-18 months after acceptance. Will consider simultaneous (only if indicated as such) submissions.
Illustration: Number of illustrations used for fiction: picture books—"every page"; young readers—15-20; middle readers—15-20. Number of illustrations used for nonfiction: picture books—"every page"; young readers—20-30; middle readers—20-30. Editorial will review ms/illustration packages; will review an illustrator's work for possible future assignments (2 or 3 samples only).
How to Contact/Illustrators: Ms/illustration packages: Ms (complete) and 2 or 3 pieces of finished art. Illustrations only: Query with samples; provide resume, promotional literature or tearsheets to be kept on file. Reports on art samples in 6-8 weeks. Original artwork returned at job's completion.
Photography: Contact: Art Director. Looking for occasional photos for specific titles. Publishes photo essays and photo concept books. To contact, photographers should provide resume and promotional literature or tearsheets to be kept on file.
Terms: Pays authors in royalties based on retail price. Pay for illustrators: by the project. Photographers paid by the project. Sends galleys to authors; dummies to illustrators, "they make the dummies for picture books." Book catalog, manuscript/artist's guidelines free on request.
Tips: Sees trends of "nonfiction and poetry books which will continue to be published widely." Illustrators: There is an "emphasis on books for babies and young children; on nonfiction." (See also Aladdin Books/Collier Books for Young Adults, Atheneum Publishers, Bradbury Press, Four Winds Press.)

*MACMILLAN CHILDREN'S BOOKS, imprint of MacMillan Publishing Company, 866 Third Ave., New York NY 10022. Contact: Submissions Editor. Publishes 30 picture books/year; 10 young readers books/year; 8 middle readers books/year; 5 young adult books/year. 5% or less of books by first-time authors; 33% from agented authors. "No primary theme—of a higher literary standard than mass market."

Close-up

Felicia Bond
Illustrator/Writer
Austin, Texas

One afternoon when Felicia Bond was five years old, she saw a buttery beam of sunlight pour into her bedroom window. That's when she knew she wanted to be an artist. "But, the representation of the sunbeam itself is not as important as the feeling it evoked, and still evokes, in me; a feeling of poignancy and time passing." She says it is still light that motivates and inspires her as an artist today.

After graduating from college in Texas, Bond moved to New York City. It wasn't long before she signed a contract with Harper & Row (now HarperCollins) to illustrate a science picture book. That was 15 years ago. In those years, she has been the author and/or illustrator of more than 15 books, including the much renowned *If You Give a Mouse a Cookie*, by Laura Numeroff. (The sequel to that book, *If You Give a Moose a Muffin*, also written by Numeroff and illustrated by Bond, came out in the fall of 1991.)

Even when illustrating other people's stories, Bond takes full creative control of the artwork. She says, "No one tells the artist what to draw or how to draw it. I invented the 'look' of Mike, the mouse in If You Give a Mouse a Cookie.*" (Though the mouse is nameless in the actual book, Bond says she named him because it makes it easier to talk about him.) "I decided what he should wear, including the polka-dot underwear! I decided what kind of cookie it should be. (I almost made it an Oreo!)"*

"I am happy I can illustrate good books written by other people," says Bond. However, when choosing projects, she admits to being selective. "I have to find something personal and exciting in every story I decide to illustrate. I turn down a story if it does not seem 'right' for me."

Though the last few years have been devoted to illustrating only, Bond has also written as well as illustrated eight books of her own. She says she didn't really have a desire to write until she was in her early 20s. But she credits her graphic mentor, Charles Schulz, as also being her verbal mentor. "I'm sure that it was reading Peanuts that taught me words could convey both humor and insight in a succinct, narrative form." *Poinsettia and Her Family*, published in 1981, was the first book she wrote. The story, about a pig named Poinsettia and her six brothers and sisters who are always in the way, is based on Bond's childhood (she also has six brothers and sisters).

The following, written by Bond, is her personal account of the creative process she experiences while writing and illustrating a picture book. She refers to the process as "The Method of the Madness":

Like most heartfelt pursuits, it takes a certain sort of mind to do this sort of thing. What follows is a brief description of my particular process in making a picture book. And believe me, if I could skip any of these steps and get away with it, I would!

• **Get ideas.** Mine come from out of nowhere and from everywhere, often or only occasionally, and at every time of the year and day. I write them *all* down. I have had ideas while driving (Quick! Pull over! Write it on the back of that old speeding ticket!), at dawn while still in bed (Quick! Find some paper in the dark! Don't step on the cat!), in the public library (Quick! Write it down on the back of my hand because once again, I've come to the library *completely unprepared*), and even while sitting at my drawing table (Quick! Write it and draw it in *such detail* that the project I originally sat down to attack is so hopelessly delayed, I can see my editor's sweat come out of the phone). I put all these pieces of paper in my sketchbook, and when I sit down to write a story, I pull all of them out. Then I usually write about something completely different.

• **Procrastinate.** This is a far more elaborate and convoluted procedure than I have space to expand on here. (However, this step can be inserted between all of the other following steps!)

• **Write.** When I finally sit down to write in earnest, I write fast and with urgency from the beginning of my story to the end, however long that takes. I take the phone off the hook.

• **Rewrite.** I am fairly self-critical and do not show my manuscript to my editor until it is as good as I think I can make it. My original story might be "inspired," but still not "work." Rewriting or revising can be very labor intensive.

• **Sketch.** I show my editor my efforts, and when we both think "go," I start sketching. I start with my primary characters and develop both their looks and personalities simultaneously. I do the same for every element of the pictures—the surroundings, the clothes, the weather, the colors and the shapes. It is a great deal of fun. I explore every possibility I can think of, and in the end go with my instincts. This is my favorite part of making a book, as it is the most flexible. Eventually, the sketches gel enough to . . .

● **Make a dummy.** I play with the text — put a phrase here . . . and . . . there. I scribble indecipherable sketches and design in my mind's eye. To prevent this from being *too* enjoyable, at this point there are usually one or two *really big problems* that involve some sort of *really big sacrifices* — of words, or a perfect page break, or a picture.

● **Start serious sketches.** I evolve my images over and over using tracing paper until they are just right. (Unfortunately, I, and many other artists I know, often miss the quirky energy of the rough sketches.) Then I trace my drawings on good paper.

● **Ta-da! Do finished art.** Scary at first, then fun, then a bit tedious. By this time, deadline panic sets in.

● **Buy special glasses for tunnel vision; then finish book.** At this point, any number of things can happen, such as my head falling off. Usually, I engage in serious diet and exercise and have a reunion with my loved ones (if I'm lucky). Also, cats start curling up on my lap again. Perhaps everyone secretly wonders if maybe I don't have much talent; otherwise, how could this process be so . . . so . . . *something*? (That's exactly why I like it!)

© 1981 by Felicia Bond

Bond wrote Poinsettia & Her Family *during one particularly lonely Christmas while living in New York City. Since she wasn't going to spend the holiday with her family in Texas, she got the idea to create a special "garland of memories" for her Christmas tree, consisting of family pictures strung together. "Poinsettia & Her Family was originally set at Christmas, and my own decorated tree became Poinsettia's." However, her editor felt the Christmas setting within the story made it too involved, and suggested taking out the tree altogether. "Then I had the idea to hang one photograph on a string around Poinsettia's neck," says Bond. "The necklace was every bit as personal to me as the garland had been."*

Fiction: All levels: adventure, anthology, animal, contemporary, fantasy, folktales, history, nature/environment, poetry, problem novels, science fiction, suspense/mystery, multicultural. Does not want to see "topic" books, stories about bunnies or kittens, "New Age" themes. Recently published *When Hugo Went to School*, by Ann Rockwell (ages 2-5, picture book); *Annabelle's Un-Birthday*, by Steven Kroll/Gail Owens (grades 1-5, storybook); *Grandpa's Mountain*, by Carolyn Reeder (grades 3-7, historical fiction).
Nonfiction: Picture books, young readers, middle readers and young adults: animal, biography, history, music/dance, nature/environment. No fixed lengths! Recently published *Eating the Plates: A Pilgrim Book of Food and Manners*, by Lucille Recht Penner (grades 1-5, nonfiction); *Duke Ellington*, by James Lincoln Collier (grades 5-9, biography); *On the Air: Behind the Scenes at a TV Newscast*, by Esther Hautzig and David Hautzig (grades 1-5, photo essay).
How to Contact/Writers: Fiction/nonfiction: Query. Submit complete ms ("only shorter works"). Submit outline/synopsis and 2 sample chapters. "For longer works, query with sample chapter and outline. All submissions must include SASE!" Reports on queries in 1 week. Publishes a book 1-2 years after acceptance.
Illustration: Average number of illustrations used for fiction: picture books—10-30; middle readers—4. Nonfiction: picture books—10-30; young readers—10-50; middle readers—5-50; young adult—0-50. Will review ms/illustration packages. Will review artwork for future assignments. Contact Art Director.
How to Contact/Illustrators: Ms/illustrations packages: Send complete ms with sample illustrations. Illustrations only: Query with samples, submit portfolio for review, drop off portfolio on specified days. Reports back only if interested. Original artwork returned at job's completion. Publishes photo essays and photo concept books. Uses color and b&w prints.
Terms: Royalties "negotiable." Offers "negotiable" advances. Pays illustrators by the project or royalty. Pays photographers by the project, per photo, royalty. Sends galleys to authors. Book catalog available for 9×12 SAE and $1.20 postage; ms guidelines available for SASE.

*MAGE PUBLISHERS INC., 1032-29th St. NW, Washington DC 20007. (202)342-1642. Book publisher. Editorial contact: A. Sepehri. Publishes 2-3 picture books/year. 100% of books by first-time authors.
Fiction: Contemporary/myth, Persian heritage. Average word length: 5,000.
Nonfiction: Persian heritage. Average word length: 5,000.
How to Contact/Writers: Fiction/nonfiction: Query. Reports on queries/ms in 3 months. Will consider simultaneous submissions.
Illustration: Number of illustrations used in fiction/nonfiction: picture book—12. Editorial will review ms/illustration packages submitted by authors/artists; ms/illustration packages. Will review artwork for possible future assignments.
How to Contact/Illustrators: Illustrations only: Send résumé and slides. Reports in 3 months. Original artwork returned at job's completion.
Terms: Pays authors in royalties. Sends galleys to authors. Book catalog free on request.

MAGINATION PRESS, Brunner/Mazel, Inc., 19 Union Square West, New York NY 10003. (212)924-3344. Book publisher. Editor-in-Chief: Susan Kent Cakars. Publishes 4-8 picture books and young reader titles/year.
Fiction: Picture Books and young readers: contemporary. "Books dealing with the therapeutic resolution of children's psychological problems."
Nonfiction: Picture Books and Young Readers: psycho therapy.
How to Contact/Writers: Fiction/nonfiction: Submit complete manuscript. Reports on queries/mss: "up to 2 months max (may be only days)." Publishes a book 1 year after acceptance.

Illustration: Number of illustrations used for fiction and nonfiction: picture books— 24-29. Reviews illustration packages. Art director, Millicent Fairhurst, will review illustrator's work for possible future assignments. Prefers b&w for text, full-color for cover.
How to Contact/Illustrators: Original artwork returned at job's completion.
Terms: Pays authors in royalties. Offers varied but low advance. Pay for illustrators: by the project, $2,000 max. Pays royalty, 2% max. Sends galleys to authors. Book catalog and manuscript guidelines free on request.

MARCH MEDIA, INC., #256, 7003 Chadwick, Brentwood TN 37027. (615)370-3148. Independent book producer/agency. President: Etta G. Wilson. 25% of books by first-time authors.
Fiction: Picture books: animal, religion. Young readers: history, religion. Middle readers: folktales. Recently produced *Natalie Jean* series, by Kersten Hamilton (7-9, fiction); *Holt and the Teddy Bear*, by Jim McCafferty (7-10).
Nonfiction: Picture books: animal, religion. Young readers: animal, history. Middle readers: biography, history, religion.
How to Contact/Writers: Fiction: Submit outline/synopsis and sample chapters. Nonfiction: submit complete ms. Reports on queries in 1 month, on ms in 2 months. Will consider simultaneous submissions.
Illustration: Editorial will review ms/illustration packages. Will review artwork for future assignments.
How to Contact/Illustrators: Ms/illustration packages: "query first." Illustrations only: send tearsheets to be kept on file. Reports back only if interested. Original art work returned at job's completion.
Terms: Method of payment: "Either royalty or fee, depending on project and publisher's requirements."
Tips: Illustrators: "Be certain you can draw children. Study book design." Looking for manuscripts that present "a unique, imaginative exploration of a situation." Recent trend reflects "more nonfiction and better art."

MEADOWBROOK PRESS, 18318 Minnetonka Blvd., Deephaven MN 55391. (612)473-5400. Book publisher. Editorial Contact: Elizabeth Weiss. Publishes 7 young reader titles/year; 4 middle reader titles/year; 2 young adult titles/year. 25% of books by first-time authors; 8% of books from agented writers.
Nonfiction: Young readers: education, hobbies, activity books. Middle readers: education, hobbies, activity books. Young adults/teens: education, hobbies, activity books. Average word length: Young readers—8,200; Middle readers—8,200.
How to Contact/Writers: Nonfiction: Query, submit outline/synopsis and sample chapters or submit complete ms. Reports on queries/mss in 1 month. Publishes a book 9 months after acceptance. Will consider simultaneous submissions.
Illustration: Number of illustrations used for nonfiction: young readers—100; middle readers—100. Editorial will review ms/illustration packages. Jennifer L. Nelson and Anne Marie Hoppe, Art Directors, will review an illustrator's work for possible use in future assignments.
How to Contact/Illustrators: Ms/illustration packages: Send "three sample chapters of ms with 1 piece of final art." Illustrations only: Send résumé and samples. Reports back in 6 weeks. Original artwork returned at job's completion.

Always include a self-addressed stamped envelope (SASE) or International Reply Coupon (IRC) with submissions.

Terms: Pays authors in royalties of 5-7½% based on retail price. Offers average advance payment of $1,000-5,000. Pay for illustrators: $100-10,000; ¼-¾% of total royalties. Sends galleys for review to authors "sometimes." Book catalog, manuscript/artist's guidelines free on request.
Tips: Illustrators: "Develop a commercial style—compare your style to that of published authors, and submit your work when it is judged 'in the ball park.' " Looking for: "A children's book by objective observers, aimed at early elementary age kids which explains how to get into, e.g., science, astronomy, magic, collecting, hobbies."

MERIWETHER PUBLISHING LTD., 885 Elkton Dr., Colorado Springs CO 80907. Book publisher. Estab. 1969. "We do most of our artwork in house; we do not publish for the children's elementary market." 75% of books by first-time authors; 5% of books from agented writers. Publishes nonfiction only—primarily how-to activity books for teens.
Nonfiction: Middle readers: activity books, religion. Young adults: activity books, how-to church activities, religion, drama/theater arts. Average length: 200 pages. Recently published *Storytelling from the Bible*, by Janet Litherland (for teens and adult, how-to book); *Contemporary Improvisation*, by Delton Horn (for teens and adults, how-to book); *Clown Skits for Everyone*, by Happy Jack Fedder (teens and adults, how-to theater arts books).
How to Contact/Writers: Nonfiction: Query or submit outline/synopsis and sample chapters. Reports on queries in 1 month. Publishes a book 6-12 months after acceptance. Will consider simultaneous submissions.
Illustration: Number of illustrations used for nonfiction: young adults—15. Uses primarily black & white artwork only. Art Director, Tom Myers, will review an illustrator's work for possible future assignments.
How to Contact/Illustrators: Ms/illustration packages: Query first. Illustrations only: Slides. Reports on art samples in 4 weeks.
Terms: Pays authors in royalties based on retail and wholesale price. Pay for illustrators: by the project; royalties based on retail or wholesale price. Sends galleys to authors. Book catalog for SAE and $1 postage; manuscript guidelines for SAE and 1 first-class stamp.
Tips: Plans "more nonfiction on communication arts subjects."

*MERRILL PUBLISHING, imprint of Macmillan Publishing Co./College Division, 445 Hutchinson Ave., Columbus OH 43235. (614)841-3700. FAX: (614)841-3701. Editor for Education: Linda Scharp. Publishes "educational books used by college students to teach them how to deal with children, children's special needs, and foundations of education. Publishes some children's literature books, and other disciplines in other divisions."
Illustration: Uses 30-40 illustrations/year for college level textbooks. Will review illustration packages. Contact Cover Designer Cathleen Norz at (614)841-3699.
How to Contact/Illustrators: Query with samples; submit portfolio for review; provide tearsheets. Reports in 1 week.
Photography: Photo Editor: Ann Vega. Uses photos of children, children with teachers at school, handicapped, children at play. Model/property release required with submissions. Uses color and b&w glossy prints and 35mm transparencies. Provide transparencies; submit portfolio for review.
Terms: Pays $300-1,000 by the project.
Tips: Wants "illustrations or photos depicting real life and some illustrations based on children's literature."

■METAMORPHOUS PRESS, Box 10616, Portland OR 97210. (503) 228-4972. Book publisher. Acquisitions Editor: Lori Stephens. Estab. 1982. Publishes 1 picture book/year; 1 young reader title/year; 1 middle reader title/year; 1 young adult title/year. 90% of

books by first-time authors; 10% of books from agented writers. Subsidy publishes 10%.
Fiction: "Metaphors for positive change."
Nonfiction: Picture books: education. Young readers: education, music/dance. Middle readers: education, music/dance, self-help/esteem. Young adults: education, music/dance, self-help/esteem.
How to Contact/Writers: Fiction: Query. Nonfiction: Query; submit outline/synopsis and sample chapters. Reports on queries in 3-4 months; on mss in 4-6 months. Publishes a book 1-2 years after acceptance. Will consider simultaneous and electronic submissions via disk or modem.
Illustration: Number of illustrations used for fiction/nonfiction: "varies." Editorial will review ms/illustration packages. Lori Stephens will review an illustrator's work for possible future assignments.
How to Contact/Illustrators: Ms/illustrations: Query. Illustrations only: "vitae with samples of range and style." Reports on art samples only if interested.
Terms: Sends galleys to authors; dummies to illustrators. Book catalog free on request.
Tips: Looks for "books that relate and illustrate the notion that we create our own realities, self-reliance and positive outlooks work best for us — creative metaphors and personal development guides given preference."

*■MIDMARCH ARTS PRESS, 300 Riverside Dr., New York NY 10025. (212)666-6990. Manager: L. Hulkower. 90% of books by first-time authors; subsidy publishes 30%. Arts/artists' themes.
Fiction: All levels: arts. Recently published *When Even the Cows Were Up*, by K. Pedigo (ages 5-9, history/coloring); *The Little Cat Who Had No Name*, by T. Reynolds (ages 7-12, fiction/picture).
Nonfiction: All levels: biography (artists), music/dance, art.
How to Contact/Writers: Nonfiction: Query. Reports on queries/mss in 3 weeks to 3 months.
Illustration: Average number of illustrations used for nonfiction: picture books — 10; middle readers — 10. Will review ms/illustration packages. Will review artwork for future assignments.
How to Contact/Illustrators: Ms/illustration packages: Query. Illustrations only: Query with samples. Reports in 3 weeks to 3 months. Original artwork returned at job's completion.
Photography: Types of photos needed "depends on book." Publishes photo essays. Uses b&w glossy prints. To contact, photographers should query with resume of credits.
Terms: Pays authors royalty. Pays illustrators royalty. Photographers paid by the project. Sends galleys to authors; dummies to illustrators. Book catalog available for 6×9 SAE and 39¢ postage; ms and artist's guidelines available for SAE and 39¢ postage.

■MOREHOUSE PUBLISHING CO., 871 Ethan Allen Hwy., Ridgefield CT 06877. (203)431-3927. FAX: (203)431-3964. Book publisher. Estab. 1884. Juvenile Books Editor: Jill Weaver. Publishes 10 picture books/year. 75% of books by first-time authors. Subsidy publishes 25%.
Fiction: All levels: religion.
Nonfiction: All levels: religion, moral message, family values. Picture books and young readers: religion.
How to Contact/Writers: Fiction/nonfiction: Submit outline/synopsis and sample chapters to Jill Weaver, Box 1321, Harrisburg PA 17105. Reports on queries in 4-6

 The solid block before a listing indicates the market subsidy publishes manuscripts.

weeks. Publishes a book 1 year after acceptance. Editorial will review ms/illustration packages.

How to Contact/Illustrators: Ms/illustration packages: 3 chapters of ms with 1 piece of final art. Illustrations only: Résumé, tearsheets. Reports on art samples in 4-6 weeks. Original artwork returned at job's completion. Send to Jill Weaver, Box 1321, Harrisburg PA 17105.

Terms: Pays authors "both royalties and outright." Offers average advance payment of $500. Sends galleys to authors. Book catalog free on request.

Tips: Writers: "Prefer authors who can do own illustrations. Be fresh, be fun, not pedantic, but let your work have a message." Illustrators: "Work hard to develop an original style." Looks for ms/illustrations "with a religious or moral value while remaining fun and entertaining."

*■JOSHUA MORRIS PUBLISHING, subsidiary of Reader's Digest, Inc., 221 Danbury Rd., Wilton CT 06897. (203)761-9999. FAX: (203)761-5655. Senior Editor: Sarah Black. "We publish mostly basic concept books and books for beginning readers. Most are in series of at least 4 and contain some kind of novelty element (i.e., lift the flap, die cut holes, book and soft toy, etc.) We publish 300-400 books per year." 5% of books by first-time authors; 5% of books from agented authors; 35% of books are subsidy published; 55% of books published on commission.

Fiction: Picture books and young readers: adventure, animal, contemporary, fantasy, folktales, health-related, history, nature/environment, religion, sports, suspense/mystery. Does not want to see poetry, short stories, science fiction. Average word length: picture books—300-400. Recently published *Read a Picture (Animals, Rhymes & Stories)*, by Burton Marks (ages 4-7, Rebus); *Alan Snow's Wonderful World*, by Alan Snow (ages 3-6, word book); *Ghostly Games*, by John Speirs, with additional text by Gill Speirs (ages 8-12, puzzle).

Nonfiction: Picture books, young readers and middle readers: activity books, animal, nature/environment, religion. Average word length: varies. Recently published *Alan Snow Complete Books (Dictionary, Atlas & Encyclopedia)*, by Alan Snow (ages 3-7, first reference); *I Wonder . . . How Many Bones Do I Have, I Wonder . . . How Does the Wind Blow*, by Andrew Langley (ages 5-8, question and answer).

How to Contact/Writers: Fiction: Query. Nonfiction: Query. Reports on queries in 1 month; reports on mss in 4 months. Publishes a book 12-18 months after acceptance. Will consider simultaneous submissions and previously published work.

Illustration: Average number of illustrations used for fiction and nonfiction "depends on book length." Will review ms/illustration packages. Will review artwork for future assignments. Contact Patricia Jennings, art director.

How to Contact/Illustrators: Ms/illustration packages: Query. Illustrations only: Send non-returnable art samples by mail; provide résumé, promotional literature or tearsheets to be kept on file. Reports back only if interested. Original artwork returned (only if requested).

Photography: Photographers should contact Patricia Jennings, art director. Uses photos of animals and children. Model/property releases required. Interested in stock photos. Publishes photo concept books. Uses 4 × 6, glossy, color prints and 4 × 5 transparencies. To contact, photographers should provide résumé, promotional literature or tearsheets to be kept on file.

Terms: Pays authors royalty, outright purchase. Offers advances. Pays illustrators by the project, royalty. Photographers paid per photo.

Tips: Best bets with this market are "innovative concept and beginning readers, and books that have a novelty element."

MOSAIC PRESS, 358 Oliver Rd., Cincinnati OH 45215. (513)761-5977. Miniature book publisher. Publisher: Miriam Irwin. Publishes less than 1 young reader title/year. 50% of books by first-time authors. "I am really not looking for children's books right now."
Fiction: Middle readers: animal, contemporary, history, problem novels, sports, spy/mystery/adventure. Average word length: middle readers—under 2,000.
Nonfiction: Middle readers: animal, biography, education, history, hobbies, music/dance, nature/environment, religion, sports. Average word length: middle readers—2,000.
How to Contact/Writers: Fiction: Query; submit complete ms. Nonfiction: Submit complete ms. Reports on queries/mss in 2 weeks. Publishes a book 4 years after acceptance. Will consider simultaneous submissions.
Illustration: Number of illustrations used for fiction: middle readers—12. Number of illustrations used for nonfiction: middle readers—8. Editorial will review ms/illustration packages. Uses black & white artwork only. Prefers to see "pen and ink under 5" tall."
How to Contact/Illustrators: Illustrations only: "photocopies of pen and ink work with SASE." Reports on art samples in 2 weeks. Original artwork returned at job's completion "after several years if requested."
Terms: Buys ms outright for $50 and 5 copies of book. Final payment is a "flat fee." Pay for illustrators: $50 and 5 copies. Book catalog is available for $3. Manuscript/artist's guidelines for business-size SAE and 2 first-class stamps.
Tips: Looks for "any type of writing that has something to say worth preserving in the form of a miniature book; that says it beautifully in very few words. Most of our children's books are bought by adults for *themselves*. Most of our books are in the $24 range, and people won't pay that much for a little book for children." Also looking for "something adults would read over and over to their children."

JOHN MUIR PUBLICATIONS, INC., P.O. Box 613, Santa Fe NM 87504-0613. (505)982-4078. Book publisher. Editorial Contact: Ken Luboff. Publishes 10 picture books/year; 10-15 middle reader nonfiction titles/year.
Nonfiction: Middle Readers: animal, biography, hobbies, nature/environment. Average word length: middle readers—12,000-15,000. Recently published *Kidding Around Series* (4 titles), by different authors (middle readers); *Extremely Weird Series* (5 titles), by Sarah Lovett.
How to Contact/Writers: Query. Reports on queries/mss in 4-6 weeks. Publishes a book 8 months after acceptance. Will consider simultaneous submissions.
Illustration: Number of illustrations used for fiction and nonfiction: picture books—25; middle readers—20-60. Reviews illustration packages. Art Production Director, Sally Blakemore, will review illustrator's work for possible future assignments.
How to Contact/Illustrators: Ms/illustration packages: query, outline and 1 chapter for illustration; 4 original finished pieces and roughs of ideas. Illustrations only: submit résumé and samples of art that have been reproduced or samples of original art for style. Original artwork returned at job's completion.
Terms: Pays authors in royalties based on wholesale price. Offers advance. Some books are paid by flat fee for illustration. Pay for Illustrators: by the project. Book catalog free on request.

NAR PUBLICATIONS, P.O. Box 233, Barryville NY 12719. (914)557-8713. Book publisher. 50% of books by first-time authors; 5% of books from agented writers.
How to Contact/Writers: Fiction/nonfiction: Query. Reports on queries in 3 weeks; mss in 1 month. Publishes book 9 months after acceptance. Will consider simultaneous and electronic submissions via disk.
Terms: Buys ms outright. Book catalog for 1 first class stamp and #10 SAE.
Tips: "We have only published two books for children. Preschool to age 8 has best chance of acceptance."

NATUREGRAPH PUBLISHER, INC., P.O. Box 1075, Happy Camp CA 96039. (916)493-5353. Contact: Barbara Brown. Publishes 4 young adult titles/year. 100% of books by first-time authors.
Nonfiction: Young adults: animal, nature/environment, native American. Average word length: young adults—70,000.
How to Contact/Writers: Nonfiction: Query. Reports on queries/mss in 2 weeks. Publishes book 18 months after acceptance.
Terms: Pays authors in royalties of 10% based on wholesale price. Sends galleys to authors. Book catalog is free on request.

*NORTH LIGHT BOOKS, 1507 Dana Ave., Cincinnati OH 45207. (513)531-2222. Book publisher. Editor: Julie Whaley. Publishes 4-8 children's books/year. 100% of books by first-time authors. Publishes art and activity books for kids aged 6-11.
Nonfiction: Picture books, young readers, middle readers and young adults: activity books, biography, history, hobbies, music/dance, nature/environment. Recently published *Paint!, Draw!, Make Gifts!* and *Make Prints!*, by Kim Solga (ages 6-11, art projects). Submit outline/synopsis and 1 sample chapter. Reports in 1 month. Publishes book 18 months to 2 years after acceptance.
Illustration: Average number of illustrations used for nonfiction: picture books—100. Will review ms/illustration packages. Will review artwork for future assignments. Contact: Julie Whaley.
How to Contact/Illustrators: Query with samples. Reports in 1 month. Original artwork returned at job's completion.
Photography: Photographers should contact Julie Whaley. Uses photos of domestic animals and nature. Model/property releases and caption required. Interested in stock photos. Uses 35mm, 2¼×2¼, 4×5 transparencies. Query with samples.
Terms: Pays author outright purchase. Offers advances. Pays illustrators by the project. Illustrators paid by the project. Photographers paid by the project or per photo. Sends galley to authors. Books catalog free.
Tips: "Learn to see things from a child's viewpoint." Author's best chance is with an art or activity book.

ODDO PUBLISHING, INC., Box 68, Fayetteville GA 30214. (404)461-7627. Book publisher. Estab. 1964. Contact: Editor. Publishes 3-6 picture books/year; 1-2 young reader titles/year; 1-2 middle reader titles/year. 10% of books by first-time authors.
Fiction: Picture books, young readers, middle readers: various categories. Average word length: picture books—500; young readers—1,000; middle readers—2,000. Recently published *Wrongway Santa*, by Rae Oetting, illustrated by Art Shardin (grades 4-6, picture book).
Nonfiction: Picture books, young readers, middle readers: various categories. Average word length: picture books—500; young readers—1,000; middle readers—2,000.
How to Contact/Writers: Fiction/nonfiction: Query; submit outline/synopsis and sample chapters. Reports on queries 1-2 weeks; on mss 8-12 weeks. Publishes a book 24 months after acceptance. Will consider simultaneous submissions.
Illustration: Number of illustrations used for fiction and nonfiction: picture books—33; young readers—33; middle readers—33. Uses color artwork only. Editorial will review all illustration packages. Will review artwork for future assginments.
How to Contact/Illustrators: Ms/illustration packages: Query first. Illustrations only: promotional literature or tearsheets to be kept on file. Reports on art samples only if interested.
Photography: Purchases photos "on a very limited basis." Uses color prints and 35mm, 2¼×2¼, or 4×5 transparencies. Provide promotional literature or tearsheets to be kept on file.

Terms: Buys ms outright; "negotiable" price. Illustrators paid by the project. Sends galleys to authors "only if necessary." Book catalog available for 9 × 12 SAE and 9 first-class stamps.

Tips: "Send simultaneous submissions. Do not be discouraged by 'no.' Keep sending to publishers." Looks for: "books that lend themselves well to illustration. Stories should have underlying educational value. Quality in story, illustration, and book construction has become increasingly important and will continue to do so. Children's books are no longer simply 'pacifiers.' 'Coping' subjects are accepted. We want children who read our books to learn something and feel good when they are finished."

*OPEN HAND PUBLISHING INC., P.O. Box 22048, Seattle WA 98122. (206)323-3868. Book publisher. Contact: Pat Andrus. Publishes 1-3 children's books/year. 50% of books by first-time authors. Multi-cultural books: African-American theme or bilingual.

Fiction: Picture books: folktales, history and African American. Young readers and middle readers: history and African-American. Young adult/teens: African-American. Average word length: picture books—32-64 pages; young readers—64 pages; middle readers—64 pages; young adult/teens—120 pages.

Nonfiction: All levels: history and African-American. Average word length: picture books—32-64 pages; young readers—64 pages; middle readers—64 pages; young adult/teens: 64-120 pages.

How to Contact/Writers: Fiction/nonfiction: Query. Reports on queries in 3 weeks; reports on mss in 5 weeks. Publishes a book 12-18 months after acceptance. Will consider simultaneous submissions.

Illustration: Average number of illustrations used for fiction and nonfiction: picture books—25; young readers—9; middle readers—9; young adults/teens—2. Will review ms/illustration packages. Will review artwork for future assignments. Contact P. Anna Johnson, publisher. Uses primarily black & white artwork only.

How to Contact/Illustrators: Ms/illustration packages: Query. Illustrations only: Query with samples. Reports in 3 weeks. Original artwork returned "depending on the book."

Terms: Pays authors royalty of 10-20% based on wholesale price. Offers advances ("only under special circumstances"). Pays illustrators by the project; commission for the work. Sends galleys to authors. Book catalog available for SAE and 1 first class stamp; ms guidelines available for SASE and 2 first class stamps.

ORCHARD BOOKS, div. and imprint of Franklin Watts, Inc., 387 Park Ave. S., New York NY 10016. (212)686-7070. Book publisher. President and Publisher: Norma Jean Sawicki. "We publish between 50 and 60 books, fiction, poetry, picture books, and photo essays." 10-25% of books by first-time authors.

Nonfiction: "We publish very selective nonfiction."

How to Contact/Writers: Fiction: Submit outline/synopsis and sample chapters; submit complete ms. Nonfiction: Submit outline/synopsis and sample chapters. Reports on queries in 2 weeks; on mss in 1 month. Average length of time between acceptance of a book-length ms and publication of work "depends on the editorial work necessary. If none, about 8 months." Will not consider simultaneous submissions.

"Picture books" are geared toward the preschool—8 year old group; "Young readers" to 5-8 year olds; "Middle readers" to 9-11 year olds; and "Young adults" to those 12 and up.

Illustration: Editorial will review ms/illustration packages. "It is better to submit ms and illustration separately unless they are by the same person, or a pairing that is part of the project such as husband and wife."

How to Contact/Illustrators: Ms/illustration packages: 3 chapters of ms with 1 piece of final art, remainder roughs. Illustrations only: "tearsheets or photocopies or photostats of the work." Reports on art samples in 1 month. Original artwork returned at job's completion.

Terms: Pays authors in royalties "industry standard" based on retail price. Sends galleys to authors; dummies to illustrators. Book catalog free on request.

OUR CHILD PRESS, 800 Maple Glen Ln., Wayne PA 19087-4797. (215)964-0606. Book publisher. Contact: Carol Hallenbeck, President. 90% of books by first-time authors.

Fiction/Nonfiction: All levels: adoption. Average word length: Open. Recently published *Chinese Eyes,* by Marjorie Ann Waybill; *Don't Call Me Marda,* by Sheila Kelly Welch; *Is That Your Sister?* by Catherine and Sherry Burin.

How to Contact/Writers: Fiction/Nonfiction: Query or submit complete manuscript. Reports on queries/mss in 2 months. Publishes a book 6-12 months after acceptance.

Illustration: Reviews ms/illustration packages. Carol Hallenbeck will review illustrator's work for possible future assignments.

How to Contact/Illustrators: Query first. Submit résumé, tearsheets and photocopies. Reports on art samples in 2 months. Original artwork returned at job's completion.

Terms: Pays authors in royalties of 5% based on wholesale price. Book catalog for SAE (business envelope) and 52¢ postage.

*RICHARD OWEN PUBLISHERS, INC., 135 Katonah Ave., Katonah NY 10536. (914)232-3903. Book publisher. Editor/Ready to Read: Janice Boland. Publishes 5 picture books/year, 5 young readers/year. 95% of books by first-time authors. Publishes "child focused, meaningful books about characters and situations with which five, six, and seven year old children can identify. We include multicultural stories that present minorities in a positive and natural way. Our stories show the diversity in America."

Fiction: Picture books, young readers: contemporary (multicultural and minorities), native American folktales, nature/environment (American animals). Does not want to see holiday, religious themes, moral teaching stories. No talking animals with personified human characterisitics. No stereotyping. Average word length: picture books – 40-80 words; young readers – 40-80 words.

Nonfiction: Picture books and young readers: animal, careers and nature/environment. No "encyclopedic" type of information stories. Average word length: picture books and young readers – 40-80 words.

How to Contact/Writers: Fiction/nonfiction: Submit complete ms. "Request guidelines first." Reports on ms in 4-6 weeks. Publishes a book 2-3 years after acceptance. Will consider simultaneous submissions.

Illustration: Average number of illustrations used for fiction and nonfiction: picture books and young readers – 8-16. Will review ms/illustration packages. Contact Janice Boland.

How to Contact/Illustrators: Ms/illustration packages: send color copies/reproductions or photos of art. Illustrations only: Send unsolicited art samples by mail; provide tearsheets; "request guidelines first." Reports in 1 month.

Photography: Photographers should contact Janice Boland. Wants photos that are child oriented; not interested in portraits." Sometimes interested in stock photos for special projects. Uses color prints. Send unsolicited photos by mail; provide tearsheets.

Terms: Pays authors royalty. Offers advances. Pays illustrators by the project. Photographers paid by the project. Ms/artist guidelines available for SASE.

Tips: "Send legible, clean copy of work with SASE and follow author guidelines. Spend lots of time reading published children's books. Listen to children, discover their lan-

Sheila Kelly Welch rendered this pencil drawing for her book, Don't Call Me Marda, *published by Our Child Press. She says of the piece, "I wanted to complement the quiet, pensive mood set by the text. I also wanted to create a sense of the boy being an integral part of the woodland scene." The book, which was Welch's first illustrating job, won an honorable mention in the 1991 Benjamin Franklin Awards, presented by Publishers Marketing Association.*

guage and their view of their world. Be interesting to them, write unique, fresh, individually voiced stories." Wants "fresh, lively, well-paced, *brief* stories that will grab and hold the attention of five, six, and seven year olds, and that they will want to reread."

*PACIFIC PRESS, P.O. Box 7000, Boise ID 83707. (208)465-2500. FAX: (208)465-2531. Book publisher. Acquisitions Editor: Marvin Moore. Publishes 2-4 picture books, 2-4 young readers, 2-4 middle readers, 4-6 young adult titles/year. 5% of books by first-time authors. Publishes books pertaining to religion, spiritual values.
Fiction: All levels: animal, health-related, religion. Does not want to see fantasy or totally non-factual stories. "We prefer true stories that are written in fiction style." Average word length: picture books—500-1,000; young readers—6,000-7,000; middle readers—25,000-33,000; young adult/teens—33,000-75,000. Recently published *Focus*

on the Edge, by Heidi Borriuk (teens); *Mystery on Colton's Island*, by Mary Duplex (ages 8-12); *Rocky and Me*, by Paul Ricchiati (ages 4-6, picture/text for pre-school).
Nonfiction: All levels: activity books, animal, health, nature/environment and religion. "All manuscripts must have a religious/spiritual/health theme." Average word length: picture books—500-1,000; young readers—6,000-7,000; middle readers—25,000-33,000; young adult/teens—33,000-80,000. Recently published *Before I Was a Kid*, by Rita Stewart (age 4-6, picture/text for preschool).
How to Contact/Writers: Fiction: Submit complete ms; submit outline/synopsis and 2 sample chapters. Nonfiction: Query; submit complete ms; submit outline/synopsis and 2 sample chapters. Reports on queries in 2 weeks; reports on mss in 2 months. Publishes a book 6-12 months after acceptance. Will consider simultaneous submissions and electronic submissions via disk or modem.
Illustration: Average number of illustrations used for fiction and nonfiction: picture books—14; middle readers—4-6. Will review ms/illustration packages. Will review artwork for future assignments. Contact: Tim Larson, book designer.
How to Contact/Illustrators: Ms/illustration packages: Submit complete package. Illustrations only: submit portfolio for review. Reports in 2 weeks. Original artwork returned at job's completion.
Terms: Pays authors royalty of 12-16% on wholesale price. Offers $300-500 advances. Pays illustrators by the project; 6% royalty on wholesale price. Sends galleys to authors. Book catalog available for 9×12 SASE. Ms guidelines available for SASE.

PANDO PUBLICATIONS, 540 Longleaf Dr., Roswell GA 30075. (404)587-3363. Book publisher. Estab. 1988. Owner: Andrew Bernstein. Publishes 2-6 middle reader titles/year; 2-6 young adult titles/year. 20% of books by first-time authors.
Nonfiction: Middle readers: animal, biography, education, history, hobbies, music/dance, nature/environment, sports. Young adults: animal, biography, education, history, hobbies, music/dance, nature/environment, sports. Average length: middle readers—175 pages; young adults—200 pages.
How to Contact/Writers: Fiction/nonfiction: Prefers full ms. Reports on queries in 1 month; on mss in 6 weeks. Publishes a book 9 months after acceptance. Will consider simultaneous submissions. "Prefers" electronic submissions via disk or modem.
Illustration: Number of illustrations used for nonfiction: middle readers—125; young adults—125. Editorial will review all illustration packages.
How to Contact/Illustrators: Ms/illustrations: Query first. Illustrations only: Tearsheets. Reports on art samples in 1 month. Original artwork returned at job's completion.
Terms: Offers average advance payment of "⅓ royalty due on first run." Illustrators paid "according to contract." Sends galleys to authors; dummies to illustrators. "Book descriptions available on request."
Tips: Writers: "Find an untapped market then write to fill the need." Illustrators: "Find an author with a good idea and writing ability. Develop the book with the author. Join a professional group to meet people—ABA, publisher's groups, as well as writer's groups and publishing auxiliary groups. Talk to printers." Looks for "how-to books, but will consider anything."

PARENTING PRESS, INC., Box 75267, Seattle WA 98125. (206)364-2900. Book publisher. Estab. 1979. Editorial Director: Shari Steelsmith. Publishes 2-3 picture books/year; 1-2 young reader titles/year; 1-2 middle reader titles/year. 40% of books by first-time authors.

Refer to the Business of Children's Writing & Illustrating for up-to-date marketing, tax and legal information.

Fiction: "We rarely publish straight fiction."
Nonfiction: Picture books: biography, education, social skills building. Young readers: education, social skills building books. Middle readers: social skills building. Average word length: picture books—500-800; young readers—1,000-2,000; middle readers—up to 10,000.
How to Contact/Writers: Fiction: "We publish educational books for children in story format. *No straight fiction.*" Nonfiction: Query. Reports on queries 4-6 weeks; mss in 1-2 months, "after requested." Publishes a book 10-11 months after acceptance. Will consider simultaneous submissions.
Illustrations: Number of illustrations used for fiction and nonfiction: picture books—14; young readers—50. Will review ms/illustration packages. "We do reserve the right to find our own illustrator, however." Editorial will review an illustrator's work for possible future assignments.
How to Contact/Illustrators: Ms/illustration packages: Query. Illustrations only: Send "résumé, samples of art/drawings (no original art); photocopies or color photocopies okay." Original artwork returned at job's completion for illustrators under contract.
Terms: Pays authors in royalties of 4% based on net. Outright purchase of ms, "negotiated on a case-by-case basis. Not common for us." Offers average advance of $150. Pay for illustrators: by the project; 4% royalty based on net. Sends galleys to authors; dummies to illustrators. Book catalog/manuscript guidelines for #10 SAE and 1 first-class stamp.
Tips: Writers: "Query publishers who already market to the same audience. We often get manuscripts (good ones) totally unsuitable to our market." Illustrators: "We pay attention to artists who are willing to submit an illustration on speculation." Looking for "social skills building books for children, books that empower children, books that encourage decision making, books that are balanced ethnically and in gender."

PAULIST PRESS, 997 Macarthur Blvd., Mahwah NJ 07430. (201)825-7300. FAX: (201)825-8345. Book publisher. Estab. 1865. Editor: Georgia J. Christo. Publishes 9-11 picture books/year; 6-7 young reader titles/year; 3-4 middle reader titles/year. 70% of books by first-time authors; 30% of books from agented writers.
Fiction: Picture books, young readers, middle readers: religious/moral. Average length: picture books—24 pages; young readers—24-32 pages; middle readers—64 pages. Recently published *A Bug From Aunt Tillie*, by Susan O'Keefe (ages 6-8, picture story book); *What Do You Do With the Rest of the Day, Mary Ann?*, by Eileen Lomasney (ages 5-7, picture book).
Nonfiction: Young readers, middle readers: religion. Recently published *Christopher Columbus: The Man who Unlocked the Secrets of the World*, by Teri Martini (ages 9-12, biography).
How to Contact/Writers: Fiction/nonfiction: Submit complete ms. Reports on queries in 1 month; on mss in 2 months. Publishes a book 12-16 months after acceptance.
Illustration: Number of illustrations used for fiction and nonfiction: picture books—12-16; young readers—12; middle readers—6-8. Editorial will review all varieties of ms/illustration packages.
How to Contact/Illustrators: Ms/illustration packages: Complete ms with 1 piece of final art, remainder roughs. Illustrations only: Résumé, tearsheets. Reports on art samples in 6 weeks. Original artwork returned at job's completion, "if requested by illustrator."
Terms: Outright purchase: $65-100/illustration. Offers average advance payment of $450-$650. Factors used to determine final payment: Color art, b&w, number of illustrations, complexity of work. Pay for separate authors and illustrators: Author paid by royalty rate; illustrator paid by flat fee, sometimes by royalty. Sends galleys to authors; dummies to illustrators.

Tips: Due to the backlog of manuscript submissions, "I will not be reading any new manuscripts until June 1992." Not interested in reviewing novels. Looking for "concept books for young readers, ages 7-9."

PELICAN PUBLISHING CO. INC., 1101 Monroe St., Gretna LA 70053. (504)368-1175. Book publisher. Estab. 1926. Editor: Nina Kooij. Publishes 6 picture books/year; 4 middle reader titles/year; 20% of books by first-time authors; 10% of books from agented writers.
Fiction: Picture books, young readers: folktales, health, history, nature/environment, religion. Middle readers: folktales, health-related, history, nature/environment, problem novels, religion, sports, suspense/mystery. Average word length: picture books—32 pages; middle readers—112 pages. Recently published *Jenny Giraffe Discovers the French Quarter*, by Cecilia Casrill Dartez (ages 5-8); *Quanah Parker: Comanche Chief*, by Rosemary K. Kissinger (ages 8-12); *Henry Hamilton in Outer Space*, by Marilyn Redmond, illustrated by Bruce Foster (ages 8-12, adventure about a Civil War ghost who stows away on a space shuttle).
Nonfiction: Young readers: biography, health, history, music/dance, nature/environment, religion. Middle readers: biography, health, history, music/dance, nature/environment, religion, sports. Recently published *Floridians All*, by George S. Fichter, illustrated by George Cardin (ages 8-12, collection of biographies on famous Florida figures).
How to Contact/Writers: Fiction/Nonfiction: Query. Reports on queries in 4-6 weeks; mss in 3-4 months. Publishes a book 12-18 months after acceptance.
Illustration: Number of illustrations used for fiction and nonfiction: picture books—16-32; middle readers—1 per chapter. Will review ms/illustration packages. Production Manager, Dana Bilbray, will review an illustrator's work for possible future assignments.
How to Contact/Illustrators: Ms/illustration packages: Query first. Illustrations only: query with samples (no originals). Reports on ms/art samples only if interested.
Terms: Pays authors in royalties; buys ms outright "rarely." Sends galleys to authors.
Tips: No anthropomorphic stories, pets stories (fiction or nonfiction), fantasy, poetry, science fiction, or romance. Writers: "Be as original as possible. Develop characters that lend themselves to series and always be thinking of new and interesting situations for those series. Give your story a strong hook—something that will appeal to a well-defined audience. There is a lot of competition out there for general themes." Looks for: "writers whose stories have specific 'hooks' and audiences, and who actively promote their work."

PERSPECTIVES PRESS, P.O. Box 90318, Indianapolis IN 46290. (317)872-3055. Book publisher. Estab. 1982. Publisher: Pat Johnston. Publishes 1-3 picture books/year; 1-3 young reader titles/year; 1-3 middle reader titles/year. 95% of books by first-time authors.
Fiction/Nonfiction: Picture books, young readers, middle readers, young adults: adoption, foster care.
How to Contact/Writers: Fiction/nonfiction: Query or submit outline/synopsis and sample chapters. Reports on queries in 2 weeks; on mss in 6 weeks. Publishes a book 6-10 months after acceptance. Will consider simultaneous submissions.
Illustration: Number of illustrations used for fiction/nonfiction: picture books—16-32; young readers—10-24; middle readers—5-8. Editorial will review ms/illustration packages. Publisher, Pat Johnston, will review illustrator's work for possible future assignments.
How to Contact/Illustrators: Reports on art samples only if interested.
Terms: Pays authors in royalties of 5-15% based on net sales. Sends galleys to authors; dummies to illustrators. Book catalog, manuscript guidelines available for #10 SAE and 2 first-class stamps.

Tips: "Do your homework! I'm amazed at the number of authors who don't bother to check that we have a very limited interest area and subsequently submit unsolicited material that is completely inappropriate for us. For children, we focus exclusively on issues of adoption and interim (foster) care; for adults we also include infertility issues."

PHILOMEL BOOKS, imprint of The Putnam & Grosset Group, 200 Madison Ave., New York NY 10016. (212)951-8700. Book publisher. Editor-in-Chief: Paula Wiseman. Editorial Director: Patricia Gauch (picture books). Editorial Contact: Laura Walsh (young reader titles). Publishes 30 picture books/year; 5-10 young reader titles/year. 20% of books by first-time authors; 80% of books from agented writers.
Fiction: Picture books: animal, fantasy, poetry, multi-cultural, history. Young readers: animal, fantasy, history. Middle readers: fantasy, history. Young adults: contemporary, fantasy, history. "Any well conceived and well written book." Average word length: "Books of quality, varying length."
Nonfiction: Picture books, young readers, middle readers, young adults: animal, biography, history. "Creative nonfiction on any subject." Average length: "not to exceed 150 pages."
How to Contact/Writers: Fiction/nonfiction: Query; submit outline/synopsis and sample chapters; all other unsolicited mss returned unopened. Reports on queries/mss in 3 months. Publishes a book 2 years after acceptance.
Illustration: Number of illustrations used for fiction: picture books—24. Will review ms/illustration packages. Art Director, Nanette Stevenson, will review an illustrator's work for possible future assignments.
How to Contact/Illustrators: Ms/illustration packages: Query first. Illustrations only: "appointment to show portfolio." Reports on art samples in 2 months. Original art work returned at job's completion.
Terms: Pays authors in advance royalties. Average advance payment "varies." Illustrators paid by advance and in royalties. Sends galleys to authors; dummies to illustrators. Books catalog, manuscript/artist's guidelines free on request.
Tips: "Discover your own voice and own story—and persevere." Looks for "something unusual, original, well-written. Fine art. Our needs change, but at this time, we are interested in receiving young fiction for the 4- to 10-year-old child. The genre (fantasy, contemporary, or historical fiction) is not so important as the story itself, and the spirited life the story allows its main character. We are also interested in receiving adolescent novels, particularly novels that contain regional spirit, such as a story about a young boy or girl written from a southern, southwestern, or northwestern perspective."

PIPPIN PRESS, 229 E. 85th St., Gracie Station, Box 92, New York NY 10028. (212)288-4920. FAX: (212)563-5703. Children's book publisher. Estab. 1987. Publisher/President: Barbara Francis. Publishes 6-8 picture books/year; 3 young reader titles/year. "Not interested in young adult books."
Fiction: Picture books, young readers, middle readers: adventure, animal, fantasy, folktales, history, nature/environment, humorous. Average word length: picture books—750-1,500; young readers—2,000-3,000; middle readers—3,000+. Recently published *Lost in the Amazon: A Miss Mallard Mystery*, by Robert Quackenbush (ages 6-9); *Scamper: A Gray Tree Squirrel*, by Edna Miller (ages 4-8, picture book); *A Spring Story*, by David Updike, illustration by Robert Andrew Parker (ages 7-10). No YA books.

Always include a self-addressed stamped envelope (SASE) or International Reply Coupon (IRC) with submissions.

Nonfiction: Picture books, young readers, middle readers: animal, biography, history, music/dance, nature/environment. Recently published *Take Me to Your Liter*, by Charles Keller, illustrated by Gregory Filling (ages 7-11, science and math jokes). No YA books.
How to Contact/Writers: Fiction/nonfiction: Query. Reports on queries in 2-3 weeks; on mss in 6-8 weeks. Publishes a book 9-18 months after acceptance. Will consider simultaneous submissions.
Illustration: Number of illustrations used for fiction: picture books—25-30; young readers—15-20; middle readers—8-10. Number of illustrations used for nonfiction: picture books—25-30; young readers—15-20; middle readers—15-20. Editorial will review an illustrator's work for possible future assignments.
How to Contact/Illustrators: Illustrations only: "Tearsheets or photocopies would be fine. I see illustrations by appointment." Reports on art samples only if interested. Original artwork returned at job's completion.
Terms: Pays authors in royalties. Pay for illustrators: Royalty. Sends galleys to authors; dummies to illustrators. "The illustrator prepares the dummy on picture books; dummies for longer books prepared by the designer are submitted to the illustrator." Book catalog available for 6×9 SAE; manuscript/artist's guidelines for #10 SAE.
Tips: "We will be publishing more transitional books, i.e. picture storybooks for ages 7 and up and more nonfiction. The market is glutted with mediocre and poor picture books. We are looking for chapter books, especially humorous ones, and will continue to publish writers and illustrators with track records."

PLAYERS PRESS, INC., Box 1132, Studio City CA 91614. (818)789-4980. Book publisher. Estab. 1965. Vice President/Editorial: R. W. Gordon. Publishes 2-10 young readers dramatic plays and musicals titles/year; 2-10 middle readers dramatic plays and musicals titles/year; 4-20 young adults dramatic plays and musicals titles/year. 35% of books by first-time authors; 1% of books from agented writers.
Fiction: "We use all categories (young readers, middle readers, young adults) but only for dramatic plays and/or musicals."
Nonfiction: "Any children's nonfiction pertaining to the entertainment industry, performing arts and how-to for the theatrical arts only."
How to Contact/Writers: Fiction/nonfiction: Submit plays or outline/synopsis and sample chapters of entertainment books. Reports on queries in 2-4 weeks; on mss in 3-4 months. Publishes a book 10 months after acceptance. No simultaneous submissions.
Illustration: Number of illustrations used for fiction: young readers—1-10; middle readers—1-8. Number of illustrations used for nonfiction: young readers—15; middle readers—2; young adults—20. Associate Editor will review an illustrator's work for possible future assignments.
How to Contact/Illustrators: Ms/illustration packages: Query first. Illustrations only: Resume, tearsheets, slides. Reports on art samples only if interested.
Terms: Pays authors in royalties of 2-20% based on retail price. Pay for illustrators: by the project; royalties range from 2-5%. Sends galleys to authors; dummies to illustrators. Book catalog available for $1.
Tips: Looks for "plays/musicals and books pertaining to the performing arts only."

CLARKSON N. POTTER INC., Random House, 201 E. 50th St., New York NY 10022. (212) 572-6166. Senior Editor: Shirley Wohl.
Fiction: Picture books: adventure, animal, contemporary, fantasy, nature/environment, suspense/mystery. Young readers and middle readers: adventure, animal, contemporary, folktales, history, nature/environment, suspense/mystery. "We do nature and picture books for children through age 11."
Nonfiction: Picture books: animal, music/dance, nature/environment, sports. "We rarely do nonfiction for children."

How to Contact/Writers: Fiction/nonfiction: *Agented work only*. Query with SASE only.
Illustrations: Will not accept unagented artwork.
Terms: Pays authors in royalties based on retail price.

*THE PRESERVATION PRESS, subsidiary of the National Trust for Historic Preservation, 1785 Massachusetts Ave., NW, Washington DC 20036. (202)673-4057. FAX: (202)673-4172. Book publisher. Director: Buckley Jeppson. Publishes 1 middle reader/year. 20% of books by first-time authors; 25% of books from agented authors; subsidy publishes 40%. Publishes books about architecture; "preservation of cultural sites and objects."
Nonfiction: Picture books, young readers, middle readers and young adults: activity books, history, architecture, American culture. Recently published *I Knew That Building!*, by D'Alelio (middle reader, activities); *What It Feels Like to Be a Building*, by Wilson (young reader, architecture).
How to Contact/Writers: Nonfiction: Submit outline/synopsis and 1 sample chapter. Reports on queries in 3 weeks; reports on mss in 2 months. Publishes a book 12-18 months after acceptance. Will consider simultaneous submissions and previously published work.
Illustration: Average number of illustrations used for nonfiction: picture books—30; young readers—20; middle readers—20; young adults—20. Will review ms/illustrations packages.
How to Contact/Illustrators: Ms/illustration packages: Submit 1-2 chapters of ms with 3-4 pieces of final art. Reports in 3-4 weeks. Original artwork returned at job's completion.
Photography: Photographers should contact Janet Walker, managing editor. Uses architectural photos—interior and exterior. Model/property releases and photo captions required. Interested in stock photos. Publishes photo essays. Uses 5×7 or 8×10 glossy, b&w prints and 35mm, $2\frac{1}{4} \times 2\frac{1}{4}$, 4×5 and 8×10 transparencies. To contact, photographers should provide résumé, business card, promotional literature and tearsheets to be kept on file.
Terms: Pays authors royalty of 5-15% based on retail price. Offers advances of $800-1,600. Pays illustrators royalty of 3-10% based on retail price. Photographers paid royalty of 5-15% based on retail price. Sends galleys to authors; dummies to illustrators. Book catalog available for 7×10 SAE and 2 first class stamps.
Tips: Looks for "an energetic, hands-on approach for kids to gain an appreciation for the variety and depth of their American cultural heritage."

THE PRESS OF MACDONALD & REINECKE, imprint of Padre Productions, Box 840, Arroyo Grande CA 93421-0840. (805)473-1947. Book publisher. Estab. 1974. Editor: Lachlan P. MacDonald. 80% of books by first-time authors; 5% of books from agented writers.
Fiction: Middle readers, young adults: fantasy, folktales, history, nature. No mystery, detective, westerns, romances. Average length: middle reader—120-140 pages.
Nonfiction: Middle readers, young adults: history, nature/environment. Average length: middle readers—120 pages.
How to Contact/Writers: Fiction: Submit outline/synopsis and sample chapters. Nonfiction: Submit complete ms. Reports on queries in 2 weeks; on mss in 4 months. Publishes a book 3 years after acceptance. Will consider simultaneous submissions.
Illustration: Number of illustrations used for fiction: middle readers—8. Number of illustrations used for nonfiction: middle readers—12. Editorial will review ms/illustration packages.
How to Contact/Illustrators: Illustrations only: Tearsheets. Reports on art samples only if interested.

Terms: Pays authors in royalties based on retail price. Other method(s) of payment: "Advance plus royalty." Illustrators paid by the project. Sends galleys to authors; dummies to illustrators. Book catalogs for 9 × 12 SAE and 52¢ in first-class stamps. Manuscript guidelines/artist's guidelines for #10 SASE.

Tips: Writers: "Concentrate on nonfiction that recognizes changes in today's audience and includes minority and gender considerations without tokenism. The Press of Mac-Donald & Reinecke is devoted to highly selected works of drama, fiction, poetry and literary nonfiction. Juveniles must be suitable for 140-page books appealing to both boys and girls in the 8-14 year range of readers." Illustrators: "There is a desperate lack of realism by illustrators who can depict proportionate bodies and anatomy. The flood of torn-paper and poster junk is appalling." Looks for: "A book of historical nonfiction of U.S. regional interest with illustrations that have 19th Century elegance and realistic character representations, about topics that still matter today."

PRICE STERN SLOAN, Suite 650, 11150 Olympic Blvd., Los Angeles CA 90064. (213)477-4118. Book publisher. Publishes 1-3 picture books/year; 5-10 young reader titles/year; 5-10 middle reader titles/year; 1-3 young adult titles/year. 65-70% of books by first-time authors; 35% of books from agented writers.

Fiction: Picture books, young readers, middle readers, young adults: adventure, anthology, animal, contemporary, health-related, history, nature/environment, sports, suspense/mystery. "No fantasy/sci-fi, religious books, or poetry." Recently published *Adventures with Barbie*, by Stephanie St. Pierre (age 7-10, fiction series); *House Full of Cats*, by Kitty Higgins (7-10, storybook); *Old MacDonald Had a Farm*, by Colin & Jacqui Hawkins (0-7, lift the flap storybook).

Nonfiction: Picture books, young readers, middle readers, young adults: activity books, animal, biography, careers, health, history, hobbies, music/dance, nature/environment, sports. No religious books or textbooks. Recently published *Barbie Party Cookbook*, (8-10, how-to cook); *City Critters Around the World*, by Amy Koss (7-11, animals/sociology); *Giants of the Insect World*, by Geoffrey Williams (7-10, science, insects).

How to Contact/Writers: Fiction/nonfiction: Query; submit outline/synopsis and 1-2 sample chapters. Reports on queries/mss in 2-3 months. Publishes a book 1 year after acceptance. Will consider simultaneous submissions and previously published work.

Illustration: Number of illustrations used for fiction/nonfiction: picture books—varies; young readers—2-7; middle readers—2-7. Editorial will review ms/illustration packages. Will review artwork for future assignments.

How to Contact/Illustrators: Ms/illustration packages: Query; submit 1-2 chapters of ms with 1-2 pieces of final art (color copies—no original work). Illustrations only: Query with samples; provide resume, business card, promotional literature or tearsheets to be kept on file. Reports in 2-3 months.

Photography: Photographers should contact Art Director. Model/property release required. Interested in stock photos. Publishes photo essays and photo concept books.

Terms: Pays authors royalty or outright purchase. Offers advances. Pays illustrators by the project. Photographers paid by the project or per photo. Sends galleys to authors; dummies to illustrators. Book catalog available for 9 × 12 SAE and $2.69 postage. Ms/artist's guidelines available.

Tips: "We don't have closed doors on any type of book. If it's good or special enough, we'll buy it. Parents are now willing to spend money on books to enhance the information a child would normally get in school."

PROMETHEUS BOOKS, 700 E. Amherst St., Buffalo NY 14215. (716)837-2475. FAX: (716)835-6901. Book publisher. Editor: Jeanne O'Day. Publishes 1 young reader title/year; 3 middle reader titles/year; 1 young adult title/year. 40% of books by first-time authors; 50% of books from agented writers.

Fiction: All levels: sex education, moral education, magic, critical thinking, science, skepticism, animal, contemporary, health, history, nature/environment. Middle readers and young adults: problem novels. Average word length: picture books—2,000; young readers—10,000; middle readers—20,000; young adult/teens—60,000. Recently published *Girls Are Girls and Boys are Boys: So What's the Difference?*, by Sol Gordon (ages 8-12, sex education).

Nonfiction: All levels: sex education, moral education, magic, critical thinking, science, skepticism, animal, biography, careers, health, history, nature/environment. Average word length: picture books—2,000; young readers—10,000; middle readers—20,000; young adult/teens—60,000. Recently published *Wonder-workers! How They Perform the Impossible*, by Joe Nickell (ages 9-14, skepticism); *How Do You Know It's True?*, by Hy Ruchlis (ages 12-15, critical thinking); *Maybe Yes, Maybe No*, by Dan Barker (ages 7-12, skepticism); *Science in a Nanosecond*, by Jim Haught (ages 10 and up, science).

How to Contact/Writers: Fiction/nonfiction: Submit complete manuscript. Reports on queries in 2 weeks; mss in 2-3 months. Publishes a book 1 year after acceptance.

Illustration: Number of illustrations used for fiction and nonfiction: picture books—40; young readers—20. Editorial will review ms/illustration packages. Editor, Jeanne O'Day, will review illustrator's work for possible future assignments.

How to Contact/Illustrators: "Prefer to have full work (manuscript and illustrations); will consider any proposal." Include résumé, photocopies. Reports on ms/art samples in 1-2 months. Original artwork returned at job's completion.

Terms: "Contact terms vary with projects." Sends galleys to author; dummies to illustrators. Book catalog is free on request.

*QUARRY PRESS, P.O. Box 1061, Kingston, Ontario K7L 4Y5 Canada. (613)548-8429. Book publisher. Publisher: Bob Hilderley. Publishes 4 picture books/year. 50% of books by first-time authors.

Fiction: Picture books: folktales. Recently published *Cathal the Giant Killer*, by Mary Alice Downie (grade 1-4, folklore); *My Underwears Inside Out*, by Diane Dawber (grade 1-4, how to write poetry).

How to Contact/Writers: Fiction: Query; submit outline/synopsis and sample chapters. Reports on queries and mss in 3 months. Publishes a book 6 months-1 year after acceptance. Will consider electronic submissions via disk or modem.

Illustration: Average number of illustrations "varies widely." Will review ms/illustration packages. Will review artwork for future assignments. Contact: Melanie Dugan, managing editor.

How to Contact/Illustrators: Ms/illustration packages: Query; submit 10 pieces of art. Illustration only: Query with samples. Reports in 3 months. Original artwork returned at job's completion.

Terms: Pays authors royalty based on retail price. Pay for illustrators varies. Sends galleys to authors; dummies to illustrators. Book catalog available for 9×12 SAE and IRC or 2 first class Canadian stamps.

Tips: "Make it easy on us. We are inundated with material, so send a clear, easy-to-read letter/manuscript. Include name, address and phone number. Make sure proposals are clear and well organized."

RANDOM HOUSE BOOKS FOR YOUNG READERS, Random House, Inc., 8th Floor, 225 Park Ave. South, New York NY 10003. (212)254-1600. Book publisher. Editor-in-Chief: Kate Klimo. 100% of books published through agents; 2% of books by first-time authors.

Fiction: Picture books: animal, easy-to-read, history, sports. Young readers: animal, easy-to-read, history, sports, spy/mystery/adventure. Middle readers: history, science, sports, spy/mystery/adventure.

Nonfiction: Picture books: animal. Young readers: animal, biography, hobbies. Middle readers: biography, history, hobbies, sports.

How to Contact/Writers: Fiction/nonfiction: submit through agent only. Publishes a book in 12-18 months. Will consider simultaneous submissions.

Illustration: Will review ms/illustration packages (through agent only). Executive Art Director, Cathy Goldsmith, will review an illustrator's work for possible future assignments.

Terms: Pays authors in royalties; sometimes buys mss outright. Sends galleys to authors. Book catalog free on request.

■**READ'N RUN BOOKS,** Subsidiary of Crumb Elbow Publishing. P.O. Box 294, Rhododendron OR 97049. (503)622-4798. Book publisher. Publisher: Michael P. Jones. Publishes 3 picture books/year; 5 young reader titles/year; 2 middle reader titles/year; 5 young adult titles/year. 50% of books by first-time authors; 2% of books from agented writers. Subsidy publishes 10%.

Fiction: Will consider all categories for all age levels. Average word length: "Open."

Nonfiction: Will consider all categories for all age levels. Average word length: "Open."

How to Contact/Writers: For fiction and nonfiction: Query. Reports on queries/mss in 2 months "or sooner depending upon work load." Publishes a book about 8 months to a year after acceptance depending on workload and previously committed projects. Will consider simultaneous submissions.

Illustration: Number of illustrations used for fiction and nonfiction: picture books—15; young readers—15; middle readers—20; young adult/teens—20. Reviews ms/illustration packages. Publisher, Michael P. Jones, will review illustrator's work for possible future assignments. "Black and white, 8×10 or 5×7 illustrations. No color work for finished artwork, but color work is great to demonstrate the artist's talents."

How to Contact/Illustrators: Query with sample chapter and several pieces of the artwork. "Artists should submit a good selection of their work, a résumé and a letter outlining their goals. Photocopies are fine." Reports on ms/art samples in 1-2 months. Original artwork returned at job's completion.

Photography: Photographers should contact Michael P. Jones. Looking for wildlife, historical, nature. Model/property release required. Photo captions optional. Publishes photo essays and photo concept books. Uses 5×7 or 8×10 b&w prints; 4×5 or 35mm transparencies. To contact, photographers should query with samples.

Terms: Pays in published copies only. Sends galleys to authors; dummies to illustrators. Book catalog available for $2. Ms/artists' guidelines available for 1 first class stamp and #10 SAE.

Tips: "Don't give up. The field can seem cruel and harsh when trying to break into the market. Roll with the punches." Wants natural history and historical books. Sees trend toward "more computer generated artwork."

*****REVIEW AND HERALD PUBLISHING ASSOCIATION,** 55 W. Oak Ridge Dr., Hagerstown MD 21740. (301)791-7000. (301)791-7102. Book publisher. Acquisitions Editor: Penny Estes Wheeler.

Nonfiction: Young readers, middle readers and young adults: health, religion. Average word length: young readers, middle readers and young adults—96 ms pages. Recently published *Money, Sex, and Other Obsessions*, by Maylan Schurch (teen, devotional); *Thank You, God, For My Body*, by Edwina Neely (preschool, healthful living); *Paint the World With Love*, by Jeannette Johnson (adult, doctrinal).

How to Contact/Writers: Nonfiction: Submit complete ms, outline/synopsis and 3 sample chapters. Reports on mss in 3 months. Will consider simultaneous submissions.

Illustration: Will review artwork for future assignments. Contact Bill Kirstein, art director. "We use all mediums and styles."

How to Contact/Illustrators: Query. Query with samples; send unsolicited art samples by mail; provide promotional literature and tearsheets. Reports in 3 weeks. Original artwork returned at job's completion (depending on contract).
Photography: Photographers should contact Asta Smith, art librarian. Uses "nature scenes, flowers, people, families, outdoors, ethnic mix." Model/property and captions required. Interested in stock photos. Uses color prints; 35mm and 4×5 transparencies. To contact, photographers should query with samples; provide promotional literature and tearsheets.
Terms: Pays illustrators by the project (range: $100-500) Photographers paid by the project (range: $100-500). Sends dummies to illustrators.

ROSEBRIER PUBLISHING CO., 1510 Perkinsville Dr., Box 106, Boone NC 28607. Independent book producer/packager. Editorial Contact: Beverly Donadio. Publishes 1 picture book/year. 50% of books by first-time authors.
Fiction: Picture books: fantasy, nature/environment. Young readers: nature/environment. Middle readers: adventure, fantasy, nature/environment, religion. No violence.
How to Contact/Writers: Fiction: submit complete ms. Reports on queries/ms in 6 months. Publishes a book 6 months after acceptance.
Illustration: Number of illustrations used in fiction: picture book—20. Editorial will review ms/illustration packages. Uses color artwork only.
How to Contact/Illustrators: Ms/illustration packages: Submit 3 chapters of ms with 1 piece of art. Illustrations only: provide tearsheets to be kept on file.
Terms: Pays authors in royalties.

THE ROSEN PUBLISHING GROUP, 29 E. 21st St., New York NY 10010. (212)777-3017. Book publisher. Estab. 1950. Editorial Contact: Ruth Rosen. Publisher: Roger Rosen. Publishes 8 middle reader titles/year; 50 young adult titles/year. 35% of books by first-time authors; 3% of books from agented writers.
Nonfiction: Young readers: contemporary, easy-to-read, sports. Middle readers: contemporary, easy-to-read, sports, psychological self-help. Young adults: contemporary, easy-to-read, sports, careers, psychological self-help. Average word length: young readers—8,000; middle readers—10,000; young adults—40,000.
How to Contact/Writers: Nonfiction: Submit outline/synopsis and sample chapters. Publishes a book 9 months after acceptance.
Illustration: Number of illustrations used for nonfiction: young readers—20; middle readers—10. Editorial will review ms/illustration packages. Roger Rosen will review an illustrator's work for possible future assignments.
How to Contact/Illustrators: Ms/illustration packages: 3 chapters of ms with 1 piece of final art. Illustrations only: Résumé, tearsheets. Original artwork returned at job's completion.
Terms: Pays authors in royalties. Sends galleys to authors. Book catalog free on request.
Tips: "Target your manuscript to a specific age group and reading level and write for established series published by the house you are approaching."

ST. ANTHONY MESSENGER PRESS, 1615 Republic St., Cincinnati OH 45210. (513)241-5615. FAX: (513)241-0399. Book publisher. Managing Editor: Lisa Biedenbach. 25% of books by first-time authors.
Nonfiction: Middle readers and young adults: religion. No fiction.
How to Contact/Writers: Nonfiction: Query, submit outline/synopsis and sample chapters. Reports on queries in 2-4 weeks; mss in 4-6 weeks. Publishes a book 12-18 months after acceptance.
Illustration: Editorial will review ms/illustration packages. "We design all covers and do most illustrations in-house." Uses primiarily b&w artwork.

Terms: Pays authors in royalties of 10-12% based on net receipts. Offers average advance payment of $600. Sends galleys to authors. Book catalog, manuscript guidelines free on request.

Tips: "We're looking for programs to be used in Catholic schools and parishes—programs that have successful track records."

ST. PAUL BOOKS AND MEDIA, Daughters of St. Paul, 50 St. Paul's Ave., Jamaica Plain MA 02130. (617)522-8911. Book publisher. Estab. 1934. Children's Editor: Sister Anne Joan, fsp. Publishes 1-2 picture books/year; 1-2 young reader titles/year; 1-2 middle reader titles/year; 1-3 young adult titles/year. 20% of books by first-time authors.

Fiction: Picture books: contemporary, religion. Young readers: adventure, anthology, contemporary, history, religion, saints. Middle readers: adventure, anthology, contemporary, history, religion, saints, devotionals. Young adults: adventure, anthology, contemporary, history, problem novels, religion. Average word length: picture books—150-300; young readers—1,500-5,000; middle readers—10,000; young adults—20,000-50,000.

Nonfiction: All levels: religion, devotionals. Average word length: picture books—200; young readers—1,500-5,000; middle readers—10,000; young adults—20,000-50,000.

How to Contact/Writers: Fiction/nonfiction: Submit outline/synopsis and sample chapters. Reports on queries in 3-8 weeks; on mss in 3 months. Publishes a book 2-3 years after acceptance. No simultaneous submissions.

Illustration: Number of illustrations used for fiction/nonfiction: picture books—8-12; young readers—8; middle readers—5; young adults—2-5. Editorial will review ms/illustration packages. Style/size of illustration "varies according to the title. Re: colors, our scanner will not take fluorescents."

How to Contact/Illustrators: Ms/illustration packages: "Outline first with art samples." Illustrations only: Résumé, slides and tearsheets. Reports on art samples in 3-8 weeks.

Photography: Photographers should contact Sister Emmanuel. Looking for children, animals—active interaction. Uses 4×5 or 8×10 b&w prints; 35mm or 4×5 transparencies.

Terms: Pays authors in royalties of 4-12% based on gross sales. Illustrations paid by the project. Photographers paid by the project, $15-200. Book catalog for 9×12 SAE and 4 first class stamps. Manuscript guidelines for legal-size SAE and 1 first class stamp.

Tips: Looking for a young adult novel that's contemporary enough to be believable and modest enough to be published by a religious press. "We are a Roman Catholic publishing house looking for manuscripts (whether fiction or nonfiction) that communicate high moral, religious and family values. Lives of saints and Bible stories welcome, as well as historical or contemporary novels for children. In Catholic circles, we are seeing a renewed interest in saints. In general, there is a high interest in allegorical fantasy, as well as stories that reflect attitudes and life situations children are deeply familiar with."

SCHOLASTIC HARDCOVER, Imprint of Scholastic Inc., 730 Broadway, New York NY 10003. (212)505-3000. Book publisher. Editorial Director, Jean Feiwel. Executive Editor: Dianne Hess. Editorial contacts are as follows: picture books: Jean Feiwel, Dianne Hess, Grace Maccarone; young readers: Dianne Hess; middle readers: Jean Teivel and Regina Griffin; young adult tales: Jean Feiwel and Regina Griffin. Publishes 40+ (in hardcover) picture books/year; 20+ young reader titles/year; 20+ middle reader titles/year; 20+ young adult titles/year. 5% of books by first-time authors; 50% of books through agents.

Fiction: Picture books/young readers/middle readers/young adult: animal, contemporary, humor, easy-to-read, fantasy, history, problem novels, romance, science fiction, sports, spy/mystery/adventure, etc.

Close-up

Jack Prelutsky
Writer/Poet
Olympia, Washington

Jack Prelutsky did not set out to be a writer or a poet. Prelutsky, born in Brooklyn and raised in the Bronx, says he had no early aspirations to be a writer.

He thought his true avocation was as a visual artist. "Over a six-month period, I had painstakingly drawn about two dozen imaginary creatures. One evening, I decided they needed poems to accompany them, and in about two hours wrote a verse for each drawing. I had no intention of publishing them, but a friend who had written a couple of children's books urged me to show them to a children's editor."

He took them to an editor at Macmillan and was told he had a natural flair for verse, but that illustration was best left to others. His first book of original poems, *A Gopher in the Garden*, was published a year later. As an example of how blithely he regarded his writing career, he didn't keep a copy of that first book. "By the time I realized I should have a copy, the title was out of print and I had to scrounge around to find one."

Prelutsky gets his ideas from everywhere. "Everything I see or hear can become a poem. I don't respond to topical events or trends, although some themes, like my book about dinosaurs, were lucky to hit the crest of waves." He says sometimes ideas literally pop into his head. "I find inspiration from everything. I wrote a poem about a boneless chicken because one day when I was in the supermarket shopping for boneless breast of chicken, I started to imagine what the rest of a boneless chicken would look like and what kind of a life it would have.

"Writing for children in general, and I think writing children's poetry in particular, is harder than writing for adults. Literature for children must be succinct, and yet presented in the most artful manner possible.

"The children's book market operates, most of the time, quite differently from the adult book market," says Prelutsky. "Adult books often explode upon the publishing scene with a lot of media hype. But most have literal shelf lives of approximately one year as hardbacks and one additional year as paperbacks before disappearing into remainder bins and the eventual exile known as 'out of print.' Children's books generally take years to establish themselves in bookstores and libraries. But once they achieve the status of a 'classic,' they will stay in print as long as they remain in the memories of parents, grandparents, teachers and librarians. Patience in this profession is an absolute necessity."

—Debbie Cinnamon

Nonfiction: Picture books/young readers/middle readers/young adult: animal, biography, education, history, hobbies, music/dance, nature/environment, religion, sports.
How to Contact/Writers: Fiction (for picture book and young reader): Submit complete mss with SASE; (for young adult and middle reader); query or submit outline/synopsis and sample chapters. Nonfiction: Query or submit outline/synopsis and sample chapters. Reports on queries in 2-4 weeks; on mss in 6-8 weeks. Publishes a book 1 year after acceptance.
Illustrations: Editorial will review ms/illustration packages. "It is not necessary for authors to supply art." Dianne Hess, senior editor, or Claire Counihan, art director, will review an illustrator's work for possible future assignments.
How to Contact/Illustrators: Illustrations only: Send tearsheets or slides. Reports in 6-8 weeks. Original artwork returned at job's completion.
Terms: Pays authors in royalties of 10% (5% if split with artist) based on retail price. Sends galleys to author; dummies to illustrator. Book catalog for postage and mailing label.
Tips: Writers: "Attend writing workshops, learn your craft, don't be afraid to revise." Illustrators: Create a finished dummy of any story and one piece of finished art to show an editor how you work."

SCHOLASTIC, INC., 730 Broadway, New York NY 10003. (212)505-3000. Book publisher. Editorial Contact: Eva Moore (young readers). Executive Editors: Ann Reit (middle readers/young adult titles); Diane Hess (picture books). 5-25% of books by first-time authors; 50% of books from agented writers.
Fiction: Picture books, middle readers: contemporary, fantasy, mystery/adventure. Young adults/teens: contemporary, romance, mystery/adventure. Average word length: middle readers—35,000; young adult/teens—45,000.
Nonfiction: Middle readers: biography, nature/environment.
How to Contact/Writers: Fiction/nonfiction: Submit outline/synopsis and sample chapters or submit complete ms. Reports on queries 1 month; mss 3 months. Publishes a book 12-18 months after acceptance.
Terms: Pays in royalties.
Tips: Writers: "Know the firm you are sending a submission to—what they publish, what they don't publish." Trends in book publishing: "Emphasis is on quality middle readers, young readers and picture books."

*SCIENTIFIC AMERICAN BOOKS, W.H. Freeman and Company, 41 Madison Ave., New York NY 10010. (212)576-9400. (212)689-2383. Book publisher. Publisher, Children's Books: Marc Gave. "Approximately 18-20 middle to YA titles are projected for our first year 1992-93." 20% of books from agented authors. Publishes science, social science, math subjects.
Fiction: "We might consider fiction with a scientific slant if there is a real purpose in presenting the material in a fictionalized context."
Nonfiction: Middle readers and young adults/teens: biography, careers, health, nature/environment, science, math, social science; all material should have a scientific slant. No books that are too similar to textbooks. Average word length: middle readers—15,000+, young adult/teens—25,000+.
How to Contact/Writers: Fiction/nonfiction: Query. Reports on queries in 2-4 weeks; reports on mss in 1-2 months. Will consider simultaneous submissions.
Illustration: Will review ms/illustration packages. Will review artwork for future assignments. Contact Bill Page, Senior Illustration Coordinator.
How to Contact/Illustrators: Ms/illustration packages: Query. Illustrations only: Query with samples; submit portfolio for review; provide tearsheets. Reports in 2-4 weeks.

© 1987 by David Neuhaus

David Neuhaus was paid a $500 advance on royalties for illustrating Helga High-Up, *published by Scholastic, Inc. in 1987. "In this piece," says Neuhaus, "I wanted to dramatize the height difference between the characters." This project led to another with Scholastic the following year.*

Photography: Photographers should contact Marc Gave, publisher, children's books. Uses scientific subjects. Model/property release required. Interested in stock photos. May publish photo essays. Uses 35mm transparencies. To contact, photographers should query with samples; submit portfolio for review; provide tearsheets.

Terms: Pays authors royalty based on net wholesale price. Offers advances. Pays illustrators by the project or by royalty. Photographers paid by the project or per photo. Sends galleys to authors. Book catalog available in spring 1992. Ms and art guidelines available for SASE.

Tips: "Study the publishers' lists to find out who is publishing what. Don't send anything out to a publisher without finding out if the publisher is interested in receiving such material." Looking for well-researched, well-written, thoughtful but lively books on a focused aspect of science, social science (anthropology, psychology—not politics, history), with lots of kid interest, for ages 9 and up.

CHARLES SCRIBNER'S SONS, Imprint of Macmillan Publishing Co., 866 Third Ave., New York NY 10940. (212)702-7885. Book publisher. Senior Vice President/Editorial Director: Clare Costello. 35% of books from agented writers.

Fiction: Picture books, young readers: adventure, animal, contemporary, fantasy, folktales, nature/environment, science. Middle readers, young adults: adventure, animal, contemporary, fantasy, folktales, history, nature/environment, problem novels, science fiction, sports, suspense/mystery. Recently published *Fox Under First Base*, by Latimer McCue (picture book); *Begin the World Again*, by Bettie Cannon (contemporary, young adult fiction); *Come Away Home*, by Alison Smith (fantasy, intermediate).
Nonfiction: Picture books: animal, nature/environment. Young readers: animal, history, nature/environment. Middle readers, young adults/teens: animal, biography, history, nature/environment. Recently published *Desert of Ice*, by Hackwell (illustrated science/environment); *Lincoln*, by Jacobs (photographic biography, intermediate); *Discovery of America*, by Faber (biography, young adult).
How to Contact/Writers: Fiction: Submit outline/synopsis and sample chapters. Nonfiction: Query. Reports on queries in 4 weeks; mss in 10-14 weeks. Publishes a book 12-18 months after acceptance, "picture books longer." Will consider simultaneous (if specified when submitted) submissions.
Illustrations: Editorial will review ms/illustration packages.
How to Contact/Illustrators: Ms/illustration packages: "Query first." Illustrations only: Send tearsheets. Reports back only if interested. Original artwork returned at job's completion.
Terms: Pays authors in royalties based on retail price. Sends galleys to authors; dummies to illustrators. Book catalog for 8×10 SAE; manuscript guidelines are for legal-size SASE.

HAROLD SHAW PUBLISHERS, 388 Gundersen Dr., Box 567, Wheaton IL 60189. (708)665-6700. Book publisher. Estab. 1967. Dir. of Editorial Services: Ramona Cramer Tucker. Publishes 2 young adult titles/year. 10% of books by first-time authors; 5% of books from agented writers.
Fiction: Young adults: adventure, problem novels. Average length: young adults—112-250 pages. Recently published *Absolutely Perfect Summer*, by Jeffrey Asher Nesbit (ages 13 and up, novel); *Hoverlight*, by Fay S. Lepka (ages 13 and up, novel); *The Sea, the Song, and the Trumpetfish*, by Fay S. Lapka (ages 13 and up, novel).
How to Contact/Writers: Reports on queries in 2-4 weeks; on mss in 4-6 weeks. Publishes a book 1 year after acceptance. Will consider simultaneous submissions.
Terms: Pays authors in royalties of 5-10% based on retail price. Sends pages to authors. Book catalog available for SAE and $1.25; manuscript guidelines for SAE and 1 first-class stamp.
Tips: No longer accepts illustrator or photographer packages. Writers: "Read your stories to children and to adults. You'll find that children are the most honest." Wants "realistic books that focus on real needs of real characters." Looks for "a very unusual story which would make us change our minds about not picking up any more children's books! It (the children's book market) is growing, but at the same time the quality of writing has been going down. There is a lot of 'fluff' on the market. Parents are now becoming more interested in books that meet needs and speak to the problems of today's world."

SHOE TREE PRESS, Imprint of Betterway Publications, Inc., Box 219, Crozet VA 22932. (804)823-5661. Book publisher. Editor: Susan Lewis. Published 9 middle reader and young adult titles in 1991. 70% of books by first-time authors. Publishes "books that kids ages 10 and up can learn from, but also enjoy."
Fiction: Middle readers: history. Young adults: contemporary, history, problem novels, sports. Average word length: middle readers—20,000-35,000; young adults—50,000-75,000. Recently published *With Secrets to Keep*, by Rose Levit (ages 12 and up, young adult contemporary).

Nonfiction: Middle readers and young adults: biography, history, sports, reference. Average word length: middle readers—30,000-45,000; young adults—35,000-75,000. Recently published *Cadets at War: The True Story of Teenage Heroism at the Battle of New Market*, by Susan Provost Beller (ages 8-12, middle grade history); *The Junior Tennis Handbook: A Complete Guide to Tennis for Juniors, Parents, and Coaches*, by Skip Singleton (ages 10 and up, sports).
How to Contact/Writers: Fiction/nonfiction: Query first please. Reports on queries in 1 month; on mss in 3 months. Publishes a book 6-12 months after acceptance. Will consider simultaneous submissions.
Illustration: Number of illustrations used for fiction and nonfiction: middle readers—12-30. Uses primarily b&w artwork. Editorial will review ms/illustration packages. Will review artwork for future assignments.
How to Contact/Illustrators: Ms/illustration packages: Query first. Illustrations only: Query with samples. Reports on art samples only if interested. Original artwork returned at job's completion.
Terms: Pays authors in royalties based on wholesale prices. Sends galleys to authors; dummies to illustrators.
Tips: "We do *not* publish picture books. Our focus has shifted to mainly nonfiction along with biographies and historical fiction." Also will consider fiction that instructs young readers in some way. "We want books that kids ages 10 and up can learn from, but also enjoy."

SKYLARK/BOOKS FOR YOUNG READERS, Imprint of Bantam Books Inc., 666 Fifth Ave., New York NY 10103. (212)765-6500. Editorial Contact: Judy Gitenstein.
Fiction: Middle readers for ages 8-12; chapter books for ages 5-8. Contemporary, fantasy, historical, humorous, mystery, adventure, multicultural themes. No short stories.
How to Contact/Writers: Fiction: Submit outline/synopsis and sample chapters; "You will get a form rejection if your ms is not for us. The number of submissions received does not allow us time to comment on them all."
Terms: Pays authors in royalties of 6-8% based on retail price.

THE SPEECH BIN, INC., 1766 Twentieth Ave., Vero Beach FL 32960. (407)770-0007. FAX: (407)770-0006. Book publisher. Contact: Jan J. Binney, Senior Editor. Publishes 10-12 books/year. 50% of books by first-time authors; less than 15% of books from agented writers. "Nearly all our books deal with treatment of children (as well as adults) who have communication disorders of speech or hearing or children who deal with family members who have such disorders (e.g., a grandparent with Alzheimer's or stroke)."
Fiction: Picture books: animal, easy-to-read, fantasy, health. Young readers, middle readers, young adult: health.
Nonfiction: Picture books, young readers, middle readers, young adults: activity books, health, textbooks. Published *Calendar Capers*, by Pamela Meza Steckbeck, illustrated by Marie M. Long (preschool-grade 5, activity book); *Acquire*, by Linda B. Collins and Sandra Sayre Chadwell (grades 4-12, word games); *Spotlight on Speech-Language Services*, by Janet M. Shaw (grades K-12, activity book).
How to Contact/Writers: Fiction/nonfiction: Query. Reports on queries in 4-6 weeks; 2-3 months on mss. Publishes a book 10-12 months after acceptance. "Will consider simultaneous submissions only if notified; too many authors fail to let us know if ms is simultaneously submitted to other publishers! We *strongly* prefer sole submissions."
Illustration: Number of illustrations used for fiction and nonfiction: picture books—50; young readers—50; middle readers—50; young adult/teens—less than 10. Editorial will review ms/illustration packages.
How to Contact/Illustrators: "Query first!" Submit résumé; tearsheets or copies also OK. Original artwork returned at job's completion.

Photography: Photographers should contact Jan J. Binney, senior editor. Looking for all ages of people, occasional scenic shots. Model/property release required. Uses glossy b&w prints, 35mm or 2¼×2¼ transparencies. To contact, photographer should provide resume, business card, promotional literature or tearsheets to be kept on file.
Terms: Pays authors in royalties. Pay for illustrators: by the project. Photographers paid by the project or per photo. Sends galleys to authors. Book catalog for 3 first class stamps and 9×12 SAE; manuscript guidelines for #10 SASE.

SRI RAMA PUBLISHING, Box 2550, Santa Cruz CA 95063. (408)426-5098. Book publisher. Estab. 1975. Secretary/Manager: Karuna K. Ault. Publishes 1 or fewer young reader titles/year.
Illustration: Illustrations used for fiction. Graphic Design Director, Josh Gitomer, will review illustrators' work for possible future assignments.
How to Contact/Illustrators: Submit several samples. Reports on art samples in 2 months. Original art work returned at job's completion.
Terms: "We are a nonprofit organization. Proceeds from our sales support an orphanage in India, so we encourage donated labor, but each case is worked out individually." Pay for illustrators: $200 minimum, $1,000 maximum. Sends galleys to authors; dummies to illustrators. Book catalog and manuscript guidelines free on request.

STANDARD PUBLISHING, 8121 Hamilton Ave., Cincinnati OH 45231. (513)931-4050. Book publisher. Director: Mark Plunkett. Publishes 25 picture books/year; 4 young reader titles/year; 8 middle reader titles/year; 4 young adult titles/year. 25% of books by first-time authors; 1% of books from agented writers. Publishes spiritual/religious books.
Fiction: Picture books: animal, contemporary, religion. Young readers: adventure, animal, contemporary, religion. Middle readers: adventure, contemporary, religion. Young adults: contemporary, religion. No poetry. Average word length: picture books—400; young readers—1,000; middle readers—25,000; young adults—40,000.
Nonfiction: Picture books, young readers: activity books, religion. Middle readers, young adults: religion. Average word length: picture books—400; young readers—1,000; middle readers—25,000; young adults—40,000.
How to Contact/Writers: Fiction/nonfiction: Query. Reports on queries in 3 weeks; on mss in 3 months. Publishes a book 18 months after acceptance. Will consider simultaneous and electronic submissions via disk or modem.
Illustration: Number of illustrations used for fiction: picture books—24; young readers—24; middle readers—12; young adults—12. Number of illustrations used for nonfiction: picture books—24. Editorial will review ms/illustration packages. Will review artwork for possible future assignments.
How to Contact/Illustrators: Ms/illustration packages: Query. Illustrations only: Query with samples. Reports on art samples in 3 weeks.
Photography: Photographers should contact Theresa Hayes. Looking for photos for bulletin covers. Model/property releases required. Uses 35mm and 2¼×2¼ transparencies. To contact, photographers should query with samples.
Terms: Pays authors in royalties of 5-12% based on wholesale price. Buys ms outright for $250-1,000. Offers average advance payment of $250. Photographers are paid $100-200 per photo. Sends galleys to authors. Book catalog available for 8½×11 SAE; manuscript guidelines for letter-size SASE.
Tips: "When writing children's books, make the vocabulary level correct for the age you plan to reach. Keep your material true to the Bible. Be accurate in quoting scriptures and references."

STAR BOOKS, INC., 408 Pearson St., Wilson NC 27893. (919)237-1591. Editorial Contact: Irene Burk Harrell. "We are still a new and growing company." All books are strongly Christian.
Fiction: Picture books and young readers: adventure, animal, contemporary, fantasy, poetry, science fiction. Middle readers: adventure, anthology, animal, contemporary, fantasy, poetry, problem novels, science fiction. Young adults: adventure, anthology, animal, contemporary, fantasy, poetry, problem novels, romance, science fiction. "Manuscripts must be somehow strongly related to the good news of Jesus Christ." Recently published *Mr. Man in the Skies*, by Dana Swoboda.
Nonfiction: All manuscripts must be strongly Christian.
How to Contact/Writers: Submit complete ms. Reports on queries in 1-2 weeks; mss in 1-2 months. Publishes a book 6 months after acceptance ("longer if extensive editing needed"). *No* simultaneous submissions.
Illustration: Editorial will review ms/illustration packages. "At present, we prefer informal black and white line art. As finances improve, we'll be interested in color."
How to Contact/Illustrators: Ms/illustration packages: send whole ms, 1-3 roughs of art. Submit art in ms packages only. Reports on art samples within a month. Original artwork returned at job's completion.
Terms: Pay: "We issue contract for the whole (ms/illustration) package." Sends galleys to authors. Book catalog/guidelines available for #10 SAE and 2 first-class stamps.
Tips: "We want biblical values, conversation that sounds real, characters that come alive, exciting stories with 'behavior modification' strengths."

STEMMER HOUSE PUBLISHERS, INC., 2627 Caves Rd., Owings Mills MD 21117. (301)363-3690. Book publisher. Estab. 1975. President: Barbara Holdridge. Publishes 1-3 picture books/year. "Sporadic" numbers of young reader/middle reader/young adult titles/year. 60% of books by first-time authors.
Fiction: Picture books: animal, ecology. Young reader/middle reader: history.
Nonfiction: Picture book: animal, music/dance. Young reader: music/dance.
How to Contact/Writers: Fiction/nonfiction: Query, submit outline/synopsis and sample chapters. Reports on queries in 6 weeks. Publishes a book 18 months after acceptance. Will consider simultaneous submissions.
Illustration: Number of illustrations used for fiction: picture books—48; young readers—24; middle readers—12. Number of illustrations used for nonfiction: picture book—48; young reader—24; middle reader—24. Will review ms/illustration packages.
How to Contact/Illustrators: Ms/illustration packages: "Query first, with several photocopied illustrations." Illustrations only: Send "tearsheets and/or slides (with SASE for return)." Reports in 2 weeks.
Terms: Pays authors in royalties of 4-6% based on wholesale price. Offers average advance payment of $300. Pay for illustrators: 4-5% royalty based on wholesale price. Sends galleys to authors. Book catalog for 9×12 SASE.
Tips: Writers: "simplicity, literary quality and originality are the keys."

*STEPPING STONE BOOKS, imprint of Random House, Inc. 225 Park Ave. S., New York NY 10003. (212)254-1600. Book publisher. Contact: Stephanie Spinner.
Fiction: Young readers: "There are no restrictions on subject matter—we just require well-written, absorbing fiction."
Illustration: Average number of illustrations used for fiction: young readers—10-15. Prefer b&w drawings.

STERLING PUBLISHING CO., INC., 387 Park Ave. South, New York NY 10016. (212)532-7160. Book publisher. Acquisitions Director: Sheila Anne Barry. Publishes 30 middle reader titles/year. 10% of books by first-time authors.

Nonfiction: Middle readers: activity books, animal, hobbies, music/dance, nature/environment, science, sports, humor, true mystery, supernatural incidents. "Since our books are highly illustrated, word length is seldom the point. Most are 96-128 pages." Recently published *Craziest Riddle Book in the World*, by Lori Miller Fox (middle readers, humor); *Simple Weather Experiments with Everyday Materials*, by Muriel Mandell (middle readers).

How to Contact/Writers: Reports on queries in 2 weeks; on mss in 6-8 weeks. Publishes a book 6-18 months after acceptance. Will consider simultaneous submissions.

Illustration: Number of illustrations used for nonfiction: middle readers—approximately 60. Editorial will review ms/illustration packages.

How to Contact/Illustrators: Ms/illustration packages: "Query first." Illustrations only: "Send sample photocopies of line drawings; also examples of some color work." Original artwork returned at job's completion "if possible, but usually held for future needs."

Terms: Pays authors in royalties of up to 10% "standard terms, no sliding scale, varies according to edition." Sends galleys to authors. Manuscript guidelines for SASE.

Tips: Looks for: "Humor, hobbies, science books for middle-school children." Also, "mysterious occurrences, activities and fun and games books."

*SUNBURST BOOKS, imprint of Farrar, Straus & Giroux, 19 Union Square West, New York NY 10003. (212)741-6900. Editor-in-Chief: Margaret Ferguson. Publishes 20 picture books, 5 middle readers, 6 young readers, and 5 young adult titles/year. 15% of books are by first-time authors; 25% of books from agented writers.

Fiction: Picture books: adventure, animal, contemporary, fantasy, folktales, history, nature/environment. Young readers: adventure, animal, contemporary, fantasy, folktales, history, nature/environment, poetry, science fiction, suspense/mystery. Middle readers: adventure, anthology, animal, contemporary, fantasy, folktales, history, nature/environment, poetry, problem novels, romance, science fiction, sports, suspense/mystery. Young adults/teens: adventure, anthology, animal, contemporary, fantasy, folktales, health-related, history, nature/environment, poetry, problem novels, romance, science fiction, sports, suspense/mystery. Recently published *Carl's Afternoon in the Park*, by Alexandra Day (ages 3 and up, picture book); *Celine*, by Brock Cole (young adult); *The Clay Marble*, by Minfong Ho (ages 10 and up, middle reader).

Nonfiction: Young readers: animal, hobbies, music/dance, nature/environment and sports. Middle readers: animal, biography, careers, history, hobbies, music/dance, nature/environment, sports. Young adults: animal, biography, careers, history, hobbies, music/dance, nature/environment, religion and sports. Does not want to see picture books.

How to Contact/Writers: Fiction: Submit complete picture book manuscript; submit outline/synopsis and 3 sample chapters. Nonfiction: Submit outline/synopsis and 3 sample chapters. Reports on queries in 2 months; reports on mss in 3 months. Publishes a book 18-24 months after acceptance. Will consider simultaneous submissions.

Illustration: Average number of illustrations used for fiction: picture books—16-20; middle readers—10. Will review ms/illustration packages. Will review artwork for future assignments. Contact Margaret Ferguson, editor-in-chief.

How to Contact/Illustrators: Ms/illustration packages: Send unsolicited art samples by mail; arrange a personal interview to show portfolio; provide promotional literature or tearsheets to be kept on file. "Do not send original art." Reports in 2 months. Original artwork returned at job's completion.

Terms: Pays authors royalty. Offers advances. Pays illustrators royalty; "flat fee for jacket illustrators." Sends galleys to authors; dummies to illustrators. Book catalog available for 7½ × 10½ SAE and 3 first class stamps. Ms/artist guidelines available for SASE.

TAB BOOKS, a division of McGraw-Hill,Inc., Blue Ridge Summit PA 17294-0850. (717)794-2191. Book Publisher. Editorial contact: Kim Tabor. Publishes 6 young reader titles/year; 6 young adult titles/year. 50% of books by first-time authors. 10% of books by agented authors.
Nonfiction: All levels: animal, hobbies, nature/environment, science, crafts.
How To Contact/Writers: Nonfiction: Query; submit outline/synopsis and sample chapters. Reports on queries in 1 month; mss in 3 months. Publishes a book 9-12 months after acceptance.
Illustration: Will review manuscript/illustration packages.
How To Contact/Illustrators: Query first; submit resume, tearsheets, photocopies. Reports back only if interested. Originals returned to artist at job's completion.
Terms: "Terms vary from project to project." Book catalog and manuscript guidelines are free on request.
Tips: Looks for "science and craft topics that are fun and educational that include activities that adult and children can work on together. Projects should be designed around inexpensive, household materials and should require under two hours for completion."

*TAMBOURINE BOOKS, imprint of William Morrow & Co. Inc., 1350 6th Ave., New York NY 10019. Book publisher. Publishes 32 picture books, 4 middle readers, 2 young adult titles/year. No primary theme for fiction or nonfiction—publishes various categories.
How to Contact/Writers: Fiction/Nonfiction: Submit complete ms. Reports on mss in 1-3 months.
Illustration: Will review ms/illustration packages. Will review artwork for future assignments. Contact Golda Laurens, art director.
How to Contact/Illustrators: Ms/illustration packages: Submit complete package. Illustrations only: submit portfolio for review; provide résumé, business card, promotional literature or tearsheets to be kept on file. Original artwork returned at job's completion.
Terms: Pays authors royalty based on retail price. Offers advances. Pays illustrators royalty. Sends galleys to authors. Book catalog available for SASE; ms and artist's guidelines available for SASE.

TEXAS CHRISTIAN UNIVERSITY PRESS, Box 30783, Fort Worth TX 76129. (817)921-7822. Book Publisher. Editorial contact: Judy Alter. Publishes 1 young adult title/year. 75% of books by first-time authors.
Fiction: Young adults/teens: history. Average word length: 35,000-50,000 words. Published *The Last Innocent Summer*, by Fowler (Y/A, novel); *Letters To Oma*, by Gurasich (Y/A, novel); *Muddy Banks*, by Tulliver (Y/A, novel).
Nonfiction: Young adults/teens; biography, history. Average word length: 35,000-50,000 words.
How To Contact/Writers: Fiction/nonfiction: Query. Reports on queries in 2 weeks; mss in 2 months. Publishes a book 1-2 years after acceptance.
Illustration: Number of illustrations used for fiction: young adults/teens-6. Editor/Art Director Tracy Row will review an illustrator's work for possible future assignments.
How To Contact/Illustrators: Reports back to artists within 1 week. Originals returned to artist at job's completion.
Terms: Pays in royalty of 10% based on wholesale price. Illustrators are paid flat fee. Book catalog is free on request. Manuscript guidelines free on request.
Tips: "We look only at historical novels set in Texas."

*TROLL ASSOCIATES, 100 Corporate Dr., Mahwah NJ 07430. Book publisher. Editor: Marian Frances.
Fiction: Picture books: animal, contemporary, folktales, history, nature/environment, poetry, sports, suspense/mystery. Young readers: adventure, animal, contemporary, folktales, history, nature/environment, poetry, science fiction, sports, suspense/mystery. Middle readers: adventure, anthology, animal, contemporary, fantasy, folktales, health-related, history, nature/environment, poetry, problem novels, romance, science fiction, sports, suspense/mystery. Young adults: problem novels, romance and suspense/mystery.
Nonfiction: Picture books: activity books, animal, biography, careers, history, hobbies, nature/environment, sports. Young Readers: activity books, animal, biography, careers, health, history, hobbies, music/dance, nature/environment, sports. Middle readers: activity books, animal, biography, careers, health, history, hobbies, music/dance, nature/environment, religion, sports. Young adults: health, music/dance.
How to Contact/Writers: Fiction: Query or submit outline/synopsis and 3 sample chapters. Nonfiction: Query. Reports in 2-4 weeks.
Illustration: Will review ms/illustration packages. Will review artwork for future assignments. Contact Marian Frances, editor.
How to Contact/Illustrators: Illustrations only: query with samples; arrange a personal interview to show portfolio; provide resume, promotional literature or tearsheets to be kept on file. Reports in 2-4 weeks.
Photography: Model/property releases required. Interested in stock photos.
Terms: Pays authors royalty or by outright purchase. Pays illustrators by the project or royalty. Photographers paid by the project.

*TROPHY BOOKS, subsidiary of HarperCollins Children's Books Group, 10 E. 53rd St., New York NY 10022. Book publisher. Editorial Director: Erin Gathrid. Publishes 6-9 chapter books, 25-30 middle grade titles, 30 picture books, 12-15 young adult titles/year. "Trophy is primarily a paperback reprint imprint."
Fiction: No subject limitations. Recently published *Melusine*, by Lynne Reid Banks (YA, mystery); *My Brother Stealing Second*, by Jim Naughton (YA, suspense); and *R-T, Margaret, and the Rats of Nimh*, by Jane Conly (middle reader, fantasy adventure).
Nonfiction: All levels: animal, biography, music/dance, nature/environment. No careers, health, hobbies, religion, textbooks. Recently published *Now is Your Time*, by Walter Dean Myers (MG/YA, historical); *The King's Day*, by Aliki (picture book, historical/bio); *Fireflies in the Night*, Judy Hawes (Let's-Read-and-Find Out Science Picture book, early science).
How to Contact/Writers: Nonfiction: Submit complete ms (for picture and chapter books); submit outline/synopsis and 3 sample chapters (for middle grade and YA). Reports on queries in 2-3 weeks; reports on mss in 4-6 weeks. Will consider simultaneous submissions, electronic submissions via disk or modem, and previously published work.
Illustration: Will review artwork for future assignments.
How to Contact/Illustrators: Illustrations only: Query with samples (no originals). Reports in 3-4 weeks.

* **The asterisk before a listing indicates the listing is new in this edition.**

Photography: Photographers should contact David Saylor, art director. Photo captions required. To contact, photographers should query with samples.
Terms: Sends galleys to authors. Ms guidelines available for SASE.

*TROUBADOR BOOKS, imprint of Price Stern Sloan , Inc., 11150 Olympic Blvd. #650, Los Angeles CA 90064. Book publisher. Editorial Assistant: Cindy Chang. Publishes 1-3 picture books/year; 5-15 young readers/year; 5-15 middle readers/year; 1-2 young adults/year. 65% of books by first-time authors; 35% of books from agented authors.
Fiction: Picture books, young readers, middle readers and young adults: adventure, animal, contemporary, health-related, history, nature/environment, problem novels, sports, suspense/mystery. Recently published *Adventures with Barbie*, by Stephanie St. Pierrer (grades 2-3, fiction); *Giants in the Insect World*, by Geoffrey Williams (ages 7-12, science/adventure); *City Critters Around the World*, by Amy Koss (ages 7-12, animals/social science).
Nonfiction: All levels: activity books, animal, careers, health, history, hobbies, music/dance, nature/environment, sports. Recently published *First Science Words*, by Q.L. Pearce (ages 6-9, science/activity/coloring); *Nature's Magic*, by Q.L. Pearce (ages 6-9, science); *Barbie Party Cookbook* (ages 8-9, cookbook/how-to).
How to Contact/Writers: Fiction/nonfiction: Query. Reports in 6-8 weeks. Publishes a book 9 months to 1 year after acceptance. Will consider simultaneous submissions, electronic submissions via disk or modem and previously published work.
Illustration: Average number of illustrations used for fiction and nonfiction: picture books—varies; young readers—3-6; middle readers—3-6. Will review ms/illustration packages. Will review artwork for future assignments. Contact Art Director.
How to Contact/Illustrators: Ms/illustration packages: Submit 1-2 chapters of ms with 1-2 color photocopies. Illustrations only: Query with samples. Provide résumé, business card, promotional literature or tearsheets to be kept on file. Reports back only if interested. Original artwork returned at job's completion ("unless it is a work for hire, in which case we own the art").
Photography: Photographers should contact art director. Uses nature/science. Model/property releases required. Interested in stock photos. To contact, photographers should query with samples. Provide résumé, business card, promotional literature or tearsheets to be kept on file.
Terms: Pays authors royalty, outright purchase. Offers advances. Pays illustrators by the project. Photographers paid by the project. Sends galleys to authors; dummies to illustrators. Book catalog available for 9×12 SAE and $2.69 postage.

*TUNDRA BOOKS OF NORTHERN NEW YORK, imprint of Tundra Books Inc. (Montreal, Canada), P.O. Box 1030, Plattsburgh NY 12901. (514)932-5434. FAX: (514)861-6426. Book publisher. Assistant Editor: Arjun Basu. Publishes 10-12 picture books/year; 1-2 young readers/year; 3-5 middle readers/year; 1-2 young adult titles/year. 10% of books by first-time authors.
Fiction: Picture books and young readers: contemporary, folktales, history, nature/environment. Middle readers: contemporary, folktales, history, nature environment, problem novels, multiethnic. Young adults: contemporary, folktales, history, nature/environment, multiethnic. "No clichés or 'trendy' subject matters. No poetry. No talking bears! No time travelling dinosaur lovers!" Recently published *The Boxing Champion*, by Roch Carrier (ages 8 and up, picture book); *How Two-Feather Was Saved from Loneliness*, by C.J. Taylor (ages 8 and up, Indian legend); *Simon in Summer*, by Gilles Tibo (ages 3 and up, picture book).
Nonfiction: Picture books: nature/environment. Young readers: history, nature/environment. Middle readers: biography, history, nature/environment. Young adults: biography. Recently published *Houses of Bark*, by Bonnie Shemie (ages 8-12, native architecture); *West Coast Chinese Boy*, by Sing Lim (ages 10 and up, autobiography); *A Child in*

Prison Camp, by Shizuye Takashima (ages 10 and up, autobiography).
How to Contact/Writers: Fiction/nonfiction: Submit outline/synopsis and sample chapters. Reports in 2 months on queries; reports on mss in 4 months. Publishes a book 1-1½ years after acceptance. Will consider simultaneous submissions.
Illustrations: Average number of illustrations used for fiction: picture books—12; middle readers—12. Average number of illustrations used for nonfiction: picture books—10-14; middle readers 12. Will review ms/illustration packages. Will review artwork for future assignments. Contact Arjun Basu, assistant editor. Uses color artwork only.
How to Contact/Illustrators: Ms/illustration packages: Send color photocopies or slides of art with ms or synopsis. Illustrations only: Provide résumé and tearsheets to be kept on file. Reports back only if interested. Original artwork returned at job's completion.
Terms: Pays authors royalty of 7-10% based on retail price. Offers advances of "approximately $1,500 for first timers." Pays illustrators royalty of 2-10% based on retail price. Sends galleys to authors (if they want); dummies to illustrators (if they want). Ms/artist's guidelines available for SASE.
Tips: "Always be on the lookout for trends: see what's big in the bookstores, at the libraries. When you've figured this out, you'll know what *not* to send out. What's in the stores now is not what will be *in* when your book comes out. We're into high quality artwork. Our motto is Children's Books as Works of Art. A lot of our illustrators are also writers. This combination works best."

TYNDALE HOUSE PUBLISHERS, 351 Executive Dr., P.O. Box 80, Wheaton IL 60189. (708)668-8300. Book publisher. Children's editorial contact: Lucille Leonard. Children's illustration contact: Marlene Muddell. Publishes approximately 25 children's titles a year. 10% of books by first-time authors. Accepts approximately 2% of solicited and unsolicited manuscripts.
Fiction/Nonfiction: Currently overstocked in all categories.
Illustration: Full-color for picture books, black and white for paperbacks, some spot illustrations for nonfiction, covers. Number of illustrations used for fiction and nonfiction: picture books—"varies." Will review ms/illustration packages.
How to Contact/Illustrators: Illustrations only: Send photocopies (color or b&w) of samples, résumé.
Terms: Pays authors fee (for some series) or royalty for manuscript with illustrations, higher for unillustrated ms. Pay for illustrators: variable fee or royalty.
Tips: "All accepted mss will appeal to evangelical Christian children and parents."

*THE VANITAS PRESS, Platslagarevägen 4 E 1, Lund, Sweden 22230. Publisher: March Laumer. Publishes 2 young adult titles/year. "All our books, at the present time, are continuations of the American 'Oz' series of novels."
Fiction: "Nothing can be considered except possible contributions to the Oz series." Young adults/teens: anthology, fantasy. Average word length: 60-100,000 words. Recently published *The Umbrellas of Oz* and *A Farewell to Oz*, by March Laumer; and *The Crown of Oz*, by Michael Michanczyk; (all for young to full adults, fantasies).
How to Contact/Writers: Query. Reports on mss in 2 weeks. Publishes book 6 months after acceptance. Will consider simultaneous submissions, electronic submissions via disk or modem, and previously published work.
Illustration: Average number of illustrations used: 15. Will review ms/illustration packages. Will review artwork for future assignments. Uses primarily black & white artwork only. "Normal single book page size: vertical orientation."
How to Contact/Illustrators: Ms/illustration packages: Query. Illustration only: Query with samples. Reports immediately. Original artwork returned at job's completion.
Terms: Pays authors percentage of profits—if any. Pays illustrators percentage of profits. "A list of publications titles can be provided."

Tips: "I would advise being willing to offer material without charge for the benefit derived from seeing one's early work in print. In much of small press publishing there simply isn't any profit to be shared; it's a 'for-the-love-of-it' operation. There's a very good chance of 'selling' us anything in the Oz-fantasy line. Otherwise, nothing." **Trends:** "I notice more concentration on pictures. Earlier, much-still-loved children's books were long, engrossable novels. Books now are wider-format, much thinner, and demand only of the reader an ability to look at pictures. Apparently reading ability is being played down."

*VICTOR BOOKS, Scripture Press, 1825 College Ave., Wheaton IL 60187. (708)668-6000. FAX: (708)668-3806. Book publisher. Senior Editor and Production Manager: Loreli Dickerson. Publishes 9 pictures books/year; 10 middle readers/year. "No young readers at this point, but open to them." 50% of books by first-time authors; 10% of books from agented authors. All books are related to Christianity.
Fiction: Picture books: adventure, animal, contemporary, religion. Young readers: adventure, animal, contemporary, religion, science fiction, sports, suspense/mystery. Middle readers: adventure, contemporary, history, religion, sports, suspense/mystery. Does not want to see stories with "Christian" animals; no holiday legends. Recently published *Dr. Drabble's Phenomenal Antigravity Dust Machine*, by Sigmund Browner and Wayne Davidson (ages 4-7, picture book); *The Reluctant Runaway*, by Jeffrey Asher Nesbit (ages 8-12, middle reader); *Creature of the Mists*, by Sigmund Browner (ages 8-12, middle reader).
Nonfiction: Picture books: biography, religion. Young readers: biography, history, religion. Middle readers: biography, history, religion, sports. No ABC books or biographies of obscure/not well-known people.
How to Contact/Writers: Fiction/nonfiction: Submit complete ms for picture books. Submit outline/synopsis and 2 sample chapters for middle readers. Reports on queries in 1 month; reports on mss in 1½ months. Publishes a book 1½ years after acceptance. Will consider simultaneous submissions.
Illustration: Average number of illustrations used for fiction and nonfiction: picture books—24; middle readers—1. Will review ms/illustration packages. Will review artwork for future assignments. Contact Paul Higdon, art director.
How to Contact/Illustrators: Ms/illustration packages: Submit complete package. Illustrations only: Submit portfolio for review. Provide résumé, promotional literature or tearsheets to be kept on file. Reports back only if interested. Does not return original artwork at job's completion.
Photography: Photographer should contact Paul Higdon, art director. Uses photos of children. Model/property releases required. Interested in stock photos. To contact, photographers should submit portfolio for review; provide résumé, promotional literature or tearsheets to be kept on file.
Terms: Pays authors royalty of 5-10% based on wholesale price, outright purchase $125-2,500. Offers advance "based on project." Pays illustrators by the project, royalty of 5% based on wholesale price. Photographers paid by the project, per photo. Sends galleys to authors. Book catalog available for 9 × 12 SAE and 2 first class stamps. Ms guidelines available for SASE.
Tips: "In general children's books I see trends toward increasingly high quality. In Christian children's books I see increasing commercial/cartoon characters—we're not interested in the latter."

VOLCANO PRESS, Box 270, Volcano CA 95689. (209)296-3345. FAX: (209)296-4515. Book publisher. President: Ruth Gottstein. Published 1 picture book in 1989; 3 in 1990.
Nonfiction: All levels: health, history, nature/environment. Will consider feminist, social issues, Pacific-rim related (Asian) material for picture books, young readers and middle readers. No fiction or poetry.

How to Contact/Writers: Nonfiction: Submit outline/synopsis and sample chapters. Reports on queries in approximately one month. Publishes a book 1 year after acceptance. "Please always enclose SASE."
Illustration: Will review artwork for future assignments.
How to Contact/Illustrators: Illustrations only: brief query with samples.
Terms: Sends galleys to authors; dummies to illustrators. Book catalog for #10 SASE.
Tips: Considers "non-racist, non-sexist types of books that are empowering to women."

VOYAGEUR PUBLISHING CO., INC., 4506 Beacon Dr., Nashville TN 37215. (615)665-2623. Book publisher. Contact: Eric Youngquist, President. Publishes 2 middle reader titles/year; 3 young adult titles/year. 50% of books by first-time authors; 50% of books from agented writers.
Fiction: Middle readers and young adults: animal, history, sports. Published *The Thong Tree*, by Haynes (grades 3-7, fiction/history); *Kentucky Frontiersmen*, by Altsheler (grades 5-10, fiction/history).
Nonfiction: Middle readers and young adults: animal, biography, history, nature/environment, sports.
How to Contact/Writers: Fiction and nonfiction: Query. Submit outline/synopsis and sample chapters. SASE. Reports on queries in 1-3 weeks. Publishes a book 6 months after acceptance.
Illustration: Number of illustrations used for fiction and nonfiction: middle readers-10; young adult/teens—6. Editorial will review ms/illustration packages. Eric Youngquist, president, or Nathaniel Kenton, editor, will review illustrator's work for possible future assignments.
How to Contact/Illustrators: Query first. "We will work with first time illustrators if they have a style that appeals to us." Submit résumé (list books that the artist has illustrated), tearsheets and "anything that will show an artist's use of color." Reports on art samples in 3 weeks. Originals "not returned if we have purchased the art."
Terms: Pays authors in royalties of 15% based on wholesale price. "Generally, we would pay royalty to the writer and purchase the artwork." Pay for illustrators: by the project. "We agree on price, then illustrator gets half of price when finished art delivered; remainder when book is released. But this is open for negotiation." Manuscript guidelines for 1 first-class stamp and #10 SAE.

■**W.W. PUBLICATIONS,** Subsidiary of American Tolkien Society, Box 373, Highland MI 48357-0373. (813)585-0985. Independent book producer. Editorial Contact: Phil Helms. 75% of books by first-time authors. Subsidy publishes 75%.
Fiction/Nonfiction: All ages: fantasy, Tolkien-related.
How to Contact/Writers: Fiction: Query. Submit outline/synopsis of complete ms. Reports on queries in 4-6 weeks; 2-3 months mss. Publishes a book 3-6 months after acceptance. Will consider simultaneous submissions.
Illustration: Reviews all illustration packages. Prefers 8½×11 b&w and ink.
How to Contact/Illustrators: Query with samples. Reports on ms/art samples in 3 months. Original art work returned at job's completion if requested.
Terms: Pays author free copies. Sends galleys to author if requested; dummies to illustrators. Book catalog for 1 first class stamp and #10 SAE.
Tips: "Tolkien oriented only."

Always include a self-addressed stamped envelope (SASE) or International Reply Coupon (IRC) with submissions.

WALKER AND CO., div. of Walker Publishing Co. Inc., 720 Fifth Ave., New York NY 10019. (212)265-3632. Book publisher. Estab. 1959. Editorial Director, Books for Young Readers: Amy C. Shields. Publishes 2-3 picture books/year; 10 young reader titles/year; 1 middle reader title/year; 15 young adult titles/year. 10-15% of books by first-time authors; 65% of books from agented writers.

Fiction: Picture books: fantasy, history. Young readers: animal, history, fantasy. Middle readers: fantasy, science fiction, history. Young adults: fantasy, history, science fiction. Recently published *Steam Train Ride*, by E.C. Mott (picture book); *Brother Night*, by V. Keller (young adult).

Nonfiction: Picture books, young readers, middle readers, young adults: animal, biography, education, history, hobbies, music/dance, nature/environment, religion, science, sports. Recently published *The Story of Things*, by S. Morrow (picture book history); *America Fights the Tide: 1942*, by John Devaney (young adult history).

How to Contact/Writers: Fiction/nonfiction: Submit outline/synopsis and sample chapters. Report on queries/mss in 2-3 months. Publishes a book 1 year after acceptance. Will consider simultaneous submissions.

Illustration: Number of illustrations used for fiction: picture books—32-48; young readers—30; middle readers—30. Number of illustrations used for nonfiction: picture books—32-48; young readers—20-30; middle readers—20-30; young adults—20-30. Editorial will review ms/illustration packages.

How to Contact/Illustrators: Ms/illustration packages: 5 chapters of ms with 1 piece of final art, remainder roughs. Illustrations only: "Tearsheets." Reports on art samples only if interested. Original artwork returned at job's completion.

Terms: Pays authors in royalties of 5-10% based on wholesale price "depends on contract." Offers average advance payment of $2,000-4,000. Pay for illustrators: By the project, $500-5,000; royalties from 50%. Sends galleys to authors. Book catalog available for 9×12 SASE; manuscript guidelines for SASE.

Tips: Writers: "Keep writing, keep trying. Don't take rejections personally and try to consider them objectively. If 10 publishers reject a work, put it aside and look at it again after a month. Can it be improved?" Illustrators: "Have a well-rounded portfolio with different styles." Looks for: "Science and nature series for young and middle readers."

WATERFRONT BOOKS, 98 Brookes Ave., Burlington VT 05401. (802)658-7477. Book publisher. Publisher: Sherrill N. Musty. 100% of books by first-time authors.

Fiction: Picture books, young readers, middle readers, young adults; mental health, family/parenting, health, special issues involving barriers to learning in children.

Nonfiction: Picture books, young readers, middle readers, young adults: education, guidance, health, mental health, social issues. "We publish books for both children and adults on any subject that helps to lower barriers to learning in children: mental health, family/parenting, education and social issues. We are now considering books for children on bettering the environment.

How to Contact/Writers: Fiction/nonfiction: Query. Reports on queries in 2 weeks; on mss in 6 weeks. Publishes a book 6 months after acceptance.

Illustration: Editorial will review ms/illustration packages.

How to Contact/Illustrators: Ms/illustration packages: Query first. Illustrations only: Résumé, tearsheets. Reports on art samples only if interested.

Terms: Pays authors in royalties of 10-15% based on wholesale price. Pays illustrators by the job. Sends galleys to authors; dummies to illustrators. Book catalog available for #10 SAE and 1 first class stamp.

Tips: "Have your manuscript thoroughly reviewed and even copy edited, if necessary. If you are writing about a special subject, have a well-qualified professional in the field review it for accuracy and appropriateness. It always helps to get some testimonials before submitting it to a publisher. The publisher then knows she/he is dealing with something worthwhile."

*WATERSTON PRODUCTIONS, INC., 1019 NW Brooks St., Bend OR 97701. (503)385-1025. Book publisher. Editor: Carey Vendrame. Publishes 3 picture books/year. 50% of books by first-time authors. "We are seeking children's stories with a regional (Northwest) feel. We want to feature Northwest writers and illustrators, but will consider all mss received."
Fiction: Picture books and young readers: various subjects including adventure, anthology, animal, contemporary, fantasy, folktales, health-related, history, nature/environment, poetry, science fiction, sports, suspense/mystery. Does not want to see "Stories that are written from an adult's perspective; stories that are cute or condescending." Average word length: picture books—200; young readers—1,500. Recently published *Letter City and the Alphabet Winds*, by Larry Kimmel (young reader); *Tea at Miss Jean's*, by Bispham Page (preschool—8 years, picture book); *Tale of Three Tractors, Jimmy the Beet Truck*, and *Big Cat the Proud*, by Molly Pearce (preschool, picture book).
Nonfiction: Picture books and young readers: activity books, animal, biography, history, nature/environment, sports. Average word length: picture books—200; young readers—1,500.
How to Contact/Writers: Fiction/nonfiction: Submit complete ms. Reports on queries/mss: 1-2 months. Publishes a book 7-9 months after acceptance. Will consider simultaneous submissions.
Illustration: Average number of illustrations used for fiction: picture books—16; young readers—16. Will review ms/illustration packages. Will review artwork for future assignments.
How to Contact/Illustrators: Ms/illustration packages: Submit complete package. Illustrations only: Send unsolicited art samples by mail. Reports in 4-6 weeks. Original artwork returned at job's completion.
Terms: Pays authors and illustrators royalty based on wholesale price or outright purchase. Offers advances. Sends galleys to authors. Book catalog available for 4 × 9½ SASE.
Tips: "Learn to view the world from a child's perspective by reading aloud to children. Browse in children's bookstores and talk with children's librarians." Wants a book that is written "from the heart—a story that presents an old idea in a new way. It must be obvious that the writer believes that a children's book requires the same skills and attention to detail as adult literature."

FRANKLIN WATTS, INC., a subsidiary of Grolier Inc., 95 Madison Ave., 11th Floor, New York NY 10016. (212)686-7070. Book publisher. Editorial contact person: Jeanne Vestal. 5% of books by first-time authors; 40% of books from agented writers.
Nonfiction: Middle readers, young adults: open categories. Average word length: middle readers—5,000; young adult/teens—16,000-35,000.
How to Contact/Writers: Query. Reports in 1 month. Publishes book 1 year after acceptance.
How to Contact/Illustrators: Query first. Original artwork returned at job's completion.

Market conditions are constantly changing! If you're still using this book and it is 1993 or later, buy the newest edition of Children's Writer's & Illustrator's Market *at your favorite bookstore or order directly from Writer's Digest Books.*

Terms: Book catalog for 10×13 SASE.
Tips: Looks for children's nonfiction grades 5-8 or 9-12.

WEIGL EDUCATIONAL PUBLISHERS, 2114 College Ave., Regina Saskatchewan S4P 1C5 Canada. (306)569-0766. Book publisher. Publisher: Linda Weigl.
Nonfiction: Young reader/middle reader/young adult: education, history, social studies. Average word length: young reader/middle reader/young adult — 64 pages.
How to Contact/Writers: Nonfiction: Submit query and résumé. Reports on queries in 1 month. Publishes a book 2 years after acceptance. Will consider simultaneous submissions.
Illustration: Number of illustrations used in nonfiction: young reader/middle reader/young adult — 20. Editorial will review ms/illustration packages.
How to Contact/Illustrators: Ms/illustration packages: "Query first." Illustrations only: Send "résumé and photocopies of completed works." Reports back only if interested or when appropriate project comes in.
Terms: Pays "either royalty or fee." Illustrators paid by the project. Sends galleys to author; sends dummies to illustrator. Book catalog free on request.
Tips: Looks for "educational material suited to a specific curriculum topic."

*ALBERT WHITMAN & COMPANY, 6340 Oakton St., Morton Grove IL 60053-2723. (708)581-0033. Book publisher. Editor-in-Chief: Kathleen Tucker. Publishes 20 picture books/year; 3 middle readers/year. 40% of books by first-time authors; 15% of books from agented authors. "We publish various categories, but we're mostly known for our concept books—books that deal with children's problems or concerns."
Fiction: Picture books: adventure, animal, contemporary, fantasy, folktales, health-related, nature/environment, poetry, sports. Young readers and middle readers: adventure, animal, contemporary, fantasy, folktales, health-related, history, nature/environment, poetry, problem novels, sports, suspense/mystery. Does not want to see "religion-oriented, ABCs, pop-up, romance, counting or any book that is supposed to be written in." Recently published *How the Ox Star Fell from Heaven*, by Lily Toy Hong (ages 5-8, picture book); *Losing Uncle Tim*, by Marykate Jordon (grades 2-6, picture book/young reader); *Speak Up, Chelsea Martin!*, by Becky Thoman Lindberg (grades 2-4/ages 7-9, young readers/middle reader).
Nonfiction: Picture books, young readers and middle readers: animal, careers, health, history, hobbies, music/dance, nature/environment, sports. Does not want to see "religion, any books that have to be written in, biographies (for now)." Recently published *Pet Mice*, by Jerome Wexler (grades 2-8, young readers/middle readers); *I Am a Jesse White Tumbler*, by Diane Schmidt (grades 2-8, young readers/middle readers); *Inspirations: Stories About Women Artists*, by Leslie Sills (ages 8 and up, middle reader).
How to Contact/Writers: Fiction/nonfiction: Submit complete ms. Reports on queries in 4-6 weeks; reports on mss in 2 months. Publishes a book 18 months after acceptance. Will consider simultaneous submissions "but let us know if it is one" and previously published work "if out of print."
Illustration: Average number of illustrations used for fiction: picture books—25; middle reader—5. Nonfiction: picture books—30; middle readers—10. Will review ms/illustration packages. Will review artwork for future assignments. Contact Editorial. Uses more color art than b&w.
How to Contact/Illustrators: Ms/illustration packages: Submit all chapters of ms with any pieces of final art. Illustrations only: Query with samples. Send unsolicited art samples by mail. Reports back only if interested. Original artwork returned at job's completion.
Photography: Photographers should contact editorial. Interested in stock photos "but seldomly!" To contact, photographers should query with samples; send unsolicited photos by mail.

Terms: Pays authors royalty. Offers advances. Pays illustrators royalty. Sends galleys to authors; dummies to illustrators. Book catalog available for 9 × 12 SAE and 5 first class stamps. Ms guidelines available for SASE.
Tips: Best bets for this market are bibliotherapy and picture book stories.

*WILLIAMSON PUBLISHING CO., Box 185, Charlotte VT 05445. (802)425-2102. Book publisher. Editorial Director: Susan Williamson. Publishes 6 picture books, 8 young readers, 8 middle readers, and 2 young adult titles/year. 80% of books by first-time authors; 20% of books from agented authors. Publishes "very successful nonfiction series (Kids Can! Series) on subjects such as nature, creative play, arts & crafts, music."
Nonfiction: Picture books: activity books, animal, history, music/dance, nature/environment, religion. Young readers, middle readers and young adults/teens: activity books, animal, health, history, music/dance, nature/environment, religion. No textbooks. Recently published *The Kids Nature Book*, by Susan Milard (ages 4-10, activity/experiential); *Kids Create!*, by Laurie Carlson (ages 4-7, art & craft); and *Kids Learn America*, by Reed & Snow (ages 7-14, informational/activity).
How to Contact/Writers: Nonfiction: Query; submit outline/synopsis and 2 sample chapters. Reports in 1-3 months. Publishes book, "depending on graphics, about 9 months" after acceptance. Will consider simultaneous submissions.
Illustration: Average number of illustrations used for nonfiction: young readers—400; middle readers—400. Uses primarily black & white artwork only.
Terms: Pays authors royalty based on wholesale price. Offers advances. Sends galleys to authors. Book catalog available for 6 × 9 SAE and 3 first class stamps; ms guidelines available for SASE.
Tips: "In nonfiction children's publishing, we are looking for authors with a depth of knowledge shared with children through a warm, embracing style—a respite in a rough world that tells not only how, but affirms that children can."

■WINSTON-DEREK PUBLISHERS, INC., Box 90883, Nashville TN 37209. (615)321-0535. Book publisher. Estab. 1972. Editorial contact as follows: picture books: Matalyn Rose Peebles; young reader titles: Maggie Ella Sims; middle reader/young adult titles: Candi Williams. Publishes 35-40 picture books/year; 25-30 young reader titles/year; 10-15 middle reader titles/year; 10-15 young adult titles/year. 50% of books by first-time authors; 5% through agents. Subsidy publishes 20% of books/year.
Fiction: Picture books: contemporary, folktales, history, religion. Young readers: adventure, folktales, history, religion. Middle readers: adventure, contemporary, folktales, history, religion, suspense/mystery. Young adults: adventure, contemporary, folktales, history, problem novels, religion, suspense/mystery. Average word length: picture book—600-1200; young reader—3,000-5,000; middle reader—2,000; young adult—10,000-40,000. Published *Matthew's Allowance*, by Christine White (ages 5-7, educational); *Saturn Storm's Broccoli Adventure*, by D. James Harrison (ages 5-7, adventure); and *Jamako and the Beanstalk*, by Fred Crump, Jr. (ages 3-6, fairy tale).
Nonfiction: Picture books: biography, careers, religion, textbooks. Young readers, middle readers and young adults: biography, careers, history, religion, textbooks/basal readers, African American biographies. Average word length: picture book—600-800; young readers—2,500-4,000; middle reader—1,000-2,500; young adult—10,000-30,000. Published *First Black Doctor in America*, by Benjamin E. Holt (grades 4-6, African-American studies); *Sprinter in Life*, by Dorothy Croman (grades 4-6, African-American studies); and *Kizito*, by Elaine M. Stone (grades 4-6, African-American studies).
How to Contact/Writers: Fiction: Query or submit outline/synopsis and sample chapters. Nonfiction: Submit complete ms. Reports on queries in 6 weeks; on mss in 8 weeks. Publishes a book 10 months after acceptance. Will consider simultaneous submissions.
Illustration: Number of illustrations used in fiction/nonfiction: picture book—20; young reader—10; middle reader—5. Editorial will review ms/illustration packages. Edi-

tor, Robert Earl, will review an illustrator's work for possible future assignments.
How to Contact/Illustrators: Ms/illustration packages: 3 chapters of ms with 1 piece of final art. Illustrations only: Send résumé and tearsheets. Reports in 3 weeks. Original art work returned at job's completion.
Terms: Pays authors in royalties of 10-15% based on wholesale price. Also pays in copies. Separate authors and illustrators: 12½% royalty to writer and 2½% royalty to illustrator. Illustrators paid $30-150 or 2½-8½% royalty. Sends galleys to author; dummies to illustrator. Book catalog for SASE; ms/artist's guidelines free on request.
Tips: Illustrators: Use "action illustrations plus send good work and variety of subjects such as male/female; b&w." Looks for: "educational, morally sound subjects, multiethnic; historical facts."

WOMEN'S PRESS, 233-517 College Street, Toronto, Ontario M6G 4A2 Canada. (416)921-2425. Book publisher. Editorial contact person: Anne Decter. Publishes 1-2 picture books/year; 0-1 middle reader titles/year; 0-1 young adult titles/year. 60% of books by first-time authors. "We give preference to authors who are Canadian citizens or those living in Canada."
Fiction: Picture books: contemporary, social issues, health and family problems. Young readers, middle readers and young adults: contemporary, problem novels. Average word length: picture books—24 pages; young readers—70-80 pages; middle readers—60-70 pages; young adult/teens—80-150 pages. Recently published *Asha's Mums*, by Elwin & Paulse (4-8, picture-issue).
Nonfiction: Picture books: environment. Young adults: sex, health.
How to Contact/Writers: Fiction/Nonfiction: Query. Reports on queries in 1 month; reports on mss in 3-6 months. Publishes a book 1 year after acceptance.
Illustration: Number of illustrations used for fiction: picture books—20+; young readers—3; middle readers—2; young adult/teens—1. Editorial will review ms/illustration packages (Canadian only).
Terms: Pays authors in royalties of 10% min. based on retail price. Sends galleys to authors; dummies to illustrators. Book catalog and/or manuscript guidelines free on request.

*WOODBINE HOUSE, 5615 Fishers Ln. Rockville MD 20852. (301)468-8800. Book publisher. Editor: Susan Stokes. Publishes 0-2 picture books/year; 0-2 young adult titles/year. 100% of books by first-time authors. "All children's books are for or about children with disabilities."
Fiction: All levels: health-related and disability-related. "No fiction unless disability-related." Average word length: picture books—24 pages. Recently published *Shelley, the Hyperactive Turtle*, by Deborah Moss (ages 5-8, picture book); *Lee, the Rabbit with Epilepsy*, by Deborah Moss (ages 5-8, picture book).
Nonfiction: All levels: disabilities. Does not want to see anything other than subjects about disabilities.
How to Contact/Writers: Fiction/nonfiction: Submit complete ms. Reports on queries in 2 weeks; reports on mss in 1-3 months. Publishes a book 18 months after acceptance. Will consider simultaneous submissions and previously published work.
Illustration: Average number of illustrations used for fiction: picture books—24. Will review ms/illustration packages.
How to Contact/Illustrators: Ms/illustration packages: Submit entire ms with 2-3 pieces of art (color photocopies OK). Reports back only if interested.
Terms: Pays authors royalty of 10-15% based on wholesale price. Offers advances of $0-5,000. Pays illustrators by the project. Sends galleys to authors. Book catalog available for 6×9 SAE and 3 first class stamps. Ms guidelines available for SASE.
Tips: "Try your book out on a couple of kids (not your own) and see whether it grabs and holds their interest." Submit books dealing with disability/chronic illness issues.

Other Book Publishers

The following book publishers are not included in this edition of *Children's Writer's & Illustrator's Market* for the reasons indicated. The phrase "did not respond" means the publisher was in the 1991 *Children's Writer's & Illustrator's Market* but did not respond to our written and phone requests for updated information for a 1992 listing.

Accent Books (no longer soliciting manuscripts)

Beyond Words Publishing (overstocked)

Branden Publishing Company (not publishing material for children)

Cloverdale Press (overstocked)

Consumer Report Books (not publishing material for children)

Dillon Press (did not respond)

Double M Press (overstocked)

Doubleday (not publishing material for children)

Eakin Publications (removed per request)

Faber and Faber, Inc. (not accepting unsolicited material)

David R. Godine, Publisher (overstocked)

Green Tiger Press (did not respond)

Maryland Historical Press (did not respond)

Misty Hill Press (did not respond)

Multnomah Press (not accepting unsolicited material)

New Day Press (did not respond)

Pocahontas Press, Inc. (not publishing material for children)

Sandlapper Publishing Co., Inc. (removed per request)

Thistledown Press Ltd. (did not respond)

Trillium Press (unresolved complaints)

Warner Juvenile Books (ceased publishing)

Magazines

Magazine editors are really roving reporters, said Elizabeth Rinck, editor of *Children's Digest* and *Children's Playmate* (both published by the Children's Better Health Institute), at the 1991 Society of Children's Book Writers regional conference in Indianapolis. What she means by this is editors are always on the lookout for a variety of fresh material. "We don't know what we want, but we recognize it when we see it," says Rinck.

When considering submissions, magazine editors concentrate on the compilation of the publication as a whole rather than the effect each story will have. Unlike book editors who depend on one subject to make one book successful over a long period of time, magazine editors don't have to be as concerned about whether one story or article will sell one issue of a magazine. Therefore, the taboos aren't as strong, and editors are more willing to take risks. Magazines are the ideal target for writers and illustrators who lack publication credits because there's more room to break in, and collecting credits is beneficial in building credibility in the children's field.

The children's magazine market

Recent times have been rough for the magazine market. Advertising revenues have dropped, circulations are down and postage rates, in addition to production costs, have increased. Though adult ad-based magazines are feeling most of the effects of these circumstances, children's magazines are not necessarily immune. *Wee Wisdom* editor Judy Gehrlein sadly announced that, after nearly 100 years in print, the magazine ceased publication after the December 1991 issue. *Pennywhistle Press* downgraded its format and is no longer interested in using freelance work. At press time, *Odyssey* magazine was in the process of being sold to Cobblestone Publishing, and *U*S*Kids* was in the process of being sold to the Children's Better Health Institute. Because of the chaos involved in ownership transfers, both publications requested not to be included this year. On the other hand, there are some big publishers who are just starting to get their feet wet in children's magazines and feel the chance they're taking at entering this field will pay off. Such new four-color magazines are *Disney Adventures* (published by the Walt Disney Company), *Faith 'n Stuff* (published by Guideposts) and *Spark* (published by F&W Publications).

In this section you will find updated listings from previous years along with a few new markets. Magazine publishers is the one section in this book that has not grown. However, it isn't any smaller than last year's, which indicates that, for the most part, kids' magazines are weathering through the tough times.

The popularity of kids' magazines

Possibly one of the reasons juvenile magazines are surviving the crunch is children find them more appealing than in the past. Today there is a much more diverse selection that covers specific interests. Also, in order to accommodate children in a visually-oriented society, publishers have snazzed up their periodicals by increasing production qualities. Parents love magazines for their children because they view reading as a desirable alternative to watching television. Some children may not be patient enough to conquer whole books, but they may be willing to flip through the pages of a magazine until something attracts them.

Children today are more worldly and have a desire to know what's going on around them. Because magazines have the advantage of timeliness, they can expose children to current events in much less time than books and at less cost (the average one-year subscription is about the same as one hardcover picture book).

Another plus for the children's magazine industry is that teachers, in an effort to promote Whole Language theory, are utilizing fact-based educational periodicals as supplements in their classrooms. As a result, it's not unusual for children to want summer subscriptions, or even their own personal subscriptions after being initially exposed to certain magazines at school.

Needs of magazines

Some of the magazines listed here are informational, while others can be described as literary, religious-oriented or special interest. A few are adult magazines with special children's sections. There are many children's magazines that are not much more than promotions for toys, movies or television shows. You're not likely to find any of these in this book because they use licensed characters and are mostly produced in-house. Also, some of these types of magazines are more interested in generating revenue than enriching a young mind, and therefore concentrate more on advertising funds than literary or educational content.

The large circulation, ad-driven publications will generally offer a better pay rate than religious or nonprofit magazines. But smaller magazines may be more open to reviewing the work of newcomers. They can provide an excellent vehicle for you to compile clippings as you work your way toward the more lucrative markets. There is a drawback, though. It's not uncommon for juvenile magazines to purchase all rights to both stories and artwork. Though work for hire is generally frowned upon among freelancers, in the end selling all rights may prove to be advantageous. All of the magazines at the Children's Better Health Institute buy all rights, as does *Highlights*. However, these magazines are very reputable, and any clips acquired through them will be valuable.

A variety of manuscripts are needed by these markets. Classic subjects considered by many magazines include stories/features about the alphabet, outer space, computers and animals (even dinosaurs). As is with books, nonfiction features are very popular—especially photo features. Also, sports stories and descriptive articles on the way things work are marketable. Though trends tend to peak and fade quickly, current needs in the general interest magazine field are solid. They include historical fiction, retold folktales, mysteries, science fiction and fantasy. Multicultural material is very high in demand—editors can't seem to find enough of it. It appears efforts are strong to supply stories and artwork which include ethnic diversity. Don't expect demands for multicultural material to subside anytime soon.

Many kids' magazines sell subscriptions via direct mail or schools, so don't be surprised if you can't find a particular publication in the bookstore or at the newsstand. Be sure to send away for a sample copy of any magazine you're interested in working with. Most listings in this section have sample copies available and will be glad to send them upon request. Editors are constantly advising freelancers to know the market they are submitting to. Becoming familiar with the theme of a magazine will save valuable time for both the freelancer submitting material and the editor who has to view the work.

Once you have determined which magazines you are interested in contacting, take another look at the listing to review their preferred method of receiving submissions. Some may wish to see an entire manuscript; others may wish to see a query letter and outline, especially for nonfiction articles (with nonfiction articles, accompanying photographs are much welcomed). If you're an artist, review the listing for the types of samples you should send to the art director.

Finally, be sure you submit your best work. Though the magazine market is a good way for children's writers and illustrators to break in, it is not a junkyard for "less-than-your-best" material.

AIM MAGAZINE, America's Intercultural Magazine, Box 20554, Chicago IL 60620. (312)874-6184. Articles Editor: Ruth Apilado. Fiction Editor: Mark Boone. Art Director: Bill Jackson. Quarterly magazine. Circ. 8,000. Readers are high school and college students, teachers, adults interested in helping, through the written word, to create a more equitable world. 15% of material aimed at juvenile audience.
Fiction: Young adults: history, "stories with social significance." Wants stories that teach children that people are more alike than they are different. Does not want to see religious fiction. Buys 20 mss/year. Average word length: 1,000-4,000. Byline given.
Nonfiction: Young adults: interview/profile, "stuff with social significance." Does not want to see religious nonfiction. Buys 20 mss/year. Average word length: 500-2,000. Byline given.
How to Contact/Writers: Fiction: Send complete ms. Nonfiction: Query with published clips. Reports on queries/mss in 1 month. Will consider simultaneous submissions.
Illustration: Buys 20 illustrations/issue. Preferred theme or style: Overcoming social injustices through nonviolent means. Will review ms/illustration packages.
How to Contact/Illustrators: Ms/illustration packages: Query first. Illustrations only: "Send examples of art, ask for a job." Reports on art samples in 2 months. Original art work returned at job's completion "if desired."
Terms: Pays on publication. Buys first North American serial rights. Pays $5-25 for assigned/unsolicited articles. Pays in contributor copies if copies are requested. Pays $5-25/b&w cover illustration. Sample copy $3.50.
Tips: "We need material of social significance, stuff that will help promote racial harmony and peace and (illustrate) the stupidity of racism."

ATALANTIK, 7630 Deer Creek Dr., Worthington OH 43085. (614)885-0550. Articles/ Fiction Editor: Prabhat K. Dutta. Art Director: Tanushree Bhattacharya. Quarterly magazine. Estab. 1980. Circ. 400. "*Atalantik* is the first Bengali (Indian language) literary magazine published from the USA. It contains poems, essays, short stories, translations, interviews, opinions, sketches, book reviews, cultural information, scientific articles, letters to the editor, serialized novels and a children's section. The special slant may be India and/or education." 10% of material aimed at juvenile audience.
Fiction: Young reader: animal. Middle readers: history, humorous, problem solving, math puzzles, travel. Young adults: history, humorous, problem solving, romance, science fiction, sports, spy/mystery/adventure, math puzzles, travel. Does not want to see: "religious, political, controversial or material without any educational value." Buys 20-40 mss/year. Average word length: 300-1,000. Byline given, "sometimes."

Nonfiction: Middle readers: history, how-to, humorous, problem solving, travel. Young adults: history, how-to, humorous, interview/profile, problem solving, travel, puzzles. Does not want to see: "religious, political, controversial or material without any educational value." Buys 20-40 mss/year. Average word length: 300-1,000. Byline given, "sometimes."
Poetry: Reviews 20-line humorous poems that rhyme; maximum of 5 submissions.
How to Contact/Writers: Fiction/nonfiction: Send complete ms. Reports on queries in 2 weeks; mss in 4 weeks. Will consider simultaneous submissions.
Illustration: Buys 4-20 illustrations/year. Prefers to review juvenile education, activities, sports, culture and recreations. Will review ms/illustration packages, including illustrator's work for possible future assignments.
How to Contact/Illustrators: Ms/illustration packages: Send "complete manuscript with final art." Illustrations only: Send "résumé with copies of previous published work." Reports only if interested.
Terms: Pays on publication. Buys all rights. Usually pays in copies for all circumstances. Sample copy $6. Writer's/illustrator's guidelines free with 1 SAE and 1 first class stamp.
Tips: Writers: "Be imaginative, thorough, flexible and educational. Most importantly, be a child."

BOYS' LIFE, Boy Scouts of America, 1325 W. Walnut Hill La., Box 152079, Irving TX 75015-2079. (214)580-2000. Articles Editor: Jeffrey Csatari. Fiction Editor: Kathleen DaGroomes. Art Director: Elizabeth Hardaway Morgan. Director of Design: Joseph P. Connolly. Monthly magazine. Estab. 1911. Circ. 1,300,000. *Boys' Life* is "a general interest magazine for boys 8 to 18 who are members of the Cub Scouts, Boy Scouts or Explorers. A general interest magazine for all boys."
Fiction: Middle readers: animal, contemporary, fantasy, history, humorous, problem-solving, science fiction, sports, spy/mystery/adventure. Does not want to see "talking animals and adult reminiscence." Buys 12 mss/year. Average word length: 500-1,500. Byline given.
Nonfiction: Average word length: 300-500. Byline given.
How to Contact/Writers: Fiction/nonfiction: Send complete ms/query. Reports on queries/mss in 2-3 weeks.
Illustration: Buys 5-7 illustrations/issue; buys 23-50 illustrations/year. Will review ms/illustration packages; illustrator's work for possible future assignments. Works on assignment only.
How to Contact/Illustrators: Ms/illustration packages: "Query first." Illustrations only: Send tearsheets. Reports on art samples only if interested. Original artwork returned at job's completion. Buys first rights.
Tips: "Study at least a year's issues to better understand type of material published."

MARION ZIMMER BRADLEY'S FANTASY MAGAZINE, Box 249, Berkeley CA 94701. (415)601-9000. Fiction Editor: Marion Bradley. Quarterly magazine. Estab. 1988. Circ. 2,000+. Publishes fantasy stories. "We are not a kiddie magazine but most of our work should not be unsuitable for bright children."
Fiction: Middle readers: fantasy. Young adults: contemporary, fantasy. Buys 50+ mss/year. Average word length: 500-5,000. Byline given. "No pen names—if a story isn't good enough to put real name on it, it's not good enough to print."
How To Contact/Writers: Send SASE for guidelines. Reports on mss in 2-3 weeks. Average length of time between acceptance of mss and publication of work is 4 months. "No simultaneous submissions. I know no one can afford to have stuff tied up so I try to report by return mail if I can't use it."
Illustration: "Must be professional illustrators. I'm occassionally willing to work with amateurs but I have limited time." Preferred theme/style: full page; double page spreads; 4 sided bleeds; ½, ⅓, ¼ page; illustration of the stories. No manuscript illustration packages.

How To Contact/Illustrators: Query. Include return address and phone number. Originals returned to artist at job's completion.
Terms: Pays on acceptance. Buys first North American serial rights. Pays 3-10¢/word for stories. Sample copies for $3.50. Writer's guidelines free on request.
Tips: "Our short-story section looks for good plot, likeable characters."

BUSINESSHIP, (formerly *THE WORLD OF BUSINE$$ KIDS*), America's Future, Lemonade Kids, Inc., Suite 330, 301 Almeria Ave., Coral Gables FL 33134. (305)445-8869. Articles Editor: Jacky Robinson. Art Director: Donn Matus. Quarterly newsletter. Estab. 1988. Circ. 75,000. "We cover stories about young entrepreneurs, how teens and preteens can become entrepreneurs, and useful information for effective business operation and management. Our goal is to help prepare America's youth for the complex and competitive world of business by sharing with them every possible business experience, the problems *and* the solutions. And while we're *serious* about business, we want them to know that business can be *fun*. 99% of material aimed at juvenile audience with one article aimed at parents in each issue."
Nonfiction: Middle readers: how-to, interview/profile, problem solving. Young adult/teens: how-to, interview/profile, problem solving. "All must relate to business;" does not want to see "any articles which do not deal with business." Buys 15 mss/year. "Our goal is 50% freelance." Average word length: 200-400. Byline: Listed as a contributing writer.
Poetry: Reviews free verse, light verse, traditional poetry; 25-50 lines.
How to Contact/Writers: Nonfiction: Send complete ms. Reports on mss in 2 months.
Terms: Pays on publication. Buys all rights. Pays 15¢ word/unsolicited articles; $35-50 for puzzles/games; $15-20 for cartoons; $5-10 for b&w/8×10 photos. Sample copies available. Writer's guidelines and sample copy available.
Tips: Looking for "any nonfiction pertaining to teens in the business world. How to choose, build, improve, market or advertise a business. When, and how, to hire (or fire) employees. Lots of profiles about successful young entrepreneurs. The latest in *any* field—entertainment, sports, medicine, etc.—where teens are making megabucks (or just movie money!). New products; book reviews on children and money; motivational articles; how-to invest/save money; news releases; tax information; stock market tips; bonds; banking; precious metals; cartoons; puzzles; poetry; games also sought."

*CAREER WORLD, Curriculum Innovations Group, 60 Revere Dr., Northbrook IL 60062. (708)205-3000. FAX: (708)564-8197. Articles Editor: Carole Rubenstein. Art Director: Kristi Simkins. Monthly (school year) magazine. Estab. 1972. A guide to careers, for students grades 7-12.
Nonfiction: Young adults: education, how-to, interview/profile, career information. Byline given. Sample copies for 9×12 SAE and 3 first class stamps.
How to Contact/Writers: Nonfiction: query with published clips.
Illustration: Buys 5-10 illustrations/year. Reviews ms/illustration packages; reviews artwork for future assignments; works on assignment only.
How to Contact/Illustrators: Submit photocopies, resumes.
Terms: Pays on publication. Buys all rights. Sample copies free for 9×12 SAE and 3 first class stamps. Writer's guidelines free, but only on assignment.

 The asterisk before a listing indicates the listing is new in this edition.

CAREERS, E.M. Guild, 1001 Avenue of the Americas, New York NY 10018. (212)354-8877. Editor-in-Chief: Mary Dalheim. Senior Editor: Don Rauf. Art Director: Roe LiBretto. Magazine published 4 times during school year (Sept., Nov., Jan., March). Circ. 600,000. This is a magazine for high school juniors and seniors, designed to prepare students for their futures.
Nonfiction: Young adults: how-to, humorous, interview/profile, problem solving. Buys 30-40 mss/year. Average word length: 1,000-1,250. Byline given.
How to Contact/Writers: Nonfiction: Query. Reports on queries/mss in 6 weeks. Will consider electronic submissions via disk or modem.
Illustration: Buys 10 illustrations/issue; buys 40 illustrations/year. Will review ms/illustration packages. Works on assignment "mostly."
How to Contact/Illustrators: Ms/illustration packages: Query first. Illustrations only: Send tearsheets, cards. Reports on art samples only if interested. Original artwork returned at job's completion.
Terms: Pays 90 days after publication. Buys first North American serial rights. Pays $250-300 assigned/unsolicited articles. Additional payment for ms/illustration packages "must be negotiated." Pays $500-1,000/color illustration; $300-700 b&w/color (inside) illustration. Sample copy $2 with SAE and $1 postage; writer's guidelines free with SAE and 1 first-class stamp.

CAT FANCY, The Magazine for Responsible Cat Owners, Fancy Publications, P.O. Box 6050, Mission Viejo CA 92690. (714)855-3045. Articles Editor: K.E. Segnar. Monthly magazine. Estab. 1965. Circ. 317,000. "Our magazine is for cat owners who want to know more about how to care for their pets in a responsible manner." 3% of material aimed at juvenile audience.
Fiction: Middle readers: animal (cat). Does not want to see stories in which cats talk. Buys 3-9 mss/year. Average word length: 750-1,000. Byline given.
Nonfiction: Middle readers: animal (cat). Buys 3-9 mss/year. Average word length: 450-1,000. Byline given.
Poetry: Reviews maximum of 64 short-line poems. "No more than 10 poems per submission please."
How To Contact/Writers: Fiction/nonfiction: Send complete ms—query is acceptable too. Reports on queries in 2 weeks; mss in 6 weeks. Average length of time between acceptance and publication of work: 4 months for juvenile material.
Illustration: Buys 3-6 illustrations/year. "Most of our illustrations are assigned or submitted with a story. We look for realistic images of cats done with pen and ink (no pencil)." Will review ms/illustration packages.
How To Contact/Illustrators: Query first or send complete ms with final art. "We only work with local artists on assignment. Ideally, the artist needs to reside in Orange County. Submit photocopies of work." Originals returned to artist at job's completion.
Terms: Pays on publication. Buys first rights and one-time rights. Pays $20-50/juvenile articles. Pays additional $45-75 for manuscript/illustration packages. $20-50/black and white (inside). Sample copies for $3.50. Writer's/artist's guidelines free for #10 SAE and 1 first class stamp.
Tips: "Our 'kids for cats' department is most open. Perhaps the most important tip I can give is: consider what 9 to 11 year olds want to know about cats and what they enjoy most about cats, and address that topic in a style appropriate for them. The entire magazine is open to freelance illustrators. We have a tremendous need for spot art."

*CHALLENGES, Curriculum Innovations Group, 60 Revere Dr., Northbrook IL 60062. (708)205-3000. FAX: (708)564-8197. Articles Editor: Carole Rubenstein. Art Director: Kristi SimKins. Monthly (school year) magazine. Estab. 1976. Includes consumer education, family matters, interpersonal skills, environment, multicultural issues—to help junior and senior high students prepare for the future.

Nonfiction: Young adult: education, how-to, problem-solving, money management, food/nutrition, clothing, family and interpersonal relations. Buys 60 mss/year.
How to Contact/Writers: Query with published clips.
Illustration: Buys 5-10 illustrations/year. Will review an illustrator's work for possible future assignments.
How to Contact/Illustrators: Submit slides, photocopies and resume.
Terms: Pays on publication. Buys all rights. Sample copies free for 9×12 SAE and 3 first class stamps. Writer's guidelines free, but only on assignment.

CHICKADEE, for Young Children from OWL, Young Naturalist Foundation, 56 The Esplanade, Ste. 306, Toronto Ontario M5E 1A7 Canada. (416)868-6001. Editor: Catherine Ripley. Art Director: Tim Davin. Magazine published 10 times/year. Estab. 1979. Circ: 130,000. *Chickadee* is a "hands-on" publication designed to interest 4-9 year olds in the world and environment around them.
Fiction: Picture material, young readers: animal, contemporary, folktales, history, humorous, problem-solving, sports, suspense/mystery/adventure. Does not want to see religious, anthropomorphic animal, romance material. Buys 8 mss/year. Average word length: 200-800. Byline given.
Nonfiction: Picture material, young readers: animal, arts/crafts, cooking, games/puzzles, how-to, humorous, interview/profile, nature/environment, travel. Does not want to see religious material. Buys 2-5 mss/year. Average word length: 20-200. Byline given.
Poetry: Maximum length: 50 lines. Limit submissions to 5 poems.
How to Contact/Writers: Fiction/nonfiction: Send complete ms. SAE and $1 money order for answer to query and return of ms. Report on queries/mss in 8 weeks. Will consider simultaneous submissions.
Illustration: Buys 3-5 illustrations/issue; buys 40 illustrations/year. Preferred theme or style: Gentle realism/humor (but not cartoons). Will review ms/illustration packages. Works on assignment only.
How to Contact/Illustrators: Ms/illustration packages: Story with sample of art. Illustrations only: Provide resume, business card, promotional literature or tearsheets to be kept on file. Reports on art samples only if interested.
Photography: Looking for animal (mammal, insect, reptile, fish, etc.) photos. Model/property releases required. Uses 35mm and 2¼×2¼ transparencies.
Write to request photo package for $1 money order, attention Robin Wilner, Photo Researcher.
Terms: Pays on acceptance. Buys all rights for mss and artwork. Buys one-time rights for photos. Pays $25-250 for assigned/unsolicited articles. Pays $500/color (cover) illustration; $50-500/b&w (inside); $100-650/color (inside). Photographers paid per photo (range: $50-450). Sample copy $4.50. Writer's guidelines free.
Tips: "Study the magazine carefully before submitting material. 'Read-to-me selection' most open to freelancers. Uses fiction stories. Kids should be main characters and should be treated with respect." (See listing for *Owl*.)

CHILD LIFE, Children's Better Health Institute, 1100 Waterway Blvd., Indianapolis IN 46202. (317)636-8881. Articles Fiction Editor: Steve Charles. Art Director: Janet Moir. Magazine published 8 times/year. Estab. 1923. Circ. 80,000. "Adventure, humor, fantasy and health-related stories with an imaginative twist are among those stories we seek. We try to open our readers' minds to their own creative potential, and we want our stories and articles to reflect and encourage this."
Fiction: Young readers: animal, contemporary, fantasy, health, history, humorous, problem-solving, science fiction, sports, suspense/mystery/adventure. Middle readers: fantasy, history, humorous, science fiction. Buys 30-35 mss/year. Average word length: 1,000. Byline given.

Close-up

Tim Davin
Art Director
Chickadee/Owl Magazines
Toronto, Canada

"I think children can read illustrations and photographs just as adults read text," says Tim Davin, art director for *Chickadee* and *Owl* magazines. Art is important as a welcome mat to reading, he says. "We use the art to tease the young reader into the text, and we are successful in that way."

Not only does Davin prefer work that creates "ripples of curiosity" about reading, but about the world, too. He includes a variety of media in each issue in order to teach there is more than one way to draw, and look at, the world around. That world includes all creatures great and small, says Davin. "In an environmental/discovery magazine, you can't be selective and only draw cute, fuzzy animals. You must appreciate the need to portray something generally considered unfriendly, like alligators or snakes, in an interesting way."

With a background in advertising and graphic design, Davin has worked in editorial positions for most of his career. His readership has ranged from general, to business-oriented, to children. To keep up, he insists, "You have to keep one thing in clear focus—your particular market." This means researching before submitting work in order to gain "understanding and appreciation for the publication you're sending to."

Children's publications require, more than others, strong visuals that can hold a child's attention for more than two seconds. "If you merely present a fleeting image, you have failed," Davin says. This advice holds true for visual work as well as marketing yourself, as he stresses the importance of presentation. "I weigh quite a bit of my decision in favor of the interview and promotional materials I receive. An artist should indicate he can handle himself professionally, that he is organized and clever."

The worst trap you can fall into is including too much in your portfolio, for Davin notes, "A lot of art people are not good editors. It's a very difficult thing to do, but you must constantly review your selections with a fresh eye. Ask yourself 'Is this a style I would be happy to recreate on an assignment?' The money cannot be your only satisfaction."

An illustration piques Davin's interest when "there is some kind of movement and story—something the visual is *saying*. Don't show me a cat standing there and looking at me," he explains. "Send me a cat leaping through the air! Give me a message that you're able to conceptualize and marry copy with your visuals."

Although many of the photos in *Chickadee* and *Owl* come from stock agencies, Davin suggests that a photographer with really good photos and an idea for an article should send them to an editor, along with a good pitch for the accompanying story. An editor, he says, has better knowledge of long-term needs of the magazine, and where such a piece might fit in. No matter what the medium, illustration or photography, art directors want to see personality through the items submitted. "I like to see a prominent direction, something the artist has developed on his own," says Davin.

A good way to be remembered after an interview is to send a clearly labeled color copy of a piece the art director liked, or something you feel is representative of your portfolio. "Then don't be discouraged," says Davin. "Send a follow-up letter in six months."

Appealing to kids is a challenge, says Davin. "We're competing now in this huge multimedia market. Kids are just blasted with videos and they have personal computers at home with wonderful graphics. You need a number of different hooks with children, and a sense of humor that speaks to the child is a good one. Never underestimate kids!"

—*Amy Tirk*

This is one of three illustrations by Marion Stuck for the story, "The Moon is Following Me," published by Chickadee. Art director Davin says this artwork "best represents the kind of illustration and quality that is appropriate for our market."

Nonfiction: Middle readers: animal, health, history, how-to, humorous, interview/profile, problem solving, travel. Average word length: 800. Byline given.

Poetry: Reviews poetry.

How to Contact/Writers: Fiction/nonfiction: Send complete ms. Reports on queries/mss in 8-10 weeks. Will consider simultaneous submissions.

Illustration: Buys 8-10 illustrations/issue; buys 65-80 illustrations/year. Preferred theme: "Need realistic styles especially." Will review an illustrator's work for possible future assignments. Works on assignment only.

How to Contact/Illustrators: Illustrations only: Send "résumé, tearsheets, photocopies and/or slides. Samples must be accompanied by SASE for response and/or return of samples." Reports on art samples in 4-6 weeks.

Terms: Editorial: Pays on publication; minimum 10¢/word; buys all rights. Pays $250/color cover; $30-70/b&w inside; $65-140 color inside. Writer's/illustrator's guidelines free with SAE and 1 first class stamp.

Tips: Illustrators: "Make sure you can draw children well and draw them accurately as far as age. Be able to illustrate a story situation. I assign poems, fiction stories and factual articles about health subjects and animals. I look for samples that portray a story, that involve children interacting with others in a variety of situations. Most of my assignments are for realistic styles, but I also use humorous, cartoony styles and unusual techniques like cut-paper, collage and woodcut."

CHILDREN'S DIGEST, Children's Better Health Institute, Box 567, Indianapolis IN 46206. (317)636-8881. Articles/Fiction Editor: Elizabeth Rinck. Art Director: Janet Moir. Magazine published 8 times/year. Estab. 1950. Circ. 125,000. For preteens; approximately 33% of content is health-related.

Fiction: Middle readers: animal, contemporary, fantasy, folktales, health, history, humorous, problem solving, science fiction, sports, suspense/mystery/adventure. Buys 25 mss/year. Average word length: 500-1,500. Byline given.

Nonfiction: Middle readers: animal, arts/crafts, biography, cooking, education, games/puzzles, health, history, how-to, humorous, interview/profile, nature/environment, problem solving, travel, sports. Buys 16-20 mss/year. Average word length: 500-1,200. Byline given.

Poetry: Maximum length: 20-25 lines.

How to Contact/Writers: Fiction/nonfiction: Send complete ms. Reports on mss in 10 weeks.

Illustration: Will review an illustrator's work for possible future assignments. Works on assignment only.

How to Contact/Illustrators: Ms/illustration packages: Query first. Illustrations only: Send résumé and/or slides or tearsheets to illustrate work; query with samples. Reports on art samples in 8-10 weeks.

Photography: Purchases photos with accompanying ms only. Model/property releases and photo captions required. Uses 35 mm transparencies.

Terms: Pays on acceptance for illustrators, publication for writers. Buys all rights for mss and artwork; one-time rights for photos. Pays 10¢/word for accepted articles. Pays $225/color (cover) illustration; $24-100/b&w (inside); $60-125/color (inside). Photographers paid per photo (range: $10-75). Sample copy 75¢. Writer's/illustrator's guidelines for SAE and 1 first-class stamp. (See listings for *Children's Playmate, Humpty Dumpty's Magazine, Turtle Magazine.*)

CHILDREN'S PLAYMATE, Children's Better Health Institute, Box 567, Indianapolis IN 46206. (317)636-8881. Articles/Fiction Editor: Elizabeth Rinck. Art Director: Steve Miller. Magazine published 8 times/year. Estab. 1929. Circ. 135,000. For children between 6 and 8 years; approximately 33% of content is health-related.

Fiction: Young readers: animal, contemporary, fantasy, folktales, history, humorous, science fiction, sports, suspense/mystery/adventure. Buys 25 mss/year. Average word length: 200-700. Byline given.
Nonfiction: Young readers: animal, arts/crafts, biography, cooking, games/puzzles, health, history, how-to, humorous, travel, sports. Buys 16-20 mss/year. Average word length: 200-700. Byline given.
Poetry: Maximum length: 20-25 lines.
How to Contact/Writers: Fiction/nonfiction: Send complete ms. Reports on mss in 8-10 weeks.
Illustration: Will review an illustrator's work for possible future assignments. Works on assignment only.
How to Contact/Illustrators: Ms/illustration packages: Query first. Illustrations only: Query with samples. Reports on art samples in 8-10 weeks.
Photography: Purchases photos with accompanying ms only. Model/property releases and photo captions required. Uses 35mm transparencies. Send completed ms with transparencies.
Terms: Pays on acceptance for illustrators, publication for writers. Buys all rights for mss and artwork; one-time rights for photos. Pays 10¢/word for assigned articles. Pays $225/color (cover) illustration; $25-100/b&w (inside); $60-125/color (inside). Photographers paid per photo (range: $10-75). Sample copy 75¢. Writer's/illustrator's guidelines for SAE and 1 first-class stamp. (See listings for *Children's Digest, Humpty Dumpty's Magazine, Turtle Magazine*.)

CHOICES, The Magazine for Personal Development and Practical Living Skills, Scholastic, Inc. 730 Broadway, New York NY 10003-9538. (212)505-3000. Editor: Laura Galen. Art Director: Joan Michaels. Monthly magazine. Estab. 1986 as *Choices* (formerly called *Coed*). "We go to teenagers in home economics and health classes. All our material has curriculum ties: Personal Development, Family Life, Careers, Food & Nutrition, Consumer Power, Child Development, Communications, Health."
Nonfiction: Buys 30 mss/year. Word length varies. Byline given (except for short items).
How to Contact/Writers: Nonfiction: Query with published clips "We don't want unsolicited manuscripts." Reports on queries in 2 weeks.
Illustration: Works on assignment only. "All art is *assigned* to go with specific articles." Pays on acceptance. Sample copy for 9 × 12 SAE and 2 first class stamps.
Tips: "*Read* the specific magazines. We receive unsolicited manuscripts and queries that do not in any way address the needs of our magazine. For example, we don't publish poetry, but we get unsolicited poetry in the mail."

CLUBHOUSE, Your Story Hour, Box 15, Berrien Springs MI 49103. (616)471-3701. Articles/Fiction Editor, Art Director: Elaine Trumbo. Bimonthly magazine. Estab. 1949. Circ. 10,000.
Fiction: Middle readers, young adults: animal, contemporary, health, history, humorous, problem solving, religious, sports. Does not want to see science fiction/fantasy/Halloween or Santa-oriented fiction. Buys 30 mss/year. Average word length: 800-1,300. Byline given.

"Picture books" are geared toward the preschool — 8 year old group; "Young readers" to 5-8 year olds; "Middle readers" to 9-11 year olds; and "Young adults" to those 12 and up.

Nonfiction: Middle readers, young adults: how-to. "We do not use articles except 200-500 word items about good health: anti—drug, tobacco, alcohol; pro—nutrition." Buys 6 mss/year. Average word length: 200-400. Byline given.
How to Contact/Writers: Fiction/nonfiction: Send complete ms. Reports on queries/mss in 6 weeks. Will consider simultaneous submissions.
Illustration: Buys 20-25 illustrations/issue; buys 120+ illustrations/year. Uses b&w artwork only. Will review an illustrator's work for possible future assignments. Works on assignment only.
How to Contact/Illustrators: Illustrations only: Send photocopies, tearsheets or prints of work which we can keep on file. Reports on art samples in 6 weeks. Originals usually not returned at job's completion, but they can be returned if desired.
Terms: Pays "about 6 months after" acceptance. Buys first and one-time rights for mss and artwork. Pays $25-35 for articles. "Writers and artists receive 2 copies free in addition to payment." Pays $30/b&w (cover) illustration; $7.50-25/b&w (inside). Sample copy for business SAE and 3 first-class stamps; writers/illustrator's guidelines free for business SAE and 1 first class stamp.
Tips: Writers: "Take children seriously—they're smarter than you think! Respect their sense of dignity, don't talk down to them and don't write stories about 'bad kids.' Illustrators: "Keep it clean, vigorous, fresh—whatever your style. Send samples we can keep on file. Black and white line art is best."

COBBLESTONE, The History Magazine for Young People, Cobblestone Publishing, Inc., 30 Grove St., Peterborough NH 03458. (603)924-7209. Articles/Fiction Editor-in-Chief: Carolyn P. Yoder. Art Director: Ann Turley. Monthly magazine. Circ. 40,000. "*Cobblestone* is theme-related. Writers should request editorial guidelines which explain procedure and list upcoming themes. Queries must relate to an upcoming theme. Fiction is not used often, although a good fiction piece offers welcome diversity. It is recommended that writers become familiar with the magazine (sample copies available)."
Fiction: Middle readers, young adults: history. Does not want to see pieces that do not relate to an upcoming theme. Buys 6-10 mss/year. Average word length: 750. Byline given.
Nonfiction: Middle readers, young adults: history, interview/profile, travel. Does not want to see material that does not relate to an upcoming theme. Buys 120 mss/year. Average word length: 300-1,000. Byline given.
How to Contact/Writers: Fiction/nonfiction: Query with published clips. Reports on queries in 5-6 months before publication; mss in 2 months before publication.
Illustration: Buys 3 illustrations/issue; buys 36 illustrations/year. Preferred theme or style: Material that is simple, clear and accurate but not too juvenile. Sophisticated sources are a must. Will review ms/illustration packages; reviews artwork for future assignments; works on assignment only.
How to Contact/Illustrators: Ms/illustration packages: Illustrations are done by assignment. Roughs required. Illustrations only: Send samples of black and white work. "Illustrators should consult issues of *Cobblestone* to familiarize themselves with our needs." Reports on art samples in 1-2 months. Original artwork returned at job's completion.
Terms: Pays on publication. Buys all rights. Pays 10-15¢ word for assigned articles. Pays $10-125/b&w (inside) illustration. Sample copy $3.95 with 7½×10½ SAE and 5 first-class stamps; writer's/illustrator's guidelines free with SAE and 1 first-class stamp.
Tips: Writers: "Submit detailed queries which show attention to historical accuracy and which offer interesting and entertaining information. Be true to your own style. Study past issues to know what we look for. All feature articles, recipes, activities, fiction and supplemental nonfiction are freelance contributions." Illustrators: "Submit black and white samples, not too juvenile. Study past issues to know what we look for. The illustra-

tion we use is generally for stories, recipes and activities." (See listing for *Faces, The Magazine About People*.)

COCHRAN'S CORNER, Cochran's Publishing Co., Box 2036, Waldorf MD 20604. (301)843-0485. Articles Editor: Ada Cochran. Fiction Editor/Art Director: Debby Thompkins. Quarterly magazine. Estab. 1986. Circ. 1,000. "Our magazine is open to most kinds of writing that is wholesome and suitable for young children to read. It is a 52-page, 8½ × 11 devoted to short stories, articles and poems. Our children's corner is reserved for children up to the age of 14. **Right now we are forced to limit our acceptance to subscribers only.**" 30% of material aimed at juvenile audience.
Fiction: Picture-oriented material: religious. Young readers: animal, fantasy, humorous, problem solving, religious. Middle readers: religious. Young adults: contemporary, history, religious, romance, science fiction. Does not want to see "anything that contains bad language or violence." Buys 150 mss/year. Average word length: 1,000 words maximum.
Nonfiction: Picture-oriented material: religious, travel. Young readers: animal, how-to, problem solving, religious, travel. Middle readers: religious, travel. Young adults: history, humorous, interview/profile, religious, travel. Does not want to see "editorials or politics." Buys 100 mss/year. Average word length: 150. Byline given.
Poetry: Reviews 20-line poetry on any subject.
How to Contact/Writers: Fiction/nonfiction: Send complete ms. Reports on mss in 3 months. Will consider simultaneous submissions.
Terms: Payment is one contributor's copy for now, but we hope as we grow to begin paying. Sample copy $5 with 9 × 11 SASE. Writer's guidelines free for SASE.
Tips: Must subscribe to be published in this market ($12/year, $20/2 years).

CRICKET MAGAZINE, Carus Corporation, P.O. Box 300, Peru IL 61354. (815)224-6656. Articles/Fiction Editor: Marianne Carus. Art Director: Ron McCutchan. Monthly magazine. Estab. 1973. Circ. 130,000. Children's literary magazine for ages 6-14.
Fiction: Picture-oriented material: animal, contemporary, fantasy, folk and fairy tales, history, humorous, problem solving, science fiction, sports, suspense/mystery/adventure. Young readers, middle readers and young adults: adventure, animal, contemporary, fantasy, folktales, history, humorous, science fiction, sports, suspense/mystery. Buys 180 mss/year. Average word length: 1,500. Byline given.
Nonfiction: Picture-oriented material: environment, history, how-to, interview/profile, natural science, problem solving, science, space, travel. Young readers, middle readers and young adults: animal, arts/crafts, biography, cooking, games/puzzles, history, how-to, humorous, nature/environment, sports. Buys 180 mss/year. Average word length: 1,000. Byline given.
Poetry: Reviews 1-page maximum length poems. Prefers 5 or less submissions.
How to Contact/Writers: Send complete ms. Do not query first. Reports on mss in 3 months. Will consider simultaneous submissions.
Illustration: Buys 35 (14 separate commissions)/issue; 425 illustrations/year. Preferred theme or style: "strong realism; strong people, especially kids; good action illustration; no cartoons. All media, but prefer other than pencil." Will review ms/illustration packages "but reserves option to re-illustrate." Will review an illustrator's work for possible future assignments.
How to Contact/Illustrators: Ms/illustrations packages: complete manuscript with sample and query. Illustrations only: provide tearsheets to be kept on file. Reports on art samples in 8 weeks. Original art work returned at job's completion.
Photography: Purchases photos with accompanying ms only. Model/property releases required. Uses b&w, glossy prints.
Terms: Pays on publication. Buys first North American and second serial rights. Buys one-time reproduction rights for artwork. Pays up to 25¢/word for unsolicited articles;

up to $3/line for poetry. Pays $500/color cover; $75-150/b&w inside. Writer's/illustrator's guidelines free with SAE and 1 first class stamp.

Tips: "Nonfiction, science, and historical articles and how-to's" most open to freelancers. Illustrators: "Edit your samples. Send only your best work or publisher's list and be able to reproduce that quality in assignments. Put name and address on *all* samples. Know a publication before you submit—does your work fit in?"

CRUSADER, Calvinist Cadet Corps, Box 7259, Grand Rapids MI 49510. (616)241-5616. Editor: G. Richard Broene. Art Director: Robert DeJonge. Magazine published 7 times/ year. Circ. 13,000. "Our magazine is for members of the Calvinist Cadet Corps—boys aged 9-14. Our purpose is to show how God is at work in their lives and in the world around them."

Fiction: Middle readers: contemporary, humorous, problem solving, religious, sports. Does not want to see fantasy, science fiction. Buys 12 mss/year. Average word length: 800-1,500.

Nonfiction: Middle readers: animal, how-to, humorous, interview/profile, problem solving, religious. Buys 6 mss/year. Average word length: 400-900.

How to Contact/Writers: Fiction/nonfiction: Send complete ms. Reports on queries in 1-3 weeks; mss in 1-5 weeks. Will consider simultaneous submissions.

Illustration: Buys 1 illustration/issue; buys 6 illustrations/year. Works on assignment only.

Terms: Pays on acceptance. Buys first rights; one-time rights; second serial (reprint rights). Pays 4-5¢/word for assigned articles; 2-5¢/word for unsolicited articles. Sample copy free with 9 × 12 SAE and 3 first-class stamps.

Tips: Publication is most open to fiction: write for a list of themes (available yearly in January).

CURRENT HEALTH I, The Beginning Guide to Health Education, 60 Revere Dr., Northbrook IL 60062-1563. (708)205-3000. Monthly (during school year Sept.-May) magazine. "For classroom use by students, this magazine is curriculum specific and requires experienced educators who can write clearly and well at fifth grade reading level."

Nonfiction: Middle readers: nature/environment, problem solving, health. Buys 60-70 mss/year. Average word length: 1,000. "Credit given in staff box."

How to Contact/Writers: Nonfiction: Query with published clips and résumé. Publishes ms 6-7 months after acceptance.

Terms: Pays on publication. Buys all rights. Pays $100-150 ("More for longer features"). Writer's guidelines available only if writer is given an assignment.

Tips: Need material about drug education, nutrition, fitness and exercise.

CURRENT HEALTH II, The Continuing Guide to Health Education, 60 Revere Dr., Northbrook IL 60062-1563. (708)205-3000. Monthly (during school year Sept.-May). "For classroom use by students, this magazine is curriculum specific and requires experienced educators who can write clearly and well at a ninth grade reading level."

Nonfiction: Young adults/teens: nature/environment, problem-solving, sports, health. Buys 70-90 mss/year. Average word length: 1,000-2,500. Byline given.

How to Contact/Writers: Nonfiction: Query with published clips and résumé. Reports on queries in 2 months. Publishes ms 6-7 months after acceptance.

Terms: Pays on publication. Buys all rights. Pays $100-150 for assigned articles, more for longer features. Writer's guidelines available only if writers are given an assignment.

Tips: Needs articles on drug education, nutrition, fitness and exercise.

DAY CARE AND EARLY EDUCATION, Human Sciences Press, 233 Spring St., New York NY 10013. (212)620-8000. Articles/Fiction Editor: Randa Nachbar. Art Director: Bill Jobson. Quarterly magazine. Circ. 2,500. Magazine uses material "involving children from birth to age 7." 5% of material aimed at juvenile audience.
Fiction: Picture material, young readers: contemporary, fantasy, humorous, problem solving. Average word length: 1,000-3,000. Byline given.
Nonfiction: Picture material, young readers: animal, how-to, humorous, problem solving. Average word length: 1,000-3,000. Byline given.
How to Contact/Writers: Fiction/nonfiction: Send complete ms. Reports on queries in 1 month; mss in 2-3 months.
Illustration: Will review ms/illustration packages.
How to Contact/Illustrators: Ms/illustration packages: Send complete ms with final art. Reports on art samples only if interested. Original artwork returned at job's completion.
Terms: Pays in 2 copies. Free sample copy; free writer's guidelines.

DISCOVERIES, Children's Ministries, 6401 The Paseo, Kansas City MO 64131. (816)333-7000. Editor: Latta Jo Knapp. Executive Editor: Mark York. Weekly tabloid. *Discoveries* is a leisure reading piece for third through sixth graders. It is published weekly by the Department of Children's Ministries of the Church of the Nazarene. "The major purposes of *Discoveries* are to: provide a leisure reading piece which will build Christian behavior and values; provide reinforcement for Biblical concepts taught in the Sunday School curriculum. The focus of the reinforcement will be life-related, with some historical appreciation. *Discoveries'* target audience is children ages 8-12 in grades three through six. The readability goal is fourth to fifth grade."
Fiction: "Fiction—stories should vividly portray definite Christian emphasis or character-building values, without being preachy. The setting, plot and action should be realistic." Average word length: 400-800. Byline given.
How to Contact/Writers: Fiction: Send complete ms. Reports on mss in 4-6 weeks.
Illustration: Preferred theme or style: Cartoon—humor should be directed to children and involve children. It should not simply be child-related from an adult viewpoint. Some full color story illustrations are assigned. Samples of art may be sent for review.
Terms: Pays on acceptance. Buys first rights; second serial (reprint rights). Pays 3.5¢/word (first rights). Contributor receives complimentary copy of publication. Writer's guidelines free with #10 SAE.
Tips: "*Discoveries* is committed to reinforcement of the Biblical concepts taught in the Sunday School curriculum. Because of this, the themes needed are mainly as follows: faith in God, obedience to God, putting God first, choosing to please God, accepting Jesus as Savior, finding God's will, choosing to do right, trusting God in hard times, prayer; trusting God to answer, Importance of Bible memorization, appreciation of Bible as God's Word to man, Christians working together, showing kindness to others, witnessing." (See listing for *Together Time*.)

*DISNEY ADVENTURES, The Walt Disney Company, 500 S. Buena Vista St., Burbank CA 91521. (818)567-5625. Articles Editor: Andrew Ragan. Fiction Editor: Suzanne Harper. Art Director: Melinda Jenkins. Photo Editor: Liz Smith. Monthly magazine. Estab. 1990. Circ. 350,000.

Always include a self-addressed stamped envelope (SASE) or International Reply Coupon (IRC) with submissions.

Fiction: Middle readers: adventure, contemporary, fantasy, humorous, science fiction, sports, suspense/mystery. Buys approx. 6-10 mss/year. Averge word length: 1,500-2,000. Byline given.

Nonfiction: Middle readers: animal, biography, games/puzzles, interview/profile, nature/environment and sports. Buys 100-150 mss/year. Average word length: 250-750. Byline given.

How to Contact/Writers: Fiction: Send complete manuscript. Nonfiction: Query with published clips. Reports in 1 month. Publishes ms 6-12 months after acceptance. Will consider simultaneous submissions and electronic submissions via disk or modem.

Illustration: Buys approx. 20 illustrations/issue; 250 illustrations/year. Reviews ms/illustration packages; reviews artwork for future assignments; works on assignment only.

How to Contact/Illustrators: Illustrations only: Provide resume, business card, promotional literature or tearsheets to be kept on file. Reports only if interested. Does not return original artwork.

Photography: Purchases photos separately. Model/property releases and captions required. Send "anything but originals—everything sent is kept on file." To contact, photographers should provide resume, business card, promotional literature or tearsheets to be kept on file. Reports only if interested.

Terms: Pays on acceptance. Buys all rights. Purchases all rights for artwork, various rights for photographs. Pays $250-750 for assigned articles. Pays illustrators $50 and up. Photographers paid $100 minimum per project, or $25 minimum per photo. Sample copies: "Buy on newsstand or order copies by calling 1-800-435-0715." Writer's guidelines for SASE.

DOLPHIN LOG, The Cousteau Society, 8440 Santa Monica Blvd., Los Angeles CA 90069. (213)656-4422. Articles Editor: Pamela Stacey. Bimonthly magazine for children ages 7-15. Circ. 110,000. Entirely nonfiction subject matter encompasses all areas of science, history and the arts which can be related to our global water system. The philosophy of the magazine is to delight, instruct and instill an environmental ethic and understanding of the interconnectedness of living organisms, including people. Of special interest are articles on ocean- or water-related themes which develop reading and comprehension skills.

Nonfiction: Picture material, middle readers: animal, environmental, ocean. Does not want to see talking animals. No dark or religious themes. Buys 15 mss/year. Average word length: 500-1,200. Byline given.

How to Contact/Writers: Do not send fiction. For nonfiction articles, query first. Reports on queries in 1 month; mss in 2 months.

Illustration: Buys 1 illustration/issue; buys 6 illustrations/year. Preferred theme or style: Biological illustration. Will review ms/illustration packages; illustrator's work for possible future assignments.

How to Contact/Illustrators: Ms/illustration packages: No original artwork, copies only. Illustrations only: Send tearsheets, slides. Reports on art samples in 8 weeks only if interested.

Terms: Pays on publication. Buys first North American serial rights; "translation rights." Pays $25-150 for assigned/unsolicited articles. Pays $25-150/b&w illustration; $25-200/color (inside). Sample copy $2 with 9 × 12 SAE and 2 first class stamps. Writer's/illustrator's guidelines free with #10 SAE and 1 first class stamp.

Tips: Writers: "Write simply and clearly and don't anthropomorphize." Illustrators: "Be scientifically accurate and don't anthropomorphize. Some background in biology is helpful, as our needs range from simple line drawings to scientific illustrations which must be researched for biological and technical accuracy."

DYNAMATH, Scholastic Inc., 730 Broadway, New York NY 10003. (212)505-3000. Fiction Editor: Jackie Glasthall. Monthly magazine. Estab. 1981. Circ. 356,000. Purpose is "to make learning math fun, challenging and uncomplicated for young minds in a very complex world."
Fiction/nonfiction: All levels: anything related to math and science topics. Byline given sometimes.
Poetry: Reviews poetry.
How To Contact/Writers: Fiction/nonfiction: Query with published clips, send manuscript. Reports on queries in 6 weeks. Average length of time between acceptance and publication of work: 4 months. Will consider simultaneous submissions and electronic submissions via disk or modem.
Illustration: Buys 4 illustrations/issue. Reviews ms/illustration packages.
How To Contact/Illustrators: Query first. Reports back in 2 months on submissions. Originals returned to artist at job's completion.
Terms: Pays on acceptance. Buys first North American serial rights.

EXPLORING, Boy Scouts of America, P.O. Box 152079, 1325 West Walnut Hill Ln., Irving TX 75015-2079. (214)580-2365. Executive Editor: Scott Daniels. Art Director: Joe Connally. Magazine published "4 times a year—not quarterly." *Exploring* is a 12 page, 4-color magazine published for members of the Boy Scouts of America's Exploring program. These members are young men and women between the ages of 14-21. Interests include careers, computers, camping, hiking, canoeing.
Nonfiction: Young adults: interview/profile, problem solving, travel. Buys 12 mss/year. Average word length: 600-1,200. Byline given.
How to Contact/Writers: Nonfiction: Query with published clips. Reports on queries/mss in 1 week.
Illustration: Buys 3 illustrations/issue; buys 12 illustrations/year. Will review an illustrator's work for possible future assignments. Works on assignment only.
How to Contact/Illustrators: Reports on art samples in 2 weeks. Original art work returned at job's completion.
Terms: Pays on acceptance. Buys first North American serial rights. Pays $300-500 for assigned/unsolicited articles. Pays $500-800/b&w (cover) illustration; $500/color (cover); $250-500/b&w (inside); $500-800/color (inside). Sample copy with 8½ × 11 SAE and 5 first-class stamps. Free writer's/illustrator's guidelines.
Tips: Looks for "short, crisp career profiles of 1,000 words with plenty of information to break out into graphics."

FACES, The Magazine About People, Cobblestone Publishing, Inc., 30 Grove St., Peterborough NH 03458. (603)924-7209. Articles/Fiction Editor-in-Chief: Carolyn P. Yoder. Art Director: Coni Porter. Magazine published 9 times/year (Sept.-May). Circ. 11,000. "Although *Faces* operates on a by-assignment basis, we welcome ideas/suggestions in outline form. All manuscripts are reviewed by the American Museum of Natural History in New York before being accepted. *Faces* is a theme-related magazine; writers should send for theme list before submitting ideas/queries."
Fiction: Middle readers, young adults: contemporary, history, religious, anthropology. Does not want to see material that does not relate to a specific upcoming theme. Buys 9 mss/year. Average word length: 750. Byline given.
Nonfiction: Middle readers, young adults: history, interview/profile, religious, travel, anthropology. Does not want to see material not related to a specific upcoming theme. Buys 63 mss/year. Average word length: 300-1,000. Byline given.
How to Contact/Writers: Fiction/nonfiction: Query with published clips. Reports on queries in 5-6 months before publication; mss 2 months before publication.
Illustration: Buys 3 illustrations/issue; buys 27 illustrations/year. Preferred theme or style: Material that is meticulously researched (most articles are written by professional

anthropologists); simple, direct style preferred, but not too juvenile. Will review ms/illustration packages. Works on assignment only.

How to Contact/Illustrators: Ms/illustration packages: Illustration is done by assignment. Roughs required. Illustrations only: Send samples of b&w work. Illustrators should consult issues of *Faces* to familiarize themselves with our needs. Reports on art samples in 1-2 months. Original artwork returned at job's completion.

Terms: Pays on publication. Buys all rights. Pays 10-15¢/word for assigned articles. Pays $10-125/b&w (inside) illustration. Sample copy $3.95 with 7½×10½ SAE and 5 first-class stamps. Writer's/illustrator's guidelines free with SAE and 1 first-class stamp.

Tips: "Writers are encouraged to study past issues of the magazine to become familiar with our style and content. Writers with anthropological and/or travel experience are particularly encouraged; *Faces* is about world cultures. All feature articles, recipes and activities are freelance contributions." Illustrators: "Submit black and white samples, not too juvenile. Study past issues to know what we look for. The illustration we use is generally for retold legends, recipes and activities." (See listing for *Cobblestone, the History Magazine for Young People*.)

*FAITH 'N STUFF, The Magazine For Kids, Guideposts Associates, Inc., 747 Third Ave., New York NY 10017. Articles Editor: Wally Metts. Fiction Editor: Lurlene McDaniel. Art Director: Mike Lyons. Photo Editor: Matt Russell. Bimonthly magazine. Estab. 1990. Circ. 85,000. "*Faith'n Stuff: The Magazine for Kids* is published bimonthly by Guideposts Associates, Inc. for kids 7-12 years old (emphasis on upper end of that age bracket). It is a Bible-based, direct mail magazine that is *fun* to read. It is *not* a Sunday school take-home paper or a miniature *Guideposts*."

*This **Faith 'n Stuff** cover is one of editor Mary Lou Carney's favorites. "These kids are having fun!" She says the cover went with the inside feature article on wheel danger as it pertains to bikes, four-wheelers and in-line skates. Though Carney claims the magazine is value-centered and Biblical-based she also says, "We are not your typical religious publication. We're bright and bold and looking for innovative kid-related ideas."*

© 1991 Guideposts Associates, Inc.

Fiction: Middle readers: adventure, animal, contemporary, fantasy, humorous, problem-solving, religious, science fiction, sports, suspense/mystery. Does not want to see preachy fiction. "We want real stories about real kids doing real things—conflicts our readers will respect; resolutions our readers will accept. Problematic. Tight. Filled with realistic dialogue and sharp imagery. No stories about 'good' children always making the right decision. If present at all, adults are minor characters and *do not* solve kids' problems for them." Buys approx. 10 mss/year. Average word length: 500-1,500. Byline given.

Nonfiction: Middle readers: animal, interview/profile. "Make nonfiction issue-oriented, controversial, thought-provoking. Something kids not only *need* to know, but *want* to know as well." Buys 10 mss/year. Average word length: 200-700. Bylines sometimes given.

How to Contact/Writers: Fiction: Send complete ms. Nonfiction: Query. Reports on queries in 6 weeks/ ms in 2 months.

Terms: Buys all rights for mss. "Features range in payment from $100-300; fiction from $75-200. We pay higher rates for stories exceptionally well-written or well-researched. Regular contributors get bigger bucks, too." Additional payment for ms/illustration packages "but we prefer to acquire our own illustrations." Sample copies are $3.25. Writer's guidelines free for SASE.

Tips: "Make your manuscript good, relevant and playful. No preachy stories about Bible-toting children. *Faith'n Stuff* is not a beginner's market. Study our magazine. (Sure, you've heard that before—but it's *necessary*!) Neatness *does* count. So do creativity and professionalism. SASE essential."

*FFA NEW HORIZONS, The Official Magazine of the National FFA Organization, National FFA Organization, 5632 Mt. Vernon Memorial Hwy., Alexandria VA 22309. (703)360-3600. FAX: (703)360-5524. Articles Editor: Andrew Markwart. Bimonthly magazine. Estab. 1952. Circ. 400,000. "*FFA New Horizons* strives to strengthen the aims and purposes of FFA by bringing to our readers living examples of how these are being fulfilled daily by individual FFA members."

Nonfiction: Young adults: animal, biography, careers, education, health, hobbies, how-to, humorous, interview/profile, nature/environment, problem-solving, sports. "All stories must be directed toward teens and have an FFA connection. Does not want to see stories that have no FFA connection at all." Average word length: 600-1,000.

How to Contact/Writers: Nonfiction: Query with published clips. Send complete ms. Reports on queries/mss in 1 month. Publishes ms 2-4 months after acceptance. Will consider simultaneous submissions and electronic submissions via disk or modem.

Illustration: Buys 6 illustrations/year. Reviews ms/illustration packages; reviews artwork for future assignments; works on assignment only.

How to Contact/Illustrators: Ms/illustration packages: Query. Illustrations only: Query with samples. Reports in 1 month. Original work not returned.

Photography: Looking for "photos that show the FFA member and that illustrate the story." Uses 5×7 color and b&w prints; 35mm transparencies. Reports in 1 month.

Terms: Pays on acceptance. Buys all rights for mss, artwork and photographs. Pay varies. Photographers paid per photo. Sample copies for 9×12 SAE and 5 first class stamps. Writer's/illustrator's/photo guidelines for SASE.

*FREE SPIRIT, News and Views On Growing Up, Free Spirit Publishing, 400 First Ave. N. #616, Minneapolis MN 55401. (612)338-2068. FAX: (612)337-5050. Articles Editor: Pamela Espeland. Bimonthly newsletter. Estab. 1986. Circ. 4,000. "Nonfiction newsletter for kids ages 9-15 on issues relevent to their lives: school, stress, self-esteem, family, friends, hobbies, personal goals, etc."

Nonfiction: Middle readers and young adults: careers, education, games/puzzles, health, hobbies, how-to, nature/environment, problem-solving, sports. No poetry. Noth-

ing religious/spiritual. Buys 12 mss/year. Average word length: 500-1,000. Byline given.
How to Contact/Writers: Nonfiction: Send complete ms. Reports on queries in 2 weeks/mss in 2 months. Publishes ms 4 months after acceptance.
Terms: Pays on publication. Buys all rights for mss. Pays $50 for unsolicited articles. Published writers get 5 copies of the issue their work appears in, *plus* $50. Sample copies for 9 × 12 SAE and 2 first class stamps.
Tips: "Before submitting your work to any publication, get a sample issue and submissions guidelines, if available. The style and format of an article can be as important as the content. Make sure the style of the article you submit is in keeping with the style of the articles they've published in the past."

THE FRIEND MAGAZINE, The Church of Jesus Christ of Latter-day Saints, 50 E. North Temple, Salt Lake City UT 84150. (801)240-2210. Managing Editor: Vivian Paulsen. Art Director: Richard Brown. Monthly magazine. Estab. 1971. Circ. 250,000. Magazine for 3-11 year olds.
Fiction: Picture material, young readers, middle readers: adventure, animal, contemporary, folktales, history, humorous, problem-solving, religious, ethnic, sports, suspense/mystery. Does not want to see controversial issues, political, horror, fantasy. Average word length: 400-1,000. Byline given.
Nonfiction: Picture material, young readers, middle readers: animal, arts/crafts, biography, cooking, games/puzzles, history, how-to, humorous, problem-solving, religious, sports. Does not want to see controversial issues, political, horror, fantasy. Buys 20 mss/year. Average word length: 400-1,000. Byline given.
Poetry: Reviews poetry. Maximum line length: 20. Maximum number of poems in a submission: 5.
How to Contact/Writers: Fiction/nonfiction: Send complete ms. Reports on mss in 2 months.
How to Contact/Illustrators: Illustrators only: Query with samples; arrange personal interview to show portfolio; provide résumé and tearsheets for files.
Terms: Pays on acceptance. Buys all rights for mss. Pays 9-11¢/word for unsolicited articles. Contributors are encouraged to send for free sample copy with 9 × 11 envelope and 85¢ postage. Free writer's guidelines.
Tips: "The *Friend* is published by The Church of Jesus Christ of Latter-day Saints for boys and girls up to twelve years of age. All submissions are carefully read by the *Friend* staff, and those not accepted are returned within two months when a self-addressed stamped envelope is enclosed. Submit seasonal material at least eight months in advance. Query letters and simultaneous submissions are not encouraged. Authors may request rights to have their work reprinted after their manuscript is published."

*THE GOLDFINCH, Iowa History for Young People, State Historical Society of Iowa, 402 Iowa Ave., Iowa City IA 52240. (319)354-3916. FAX: (319)335-3924. Editor: Deborah Gore. Quarterly magazine. Estab. 1980. Circ. 2,500. "The award-winning *Goldfinch* consists of 10 to 12 nonfiction articles, short fiction, poetry and activities per issue. Each

* *The asterisk before a listing indicates the listing is new in this edition.*

magazine focuses on an aspect or theme of history that occurred in or affected Iowa."

Fiction: Middle readers: adventure, animal, folktales, history. Fiction only on spec. Buys approx. 4 mss/year. Average word length: 500-1,500. Byline given.

Nonfiction: Middle readers: arts/crafts, biography, games/puzzles, history, how-to, interview/profile, travel. Uses 20-30 mss/year. Average word length: 500-1,500. Byline given.

Poetry: Reviews poetry. No minimum or maximum word length; no maximum number of submissions.

How to Contact/Writers: Fiction/nonfiction: Query with published clips. Reports on queries/mss in 2-4 weeks. Publishes ms 1 month-1 year after acceptance. Will consider electronic submissions via disk or modem.

Illustration: Buys 4 illustrations/issue; 20 illustrations/year. Uses b&w artwork only. Prefers cartoon, line drawing. Reviews ms/illustration packages; reviews artwork for future assignments; works on assignment only.

How to Contact/Illustrators: Ms/illustration packages: Query. Illustrations only: Query with samples. Reports in 2-4 weeks. Original work returned upon job's completion.

Photography: Types of photos used vary with subject. Model/property releases required with submissions. Uses b&w prints; 35mm transparencies. Query with samples. Reports in 2-4 weeks.

Terms: Pays on acceptance (artwork only). Buys all rights. Payment for manuscripts is in copies at this time. Pays illustrators $10-150. Photographers paid per photo (range: $10-100). Sample copies are $3. Writer's/illustrator's/photo guidelines free for SASE.

Tips: "The editor researches the topic and determines the articles. Writers, most of whom live in Iowa, work from primary and secondary research materials to write pieces. The presentation is aimed at children 8-14 and the writing of E.B. White is a model for the prose."

GUIDE MAGAZINE, Review and Herald Publishing Association, 55 West Oak Ridge Dr., Hagerstown MD 21740. (301)791-7000. Articles Editor: Jeannette Johnson. Art Director: Bill Kirstein. Weekly magazine. Estab. 1953. Circ. 42,000. "Ours is a weekly Christian journal written for 10- to 14-year-olds, presenting true stories relevant to the needs of today's young person, emphasizing positive aspects of Christian living."

Fiction: Young adults: Animal, contemporary, history, humorous, problem solving, religious, character-building. "We like 'true-to-life,' that is, based on true happenings."

Nonfiction: Young adults: animal, history, how-to, humorous, interview/profile, problem solving, religious, character-building. Does not want to see violence, hunting nonfiction. Buys 300+ mss/year. Average word length: 500-600 minimum, 1,200-1,500 maximum. Byline given.

How to Contact/Writers: Nonfiction: Send complete ms. Reports in 1-2 weeks. Will consider simultaneous and electronic submissions via disk or modem. "We can only pay half of the regular amount for simultaneous submissions."

Illustration: Buys 4-6 illustrations/issue; buys 350+ illustrations/year. Works on assignment only.

How to Contact/Illustrators: Ms/illustration packages: "art is by assignment only. Glad to look at portfolios." Artists interested in illustrations only: "Send tearsheets and slides." Original artwork returned at job's completion.

Terms: Pays on acceptance. Buys first North American serial rights; first rights; one-time rights; second serial (reprint rights) simultaneous rights. Pays 4¢/word/assigned articles; 3-4¢/word/unsolicited articles. "Writer receives several complimentary copies of issue in which work appears." Pays $150-250/b&w (cover) illustration; $175-300/color (cover); $125-175/b&w (inside); 150-175/color (inside). Sample copy free with 5 × 9 SAE and 2 first-class stamps; writer's/illustrator's guidelines for SASE.

HICALL, Gospel Publishing House, 1445 Boonville Ave., Springfield MO 65802-1894. (417)862-2781, ext. 4349. Articles/Fiction Editor: Deanna Harris. Art Director: Jeff Jansen. Quarterly newsletter (Sunday school take-home paper). Estab. 1920. Circ. 80,000. "Slant articles toward the 15- to 17-year-old teen. We are a Christian publication, so all articles should focus on the Christian's responses to life. Fiction should be realistic, not syrupy nor too graphic. Fiction should have a Christian slant also."
Fiction: Young adults: adventure, contemporary, fantasy, history, humorous, problem-solving, religious, romance, sports. Also wants fiction based on true stories. Buys 100 mss/year. Average word length 1,000-1,500. Byline given.
Nonfiction: Young adults: animal, biography, careers, education, games/puzzles, health, history, hobbies, how-to, humorous, nature/environment, problem solving, religious, sports. Buys 25 mss/year. Average word length: 1,000. Byline given.
Poetry: Reviews 20-line poetry. Limit submissions to 5 poems.
How to Contact/Writers: Fiction/nonfiction: Send complete ms. Do *not* send query letters. Reports on mss in 4-6 weeks. Will consider simultaneous submissions.
Illustration: Buys 10-30 illustrations/year. Uses color artwork only. "Freelance art used only when in-house art department has a work overload." Prefers to review "realistic, cartoon, youth-oriented styles." Will review an illustrator's work for possible future assignments. Works on assignment only. "Any art sent will be referred to the art department. Art department will assign freelance art."
How to Contact/Illustrators: Illustrations only: Query with samples; send "tearsheets, slides, photos. Résumé helpful." Reports in 4-6 weeks.
Photography: "Teen photo that look spontaneous. Professional and urban photos urgently needed." Uses color prints, 35mm, 2¼ × 2¼, 4 × 5 transparencies. To contact, send unsolicited photos by mail.
Terms: Pays on acceptance. For mss, buys first North American serial rights, first rights, one-time rights, second serial (reprint rights), simultaneous rights. For artwork, buys one-time rights for cartoons, all rights for assigned illustrations; one-time rights for photos. Pays 4¢/word/assigned articles; 2-3¢/word/unsolicited articles. Pays $35/b&w cover photo; $50/color cover photo; $25/b&w inside photo; $35/color inside photo. Sample copy free with 6 × 9 SASE. Writer's guidelines free with SASE.

HIGH ADVENTURE, Assemblies of God, 1445 Boonville Ave., Springfield MO 65802. (417)862-2781, Ext. 4181. FAX: (417)862-8558. Editor: Marshall Bruner. Quarterly magazine. Circ. 86,000. Estab. 1971. Magazine is designed to provide boys with worthwhile, enjoyable, leisure reading; to challenge them in narrative form to higher ideals and greater spiritual dedication; and to perpetuate the spirit of Royal Rangers through stories, ideas and illustrations. 75% of material aimed at juvenile audience.
Fiction: Buys 100 mss/year. Average word length: 1,000. Byline given.
Nonfiction: Articles: Christian living, devotional, Holy Spirit, salvation, self-help; biography; missionary stories; news items; testimonies.
How to Contact/Writers: Fiction/nonfiction: Send complete ms. Include Social Security number with submission. Reports on queries in 6-8 weeks. Will consider simultaneous submissions. Will review ms/illustration packages.
How to Contact/Illustrators: Ms/illustration packages: Send complete ms with final art. Illustrations only: "Most of our artwork is done in-house."
Terms: Pays on acceptance. Buys first rights. Pays 2-3¢/word for unsolicited articles. Sample copy free with 8½ × 11 SASE. Free writer's/illustrator's guidelines.

Refer to the Business of Children's Writing & Illustrating for up-to-date marketing, tax and legal information.

HIGHLIGHTS FOR CHILDREN, 803 Church St., Honesdale PA 18431. (717)253-1080. Manuscript Coordinator: Beth Troop. Art Director: Rosanne Guararra. Monthly (July-August issue combined) magazine. Estab. 1946. Circ. 2.8 million. Our motto is "Fun With a Purpose." We are looking for quality fiction and nonfiction that appeals to children, encourages them to read, and reinforces positive values. All art is done on assignment.

Fiction: Picture-oriented material: animal, contemporary, fantasy, history, humorous, problem solving. Young readers, middle readers: animal, contemporary, fantasy, history, humorous, problem solving, science fiction, sports, mystery/adventure. Does not want to see: war, crime, violence. Buys 150+ mss/year. Average word length: 400-800. Byline given.

Nonfiction: Picture-oriented material: animal, history, how-to, humorous, problem solving. Young readers, middle readers: animal, history, how-to, humorous, interview/profile, problem solving, foreign, science, nature, arts, sports. Does not want to see: trendy topics, fads, personalities who would not be good role models for children, guns, war, crime, violence. Buys 75+ mss/year. Maximum word length: 900. Byline given.

How to Contact/Writers: Send complete ms. Reports on queries in 4 weeks; mss in 4 weeks.

Illustration: Preferred theme or style: Realistic, some stylization, cartoon style acceptable. Works on assignment only.

How to Contact/Illustrators: Ms/illustration packages: Art is done on assignment only. Illustrations only: Photocopies, tearsheets, or slides. Résumé optional. Reports on art samples in 4 weeks.

Terms: Pays on acceptance. Buys all rights. Pays 14¢/word and up for unsolicited articles. "Illustration fees vary on size of job. Median range: $350-600. Pays more for covers." Writer's/illustrator's guidelines free on request.

Tips: Writers: "Analyze several issues of the magazines you want to write for. Send for writer's guidelines." Illustrators: "Fresh, imaginative work presented in a professional portfolio encouraged. Flexibility in working relationships a plus. Illustrators presenting their work need not confine themselves to just children's illustrations as long as work can translate to our needs. We also use animal illustrations, real and imaginary. We need party plans, crafts and puzzles—any activity that will stimulate children mentally and creatively. We are always looking for imaginative cover subjects."

HOBSON'S CHOICE, (formerly *Starwind*), Box 98, Ripley OH 45167. (513)392-4549. Editor: David F. Powell. Monthly magazine. Estab. 1974. Circ. 2,000. "*Hobson's Choice* is a science fiction magazine which also publishes science and technology-related nonfiction along with the stories. Although the magazine is not specifically aimed at children, we do number teenagers among our readers. Such readers are the type who might enjoy reading science fiction (both young adult and adult), attending science fiction conventions, using computers, and be interested in such things as astronomy, the space program, etc."

Fiction: Young adults: fantasy, folktales, science fiction. Buys 12-15 mss/year. Average word length 2,000-10,000.

Nonfiction: Young adults: biography, careers, education, games/puzzles, how-to (science), interview/profile, travel, informational science book review. Does not want to see crafts. Buys 8-10 mss/year. Average word length: 1,500-5,000. Byline given.

How to Contact/Writers: Fiction: Send complete ms. Nonfiction: query first. Reports on queries/mss in 2-3 months. Will consider submissions via disk (Macintosh MacWrite, WriteNow, IBM PC or compatible on 3½ disks.

Illustration: Buys 2-5 illustrations/issue; buys 20-30 illustrations/year. Uses b&w artwork only. Prefers to review "science fiction, fantasy or technical illustration." Will review ms/illustration packages.

How to Contact/Illustrators: Ms/illustration packages: "Would like to see clips to keep on file (b&w only, preferably photocopies)." Illustrations only: Provide tearsheets to be kept on file. "If we have an assignment for an artist, we will contact him/her with the ms we want illustrated. We like to see roughs before giving the go-ahead for final artwork." Reports in 2-3 months. Original artwork returned at job's completion, "sometimes, if requested. We prefer to retain originals, but a high-quality PMT or Velox is fine if artist wants to keep artwork."

Photography: Purchases photos with accompanying ms only. Uses b&w prints.

Terms: Pays 50% on acceptance (for art), 50% on publication. Pays 25% on acceptance (for writing), 75% on publication. Buys first North American serial rights; second serial (reprint rights). Buys first rights for artwork and photographs. Pays $5-100/article. Payment for illustrations: Pays $30-50/b&w cover; $10-25/b&w inside. Sample copy $1.75; writer's/illustrator's guidelines free with business-size SAE and 1 first class stamp. "Specify fiction or nonfiction guidelines, or both." Tip sheet package for $1 and business-size envelope with 2 first class stamps (includes all guidelines and tips on writing science fiction and science nonfiction).

Tips: Writers: "Read lots of children's writing in general, especially specific genre if you're writing a genre story. (SF, romance, mystery, etc.). We list upcoming needs in our guidelines; writers can study these to get an idea of what we're looking for." Illustrators: "Study illustrations in back issues of magazines you're interested in illustrating for, and be able to work in a genre style if that's the type of magazine you want to publish your work. Everything is open to freelancers, as almost all our artwork is done out-of-house. (We occasionally use public domain illustrations, copyright-free illustrations and photographs.)"

THE HOME ALTAR, Meditations for Families with Children, Augsburg Fortress, 426 S. Fifth St., Box 1209, Minneapolis MN 55440. Articles/Fiction Editor: M. Elaine Dunham, Box 590179, San Francisco CA 94159-0179. Quarterly magazine. Circ. approx. 70,000. This is a booklet of daily devotions, used primarily by Lutheran families. Each day's reading focuses on a specific Bible passage. 98% of material aimed at juvenile audience.

Fiction: Young readers, middle readers: contemporary, folktales, problem-solving, religious. Buys 365 mss/year. Average word length: 125-170. Byline given.

Nonfiction: Young readers, middle readers: interview/profile, problem solving, religious. Average word length: 125-170. Byline given.

How to Contact/Writers: Fiction/nonfiction: Query with published clips.

Illustration: Buys 100 illustrations/year. Works on assignment only.

How to Contact/Illustrators: Reports on art samples only if interested.

Terms: Pays on acceptance. Buys all rights. Pays $10 for assigned articles. Free writer's guidelines for 6×9 SAE and 98¢ postage.

HOPSCOTCH, The Magazine for Girls, Hopscotch, Inc., Box 1292, Saratoga Springs NY 12866. (518)587-2268. Articles/Fiction/Art Director: Donald P. Evans. Bimonthly magazine. Estab. 1989. Circ. 7,000. For girls from 6 to 12 years, featuring traditional subjects—pets, games, hobbies, nature, science, sports etc.—with an emphasis on articles that show girls actively involved in unusual and/or worthwhile activities."

Fiction: Young readers and middle readers: animal, contemporary, fantasy, folktales, health, history, humorous, problem solving, science fiction, sports, suspense/mystery/adventure. Does not want to see stories dealing with dating, sex, fashion, hard rock music. Buys 24 mss/year. Average word length: 300-1,100. Byline given.

Nonfiction: Young readers and middle readers: animal, arts/crafts, biography, careers, cooking, education, games/puzzles, health, history, hobbies, how-to, humorous, interview/profile, nature/environment, problem solving, travel, sports. Does not want to see pieces dealing with dating, sex, fashion, hard rock music. Buys 36 mss/year. Average word length: 400-1,100. Byline given.

Poetry: Reviews traditional, wholesome, humorous poems. Maximum word length: 400; maximum line length: 40. Will accept 6 submissions/author.

How to Contact/Writers: Fiction: Send complete ms. Nonfiction: Query, send complete ms. Reports on queries/mss in 2 weeks. Publishes ms 6 months after acceptance. Will consider simultaneous submissions.

Illustration: Buys 4-8 illustrations/issue; buys 24-48 illustrations/year. "Generally, the illustrations are assigned after we have purchased a piece (usually fiction). Occasionally, we will use a painting—in any given medium—for the cover, and these are usually seasonal." Uses b&w artwork only for inside; color for cover. Will review all varieties of ms/illustration packages.

How to Contact/Illustrators: Query first or send complete ms with final art. Illustrations only: Query with samples. Reports on art samples in 2 weeks. Original artwork returned at job's completion.

Photography: Purchases photos separately (cover only) and with accompanying ms only. Looking for photos to accompany article. Model/property releases required. Uses 5×7, b&w prints; 35mm transparencies.

Terms: Pays on acceptance. For mss, artwork and photos, buys first North American serial rights; second serial (reprint rights). Pays $40-100 for assigned articles; $30-80 for unsolicited articles. "We always send a copy of the issue to the writer or illustrator." Text and art are treated separately. Pays $150-200/color cover; $25-50/b&w inside. Photographers paid per photo (range: $10-20; $150 for color cover photo). Sample copy for $3 and 9×12 SASE. Writer's/illustrator's guidelines free for #10 SASE.

Tips: "Please look at our guidelines and our magazine . . . and remember, we use far more nonfiction than fiction. Most welcome is the article that has a girl or girls directly involved in an interesting and/or worthwhile activity. If decent photos accompany the piece, it stands an even better chance of being accepted. We believe it is the responsibility of the contributor to come up with photos. Please remember, our readers are 6-12 years—most are 7-10—and your text should reflect that."

HUMPTY DUMPTY'S MAGAZINE, Children's Better Health Institute (div. Benjamin Franklin Literary & Medical Soc.), 1100 Waterway Blvd., Box 567, Indianapolis IN 46206. (317)636-8881. Editor: Christine French Clark. Art Director: Larry Simmons. Magazine published 8 times/year—Jan/Feb; Mar; April/May; June; July/Aug; Sept; Oct/Nov; Dec. *HDM* is edited for kindergarten children, approximately ages 4-6. It includes fiction (easy-to-reads; read alouds; rhyming stories; rebus stories), nonfiction articles (some with photo illustrations), poems, crafts, recipes and puzzles. Much of the content encourages development of better health habits. We especially need material promoting fitness. "All but 2 pages aimed at the juvenile market. The remainder may be seasonal and/or more general."

Fiction: Picture-oriented material: animal, contemporary, fantasy, humorous, sports, health-related. Young readers: animal, contemporary, fantasy, humorous, science fiction, sports, suspense/mystery/adventure, health-related. Does not want to see bunny-rabbits-with-carrot-pies stories! Also, talking inanimate objects are very difficult to do well. Beginners (and maybe everyone) should avoid these. Buys 35-50 mss/year. Maximum word length: 700. Byline given.

Nonfiction: Picture-oriented material, young readers: animal, how-to, humorous, interview/profile, health-related. Does not want to see long, boring, encyclopedia rehashes. "We're open to almost any subject (although most of our nonfiction has a health angle), but it must be presented creatively. Don't just string together some facts." Looks for a fresh approach. Buys 6-10 mss/year. Prefers very short nonfiction pieces—500 words maximum. Byline given.

How to Contact/Writers: Send complete ms. Nonfiction: Send complete ms with bibliography if applicable. "No queries, please!" Reports on mss in 8-10 weeks.
Illustration: Buys 13-16 illustrations/issue; buys 90-120 illustrations/year. Preferred theme or style: Realistic or cartoon. Will review ms/illustration packages. Works on assignment only.
How to Contact/Illustrators: Ms/illustration packages: Send slides, printed pieces or photocopies. Illustrations only: Send slides, printed pieces or photocopies. Reports on art samples only if interested.
Terms: Writers: Pays on publication. Artists: Pays within 6-8 weeks. Buys all rights. "One-time book rights may be returned if author can provide name of interested book publisher and tentative date of publication." Pays about 10¢/word for unsolicited stories/articles; payment varies for poems and activities. Up to 10 complimentary issues are provided to author with check. Pays $250/color cover illustration; $30-70 per page b&w (inside); $55-110/2-color (inside); $65-140/color (inside). Sample copy for 75¢. Writer's/illustrator's guidelines free with SASE.
Tips: Writers: "Study current issues and guidelines. Observe, especially, word lengths and adhere to requirements. It's sometimes easier to break in with recipe or craft ideas, but submit what you do best. Don't send your first, second, or even third drafts. Polish your piece until it's as perfect as you can make it." Illustrators: "Please study the magazine before contacting us. Your art must have appeal to three- to seven-year-olds." (See listings for *Children's Digest, Children's Playmate, Turtle Magazine.*)

*INSTRUCTOR MAGAZINE, Scholastic, Inc., 730 Broadway, New York NY 10003. (212)505-4927. FAX: (212)260-8595. Art Director: Drew Hires. Magazine published 9 times/year. Estab. 1891. Circ. 300,000. "*Instructor*'s primary audience is teachers grades K-8. Features and regular columns offer practical and professional information for educators."
Nonfiction: Young readers and middle readers: animal, arts/crafts, biography, careers, cooking, education, fashion, games/puzzles, health, history, hobbies, how-to, humorous, interview/profiles, nature/environment, problem-solving, religion, travel, sports. Buys fewer than 10 mss/year. Written for kids. Byline sometimes given.
Poetry: Reviews poetry.
How to Contact/Writers: Fiction/nonfiction: Send complete ms. Reports in 4-6 weeks. Publishes ms 3 months to 1 year after acceptance. Will consider electronic submissions via disk or modem.
Illustrations: Buys 19 illustrations/issue. Uses color artwork only. Prefers friendly/modern illustrations. Reviews artwork for future assignments; works on assignment only.
How to Contact/Illustrators: Ms/illustration packages: Query. Illustration only: Query with samples. Reports back only if interested. Original work returned upon job's completion (if requested).
Photography: Looking for photos on education. Model/property releases required; photo captions "helpful." To contact, query with samples. Reports back only if interested.
Terms: Pays on publication. Buys one-time rights for mss. Pays $20 and for assigned articles. "Published authors receive a complementary copy." Writer's guidelines for SASE.
Tips: "We're not a children's magazine."

INTERNATIONAL GYMNAST, Sundbysports, Inc., 225 Brooks, Box 2450, Oceanside CA 92054. (619)722-0030. Editor: Dwight Normile. Monthly publication. "We are a magazine about gymnasts for ages 9 and up."
Fiction: Young adults: problem solving and sports stories for gymnasts.
Nonfiction: Young adults: biography, health, interview/profile, sports. Gymnastics material only.

How to Contact/Writers: Query with published clips. Will consider simultaneous submissions (please advise).
Illustration: Will review ms/illustration packages. Uses b&w artwork only, but "very rarely." Usually prefers cartoons—8½×11 camera ready.
How to Contact/Illustrators: Ms/illustration packages: query first. Illustrations only: send slides or prints.
Photography: Looking for clear action/personality photos. Photo captions required. Uses 5×7 or 8×10, b&w, glossy prints; 35mm transparencies. To contact, send unsolicited photos by mail.
Terms: Pays on publication by arrangement. Buys one-time rights for mss, artwork and photos. Pays $15-25 for articles. Pays illustrators per b&w inside photo (range: $10-15). Photographers paid per photo (range: $5-50).
Tips: "For us, gymnastics knowledge is necessary. Standard kidstuff with tenuous gym orientation doesn't cut it."

JACK AND JILL, Children's Better Health Institute, 1100 Waterway Blvd., Indianapolis IN 46206. (317)636-8881. Articles, Fiction Editor: Steve Charles. Art Director: Ed Cortese. Magazine published 8 times/year. Estab. 1938. Circ. 360,000. "Write entertaining and imaginative stories *for* kids, not just *about* them. Writers should understand what is funny to kids, what's important to them, what excites them. Don't write from an adult "kids are so cute" perspective. We're also looking for health and healthy lifestyle stories and articles, but don't be preachy."
Fiction: Young readers: animal, contemporary, fantasy, history, humorous, problem solving. Middle readers: contemporary, humorous. Buys 30-35 mss/year. Average word length: 900. Byline given.
Nonfiction: Young readers: animal, history, how-to, humorous, interview/profile, problem solving, travel. Buys 8-10 mss/year. Average word length: 1,000. Byline given.
Poetry: Reviews poetry.
How to Contact/Writers: Fiction/nonfiction: Send complete ms. Reports on queries in 2 weeks; mss in 8-10 weeks. Will consider simultaneous submissions.
Terms: Pays on publication; minimum 10¢/word. Buys all rights.

JUNIOR TRAILS, Gospel Publishing House, 1445 Boonville Ave., Springfield MO 65802. (417)862-2781. Articles/Fiction Editor: Sinda S. Zinn. Quarterly magazine. Circ. 70,000. Junior Trails is an 8-page take-home paper for fifth and sixth graders. Its articles consist of fiction stories of a contemporary or historical nature. The stories have a moral slant to show how modern-day people can work out problems in acceptable ways, or give examples in history from which we can learn.
Fiction: Middle readers: contemporary, history, humorous, problem solving, religious, adventure. Does not want to see science fiction, mythology, ghosts and witchcraft. Buys 100 mss/year. Average word length: 800-1,500. Byline given.
Nonfiction: Middle readers: animal, arts/crafts, biography, history, humorous, nature/environment, problem solving, religious, travel. Buys 30 mss/year. Average word length: 300-800. Byline given.
Poetry: Wants to see poetry with a religious emphasis.
How to Contact/Writers: Fiction/nonfiction: Send complete ms. Reports on queries in 2 weeks; mss in 4-6 weeks. Will consider simultaneous submissions.
Illustration: Uses color artwork only. Reviews artwork for future assignments.
How to Contact/Illustrators: Illustrations only: provide résumé, business card, promotional literature or tearsheets to be kept on file; or arrange personal interview to show portfolio.
Photography: Uses 2¼×2¼ transparencies. To contact, photographers should query with samples; provide résumé, business card, promotional literature or tearsheets to be kept on file.

Terms: Pays on acceptance. For mss, buys first rights; one-time rights; second serial (reprint rights); first North American serial rights. Buys all rights to artwork; one-time rights to photographs. Pays 2-3¢/word for unsolicited articles. Photographers paid per photo (range: $25-60). Sample copy free with 9 × 12 SASE.
Tips: "Avoid trite, overused plots and themes. Make children be children—not babies or super, adult-like people. Let your characters weave the story. Don't fill up space with unnecessary details. We are always in need of good fiction stories." Looks for: "fiction that presents believable characters working out their problems according to Bible principles. Present Christianity in action without being preachy; articles with reader appeal, emphasizing some phase of Christian living, presented in a down-to-earth manner; biography or missionary material using fiction technique; historical, scientific or nature material with a spiritual lesson; fillers that are brief, purposeful, usually containing an anecdote, and always with a strong evangelical emphasis."

KEYNOTER, Key Club International, 3636 Woodview Trace, Indianapolis IN 46268. (317)875-8755. Articles Editor: Tamara P. Burley. Art Director: James Patterson. Monthly magazine. Estab. 1915. Circ. 133,000. "As the official magazine of the world's largest high school service organization, we publish nonfiction articles that interest teenagers and help our readers become better students, citizens and leaders."
Nonfiction: Young adults: how-to, humorous, problem solving. Does not want to see first-person accounts; short stories. Buys 15 mss/year. Average word length: 1,800-2,500. Byline given.
How to Contact/Writers: Nonfiction: Query. Reports on queries/mss in 1 month. Will consider simultaneous submissions.
Illustration: Buys 2-3 illustrations/issue; buys 15 illustrations/year. Will review ms/illustration packages. Works on assignment only.
How to Contact/Illustrators: Ms/illustration packages: "Because of our publishing schedule, we prefer to work with illustrators/photographers within Indianapolis market." Reports on art samples only if interested. Original artwork returned at job's completion if requested.
Terms: Pays on acceptance. Buys first North American serial rights. Pays $75-300 for assigned/unsolicited articles. Sample copy free with 8½ × 11 SAE and 65¢ postage. Writer's guidelines free with SAE and 1 first-class stamp.
Tips: "We are looking for light or humorous nonfiction, self help articles." Also looking for articles about education reform, national concerns, trends, teen trends in music, fashion, clothes, ideologies, etc.

KID CITY, Children's Television Workshop, 1 Lincoln Plaza, New York NY 10023. (212)595-3456. Articles editor: Maureen Hunter-Bone; Fiction editor: Lisa Rao; Art director: Michele Weisman. Monthly magazine. Estab. 1971. Circ. 330,000+.
Fiction: Middle readers: animal, contemporary, history, humorous, science fiction, sports, spy/mystery/adventure. Does not want to see "cutesy, overly moralistic, preachy material." Buys 3-4 mss/year. Average word length: 200-500. Byline given.
Nonfiction: Middle readers: animal, nature/environment, sports. Does not want to see puzzle and games submissions. Buys 12 mss/year. Average word length: 200-500. Byline given.
How to Contact/Writers: Fiction: Send complete ms. Nonfiction: Query or send complete ms. Reports on queries/mss in 4 weeks. Will consider simultaneous submissions (if notified).
Illustration: Buys 5+ illustrations/issue; 50-60 illustrations/year. Works on assignment only.
How to Contact/Illustrators: Artists send samples. Reports back only if interested. Originals returned to artist at job's completion.

Terms: Pays on acceptance. Buys all rights. Pays $75-300 for assigned/unsolicited articles. Pays $300-400 per page for inside color illustrations. Writer's guidelines free with SASE. Sample copy with 8×11 SASE and $1.50.
Tips: Writers: "Use concrete, colorful, direct language. We use short-short stories—2 pages, 100 lines at 45 characters per line." Illustrators: "Avoid the cute. Use hot colors. Don't make kids you illustrate look like kewpie dolls. Don't be afraid of detail. Use a sense of humor. Send lots of sample cards to art directors. Write or call to bring in portfolios." (See listing for *3-2-1 Contact*.)

LADYBUG, THE MAGAZINE FOR YOUNG CHILDREN, P.O. Box 300, 315 Fifth Street, Peru IL 61354. (815)224-6643. Editor-in-Chief: Marianne Carus. Associate Editor: Paula Morrow. Art Director: Ron McCutchan. Monthly magazine. Estab. 1990. Circ. 130,000. Literary magazine for children 2-7, with stories, poems, activities, songs and picture stories.
Fiction: Picture-oriented and young readers: adventure, animal, contemporary, fantasy, folktales, humorous, picture book texts. "Open to any easy fiction stories." Buys 50 mss/year. Average word length 300-750 words. Byline given.
Nonfiction: Picture-oriented and young readers: animal, arts/crafts, games/puzzles, how-to, humorous, nature/environment. "Nonfiction in *Ladybug* will not be in article form, but rather in pictures with short captions." Buys 35 mss/year.
Poetry: Reviews 20-line maximum length poems; limit submissions to 5 poems. Uses lyrical, humorous, simple language.
How to Contact/Writers: Fiction/nonfiction: Send complete ms. Queries not accepted. Reports on mss in 3 months. Publishes ms up to 2 years after acceptance. Will consider simultaneous submissions.
Illustration: Buys 12 illustrations/issue; 145 illustrations/year. Uses color artwork only. Prefers "bright colors; all media, but use watercolor and acrylics most often; same size as magazine is preferred but not required." Reviews ms/illustration packages.
How to Contact/Illustrators: Ms/illustrations packages: "Manuscript with one or two rough sketches and some examples of finished artwork from other projects." Illustrations only: To contact, query with samples; submit portfolio for review. "Tearsheets, good quality photocopies, C-prints; slides are somewhat less useful, but OK." Reports on art samples in 2 months. Original artwork returned at job's completion.
Terms: Pays on publication. For mss, buys first North American serial rights; second serial (reprint rights). Buys one-time reproduction rights for artwork. Pays up to 25¢/word. Pays $750 for color (cover) illustration, $200-300 for color (inside) illustration. Sample copy for $2. Writer's/illustrator's guidelines free for #10 SAE and 1 first class stamp.
Tips: Writers: "Read copies of back issues and current issues. Set a manuscript aside for a few weeks, then reread before sending it off. Adhere to specified word limits." Illustrators: "Include examples, where possible, of children, animals, and—mostly important—action and narrative (i.e., several scenes from a story, showing continuity and an ability to maintain interest)." Has a need for "well-written read-aloud stories."

LIGHTHOUSE, Lighthouse Publications, Box 1377, Auburn WA 98071-1377. Editor/Publisher: Tim Clinton. Bimonthly magazine. Estab. 1986. Circ. 300. Magazine contains timeless stories and poetry for family reading. 25% of material aimed at juvenile audience.

Always include a self-addressed stamped envelope (SASE) or International Reply Coupon (IRC) with submissions.

Fiction: Young readers, middle readers, young adults: animal, contemporary, humorous, problem-solving, sports, mystery/suspense. Does not want to see anything not "G-rated," any story with a message that is not subtly handled. Buys 18 mss/year. Average word length: 2,000. Byline given.
Poetry: Reviews poetry. Maximum line length: 50. Maximum number of submissions: 5.
How to Contact/Writers: Fiction: Send complete ms and SASE with sufficient postage for return of ms. Reports on mss in 2 months.
Terms: Pays on publication. Buys first North American serial rights; first rights. Sample copy for $3 (includes guidelines). Writer's guidelines free with regular SAE and 1 first-class stamp.
Tips: "All sections are open to freelance writers—just follow the guidelines and stay in the categories listed above."

LISTEN, Celebrating Positive Choices, 1350 North Kings Rd., Nampa ID 83687. (208)465-2500. Monthly magazine. Circ. 100,000. *Listen* offers positive alternatives to drug use for its teenage readers.
Fiction: Young adults: contemporary, humorous, problem solving. Buys 12 mss/year. Average word length: 1,200-1,500. Byline given.
Nonfiction: Young adults: how-to, interview/profile, problem solving. Buys 50 mss/year. Average word length: 1,200-1,500. Byline given.
How to Contact/Writers: Fiction/nonfiction: Send complete ms. Reports on queries/mss in 2 months.
Terms: Pays on acceptance. Buys first North American serial rights. Pays $150 for assigned articles; $100 for unsolicited articles. Sample copy for $2 and SASE. Writer's guidelines free with SASE.
Tips: *Listen* is a magazine for teenagers. It encourages development of good habits and high ideals of physical, social and mental health. It bases its editorial philosophy of primary drug prevention on total abstinence from alcohol and other drugs. Because it is used extensively in public high school classes, it does not accept articles and stories with overt religious emphasis. Four specific purposes guide the editors in selecting materials for *Listen*: 1) To portray a positive lifestyle and to foster skills and values that will help teenagers deal with contemporary problems, including smoking, drinking and using drugs. This is *Listen*'s primary purpose. 2) To offer positive alternatives to a lifestyle of drug use of any kind. 3) To present scientifically accurate information about the nature and effects of tobacco, alcohol and other drugs. 4) To report medical research, community programs and educational efforts which are solving problems connected with smoking, alcohol and other drugs. Articles should offer their readers activities that increase one's sense of self-worth through achievement and/or involvement in helping others. They are often categorized by three kinds of focus: 1) Hobbies. 2) Recreation. 3) Community Service. Cartoons: May be slanted against using tobacco, alcohol and other drugs; or may be of general interest to teenagers. Pays $15 each.

MY FRIEND, A Magazine for Children, Daughters of St. Paul/St. Paul Books and Media, 50 St. Paul's Ave., Jamaica Plain, Boston MA 02130. (617)522-8911. Articles/Fiction Editor: Sister Anne Joan, fsp. Art Director: Sister M. Joseph, fsp. Magazine published 10 times/year. Estab. 1979. Circ. 17,000. "*My Friend* is a magazine of inspiration and entertainment for a predominantly Catholic readership. We reach ages 6-12."
Fiction: Picture-oriented material: animal, contemporary, religious. Young readers: contemporary, fantasy, history, humorous, problem solving, religious, sports, adventure. Middle readers: contemporary, history, humorous, problem solving, religious, science fiction, sports, adventure. Young adults: religious. Does not want to see poetry, animals as main characters in religious story, stories whose basic thrust would be incompatible with Catholic values. Buys 50 mss/year. Average word length: 450-750. Byline given.

illustrated by Charles Jordan

This illustration by Charles Jordan accompanied an article in My Friend entitled "Learning to Be Me." Jordan wished to convey a younger brother's feeling of rejection as his father gives his older brother all of his attention. "With this piece," he says, "I was able to show a more realistic style, different from the cartoon-like work I usually do." Jordan was paid $125 for the assignment.

Nonfiction: Picture-oriented material: animal, religious. Young readers: history, how-to, humorous, interview/profile, science religious. Middle readers: history, interview/profile, problem solving, science religious. Does not want to see material that is not compatible with Catholic values; "new age" material. Buys 10 mss/year. Average word length: 450-750. Byline given.

How to Contact/Writers: Fiction/nonfiction: Send complete ms. Reports on queries in 3 weeks; mss in 3-4 weeks.

Illustration: Buys 8 illustrations/issue; buys 60-80 illustrations/year. Preferred theme or style: Realistic depictions of children, but open to variety! "We'd just like to hear from more illustrators who can do *humans*! (We see enough of funny cats, mice, etc.)" Looking for a "Bible stories" artist, too. Will review ms/illustration packages.

How to Contact/Illustrators: Ms/illustration packages: Send complete ms with copy of final art. Reports on art samples in 3-4 weeks. Original artwork returned at job's completion.

Terms: Pays on publication. Buys one-time rights. Pays $20-150 per story. Sample copy free with 9 × 12 SAE and 4 first-class stamps. Writer's/illustrator's guidelines free with SAE and 1 first-class stamp.

Tips: Writers: "Right now, we're especially looking for science articles and stories that would appeal to boys. We are not interested in poetry unless it is humorous." Illustrators: "Please contact us! For the most part, we need illustrations for fiction stories."

NATIONAL GEOGRAPHIC WORLD, National Geographic Society, 17th and M Streets NW, Washington DC 20036. (202)857-7000. Editor: Pat Robbins. Photo Editor: Chuck Herron. Art Director: Ursula Vosseler. Monthly magazine. Circ. 1.2 million. *"National Geographic World* features factual stories on outdoor adventure, natural history, sports, science and history for children ages 8 and older. Full-color photographs are used to attract young readers and the text easily guides them through the story." Does not publish fiction.
Nonfiction: Middle readers, young adults: animal, history, humorous, nature/environment, sports, foreign. *"World* does not publish manuscripts from outside writers. Story ideas that lend themselves to photo stories will be considered. All writing is done by staff." Picture material: animal, history, how-to, travel. Average word length: 90-600.
How to Contact/Writers: Nonfiction: Query only—no ms please. Reports on queries in 6-8 weeks.
Illustration: Assignment only.
How to Contact/Illustrators: Illustrations only: Query with samples; arrange personal interview to show portfolio.
Photography: Purchases photos separately. Looking for "imaginative, eye-catching action transparencies." Model/property releases and photo captions required. Uses 35mm transparencies. To contact, photographers should query with proposal and outline of photo possibilities.
Terms: Pays on publication. Buys one-time rights for mss, artwork and photos. Pays $600 for color (cover), $100-300 for color (inside) photos. Photographers are paid per published page. Free sample copy; contributor's guidelines available free.
Tips: "All *World* stories are written by staff. For *World*, the story proposal is the way to break in. Think through the focus of the story and outline what action photos are available. Keep in mind that *World* is a visual magazine. A story will work best if it has a very tight focus and if the photos show children interacting with their surroundings as well as with each other."

NATURE FRIEND MAGAZINE, Pilgrim Publishers, 22777 State Road 119, Goshen IN 46526. (219)534-2245. Articles Editor: Stanley Brubaker. Monthly magazine. Estab. 1983. Circ. 11,000. "See our writer's guide *before* submitting articles."
Nonfiction: Picture-oriented material: animal, nature. Young readers: animal, nature. Middle readers: animal, nature. Young adult: animal, nature. Does not want to see evolutionary material. Buys 50-80 mss/year. Average word length: 350-1,500. Byline given.
How to Contact/Writers: Nonfiction: Send complete ms. Reports on mss in 1-4 months. Will consider simultaneous submissions.
Illustration: Buys 10 illustrations/year. See samples of magazine for styles of art used. Will review ms/illustration packages.
Terms: Pays on publication. Buys one-time rights. Pays $15-60. Payment for ms/illustration packages: $15-40. Payment for illustrations: $15-80/b&w inside. Two sample copies for $2 with 7×10 SAE and 85¢ postage. Writer's/illustrator's guidelines for $1.
Tips: Looks for "main articles, puzzles and simple nature and science projects."

NEW ERA MAGAZINE, Official Publication for Youth of the Church of Jesus Christ of Latter-Day Saints, 50 E. North Temple Street, Salt Lake City UT 84150. (801)240-2951. Articles/Fiction Editor: Richard M. Romney. Art Director: B. Lee Shaw. Monthly magazine. Estab. 1971. Circ. 200,000. General interest religious publication for youth ages 12-18 who are members of The Church of Jesus Christ of Latter-Day Saints ("Mormons").

Fiction: Young adults: contemporary, humorous, problem solving, religious, romance, science fiction. "All material must relate to 'Mormon' point of view." Does not want to see formula pieces, articles not sensitive to an LDS audience. Buys 20 mss/year. Average word length: 250-2,500. Byline given.

Nonfiction: Young adults: biography, careers, education, fashion, games/puzzles, humorous, interview/profile, problem-solving, religion, travel, sports; "general interest articles by, about and for young Mormons. Does not want to see formula pieces, articles not adapted to our specific voice and our audience." Buys 150-200 mss/year. Average word length: 250-2,000. Byline given.

Poetry: Reviews "30-line maximum" poems. Will accept 10 submissions/author.

How to Contact/Writers: Fiction/nonfiction: Query. Reports on queries/mss in 6-8 weeks. Publishes ms 1 year or more after acceptance. Will consider electronic submissions via disk.

Illustration: Buys 5 illustrations/issue; buys 50-60 illustrations/year. "We buy only from our pool of illustrators. We use all styles and mediums." Works on assignment only.

How to Contact/Illustrators: Illustrations only: Submit portfolio for review; provide resume, business card, promotional literature and tearsheets to be kept on file. Reports on art samples in 6-8 weeks. Original artwork returned at job's completion.

Terms: Pays on acceptance. For mss, buys first rights; other rights ("right to publish again in other church usage"). Buys all or one-time rights for artwork and photos. Pays $25-375 for articles. Pays illustrators and photographers "by specific arrangements." Sample copy for $1. Writer's guidelines free for SAE (business envelope and 1 first class stamp).

Tips: Open to "first-person and true-life experiences. Tell what happened in a conversational style."

NICKELODEON, MTV Networks, 1775 Broadway, New York NY 10019. (This market did not respond to requests to be listed.)

NOAH'S ARK, A Newspaper for Jewish Children, 8323 Southwest Freeway, #250, Houston TX 77074. (713)771-7143. Articles/Fiction Editor: Debbie Israel Dubin. Art Director: Nachman. Monthly tabloid. Circ. 450,000. All submissions must have Jewish content and positive Jewish values. The newspaper is sent to more than 400 religious schools and submissions must be appropriate for educational use as well.

Fiction: Young readers, middle readers: contemporary, history, religious, sports. Does not want to see Christian and secular material. Buys 3 mss/year. Average word length: 650. Byline given.

Nonfiction: Young readers, middle readers: history, how-to, humorous, interview/profile, problem solving, religious, travel. Does not want to see secular, Christian nonfiction. Buys 1 ms/year, "only because more not submitted." Average word length: 500. Byline given.

How to Contact/Writers: Fiction/nonfiction: Send complete ms. Report on mss 6-8 weeks.

Terms: Pays on acceptance. Buys first North American serial rights. Pays 5¢/word for unsolicited articles. Sample copy free with #10 SAE and 1 first-class stamp. Writer's guidelines free with SASE.

Tips: "Send appropriate material. We receive mostly inappropriate submissions; very few submissions have Jewish values as required."

"Picture books" are geared toward the preschool—8 year old group; "Young readers" to 5-8 year olds; "Middle readers" to 9-11 year olds; and "Young adults" to those 12 and up.

ON THE LINE, Mennonite Publishing House, 616 Walnut Ave., Scottdale PA 15683. (412)887-8500. Editor: Mary Clemens Meyer. "Monthly in weekly parts" magazine. Estab. 1970. Circ. 10,000.
Fiction: Young adults: contemporary, history, humorous, problem-solving, religious, sports and suspense/mystery. "No fantasy or fiction with animal characters." Buys 60 mss/year. Average word length: 900-1,200. Byline given.
Nonfiction: Middle readers, young adults: animal, arts/crafts, biography, cooking, games/puzzles, health, history, hobbies, how-to, humorous, nature/environment, problem-solving. Does not want to see articles written from an adult perspective. Average word length: 200-600. Byline given.
Poetry: Wants to see light verse, humorous poetry. Maximum line length: 24 lines.
How to Contact/Writers: Fiction/nonfiction: Send complete ms. Reports on queries/mss in 1 month. Will consider simultaneous submissions.
Illustration: Buys 1-2 illustrations/issue; buys 52 illustrations/year. "Illustrations are done on assignment only, to accompany our stories and articles—our need for new artists is very limited."
How to Contact/Illustrators: Illustrations only: "Prefer samples they do not want returned; these stay in our files." Reports on art samples only if interested. Original art work returned at job's completion.
Photography: Looking for photography showing ages 12-14, both sexes, good mix of races, wholesome fun. Uses 8 × 10 glossy b&w prints. To contact, photographers should send unsolicited photos by mail.
Terms: Pays on acceptance. For mss buys one-time rights; second serial (reprint rights). Buys one-time rights for artwork and photos. Pays 2-5¢/word for assigned/unsolicited articles. Pays $25-50/color (inside) illustration. Photographers are paid per photo, $15-50 (cover). Sample copy free with 7 × 10 SAE. Free writer's guidelines.
Tips: "We will be focusing on the 12 and 13 age group of our 10-14 audience. (Focus was somewhat younger before.)"

OWL MAGAZINE, The Discovery Magazine for Children, Young Naturalist Foundation, Ste. 306, 56 The Esplanade, Toronto Ontario M5E 1A7 Canada. (416)868-6001. Editor: Debora Pearson. Managing Editor: Deena Waisberg. Art Director: Tim Davin. Magazine published 10 times/year. Circ. 160,000. "*Owl* helps children over eight discover and enjoy the world of science and nature. We look for articles that are fun to read, that inform from a child's perspective, and that motivate hands-on interaction. *Owl* explores the reader's many interests in the natural world in a scientific, but always entertaining, way."
Fiction: Middle readers, young adults: animal, contemporary, fantasy, humorous, science fiction, sports, suspense/mystery/adventure. Does not want to see romance, religion, anthropomorphizing. Average word length: 500-1,000. Byline given. "We publish only 3-4 pieces of fiction per year."
Nonfiction: Middle readers, young adults: animal, biology, high-tech, humor, interview/profile, travel. Does not want to see religious topics, anthropomorphizing. Buys 20 mss/year. Average word length: 200-1,500. Byline given.
How to Contact/Writers: Fiction/nonfiction: Query with published clips. Report on queries in 4-6 weeks; mss in 6-8 weeks.
Illustration: Buys 3-5 illustrations/issue; buys 40-50 illustrations/year. Uses color artwork only. Preferred theme or style: lively, involving, fun, with emotional impact and appeal. "We use a range of styles." Works on assignment only.
How to Contact/Illustrators: Illustrations only: Send tearsheets and slides. Reports on art samples only if interested. Original artwork returned at job's completion.
Photography: Looking for shots of animals and nature. "Label the photos." Uses 2¼ × 2¼ and 35mm transparencies. To contact, photographers should query with samples.

Terms: Pays on acceptance. For mss, artwork and photos buys first North American and world rights. Pays $200-500 (Canadian) for assigned/unsolicited articles. Pays up to $650 (Canadian) for illustrations. Photographers are paid per photo. Sample copy $3.25. Free writer's guidelines.
Tips: Writers: "Talk to kids and find out what they're interested in; make sure your research is thorough and find good consultants who are doing up-to-the-minute research. Be sure to read the magazine carefully to become familiar with *Owl*'s style." Illustrators: "Talk to kids and find out what work appeals to them. Look through *Owl* to see what styles we prefer." (See listing for *Chickadee*.)

PIONEER, Brotherhood Commission, SBC, 1548 Poplar Ave., Memphis TN 38104. (901)272-2461. Articles Editor: Jene C. Smith. Monthly magazine. Circ. 30,000. Magazine contains boy interests, sports, crafts, sports personalities, religious.
Nonfiction: Young adults: animal, arts/crafts, biography, careers, education, fashion, games/puzzles, health, hobbies, how-to, nature/environment, sports. Buys 15 mss/year. Average word length: 400-600. Byline given.
How to Contact/Writers: Nonfiction: Send complete ms. Reports on queries in 1 month; mss in 2 months. Will consider simultaneous submissions.
Illustration: Buys 1-2 illustrations/issue; buys 12 illustrations/year. Will review ms/illustration packages.
How to Contact/Illustrators: Ms/illustration packages: Send complete ms with final art. Illustrations only: Provide resume, business card, promotional literature or tearsheets to be kept on file.
Terms: Pays on acceptance. Buys one-time and reprint rights. Pays $25-35 for articles. Sample copy free with #10 SAE and 3 first-class stamps. Writer's/illustrator's guidelines free with SAE and 1 first-class stamp.
Tips: Wants to see "teenagers in sports, nature, health, hobbies—no preachy articles."

POCKETS, Devotional Magazine for Children, The Upper Room, 1908 Grand, Box 189, Nashville TN 37202. (615)340-7333. Articles/Fiction Editor: Janet R. McNish. Art Director: Chris Schechner, Ste. 206, 3100 Carlisle Plaza, Dallas TX 75204. Magazine published 11 times/year. Estab. 1981. Circ. 72,000. Stories should help children 6 to 12 experience a Christian lifestyle that is not always a neatly wrapped moral package, but is open to the continuing revelation of God's will.
Fiction: Young readers, middle readers: contemporary, fantasy, history, religious, "retold Bible stories." Does not want to see violence. Buys 26-30 mss/year. Average word length: 800-2,000. Byline given.
Nonfiction: Young readers, middle readers: history, interview/profile, religious, "communication activities." Does not want to see how-to articles. Our nonfiction reads like a story. History is in form of role-model stories as is profile. Buys 10 mss/year. Average word length: 800-2,000. Byline given.
How to Contact/Writers: Fiction/nonfiction: Send complete ms. Report on mss in 4 weeks. Will consider simultaneous submissions.
Illustration: Buys 30 illustrations/issue. Preferred theme or style: varied; both 4-color and 2-color. Will review ms/illustration packages. Works on assignment only.
How to Contact/Illustrators: Ms/illustration packages: No final art. Illustrations only: Send résumé, tearsheets, slides to Chris Schechner, Ste. 206, 3100 Carlisle Plaza, Dallas TX 75204. Reports on art samples only if interested. Original artwork returned at job's completion.
Terms: Pays on acceptance. Buys first North American rights. Pays $250 for assigned articles; 12¢/word for unsolicited articles. Pays $500/color (cover) illustration; $50-500/color (inside). Sample copy free with 7×9 SAE and 4 first-class stamps. Writer's/illustrator's guidelines free with SAE and 1 first-class stamp.

Close-up

Anni Matsick
Illustrator
State College, Pennsylvania

People kept telling Anni Matsick she should be a children's illustrator. "I didn't train to be an illustrator. In fact, my formal education was strictly fine art, but the things I did for fun, such as doodling and making humorous cards caused others to remark that I ought to look into the field."

Matsick heard this many times from valued friends, but it wasn't until a friend asked her to help with a picture book project that she realized she wanted to specialize in illustrating for children. "I did the dummy for the book and we came very close to publication. After that, I was hooked."

Even though she did not begin her art career as an illustrator, she says her background has helped her, especially in the way she looks at each assignment. "I ask myself what is the best, most personal, unique way I can bring this story, feature or puzzle to life? Should I use an unusual perspective? What about composition? Content? These are the things a painter thinks about."

Matsick's work appears regularly in national children's magazines, including *Pockets*, *Child Life*, and a number of special publications for *Highlights*. Always looking for new opportunities, Matsick recently completed her first picture book (*Mirror Magic*, by Seymour Simon) for Bell Books, an imprint of Boyds Mills Press (the book publishing arm of Highlights for Children, Inc.).

"I'd like to do more books," she says. "Your work has a substantially longer life in book form. But with magazines there is variety, spontaneity. I already do work for quite a few magazines and I would not want to cut that off."

Matsick works in watercolor with ink or pencil and tends to aim most of her work to a 6-to-12-year-old audience. She tries to look for ways to include humor in many of her assignments, but beyond this, "I let the story or feature lead me. The nature of the story—some are light, some have a strong moral lesson, some are humorous—determines which style will best fit the piece."

Most magazine assignments, she says, involve both a rough and a final illustration. When an art director contacts you for an assignment (assuming you have made first contact by sending samples), you'll usually be given a date for the roughs, a date finals are due, a description of the project and what it pays, she explains. Then you'll get the story and a layout either by fax or overnight express. In general, you'll have a two-to-four week lead time to complete the assignment. The content and composition is often left to the illustrator and most art directors are open to your suggestions on how best to handle the work. And, Matsick adds, "if you care about your work arriving on time and in good condition, use an overnight carrier to send your finished artwork."

While the ability to use humor in your illustration is a plus, Matsick says illustrators interested in drawing for children should study them. "Look at kids," she says. "Go to Disneyworld, if you can. Walk around in a big city. These are great places to see children from all over the world." Knowing how to draw children from different ethnic backgrounds and of different ages is important, she says, especially if you are interested in the education market.

Matsick got her experience drawing children during the years when she set up her easel at art fairs to do quick portraits. She also has the added advantage of watching her young son, Amos. She uses him to act out gestures and has "turned him into all sorts of children—boys, girls, all ages."

To be a successful freelance illustrator, you need more than talent, she says. "A good phone personality is vital. You want to sound natural, but be positive, conveying enthusiasm and interest. On paper, you want to appear crisp, direct and your communications skills in general must be up to par."

Matsick built her business slowly, starting in a spare room and working up to a skylit studio. As her business grew, she added professionally designed stationery, an answering machine, copier and, more recently, a fax machine. She says the fax is very useful—it helps her get jobs that require a quick turn-around—but it's best to invest in equipment one piece at a time. The money should come first, she warns, before adding the trappings.

—Robin Gee

Matsick was paid $500 for this cover illustration for Pockets. Rendered in sepia ink and watercolor, it was intended to convey "a spirit of fun." The illustration appeared in the Graphic Artists Guild Directory of Illustration #6 and continues to draw response from major publishers and art agencies.

© Anni Matsick 1989

Tips: "Ask for our themes first. They are set yearly in the fall. Also, we are looking for articles about real children involved in environment, peace, or similar activities."

P3, The P3 Foundation, Inc., P.O. Box 52, Montgomery VT 05470. (This market declined to be listed.)

RACING FOR KIDS, Griggs Publishing Company, Inc., P.O. Box 500, Concord NC 28026. (This market did not respond to requests to be listed.)

R-A-D-A-R, Standard Publishing, 8121 Hamilton Ave., Cincinnati OH 45231. (513)931-4050. Articles/Fiction Editor: Margaret Williams. Weekly magazine. Circ. 150,000. *R-A-D-A-R* is a weekly take-home paper for boys and girls who are in grades 3-6. Our goal is to reach these children with the truth of God's Word, and to help them make it the guide of their lives. Many of our features, including our stories, now correlate with the Sunday school lesson themes. Send for a quarterly theme list and sample copies of *R-A-D-A-R*. Keep in mind that others will be submitting stories for the same themes—this is not an assignment.
Fiction: Middle readers: animal, contemporary, history, humorous, problem solving, religious, sports, suspense/mystery/adventure. Does not want to see fantasy or science fiction. Buys 150 mss/year. Average word length: 400-1,000. Byline given.
Nonfiction: Middle readers: animal, history, how-to, humorous, interview/profile, problem solving, religious, travel. Buys 50 mss/year. Average word length: 400-1,000. Byline given.
Poetry: Reviews poetry. Maximum line length: 16.
How to Contact/Writers: Fiction/nonfiction: Send complete ms. Reports on queries/mss 6-8 weeks. Will consider simultaneous submissions, (but prefer not to). Reprint submissions must be retyped.
Illustration: Will review all illustration packages. Works on assignment only; there have been a few exceptions to this.
How to Contact/Illustrators: Illustrations only: Send résumé, tearsheets, business card or promotional literature; samples of art can be photocopied. Reports on art samples only if interested.
Photography: Purchases photos from freelancers. Model/property releases required. Send résumé, business card, promotional literature or tearsheets to be kept on file.
Terms: Pays on acceptance. Buys first rights, one-time rights, second serial, first North American; all rights to art. Pays 3-7¢/word for unsolicited articles, few are assigned. Contributor copies given "not as payment, but all contributors receive copies of their art/articles." Pays $70-125 for color illustrations; $125-150 for color cover; $40-60 for line art only. Photographers paid $125 maximum per photo. Sample copy and writer's guidelines free with 9⅜ × 4¼ SAE and 1 first-class stamp. (See listing for *Straight.*)
Tips: "Write about current topics, issues that elementary-age children are dealing with. Keep illustrations/photos current."

RANGER RICK, National Wildlife Federation, 8925 Leesburg Pike, Vienna VA 22184. (703)790-4000. Editor: Gerald Bishop. Art Director: Donna Miller. Monthly magazine. Circ. 850,000. "Our audience ranges from ages six to twelve, though we aim the reading level of most material at nine-year-olds or fourth graders."
Fiction: Middle readers: animal, fantasy, humorous, science fiction. Buys 4-6 mss/year. Average word length: 900. Byline given.
Nonfiction: Middle readers: animal, humorous. Buys 20-30 mss/year. Average word length: 900. Byline given.
How to Contact/Writers: Fiction: Query with published clips; send complete ms. Nonfiction: Query with published clips. Reports on queries/mss in 6 weeks.

Illustration: Buys 6-8 illustrations/issue; buys 75-100 illustrations/year. Preferred theme or style: nature, wildlife. Will review an illustrator's work for possible future assignments. Works on assignment only.

How to Contact/Illustrators: Illustrations only: Send résumé, tearsheets. Reports on art samples in 6 weeks. Original artwork returned at job's completion.

Terms: Pays on acceptance. Buys all rights (first North American serial rights negotiable). Pays up to $550 for full-length of best quality. For illustrations, buys one-time rights. Pays $250-1,000 for color (inside, per page) illustration. Sample copy $2. Writer's guidelines free with SASE.

Tips: "Fiction and nonfiction articles may be written on any aspect of wildlife, nature, outdoor adventure and discovery, domestic animals with a 'wild' connection (such as domestic pigs and wild boars), science, conservation, or related subjects. To find out what subjects have been covered recently, consult our annual indexes and the *Children's Magazine Guide*. These are available in many libraries. The National Wildlife Federation (NWF) discourages the keeping of wildlife as pets, so the keeping of such pets should not be featured in your copy. Avoid stereotyping of any group. For instance, girls can enjoy nature and the outdoors as much as boys can, and mothers can be just as knowledgeable as fathers. The only way you can write successfully for *Ranger Rick* is to know the kinds of subjects and approaches we like. And the only way you can do that is to read the magazine. Recent issues can be found in most libraries or are available from our office for $2 a copy."

SCHOLASTIC MATH MAGAZINE, Scholastic, Inc., 730 Broadway, New York NY 10003. (212)505-3135. FAX: (212)505-3377. Editor: Tracey Randinelli. Artist: Leah Bossio. Art Director: Joan Michael. Magazine published 14 times/year; September-May. Estab. 1980. Circ. 307,000. "We are a math magazine for 7, 8, 9 grade classrooms. We present math in current, relevant, high-interest topics. Math skills we focus on include whole number, fraction, and decimal computation, percentages, ratios, proportions and geometry."

Fiction: Young adults: problem-solving. Buys 14 mss/year "in the form of word problems." Average line length 80-100.

Nonfiction: Young adults: cooking, fashion, games/puzzles, problem solving. Does not want to see "anything dealing with *very* controversial issues—i.e., teenage pregnancy, AIDS, etc." Buys 20 mss/year. Average line length 80-100. Byline given.

How to Contact/Writers: Fiction/nonfiction: Query. Reports on queries/mss in 1 month. Will consider simultaneous submissions.

Illustration: Buys 4 illustrations/issue; 56 illustrations/year. Prefers to review "humorous, young adult sophistication" types of art. Will review ms/illustration packages. Works on assignment only.

How to Contact/Illustrators: Ms/illustration packages: "Query first." Illustrations only: Query with samples; submit portfolio for review. Reports back only if interested. Original artwork returned at job's completion.

Terms: Pays on publication. Buys all rights for mss. Pays $50-350/assigned article. Photographers are paid by the project.

Tips: "For our magazine, stories dealing with math concepts and applications in the real world are sought."

*SCHOOL MAGAZINE, (BLAST OFF!, COUNTDOWN, ORBIT, TOUCHDOWN), New South Wales Dept. of Education, Box A242, Sydney NSW 2000 Australia. (02)261-7231. Acting Editor: Jonathan Shaw. 4 monthly magazines. Circ. 305,000. *School Magazine* is a literary magazine that is issued free to all N.S.W. primary public schools. Private schools and individuals subscribe for a small fee. We include stories, plays and poems. The 4 magazines issued each month are graded according to age level, 8-12 years.

Fiction: Young readers: animal, contemporary, fantasy, humorous. Middle readers: animal, contemporary, fantasy, history, humorous, problem solving, romance, science fiction, suspense/mystery/adventure. Buys 30 mss/year. Average word length: 500-2,500. Byline given.
Poetry: Maximum length length: 150 lines. Limit submissions to 10 poems.
How to Contact/Writers: Fiction: Send complete ms. SASE (IRC) for return of ms. Reports on queries in 2 months. Publishes ms 6 months after acceptance.
Terms: Pays on acceptance. Buys first Australian serial rights. "Pays $133 per thousand words." Free sample copy.
Tips: "Subscribe to *School Magazine*—read as much children's literature as possible. Fantasy, real-life both acceptable for fiction. Good quality is the main criterion."

*SCHOOL MATES, USCF's Magazine For Beginning Chess Players, United States Chess Federation, 186 Rt. 9W, New Windsor NY 12553. (914)562-8350. FAX (914)561-CHES. Editor-in-Chief: Jennie Simon. Bimonthly magazine. Estab. 1987. Circ. 6,000. Magazine for beginning chess players. Offers instruction articles, features on famous players, scholastic chess coverage, games, puzzles, occasional fiction, listing of chess tournaments.
Fiction: Young readers, middle readers, and young adults: problem-solving (chess related). Average word length: 1,000-5,000 words.
Poetry: "We've just begun to consider publishing poetry." Wants to see poetry about chess!!
How to Contact/Writers: Send complete ms. Reports on queries in 1 month/mss in 2 months.
Illustration: Buys 2-3 illustrations/year. Prefers b&w, ink preferably, cartoons OK. Reviews ms/illustration packages; reviews artwork for future assignments.
How to Contact/Illustrators: Query first. Reports back only if interested.
Terms: Pays on publication. Buys one-time rights. Sometimes pays with contributor copies. "When the writer/illustrator fees are more than we (as a not-for-profit company) can afford to pay, we make this type of prior arrangement (paying in copies)." Pays $50-75/b&w cover; $25-45/b&w inside. Sample copies are free for 9×12 SAE and 2 first class stamps. Writer's guidelines free on request.

*SCIENCE WEEKLY, Science Weekly Inc., Suite 202, 2141 Industrial Pkwy., Silver Spring MD 20904. (301)680-8004. FAX: (301)680-9240. Biweekly magazine. Estab. 1984. Circ. 250,000.
Nonfiction: All levels: education, problem-solving, science/math education. "Call for more information on freelancing needs."
Terms: Pays on publication. "Call for more information, writer's guidelines and training workshop."

SCIENCELAND, To Nurture Scientific Thinking, Scienceland Inc., 501 Fifth Ave. #2108, New York NY 10017-6102. (212)490-2180. FAX: (212)986-2077. Editor/Art Director: Al Matano. Magazine published 8 times/year. Estab. 1977. Circ. 16,000. This is

✴ *The asterisk before a listing indicates the listing is new in this edition.*

"a content reading picture-book for K-3rd grade to encourage beginning readers; for teachers and parents."

Nonfiction: Picture-oriented material and young readers: animal, art/crafts, biography, careers, cooking, education, games/puzzles, health, history, how-to, nature/environment, problem solving. Does not want to see "unillustrated material."

Poetry: Reviews poetry. Maximum length: 12 lines.

How to Contact/Writers: Not interested in stories. *Must* be picture or full-color illustrated stories.

Illustration: Prefers to review "detailed, realistic, full color art. No abstracts." Uses "predominantly" color artwork. Will review ms/illustration packages; reviews artwork for future assignments.

How to Contact/Illustrators: Ms/illustration packages: "Query first." Illustrations only: Send unsolicited art by mail; provide resume, promotional literature or tearsheets to be kept on file. Reports back in 3-4 weeks. Original artwork returned at job's completion, "depending on material."

Photography: Wants to see "physical and natural science photos with children in scenes whenever possible." Model/property release and photo captions required. Uses 35mm transparencies. To contact, photographer should submit portfolio for review; provide resume, promotional literature or tearsheets to be kept on file.

Terms: Pays on publication. Buys first rights for mss, artwork and photos. Payment for ms/illustration packages: $50-500. Payment for illustrations: $25-300 color cover; $25-300 color inside. Photographers paid by the project. Sample copy free with 9 × 12 SASE.

Tips: "Must be top notch illustrator or photographer. No amateurs."

SEVENTEEN MAGAZINE, News America, 850 Third Ave., New York NY 10022. (212)759-8100. Managing Editor: Roberta Myers. Articles Editor: Sarah Patton. Fiction Editor: Adrian Nicole LeBlanc. Art Director: Annie Demchick. Monthly magazine. Estab. 1944. Circ. 1,750,000. "General-interest magazine for teenage girls."

Fiction: Young adults: animal, contemporary, fantasy, history, humorous, problem-solving, religious, romance, science fiction, sports, spy/mystery/adventure, adult. "We consider all good literary short fiction." Buys 12-20 mss/year. Average word length 900-3,000. Byline given.

Nonfiction: Young adults: animal, history, how-to, humorous, interview/profile, problem solving, religious, travel. Buys 150 mss/year. Word length: Lengths vary from 800-1,000 words for short features and monthly columns to 2,500 words for major articles. Byline given.

Poetry: Reviews poetry "only by teenagers younger than 21."

How to Contact/Writers; Fiction: Send complete ms. Nonfiction: Query with published clips or send complete ms. Reports on queries/mss in 3 weeks. Will consider simultaneous submissions.

Illustration: 1 illustration per short story. Will review ms/illustration packages. Illustrators paid by the project. Writer's guidelines for business-size envelope and 1 first-class stamp.

*SHARING THE VICTORY, Fellowship of Christian Athletes, 8701 Leeds, Kansas City MO 64129. (816)921-0909. FAX: (816)921-8755. Articles Editor: John Dodderidge. Art Director: Frank Grey. Photo Editor: John Dodderidge. Monthly magazine. Estab. 1982. Circ. 55,000. "Purpose is to present to coaches and athletes, and all whom they influence, the challenge and adventure of receiving Jesus Christ as Savior and Lord."

Nonfiction: Young adults: interview/profile, sports. Buys 20-25 mss/year. Average word length: 400-900. Byline given.

Poetry: Reviews poetry. Maximum word length 50-75.

How to Contact/Writers: Nonfiction: Query with published clips. Reports in 3 weeks. Publishes ms 3 months after acceptance. Will consider simultaneous submissions, electronic submissions via disk or modem and previously published work.

Photography: Purchases photos separately. Looking for photos of sports action. Uses color, b&w prints and 35mm transparencies.

Terms: Pays on publication. Buys first rights and second serial (reprint rights). Pays $50-250 for assigned and unsolicited articles. Photographers paid per photo (range: $50-300). Sample copies for 9 × 12 SASE and $1. Writer's/photo guidelines for SASE.

Tips: "Be specific—write short. Take quality photos that are useable." Wants interviews and features. Interested in colorful sports photos.

SHOFAR, 43 Northcote Dr., Melville NY 11747. (516)643-4598. Managing Editor: Gerald H. Grayson. Magazine published monthly Oct. through May—double issues Dec./Jan. and April/May. Circ. 17,000. For Jewish children ages 9-13.

Fiction: Middle readers: cartoons, contemporary, humorous, poetry, puzzles, religious, sports. All material must be on a Jewish theme. Buys 10-20 mss/year. Average word length: 500-700. Byline given.

Nonfiction: Middle readers: history, humorous, interview/profile, religious. Buys 10-20 mss/year. Average word length: 500-1,000. Byline given.

How to Contact/Writers: Fiction/nonfiction: Send complete ms (preferred). Queries welcome. Submit holiday theme pieces at least 4 months in advance. Will consider simultaneous and electronic submissions via disk or modem (only Macintosh).

Illustration: Buys 3-4 illustrations/issue; buys 15-20 illustrations/year. Works on assignment only.

How to Contact/Illustrators: Ms/illustration packages: Query first. Illustrations only: Send tearsheets. Works on assignment only. Reports on art samples only if interested. Original artwork returned at job's completion.

Terms: Buys first North American serial rights or first serial rights. Pays on publication. Pays 7¢/word plus 5 contributor's copies. Photos purchased with mss at additional fees. Pays $25-100/b&w cover illustration; $50-150/color (cover). Sample copy free with 9 × 12 SAE and 3 first-class stamps. Free writer's/illustrator's guidelines.

SING OUT!, The Folk Song Magazine, Sing Out! Corp., Box 5253, 125 E. 3rd St., Bethlehem PA 18015-5253. (215)865-5366. Editor: Mark D. Moss. Contributing Editor: Jeff Eilenberg. Managing Director: Diane C. Petro. Quarterly magazine. Estab. 1950. Circ. 6,000 member; 2,500 newstand. Readers are "a diverse group of music lovers, who believe in preserving the folk music of America as well as the native music of all countries. Additionally, *Sing Out!* explores the new musical fusions being created daily by rising new troubadors." 20% (Kidsbeat column) of material aimed at juvenile audience.

Fiction: Middle readers, young adults: storytelling. "We have a storytelling column, Endless Tale."

Nonfiction: Picture-oriented material: music. Young readers: music. Middle readers: history, interview/profile, music. Young adults: history, how-to, humorous, interview/profile, religious, music. Does not want to see "non-music material."

How to Contact/Writers: Fiction/nonfiction: "Query first." Will consider simultaneous and electronic submissions via disk or modem.

Illustration: Prefers to review "music-oriented themes—folk preferred." Will review ms/illustration packages.

How to Contact/Illustrators: Ms/illustration packages: "Query first and foremost!" Illustrations only: Send tearsheets. Reports only if interested.

Terms: Pays on publication. Buys first North American serial rights or first rights. Pay is "negotiable." Writer's/illustrator's guidelines free with SASE.

Tips: "Be as pertinent as possible to folk music needs and interests. We accept many freelance reviews of artists and their work."

THE SINGLE PARENT, Journal of Parents Without Partners, Inc., Parents Without Partners, Inc., 8807 Colesville Rd., Silver Spring MD 20910. (301)588-9354. FAX: (301)588-9216. Articles/Fiction Editor/Art Director: Rene McDonald. Bimonthly magazine. Estab. 1957. Circ. 125,000. Members of PWP are single parents who are divorced, widowed or never married. "All our material is related to this basic fact. We look at the positive side of our situation and are interested in all aspects of parenting, and the particular situation of single parenting." 10% of material aimed at juvenile audience.

Fiction: All levels: contemporary, humorous, problem solving, suspense/mystery/adventure. Does not want to see "downers" or sports, romance, or anthropomorphic material. Buys 12 mss/year. Average word length: 800-1,500. Byline given.

Nonfiction: Picture-oriented material: careers, cooking, games/puzzles, health, humorous, problem-solving. Young readers, young adults: careers, cooking, education, health, history, humorous, interview/profile, problem-solving. Middle readers: careers, cooking, education, health, history. "We do not ordinarily use nonfiction aimed at children, but could be persuaded by a particularly good piece." Does not want to see material unrelated to single-parent children and families. Average word length: 800-1,800. Byline given.

How to Contact/Writers: Fiction/nonfiction: Send complete ms. Reports on queries/mss in 6 weeks. Will consider simultaneous submissions. Scannable manuscripts are required.

Illustration: Buys 4-6 illustrations/issue. Preferred theme or style: Line art, sometimes with mechanicals. "Must fit trim size—8¼ × 10¾." No special preference for style, but leans toward realistic. Will review ms/illustration packages. Works on assignment only.

How to Contact/Illustrators: Ms/illustration packages: Send complete ms with final art with prepaid return envelope. Illustrations only: Send nonreturnable samples in

Sonia Safier-Kerzner received $140 for this pen and ink illustration used with a short story in **Single Parent** *magazine. The story, entitled "What's in a Name?" is about a young girl who feels "different." Safier-Kerzner says she wanted the mood of her artwork to convey hesitance, awkwardness and some sadness. "Single Parent gives its illustrators great conceptual freedom," she says. "When the end product—the printed piece—produces well and conveys the message I want it to, it gives me great satisfaction."*

© 1991 by Sonia Safier-Kerzner

whatever form the artist prefers. Reports on art samples only if interested. Original artwork returned at job's completion.

Photography: Wants to see "children with one parent, children interacting, including angrily." Model/property release required. Uses 8×10 b&w prints, 35mm transparencies. To contact, photographer should query with samples; provide resume, business card and tearsheets.

Terms: Pays on publication. Buys one-time rights to mss, artwork and photos. Pays $35-125 for unsolicited stories. Pays $125/color (cover) illustration; $50-75/b&w (inside); $50-75/color (inside). Sample copy $1.25 (first class postage). Writer's/illustrator's guidelines free with SASE.

Tips: Writers: "Study your target; do not submit material if you've never seen the magazine. In stories where the protagonist undergoes a behavior change, build up a credible reason for it. 'Comes to realize' is not a credible reason. Be aware of the age you are writing about and for. Include less fluff and more substance in attractive formats. We are overstocked at the moment with children's stories, but still buy one occasionally that we're unable to resist. Our greatest need is for articles for adults, in particular, articles on parenting from the single father's perspective." Illustrators: "Get examples of your work to as many editors as possible, but remember, there are hundreds of others doing the same thing. All samples are reviewed, and I put those that appeal to me in a separate file as potential illustrators for the magazine. To get into the 'may call on' file, provide me with nonreturnable samples that illustrate the broadest range of your work—I may not appreciate your cartoon style, but think your realistic style is super or vice versa."

SKIPPING STONES, A Multi-Cultural Children's Quarterly, P.O. Box 3939, Eugene OR 97403. (503)342-4956. Managing Editor: Arun N. Toké. Quarterly magazine. Estab. 1988. Circ. 3,000. "*Skipping Stones* is a multi-cultural nonprofit children's magazine designed to encourage cooperation, creativity and celebration of cultural and environmental richness. We encourage submissions by minorities and under-represented populations."

Nonfiction: All age groups: animal, nature/environment, problem-solving, religious, travel, and multicultural and environmental awareness. Does not want to see preaching or abusive language. Average word length: 300 words. Byline given.

How to Contact/Writers: Query. For nonfiction, send complete ms. Reports on queries in 2 months. Will consider simultaneous submissions. Please include your name on each page.

Illustration: Prefers b&w drawings especially by young adults. Will consider all illustration packages. B&w photos also welcome.

How to Contact/Illustrators: Submit complete ms with final art. Submit tearsheets. Reports back in 2 months (only if interested). Original artwork returned at job's completion.

Terms: No payment; just a copy of the magazine containing work. Acquires one-time rights. Sample copy for $4 with SAE and 4 first class stamps. Writer's/illustrator's guidelines for 1 first class stamp and 4×9 SAE.

Tips: Wants material "meant for children," with multi-cultural or environmental awareness theme. "Think, live and write as if you were a child. Let the 'inner child' within you speak out—naturally, uninhibited." Wants "material that gives insight on cultural celebrations, lifestyle, custom and tradition, glimpse of daily life in other countries and cultures. Photos, songs, artwork are most welcome if they illustrate/highlight the points. Translations are welcome if new submission is in a language other than English. In 1992, we will be publishing two special issues on the themes of women (and Girl Child) around the world and native societies in the Americas. We're seeking materials for these two themes."

*SPARK! Creative Fun for Kids, F&W Publications, 1507 Dana Ave., Cincinnati OH 45207. (513)531-2222. FAX: (513)531-1843. Editorial Director: Michael Ward. Art Director: Stephanie Redman. Monthly magazine. Estab. 1991. Circ. 80,000. "Publication devoted to nurturing creativity in 6- to 11-year-old children; publish art and writing projects that kids can do on their own or with minimal help from their parents."
Fiction: Young readers and middle readers: adventure, fantasy, folktales, humorous, problem-solving, sports. Buys approx. 15-20 mss/year. Average word length: 300-800 words. Byline given.
Nonfiction: Young readers, middle readers: arts/crafts and how-to. Buys 60-70 mss/year. Average word length: 250-500. Byline given.
Poetry: Maximum length: 100 words.
How to Contact/Writers: Fiction/nonfiction: Query with published clips. Reports in 4 weeks. Publishes ms 3 months after acceptance. Will consider simultaneous submissions and previously published work.
Illustration: Buys 5-7 illustrations/issue; 40 illustrations/year. Reviews ms/illustration packages; review artwork for future assignments; works on assignment only.
How to Contact/Illustrators: Illustrations only: provide resume and tearsheets. Reports back only if interested. Original work returned upon job's completion.
Terms: Pays on acceptance. Buys first North American serial rights. Purchases first North American rights for artwork. Pays $50-250 for articles. Sample copies for $2.50 and SASE. Writer's guidelines free for SASE.
Tips: "Writers should understand the developmental levels of kids 4-11, and know how to structure articles and projects to meet their needs." Seeking "articles that describe, step-by-step, and illustrate creative projects for kids. Query with the entire articles and photos of the projects."

SPORTS ILLUSTRATED FOR KIDS, Time Inc. Magazine Company, 1271 Avenue of the Americas, New York NY 10020. (This market did not respond to requests to be listed.)

STORY FRIENDS, Mennonite Publishing House, 616 Walnut Ave., Scottdale PA 15683. (412)887-5181. FAX: (412)887-3111. Editor: Marjorie Waybill. Art Director: Jim Butti. "Monthly in weekly issues magazine." Estab. 1905. Circ. 10,000. Story paper that reinforces Christian values for children ages 4-9.
Fiction: Young readers: contemporary, humorous, problem solving, religious, relationships. Buys 45 mss/year. Average word length: 300-800. Byline given.
Nonfiction: Picture-oriented and young readers: interview/profile, nature/environment. Buys 10 mss/year. Average word length: 300-800. Byline given.
Poetry: "I like variety—some long story poems and some four-lines."
How to Contact/Writers: Fiction/nonfiction: Send complete ms. Reports on mss in 2-3 weeks. Will consider simultaneous submissions.
Illustration: Works on assignment only.
Terms: Writer's guidelines free with SAE and 2 first class stamps.

Always include a self-addressed stamped envelope (SASE) or International Reply Coupon (IRC) with submissions.

STRAIGHT, Standard Publishing, 8121 Hamilton Ave., Cincinnati OH 45231. (513)931-4050. Articles/Fiction Editor: Carla J. Crane. "Quarterly in weekly parts" magazine. Circ. 60,000. *Straight* is a magazine designed for today's Christian teenagers.

Fiction: Young adults: contemporary, humorous, problem-solving, religious, sports. Does not want to see science fiction, fantasy, historical. Buys 100-115 mss/year. Average word length: 1,100-1,500. Byline given.

Nonfiction: Young adults: careers, how-to, humorous, interview/profile, nature/environment, problem solving, religious. Does not want to see devotionals. Buys 24-30 mss/year. Average word length: 500-1,000. Byline given.

Poetry: Reviews poetry from teenagers only.

How to Contact/Writers: Fiction/nonfiction: Query or send complete ms. Report on queries in 1-2 weeks; mss in 4-6 weeks. Will consider simultaneous submissions.

Illustration: Buys 40-45 illustrations/year. Uses color artwork only. Preferred theme or style: Realistic, cartoon (full-color only). Will review ms/illustration packages "on occasion." Works on assignment only.

How to Contact/Illustrators: Ms/illustration packages: Query first. Illustrations only: Submit portfolio for review; provide resume, business card, promotional literature or tearsheets.

Photography: Purchases photos separately. Looking for contemporary teenagers. Model/property release required. Uses 5 × 7 or 8 × 10 b&w prints and 35mm transparencies. To contact, photographer should send unsolicited photos by mail.

Terms: Pays on acceptance. For mss buys first North American rights; second serial (reprint rights). Buys full rights for artwork; one-time rights for photos. Pays 3-7¢ per word for articles. Pays illustrators $150-250/color inside. Photographers paid per photo (range: $50-125). Sample copy free with business SASE. Writer's/illustrator's guidelines free with business SASE.

Tips: "The main characters should be contemporary teens who cope with modern-day problems using Christian principles. Stories should be uplifting, positive and character-building, but not preachy. Conflicts must be resolved realistically, with thought-provoking and honest endings. Accepted length is 1,100 to 1,500 words. Nonfiction is accepted. We use devotional pieces, articles on current issues from a Christian point of view, and humor. Nonfiction pieces should concern topics of interest to teens, including school, family life, recreation, friends, part-time jobs, dating and music." (See listing for *R-A-D-A-R*.)

SUPERSCIENCE BLUE, Scholastic, Inc., 730 Broadway, New York NY 10003. (212)505-3000. Editor: Lorraine Hopping Egan. Art Director: Susan Kass. Monthly (during school year) magazine. Estab. 1989. Circ. 375,000. "News and hands-on science for children in grades 4-6. Designed for use in a class setting; distributed by teacher. Articles make science fun and interesting for a broad audience of children. Issues are theme-based."

Nonfiction: Middle readers: animal, how-to (science experiments), nature/environment, problem solving, science topics. Does not want to see "general nature stories. Our focus is science with a *news* or *hands-on* slant. Write for editorial calendar." Buys 10-20 mss/year. Average word length: 250-600. Byline sometimes given.

How to Contact/Writers: Nonfiction: Query with published clips. (Most freelance articles are assigned.) Reports on queries in 4-6 weeks. Publishes ms 4 months after acceptance.

Illustration: Buys 2-3 illustrations/issue; 10-12 illustrations/year. Works on assignment only.

How to Contact/Illustrators: Illustrations only: Send résumé and tearsheets. Reports on art samples only if interested. Original artwork returned at job's completion.
Terms: Pays on acceptance. Buys all rights. Pays $150-450. Illustrations only: $75+/ b&w (inside); $150-1,200/color (inside) (complicated spreads only). Writer's guidelines free on request.
Tips: Looks for "news articles and photo essays. Good journalism means always going to *primary* sources—interview scientists in the field, for example, and *quote* them for a more lively article."

TAKE 5, Back to the Bible, P.O. Box 82808, Lincoln NE 68501. (402)474-4567. Editor: Marcia Claesson. Quarterly devotional. Circ. approx. 25,000.
Nonfiction: Young adults: Commentaries on specific Bible passages. By assignment only. Writer's must agree with Statement of Faith. Average word length: 200.
How to Contact/Writers: Send samples of devotionals. Reports in 2 weeks.
Terms: Buys first rights. Pays $15.

'TEEN MAGAZINE, Petersen Publishing Co., 8490 Sunset Blvd., Los Angeles CA 90069. (213)854-2950. Editor: Roxanne Camron. Fiction Editor: Karle Dickerson. Art Director: Laurel Finnerty. Monthly magazine. Estab. 1957. Circ. 1,100,000. "We are a pure junior high and senior high female audience. *'TEEN* teens are upbeat and want to be informed."
Fiction: Young adults: humorous, problem-solving, romance and spy/mystery/adventure. Does not want to see "that which does not apply to our market—i.e., science fiction, history, religious, adult-oriented." Buys 12 mss/year. Length for fiction: 10-15 pages typewritten, double-spaced.
Nonfiction: Young adults: animal, how-to, humorous, interview/profile, problem solving and young girl topics. Does not want to see adult oriented, adult point of view." Buys 25 mss/year. Length for articles: 10-20 pages typewritten, double-spaced. Byline given.
How to Contact/Writers: Fiction/nonfiction: Query. Reports on queries/mss in 10 weeks. Will consider electronic submissions via disk or modem.
Illustration: Buys 0-4 illustrations/issue. Preferred theme or style: "Various styles for variation. Use a lot of b&w illustration. Light, upbeat." Will review ms/illustration packages; illustrator's work for possible future assignments.
How to Contact/Illustrators: Ms/illustration packages: "Query first." Illustrations only: "Want to see samples whether it be tearsheets, slides, finished pieces showing the style."
Terms: Pays on acceptance. Buys all rights. Pays $25-400 for assigned articles. Pays $25-250/b&w inside; $100-400/color inside. Writer's/illustrator's guidelines free with SASE.
Tips: Illustrators: "Present professional finished work. Get familiar with magazine and send samples that would be compatible with the style of publication." There is a need for artwork with "fiction/specialty articles. Send samples or promotional materials on a regular basis."

TEEN POWER, Scripture Press Publications, Inc., Box 632, Glen Ellyn IL 60138. (708)668-3806. Editor: Amy J. Swanson. Quarterly magazine. Estab. 1965. "*Teen Power* is an eight-page Sunday School take-home paper aimed at 11-16 year olds in a conservative Christian audience. Its primary objective is to help readers see how principles for Christian living can be applied to everyday life."
Fiction: Young adults: contemporary, humorous, problem solving, religious, sports. Do not want to see "unrealistic stories with tacked-on morals. Fiction should be true-to-life and have a clear, spiritual take-away value." Buys 50 mss/year. Average word length: 400-1,200. Byline given.

Nonfiction: Young adults: how-to, humorous, interview/profile, problem-solving religion. Does not want to see "articles with no connection to Christian principles." Buys 30 mss/year. Average word length: 250-700. Byline given.
How To Contact/Writers: Fiction/nonfiction: Send complete ms. Reports on mss in 2 months. Average length of time between acceptance and publication of work: "at least one year." Will consider simultaneous submissions.
Terms: Pays on acceptance. Buys one-time rights. Pays $20-120/unsolicited articles. Sample copies and writer's guidelines for #10 SAE and 1 first class stamp.

3-2-1 CONTACT, Children's Television Workshop, One Lincoln Plaza, New York NY 10023. (212)595-3456. Articles Editor: Jonathan Rosenbloom. Fiction Editor: Curtis Slepian. Art Director: Al Nagy. Magazine published 10 times/year. Estab. 1979. Circ. 440,000. This is a science and technology magazine for 8-14 year olds. Features cover all areas of science and nature.
Fiction: "Our fiction piece is an on-going series called "The Time Team." So far it has been written in-house."
Nonfiction: Middle readers: animal, how-to, interview/profile. Young adults: animal, how-to, interview/profile. Does not want to see religion, travel or history. Buys 20 mss/year. Average word length: 750-1,000. Byline given.
How to Contact/Writers: Fiction/nonfiction: Query with published clips. Reports on queries in 3 weeks.
Illustration: Buys 15 illustrations/issue; buys 150 illustrations/year. Works on assignment only.
How to Contact/Illustrators: Illustrations only: Send tearsheets. Reports on art samples only if interested. Original artwork returned at job's completion.
Terms: Pays on acceptance. Pays $100-600 for assigned/unsolicited articles. Pays $500-1,000/color (cover) illustration; $150-300/b&w (inside); $175-350/color (inside). Sample copy for $1.75 and 8 × 14 SASE; writer's/illustrator's guidelines free with 8½ × 11 SASE.
Tips: Looks for "features. We do not want articles based on library research. We want on-the-spot interviews about what's happening in science now." (See listing for *Kid City*.)

TOGETHER TIME, Children's Ministries, 6401 The Paseo, Kansas City MO 64131. Editor: Lynda T. Boardman. Executive Editor: Mark A. York. Weekly tabloid. "*Together Time* is a take-home reading piece for 3 and 4 year-olds and their parents. The major purposes of *Together Time* are to provide a home-reading piece to help parents build Christian behavior and values in their children, and to provide life-related home reinforcement for Biblical concepts taught in the Sunday School curriculum."
Fiction: Picture material: religious. "Fiction stories should have definite Christian emphasis or character-building values, without being preachy. The setting, plot and action should be realistic." Average word length: 150-200. Byline given.
Nonfiction: Picture-oriented material: religion.
Poetry: Maximum line length: 4-8 lines.
Photography: Purchases photos separately. Uses 35mm transparencies. To contact, photographers should send unsolicited photos by mail.
How to Contact/Writers: Fiction: Send complete ms. Reports on mss in 10-12 weeks.
Terms: Pays on acceptance. Buys all rights and first rights. Pays 5¢/word for multi-use rights; 3-5¢/word for first rights. Complimentary copy mailed to contributor. Writer's guidelines free with #10 SASE.
Tips: "*Together Time* is planned to reinforce the Biblical concepts taught in the Sunday School curriculum. Because of this, the basic themes needed are as follows: security in knowing there is a God, God is creator and giver of good gifts, Jesus is God's son, Jesus is a friend and helper, the Bible is God's special book, introduction to God's love and forgiveness, asking forgiveness (from parents, teacher, friends and God), expressing

simple prayers, church is a special place where we learn about God, each person is special and loved by God, accept failure without losing self-confidence, desire to be like Jesus, desire to be helpful, appreciate God's world, appreciate community helpers." (See listing for *Discoveries*.)

TOUCH, Calvinettes, Box 7259, Grand Rapids MI 49510. (616)241-5616. Editor: Joanne Ilbrink. Managing Editor: Carol Smith. Art Director: Chris Cook. Monthly (with combined issues May/June, July/Aug.) magazine. Circ. 15,200. "*Touch* is designed to help girls ages 9-14 see how God is at work in their lives and in the world around them."
Fiction: Middle readers: animal, contemporary, history, humorous, problem solving, religious, romance. Does not want to see unrealistic stories and those with trite, easy endings. Buys 40 mss/year. Average word length: 400-1,000. Byline given.
Nonfiction: Middle readers: how-to, humorous, interview/profile, problem solving, religious. Buys 5 mss/year. Average word length: 200-800. Byline given.
How to Contact/Writers: Fiction/nonfiction: Send complete ms. Report on mss in 4 months. Will consider simultaneous submissions.
Illustration: Buys 1-2 illustrations/issue; buys 10-15 illustrations/year. Prefers illustrations to go with stories. Will review ms/illustration packages. Works on assignment only.
How to Contact/Illustrators: Ms/illustration packages: "We would prefer to consider finished art with a ms." Illustrations only: "A sample of work could be submitted in tearsheets or rough drafts." Reports on art samples only if interested.
Terms: Pays on publication. Buys first North American serial rights; first rights; second serial (reprint rights); simultaneous rights. Pays $20-50 for assigned articles; $5-30 for unsolicited articles. "We send complimentary copies in addition to pay." Additional payment for ms/illustration packages: $5-20. Pays $25-50/b&w (cover) illustration; $15-25/b&w (inside) illustration. Writer's guidelines free with SASE.
Tips: Writers: "The stories should be current, deal with adolescent problems and joys, and help girls see God at work in their lives through humor as well as problem solving." Illustrators: Write for guidelines and our biannual update. It is difficult working with artists who are not local."

TQ, Teen Quest, Good News Broadcasting Assoc., Box 82808, Lincoln NE 68501. (402)474-4567. FAX: (402)474-4519. Managing Editor: Lisa Thompson. Art Director: Victoria Valentine. Monthly (combined July/August issue) magazine. Estab. 1947. Circ. 55,000. "Ours is a magazine for Christian teenagers. Articles and fiction purchased from freelancers must have a Christian basis, be relevant to contemporary teen culture, and be written in a style understandable and attractive to teenagers. Artwork must be likewise appropriate."
Fiction: Young adults: contemporary, fantasy, humorous, problem solving, religious, romance, science fiction, sports, suspense/mystery/adventure. Buys 40 mss/year. Average word length: 1,500-3,000. Byline given.
Nonfiction: Young adults: how-to, humorous, interview/profile, problem solving, religious, travel. Buys 30 mss/year. Average word length: 500-2,000. Byline given.
How to Contact/Writers: Fiction/nonfiction: Query. Reports on queries in 6 weeks; mss in 6-8 weeks. Will consider simultaneous submissions (indicate so).
Illustration: Buys 5 illustrations/issue; buys 50 illustrations/year. Preferred theme or style: "Realistic, somewhat contemporary, but not too far out of the mainstream." Works on assignment only.
How to Contact/Illustrators: Ms/illustration packages: Query only. Illustrations only: Send tearsheets. Reports on art samples only if interested. Original artwork returned at job's completion.
Terms: Pays on completion of assignment. Buys one-time rights. Pays 10-15¢/word for assigned articles; 7-12¢/word for unsolicited articles. Sample copy for 10 × 12 SAE and

5 first-class stamps; writer's/illustrator's guidelines for business-size envelope and 1 first-class stamp.

Tips: Fiction: be current; Christian message without being "preachy." "Most stories we buy will center on the lives and problems of 14 to 17 year-old characters. The problems involved should be common to teens (dating, family, alcohol and drugs, peer pressure, school, sex, talking about one's faith to nonbelievers, standing up for convictions, etc.) in which the resolution (or lack of it) is true to our reader's experiences. In other words, no happily-ever-after endings, last-page spiritual conversions or pat answers to complex problems. We're interested in the everyday (though still profound) experiences of teen life—stay away from sensationalism."

TURTLE MAGAZINE, For Preschool Kids, Ben Franklin Literary & Medical Society, Children's Better Health Institute, Box 567, Indianapolis IN 46206. (317)636-8881. Editor: Christine Clark. Art Director: Bart Rivers. Monthly/bimonthly magazine, Jan./Feb., March, April/May, June, July/August, Sept., Oct./Nov., Dec. Circ. approx. 550,000. *Turtle* uses bedtime or naptime stories that can be read to the child. Also used are poems and health-related articles. All but 2 pages aimed at juvenile audience.

Fiction: Picture-oriented material: animal, contemporary, health-related. "Need stories featuring the Turtle character, PokeyToes (study current issues for a feel of what the character is like). Also needs action rhymes to foster creative movement." Does not want to see stories about monsters or scary things. Avoid stories in which the characters indulge in unhealthy activities like eating junk food. Buys 50 mss/year. Average word length: 200-600. Byline given.

Nonfiction: Picture-oriented material: animal, contemporary, health. Buys 20 mss/year. Average word length: 200-600. Byline given.

How to Contact/Writers: Fiction/nonfiction: Send complete ms. Reports on mss in 8-10 weeks.

Illustration: Buys 20-25 illustrations/issue; 160-200 illustrations/year. Prefers "realistic and humorous illustration."

Terms: Pays 10¢/word for articles. Pays $250/color (cover) illustration, $30-70/b&w (inside); $65-140/color (inside). Sample copy 75¢. Writer's/illustrator's guidelines free with SAE and 1 first-class stamp.

Tips: "We're beginning to edit *Turtle* more for the very young preschooler, so we're looking for stories and articles that are written more simply than those we've used in the past. Our need for health-related material, especially features that encourage fitness, is ongoing. Health subjects must be age-appropriate. When writing about them, think creatively and lighten up! Fight the tendency to become boringly pedantic. Nobody—not even young kids—likes being lectured. Always keep in mind that in order for a story or article to educate preschoolers, it first must be truly entertaining—warm and engaging, exciting, or genuinely funny. Understand that writing for *Turtle* is a difficult challenge." (See listings for *Children's Digest, Children's Playmate, Child Life, Humpty Dumpty's Magazine, Jack and Jill*.)

VENTURE, Christian Service Brigade, Box 150, Wheaton IL 60189. (708)665-0630. Articles/Fiction Editor: Deborah Christensen. Art Director: Robert Fine. Bimonthly magazine. Estab. 1937. Circ. 23,000. The magazine is designed "to speak to the concerns of boys from a biblical perspective. To provide wholesome, entertaining reading for boys."

Fiction: Middle readers, young adults: contemporary, humorous, problem-solving, religious, sports, suspense/mystery/adventure. Does not want to see fantasy, romance, science fiction. Buys 12 mss/year. Average word length: 1,000-1,500. Byline given.

Nonfiction: Middle readers, young adults: animal, how-to, humorous, interview/profile, problem solving, religious, travel. Buys 3 mss/year. Average word length: 1,000-1,500. Byline given.

How to Contact/Writers: Fiction/nonfiction: send complete ms. Reports on queries in 1 week; mss in 2 weeks. Will consider simultaneous submissions.
Illustration: Buys 3 illustrations/issue; buys 18 illustrations/year. Will review ms/illustration packages.
How to Contact/Illustrators: Ms/illustration packages: send complete ms. Illustrations only: Send tearsheets, slides. Reports on art samples in 2 weeks. Original artwork returned at job's completion.
Terms: Pays on publication. Buys first North American serial rights; first rights; one-time rights; second serial (reprint rights). Pays $75-150 for assigned articles; $30-100 for unsolicited articles. Pays $35-125/b&w (cover) illustration; $35-50/b&w (inside) illustration. Sample copy $1.85 with 9×12 SAE and 98¢ postage affixed. Writer's/illustrator's guidelines free with SAE and 1 first class stamp.

VOICE, Scholastic, Inc., 730 Broadway, New York NY 10003. (212)505-3000. Fiction Editor: Forrest Stone. Art Director: Joy Makon. Biweekly "during school year (16 issues/year)" magazine. Estab. 1946. Circ. 250,000. *Voice* is "a language-arts magazine for junior high and high school students."
Fiction: Young adults: contemporary, fantasy, history, humorous, problem-solving, romance, science fiction, sports, spy/mystery/adventure, poetry and drama. Does not want to see "anything over 3,000 words unless writer is quite established." Buys 10 mss/year. Average word length: up to 3,000. Byline given.
Nonfiction: Young adults: humorous, problem solving and travel. Buys 5 mss/year. Average word length: up to 1,000. Byline given.
Poetry: Reviews "good" poetry; send no more than 10 submissions.
How to Contact/Writers: Fiction: Send complete ms. Nonfiction: Query with published clips. Reports on queries in 2-4 weeks; mss in 1-3 months. Will consider simultaneous submissions.
Terms: Pays on publication. Pays $100-500 for assigned and unsolicited articles.

WITH, Faith & Life Press, Mennonite Publishing House, Box 347, 722 Main, Newton KS 67114. (316)283-5100. Published 8 times a year. Circ. 5,000. Magazine published for teenagers, ages 15-18, in Mennonite congregations. We deal with issues affecting teens and try to help them make choices reflecting an Anabaptist-Mennonite faith.
Fiction: Young adults: contemporary, fantasy, folktales, humorous, problem solving, religious, sports. Buys 10 mss/year. Average word length: 1,000-2,000. Byline given.
Nonfiction: Young adults: first-person teen personal experience (as-told-to), careers, how-to, humorous, nature/environment, problem-solving, religious. Buys 15-20 mss/year. Average word length: 500-1,500. Byline given.
Poetry: Wants to see religious, humorous, nature. Maximum word length: 50.
How to Contact/Writers: Send complete ms. Query on first-person teen personal experience stories. Reports on queries in 1 month; mss in 3 months. Will consider simultaneous submissions.
Illustration: Buys 6-8 illustrations/issue; buys 50-60 illustrations/year. Uses b&w and 2-color artwork only. Preferred theme or style: Candids/interracial. Will review ms/illustration packages.
How to Contact/Illustrators: Ms/illustration packages: Query first. Illustrations only: Send 8×10 b&w prints. Reports on art samples in 1 month. Original art work returned at job's completion.
Photography: Looking for teens (ages 15-18), ethnic minorities, candids. Uses 8×10 b&w glossy prints. To contact, photographers should send unsolicited photos by mail.
Terms: Pays on acceptance. For mss buys one-time rights; second serial (reprint rights). Buys one-time rights for artwork and photos. Pays 4¢/word for unsolicited unpublished manuscripts; 2¢/word for reprints. Will pay more for assigned as-told-to stories. Pays $25-50/b&w (cover) illustration; $20-35/b&w (inside) illustration. Photographers are

Close-up

Deborah Christensen
Managing Editor
Venture
Wheaton, Illinois

The magazine's mission sounds simple enough—to speak to the concerns of boys from a biblical perspective, and to provide wholesome, entertaining reading for boys. But simplicity can be deceptive. According to Deborah Christensen, managing editor of *Venture* magazine, oversimplification is the trap too many freelance writers get caught in when incorporating Christian themes into their work.

"We receive mostly inspirational stories where the problem is all fixed up at the end. And that's just not the way life is," she says. "A lot of the pieces we receive don't show how Christianity is woven through the life of the character, making it a natural part of daily life . . . life is a process, and sometimes the loose ends aren't always wrapped up."

Venture was launched in 1959 as a magazine for members of the Christian Service Brigade. The Brigade, a non-denominational organization, sponsors boys clubs through churches throughout the United States and Canada. Some 20,000 boys, ages 8 to 18, receive the bimonthly publication. *Venture* is designed to reinforce the Christian principles Brigade members are encouraged to live by—community service and devotion to God and family—and to provide role models for Christian leadership.

Working these principles into fiction and nonfiction pieces that entertain *Venture* readers without heavy-handed morality is the tricky part, according to Christensen. "Very few writers can do that," she says. "We don't want tacked-on lessons, and we don't want (writers) to sermonize. We want them to show Christianity is woven into every area of your life, and not just something you sit down and pray about." She cites the example of a recently-published short story which incorporated Christian values and reflected the complexity of the life choices boys face: "The character had come to a conclusion about the way he wanted to live his life, but it was still a struggle. It wasn't 'happily-ever-after.' Through circumstances he had reached some decisions on a course to take, but the problem wasn't solved yet."

Complex, and even controversial, issues are not off limits to *Venture* freelancers. Previous issues have handled such heavyweight subjects as suicide. Christensen says she wants that trend to continue. "I want to start dealing with the things kids face that I didn't face when I was in junior high and high school 20 years ago, such as drugs and gangs." Also, she says she wouldn't mind lightly touching on sexual issues by promoting abstinence among boys. Christensen does encourage writers to exercise caution with these types of issues. "The magazine comes into the home and parents read it too, so we have to strike that delicate balance between meeting the needs of the boys and yet not offending the parents."

Articles and short stories dealing with "the big stuff" are by no means all Christensen looks for in manuscripts. Much of the material published in *Venture* deals with the more routine aspects of boys' lives—stories about sports and adventure, self-discipline, prayer, getting along with parents and discipling and growing in Christ. Christensen adds too few writers submit humorous pieces. "I know humor is hard to write, but boys like humor. If you're gearing for that junior high age, they have really bizarre senses of humor. What we really need is somebody who can creatively incorporate humor with issues of the day, and in a wide range of subject matter."

Venture publishes roughly 12 fiction and 3 nonfiction freelance pieces a year, which Christensen selects from the stacks of some 1,300 manuscripts she receives annually. She says she looks for pieces which exhibit conflict and resolution, and have Christian principles woven into the fabric of the character and his circumstances. Strong writing skills are critical, she says. "The reason we are most likely to reject something is poor writing. If the writer cannot write, I just don't get past the first page."

Venture assigns 18 to 24 projects to outside illustrators each year. Christensen says freelancers are welcome to submit samples (or photocopies of samples) of their work to the art director, who keeps them on file and makes assignments on an as-needed basis. The magazine's interior art consists of line drawings and black-and-white photography. Cover art is primarily black-and-white photography, although Christensen says they have used illustrations on the cover "on occasion."

—Anne Bowling

Steve Miller illustrated this pencil and ink/airbrush piece for Venture. According to Christensen, "The quality of Mr. Miller's work is exceptional. He captures the water and the distortions that water causes with reality. Too often the work we get doesn't compare with the samples that are sent. This piece met our hopes—so much so that this is one of the very few illustrations that we have used for a cover."

VENTURE

SHARK!
TWO BOYS' ENCOUNTER
WITH A GREAT WHITE

Meet Michael Johnson
RANKED NO. 1 IN THE WORLD
IN BOTH THE 200- AND THE 400-METER DASH

paid per photo (range: $20-50 cover only). Sample copy for 9 × 12 SAE and $1.21 postage. Writer's/illustrator's guidelines free with SASE.
Tips: "We're hungry for stuff that makes teens laugh—fiction, nonfiction, and cartoons. It doesn't have to be religious, but must be wholesome."

WONDER TIME, Beacon Hill Press, 6401 The Paseo, Kansas City MO 64131. (816)333-7000. Editor: Evelyn Beals. Weekly magazine. Circ. 45,000. "*Wonder Time* is a full-color story paper for first and second graders. It is designed to connect Sunday School learning with the daily living experiences and growth of the primary child. Since *Wonder Time's* target audience is children ages six to eight, the readability goal is to encourage beginning readers to read for themselves. The major purposes of *Wonder Time* are to: Provide a life-related paper which will build Christian values and encourage ethical behavior and provide reinforcement for the biblical concepts taught in the Word Action Sunday School curriculum."
Fiction: Young readers: problem-solving, religious. Buys 52 mss/year. Average word length: 400-550. Byline given.
Poetry: Reviews religious poetry of 4-8 lines.
How to Contact/Writers: Fiction/nonfiction: Send complete ms. Reports on queries/mss in 6-8 weeks. Will consider simultaneous submissions.
Illustration: Buys 10-15 illustrations/year. Will review illustration packages. Works on assignment only.
How to Contact/Illustrators: Ms/illustration packages: Ms with sketch. Illustrations only: Samples of work. Reports on art samples only if interested.
Terms: Pays a minimum of $25 per story for rights which allow the publisher to print the story multiple times in the same publication without repayment. Sends complimentary contributor's copies of publication. Sample copy and writer's guidelines with 9½ × 12 SAE and 2 first class stamps.
Tips: "These basic themes reappear regularly: faith in God; putting God first; choosing to please God; understanding that Jesus is God's Son and our Savior; choosing to do right; asking forgiveness; trusting God in hard times; prayer: trusting God to answer; appreciation of the Bible as God's word to man; importance of Bible memorization; understanding both meanings of church: a place where we worship God, a fellowship of God's people working together; understanding each person's value to God and to others; showing love and kindness to others; enriching family life, including non-traditional family units; addressing current problems which children may face."

YABA FRAMEWORK, Young American Bowling Alliance, 5301 South 76th St., Greendale WI 53129. (414)421-4700. Editor: Laura Plizka. Tabloid published 6 times/bowling season. Estab. 1987. Circ. 600,000. "Our audience is youth bowlers between the ages of 3-21. Our paper is predominantly nonfiction news regarding our membership, leagues and tournaments. On occasion we use puzzles, fiction and cartoons." 85% of material directed to children.
Nonfiction: Does not want to see "anything not pertaining to YABA sanctioned leagues or tournaments." Average word length: 500-1,500. Byline sometimes given.
How to Contact/Writers: Nonfiction: Query. Reports on queries in 2 weeks. Will consider simultaneous submissions.
Illustration: Buys 1 illustration/issue; 3 illustrations/year. Preferred theme or style: "Relating to youth bowling." Works on assignment only.
How to Contact/Illustrators: Ms/illustration packages: "Query first." Illustrations only: Send tearsheets. Reports on art samples only if interested. Original artwork returned at job's completion "if requested."
Terms: Pays on publication. Buys first North American serial rights. Pays $40-50/assigned articles. Sample copy for 9 × 12 SAE; writer's/illustrator's guidelines free with SASE.

THE YOUNG CRUSADER, National WCTU, 1730 Chicago Ave., Evanston IL 60201. (708)864-1396. Managing Editor: Michael C. Vitucci. Monthly magazine. Estab. 1900. Circ. 3,500. The magazine is geared to the 8-12 year old child. It stresses high morals and good character. Nature and informational stories are also used. Above all, the stories should not be preachy or religious as the magazine is used in public schools.

Fiction: Middle readers: contemporary, problem-solving, positive character building. Does not want to see preachy, religious-type stories. Buys 4 mss/year. Average word length: 550-650. Byline given.

Nonfiction: Middle readers: animal, history, interview/profile, problem solving, travel. Buys 10 mss/year. Average word length: 550-650. Byline given.

How to Contact/Writers: Fiction/nonfiction: Send complete ms. Will consider simultaneous submissions. "I require submissions to be copies. If used, I will publish; if not used, the manuscript will be destroyed."

Terms: Pays on publication. Buys second serial (reprint rights); simultaneous rights. Pays ½¢/word for assigned/unsolicited articles. Free sample copy.

Tips: "Don't write down to the child. Writers often underestimate their audience." **Looks for:** "nonfiction stories stressing good character and high morals."

YOUNG JUDAEAN, Hadassah Zionist Youth Commission, 50 W. 58th St., New York NY 10019. (212)303-8250. Editor: Ira Weiss. Published 3 times a year (fall, winter, spring). Estab. 1910. Circ. 4,000. "Magazine is intended for members—age 9-12—of Young Judaea, which is the Zionist-oriented youth movement sponsored by the Hadassah Women's Organization."

Fiction: Middle readers: contemporary, fantasy, history, humorous, science fiction, sports and spy/mystery/adventure. Does not want to see "any material that does *not* relate to Jewish themes. Also, no material whose Jewishness is theological rather than cultural." Buys 10-15 mss/year. Average word length: 500-1,500. Byline given.

Nonfiction: Middle readers, young adults: history, how-to, humorous, interview/profile, problem solving and travel. Does not want to see "anything that preaches a particular theological outlook. Anything that is *not* related to Jewish life." Buys 30 mss/year. Average word length: 500-1,500. Byline given.

How to Contact/Writers: Fiction: Send complete ms. Nonfiction: Send complete ms or query.

Illustration: Buys 6 illustrations/issue. Preferred theme or style: "Lively and anecdotal." Will review ms/illustration packages; illustrator's work for possible future assignments.

How to Contact/Illustrators: Ms/illustration packages: Send complete ms with final art. Illustrations only: Send tearsheets. Original artwork returned at job's completion "if requested."

Terms: Pays on publication. Buys first North American serial rights. Pays $20-50 for assigned articles; $20-50 for unsolicited articles. Additional payment for ms/illustration packages is "manuscript plus $20 per illustration." Pays $20-40/b&w cover illustration, $20-30 b&w inside illustration. Sample copy $1 with SASE; free writer's/illustrator's guidelines.

Market conditions are constantly changing! If you're still using this book and it is 1993 or later, buy the newest edition of Children's Writer's & Illustrator's Market at your favorite bookstore or order directly from Writer's Digest Books.

YOUNG SALVATIONIST, The Salvation Army, 615 Slaters Lane, Alexandria VA 22314. (201)239-0606. Articles Editor: Captain M. Lesa Salyer. Monthly magazine. Estab. 1984. Circ. 50,000. "We accept material with clear Christian content written for high school age teenagers. *Young Salvationist* is published for teenage members of The Salvation Army, a fundamental, activist denomination of the Christian Church."
Fiction: Young adults: religious. Buys 12-20 mss/year. Average word length: 750-1,200. Byline given.
Nonfiction: Young adults: religious. Buys 40-50 mss/year. Average word length: 750-1,200. Byline given.
Poetry: Reviews 16-20 line poetry dealing with a Christian theme. Send no more than 6 submissions.
How to Contact/Writers: Fiction/nonfiction: Query with published clips or send complete ms. Reports on queries in 2-3 weeks; mss in 1 month. Will consider simultaneous submissions.
Illustration: Buys 2-3 illustrations/issue; 20-30 illustrations/year. Will review ms/illustration packages.
How to Contact/Illustrators: Ms/illustration packages: "Query or send manuscript with art." Reports on artwork in 2-3 weeks (with SASE). Original artwork returned at job's completion "if requested."
Terms: Pays on acceptance. Buys first North American serial rights, first rights, one-time rights, second serial (reprint rights) simultaneous rights. Pays $40/assigned articles (depends on length); $25 for unsolicited articles (depends on length). Pays $100-150 color (cover) illustration; $50-100 b&w (inside) illustration; $100-150 color (inside) illustration. Sample copy for 9×12 SAE and 3 first class stamps. Writer's/illustrator's guidelines free for #10 SASE.
Tips: Writers: "Write for our themes." Looking for "nonfiction articles to fit themes."

YOUTH UPDATE, St. Anthony Messenger Press, 1615 Republic St., Cincinnati OH 45210. (513)241-5615. Articles Editor: Carol Ann Morrow. Art Director: Julie Lonneman. Monthly newsletter. Estab. 1982. Circ. 32,000. "Each issue focuses on one topic only. *Youth Update* addresses the faith and Christian life questions of young people and is designed to attract, instruct, guide and challenge its audience by applying the gospel to modern problems and situations. The students who read *Youth Update* vary in their religious education and reading ability. Write for the average high school student. This student is 15-years-old with a C+ average. Assume that they have paid attention to religious instruction and remember a little of what 'sister' said. Aim more toward 'table talk than teacher talk.' "
Nonfiction: Young adults: religious. Does not want to see travel material. Buys 12 mss/year. Average word length: 2,300-2,400. Byline given.
How to Contact/Writers: Nonfiction: Query. Reports on queries/mss in 6 weeks. Will consider computer printout and electronic submissions via disk.
Terms: Pays on acceptance. Buys first North American serial rights. Pays $325-400 for assigned/unsolicited articles. Sample copy free with #10 SAE and 1 first class stamp.
Tips: "Read the newsletter yourself—3 issues at least. In the past, our publication has dealt with a variety of topics including: dating, Lent, teenage pregnancy, baptism, loneliness, rock and roll, confirmation and the Bible. When writing, use the *New American Bible* as translation. More interested in church-related topics."

ZILLIONS: Consumer Reports for Kids, Consumers Union, 101 Truman Ave., Yonkers NY 10703-1057. Editor: Jeanne Kiefer. Art Director: Rob Jenter. Bimonthly magazine. Estab. 1990 (1980 as *Penny Power*). Circ. 275,000. "Consumer Education—advice on buying, saving, product tests, coping skills, media reviews, advertising smarts, health, ecology. Audience—kids 8-14."

Nonfiction: Middle readers and young adults: how-to, nature/environment, problem solving, sports advice, consumer education, health. "All articles are assigned—no submissions accepted." Buys 12+ mss/year. Average word length: 1,000-1,500.

How to Contact/Writers: Query with published clips. Publishes ms 3 months after acceptance.

Illustration: Buys 5 illustrations/issue. Prefers humorous, all 4-color. Reviews ms/illustration packages. Works on assignment only.

How to Contact/Illustrators: Ms/illustrations packages: query only. Illustrations only: send tearsheets. Reports on art samples only if interested. Original artwork returned at job's completion.

Terms: Pays on acceptance. Buys all rights. Pays $500-1,000 for assigned articles. Pays $1,000-1,500/color (cover); $500-1,500/color (inside). Sample copy and writer's guidelines free on request.

Other Magazine Publishers

The following magazine publishers are not included in this edition of *Children's Writer's & Illustrator's Market* for the reasons indicated. The phrase "did not respond" means the publisher was in the 1991 *Children's Writer's & Illustrator's Market* but did not respond to our written and phone requests for updated information for a 1992 listing.

Animal Tales (did not respond)

Delirium (did not respond)

Friend (ceased publishing)

Group (removed per request)

Insights (receiving too much inappropriate material)

Mad Magazine (removed per request)

Odyssey (requested removal due to change of ownership)

Pennywhistle Press (no longer using freelance work)

Scope (not accepting unsolicited material)

Six Lakes Arts (removed per request)

Teen Dream (receiving too much inappropriate material)

Tyro Magazine (ceased publishing)

U*S*Kids (requested removal due to change of ownership)

Wee Wisdom (ceased publishing)

Young American (did not respond)

Audiovisual Markets

Videocassette recorders (VCRs) can now be found in millions of homes, as well as thousands of schools. With them comes a new means of entertaining and educating children. Because of this, video products are no longer sidelines in the children's market.

It used to be that video stores were the only place to buy videos, but now they are prominent items in books and toy stores as well. Also, people are purchasing reasonably-priced videos rather than renting them, and children's videos make up a major percentage of these purchases.

Though children's entertainment videos can be considered "babysitters," parents are equally interested in the educational advantages. For example, the mass market audience has responded strongly to interactive videos, or, read-alongs for children. One such series (new this year) is the Bank Street Read-Along Story Videos, which combines live action with computer animation. In the Bank Street story videos, each story is told twice. The second version includes words printed on the screen so kids can read along.

New in this ever-expanding technological field are laser videodiscs, which are as much a threat to videotapes as compact discs were to records. They have clearer pictures than videotapes and digital sound. Laser videodiscs do not wear out, and therefore are good for repeated playing and are virtually childproof. They're used alone or in conjunction with a personal computer, making for an interactive teaching system.

The prognosis is good for the future of children's audiovisual products. Video production companies are just now starting to recognize the profit potential of the children's market. Many such production companies are included in this section and have a range of writing and animation needs that include educational and entertainment subjects. Educational films may not pay quite as much as those destined for entertainment distribution, but they are a good way to break in. Notice that video isn't the only format produced by production houses. Writers and illustrators may find themselves working on film projects, filmstrips or multi-media productions.

Be aware that audiovisual media rely more on the "visual" to tell the story. The script itself plays a secondary role and explains only what the visual message doesn't make clear to viewers. Thus, these markets may be more open to work-for-hire artists with specific skills, such as in animation, storyboarding and video graphics.

AERIAL IMAGE VIDEO SERVICES, #203, 101 W. 31 St., New York NY 10001. (212)279-6026, (800)237-4259. FAX: (212)279-6229. President: John Stapsy. Estab. 1979. Type of company: Video production and post production, and audio production and post production. Uses videotapes and audio. (For list of recent productions consult the Random House catalog of children's videos.)
Children's Writing: Does not accept unsolicited material. Submissions returned with proper SASE. Reports in "days."
Children's Illustration/Animation: Does not accept unsolicited material. Hires illustrators for: computer and hand animation, storyboarding, live action and comprehensives. Types of animation produced: cel animation, clay animation, stop motion, special

effects, 3-D, computer animation, video graphics, motion control and live action. Submission method: send cover letter, résumé and demo tape. Art samples returned with proper SASE. Reports in "weeks." Pays "per project."
Tips: When reviewing a portfolio/samples, looks for "application to a project, general talent and interests based on examples."

*BALL & CHAIN, 164 Fairfield Ave., Stamford CT 06902. (203)324-0018. Owner: Chuck Jensen. Estab. 1978. Animation studio. Uses films, videotapes.
Children's Writing: Needs: animation scripts. To submit, query. Submissions are filed.
Illustration: Hires illustrators for animation. Types of animation produced: cel animation, special effects, motion control, live action. To submit, send demo tape. Art samples are filed.

*BENNU PRODUCTIONS INC., 626 McLean Ave., Yonkers NY 10705. (914)964-1828. FAX: (914)964-2914. Producer: Wayne J. Keeley. Estab. 1985. Film and video production house. Audience: General public, businesses, schools, etc. Uses multimedia productions, films and videotapes. Recent children's productions: "Say No to Strangers," written by Wayne J. Keeley (video safety program for children); "Save Our Planet" written by Wayne J. Keeley/Chris Austermann (environmental educational video for junior/senior high). 25% of writing by freelancers; 25% of illustrating/animating by freelancers.
Children's Writing: Needs: Educational material on all relevant topics for all age levels. Subjects include: substance abuse, environment, history, health, science, art, etc. To submit, query. Submissions returned with proper SASE. Reports back only if interested. Pay varies.
Illustration: Hires illustrators for animation (computer and graphic), storyboarding, character development, live action, comprehensives, pencil testing. Types of animation produced: special effects, computer animation, video graphics, live action. To submit, send cover letter, résumé, demo tape (VHS) and business card. Art samples returned with proper SASE. Reports back only if interested. Pay varies.
Tips: "Educationally stimulating material should be submitted." Looks for "creativity, innovation, flexibility."

*BES CREATIVE, a division of BES Teleproductions, 6829-E Atmore Rd., Richmond VA 23225. (804)276-5110. Executive Producer: Carolyn McCulley. Director of Animation: Ed Lazor. Estab. 1973. Full service production company within digital post-production facility. Uses films, videotapes. "We simply produce the creative concepts developed by others."
Illustration: Types of animation produced: cel animation, clay animation, special effects, computer animation, video graphics, live action. To submit send cover letter, demo tape, proposal. Pays varies per project.

CLEARVUE, 6465 N. Avondale, Chicago IL 60631. (312)775-9433. President: Mark Ventling (for scripts); V.P. Editorial: Howard Rosemorm (for illustration/animation). Estab. 1969. Type of company: production house. Audience: educational pre-school through

✱ *The asterisk before a listing indicates the listing is new in this edition.*

high school. Uses film strips, slide sets, videotapes. 30% of writing is by freelancers; 70% of illustrating/animating is by freelancers.

Children's Writing: Needs: educational material; preschool, 5-8, 9-11, 12 and older. Submission method: query with synopsis. Submissions are returned. Reports in 2 weeks. Guidelines/catalog free. Buys material outright.

Children's Illustration/Animation: Hires illustrators for: animation, storyboarding. Types of animation produced: cel animation. Art samples returned. Reports in 2 weeks. Guidelines/catalog free. Pay: "open."

Tips: "Programs must be designed for educational market—not home or retail."

DIMENSION FILMS, 15007 Gault St., Van Nuys CA 91405. (818)997-8065. President: Gary Goldsmith. Estab. 1962. Production house. Audience: schools and libraries. Uses film strips, films, videotapes. 10% of writing is by freelancers; 100% of illustrating/ animating is by freelancers.

Children's Writing: Needs: educational material and documentaries for Kindergarten-12th-grade audience. Submission method: query. Submissions filed. Reports in a matter of weeks. "Prefer phone calls" for guidelines. Pays in accordance with Writer's Guild standards.

Children's Illustration/Animation: Hires illustrators for storyboarding, comprehensives. Types of animation produced: cel animation, video graphics, live action. Submission method: send cover letter and résumé. Reports in a matter of weeks. "Call for guidelines." Pays $30-60/frame.

Tips: Illustrators/animators: looking for "imagination, clarity and purpose." Portfolio should show "strong composition; action in stillness."

EDUCATIONAL VIDEO NETWORK, 1401 19th St., Huntsville TX 77340. (409)295-5767. Editor: Gary Edmondson. Estab. 1954. Production house. Audience: educational (school). Uses videotapes. 20% of writing by freelancers; 20% of illustrating/animating is by freelancers.

Children's Writing: Needs: "Educational material" for ages 9-11 and 12-18. Submission method: script with video or animation. Submissions returned with proper SASE. Reports in 1 month. Guidelines/catalog free. Pays writers in royalties or buys material outright.

Children's Illustration/Animation: Hires illustrators for: acetate cels, animation. Types of animation produced: cel animation stills, video graphics, live action. Submission method: send cover letter and VHS demo tape. Art samples returned with proper SASE. Reports in 1 month. Guidelines/catalog free.

Tips: "Materials should fill a curriculum need in grades 6-12." Writers/scriptwriters: "Work must be of professional quality adaptable to video format." Illustrators/animators: Looks for "creativity." "More live-action is being demanded. Go to school library and ask to review most popular A-V titles."

*FINE ART PRODUCTIONS, 67 Maple St., Newburgh NY 12550. (914)561-5866. Director: Richie Suraci. Estab. 1989. "We cover every aspect of the film, video, publishing and entertainment industry." Audience: All viewers. Uses film strips, films, slide sets, videotapes, multimedia productions, any format needed. Recent children's productions: "1991 Great Hudson River Revival," written by Richie Suraci and others; illustrated by various artists. (35mm film and print on environment, clearwater sailing ship.) "Wheel and Rock to Woodstock Bike Tour," written and illustrated by various artists; (Film, print, video on exercise, health, music and volunteerism.) Percent of freelance illustrators/animators used varies.

Children's Writing: To submit, query with synopsis, or submit synopsis/outline, completed script, résumé. Submissions are filed, or returned with proper SASE. Reports in 1 month if interested. Pay is negotiated.

Illustration: Hires illustrators for animation, storyboarding, character development, live action, comprehensives, pencil testing. Types of animation produced: cel animation, clay animation, stop motion, special effects, computer animation, video graphics, motion control, live action. To submit, send cover letter, résumé, demo tape (VHS or ¾"), b&w print samples, color print samples, tearsheets, business card. Art samples are filed, or returned with proper SASE. Reports in 1 month if interested. Guidelines/catalog for SAE. Pay is negotiated.

*JOHN GATI FILM EFFECTS, INC., Suite 832, 154 West 57th St., New York NY 10019. (212)582-9060. Director/Producer: John Gati. Estab. 1982. Animation studio and production house. Audience: Children from 9-12, and all ages. Uses film, videotapes. 100% of writing is by freelancers; 100% of illustrating/animating is by freelancers.
Children's Writing: Needs: "Animation and educational materials for ages 9-11 and 12 and older." Submission method: submit synopsis/outline and/or completed script. Submissions returned with proper SASE. Reports in a matter of weeks.
Children's Illustration/Animation: Types of animation produced: stop motion, special effects, motion control, puppets. Art samples returned with proper SASE. Guidelines/catalog free. Pays "according to projects."
Tips: Wants illustrators/animators interested in "puppet design, development and building for stop motion cinematography." Illustrator/animators: Looks for "educational video, cable and educational broadcast quality."

*GLYN/NET, INC., 155 West 23rd St., 12th Fl., New York NY 10011. (212)691-9300. FAX: (212)691-9805. Executive Producer: Patrice Samara. Estab. 1968. Production house. Audience: Theme park entertainment, business video, TV and home video. Uses multimedia productions, videotapes. Recent children's productions: "Muppet Babies Video Story Books" with Jim Henson; illustrated by various artists (moral tales for 2 and up); "Ben Vereen's Kids Sing Along," written by Dennis Scott (series of participatory videos for ages 2 and up). 25% of writing is by freelancers; 100% of illustrating/animating is by freelancers.
Children's Writing: Needs: scripts, educational material, home videos for all ages. To submit, query with synopsis. "Do not call." Submissions are filed. Submissions cannot be returned. Reports in 1 month only if interested. Pays royalty (occasionally), buys material outright.
Illustration: Hires illustrators for animation, storyboarding, live action. Types of animation produced: stop motion, special effects, computer animation, video graphics, motion control, live action. Art samples are filed. Reports in 1 month if interested. Pay varies.

*GREY FALCON HOUSE, Suite 443, 496-A Hudson St., New York NY 10014. (212)777-9042. FAX: (212)691-8661. President: Ann Grifalconi. Estab. 1972. Production house. Uses films strips, multimedia productions, films, videotapes. Recent children's productions: "The Underwear Champ" (film strips/video cassettes, the fictional story of how commercials are made for ages 9-14). "The Village of Round and Square Houses" (filmstrip and video cassettes about African village and myth). 50% of writing is by freelancers; 50% of illustrating/animating is by freelancers.
Children's Writing: Needs: new material on world subjects and folklores, myths; mostly fiction (7 and older). To submit, query with résumé. Submissions are filed, or returned with proper SASE. Reports back only if interested. Pay varies.
Illustration: Hires illustrators for animation. Types of animation produced: cel animation, clay animation, stop motion, special effects, computer animation, video graphics, motion control, live action. To submit, send résumé, b&w print samples, business card. Art samples are filed.

*HOME, INC., 731 Harrison Ave., Boston MA 02118. (617)266-1386. Director: Alan Michel. Estab. 1974. Nonprofit video production and post production facility which produces some teen television programming for the local Boston market. Audience: teenagers, teachers, instructors, education administrators, parents, social workers and court intervention professionals. Uses videotapes. Recent children's productions: "Going to Court," written by Ken Cheeseman; graphics: Alan Michel (¾" videotape puppet drama explaining the court for ages 3 through teens). "Stand Back from Crack," written by Young Nation; graphics: Alan Michel (¾" videotape, anti drug public service video for teen and pre-teen). 90% of writing is by freelancers; 15% of illustrating/animating is by freelancers.
Children's Writing: Needs: scripts, curriculum, educational support material for videos, proposal writing for elementary through high school. Subjects include social or cultural content/sometimes career or health care oriented. To submit, send synopsis/outline and résumé. Submissions are filed and cannot be returned. Reports back only if interested. Payment negotiated/commissioned.
Illustration: Hires illustrators for storyboarding and graphics. Types of animation produced: special effects, computer animation and video graphics. To submit send cover letter, résumé, VHS demo tape, b&w and color print samples. Samples are filed and not returned. Reports back only if interested. Payment negotiated. Pays $250-4,000/project for specialized animation.
Tips: "We look for cooperative associates who have a committment to quality and to their profession. This includes their presentation and follow-through in their dealings with us prior to project engagement."

*I.N.I. ENTERTAINMENT GROUP, INC., Suite 700, 11150 Olympic Blvd., Los Angeles CA 90064. (213)479-6755. FAX: (213)479-3475. President: Irv Holender. Director of Advertising: Linda Krasnoff. Estab. 1985. Producer/International Distributor. Audience: children of all ages. Uses films. Recent children's productions: "The Adventures of Oliver Twist," screenplay written by Fernando Ruiz (updated version of the Dickens tale for ages 4-12); "Alice Through the Looking Glass," screenplay written by James Brewer (updated and upbeat version of Carroll's for ages 4-12). 100% of writing is by freelancers; 100% of illustrating/animating is by freelancers.
Children's Writing: Needs: animation scripts/scripts. "Anything from fantasy to fable." To submit, query with synopsis. Submit synopsis/outline, completed script, résumé. Submissions returned with proper SASE. Reports back only if interested. Pay varies.
Illustration: Type of animation produced: computer animation. To submit, send cover letter, résumé, demo tape (VHS), color print samples, business card. Art samples are filed, returned with proper SASE or not returned. Reports back only if interested.
Tips: "We are gearing to work with fairytales or classic stories. We look for concise retelling of older narratives with slight modifications in the storyline, while at the same time introducing children to stories that they would not necessarily be familiar with. We don't hire illustrators for animation. We hire the studio. The illustrators that we hire are used to create the advertising art."

*KENSINGTON FALLS ANIMATION, Suite 200, 2921 Duss Ave., Ambridge PA 15003. (412)266-0329. FAX: (412)266-4016. Producer: Michael Schwab. Estab. 1979. Animation studio. Audience: Entertainment, educational. Uses film strips, slide sets, films, videotapes. 100% of writing is by freelancers; 100% of illustrating/animating is by freelancers.
Children's Writing: Needs: animation scripts, educational material. To submit, query with résumé. Submissions are filed. Reports back only if interested. Guidelines/catalog free on request. Writers paid in accordance with Writer's Guild standards.
Illustration: Hires illustrators for character animation, storyboarding, character development, pencil testing. Types of animation produced: cel animation. To submit, send

cover letter, résumé, demo tape (VHS or ¾"). Art samples returned with proper SASE. Guidelines/catalog free on request. Pays: $10-50/hour for storyboarding/comp work; $20-50/hour for animation work.
Tips: "We offer apprenticeships."

*KJD TELEPRODUCTIONS, 30 Whyte Dr., Voorhees NJ 08043. (609)751-3500. FAX: (609)751-7729. President: Larry Scott. Creative Director: Kim Davis. Estab. 1989. Location production services (Betacam Sp) plus interformat edit and computer animation. Audience: industrial and broadcast. Uses slide sets, multimedia productions, videotapes. Recent children's productions: "Kidstuff," written by Barbara Daye; illustrated by Larry Scott (educational vignettes for ages 6-16). 10% of writing is by freelancers; 25% of animating/illustrating by freelancers.
Children's Writing: Needs: animation. To submit, query. Submissions are filed. Reports in 2 weeks. Pays royalty, outright purchase.
Illustration: Hires illustrators for animation. Types of animation produced: computer animation. To submit, send cover letter, résumé, demo tape (VHS or ¾"), b&w print samples, tearsheets, business card. Art samples are filed. Reports in 2 weeks. Pay varies.

MARSHMEDIA, P.O. Box 8082, Shawnee Mission KS 66208. (816)523-1059. FAX: (816)333-7421. Production Director: Joan K. Marsh. Estab. 1969. Production and marketing house. Audience: grades K-12. 100% of writing is by freelancers; 100% of illustrating/animating is by freelancers.
Children's Writing: Needs: educational materials—filmstrip video scripts and book texts for grades K-12. Subjects include: "health, drug education, guidance, safety, nutrition." Submission method: query with synopsis and submit completed scripts, résumé. Submissions returned with proper SASE. Reports back only if interested. Buys material outright.
Children's Illustration/Animation: Submission method: send résumé and VHS demo tape. Art samples returned with proper SASE. Reports in 1 month.

*NATIONAL GALLERY OF ART, Education Dept., Washington DC 20565. FAX: (202)-789-2681. Coordinator of Teacher Materials: Janna Eggebeen. Estab. 1941. Museum. Audience: teachers and students. Uses film strips, slide sets, videotapes, reproductions. Recent children's productions: "The Magic Picture Frame," written by Maura Clarkin; (reproductions of paintings for NGA Museum Guide for ages 7-10). 75% of writing is by freelancers.
Children's Writing: Needs: educational material for all levels. Subjects include knowledge of art-making and art history. To submit, send résumé. Submissions are filed. Reports back only if interested. Guidelines/catalog not available. Buys material outright.

*NEW & UNIQUE VIDEOS, 2336 Sumac Dr., San Diego CA 92105. (619)282-6126. FAX: (619)283-8264. Acquisitions Manager: Candy Love. Estab. 1985. Video production and distribution services. "Audience varies with each title." Uses films and videotapes. Recent children's productions: "Battle at Durango: The First-Ever World Mountain Bike Championships," written by Patricia Mooney; produced by Mark Schulze. (VHS video mountain bike race documentary for 12 and over) "John Howard's Lessons In Cycling," written by John Howard; direction and camera by Mark Schulze. (VHS video on cycling for 12 and over.) 50% of writing is by freelancers; 85% of illustrating/animating is by freelancers.
Children's Writing: Needs: video scripts and/or completed videotape productions whose intended audiences may range from 1 and older. "Any subject matter focusing on a Special Interest that can be considered 'new and unique.' " To submit, query. Submissions are returned with proper SASE. Reports in 2-3 weeks. Payment negotiable.

Illustration: Hires illustrators for film or video animation. Types of animation produced: computer animation and video graphics. To submit, send cover letter. Art samples returned with proper SASE. Reports back in 2-3 weeks. Payment negotiable.

Tips: "As more and more video players appear in homes across the world, and as the interest in Special Interest videos climbs, the demand for more original productions is rising meteorically."

NTC PUBLISHING GROUP, 4255 W. Touhy Ave., Lincolnwood IL 60646. (708)679-5500. FAX: (708)679-2494. Editorial Director: Michael Ross. Art Director: Karen Christoffersen. Estab. 1960. Type of company: publisher. Audience: all ages. Uses film strips, multimedia productions, videotapes, books and audiocassettes. Recent children's production: *Let's Learn English Picture Dictionary*, (versions in Spanish, French, German and Italian); illustrations by Marlene Goodman. For ages 7-11. 40% of writing is by freelancers; 50% of illustrating/animating is by freelancers.

Children's Writing: Needs: educational material for ages 5-14. Subjects include: "mostly foreign language, travel and English." Submission method: submit synopsis/outline, completed script, résumé and samples. Submission returned with proper SASE only. Reports in 2 months. Guidelines/catalog free. Pays writers in royalties or buys material outright – "depends on project."

Children's Illustration/Animation: Hires illustrators for character development, comprehensives, pencil testing. Types of animation produced: stop motion, video graphics. Submission method: send cover letter, résumé, color print samples, tearsheets, business card. Art samples returned with proper SASE. Reports in 8 weeks. Guidelines/catalog free.

Tips: Looking for "experienced professionals only with proven track record in the *educational* field."

OLIVE JAR ANIMATION, 44 Write Pl., Brookline MA 02146. (612)566-6699. FAX: (617)566-0689. Executive Producer: Fred MacDonald. Estab. 1984. Type of company: animation studio. Audience: all ages. Uses films, videotapes. 75% of writing is by freelancers; 75% of illustrating/animating is by freelancers.

Illustration: Hires illustrators for animation (all types), storyboarding, pencil testing, design, ink paint, sculpture, illustration. Types of animation produced: cel animation, clay animation, stop motion, special effects. Submission method: send cover letter, résumé, demo tape, b&w print samples, color print samples, tearsheets, business card. Art samples are filed. Reports back only if interested. Pays $7-12/hour for animation work; $7-12/cel for animation work; $7-15 project for animation work; $7-15/hour for specialized animation work; $7-15/frame or cel; $7-12/project for specialized animation.

Tips: Looks for "someone who is really good at a particular style or direction as well as people who work in a variety of mediums. Attitude is as important as talent. The ability to work with others is very important."

*SEA STUDIOS, INC., 810 Cannery Row, Monterey CA 93940. (408)649-5152. FAX: (408)649-1380. Office Manager: Cindy Ignacio. Estab. 1985. Natural history video production company. Audience: general. Uses multimedia productions, videotapes. 50% of writing is by freelancers; 50% of illustrating/animating is by freelancers.

Children's Writing: Needs: educational material – target age dependent on project. To submit, send résumé (no phone calls please). Submissions returned with proper SASE. Reports back only if interested. Pay negotiable.

Illustration: To submit, send cover letter, résumé (no phone calls please). Art samples returned with proper SASE. Reports back only if interested.

*SHADOW PLAY RECORDS & VIDEO, P.O. Box 180476, Austin TX 78718. (512)345-4664. FAX: (512)345-9734. President: Peter J. Markham. Estab. 1984. Children's music publisher. Audience: families with children ages 3-10. Uses videotapes. Recent children's productions: "Joe's First Video," written by Joe Scruggs; illustrated by various artists (VHS children's music videos for preschool-10 years). 5% of writing is by freelancers; 100% of illustrating/animating by freelancers.
Children's Writing: Needs: poems or lyrics for children's songs. To submit, send query. No unsolicited submissions accepted! Submissions returned with proper SASE. Reports in 6 weeks. Pays royalty or buys material outright.
Illustration: Hires illustrators for animation, storyboarding, live action, pencil testing. Types of animation produced: cel animation, clay animation, stop motion, special effects, computer animation, video graphics, live action. To submit, send cover letter, résumé, demo tape (VHS), color print samples, business card. Art samples returned with proper SASE. Reports in 6 weeks. Pay varies by project and ability of artist.

*A.J. SHALLECK PRODUCTIONS, INC., Suite 4L, 350 East 62nd St., New York NY 10021. (212)421-2252. FAX: (212)832-7974. President; Alan J. Shalleck. Estab. 1981. Production house. Audience: pre-K-3rd grade. Uses multimedia productions, films, videotapes. Recent children's productions: "Classic Fairy Tales (Red Riding Hood, etc.)", written by various authors; illustrated by Troll Books (storybook animation of class and original stories for pre-K-3rd grade). "Curious George," written by Margret Rey and A. Shalleck; illustrated by various animators (video cassette for pre-K-3rd grade).
Children's Writing: Needs: vary with project; pre-K-3rd grade. To submit, query. Submissions are filed. Buys material outright.
Illustration: Hires illustrators for animation, storyboarding. Types of animation produced: video graphics, storybook animation. To submit, send coverletter, résumé, demo tape (VHS). Samples are returned with proper SASE.

*SISU HOME ENTERTAINMENT, #402, 20 West 38th St., New York NY 10018. (212)768-2197. FAX: (212)768-7413. President: Haim Scheinger. Estab. 1988. Video and audio manufacturers (production, distribution). Audience: Children (educational and entertainment videos). Uses videotapes and audio. Recent children's production: "Lovely Butterfly—Chanuka," written by IETV (Israel Educational TV), illustrated by IETV (Jewish Holiday-Program for ages 2-5). 25% of writing by freelancers.
Children's Writing: Needs are for publicity writing—all ages. To submit, arrange interview.
Illustration: Types of animation produced: clay animation, video graphics. To submit, send résumé. Art samples filed. Reports back only if interested.

*STILES-BISHOP PRODUCTIONS INC., 3255 Bennett Dr., Los Angeles CA 90068. (213)466-0701. FAX: (213)466-5496. Contact: Katy Bishop. Estab. 1974. Production house. Audience: children. Uses videotapes and books. Recent children's productions: "The Cinnamon Bear" (audiotape and books of children's Christmas story for ages 2-10). 50% of writing is by freelancers; 100% of illustrating/animating is by freelancers.
Children's Writing: Needs: children's fiction for ages 2-11. Subjects include: all genres. To submit, send synopsis/outline, completed script, résumé, book. Submissions cannot be returned. Reports back only if interested. Pays negotiable royalty.
Illustration: Hires illustrators for animation and books. Types of animation produced: cel animation, computer animation, live action. To submit, send cover letter, résumé, VHS or ¾" demo tape, color print samples. Art samples are not returned. Reports back only if interested. Payment negotiable.

TREEHAUS COMMUNICATIONS, INC., 906 W. Loveland Ave., P.O. Box 249, Loveland OH 45140. (513)683-5716. President: Gerard A. Pottebaum. Estab. 1968. Type of company: production house. Audience: preschool through adults. Uses film strips, multimedia productions, videotapes. Recent children's production: *Seeds of Self-Esteem* series, written by Dr. Robert Brooks, Jane Ward and Gerard A. Pottebaum, includes two books for teachers, four in-service teacher training videos and 27 posters for children from primary grades through junior high school, distributed by American Guidance Service, Inc. 30% of writing is by freelancers; 30% of illustrating/animating is by freelancers.
Children's Writing: Needs: educational material/documentaries, for all ages. Subjects include: "social studies, religious education, documentaries on all subjects, but primarily about people who live ordinary lives in extraordinary ways." Submission method: query with synopsis. Submissions returned with proper SASE. Reports in 1 month. Guidelines/catalog for SAE. Pays writers in accordance with Writer's Guild standards.
Tips: Illustrators/animators: "Be informed about movements and needs in education, multi-cultural sensitivity." Looks for "social values, originality, competency in subject, global awareness."

BILL WADSWORTH PRODUCTIONS, 2520 Longview, #308, Austin TX 78705. (512)478-2971. Director: Bill Wadsworth. Estab. 1978. Production house. Audience: K-12. Uses films, videotapes. Children's productions: *Tailypo*, written by Bill Wadsworth, 16mm Folk Tale aimed at elementary age; *Another Half*, written by Bill Wadsworth, 16mm gender role pressures aimed at ages 11-17; *First Things First*, written by Bill Wadsworth, 16mm on sexuality education aimed at ages 11-17.
Children's Writing: No needs at this time. "In future, grades 3-8." Subject matter varies. Submission method: query. Submissions are not returned. Reports back only if interested. Pay is negotiated.
Illustration: Hires illustrators periodically on freelance basis for: animation, storyboarding. Types of animation produced: cut out. Submission method: send cover letter, résumé, business card. Art samples are filed or not returned.

Audiotapes

In recent years, efforts have been made to promote children's audiovisual products, both spoken-word and musical. Those efforts have paid off, for today children's cassettes and book/cassette packages make up a significant presence in most bookstore and library inventories.

There are many indicators that the popularity of audiotapes is more than a passing fad. The art of storytelling is becoming more popular, so much that large storytelling festivals are held each year throughout the country—the largest being each October in Jonesborough, Tennessee. Most large publishers house audio departments and produce cassettes from their own backlists. Spoken word cassette/book packages are loved by children who enjoy having stories read to them (with today's two-career families, parents don't have as much time to read to their kids). Book/cassette packages also expedite the development of reading skills among children by allowing them to read the book simultaneously with the recorded narration. Though story tapes aren't produced with the intention of being a replacement for reading, they do make an excellent supplement. One trend in story tapes is for celebrities such as Robin Williams, Judy Collins, Meryl Streep and Jack Nicholson to do the narrations. Also, established authors are recording their own creations. In autumn 1991, Listening Library released *Something Big Has Been Here*, where poet Jack Prelutsky (see close-up in book publishers section, page 125) reads and sings a selection of his poems. Shel Silverstein is another author who has transferred his stories to best-selling audiocassettes.

Producers of children's music tapes are striving to record contemporary material tackling modern day issues (such as drug prevention), and with the same production qualities as recorded material for adults. Even grown-ups like to listen to some of the music currently being produced for children. This is no accident. Adults are more likely to purchase children's music they find tolerable—in other words, music they can bear to listen to over and over again (that's usually the way kids like to play it).

Flashier packaging is evident in audiocassettes in order to make them more appealing. Also, with the saturation of compact disc players in households nationwide, it is foreseen the majority of children's audio packages will soon be available on compact disc.

Represented in this section are book publishers, sheet music publishers and recording companies looking for good story material and unique children's music to record. There are some that are interested in reviewing both. Study each listing to determine what subject matter is preferred and what age levels material should be geared to. Pay rates will, for the most part, be based on royalties for writers and songwriters or, for recording musicians, on recording contracts.

*AMERICAN MELODY, P.O. Box 270, Guilford CT 06437. (203)457-0881. President: Phil Rosenthal. Music publisher, record company (American Melody), recording studio, book publisher. Estab. 1985.
Music: Releases 4 LPs/year. Member of BMI. Publishes 10 children's songs/year; records 30 children's songs/year. Works with composers, lyricists, team collaborators. For

music published pays standard royalty of 50%; for songs recorded pays musicians/artists on record contract, musicians on salary for inhouse studio work, and songwriters on royalty contract. Call first and obtain permission to submit material. Submit demo cassette. SASE/IRC for return of submission. Reports in 1 month. Recently recorded songs: *The Bremen Town Song*, by Max Showalter and Peter Walker, recorded by Max Showalter on American Melody label (folk music for ages 2-10); *Calico Pie*, by Phil Rosenthal, recorded by Phil Rosenthal on American Melody label (bluegrass music for ages 1-8).

Music Tips: "Submit as nice a demo as possible, with lyrics understandable."

Stories: "Plan to publish 2 book/cassette packages/year, beginning in 1992." 100% of stories are fiction. Will consider all kinds of genres for ages 2-10. For nonfiction, considers biography and history. Authors are paid royalties based on wholesale price. Submit both cassette tape and manuscript. Reports on queries/mss in 1 month. Catalog is free on request. Recently recorded story tapes: *The Gold Dog*, by Lev Ustinov, narrated by Max Showalter (fairy tales for ages 4-12); *Tales from the First World*, written and narrated by Sylvia and Jeff McQuillan (adaptations of folktales for ages 2-12).

BRENTWOOD MUSIC, INC., 316 Southgate Court, Brentwood TN 37027. (615)373-3950. FAX: (615)373-0386. Contact: Product Development—Children's Division. Music publisher, book publisher, record company, children's video. Estab. 1980.
Music: Releases 40 cassettes/year; 24-30 CDs/year. Member of ASCAP, BMI and SESAC. Publishes 60-120 children's songs/year. Works with composers. For music published pays standard royalty of 50% of net receipts. Submit demo cassette tape by mail; unsolicited submissions OK; 2 songs and lyric sheet or lead sheet. "No music can be returned unless you include a self addressed, stamped envelope. Do not send stamps or postage only. If you want it back, send an *envelope* big enough to hold all material and the *proper* postage. No exceptions." Reports in 3-6 months.
Stories: Will consider fictional animal, fantasy or adventure aimed at preschool through 3rd or 4th grades. Author's pay is negotiable, depending on project. Query. Reports in 1 week.

CHILDREN'S LEARNING CENTER, 117 W. Rockland Rd, P.O. Box 615, Libertyville IL 60048. (708)362-4060. FAX: (708)362-4653. President: Perry Johnson. Music publisher and record company (Dharma, Future). Estab. 1968.
Music: Releases 3 singles/year; 5 12-inch singles/year; 3 LPs/year; 1 CD/year. Member of BMI. Publishes 5 children's songs/year. Works with team collaborators. For music published pays standard royalty of 50%; for songs recorded pays songwriters on royalty contract (percentage royalty paid). Making contact: Submit up to 5 cassette demo tapes and lyric sheets by mail; unsolicited submissions OK. SASE or IRC's for return of unsolicited submissions. Reports in 6 months. Recently recorded songs: "Who Are You," recorded by Bill Hooper (sing along); "Alligator," recorded by Bill Hooper (body movements); and "Race Around Your Body," recorded by Bill Hooper (sing along).
Stories: Publishes 1 book/cassette package/year; ages 3-8. Any genre nonfiction. Authors are paid in royalties 50% minimum. Making contact: Submit cassette tape of story. Reports on queries/mss 6 months. Recently recorded story tape: "Active Music for Children," by Bill Hooper (ages 3-8, learning).

THE CHRISTIAN SCIENCE PUBLISHING SOCIETY, One Norway Street, Boston MA 02115. (617)450-2033. FAX: (617)450-2017. General Publications Product Manager: Rhoda M. Ford. Book publisher "but we do issue some recordings." Estab. 1898.
Music: Releases 2 audio cassettes/year; 1 CD/year. Hires staff writers for children's music. Works with team collaborators. Submit demo cassette tape by mail; unsolicited submissions OK. Send cover letter with proposal, references, résumé. Does not return unsolicited submissions. Reports in 2 months.

Stories: Publishes 1-2 book/cassette packages/year; 1 audio tape/year. 100% of stories are nonfiction. Will consider nonfiction for beginning readers, juveniles, teens based on the Bible (King James Version). Authors are paid royalty or outright purchase of manuscript, "negotiated with contract." Submit outline/synopsis and sample chapters. Include Social Security number with submission. Reports on queries/mss in 2 months. Trade Kit available.
Tips: "Since we are part of The First Church of Christ, Scientist, all our publications are in harmony with the teachings of Christian Science."

*THE CUTTING CORPORATION, 4940 Hampden Lane, Bethesda MD 20814. (301)654-2887. Children's audio book producer. Estab. 1971.
Stories: Publishes 10 audio tapes/year. 100% of stories are fiction. Will consider adventure, fantasy, fairy tales. Story tapes aimed at ages 3-8. For nonfiction, considers history. Story tapes aimed at ages 3-8. Authors are paid by outright purchase of manuscript. Submit casssette tape of story. Reports on queries in 1 week; on mss in 1 month. Recently recorded story tapes: *Frolics Dance*, by Soundprints Corporation, narrated by Tom Chapin (ages 5-8, animal); *Beaver at Long Pond*, by Soundprints Corporation, narrated by Red Grammer (ages 5-8, nature).

*DAVENPORT FILMS, Rt. 1 Box 527, Delaplane VA 22025. (703)592-3701. FAX: (703)592-3717. Director of Distribution: B.J. Fleming Williams. Film and video producers and distributors. Estab. 1970.
Stories: Publishes 1/year. 100% of stories are fiction. Will consider animal, fantasy and adventure stories aimed at K-adult. Authors are paid by outright purchase of ms. Reports on queries in 1 week. Catalog is free on request. Recently recorded: *Ashpet*, narrated by Louise Anderson (ages 8-adult, folk/fairy tales); *Soldier Jack*, narrated by Gary Slemp (7-adult, folk/fairy tales).

*DISCOVERY MUSIC, 5554 Calhoun Ave., Van Nuys CA 91401. (818)782-7818. FAX: (818)782-7817. Director of Publicity and Artist Mgmt.: Kym Pahoundis. Record company (Discovery Music). Estab. 1985.
Music: Releases 2-3 LPs and 2-3 CDs/year. Records approximately 45 songs/year. For songs recorded pays musicians/artists on record contract, musicians on salary for in-house studio work, songwriters on royalty contract (percentage royalty). Submit demo tape by mail; unsolicited submissions OK. Submit demo cassette with cover letter. Cannot return material. Reporting on submissions "varies." Recently recorded songs: *Polka Dot Polka*, by Joanie Bartels and Chris Rhyne, recorded by Discovery Music on Discovery Music label (children's music for ages 3-8); *Dinosaur Rock-n-Roll*, by Joanie Bartels and Chris Rhyne, recorded by Discovery music on Discovery Music label (children's music for ages 3-8).

*DOVE AUDIO, 301 N. Cañon Dr., Beverly Hills CA 90210. (213)273-7722. FAX: (213)273-0365. Customer Service Supervisor: Maryann Camarillo. Audio book publisher. Estab. 1985.

* *The asterisk before a listing indicates the listing is new in this edition.*

Stories: Publishes approx. 100/year (audiotapes only). 50% of stories are fiction; 50% nonfiction. Submit through agent only. Reports in 2 weeks. Catalog is free on request. Recently recorded story tapes include *Ryan White: My Own Story*, by Ryan White, narrated by Lukas Haas (ages 8 and up, biography).

*DUTTON CHILDREN'S BOOKS, 375 Hudson St., New York NY 10014. (212)366-2600. FAX: (212)366-2011. Senior Vice President and Publisher: Christopher Franceschelli. Book publisher.
Stories: Publishes 3 book/cassette packages/year. 100% of stories are fiction. Will consider animal and fantasy. Story tapes aimed at ages 2-10. Authors are paid 5-12% royalties based on retail price; outright purchase of $2,000-20,000; royalty inclusive. Average advance $3,000. Submit outline/synopsis and sample chapters through agent. Reports on queries in 3 weeks; on mss in 6 months. Catalog is available for 8×11 SAE and 8 first class stamps. Ms guidelines available for #10 SAE and 1 first class stamp. Recent children's story tapes include *Noah's Ark*, narrated by James Earl Jones.
Story Tips: "Do not call publisher. Get agent. Celebrity readers sell."

*EARTH MOTHER PRODUCTIONS, INC., P.O. Box 43204, Tucson AZ 85733. (602)575-5114. FAX: (602)886-3162. Vice-President: Tim Ballingham. Record company (Earth Mother Productions). Estab. 1987.
Music: Releases 2 singles and 2 CDs/year. Member of BMI. Records 20 children's songs/year. Works with composers and/or lyricists. For songs recorded pays musicians/artists on record contract, musicians on salary for inhouse studio work, mechanical licensing—royalty rate statutory. Submit demo tape by mail; unsolicited submissions OK. Submit demo cassette with lyric and lead sheet. Reports in 6 weeks. Recently recorded songs: *Night-Herding Song*, by John A. Lomax, Alan Lomax, Harry Stephens, recorded by Pamela Ballingham on Earth Mother Productions (lullaby for birth and up); and *Voyager for Dreamers*, written and recorded by Pamela Ballingham on Earth Mother Productions (lullaby for birth and up).
Music Tips: "Besides being fun, today's music must have quality of sound, be relevant, and have consciousness without being preachy."

*ROY EATON MUSIC INC., 595 Main St., Roosevelt Island NY 10044. (212)980-9046. FAX: (212)980-9068. President: Roy Eaton. Music publisher, TV and radio music production company. Estab. 1982.
Music: Member of BMI. Hires staff writers for children's music. Works with composers, lyricists, team collaborators. For music published pays standard royalty of 50%. Write or call for permission to submit material. Submit demo cassettte with lyric sheet.

*FINE ART PRODUCTIONS, 67 Maple St., Newburgh NY 12550. (914)561-5866. Contact: Richie Suraci. Music publisher, record company, book publisher. Estab. 1989.
Music: Member of ASCAP and BMI. Publishes and records 1-12 children's songs/year. Hires staff writers for children's music. Works with composers, lyricists, team collaborators. For music published pays standard royalty of 50% or other amount; for songs recorded pays musicians/artists on record contract, musicians on salary for inhouse studio work, songwriters on varying royalty contract. Submit demo tape by mail; unsolicited submissions OK. Submit demo cassette. Not neccessary to include lyric or lead sheets. SASE/IRC for return of submission. Reports in 2 months.
Stories: Publishes 1 book/cassette package and 1 audio tape/year. 50% of stories are fiction; 50% nonfiction. Will consider all genres for all age groups. Authors are paid varying royalty on wholesale or retail price. Submit complete ms, outline/synopsis and sample chapters, both cassette tape and manuscript. Reports in 2-3 months. Catalog is available for $3, large SAE and 52¢ stamps. Ms guidelines free with SASE.

FRONTLINE MUSIC GROUP/FMG BOOKS, Box 28450, Santa Ana CA 92799. (714)660-3888. FAX: (714)660-3899. Executive Vice President: Brian Tong. Music publisher, record company, book publisher. Record labels include Alma, Vineyard, Asaph, Frontline Kids. Estab. 1985.
Music: Releases 80-100 singles/year; 40-50 LPs/year; 40-50 CDs/year. Member of ASCAP and BMI. Publishes and records 50-60 children's songs/year. Hires staff writers for children's music. Works with composers, lyricists, team collaborators. For music published pays standard royalty of 50%; for songs recorded pays musicians/artists on record contract, musicians on salary for inhouse studio work, and songwriters on royalty contract. Submit cassette demo tape and lyric sheet by mail—unsolicited submissions OK. Requirements: only Christian material, no fantasy stuff. SASE for return of submissions. Reports in 3-4 weeks.
Tips: Songwriters: "Submit fresh material that is relevant to today's issues. Trends in children's music: "Age groupings are becoming more specialized. There is a distinct difference in likes and dislikes between 6-10 and 10-13 year olds and 14-16 year olds."
Stories: Publishes 2-4 book/cassette packages/year. 100% of stories are fiction. Will consider fictional animal, fantasy, history, sports and suspense/mystery/adventure stories aimed at all juvenile audiences "if Christian." Will consider nonfictional Bible stories aimed at all juvenile audiences. Authors are paid in royalties based on retail price. Submit complete ms. SASE for return of ms. Reports on queries in 4-6 weeks; mss in 6-8 weeks. Book catalog, ms guidelines not available.
Tips: Writers: "Be unusual." Trends in children's reading material: "More sophistication."

GORDON MUSIC CO. INC./PARIS RECORDS, P.O. Box 2250, Canoga Park CA 91306. (818)883-8224. Owner: Jeff Gordon. Music publisher, record company. Estab. 1950.
Music: Releases 3-4 CDs/year. Member of ASCAP and BMI. Publishes 6-8 children's songs/year; records 10-15 children's songs/year. Works with composers, lyricists, team collaborators. For music published pays standard royalty of 50%; for songs recorded, arrangement made between artist and company. Call first and obtain permission to submit. Submit 3-4 videocassette tapes, lyric and lead sheets. Does not return unsolicited submissions. Recently recorded children's songs: *Izzy, the Pest of the West*, recorded by Champ on Paris label.

HARCOURT BRACE JOVANOVICH, PUBLISHERS, 1250 Sixth Avenue, San Diego CA 92101. (619)699-6810. FAX: (619)699-6777. Director: Louise A. Howton. Book publisher.
Music: Works with composers, lyrists, team collaborators. "We only publish book-and-cassette packages of our most successful back-list titles, and so accept no submissions. All our artists are solicited." Reports in 4-8 weeks.
Tips: "Our children's book-and-cassette program is very limited at this time, and we're not apt to work with unknowns. We select musicians we feel are qualified, and approach them with our project. We are not yet looking for unsolicited submissions."
Stories: Publishes 3 book/cassette packages/year. 100% of stories are fiction aimed at ages 3-10. Method of payment "determined from our history with artist and individual project." Submit complete manuscript, outline/synopsis and sample chapters; submit through agent only. Reports on queries in 2-4 weeks; reports on mss in 1-2 months. Book catalog for 9 × 12 SAE and 3 first class stamps.

*DURKIN HAYES PUBLISHING, One Colomba Dr., Niagara Falls NY 14305. (716)298-5150. FAX: (716)298-5607. Development Manager: Patrick Hayes. Book publisher, audio book publisher. Estab. 1980.
Stories: Publishes 6 book/cassette packages/year; 28 audio tapes/year. 90% of stories are fiction; 10% nonfiction. Will consider any genre of fiction aimed at children to

adults. For nonfiction considers biography, sports aimed at children to adults. Authors are paid 5-10% royalty based on wholesale price. Average advance $2,000. Submit outline/synopsis and sample chapters; cassette tape of story; both cassette tape and manuscript. Reports in 3 months. Catalog free for SAE. Ms guidelines free for SASE.

BOB HINKLE MANAGEMENT, INC., (formerly The Children's Group), 17 Cadman Plaza West, Brooklyn NY 11201. (718)838-2544. FAX: (718)858-8976. President: Bob Hinkle. Vice President: John Scilipote. Children's Entertainment/Media Company: Personal management, product development, international consultation, concert promotion. Estab. 1988.
Music: Works with composers, lyricists, team collaborators. Submit cassette, VHS or ¾" videocassette and lyric sheet. Requirements: "Call to talk with us about who's recording and how the caller's material may fit those recording." Does not return unsolicited material. Reports in a matter of weeks.
Tips: Songwriters: "As an artist manager, a submission should be appropriate to the artist(s) in mind." Trends in children's music: "Becoming more sophisticated. Selling more. Careers developing just as in rock, pop, jazz, etc."

*HOME, INC., 731 Harrison Ave., Boston MA 02118 (617)266-1386. Director: Alan Michel. Nonprofit video production company. Estab. 1973.
Music: Paymaster through to AFTRA/SAG. Works with composers, lyricists, team collaborators. For music published pay negotiated on a project by project basis. Submit demo tape by mail; unsolicited submissions OK. Submit demo cassette with 3-6 songs. "I am usually looking for versatility and range in demos submitted." Cannot return material. Reports back only if interested in the work. Recently recorded songs: *Going to Court*, music only by Don Dinicola, recorded by Don Dinicola used on video tape as sound track (country for preschool-preteen); *Stand Back From Crack*, by Young Nation, recorded by Frank King used on video tape (rap for teen).
Music Tips: "We are not a publisher or record company. We work with independent publishers who are attempting to meet some social need through communications. We specialize in developing teen and preteen related programming."
Stories: Publishes 5 videos/year. 100% of stories are fiction. Will consider drama, music videos, public service announcements, training for preteens and teens. For nonfiction, considers animal, education and others as may be needed. Payment negotiated. Submit outline/synopsis and sample chapters with résumé. If interested, reports in 2-3 weeks (if solicited only).

KIDZ & COMPANY, Suite 105, 831 SW Vista, Portland OR 97205. (503)227-3591. Contact: Sandra Louise. Estab. 1983.
Music: Releases 6 singles/year; 6 12-inch singles/year. Records 6 children's songs/year. Hires staff writers for children's music. Works with composers, lyricists, team collaborators. For music published pays standard royalty of 50%. Submit demo cassette tape by mail; unsolicited submissions OK.

*MAMA-T ARTISTS/THE FOLKTELLERS, P.O. Box 2898, Asheville NC 28802. (704)258-1113. Contact: Amy D. Mozingo. Inhouse publisher of storytelling tapes. Estab. 1981.
Stories: Publishes audio tapes only. 75% of stories are fiction; 25% nonfiction. Will consider all genres for varying age groups. Authors are paid 2-8% royalties based on retail price; outright purchase of $1,000 (so far have only done once). Average advance $100. Submit complete ms—"we do all performing ourselves." Reports on queries/mss in 2-3 weeks. Catalog is free on request. Recently recorded story tapes: *Tales to Grow On*, narrated by The Folktellers (traditional and contemporary stories for K-3rd grade and 4-5th grade).

*MELODY HOUSE, INC., 819 NW 92nd St., Oklahoma City OK 73114. (405)840-3383. FAX: (405)840-3384. President: Stephen Fite. Record company (Melody House). Estab. 1972.
Music: Releases 6 LPs/year. Records 72 children's songs/year. Works with composers, lyricists, team collaborators. For songs recorded pays musicians on salary for inhouse studio work, or standard mechanical royalty per song. Submit demo tape by mail; unsolicited submissions OK. Submit demo cassette (5 songs or more) with lyric and lead sheets. SASE/IRC for return of submission. Reports in 2 months. Recently recorded songs: *Blues for My Blue Sky*, by Stephen Fite, recorded by Al Rasso on Melody House label (rhythm and blues for ages 4-8); *What A Beautiful World*, by Al Rasso, recorded by Stephen Fite on Melody House label (ballad for ages 4-8).
Music Tips: "The music and the lyrics should reach out and grab the child's attention. Children are much more sophisticated in their listening than their parents were at the same age. Children's music is definitely taking on the characteristics of the pop market with the sounds and even the hype in some cases. Even some of the messages are now touching on issues such as divorce/separation, the environment and social consciousness, both in the U.S. and the world."

*NEW DAY PRESS, 2355 E. 89th St., Cleveland OH 44106. (216)795-7070. Chair, Editorial Committee: Charlotte Durant. Book publisher. Estab. 1972.
Stories: Publishes "1 or less" book/cassette packages/year. 50% of stories are fiction; 50% are nonfiction. Will consider historical African-American fiction and nonfiction only aimed at 6-12 year olds. Buys mss outright for $100. Query. Book catalog free on request. Recently recorded story tape: *Fireside Tales*, written by Mary Shepard-Moore and narrated by Carolyn Gordon (African-American History for 6-12 year olds).

*NEW YORK SOUND & MUSIC, INC., #2108, 875 Avenue of the Americas, New York NY 10001. (212)279-6227. FAX: (212)279-6229. President: Matthew Kaplowitz. Music publisher, book publisher, audio/video production company. Estab. 1974.
Music: Member of ASCAP and BMI. Publishes and records 50-100 children's songs/year. Works with composers, lyricists, team collaborators. Pay for music published varies with project. For songs recorded pays musicians/artists on record contract, songwriters on royalty contract. Write for permission to submit material. Submit demo cassette, not necessary to include lyric or lead sheets. Cannot return material. Recently published and recorded songs: *Me & You*, by Matthew Kaplowitz and Don Cornelius, recorded by The Syreens on NVS label (children's music video about human rights for ages 6-adult); *I Love Animals*, by Matthew Kaplowitz and Don Cornelius, recorded by studio musicians/singers on NVS label (contemporary music for ages 5-adult).
Music Tips: "We are seeing a trend toward eclectic rather than tightly stylized material."
Stories: Publishes 10-15 book/cassette packages and 22-25 audio tapes/year. 75% of stories are fiction; 25% nonfiction. Authors are paid varying royalty; outright purchase. Query. Recently recorded and published story tapes: *Echo Canyon*, by Matthew Kaplowitz, narrated by Annie Wormbog and Rebecca Potrost (children's adventure for ages 6-10); *I Can't Stop Laughin'*, by Matthew Kaplowitz (fantasy adventure for ages 6-10).

PETER PAN INDUSTRIES, 88 St. Francis St., Newark NJ 07105. (201)344-4214. FAX: (201)344-0465. Vice President of Sales: Shelly Rudin. Music publisher, record company. Record labels include Parade Music, Compose Music, Peter Pan. Estab. 1927.
Music: Releases 20 singles/year; 10 12-inch singles; 45 LPs/year; 45 CDs/year. Member of ASCAP and BMI. Publishes 50 children's songs/year; records 80-90 songs/year. Works with composers, lyricists, team collaborators. For music published pays standard royalty of 50%; for songs recorded pays musicians/artists on record contract, songwriters on royalty contract. Making contact: Submit a 15 IPS reel-to-reel demo tape or VHS

videocassette by mail—unsolicited submissions OK. SASE (or SAE and IRCs) for return of submissions. Reports in 4-6 weeks.

Stories: Publishes 12 book/cassette packages/year. 90% of stories are fiction; 10% nonfiction. Will consider all genres of fiction and nonfiction aimed at 6 month olds to 9 year olds. Authors are paid in royalties based on wholesale price. Making contact: Query. Reports on queries in 4-6 weeks. Book catalog, manuscript guidelines free on request.

Tips: "Tough business but rewarding. Lullabies are very popular."

*PLANETARY PLAYTHINGS, P.O. Box 66, Boulder Creek CA 95006. (408)372-3100. FAX: (408)338-9861. Vice President: Howard Martin. Music publisher, book publisher, record company. Estab. 1989.

Music: Releases 3 LPs and 3 CDs/year. Member of ASCAP. Publishes and records 2 children's songs/year. Works with composers. For music published pays standard royalty of 50%; for songs recorded pays musicians on salary for inhouse studio work. Call first and obtain permission to submit material. Submit demo cassette. Cannot return material. Reports in 1 month. Recently published and recorded songs: *Heart Way*, written and recorded by Deborah Razman on Planetary Productions label (relaxation for ages 3-7); *Heart Zones*, written and recorded by Doc Lew Childre on Planetary Productions label (stress reduction, learning enhancement ages 5-21).

Stories: Publishes 8 book/cassette packages/year. 70% of stories are fiction; 30% nonfiction. Will consider adventure stories aimed at 5 to teen audience. For nonfiction, considers education aimed at teen audience. Submit query. Reports on queries in 1 month; on mss in 2 months. Catalog is free on request.

Tips: "We are a consortium of 40 artists, writers, musicians, educators and business professionals who have common ownership of the business. All of our books and tapes are created inhouse. We do not usually publish works by outside people but we are open to sharing ideas and having contact with others in the industry. If you have any questions, please call 1-800-372-3100."

RHYTHMS PRODUCTIONS/TOM THUMB MUSIC, Box 34485, Los Angeles CA 90034. (213)836-4678. President: R.S. White. Record company, cassette and book packagers. Record label, Tom Thumb—Rhythms Productions. Estab. 1955.

Music: Releases 4-6 LPs/year. Member of ASCAP. Records 4 albums/year. Works with composers and lyricists. For songs recorded pays musicians/artists on record contract, songwriters on royalty contract. Submit a cassette demo tape or VHS videotape by mail—unsolicited submissions OK. Requirements: "We accept musical stories. Must be produced in demo form, and must have educational content or be educationally oriented." Reports in 2 months. Recently recorded: *The Adventures of Mr. Windbag*, written by Ruth and David White (6 book and cassette packages), all on Tom Thumb label.

*A.J. SHALLECK PRODUCTIONS, INC., Suite 4L, 350 East 62 St., New York NY 10021. (212)421-2252. FAX: (212)832-7974. President: Alan J. Shalleck. Audio visual production house, children's home video/film. Estab. 1981.

Music: Hires staff writers for children's music. Works with composers, lyricists, team collaborators.

Stories: Publishes 5-15 book/cassette packages and audio tapes/year. 100% of stories are fiction. Will consider various genres for appropriate age group; pre-K-3rd grade. Authors are paid by outright purchase. Average advance $500-1,000. Query. Recently recorded story tapes: *Classic Titles* (Goldilocks, Henny Penny, etc.), by various authors, narrated by Fred Newman (classic and original stories for pre-K-3rd grade); *Curious George Various*, by Margret Rey and A. Shalleck (children's fiction for pre-K-3rd grade).

Story Tips: "We are noticing more stories involving present social problems."

SILVER BURDETT & GINN, 250 James St., Morristown NJ 07960-1918. (201)285-8003. Music Editor: Donald Scafuri. Music textbook publisher, grades K-8 (each grade package contains a set of recordings). Estab. 1867.
Music: Member of ASCAP. Publishes and records 200 songs/year. Hires staff writers for children's music. Works with composers, lyricists, team collaborators. For music published pays standard mechanical royalty rate; $400 set fee per song (melody and lyrics). Write first and obtain permission to submit a cassette tape and lead sheet. SASE. Reports in 3 months.
Tips: "Songs should reflect the appropriate vocal range, rhythmic sophistication and style for a particular age level. Lyrics should also be age appropriate. The songwriter should become familiar with those types of songs that are most successful in a classroom setting. (Styles could include pop, folk, 2-or 3-part choral.)"

SIMON & SCHUSTER CHILDREN'S BOOKS, 1230 Avenue of the Americas, New York NY 10020. (212)698-7257. FAX: (212)698-7677. Vice President, Editor-in-Chief: Grace Clarke. Vice President, Marketing Director: Ken Geist. Book publisher. Estab. 1927.
Stories: Publishes 4 book/cassette packages/year. 100% of stories are fiction. "Story-tapes are developed using Simon & Schuster best selling and award winning children's books." Books aimed at 3-8 year olds. Pays authors in royalties of 2%. Submit through agent only. Book catalog free on request. Recently recorded story tapes: *Teddy Bear's Picnic*, by Jimmy Kennedy, and narrated by the Bearcats (Green Tiger Press). New book and cassette package includes *Chicka Chicka Boom Boom*, performed by Ray Charles.

***SONG WIZARD RECORDS**, P.O. Box 931029, Los Angeles CA 90093. (213)461-8848. FAX: (213)461-0936. Owner: Dave Kinnoin. Record company. Record label Song Wizard Records. Estab. 1987.
Music: Releases 1 cassette/year. Member of ASCAP. Records 13 songs/year. Works with composers, lyricists and team collaborators. For songs recorded pays songwriters on royalty contract (negotiable). Write for permission to submit material. Submit demo cassette with 3 songs and lyric sheet. "Put name, address, phone number and copyright notice on all pieces of submission." SASE/IRC for return of submission. Reports in 6 months or sooner. Recently recorded songs: "Fun-A-Rooey," written and recorded by Dave Kinnoin on Song Wizard Records label (pop rock for ages 2-8); "Daring Dewey," written and recorded by Dave Kinnoin on Song Wizard Records label (pop rock for ages 5-12).
Music Tips: "Be startlingly fresh with pure rhymes and poetic devices that live happily with singability. Songs have to be extra good because competition is strong. If someone sends me a song that is so amazing I can't refuse it, I'll record it or pass it to someone else who may."

***SOUND PUBLICATIONS, INC.**, Suite 108, 10 E 22nd St., Lombard IL 60148. (708)916-7071. FAX: (708)916-1999. Vice President: Cheryl Basilico. Audio cassette package publisher. Estab. 1991.
Music: Publishes and records 140 children's songs/year. Works with composers, team collaborators. For music published pays special publishing and distribution package; for songs recorded pays all recording and production costs. Call or write for permission to submit material. Submit demo cassette with personal bio and letter of recommendation, 3-5 songs, lyric sheet. "Music is to be educational." Cannot return material. Reports in 1 month. Recently published and recorded songs: *Hop Little Bunny*, by Bill Hooper, recorded by Bill Hooper on Sound Publications label (educational music for ages 2-5); *Ostrich Song*, written and recorded by Bill Hooper on Sound Publications (educational music for ages 2-5).

Music Tips: "If you have not performed your songs for a group of children, do so before expecting them to react to your efforts. Music must be more than entertainment. A creative way of presenting education is essential."
Stories: Publishes 6 book/cassette packages. 100% of stories are fiction. Considers all genres for ages 12 and under. Authors are paid special publishing and distribution package. Submit both cassette tape and manuscript. Reports in 1 month.
Story Tips: "Morals are the hardest thing to teach a child. Do it in a way that is understandable and you will be successful."

*SOUNDPRINTS, a Division of Trudy Management Corporation, 165 Water St., P.O. Box 679, Norwalk CT 06856. (203)838-6009. Editor: Dorothy Shillinglaw. Book publisher. Estab. 1988.
Stories: Publishes 2-3 book/cassette packages/year. 100% of stories are fiction. Will consider realistic animal stories for preschool-3rd grade. For nonfiction, considers animal for preschool-3rd grade. Authors are paid royalties based on wholesale price. Query with SASE. Reports in 2 weeks on queries; 1 month on mss. Catalog free on request. Ms guidelines free with SASE. Recently published and recorded story tapes: *Jackrabbit and the Prairie Fire*, by Susan Saunders, narrated by Peter Thomas (black-tailed jackrabbit on the Great Plains for preschool-3rd grade); *Seasons of a Red Fox*, by Susan Saunders, narrated by Peter Thomas (the first year in the life of a red fox for preschool-3rd grade).
Tips: "Be realistic. Much of what I get is not worth reading."

TEXAS STAR INTERNATIONAL/LONNY TUNES MUSIC, B.M.I., P.O. Box 460086, Garland TX 75046. President: Lonny Schonfeld. Music publisher, record company. Record labels include Lollipop Farm. Estab. 1987.
Music: Releases 2 singles and 2 LPs/year. Member of BMI. Publishes and records 3-6 children's songs/year. Works with composers, team collaborators. For music published pays standard royalty of 50%. For songs recorded pays musicians on salary for inhouse studio work. Submit demo cassette tape with no more than 3 songs and lyric sheet by mail. Looking for "stories and songs with 'positive' endings." Reports in 6-8 weeks.
Stories: Publishes 2 audiotapes/year. 100% of stories are fiction. Will consider fictional animal, fantasy, everyday life occurrences (kids, ages 2-12). Authors are paid in royalties. BMI method of payment: 50% of publishing rights. Submit cassette tape of story. Reports on queries/mss in 6-8 weeks. Manuscript guidelines for legal size SAE and 1 first class stamp.

*TLC BOOKS & GAMES, INC., P.O. Box 58, Somers CT 06071. (203)763-0770. FAX: (203)763-3038. Vice President: Mary Fedus. Book publisher. Estab. 1988.
Music: Hires staff writers for children's music. Works with composers, lyricists. Submit demo tape by mail; unsolicited submissions OK. Submit demo cassette with lyric sheet. SASE/IRC for return of submission. Reports in 1 week.
Stories: Publishes 4 book/cassette packages/year. 100% of stories are fiction. Will consider self-esteem issues for ages 4-8. Authors are paid by individual arrangement. Submit complete ms and cassette tape of story. Reports in 1 week. Catalog free on request. Recently published story tapes: *Caterpillar Had a Dream*, written and narrated by Jaye Bartlett, (poetry, self-esteem for ages 2-7); *Freddy the Elephant*, the Story of a Sensitive Leader, narrated by Jaye Bartlett (poetry, self-esteem for ages 4-8).

*TRENNA PRODUCTIONS, P.O. Box 2484, Malibu CA 90265. (213)457-2583. FAX: (213)457-6998. President: Trenna Daniells. Children's audio story cassette publisher. Estab. 1981.
Music: Releases 4 LPs/year. Works with composers. For music published pays per project. Submit demo tape by mail; unsolicited submissions OK. Submit demo cassette.

SASE/IRC for return of submission. Recently recorded music: *Be True To Yourself*, by composer Jimmy Hammer, recorded by Trenna Daniells on Trenna Productions (for ages 4-9); *No More Nightmares*, by composer Jimmy Hammer, recorded by Trenna Daniells on Trenna Productions (ages 4-9).

*UPSTREAM PRODUCTIONS, 35 Page Ave., P.O. Box 8843, Asheville NC 28814. (704)258-9713. FAX: (704)258-9727. Owner: Steven Heller. Music composer and producer and record company. Estab. 1982.
Music: Releases 1-3 LPs and 1-3 CDs/year. Member of ASCAP and BMI. Publishes and records 5-8 children's songs/year. Works with composers and lyricists. For music published pays standard royalty of 50%. "Submit letter first for cassette request. Cassettes should have 1-3 songs." Cassettes not returned.

WATCHESGRO MUSIC PUBLISHING CO., BMI. Watch Us Climb, ASCAP. Box 1794, Big Bear City CA 92314. (714)585-4645. President: Eddie Lee Carr. Music publisher, record company. Record labels include Interstate 20 Records, Tracker Records. Estab. 1970.
Music: Releases 10 singles/year; 5 12-inch singles/year; 1 LP/year; 1 CD/year. Publishes 15 children's songs/year; records 4 children's songs/year. Works with composers, lyricists. For music published pays standard royalty of 50%; for songs recorded pays musicians/artists on record contract, musicians on salary for inhouse studio work. Write or call first and obtain permission to submit a cassette tape. Does not return unsolicited material. Reports in 1 week.

*WE LIKE KIDS!, produced by KTOO-FM, 224 4th St., Juneau AK 99801. (907)586-1670. FAX: (907)586-3612. Producers: Jeff Brown or Judy Hall. Producer of nationwide children's radio show.
Music: Releases 50+ programs/year. Member of Children's Music Network; National Association for the Preservation and Perpetuation of Storytelling. Submit demo tape by mail; unsolicited submissions OK. Submit demo cassette vinyl, CD.
Music Tips: "The best advice we could give to anyone submitting songs for possible airplay is to make certain that they give their best performance and record it in the best way possible. A mix of well-honed songwriting skills, an awareness of a variety of international musical styles, and the advent of home studios have all added up to a delightful abundance of quality songs and stories for children."
Stories: "Our show is based on themes most of the time. Send us your stories." Ms guidelines free with SASE (newsletter also available).

WORLD LIBRARY PUBLICATIONS INC., 3815 N. Willow Dr., Schiller Park IL 60176. (708)678-0621. Editorial Director: Nicholas T. Freund. Music publisher. Estab. 1945.
Music: Publishes 10-12 children's songs/year. Works with composers. For music published pays 10% of sales. Making contact: Submit demo cassette tape and lead sheet by mail; unsolicited submissions OK. "Should be religious. We are primarily a Roman Catholic publisher." Reports in 3 months. Published children's songs: "Let the Children Come to Me," written and recorded by James V. Marchconda on WLP cassette 7845 label (religious/catechetical); "Gather You Children," written by Peter Finn and James Chepponis (religious/catechetical); and "Mass of the Children of God," written by James V. Marchionda on WLP Cassette 7664 label (liturgical).

Scriptwriter's Markets

There are rumors that children are less discriminating than adults, and therefore not as picky about the plays they view. The reality is children are about the cruelest critics there are. Most adults will sit patiently and watch a dull play just to be polite, but for the most part, kids don't care about being polite and are less inhibited at visibly expressing their dissatisfaction. One way to assure against a bored audience is to use plenty of rhythm, repetition and effective dramatic action. Avoid using subplots and unnecessary dialogue, which will add to the length of the play. Most plays for children average less than an hour. For more tips on hooking a young audience, read Michael Maschinot's article, "Writing Plays for Young Audiences" in the July 1991 *Writer's Digest*.

"Fourth wall" plays, or plays where actors perform as if they are not aware of the audience, are still the standard in this field. But because of the competition of movies and television, interactive plays which involve the audience are gaining more acceptance.

The U.S. population is comprised of a multitude of ethnic subcultures. Be aware of this when writing plays for children. You might have a better chance at selling a script if it reflects racial diversity.

Since many theater groups produce plays with limited budgets, scripts containing elaborate staging and costumes might not meet their needs. Also, many children's plays are touring productions that consist of three to six actors. There might be more characters in your play than available actors, so think about how the roles can be doubled up. Also, touring theaters want simple sets that can be easily transported. To become more familiar with the types of plays the listed markets are looking for, contact them about their specific needs. Some will have catalogs available.

Plays using adult roles *and* plays with children's roles are being solicited by the markets in this section. Note the listings contain percentages of how many plays produced are for adult roles, and how many are for children's roles.

Payment for playwrights usually comes in the form of royalties, outright payments or a combination of both. The pay scale isn't going to be quite as high as screenplay rates, but playwrights *do* benefit by getting to watch their work performed live by a variety of groups employing a multitude of interpretations.

*ART EXTENSIONS THEATER, 11144 Weddington, N. Hollywood CA 91601. (818)760-8675. FAX: (818)508-8613. Artistic Director: Maureen Kennedy Samuels. Estab. 1991. Produces 2 children's plays/year; 1 children's musical/year. Small budget. Equity waiver. 90% of plays/musicals written for adult roles; 10% for juvenile roles. Recently produced plays: *Cirquedula — Working without Annette*, (by Debbie Devine) about fear of change for ages 7-12. Will consider simultaneous submissions and previously performed work. Submission method: query with synopsis, character breakdown and set description, submit complete ms and score. Reports in 2 weeks. Pays writers in royalties of 5-10%; pays $10-25/performance. SASE for return of submission.

*ARTREACH TOURING THEATRE, 3074 Madison Rd., Cincinnati OH 45209. (513)871-2300. FAX: (513)871-2501. Artistic Director: Kathryn Schultz Miller. Estab. 1976. "ArtReach has cast requirement of 3: 2 men and 1 woman. Sets must look big but fit in

large van." Professional theater. Recently produced plays: *Young Cherokee*, by Kathryn Schultz Miller—history and culture of early Cherokee tribe as seen through the eyes of a young brave, for primary students and family audiences; *The Trail of Tears*, by Kathryn Schultz Miller—a companion play to *Young Cherokee* depicting story of Cherokee removal and unjust destruction of their culture, for intermediate through adult audiences. Does not want to see musicals, holiday plays, TV type scripts (about drugs, child abuse etc.) or fractured fairy tales. Will consider simultaneous submissions and previously performed work. Submission method: query with synopsis, character breakdown and set description. Reports in 10 days to 6 weeks. Author retains rights. Pays writers in royalties. SASE for return of submission.
Tips: "Type script in professional form found in *Writer's Market*. Do not submit plays that are less than 45 pages long. Look to history, culture or literature as resources."

BAKER'S PLAYS, 100 Chauncy St., Boston MA 02111. (617)482-1280. FAX: (617)482-7613. Editor: John B. Welch. Estab. 1845. Publishes 5-8 children's plays/year; 2-4 children's musicals/year. 80% of plays/musicals written for adult roles; 20% for juvenile roles. Subject matter: "Touring shows for 5-8 year olds, full lengths for family audience and full lengths for teens." Submission method: Submit complete ms, score and tape of songs. Reports in 4 months. Rights obtained on mss: worldwide rights. Pays writers in royalties (amount varies) or $10-100/performance.
Tips: "Looking for writers for the theater, not frustrated poets or novelists." Wants "honest, committed material dealing with today's issues."

*CALIFORNIA THEATRE CENTER, P.O. Box 2007, Sunnyvale CA 94087. (408)245-2979. FAX: (408)245-0235. Artistic Director: Gayle Cornelison. Estab. 1976. Produces 15-30 children's plays/year. "For our professional company, we usually need scripts with 5-6 actors. For our summer training program for young people, we do scripts with large casts (20-30)." "Professional productions year-round; Summer Equity and Summer Amateur Training productions." 75% of plays/musicals written for adult roles; 25% for juvenile roles. Recently produced plays: *King of the Golden River*, by James Still (based on short story by John Ruskin)—adventure fantasy; *Maggie Magalita*, by Wendy Kesselman (young Hispanic girl coming of age)—4th grade and up. Does not want to see "cutesy; patronizing scripts." Will consider simultaneous submissions and previously performed work. Submission method: submit complete ms and tape. Reports in months. Rights vary. Pays writers in royalties. SASE for return of submissions.
Tips: "Approach the young audience with respect toward what they're interested in and capable of understanding."

CHILDREN'S STORY SCRIPTS, Baymax Productions, Suite 130, 2219 W. Olive Ave., Burbank CA 91506. (818)563-6105. FAX: (818)563-2968. Editor: Deedra Bébout. Estab. 1990. Produces 3-10 children's scripts/year. "Except for small movements and occasionally standing up, children remain seated in Readers Theatre fashion." Publishes scripts sold to schools, camps, churches, scouts, hotels, cruise lines, etc. Wherever there's a program to teach to or entertain children. "All roles read by children except K-2 scripts. Then kids have easy lines, leader reads the narration." Subject matter: Scripts on all subjects. Targeted age range—K-8th grade, 5-13 years old. Recently published: *Antonio's Magic Colors*, by Irene Schmidt—mixing primary colors, for grades K-2; *Memories of the Pony Express*, by Sharon Gill Askelson—Pony Express, for grades 5-8. No "sweet,

Always include a self-addressed stamped envelope (SASE) or International Reply Coupon (IRC) with submissions.

syrupy, predictable stories." Accepts simultaneous submissions. Submission method: submit complete ms. Reports in 2 weeks. Rights obtained on mss: All rights; authors retain copyrights. Pays writers in royalties; 10-15% on sliding scale, based on retail price. SASE for return of submission.

Tips: "Children's Story Scripts are essentially *prose* stories broken into parts. Descriptive narration is mixed with character dialogue. The scripts are meant to be read aloud. All the children enter at the beginning and remain in place throughout the performance. We do not hit the kids over the head with the moral or purpose of a script. We provide discussion questions which can be used after the performance to address the purpose of the story. Writer's guidelines packet available for business-sized SASE with two first-class stamps. Guidelines explain what Children's Story Scripts are, give four-page examples from two different scripts, give list of suggested topics for scripts."

CIRCA '21 DINNER THEATRE, P.O. Box 3784, Rock Island IL 61204-3784. (309)786-2667. Producer: Dennis Hitchcock. Estab. 1977. Produces 2-3 children's plays/year; 1-2 children's musicals/year. "Prefer a cast no larger than 12." Produces children's plays for professional productions. 95% of plays/musicals written for adult roles; 5% written for juvenile roles. Submission method: query with synopsis, character breakdown, tape and set description. Reports in 3 months. Payment negotiable.

*I.E. CLARK, INC., P.O. Box 246, Schulenburg TX 78956. FAX: (409)743-4765. Estab. 1956. Publishes 3 children's plays/year; 1 or 2 children's musicals/year. Medium to large casts preferred. Publishes plays for all ages. Recently published plays: *Wind of a Thousand Tales*, by John Glore (a young girl who doesn't believe in fairy tales) for ages 5-12; *Rock'n'Roll Santa*, by R. Eugene Jackson (Santa's reindeer form a rock band) for ages 4-16. Does not want to see plays that have not been produced. Will consider simultaneous submissions and previously performed work. Submission method: submit complete ms and audio or video tape. Reports in 6-8 months. Purchases all rights. Pays writers in negotiable royalties. SASE for return of submission.

Tips: "We publish only high quality literary works."

*COMMUNITY CHILDREN'S THEATRE OF KANSAS CITY INC., 8021 E 129th Terrace, Grandview MO 64030. (816)761-5775. Contact: Blanche Sellens. Estab. 1951. Produces 5 children's plays/year. Prefer casts of between 6-8. Produces children's plays for amateur productions. Produce plays for ages K-6. Recently produced plays: *Red Versus the Wolf*, by Judy Wolferman — musical for K-6 audience. Submission method: query first, then submit complete ms. Reports in a matter of months. "Winning script is performed by one of the units for two years."

Tips: "Write for guidelines and details for The Margaret Bartle Annual Playwriting Award."

CONTEMPORARY DRAMA SERVICE, Division of Meriwether Publishing Ltd., 885 Elkton Dr., Colorado Springs CO 80907. (719)594-4422. FAX: (719)594-9916. Editor: Arthur Zapel. Estab. 1979. Publishes 35-40 children's plays/year; 3 children's musicals/year. 15% of plays/musicals written for adult roles; 85% for juvenile roles. Recently published plays: *Phantom of the Opr'y*, by Tim Kelly and Vigilant and Castle — a comedy version of the classic "Phantom" story put to music for all ages — mostly adults; *The Little Stars of Bethlehem*, by Janet Meili — a fantasy Christmas story for child performers for children and adults. "We do not publish plays for elementary level except for church plays for Christmas and Easter. All of our secular plays are for teens or college level." Submission method: query with synopsis, character breakdown and set description; "query first if a musical." Rights obtained on mss: all first rights. Payment varies according to type: royalty or purchase. SASE for return of submission.

Close-up

Kathryn Schultz Miller
Artistic Director
ArtReach Touring Theatre
Cincinnati, Ohio

"The company was pretty much born at the prover-
bial kitchen table," says Kathryn Schultz Miller
about the inception of ArtReach Touring Theatre.
Miller and several college friends founded the
company in 1976 with the intention of producing a
Shakespeare festival every summer, an adult series
throughout the year, and a children's series to be
performed in schools. The latter project ultimately became ArtReach's primary
focus.

"It was the children's series that ended up being the most lucrative for us,"
says Miller. "It's the one that survived and that was the direction I was going
in, so I ended up at that end of the company." Miller writes and produces plays
for ArtReach, which performs approximately 1,000 shows per year. Based in
Cincinnati, Ohio, the company tours nationally and includes actors and directors from all over the United States.

Miller began her career writing story theater (mini-plays and vignettes), but
has since graduated into writing and producing full-length productions. "We
are very committed to doing plays that have beginnings, middles and ends. We
want the play to be a full experience. We are not interested in story theater or
vignettes of any kind. We look for very strong storylines and reasons for doing
shows."

With such specific requirements, ArtReach may be a difficult market for the
freelance writer of children's scripts to break into. "I really have to be given a
good reason to look at a script that is not developed through the company,"
says Miller. "I think you'll find this with touring theaters in general. We use
only three actors, but the show must look big. (The writer) can send me a script
that might have more than three characters, but there has to be a way that I
can break that down." Although plays produced by ArtReach must be written
for a minimal number of characters, they must be long enough to translate into
an hour's worth of performance and generalized enough in terms of subject
material and age range.

Miller prefers stories with classic backgrounds and literary value. "I don't
like didactic stories. We do not want to teach traffic safety or dental hygiene. I
think people who are in theater for children should consider themselves theater
people before teachers." Miller views children's theater as being more than
just entertainment, however. "I see it as a way to really communicate artistically
and to look at life in different ways. We actually try to stay away from shows

that are just entertaining. We are doing 'Sword in the Stone' this year, which is a lot of fun. It involves magic tricks and audience participation, but it also involves the idea of a boy coming to understand what power and battle mean. We want kids to think about these things without telling them what they should think. We want to trigger their thought processes."

When reviewing freelance manuscript packages, Miller says she prefers to first see a cover letter with a brief résumé listing any previous work produced by other theaters, as well as any awards won. She then looks at the play itself to determine whether the subject material and length are suitable for ArtReach's needs. "Generally, if I find something that I really like but have difficulty putting into a season, I'll send a note saying that I'm interested in the writing, and request the writer try us again," says Miller.

As an author of more than ten children's plays, Miller understands what *does* and *does not* work in children's theater. Rendering a story as honestly as possible, she says, is of fundamental importance. "You can present anything to kids. You don't have to soup it up with a lot of props and funniness. In fact, that is what really loses kids' attention. I think the trend in children's theater is going toward more serious stories. Children have always been very savvy—I just don't think there were a lot of serious people in theater who were making real plays for kids."

—Roseann Shaughnessy

THE COTERIE, 2450 Grand, Kansas City MO 64108. (816)474-6785. FAX: (816)545-6500. Artistic Director: Jeff Church. Estab. 1979. Produces 7 children's plays/year; 2 children's musicals/year. "Prefer casts of between 5-7, no larger than 15. Props and staging should be relatively simple." Produces children's plays for professional productions. 80% of plays/musicals written for adult roles; 20% for juvenile roles. "We do *not* produce puppet shows, although we may use puppets in our plays. We produce original plays, musicals and literary adaptations for ages 5 through adult." Recently produced plays: *Amelia Lives*, by Laura Annawyn Shamas—one-woman show on Amelia Earhart for 6th grade through adult audience; *Dinosaurus*, by Ed Mast and Lenore Bensinger—Mobil Oil workers discover cavern of dinosaurs, for ages 5 through adult audience. "We do *not* want to see 'camp' adaptations of fairytales." Submission method: query with synopsis, character breakdown and set description. Reports in a matter of months. Rights obtained on mss: "negotiable." Pays writers in royalties; buys material outright for $500-1,500; pays $15-35/performance. SASE for return of submission.
Tips: There are "smaller casts, simpler staging requirements, strong thematic, character and plot development, 'risky' issues; (i.e. teen pregnancy, substance abuse, race relations, etc.). There is a need for non-condescending material for younger age groups (5-8) and for middle school (ages 9-13). Fairytales are fine, but they should be straightforward and non-condescending."

*CREEDE REPERTORY THEATRE, P.O. Box 269, Creede CO 81130. (719)658-2541. FAX: (719)658-2343. Artistic Director: Richard Baxter. Estab. 1966. Produces 1-2 children's plays/year. Limited to 4-6 cast members and must be able to tour. Produces children's plays for summer, school or professional productions. 100% of plays/musicals written for adult roles. Publishes plays for ages K-12. Recently produced plays: *Prairie Dog Tales*, by Ric Averill and the Seem-to-Be Players—country western folktales for ages K-6; *Tortilla Soup*, by Joe Hayes—fables of New Mexico for ages K-12. Will consider simultaneous submissions and previously performed work. Query first, submit complete ms and score, or query with synopsis, character breakdown and set description. Reports in 12 months. Pays writers in 5% royalties; pays $25-30 per performance.

DRAMATIC PUBLISHING, INC., 311 Washington St., Woodstock IL 60098. (815)338-7170. FAX: (815)338-8981. Estab. 1885. Publishes plays and musicals for children and young adults. Recently published plays/musicals: *A Thousand Cranes*, written by Kathryn Schultz Miller—the after effects of bombing Hiroshima on a young girl for 10-16 yrs. audience. *The Trial of Goldilocks* (operetta), written by Joseph Robinette and Robert Chauls—using differing points of view to examine an event for 5-10 yrs. audience. Submission method: send script, (with a cassette if a musical) and include an SASE if wish to have ms returned. Reports in 3-4 months. Pays writers in royalties.
Tips: Scripts should be from ½ to 1½ hours long, and not didactic or condescending. Original plays dealing with hopes, joys and fears of today's children are preferred to adaptations of old classics.

ELDRIDGE PUBLISHING CO. INC., P.O. Box 216, Franklin OH 45005. (513)746-6531. Editor: Nancy Vorhis. Estab. 1906. Publishes approximately 15 children's plays/year (5-8 for elementary; 10-12 for junior and senior high); 2-3 children's musicals/year. Prefers simple staging; flexible cast size. We "publish for middle, junior and high school, all genres." Published plays: *I Am a Star*, by Billy St. John—teen soap opera star goes undercover as a "nerdy" type student at a high school to prove she can really act for high school audience; *Every Baby-Sitter's Nightmare*, by Craig Sodaro—imagine everything that can go wrong while babysitting 3 wild children, for junior high school audience. Does not want to see "anything suggestive; anything with a subject matter that is too mature." Submission method: submit complete ms, score and tape of songs (if a musical). Reports in 2 months. Rights obtained on mss: all dramatic rights. Pays writers 10% of copy sales or 35% of royalties; buys material outright for $150-300.
Tips: "We always need material which offers flexible casting; parts which can be played by boys or girls or 'group' parts which may include one or several students. We like upbeat themes with humor and physical action."

*ENCORE PERFORMANCE PUBLISHING, P.O. Box 692, Orem UT 84059. (800)927-1605. Estab. 1978. Publishes 10-15 children's plays/year; 6-10 children's musicals/year. Prefers equal male/female ratio if possible. Adaptations for K-12 and older. Recently published plays: *Commedia Pinocchio*, by Lane Riosley—stylized—small cast classic adaptation for K-12 audience; *The Reluctant Dragon*, by Jim Geisel—classic adaptation for K-12 audience. Will only consider previously performed work. Looking for issue plays and unusual fairy tale adaptations. Submission method: query first. Purchases all publication and production rights. Author retains copyright. Pays writers in royalties (50%). SASE for return of submission.

*THE FREELANCE PRESS, Box 548, Dover MA 02030. (508)785-1260. Estab. 1979. Produces 3 musicals and/or plays/year. Casts are comprised of young people, ages 8-15, and number 25-30. "We publish original musicals on contemporary topics for children and adaptations of children's classics (e.g., Velveteen Rabbit, Rip Van Winkle)." Recently published plays: *Velveteen Rabbit*, based on story of same name for ages 8-11; *Monopoly*, 3 young people walk through board game, the winner gets to choose where he/she wants to live (ages 11-15). No plays for adult performers. Will consider simultaneous submissions and previously performed work. Submit complete ms and score with SASE. Reports in 3 months. Pays writers 10% royalties. SASE for return of submission.

SAMUEL FRENCH, INC., 45 W. 25th St., New York NY 10010. (212)206-8990. FAX: (212)206-1429. Editor: Lawrence Harbison. Estab. 1830. Publishes 2 or 3 children's plays/year; "variable number of musicals." Subject matter: "All genres, all ages. No

puppet plays. No adaptations of any of those old 'fairy tales.' No 'Once Upon a time, long ago and far away.' No kings, princesses, fairies, trolls, etc." Submission method: submit complete ms and demo tape (if a musical). Reports in 2-8 months. Rights obtained on mss: "Publication rights, amateur and professional production rights, option to publish next 3 plays." Pay for writers: "book royalty 10%; professional production royalty: 90%; amateur production royalty: 80%." SASE for return of submissions.
Tips: "Children's theater is a very tiny market, as most groups perform plays they have created themselves or have commissioned."

THE GREAT AMERICAN CHILDREN'S THEATRE COMPANY, P.O. Box 92123, Milwaukee WI 53202. (414)276-4230. FAX: (414)276-2214. Artistic Director: Teri Solomon Mitze. Estab. 1975. Produces 2 children's plays/year. Produces children's plays for professional productions; 100% written for adult roles. Recently produced plays: *The Secret Garden*, by Brett Reynolds—children's classic for ages K-8; *Charlie & the Chocolate Factory*, by Richard R. George—children's classic for ages K-8. Will consider previously performed work. Submission method: query with synopsis, character breakdown and set description. Reports in weeks. Rights and payment negotiable.

*HAYES SCHOOL PUBLISHING CO. INC., 321 Pennwood Ave., Wilkinsburg PA 15221. (412)371-2373. FAX: (412)371-6408. Estab. 1940. Wants to see supplementary teaching aids for grades K-12. Will consider simultaneous and electronic submissions. Query first with synopsis, character breakdown and set description, or with complete ms and score. Reports in 3-4 weeks. Purchases all rights. Pays writers by outright purchase. SASE for return of submissions.

HONOLULU THEATRE FOR YOUTH, 2846 Ualena St., Honolulu HI 96819. (808)839-9885. FAX: (808)839-7018. Artistic Director: Pamela Sterling. Estab. 1955. Produces 6 children's plays/year. Subject matter: Looks for plays "celebrating cultures of the Pacific Rim, especially. Also, plays that deal with issues of concern to today's young audiences (varying in age from 6-18)." Submission method: query first with cast requirements and synopsis. SASE required for each script requested.
Tips: "Adaptations of published fiction for children to play form are the most frequently accepted types; queries could produce commissions to proceed with an adaptation, or possibly even an original work if it meets our needs and agrees with our philosophy."

THE NEW CONSERVATORY CHILDREN'S THEATRE COMPANY & SCHOOL, 25 Van Ness Ave., San Francisco CA 94102. (415)861-4914. Executive Director: Ed Decker. Estab. 1981. Produces 6-10 children's plays/year; 1-2 children's musicals/year. Youth ages 4-19, a limited budget. Produces children's plays for "A professional theater arts training program for youths ages 4-19 during the school year and a summer session. The New Conservatory also produces educational plays for its touring company." 100% written for juvenile roles. Produced: *Gunplay*, by Dylan Russell—explores the epidemic of young people and handgun violence for teen and young adult audience; *You Are, I Am*, by Rachel LePell—deals with issues of prejudice and racism in a junior high school setting for ages 9-19. "We do not want to see any preachy or didactic material." Submission method: query with synopsis, character breakdown and set description, or submit complete ms and score. Reports in 3 months. Rights obtained on mss: "negotiable." Pays writers in royalties. SASE for return of submission.
Tips: Trends: "Addressing socially relevant issues for young people and their families."

*NEW PLAYS INCORPORATED, P.O. Box 5074, Charlottesville VA 22905. (804)977-4969. Artistic Director: Patricia Whitton. Estab. 1964. Publishes 4 plays/year; 1 or 2 children's musicals/year. Publishes "Generally material for kindergarten through junior high." Recently published *Round Pegs Square Pegs*, by Mary Hall Surface—conflict resolution for ages 6-11; *The Rematch of the Tortoise and the Hare*, by Bill Stevens—concert piece for chamber orchestra and 5 actors for family audience. Does not want to see "adaptations of titles I already have. No unproduced plays; junior high improvisations." Will consider simultaneous submissions and previously performed work. Submissions method: submit complete ms and score. Reports in 2 months. Purchases exclusive rights to sell acting scripts. Pays writers in royalties (50% of production royalties; 10% of script sales). SASE for return of submission.

NEW YORK STATE THEATRE INSTITUTE, P.A.C. 266 1400 Washington Ave., Albany NY 12222. (518)443-5222. FAX: (518)442-5318. Producing Director: Patricia B. Snyder. Estab. 1976. Produces 1-2 children's plays and 1-2 children's musicals/year. Produces family plays for professional theater. 90% of plays/musicals are written for adult roles; 10% for juvenile roles. Does not want to see plays for children only. Submission method: submit complete ms and tape of songs (if a musical). Reports in 2-3 months. Rights obtained on mss: "varies." Pay for writers: "fees vary in nature and in degree." SASE for return of submission.
Tips: Writers should be mindful of "audience *sophistication*!"

*THE OPEN EYE: NEW STAGINGS, 270 West 89th St., New York NY 10024. (212)769-4142. Artistic Director: Amie Brockway. Estab. 1972 (theater). Produces plays for a family audience. Most productions are with music, but are not musicals. "Casts are usually limited to six performers because of economic reasons. Technical requirements are kept to a minimum for touring purposes." Professional productions using members of Actor's Equity Association. 100% of plays/musicals written for adult roles. Recently produced plays: *A Woman Called Truth*, by Sandra Fenichel Asher (a play celebrating the life of Sojourner Truth)—ages 8 through adult; *Eagle or Sun*, by Sabina Berman (the conquest of Mexico from the Aztec point of view)—ages 8 through adult. "No videos or cassettes. We accept only one script per playwright per year." Will consider previously performed work. Submit complete ms and score. Reports in 3-6 months. Rights agreement negotiated with author. Pays writers by one time fee or royalty negotiated with publisher. SASE for return of submission.
Tips: "We are seeing a trend toward plays that are appropriate for a family audience and that address today's multicultural concerns."

PIONEER DRAMA SERVICE, P.O. Box 22555, Denver CO 80222. (303)759-4297. FAX: (303)759-0475. Editor: Steven Fendrich. Estab. 1960. Publishes 7 children's plays/year; 2 children's musicals/year. Subject matter: Publishes plays for ages 9-high school. Recently published plays/musicals: *Nutcracker*, by Patrick R. Dorn and Bill Francoeur—unique Christmas musical for ages 10 and up; *The Empty Chair*, by Tim Kelly—one-act anti-drug drama for teens and up; *A Little Bit of Magic*, by Gail and Grant Golden—small cast musical ideal for touring for audiences 5 and up; casts 10 and up. Does not want to see "script, scores, tapes, pics and reviews." Submission method: query with synopsis, character breakdown and set description. Reports in 2 months. Rights obtained on mss: all rights. Pays writers in royalties (10% on sales, 50% royalties on productions); or buys material outright for $200-1,000.

PLAYERS PRESS, INC., P.O. Box 1132, Studio City CA 91614-0132. (818)789-4980. Vice President: R. W. Gordon. Estab. 1965. Publishes 5-25 children's plays/year; 2-15 children's musicals/year. Subject matter: "We publish for all age groups." Recently published plays/musicals: *Rapunzel N' the Witch*, by William-Alan Landes—musical for grades for 4-12. Submission method: query with synopsis, character breakdown and set description; include #10 envelope SASE with query. Reports in 6-9 months. Rights obtained on mss: stage, screen, TV rights. Payment varies; outright purchases are available upon written request.

Tips: "Entertainment quality is on the upswing and needs to be directed at the world, no longer just the USA."

THE PLAYHOUSE JR., (formerly Pittsburgh Playhouse Jr.), 222 Craft Ave., Pittsburgh PA 15213. (412)621-4445. Director: Wayne Brinda. Estab. 1949. Produces 5 children's plays/year including 1 children's musical/year. Produces children's plays for semi-professional with a college theater department: 99% of plays/musicals written for adult roles; 1% written for juvenile roles. Does not want to see "strong social problem plays." Submission method: query with synopsis, character breakdown and set description; first drafts. Reports in 3 weeks. Rights obtained on mss: "performance rights — negotiable." Pays writers commission/royalty.

PLAYS, THE DRAMA MAGAZINE FOR YOUNG PEOPLE, 120 Boylston St., Boston MA 02116. (617)423-3157. Managing Editor: Elizabeth Preston. Estab. 1941. Publishes 70-75 children's plays/year. "Props and staging should not be overly elaborate or costly. Our plays are performed by children in school." 100% of plays written for juvenile roles. Subject matter: Audience is lower grades through junior/senior high. Recently published plays: *Moonlight Is When*, by Kay Arthur, about a shy young researcher who finds romance in an unexpected place — the Museum of Natural History; *Express to Valley Forge*, by Earl J. Dias, about a courageous patriot who saves the day for George Washington's army; and *Kidnapped*, a dramatization of the Herman Melville classic, adapted by Adele Thane. Send "nothing downbeat — no plays about drugs, sex or other 'heavy' topics." Submission methods: query first on adaptations of folk tales and classics; otherwise submit complete ms. Reports in 2-3 weeks. Rights obtained on mss: all rights. Pay rates vary, on acceptance. Guidelines available; send SASE. Sample copy $3.
Tips: "Above all, plays must be entertaining for young people with plenty of action and a satisfying conclusion."

PLAYS FOR YOUNG AUDIENCES, P.O. Box 22555, Denver CO 80222. (303)759-4297. FAX: (303)759-0475. Editor: Steven Fendrich. Estab. 1989. Publishes 3 children's plays/year; 1 children's musical/year. Subject matter: Publishes plays for preschool-8th grade audience. Recently produced plays: *A Little Bit of Magic*, by Gail and Grant Golden — audiences pre-school and up, casting 10 and up — small cast musical, ideal for touring; *The Dancing Snowman*, by R. Eugene Jackson and Carl Alette, audiences pre-school and up, cast-10 and up — musical; *Nutcracker*, by Patrick R. Dorn and Bill Francoeur, ages 10 and up — unique Christmas musical. Does not want to see script, score, tape, pictures and reviews. Submission method: query first; query with synopsis, character breakdown and set description. Reports in 2 months. Rights obtained on mss: all rights. Pays writers in royalties of 10% in sales, 50% on productions; or buys material outright for $200-1,000.

STAGE ONE: THE LOUISVILLE CHILDREN'S THEATRE, 425 W. Market, Louisville KY 40202. (502)589-5946. FAX: (502)589-5779. Producing Director: Moses Goldberg. Estab. 1946. Produces 10 children's plays/year 1-3 children's musicals/year. Stage One is an equity company producing children's plays for professional productions. 100% of plays/musicals written for adult roles. "Sometimes do use students in selected productions." Recently produced plays: *Bridge to Terabithia*, by Katherine Patason, Stephanie Tulan, music by Steven Leibman — deals with friendship and the acceptance of tragedy, for 9 year old through adult audience; *Babar*, by Thomas Olson (adaptation) — story about the adventures of an elephant for 4-12 year old audience. Submission method: submit complete ms, score and tape of songs (if a musical); include the author's résumé if desired. Reports in 3-4 months. Pays writers in royalties or per performance.
Tips: Looking for "stageworthy and respectful dramatizations of the classic tales of childhood, both ancient and modern; plays relevant to the lives of young people and

their families; and plays directly related to the school curriculum."

TADA!, 120 West 28th St., New York NY 10001. (212)627-1732. Co-Artistic Directors: Janine Trevens and James Learned. Estab. 1984. Produces 3-4 children's plays/year; 3-4 children's musicals/year. "All actors are children, ages 6-17." Produces children's plays for professional, year-round theater. 100% of plays/musicals written for juvenile roles. Recently produced plays: *The Gift of Winter*, book by Michael Slade, music by David Evans, lyrics by Faye Greenberg—how the very first snowfall came to happen for 2 through adults; *Rabbit Sense*, book by Davidson Lloyd, music by John Kroner, lyrics by Gary Gardner—several Brer Rabbit stories told with new relevance by weaving them through a modern day story in an urban setting for 2 through adults. Submission method: query with synopsis, character breakdown and set description; submit complete ms, score and tape of songs (if a musical). Reports in 3 months. Rights obtained on mss: "Depends on the piece." Pays writers in royalties. SASE for return of submissions.
Tips: "Too many authors are writing productions, not plays. Our company is multi-racial and city-oriented. We are not interested in fairy tales."

THEATRE FOR YOUNG AMERICA, 7204 W. 80th St., Overland Park KS 66204. (913)648-4600. Artistic Director: Gene Mackey. Estab. 1974. Produces 10 children's plays/year; 3-5 children's musicals/year. We use a "small cast (4-7), open thrust stage." Theatre for Young America is a professional equity company. 80% of plays/musicals written for adult roles; 20% for juvenile roles. Recently produced plays: *The Wizard of Oz*, by Jim Eiler and Jeanne Bargy—for ages 6 and up; *A Partridge in a Pear Tree*, by Lowell Swortzell—deals with the 12 days of Christmas, for ages 6 and up; *Three Billy Goats Gruff*, by Gene Mackey and Molly Jessup—Norwegian folk tales, for ages 6 and up. Submission method: query with synopsis, character breakdown and set description. Reports in 2 months. Rights obtained on mss: "production, tour rights in local area." Pays writers in royalties or $10-50/per performance.
Tips: Looking for "cross-cultural material that respects the intelligence, sensitivity and taste of the child audience."

*THEATREWORKS/USA, 890 Bwy, New York NY 10003. (212)677-5959. Artistic Director: Jay Harnick. Estab. 1960. Produces 4 musicals/year. Cast of 5 actors. Play should be 1 hour long, tourable. Professional children's theatre comprised of adult equity actors. 100% of musicals are written for adult roles. Recently produced musicals: *Harriet the Spy*, by James Still/Kim Olan/Alison Hubbard (adaptation of Louise Fitzhugh book)—grades 4-8; *Harold and the Purple Crayon*, by Jane Shepard/Jon Ehrlich/Robin Pagerbin (adaptations of picture book by Crockett Johnson)—ages K-3. No fractured, typical "kiddy theatre" fairy tales. Will consider previously performed work. Query first with synopsis, character breakdown and set description. Reports in 6 months. Pays writers 6% royalties. SASE for return of submission.

THE YOUNG COMPANY, P.O. Box 225, Milford NH 03055. (603)673-4005. Literary Manager: Blair Hundertmark. Estab. 1984. Produces 10-12 children's plays/year; 1-2 children's musicals/year. "Scripts should not be longer than an hour, small cast preferred; very small production budgets, so use imagination." The Young Company is a professional training program associated with American Stage Festival. Does not want to see condescending material. Submission method: Query with synopsis, character breakdown and sample score. Rights obtained on mss: first production credit on all future materials. Pays small fee and housing for rehearsals.
Tips: Looks for "concise and legible presentation, songs that further dramatic action. Develop material with strong marketing possibilities. See your work in front of an audience and be prepared to change it if your audience doesn't 'get it.' Don't condescend to your audience. Tell them a *story*."

Special Markets

Over 90% of children's-only bookstores carry ancillary products such as posters, coloring books, greeting cards, puzzles and games in their inventories. Booksellers have discovered sidelines are valuable in a couple of different ways: First, they act as bait to lure customers who might not visit the bookstore if it only carried books. Prominently displayed sidelines increase the visual attractiveness and enhance the image of a bookstore. As a result, the more inviting atmosphere is more likely to draw people in. Second, booksellers like selling sidelines because they offer a higher margin of profit than books, therefore making them a good source of supplemental revenue. Bookstore owners are especially interested in sidelines which are book-related or education-oriented.

What follows is a list of special markets that produce various sidelines for children and are interested in using the services of freelancers. Sidelines consist of a potpourri of products, so needs among these markets may greatly vary. Read through the listing carefully to determine subject needs and methods of submission. If more specific guidelines are available from the company, write to request them. Conforming to detailed submission procedures will increase your chances of selling to these markets.

*ARISTOPLAY, LTD., P.O. Box 7529, Ann Arbor MI 48107. (313)995-4353. FAX: (313)995-4611. Editor: Jan Barney Newman. Art Director: Jack Thompson. Estab. 1980. 10% of material written by freelancers; 50% illustrated by freelancers. Buys 2 freelance projects/year; receives 100 submissions/year. Produces various materials—all educational subjects.
Making Contact & Terms: Submit seasonal special games 1 year in advance. "We do not accept unsolicited submissions. A descriptive letter required. We buy copyright." Pays half on acceptance; half on publication. Pays $1,500-5,000 for games.
Tips: Target age group 4-14. "We are an educational game company. Writers and illustrators working for us must be willing to research the subject and period of focus."

A/V CONCEPTS CORP., 30 Montauk Blvd., Oakdale NY 11769. (516)567-7227. FAX: (516)567-8745. Art Director: Philip Solimene. Estab. 1969. 100% of material written and illustrated by freelancers. Buys 23 freelance projects/year; receives 100 submissions/year. Children's educational publications. Cartoonists: looks for "super hero-like characters in 4-color and b&w."
Making Contact & Terms: Reports in 10 days. Purchases all rights. Pays on publication. Writer's/illustrator's guidelines for SASE.
Tips: Target age group: K-12.

*THE AVALON HILL GAME CO., 4517 Harford Rd., Baltimore MD 21214. (301)254-9200. FAX: (301)254-0991. Editor: A. Eric Dott. Art Director: Jean Baer. Estab. 1958. 50% of material written and illustrated by freelancers. Buys 50 freelance projects/year; receives 500 submissions annually. Produces comic books (*Tales From the Floating Vagabond*) and an extensive line of games.
Making Contact & Terms: Submit seasonal special games 1 year in advance; seasonal comic books 9 months in advance. SASE. Reports in 6 weeks. Buys all rights on accepted material. Pays on acceptance and publication.

Tips: Seeks creative writing about adventure, strategy board and computer games. Target market is "above-average, intelligent teens."

bePUZZLED/LOMBARD MARKETING, INC., 45 Wintonbury Avenue, Bloomfield CT 06002. (203)286-4226. FAX: (203)286-4229. Editor/Art Director: Luci Seccareccia. Estab. 1987. 100% of material written and illustrated by freelancers. Buys 10 freelance projects/year. Puzzles and/or games: mystery jigsaw puzzle games. Needs "to be announced via mail to list of interested freelancers."
Making Contact & Terms: Submit special puzzles in March-April for Christmas. Reports in 2-6 weeks. Material copyrighted. Purchases all rights. Pays on acceptance. Pay for puzzles $200-1,000. Writer's guideline sheet for #10 SAE and 2 first-class stamps.
Tips: Target age group: 4-6 years; 7-10 years; ages 12-adult.

BRILLIANT ENTERPRISES, 117 W. Valerio St., Santa Barbara CA 93101. Art Director: Ashleigh Brilliant. Estab. 1967. Greeting cards: wide range of humorous concepts. Greeting cards: unrhymed.
Making Contact & Terms: Reports in 3 weeks. Material copyrighted. Purchases all rights. Pays on acceptance. Pay for greeting cards $40 minimum. Writer's/illustrator's guideline sheet for $2 and SAE.

*COLLECTOR'S GALLERY, P.O. Box 410, Long Lake MN 55356. (612)476-0241. FAX: (612)476-6799. Editor: Polly McCrea. Estab. 1980. 15% of material illustrated by freelancers. Buys 4 freelance projects/year; receives 35 submissions/year. Produces make-your-own greeting card kits and activity pads with games which can be played over and over (example: jumbo tic tac toe). "I'm not looking for freelance artwork at this time, but am interested in children's game materials."
Making Contact & Terms: Submit seasonal special games and puzzles 6-9 months in advance. SASE. Reports in 3-4 weeks. Buy all rights on accepted material. Pays on acceptance. Pays $30-75 for puzzles. Illustrator's guidelines for SASE.
Tips: "Small activity games played with paper and pen, that can go on small notepads sell best." Target age group: 6-12.

COLORMORE, INC., P.O. Box 111249, Carrollton TX 75011-1249. (316)636-9326. President: Susan C. Koch. Estab. 1987. 50% of material written and illustrated by freelancers. Buys 3 freelance projects/year; receives 50 submissions/year. Greeting card line(s): "color-your own postcards and seasonal cards." Coloring books: "travel-related/geography/social studies." Illustrators: looks for "color-your own postcards with Texas themes."
Making Contact & Terms: Submit greeting cards 12 months in advance, special coloring books 12 months in advance. SASE. Reports in 6 weeks. Material copyrighted. Buys all rights. Pays on publication. Pay for greeting cards "varies"; pay for coloring books is within a 5-8% royalty range. Writer's/illustrator's guideline sheets for legal-size SAE and 1 first class stamp.
Tips: Target age group: 5-10 years.

*CONTEMPORARY DESIGNS, 213 Main St., Gilbert IA 50105. (515)232-5188. FAX: (515)232-3380. Editor and Art Director: Sallie Abelson. Estab. 1977. 25% of material is written by freelancers; 20% illustrated by freelancers. Buys 50 freelance projects/year; receives 150 submissions/year. Publishes greeting cards, coloring books and puzzles and/or games. "Greeting cards should be funny—for children who go to camp."

*Refer to the Business of Children's Writing & Illustrating
for up-to-date marketing, tax and legal information.*

Making Contact & Terms: Submit seasonal material 1 year in advance. SASE. Reports in 1 month. Buys all rights on accepted material. Pays on acceptance. Pays $40 for greeting cards; negotiable amount for coloring books and puzzles. Writer's/illustrator's guidelines for SASE.

Tips: "Greeting cards for campers and Jewish markets only. Puzzles, games and coloring books should be Judaic."

CREATE-A-CRAFT, Box 330008, Fort Worth TX 76163-0008. (817)292-1855. Editor: Mitchell Lee. Estab. 1967. Produces greeting cards, giftwrap, games, calendars, posters, stationery and paper tableware products for all ages. Works with 3 freelance artists/year. Buys 3-5 designs/illustrations/year. Prefers artists with experience in cartooning. Works on assignment only. Buys freelance designs/illustrations mainly for greetings cards and t-shirts. Also uses freelance artists for calligraphy, P-O-P displays, paste-up and mechanicals. Considers pen & ink, watercolor, acrylics and colored pencil. Prefers humorous and "cartoons that will appeal to families. Must be cute, appealing, etc. No religious, sexual implications or off-beat humor." Produces material for all holidays and seasons; submit 6 months before holiday.

Making Contact & Terms: For guidelines and sample cards, send $2.50 and #10 SASE. Contact only through artist's agent. Samples are filed. Samples not filed are not returned. Reports only if interested. Write to schedule an appointment to show a portfolio, which should include original/final art, final reproduction/product, slides, tearsheets, color and b&w. Original artwork is not returned to the artist after job's completion. "Payment depends upon the assignment, amount of work involved, production costs, etc. involved in the project." Buys all rights.

Tips: "Demonstrate an ability to follow directions exactly. Too many submit artwork that has no relationship to what we produce."

ECLIPSE COMICS, P.O. Box 1099, Forestville CA 95436. (707)887-1521. FAX: (707)887-7128. Editor-in-Chief: Catherine Yronwode. Art Director: Chris Pitzer. Estab. 1978. 100% of material written and illustrated by freelancers. Buys "approximately 100" freelance projects/year; receives 500 submissions/year. Comic books: looks for "realistic art and stories that appeal to a broad spectrum and a variety of ages. Doesn't want to see pornography, sexist exploitation, racist stories." Writers: "All material submitted should be in (brief) outline form with 5-6 sample pages of script." Illustrators: "We will only look at samples of continuity art and cover illustrations; display pieces are not needed."

Making Contact & Terms: SASE. Pays on acceptance. Pay for comic books "varies; writer and artist split 8% royalty." Guideline sheets for #10 SAE and 1 first class stamp; guidelines and a sample comic for $1.75 and 9×12 SAE.

EPHEMERA BUTTONS, P.O. Box 490, Phoenix OR 97535. Editor: Ed Polish. Estab. 1980. 90% of material written and 10% illustrated by freelancers. Buys over 200 freelance projects/year; receives over 2,000 submissions/year. Novelty pin back buttons with slogans and art. Need simple and bold line art that would work on a button.

Making Contact & Terms: SASE for return of submission. Reports in 3 weeks. Material copyrighted. Pays on publication. Pays $25 per slogan or design. Guideline sheets for #10 SAE and 1 first class stamp.

Tips: Looks for "very silly and outrageously funny slogans. We also are looking for provocative, irreverent and outrageously funny *adult* humor."

FANTAGRAPHICS BOOKS, INC., 7563 Lake City Way NE, Seattle WA 98115. (206)524-1967. FAX: (206)524-2104. Submissions Editor: Robert Boyd. Art Director: Dale Yarger. 100% of material written and illustrated by freelancers. Estab. 1975. Buys 10-15 freelance projects/year; receives 300+ submissions/year. Comic books: "We print comics of quality mostly aimed at adults, but a few for younger readers. We like projects

that come wholly from the creator (writer and artist); any subject or style they use is fine. The only thing an illustrator should be aware of is that we rarely print comics in color; we prefer black-and-white art."
Making Contact & Terms: Submit seasonal comic books 9 months in advance. Reports in 6 weeks. Purchases one-time rights. Pays on publication. Pays 4% minimum for comic books. Guideline sheets for #10 SASE.

*FAX-PAX USA, INC., 37 Jerome Ave., Bloomfield CT 06002. (203)242-3333. FAX: (203)242-7102. Editor: Stacey L. Savin. Estab. 1990. 50% of material written by freelancers; 50% illustrated by freelancers. Buys 1 freelance project/year. Publishes educational picture cards. Needs include U.S. History. Uses rhymed verse.
Making Contact & Terms: Buys all rights. Pays on publication. Cannot return material.
Tips: "Nursery rhymes, fables and ABC's sell best." Target ages 1-10.

*FOR KIDS' SAKE PUBLISHERS, P.O. Box 70182, Eugene OR 97401-0111. Editor: Patrick G. Harrison. Estab. 1989. 90% of material written by freelancers; 100% illustrated by freelancers. Produces coloring books (illustrated children's poems suitable for coloring; environmental and inspiring themes) and posters (simple, but appealing to the child's heart in all of us). "Need writers of children's poems suitable for coloring with environmental and inspiring themes. Need illustrators interested in doing coloring book style drawings." Uses rhymed verse.
Making Contact & Terms: Submit seasonal special coloring books 1 year in advance. SASE. Reports in 2 months. Buys all rights (but negotiable). Pays on publication (with small advance). Pays $25 minimum for coloring books + % royalty. Pays "per illustrated poem. If poet and illustrator are 2 people: split pay and royalty." Writer's/illustrator's guidelines for $2 or 9×12 SASE (75¢ postage).
Tips: Wants illustrated poems suitable for coloring. Target age group 8-12. "We look for coloring books that combine poetry and art."

*GREAT AMERICAN PUZZLE FACTORY, INC., 16 South Main St., S. Norwalk CT 06854. (203)838-4240. FAX: (203)838-2065. Art Director: Pat Duncan. Estab. 1976. 100% illustrated by freelancers. Buys 30 freelance projects/year; receives 300 submissions/year. Produces puzzles.
Making Contact & Terms: Not interested in seasonal. SASE. Reports in 2 weeks. Rights vary. Pays on publication. Pay varies.
Tips: Wants "whimsical, fantasy" material. Target age group: 4-12.

*HIGHLIGHTS FOR CHILDREN, Hidden Pictures, Puzzlemania, Activity Books, 803 Church St., Honesdale PA 18431. (717)253-1080. FAX: (717)253-0179. Editor: Kent L. Brown Jr. Art Director: Rosanne Guararra. Estab. 1946. 90% of materials freelance written and illustrated. Receives 7,000-8,000 submissions annually. Needs "independent activities targeting children 5-12 years in age. We favor visually stimulating puzzles free of violent themes."
Making Contact & Terms: Special puzzle submissions accepted year-round. SASE for return of submission. Reports in 1-2 months. Purchases all rights. Pays on acceptance. Writer's guidelines for SASE.
Tips: Looking for "codes, matching, crosswords, dot-to-dots, math and logic puzzles, hidden pictures, mazes, quizzes, riddles." Illustrators: "In illustration almost any range of art is accepted these days. Children are more sophisticated now in terms of graphics and design—the illustrator should be aware of this."

INTERCONTINENTAL GREETINGS LTD., 176 Madison Ave., New York NY 10016. (212)683-5830. Contact: Robin Lipner. Estab. 1964. 100% of material freelance written and illustrated. Bought over 200 freelance projects last year. Received "thousands" of

submissions last year. Produces greeting cards and scholastic products (notebooks, pencil cases). Needs "humorous writing for greeting cards only. Greeting card (style) artwork in series of three or more. We use very little writing except for humor."
Making Contact & Terms: Accepts seasonal/holiday material year-round. SASE for return of submissions. Reports in 1 month. Purchases world rights under contract (for 2 years). Pays on publication. Pays $30-100 for greeting cards (per usage) and $80-200 for puzzles (per usage). "We hope to use each piece 2-20 times." Writer's/illustrator's guidelines available for SASE.
Tips: Target age group for juvenile cards: ages 1-10. Illustrators: "Use clean colors, not muddy or dark."

*KINGDOM PUZZLES, 7231 Vanalden Ave., Reseda CA 91335-4119. (818)705-4572. FAX: (818)705-4572. Owner: M. Oldenkamp. Estab. 1987. Produces puzzles.
Making Contact & Terms: Submit seasonal puzzles 1 year in advance. SASE. Reports in 2 months. Pay varies.
Tips: Wants "wildlife, nature" material for children and adults.

*LAMONT PUBLISHING, P.O. Box 412, Ashland OH 44805-0412. (419)281-5105. FAX: (419)281-4223. Editor: Peter Brick. Art Director: George Lamont. Estab. 1974. 100% of material written and illustrated by freelancers. Buys 37 freelance projects/year; receives 400-500 submissions/year. Produces greeting cards and coloring books. Wants children's illustrations suitable for picture books. Uses unrhymed verse.
Making Contact & Terms: Submit seasonal greeting cards 1 year in advance; special coloring books 6 months in advance. SASE. Reports in 3 weeks. Buys all rights. Writer's guidelines for SASE.
Tips: Target age group: 4-16 years.

*MAYFAIR GAMES, 5641 Howard St., Niles IL 60648. (708)647-9650. FAX: (708)647-0939. Editorial Director: Jim Musser. Art Director: Mari Paz Cabardo. Estab. 1981. 100% of material is written and illustrated by freelancers. Buys 25 freelance projects/year; receives 100 submissions/year. Produces games under DC Heroes license and role playing and strategy games for teens and adults.
Making Contact & Terms: SASE. Reports in 2 months. Pays on acceptance and publication. Writer's guideline sheet for SASE.
Tips: Target age group: 14-40 years.

*DAVID MEKELBURG & FRIENDS, 1222 N. Fair Oaks Ave., Los Angeles CA 91103. (818)798-3633. FAX: (818)798-7385. Editor: Richard Crawford. Estab. 1988. 10% of material illustrated by freelancers. Buys 5 freelance projects/year. Material produced includes greeting cards.
Making Contact & Terms: Submit seasonal greeting cards 1 year in advance. SASE. Reports in 1 week. Pays on publication.

*NORTHWEST CORNER, INC., 1011 92 Ave. NE, Bellevue WA 98004. (206)451-3292. FAX: (206)455-9512. Editor: Shar Freeman. Estab. 1977. 50% of material is written by freelancers. Produces games and puzzles.
Making Contact & Terms: Submit seasonal/holiday special games and puzzles 1 year in advance. SASE. Pays on publication. Pay "depends on the project."
Tips: Specializes in wooden games, "however we are not limited to that." Target age group: 6-106. Sees trend toward educational games.

*PEACEABLE KINGDOM PRESS, 1051 Folger Ave., Berkeley CA 94710. (510)644-9801. FAX: (510)644-9805. Art Director: Olivia Hurd. Estab. 1983. 100% of material illustrated by freelancers. Buys 60 freelance projects/year; receives 100 submissions/year.

Produces posters and greeting cards. Uses images from classic children's books.
Making Contact & Terms: Submit seasonal posters and greeting cards 6 months in advance. Cannot return material. Reports in 1 week. Buys rights to distribution worldwide. Pays on publication with advance. Pays 5-10% of wholesale for greeting cards.
Tips: "We only choose from illustrations that are from published children's book illustrators."

PRICE STERN SLOAN, Suite 650, 11150 Olympic Blvd., Los Angeles CA 90064. Editor: Wendy Baker Vinitsky. Estab. 1964. 90% of material written and illustrated by freelancers. Buys 50 freelance projects/year; receives hundreds of submissions/year. Publishes "activity books and board books."
Making Contact & Terms: SASE. Reports in 4-6 weeks. Rights purchased: "depends on project." Payment depends on project. Writer's/illustrator's guidelines for business-size SAE and 1 first-class stamp. "Seasonal (fall or spring issue) catalog available with SASE and 4 first class stamps."
Tips: Target age group: preschool-YA. Trend toward "children's nonfiction."

*RIVERCREST INDUSTRIES, P.O. 771662, Houston TX 77215. (713)789-5394. FAX: (713)789-9666. Editor: Harry Capers. Estab. 1981. 100% of material airbrushed by freelancers. Buys 2 freelance projects/year. Produces games and books. Interested in someone to handle airbrush on completed illustrations.
Making Contact & Terms: SASE. Pays on acceptance.
Tips: Produces holiday games and juvenile books. Target age groups 2-7 for books; 6-adult for games.

STANDARD PUBLISHING, 8121 Hamilton Ave., Cincinnati OH 45231. (513)931-4050. FAX: (513)931-0904. Contact: Children's Book Editor. Estab. 1866. 100% of material illustrated by freelancers. Buys 75 freelance projects/year; receives 1,200 submissions/year. Publishes religious/value-oriented material.
Making Contact & Terms: Submit seasonal books, games and puzzles 12-18 months in advance. SASE. Reports in 3 months. Material copyrighted. Buys all rights. Pays on acceptance. Writer's guidelines for SAE and 1 first class stamp.
Tips: Looks for "Bible-oriented" material, for a preschool-6th grade audience.

WARNER PRESS, P.O. Box 2499, Anderson IN 46018. Editor: Cindy Maddox. Art Director: Dianne Deckert. Estab. 1880. 60% of material written by freelancers; 75% illustrated by freelancers. Publishes children's birthday cards, coloring and activity books, all religious-oriented. "Need fun, up-to-date stories for coloring books, with religious emphasis. Also considering activity books for Sunday school classroom use."
Making Contact & Terms: Submit seasonal greeting cards and coloring books 18 months in advance. Reports in 6 weeks. Material copyrighted. Buys all rights. Pays on acceptance.

Young Writer's/ Illustrator's Markets

This book caters to all ages, and in recognition of the fact children and teens can be writers and illustrators too, markets that solicit work *by* creative kids are included in this section.

Some of the magazines in this section are exclusively for children; others are adult magazines that have set aside special sections to feature the work of younger writers and illustrators. Since most juvenile magazines are distributed through schools, churches and home subscriptions, some of the smaller, literary magazines here may not be easily found in the bookstore or library. In such a case, you may need to contact the magazine to see if a sample copy is available, and what the cost might be. It is important for writers and artists to be familiar with the editorial needs of magazines they are interested in submitting to.

Be advised that it is important to send a self-addressed stamped envelope (SASE) with proper postage affixed with each submission. This way, if the market is not interested in your work, they will send it back to you. If you do not send the SASE with your submission, you probably won't get your work back. If your work is rejected the first time you send it out, be assured you are not the first one this has happened to. Many of our best known writers and artists were turned down more times than they can count at the beginning of their careers, yet went on to be successful at their craft. The key to becoming published lies in persistence as well as talent. Keep sending out stories and artwork as you continue to improve your craft. Someday, an editor may decide your work is just what he needs.

As the adult writers and artists have been advised in other parts of this book, refer to the Business of Children's Writing & Illustrating at the beginning of this book if you're not sure what steps to take when submitting your work. Best of luck in your writing or art career!

THE ACORN, 1530 7th St., Rock Island IL 61201. (309)788-3980. Newsletter. Estab. 1989. Audience consists of "kindergarten-12th grade, teachers and other adult writers." Purpose in publishing works by children: to expose children's manuscripts to others and provide a format for those who might not have one. Children must be K-12 (put grade on manuscripts).
Magazines: 99% of magazine written by children. Uses 3 fiction pieces (500 words), 2 nonfiction pieces (500 words), 6 pieces of poetry (32 lines). Pays 1 copy of the issue the work is in. Sample copy $1. Subscription $10 for 6 issues. Submit mss to Betty Mowery, editor. Send complete ms. Will accept typewritten, legibly handwritten and/or computer printout. SASE. Reports in 1 week.
Artwork: Publishes artwork by children. Looks for "all types; size 4×5. Use black ink in artwork." Pays in 1 copy of issue the work is in. Submit artwork either with manuscript or separately to Betty Mowery. SASE. Responds in 1 week.
Tips: "My biggest problem is not having names on the manuscript. If the manuscript gets separated from the cover letter, there is no way to know whom to respond to. Also, adults who submit will often go over word limit—we are a small publication and cannot handle more than wordage previously stated. I will use occasional articles by adults, but

it must relate to something that will help children with their writing—submitting or publishing. Manuscripts without SASE will not be returned."

*BOODLE, P.O. 1049, Portland IN 47371. (219)726-8141. Magazine published quarterly. "Each quarterly issue offers children a special invitation to read stories and poems written by others. Children can learn from the ideas in these stories and the techniques of sharing ideas in picures and written form. Audience is ages 6-12. We hope that publishing children's writing will enhance the self-esteem of the authors and motivate other children to try expressing themselves in this form." Submission requirements: "We ask that authors include grade when written, current grade, name of school, and a statement from parent or teacher that the work is original."
Magazines: 95% of magazine written by children. Uses 12 short stories (100-500 words), 1 mostly animal nonfiction piece (100-500 words), 25 poems (50-500 words), 2 puzzles and mazes (50-500 words). Pays 2 copies of issue. Submit mss to Mavis Catalfio, editor. Submit complete ms. Will accept typewritten and legibly handwritten mss. Include SASE.
Artwork: Wants "mazes, cartoons, drawings of animals or seasons or sports which will likely match a story or poem we publish." Pays 2 copies of issue. "Drawings should be done in black ink or marker." Submit artwork to Mavis Catalfio. Reports in 2 months.
Tips: "Submit seasonal materials at least 6 months in advance. We love humor and offbeat stories. We seldom publish sad or depressing stories about death or serious illness."

BOYS' LIFE, 1325 Walnut Hill Ln., Box 152079, Irving TX 75015-2079. (214)580-2000. Magazine published monthly. Audience consists of boys 8-18. Requirements to be met before work is published: must be 18 or under.
Magazines: One page, which does not run every month, is written by children. Uses fiction stories (500 words or less); nonfiction pieces (500 words or less); poetry. "We pay $25 for mss that are published in our Readers' Page column." Submit mss to special features editor. Will accept typewritten, legibly handwritten, computer printout mss. "We do not acknowledge receipt of ms."

CHALK TALK MAGAZINE, Chalk Talk Publishing, 1550 Mills Rd., RR2, Sidney, BC V8L351 Canada. (604) 656-1858. Monthly magazine. Estab. 1988. "*Chalk Talk* gives children the opportunity to become published authors and inspires an enthusiasm for the written word. It is written by children for children."
Magazine: Submissions welcome from all children ages 5 to 14. The magazine contains "fun and imaginative stories and poems, true life experiences, book reviews, ecology news and concerns, and contains something different every month. Send in as many contributions as you like at one time and as often as you wish." SASE for return of ms. Contributors are not paid for their submissions.
Artwork: "Artwork reproduces best from plain paper drawn in dark crayon, felt, pen or pencil."

*CHICKADEE MAGAZINE, Suite 306, 56 The Esplanade, Toronto, Ontario M5E 1A7 Canada. (416)868-6001. Magazine published 10 times/year. "*Chickadee* is for children aged 3-9. It's purpose is to entertain and educate children about science and nature in the world around them." "*Chickadee* publishes children's drawings to promote creativity and to give all ages of readers the chance to express themselves. Drawings must follow the topics that are given each month."

CHILDREN'S ALBUM EGW PUBLISHING, Box 6086, Concord CA 94524. (415)671-9852. Magazine published bi-monthly. Audience consists of children ages 8-14. "*Children's Album* is a collection of creative thoughts and expressions dedicated to nurturing a child's positive self-image, to enlightening—without preference to age—with individuality, wisdom, and infinite imagination, to learning through fun, and to reminding—lest an adult forget what it is like to think as a child." Writer's guidelines available on request.

Magazines: 80% of magazine written by children. Uses 10 short stories (500-700 words), 10 poems (length varies). Pays in 1 year subscription. Submit mss to Margo Lemas, editor. Send query; submit complete ms. Will accept typewritten, legibly handwritten mss. SASE. Reports in 2-4 weeks.

Artwork: Publishes artwork and photos by children; submit artwork on 8½×11 paper. Pays in 1 year subscription. SASE. Reports in 2-4 weeks.

CHILDREN'S DIGEST, Box 567, Indianapolis IN 46206. (317)636-8881. Magazine. Published 8 times/year. Audience consists of preteens. Purpose in publishing works by children: to encourage children to express themselves through writing. Requirements to be met before work is published: require proof of originality before publishing stories. Writer's guidelines available on request.

Magazines: 10% of magazine written by children. Uses 1 fiction story (about 200 words), 6-7 poems, 15-20 riddles, 7-10 letters/issue. "There is no payment for manuscripts submitted by readers." Submit mss to *Children's Digest* (Elizabeth A. Rinck, editor). Submit complete ms. Will accept typewritten, legibly handwritten, computer printout mss. "Readers whose material is accepted will be notified by letter. Sorry, no materials can be returned."

CHILDREN'S PLAYMATE, Box 567, Indianapolis IN 46206. (317)636-8881. Magazine. Estab. 1928. Audience consists of children between 6 and 8 years of age. Purpose in publishing works by children: to encourage children to write. Writer's guidelines available on request.

Magazines: 10% of magazine written by children. Uses 6-7 poems, 8-10 jokes, 8-10 riddles/issue. "There is no payment for manuscripts submitted by children." Submit mss to *Children's Playmate* (Elizabeth A. Rinck, editor). Submit complete ms. Will accept typewritten, legibly handwritten, computer printout mss. "If a child's work is published, he/she will be notified by a letter. No material may be returned."

Artwork: Publishes artwork by children. "Prefers dark-colored line drawings on white paper. No payment for children's artwork published." Submit artwork to *Children's Playmate*.

CLUBHOUSE, Box 15, Berrien Springs MI 49103. (616)471-9009. Director of Publications: Elaine Trumbo. Magazine. Estab. 1949. Publishes 1 section by kids in each issue, bimonthly. "Audience consists of kids 9-14; philosophy is God loves kids, kids are neat people." Purpose in publishing works by children: encouragement; demonstration of talent. Requirements to be met before work is published: age 9-14; parent's note verifying originality.

Magazines: ¹⁄₁₆th of magazine written by children. Uses adventure, historical, everyday life experience (fiction/nonfiction-1,200 words); health-related short articles; poetry (4-24 lines of "mostly mood pieces and humor"). Payment for ms: prizes for children, money for adult authors. Query. Will accept typewritten, legibly handwritten, computer printout mss. "Will not be returned without SASE." Reports in 6 weeks.

Artwork: Publishes artwork by children. Looks for all types of artwork-white paper, black pen. Pays in prizes for kids. Send black pen on white paper to Elaine Trumbo, editor. SASE—"won't be returned without SASE."

Tips: "All items submitted by kids are held in a file and used when possible. We normally suggest they do not ask for return of the item."

Close-up

Mavis Catalfio
Editor
Boodle

"Our goal is to be upbeat," says Mavis Catalfio, cofounder and editor of *Boodle*, a quarterly magazine of stories, poems, pictures and puzzles "for kids by kids." The idea for *Boodle* began when work Catalfio found outstanding in a young author/illustrator program was rejected by existing children's markets. With support from a local newspaper publisher, Catalfio and Liz Lawson, *Boodle*'s art director, launched the magazine in 1989.

Since then, they have published work by students in over 15 different states. "We want to reach student writers and illustrators across the country," Catalfio says. She hopes *Boodle* inspires readers to write and/or illustrate their own material. "Our selections tend to be less 'literary' than some other magazines. We hope children will read *Boodle* and think, 'Hey, I can do that.' And we hope they follow through and write to us."

In the 300-500 text submissions for each issue, Catalfio seeks original, humorous stories and poems: "We select material that is light-hearted and witty. Also, stories with unusual plots or unusual animals are more likely to be accepted. We follow a seasonal theme, focusing on appropriate weather, holidays, sports and leisure activities. We receive so much seasonal material, competition for publication is strongest here. More unusual subjects have a better chance for inclusion." She adds that students should submit seasonal work at least six months in advance.

Students should also note that only black-and-white artwork is accepted, and "all artwork we publish accompanies a specific story. So, a combination of art and text submitted together has an advantage," says Catalfio. However, they will match art from one contributor with a story from another. "Stories about animals, sports and school are frequently matched with illustrations, so artists who wish to submit only illustrations should focus on these topics," she says.

"We receive many envelopes from teachers who were pleased with the way a creative writing assignment turned out. In each, we try to find a 'shining star' that we can publish, but teachers should be aware that many others across the country are using the same textbook suggestions for language arts development," says Catalfio. For this reason, she prefers single submissions from either a student or a teacher who has done some preliminary selection.

Catalfio does not want very long stories or stories with long-winded conversations. She is also disappointed when students do not follow *Boodle*'s guidelines. "We are inconvenienced when students do not include a title or complete information about themselves," she says, stressing that students who want a reply must include a self-addressed, stamped envelope.

Young writers and artists should read *Boodle* to see what kind of material is published. "But do not try to write the same type of material you read. Try to think of something different. What kind of story would you like to have read, but didn't find?" Catalfio asks. Overall, she says, "the surest way to get your story or poem published is to make me smile or laugh when I read it."

— Christine Martin

CREATIVE KIDS, Box 6448, Mobile AL 36660. (205)478-4700. Editor/Publisher: Fay L. Gold. Magazine published 8 times/year (Oct.-May). Estab. 1979. "All of our material is by children, for children." Purpose in publishing works by children: to "create a product that is good enough for publication and to offer an opportunity for children to see their work in print." Requirements to be met before work is published: ages 5-18 — must have statement by teacher or parent verifying originality. Writer's guidelines available on request. SASE required.

Magazines: Uses "about 6" fiction stories (200-750 words); "about 6" nonfiction stories (200-750 words); poetry, plays, ideas to share 200-750 words/issue. Pays in free magazine. Submit mss to Fay L. Gold, editor. Will accept typewritten, legibly handwritten mss. Reports in 1 month. SASE required.

Artwork: Publishes artwork by children. Looks for "any kind of drawing, cartoon, or painting." Pays in "free magazine." Send original or a photo of the work to Fay L. Gold, editor. No photocopies. Reports in 1 month. SASE required.

Tips: "*Creative Kids* is a magazine by kids, for kids. The work represents children's ideas, questions, fears, concerns and pleasures. The material never contains racist, sexist or violent expression. The purpose is to encourage youngsters to create a product that is good enough for publication. A person may submit one or more pieces of work. Each piece must be labeled with the student's name, birth date, grade, school, home address, and school address. Include a photograph, if possible. Recent school pictures are best. Material submitted to *Creative Kids* must not be under consideration by any other publication. Items should be carefully prepared, proofread and double checked. All activities requiring solutions must be accompanied by the correct answers. We're looking for current topics of interest: nutrition, ecology, cleaner environment, etc."

ESSENTIAL NEWS, (formerly *Bear Essential News for Kids*), P.O. Box 26908. Tempe AZ 85285-6908. (602)345-READ. Newspaper published monthly. Audience consists of children, grades 4-8, their families and educational community. Philosophy is to "stimulate a positive attitude toward learning and experiencing. Support kids' creativity. Emphasize genuine, self-esteem building content. Our purpose is to be a leader in unlocking the potential of today's children and developing their self-esteem." Students must be grades 4-8, and may submit original work from any major market as an *Essential News* correspondent. Writer's guidelines available on request.

Magazines: Nonfiction news and features (uses 10 pieces per zone (75-100 words); also uses for each issue: short poems (10-15/zone), letters to the editor (6-10/zone, 50 words), and reviews (4-6/zone, 75-100 words). Pays free copy. Children submit mss to

Always include a self-addressed stamped envelope (SASE) or International Reply Coupon (IRC) with submissions.

Janet Cooper, Cub Reporter/Program Director. Submit complete manuscript. Will accept typewritten, legibly handwritten and/or floppy disk (Mac). Reports in 2 months. Sample issue $1.
Artwork: Publishes artwork and photos by children. Pays free copy. Submit artwork to Janet Cooper.

FREE SPIRIT PUBLISHING INC., Suite 616, 400 First Ave. North, Minneapolis MN 55401. (612)338-2068. Publishes 3-8 books/year since starting in 1983 and a newsletter for 9-15 year-olds, 5 times/year. "We specialize in SELF-HELP FOR KIDS™. Our main interests include the development of self-esteem, self-awareness, creative thinking and problem solving abilities, assertiveness, and making a difference in the world. Children have a lot to share with each other. They also can reach and teach each other in ways adults cannot. Additionally, we publish the work of young people in the newsletter. Children only need an adult's signature assuring authenticity for the cartoon and writing contests we sponsor." Writer's guidelines available on request (specify student guidelines).
Books: Publishes psychology, self-help, how-to, education. Pays advance and royalties. Submit mss to Judy Galbraith, publisher. Send query. Will accept typewritten mss. Reports in 3-4 months.
Magazines: 20% of magazine written by children. Uses 2-5 nonfiction articles and survey responses. Word length: 100-800. Payment for children's articles: "A T-shirt and 3 copies of the newsletter in which they're published. Contest winners receive money and books." Submit complete ms. to Elizabeth Salzmann, editorial assistant. Will accept typewritten, legibly handwritten mss. Reports in 2 months.
Artwork: "We run a cartoon contest annually. Write for details." Contest winners receive a cash prize, and their entries are published. Winners also get a T-shirt and a book. Request rules and entry form in September or October (contest deadline is 1 November).

FUTURIFIC, INC., the Foundation for Optimism, Futurific, 280 Madison Ave., New York NY 10016. Publisher: B. Szent-Miklosy. (212)684-4913. Magazine published monthly. Audience consists of people interested in an accurate report of what is ahead. "We do not discriminate by age. We look for the visionary in all people. They must say what will be. No advice or 'may-be.'" Sample copy for $3 postage and handling. Writer's guidelines available on request.
Magazines: Submit mss to B. Szent-Miklosy, publisher. Will accept typewritten, legibly handwritten, computer printout, 5½ inch Word Perfect diskette, mss. Will also accept disk submissions (5½ inch Word perfect diskette).
Artwork: Publishes artwork by children. Looks for "what the future will look like." Pay is negotiable. Send b&w drawings or photos. Submit artwork to B. Szent-Miklosy, publisher.

*THE GOLDFINCH, 402 Iowa Ave., Iowa City IA 52240. (319)335-3916. Magazine published quarterly. Audience is fifth and sixth graders. "Magazine supports creative work by children: research, art, writing." Submitted work must go with the historical theme of each issue.
Magazines: 10-20% written by children. Uses at least 1 nonfiction essay, poem, story/issue (500 words). Pays complementary copies. Submit mss to Deborah Gore, editor. Submit complete ms. Will accept typewritten, legibly handwritten, computer disk (Apple) mss. Reports in 1 month.
Artwork: Publishes artwork/photogrphs by children. Art and photos must be black and white. Pays complementary copies. Query first to Deborah Gore.

*HIGH SCHOOL WRITER, P.O. Box 718, Grand Rapids MN 55744. (218)326-8025. Magazine published monthly during the school year. "The *High School Writer* is a magazine written by students *for* students. All submissions must exceed usual and customary standards of decency." Purpose in publishing works by children: "To provide a real audience for student writers—and text for study." Submissions by junior high and middle school students accepted for our junior edition. Senior high students' works are accepted for our senior high edition. Students attending schools that subscribe to our publication are eligible to submit their work." Writer's guidelines available on request.
Magazines: Uses fiction, nonfiction and poetry. Submit mss to Roxanne Kain, editor. Submit complete ms, teacher must submit. Will accept typewritten, computer generated (good quality) mss.
Tips: "Submissions should not be sent without first obtaining a copy of our guidelines. Also, submissions will not be considered unless student's school subscribes."

HIGHLIGHTS FOR CHILDREN, 803 Church St., Honesdale PA 18431. (717)253-1080. Magazine published monthly (July-August issue combined). "We strive to provide wholesome, stimulating, entertaining material that will encourage children to read. Our audience is children 2-12." Purpose in publishing works by children: to encourage children's creative expression. Requirements to be met before work is published: age limit is 15.
Magazines: 15-20% of magazine written by children. Features which occur occasionally: "What Are Your Favorite Books?" (8-10 per year), Recipes (8-10 per year), "Science Letters" (15-20 per year). Special features which invite children's submissions on a specific topic: "Tell the Story" (15-20 per year), "You're the Reporter" (8-10 per year), "Your Ideas, Please" (8-10 per year), "Endings to Unfinished Stories" (8-10 per year). Submit complete mss to the Editor. Will accept typewritten, legibly handwritten, computer printout mss. Responds in 3-6 weeks.
Artwork: Publishes artwork by children. No cartoon or comic book characters. No commercial products. Submit black-and-white artwork for "Our Own Pages." Color for others. Features include "Creatures Nobody Has Ever Seen" (5-8 per year) and "Illustration Job" (18-20 per year). Responds in 3-6 weeks.

*INTERNATIONAL READERS' NEWSLETTER, Perfection Learning Corporations, 10520 New York Ave., Des Moines IA 50322. (515)278-0133. Newsletter published quarterly. "The Perfection Learning Corporation believes that dialogue within a literary community allows readers to celebrate their reading and share new insights about themselves, their friends, their families, and their world. Therefore, the *International Readers' Newsletter* will provide a forum for students to engage in literary talk with other students. This publication will help make learning a social and interactive activity. The *IRN* invites students to submit written and visual responses to fiction or nonfiction. Published responses will express students' feelings and ideas in their own voices."
Magazines: Uses 20-25 essays (1 typed page preferred). Publishes personal reactions to literature in the form of essays, dialogues, poetry, literary letters, etc. Submission requirements: writing will be considered it it meets the following guidelines: "Writing must be original responses to fiction or nonfiction. Include the title and author of the reading or film you are responding to. Fill out a copy of the Permission to Publish form (can be obtained from copy of newsletter) and attach to each writing submitted. Writers are limited to four submissions per year." Submit mss to Kathie O'Sell, newsletter coordinator. Student or teacher may submit. Acknowledges receipt in 1 month.
Artwork: Publishes artwork/photographs by children. "Visual interpretations of fiction or nonfiction (cartoons, scenes, collages, etc.) will be considered." Submission requirements: Artwork will be considered if it meets the following guidelines: Artwork is clearly connected to a specific fiction or nonfiction piece; artwork is done on white paper with black ink or charcoal; original work must be sent—no copies, please. (We regret that

we will not be able to return your work); artwork is received in good condition. Do not bend or fold the artwork; Permission to Publish form is included with your artwork (can be obtained from copy of newsletter)." Submit artwork/photos to Kathie O'Sell, newsletter coordinator. Acknowledges receipt in 1 month. Please call for additional information.

*KIDSART, P.O. Box 274, Mt. Shasta CA 96067. (916)926-5076. Newsletter published quarterly. Publishes "hands-on art projects, open-ended art lessons, art history, lots of child-made art to illustrate." Purpose in publishing works by children: to "provide achievable models for kids—give young artists a forum for their work." Before publishing works "We always phone before publication to be sure it's OK with their folks, name's spelled correctly, etc."
Artwork: Publishes artwork/photographs by children. Any submissions by children welcomed. Pays free copies of published work. Submit artwork/photos to Kim Solga, editor. SASE desired, but not required. Reports in 3-4 weeks.

LIFEPRINTS, Blindskills, P.O. Box 5181, Salem OR 97304. (503)581-4224. Magazine published quarterly. Estab. 1983. Includes blind and visually impaired successes.
Magazines: Uses nonfiction anecdotal material. We do not pay; nonprofit. Editor: Carol M. McCarl. Will accept manuscripts in typed, brailled, or in cassette formats. Query or submit complete ms. SASE. A small honorarium is awarded to students whose articles are published in *Lifeprints*. Articles published in *Lifeprints* are written for visually impaired or blind persons.

*THE MCGUFFEY WRITER, 5128 Westgate Dr., Oxford OH 45056. (513)523-5565. Magazine published 3 times per year. "We publish poems and stories by children that compel the editors to read them to the end because of extraordinary originality of content or facility with language given the age of the child author." Purpose in publishing works by children: to reward by recognition those who strive to create in words and/or drawings and to motivate other children to try to meet a standard set in a sense by their peers. Requirements: be in grades K-12, no geographic restriction, originality must be attested to by adult parent or teacher. Writer's guidelines available on request.
Magazines: Uses 3-4 fiction short stories (800-2,000 words), 5-8 poems (varying length). Pays 2 free copies. Submit mss to Submissions Editor. Teacher submission preferred. "Send copy—we do not return submissions." Will accept typewritten form and legible handwriting. Responds in 3 months.
Artwork: Publishes black & white illustrations to fit 7½×8 page—any theme. Pays 2 contributor copies. Submit art and photographs to Linda Sheppard, art editor. Responds in 3 months.

MERLYN'S PEN: The National Magazine of Student Writing, Box 1058, East Greenwich RI 02818. (401)885-5175. Magazine. Published every 2 months during the school year, September to May. "We publish 150 manuscripts annually by students in grades 7-10. The entire magazine is dedicated to young adults' writing. Our audience is classrooms, libraries and students from grades 7-10." Requirements to be met before work is published: writers must be in grades 7-10 and must follow submission guidelines for preparing their manuscripts. When a student is accepted, he/she, a parent and a teacher must sign a statement of originality.
Magazines: Uses 6-8 short stories, plays (fiction); 2-3 nonfiction essays; poetry; letters to the editor; editorials; reviews of previously published works; reviews of books, music, movies. No word limit on any material. Pays for ms in three copies of the issue and a paperback copy of *The Elements of Style* (a writer's handbook). Also, a discount is offered for additional copies of the issue. Submit complete ms. Will only accept typewrit-

ten mss. "All rejected manuscripts have an editor's constructive critical comment in the margin." Reports in 11 weeks.
Artwork: Publishes artwork by young adults, grades 7-10. Looks for black and white line drawings, cartoons, color art for cover. Pays in 3 copies of the issue to the artist, and a discount is offered for additional copies. Send unmatted original artwork. Reports in 11 weeks.
Tips: "All manuscripts and artwork must be submitted with a cover sheet listing: name, age and grade, home address, home phone number, school name, school phone number, school address, teacher's name and principal's name. SASE must be large enough and carry enough postage for return."

MY FRIEND, 50 St. Paul's Ave., Jamaica Plain, Boston MA 02130. (617)522-8911. Magazine published 10 times/year. Audience consists of children ages 6-12, primarily Roman Catholics. Purpose in publishing works by children: to stimulate reader participation and to encourage young Catholic writers. Requirements to be met before work is published: we accept work from children ages 6-16. Requirements regarding originality included in guidelines. Writer's guidelines available for SASE.
Tips: "Our 'Junior Reporter' feature gives young writers the chance to do active research on a variety of topics. Children may ask for an 'assignment' or suggest topics they'd be willing to research and write on. This would be mainly where our interest in children's writing would lie."

THE MYTHIC CIRCLE, Mythopoeic Society, Box 6707, Altadena CA 91001. Editor: Tina Cooper and Christine Lowentrout. Art Director: Lynn Maudlin. Magazine published quarterly. Circ. 150. Fantasy writer's workshop in print featuring reader comments in each issue. 5% of publication aimed at juvenile market.
Nonfiction: How-to, interview/profile. "We are just starting with nonfiction—dedicated to how to write and publish." Buys maximum of 4 mss/year. Average word length: 250-2,000. Byline given.
How to Contact/Writers: Fiction: send complete ms. Nonfiction: query. SASE (IRC) for answer to query and return of ms. Reports on queries/mss in 1 month. Will consider photocopied, computer printout (dark dot matrix) and electronic submissions via disk (query for details).
Artwork: Buys 10 illustrations/issue; buys 30 illustrations/year. Preferred theme or style: fantasy, soft science fiction. Reports on art samples in 3-6 weeks. Original artwork returned at job's completion (only if postage paid).
Terms: Pays on publication. Buys one-time rights. Pays in contributor copies. Sample copy $5. Writer's guidelines free with SAE and 1 first-class stamp.
Tips: "We are a good outlet for a story that hasn't sold but 'should' have—good feedback and tips on improvement. *We do have a 'Mythopoeic Youth' section with stories and art by those under 18 years.*"

*NATIONAL GEOGRAPHIC WORLD, 17th and M St. NW, Washington DC 20036. (202)857-7000. Magazine published monthly. Picture magazine for ages 8 and older.
Artwork: Publishes art, letters, poems, games, riddles, jokes and craft ideas by children in mailbag section only. Send by mail to: Mailbag. "Sorry, but *World* cannot acknowledge or return your contributions."

*PANDORA (Pandora All Youth Issue), 2844 Grayson, Ferndale MI 48220. Magazine published yearly. Purpose in publishing works by children: "to provide a showcase for young writers who have something special to express. Also, to provide young readers with material to enjoy that is accessible as it is by their peers. Our annual publication looks for work by writers not yet graduated from high school. We assume all work is original. If we had doubts we would contact the author first and query. Then, if necessary, we might contact parents." Writer's guidelines available on request.

Magazines: Uses 8-12 science fiction and fantasy stories, 2 essays and reviews related to above, and 6-8 science fiction and fantasy poems per issue. Pays "on publication, 1-2¢ per word fiction; poetry varies, as does non-fiction." Submit mss to Meg MacDonald, editor. Submit complete ms. Teacher may submit (individual or batches). Will accept typewritten form and legible handwriting. SASE. Responds in 3-6 months.

Artwork: Publishes artwork and photography by children. Looks for science fiction, fantasy; b&w medium — 4 × 6 or reducible to that size. Pays on publication; rates vary. Submit art and photographs to Polly Vedder, art editor. SASE. Responds in 3-6 months.

THE PIKESTAFF FORUM, P.O. Box 127, Normal IL 61761. (309)452-4831. Magazine published annually; "we hope to eventually get out two issues per year." "The basic audience of *The Pikestaff Forum* is adult; in each issue we have a Young Writers feature publishing writing and artwork by young people aged 7 through 17. Purpose in publishing works by children: Our purpose is twofold: (1) to put excellent writing by young people before the general public, and (2) to encourage young people in developing their self-confidence and powers of literary expression. Requirements to be met before work is published: Work must be by young people aged 7 through 17; it must be original, previously unpublished, and submitted by the authors themselves (we do *not* wish parents or teachers to submit the work); the person's age at the time the piece was written must be stated." Writer's guidelines available on request.

Magazines: 10% of magazine written by children. Uses 1-3 fiction stories, 7-10 poems/issue. Poetry always welcome. Author or artist receives three free copies of the issue in which the work appears, and has the option of purchasing additional copies at a 50% discount. Submit mss to Robert D. Sutherland, editor/publisher. Submit complete ms. Will accept typewritten, legibly handwritten, computer printout mss.

Artwork: Publishes artwork by children. No restrictions on subject matter; "should be free-standing and interesting (thought-provoking). *Black and white only* (dark image); we cannot handle color work with our format." Artist receives three free copies of the issue in which the work appears, and has the option of purchasing additional copies at a 50% discount off cover price. In black and white, clearly marked with artist's name, address and age at the time the work was created. Submit artwork to Robert D. Sutherland, editor/publisher. Reports in 3 months. "We do not wish teachers to submit for their students, and we do not wish to see batches of works which are simply the product of school assignments."

PURPLE COW, The Newspaper for Teens and Young Adults, 1431 Woodmont Ln., Atlanta GA 30318. (404)350-9355. Newspaper published monthly. "All of our articles are written *by* teens. Our target market is teenagers and youth adults (ages 12-19). Our philosophy is to give teens quality reading material, positive messages, and a healthy means of communications within the community. Our articles are predominately written by an area teen board, which are a representative group of writers from all local high schools. Freelance work *is* accepted on college and career issues." Writer's guidelines available on request.

Magazines: Uses 15 nonfiction stories/issue (200-700 word length). Payments range from $10-25. Pays on publication; writer retains all rights. Submit mss to editor. Submit complete ms. Will accept typewritten mss.

Artwork: Publishes artwork by children. Looks for music, comics, issue-related. Submit artwork to Melissa Goldman, editor.

Tips: "Please note that there are additional Purple Cows in Birmingham, Dallas and Charlotte. You may feel free to approach these publications separately. These publications have acceptance policies similar to those of the Atlanta Purple Cow."

REFLECTIONS, Box 368, Duncan Falls OH 43734. (614)674-5209. Magazine. Published January and June. Purpose in publishing works by children: to encourage writing. Requirements to be met before work is published: statement of originality signed by teacher or parent. Writer's guidelines available on request (with SASE).
Magazines: 100% of magazine written by children. Uses 1-3 fiction stories (1,000-2,000 words); 1-3 nonfiction articles (1,000-2,000 words); poetry. Pays in contributor's copy. Editor: Dean Harper. Submit complete ms. Will accept typewritten, legibly handwritten, computer printout mss. "Please include your name, age, school, address, and your teacher's name. Be certain to include a self-addressed stamped envelope with your manuscripts. Make the statement that this is your own original work, then date it and sign your name. Your teacher or parent should also sign it." Reports in 2 weeks.
Artwork: Publishes artwork by children. Pays in contributor's copy. Editor: Dean Harper. SASE. Reports in 2 weeks.

*SHOFAR MAGAZINE, 43 Northcote Dr., Melville NY 11747. (516)643-4598. Magazine.
Magazines: 10-20% of magazine written by young people. Uses fiction/nonfiction (500-750 words), Kids Page items (50-150 words). Pays 7-10¢/word. Submit mss to Gerald Grayson, managing editor. Submit complete ms. Will accept typewritten, legibly handwritten mss and computer disk (Mac only). SASE. Reports in 4-6 weeks.
Artwork/Photography: Publishes artwork and photography by children. Pays "by the piece, depending on size and quantity." Submit original with SASE. Reports in 4-6 weeks.

SKIPPING STONES, Multicultural Children's Quarterly, Box 3939, Eugene OR 97403. (503)342-4956. Articles Editor: Arun N. Toke. Fiction Editor: Amy Klauke. Quarterly magazine. Estab. 1988. Circulation 3,000-4,000. "*Skipping Stones* is a multicultural, nonprofit, children's magazine to encourage cooperation, creativity and celebration of cultural and environmental richness. It offers itself as a creative forum for communication among children from different lands and backgrounds."
Magazine: Fiction accepted only by young writers (under 19 years of age). Word length for fiction: 2 pages. Byline given.
Poetry: Publishes poetry by young, unpublished writers.
How to Contact/Writers: Send complete manuscript. Reports on queries in 1 month; on ms in 2 months. Accepts simultaneous submissions.
Artwork: Will review all varieties of manuscript/illustration packages. Reports back to artists in 2 months.
Terms: "We are not able to pay cash. We are glad to give a few copies of the magazine in which your contribution is published." Sample copy for $4 and 8½ × 11 SAE with 4 first class stamps.
Tips: "Think, live and write as if you were a child. Let the 'inner child' within you speak out — naturally, uninhibited." Wants "material that gives insight on cultural celebrations, lifestyle, custom and tradition, glimpse of daily life in other countries and cultures. Photos, songs, artwork are most welcome if they illustrate/highlight the points. We are doing 2 special features for the summer of 1992. We are also looking for material from Eastern Europe."

SKYLARK, 2233 171st St., Hammond IN 46323. (219)932-6360. Editor: Pamela Hunter. Children's Editor: Cheryl Dipple. Annual magazine. Circ. 500-750. 15% of material aimed at juvenile audience. Presently accepting material *by* children. "*Skylark* wishes to provide a vehicle for creative writing of all kinds, by all ages, especially in our area which has not ordinarily provided such an outlet. Children need a place to have their work published alongside that of adults." Parent or teacher verification required. Writer's guidelines available upon request.

Magazines: Uses animal, friends, families, life experiences, mystery. Does not want to see material about Satan worship, graphic sex. Uses 3 fiction stories (1,200 words max.), 4 nonfiction stories (1,200 words max.), 25 poems, (20 words max.). Pay in contributor's copies. Submit ms to Children's Editor. Submit complete ms. Will accept typewritten ms. SASE. Reports in 6 months. Byline given.
Artwork: Publishes artwork/photos by children. Looks for "photos of animals, landscapes and sports, and artwork to go along with text." Pay in contributor's copies. Use pen, black on white paper, 8½×11, unlined. Submit artwork/photos to Children's Editor. SASE. Reports in 6 months.

THE SOW'S EAR POETRY JOURNAL, 245 McDowell St., Bristol TN 37620. (615)764-·1625. Magazine published quarterly. "Our audience includes serious poets throughout the USA. We publish school-aged poets in each issue to encourage young writers and to show our older audience that able young poets are writing. We request young poets to furnish age, grade, school and list of any previous publication." Writer's guidelines available on request.
Magazines: 3% of magazine written by children. Uses 1-5 poems (1 page). Pays 1 copy. Submit complete ms. Will accept typewritten, legibly handwritten mss. SASE. Reports in 3 months.
Artwork: Publishes artwork and photographs by children. "Prefer line drawings. Any subject or size that may be easily reduced or enlarged. Must be black & white." Pays 1 copy. Submit artwork to Mary Calhoun, Graphics Editor. SASE. Reports in 4 months.

*SPRING TIDES, 824 Stillwood Dr., Savannah GA 31419. (912)925-8800. Annual magazine. Audience consists of children 5-12 years old. Purpose in publishing works by children: to encourage writing. Writers guidelines available on request.
Magazines: Uses 12-24 pieces of material per issue. Submit complete ms. Will accept typewritten mss. SASE.
Artwork: Publishes artwork by children. "We have so far used only local children's artwork because of the complications of keeping and returning pieces."

STONE SOUP, The Magazine by Children, Children's Art Foundation, Box 83, Santa Cruz CA 95063. (408)426-5557. Articles/Fiction Editor, Art Director: Ms. Gerry Mandel. Magazine published 5 times/year. Circ. 13,000. "We publish fiction, poetry and artwork by children through age 13. Our preference is for work based on personal experiences and close observation of the world." Writer's guidelines available upon request.
Magazines: 100% of magazine written by children. Uses animal, contemporary, fantasy, history, problem solving, science fiction, sports, spy/mystery/adventure fiction stories. Uses 5-10 fiction stories (100-2,500 words), 5-10 nonfiction stories (100-2,500 words), 2-4 poems. Does not want to see classroom assignments and formula writing. Buys 50 mss/year. Byline given. Pays on acceptance. Buys all rights. Pays $10 each for stories and poems, $15 for book reviews. Contributors also receive 2 copies. Sample copy $2. Free writer's guidelines. "We don't publish straight nonfiction, but we do publish stories based on real events and experiences." Send complete ms. Will accept typewritten, legibly handwritten mss. SASE. Reports in 1 month.
Artwork: Publishes any type, size or color artwork/photos by children. Pays $8 for b&w illustrations. Contributors receive 2 copies. Sample copy $2. Free illustrator's guidelines. Send originals if possible. SASE. Reports in 1 month. Original artwork returned at job's completion. All artwork must be by children through age 13.

STRAIGHT MAGAZINE, Standard Publishing, 8121 Hamilton Ave., Cincinnati OH 45231. (513)931-4050. Magazine published weekly. Estab. 1951. Magazine includes fiction pieces and articles for Christian teens 13-19 years old to inform, encourage and

uplift them. Purpose in publishing works by children: to provide them with an opportunity to express themselves. Requirements to be met before work is published: must submit their birth date and Social Security number (if they have one). Writer's guidelines available on request, "included in regular guidelines."
Magazines: 15% of magazine written by children. Uses fiction (500-1,000 words); personal experience pieces (500-700 words); poetry (approx. 1 poem per issue). Pays flat fee for poetry; per word for stories/articles. Submit mss to Carla J. Crane, editor. Submit complete ms. Will accept typewritten and computer printout mss. Reports in 4-6 weeks.
Artwork: Publishes artwork by children. Looks for "anything that will fit our format." Pays flat rate. Submit artwork to Carla Crane, editor. Reports in 4-6 weeks.

SUNSHINE MAGAZINE, Henrichs Publications, Inc., P.O. Box 40, Sunshine Park, Litchfield IL 62056. (217)324-3425. Magazine published monthly. Goal is to "to promote goodwill, a positive attitude and a cheerful, wholesome approach to everyday living. Audience is all the family." Purpose in publishing works by children: "to encourage writing, reading and communication among children."
Magazines: "Two pages/issue written by children. Submit complete ms." Uses fiction, nonfiction and poetry (up to 200 words). Pays in copies. Submit mss to Peggy Kuethe, associate editor. Submit complete ms. Will accept typewritten, legibly handwritten, computer printout mss. SASE. Reports in 3 months.

*TEXAS HISTORIAN, Texas State Historical Association, 2/306 Sid Richardson Hall, Univ. Station, Austin TX 78731. (512)471-1525. Articles Editor: David De Boe. Magazine published 5 times a year in January, March, May, September and November. Estab. 1940. Circ. 2,200. "The *Texas Historian* is the official publication of the Junior Historians of Texas. Articles accepted for publication must be written by members of the Junior Historians of Texas." 75% of material directed to children.
Nonfiction: Young adult: history. Average word length: 2,500.

THUMBPRINTS, 928 Gibbs St., Caro MI 48723. (517)673-6653. Newsletter published monthly. "Our newsletter is designed to be of interest to writers and allow writers a place to obtain a byline." Purpose in publishing works by children: to encourage them to seek publication of their work. Statement of originality required. Writer's guidelines available on request, "same guidelines as for adults."
Newsletter: Percentage of newsletter written by children "varies from month to month." Pays in copies. Submit ms to Janet Ihle, editor. Submit complete ms or have teacher submit. Will accept typewritten and computer printout mss. Reports in 6-8 weeks.
Artwork: Publishes artwork by children. Looks for art that expresses our monthly theme. Pays in copies. Send pencil or ink line drawings no larger than 3 × 4. Submit artwork to Janet Ihle, editor. SASE. Reports in 3 months.
Tips: "We look forward to well written articles and poems by children. It's encouraging to all writers when children write and are published."

TURTLE, Ben Franklin Literary & Medical Society, Children's Better Health Institute, 1100 Waterway Blvd., Box 567, Indianapolis IN 46206. (317)636-8881. Magazine. "*Turtle* is generally a health-related magazine geared toward children from ages 2-5. Purpose in publishing works by children: we enjoy giving children the opportunity to exercise their creativity." Requirements to be met before work is published: for ages 2-5, publishes artwork or pictures that you have drawn or colored all by yourself. Writer's guidelines available on request.
Artwork: Publishes artwork by children. There is no payment for children's artwork. All artwork must have the child's name, age and complete address on it. Submit artwork

Here's a colorful, exciting new way to stimulate young imaginations.

Subscribe to SPARK! today and save 40% off the newsstand price!

Use the order form on the reverse side, or call 800-777-1101 and charge your Visa or MasterCard.

to *Turtle* Magazine Editorial Director: Christine Clark. "No artwork can be returned."

WHOLE NOTES, P.O. Box 1374, Las Cruces NM 88004. (505)382-7446. Magazine published twice yearly. "We look for original, fresh perceptions in writing. General audience. We try to recognize excellence in creative writing by children as a way to encourage and promote imaginative thinking." Writer's guidelines available on request.
Magazines: Every fourth issue is 100% by children. Uses 1-3 fiction short, short stories—any kind (length open), 30 poems/issue (length open). Pays 2 complimentary copies. Submit mss to Nancy Peters Hastings, editor. Submit complete ms. Will accept typewritten, legibly handwritten mss. SASE. Reports in 3 weeks.
Artwork: Publishes artwork and photographs by children. Looks for black and white line drawings which can easily be reproduced; b&w photos. Pays complimentary copy of issue. Send clear photocopy. Submit artwork to Nancy Peters Hastings, editor. SASE. Reports in 3 weeks.
Tips: Sample issue is $3.

WOMBAT: A JOURNAL OF YOUNG PEOPLE'S WRITING AND ART, 365 Ashton Dr., Athens GA 30606. (404)549-4875. Published 4 times a year. "Illiteracy in a free society is an unnecessary danger which can and must be remedied. *Wombat*, by being available to young people and their parents and teachers, is one small incentive for young people to put forth the effort to learn to read and write (and draw) better, to communicate better, to comprehend better and—hopefully—consequently, to someday possess greater discernment, judgment and wisdom as a result." Purpose in publishing works by children: to serve as an incentive, to encourage them to work hard at their reading, writing and—yes—drawing/art skills, to reward their efforts. Requirements to be met before work is published: ages 6-16; all geographic regions; statement that work is original.
Magazines: 95% of magazine written by children. Have one 2-4 page "Guest Adult Article" in most issues/when available (submitted). Uses poetry, any kind of fiction (3,000 words maximum, shorter preferred) but avoid extreme violence, religion or sex (approaching pornography); uses any kind of nonfiction of interest to 6-16 year olds (3,000-4,000 words); cartoons, puzzles and solutions, jokes and games and solutions. Pays in copies and frameable certificates. Submit mss to Publisher: Jacquelin Howe. Submit complete ms. Teacher can submit; parents, librarians, students can submit. Will accept typewritten, legibly handwritten, computer printout mss. Responds in 1-2 weeks with SASE; up to 1 year with seasonal or holiday works (past season or holiday). Written work is not returned. SASE permits *Wombat* to notify sender of receipt of work.
Artwork: Publishes artwork by children. Looks for: works on paper, not canvas. Photocopies OK if clear and/or reworked for clarity and strong line definition by the artist. Pays in copies and frameable certificates. Submit artwork to Publisher: Jacquelin Howe. "Artwork, only, will be returned if requested and accompanied by appropriate sized envelope, stamped with sufficient postage."
Tips: *"Wombat* is, unfortunately, on 'hold' probably throughout this entire school year; therefore, we are asking people to please query as to when/if we will resume publication, before subscribing or submitting works to *Wombat* right now."

WRITING, 60 Revere Drive, Northbrook IL 60062. (708)205-3000. Magazine published monthly (September-May). Purpose is "to teach students to write and write well; grades 7-12. Should indicate age, address, school and teacher with submission. No formal guidelines; but letter is sent if request received."
Magazines: Small percentage of magazine written by children. Uses 1-10 mss/issue. No pay for student writing. Submit mss to Alan Lenhoff, editor. Submit complete ms; either child or teacher may submit. Prefer typewritten mss. SASE.

YOUNG VOICES MAGAZINE, P.O. Box 2321, Olympia WA 98507. (206)357-4683. Magazine published bimonthly. "Young Voices is by elementary and middle school/junior high students for people interested in their work." Writer's guidelines available on request.

Magazines: Uses 20 fiction stories, 2 reviews, 15 poems per issue. Pays $3-5 on acceptance. Submit mss to Steve Charak, Editor/Publisher. Submit complete ms. Will accept typewritten, legibly handwritten mss. SASE. Reports in 3 months.

Artwork: Publishes artwork by children. "Prefer work that will show up in black and white." Pays $3-5 on acceptance. Submit artwork to Steve Charak. Reports in 3 months.

Contests & Awards

Publication is not the only way to get your work recognized. Contests really can be viable vehicles to gain recognition in the industry. Placing in a contest or winning an award truly validates the time spent on a craft, including writing and illustrating. Even for those who don't place, many competitions offer the chance to obtain valuable feedback from judges and other established writers or artists.

Not all of these contests are geared strictly for professionals. Many are designed for "amateurs" who haven't yet been published. Still others are open only to students. Contests for students in this section are marked with a double dagger (‡).

Be sure to study the guidelines and requirements for each contest. Regard entry deadlines as gospel and note whether manuscripts and artwork should be unpublished or previously published. Also, be aware that awards vary with each contest. Where one contest may award a significant monetary amount, another may award a certificate or medal instead of money.

You will notice that some contests require nominations. For published authors, competitions provide an excellent means for promoting your work. If your book is eligible for a contest or award, have the appropriate people at your publishing company nominate or enter your work for consideration. Then make sure enough copies of your work are sent to the contest judges and any other necessary people affiliated with the competition.

Read through the listings that interest you, then send away for more information to acquire specifics about the types of written or illustrated material reviewed, word length and any qualifications you should know about, such as who retains the rights to prize-winning material.

*JANE ADDAMS CHILDREN'S BOOK AWARD, Jane Addams Peace Association, % Jean Gore, 980 Lincoln Place, Boulder CO 80302. (212)682-8830. Contest/Award Director: Jean Gore. Annual contest/award. Estab. 1953. "The Jane Addams Children's Book Award is presented annually for a book that most effectively promotes the cause of peace, social justice, world community, and the equality of the sexes and all races." Previously published submissions only; year previous to year the award is presented. Deadline for entries: April 1. SASE for contest/award rules and entry forms. No entry fee. Awards a certificate to the author and seals for book jackets to the publisher (at cost). Judging by a committee of children's librarians. Works displayed at an award ceremony.

AIM Magazine Short Story Contest, P.O. Box 20554, Chicago IL 60620. (312)874-6184. Contest Directors: Ruth Apilado, Mark Boone. Annual contest. Estab. 1983. Purpose of the contest: "We solicit stories with social significance. Youngsters can be made aware of social problems through the written word and hopefully they will try solving them." Unpublished submissions only. Deadline for entries: August. SASE for contest rules and entry forms. SASE for return of work. No entry fee. Awards $100. Judging by members of staff. Contest open to everyone. Subscription rate $8/year. Single copy $2.

‡AMERICA & ME ESSAY CONTEST, Farm Bureau Insurance, 7373 W. Saginaw, Box 30400, Lansing MI 48909. (517)323-7000. Communications/Advertising Technician: Blythe Redman. Annual contest/award. Estab. 1968. Purpose of the contest/award: to give Michigan 8th graders the opportunity to express their thoughts/feelings on America and their roles in America. Unpublished submissions only. Deadline for entries: mid-November. SASE for contest/award rules and entry forms. "We have a school mailing list. Any school located in Michigan is eligible to participate." Entries not returned. No entry fee. Awards savings bonds and plaques for state top ten ($500-1,000), certificates and plaques for top 3 winners from each school. Judging by home office employee volunteers. Requirements for entrants: "participants must work through their schools or our agents' sponsoring schools. No individual submissions will be accepted. Top ten essays and excerpts from other essays are published in booklet form following the contest. State capital/schools receive copies."

‡AMHA MORGAN ART CONTEST, American Morgan Horse Assoc., Box 960, Shelburne VT 05482. (802)985-4944. Communications Director: Tracey Holloway. Annual contest/award. The art contest consists of three categories: Morgan art (pencil sketches, oils, water colors, paintbrush), Morgan cartoons, Morgan speciality pieces (sculptures, carvings). Unpublished submissions only. Deadline for entries: December. Contest/award rules and entry forms sent upon request. Entries not returned. Entry fee is $2. Awards $50 first prize and AMHA ribbons to top 5 places in 3 divisions. "All work submitted becomes property of The American Morgan Horse Association. Selected works may be used for promotional purposes by the AMHA." Requirements for entrants: "We consider all work submitted." Works displayed at the annual convention. **Tips:** This year the Morgan Horse Association, Inc. will be sponsoring two judgings. The first will be divided into three age groups: 13 years and under, 14-21 years and adult. The second judging will be divided into three categories and open to all ages. The top 5 places will receive official Art Contest Ribbons. Each art piece must be matted, have its own application form and its own entry fee.

*‡BAKER'S PLAYS HIGH SCHOOL PLAYWRITING CONTEST, Baker's Plays, 100 Chauncy St., Boston MA 02111. (617)482-1280. Contest Director: Raymond Pape. Annual contest. Estab. 1990. "To acknowledge playwrights at the high school level and to insure the future of American Theatre by encouraging and supporting those who are its cornerstone: young playwrights." Unpublished submissions only. Deadline for entries: January 31. SASE for contest rules and entry forms. No entry fee. Awards $500 to the first place playwright and Baker's Plays will publish the play under the Best Plays from the High School Series. $250 to the second place playwright with an honorable mention and $100 to the third place playwright with an honorable mention in the series. Judged anonymously. Open to any high school student. The first place playwright will have his/her play published in an acting edition the September following the contest. The work will be described in the Baker's Plays Catalogue, which is distributed to 65,000 prospective producing organizations. "Plays must be accompanied by the signature of a sponsoring high school drama or English teacher, and it is recommended that the play receive a production or a public reading prior to the submission. Please include a SASE."

MARGARET BARTLE ANNUAL PLAYWRITING AWARD, Community Children's Theatre of Kansas City, 8021 E. 129th Terrace, Grandview MO 64030. (816)761-5775. Chairperson: Mrs. E. Morley Sellens. Annual contest/award. Unpublished submissions only.

✝ *The double dagger before a listing indicates the contest is for students.*

Deadline for entries: end of January. SASE for contest/award rules and entry forms. SASE for return of entries. No entry fee. Awards $500. Judging by a committee of five. "Winning play is produced by one of the troups for two years."

THE IRMA SIMONTON BLACK BOOK AWARD, Bank Street College of Education, 610 West 112th Street, New York NY 10025. (212)222-6700. Contact: Linda Greengrass. Annual award. Estab. 1972. Purpose of the award: "The award is given each spring for a book for young children, published in the previous year, for excellence of both text and illustrations." Entries must have been published during the previous calendar year. Deadline for entries: January after book is published. "Publishers submit books to us by sending them here to me at the Bank Street library. Authors may ask their publishers to submit their books. Out of these, three to five books are chosen by a committee of older children and adults. These books are then presented to children in selected second, third and fourth grade classes here and at a few other cooperating schools on the east coast. These children are the final judges who pick the actual award. The award is a scroll (one each for the author and illustrator, if they're different) with the recipient's name and a gold seal designed by Maurice Sendak."

BOOK OF THE YEAR FOR CHILDREN, Canadian Library Association, Ste. 602, 200 Elgin St., Ottawa ON K2P 1L5 Canada. (613)232-9625. Chairperson, Canadian Association of Children's Librarians. Annual contest/award. Estab. 1947. "The main purpose of the award is to encourage writing and publishing in Canada of good books for children up to and including age 14. If, in any year, no book is deemed to be of award calibre, the award shall not be made that year. To merit consideration, the book must have been published in Canada and its author must be a Canadian citizen or a permanent resident of Canada." Previously published submissions only; must be published between January 1 and December 1. Deadline for entries: January 1. SASE for contest/award rules and entry forms. Entries not returned. No entry fee. Awards a medal. Judging by committee of members of the Canadian Association of Children's Librarians. Requirements for entrants: Contest open only to Canadian authors or residents of Canada. "Winning books are on display at CLA headquarters."

BOOK PUBLISHERS OF TEXAS, Children's/Young People's Award, The Texas Institute of Letters, P.O. Box 9032, Wichita Falls TX 76308-9032. (817)692-6611 ext. 4123. Contact: James Hoggard. Send to above address for list of judges to whom entries should be submitted. Annual award. Purpose of the award: "To recognize notable achievement by a Texas writer of books for children or young people or by a writer whose work deals with a Texas subect. The award goes to the author of the winning book, a work published during the calendar year before the award is given. Judges list available each October. Deadline is first postally operative day of January." Previously published submissions only. SASE for award rules and entry forms. No entry fee. Awards $250. Judging by a panel of three judges selected by the TIL Council. Requirements for entrants: The writer must have lived in Texas for two consecutive years at some time, or the work must have a Texas theme.

THE BOSTON GLOBE-HORN BOOK AWARDS, The Boston Globe & The Horn Book, Inc., The Horn Book, 14 Beacon St., Boston MA 02108. (617)227-1555. Contest/Award Directors: Stephanie Loer and Anita Silvey. Writing Contact: Stephanie Loer, children's book editor for *The Boston Globe*, 298 North St., Medfield MA 02052. Annual contest/award. Estab. 1967. "Awards are for picture books, nonfiction and fiction. Up to three honor books may be chosen for each category." Books must be published between July 1, 1991 through June 30, 1992. Deadline for entries: May 1. "Publishers usually nominate books." Award winners receive $500 and silver engraved bowl, honor book winners receive a silver plate." Judging by three judges involved in children's book field who are chosen by Anita Silvey, editor-in-chief for *The Horn Book* and Stephanie Loer, children's book editor for *The Boston Globe*. "*The Horn Book* publishes speeches given at awards ceremonies. The book must be available/distributed in the U.S. The awards are given at the fall conference of the New England Round Table of Children's Librarians."

BUCKEYE CHILDREN'S BOOK AWARD, State Library of Ohio, 65 S. Front St., Columbus OH 43266-0334. (614)644-7061. Dr. Evelyn Freeman, Chairperson. Correspondence should be sent to Floyd C. Dickman at the above address. Award every two years. Estab. 1981. Purpose of the award: "The Buckeye Children's Book Award Program was designed to encourage children to read literature critically, to promote teacher and librarian involvement in children's literature programs, and to commend authors of such literature, as well as to promote the use of libraries. Awards are presented in the following three categories: Grades K-2, Grades 3-5 and Grades 6-8." Previously published submissions only. The book must have been originally copyrighted in the United States within the last three years preceding the nomination year. Deadline for entries: February 1. "The nominees are submitted by this date during the even year and the votes are submitted by this date during the odd year. This award is nominated and voted upon by children in Ohio. It is based upon criteria established in our bylaws. The winning authors are awarded a special plaque honoring them at a special banquet given by one of the sponsoring organizations. The BCBA Board oversees the tallying of the votes and announces the winners. The book must have been written by an author, a citizen of the United States and originally copyrighted in the U.S. within the last three years preceding the nomination year. The award-winning books are displayed in a historical display housed at the Columbus Metropolitan Library in Columbus, OH."

*1992 BYLINE CHILDREN'S ARTICLE CONTEST, *Byline* Magazine, P.O. Box 130596, Edmond OK 73013. (405)348-5591. Publisher: Marcia Preston. Estab. 1981. Nonfiction on any subject appropriate for a children's magazine. Unpublished submissions only. Deadline for entries: April 10. SASE for contest/award rules and entry forms. Entry fee is $4. 1st prize: $40; 2nd prize: $25; 3rd prize $15. Judging by qualified editors and writers. Winner's list published in magazine dated 3 months past deadline. Only student entries (winners) are published.

*1992 BYLINE CHILDREN'S FICTION CONTEST, *Byline* Magazine, P.O. Box 130596, Edmond OK 73013. (405)348-5591. Publisher: Marcia Preston. Estab. 1981. For a short story or picture book for kids ages 2-12. *(No need to send art for books.) Unpublished submissions only. Deadline for entries: June 1. SASE for contest/award rules and entry forms. Entry fee $4. 1st prize: $50; 2nd prize: $30; 3rd prize: $15. Judging by qualified writers and editors. Winner's list published in magazine dated 3 months past deadline. Only student entries (winners) are published.

*‡BYLINE MAGAZINE STUDENT PAGE, P.O. Box 130596, Edmond OK 73013. (405)348-5591. Contest/Award Director: Marcia Preston, publisher. Estab. 1981. "We offer student writing contests on a monthly basis, September through June, with cash prizes and publication of top entries." Previously unpublished submissions only. Deadline for entries varies. Entry fee varies. Awards cash and publication. Judging by qualified editors and writers. "We publish top entries in student contests. Winners' list published in mag dated 3 months past deadline. Only student entries (winners) are published."

CALDECOTT AWARD, Association for Library Service to Children, division of the American Library Association, 50 E. Huron, Chicago IL 60611. (312)280-2163. Executive Director ALSC: Susan Roman. Annual contest/award. Estab. 1938. Purpose of the contest/award: to honor the artist of the most distinguished picture book for children published in the U.S. Must be published year preceding award. Deadline for entries: December. SASE for contest/award rules and entry forms. Entries not returned. No entry fee. "Medal given at ALA Annual Conference during the Newbery/Caldecott Banquet."

CANADA COUNCIL GOVERNOR GENERAL'S LITERARY AWARDS, 99 Metcalfe St., P.O. Box 1047, Ottawa, Ontario K1P 5V8 Canada. (613)598-4376. Officer, Writing and Publishing Section: Josiane Polidori. Annual contest/award. Estab. 1937. Purpose of contest/award: to encourage Canadian authors and illustrators of books for young people as well as to recognize the importance of their contribution to literary activity. Award categories include children's text and children's illustration. Must be published between October 1 and September 30. Eligible books are submitted by publishers (5 copies must be sent to Canada Council). All books must be received by September 30. Submission forms available on request. Entries not returned. No entry fee. Awards $10,000 (Canadian). Judging by practicing writers, illustrators plus librarian or critic. Contest open to Canadian writers and illustrators only.

*‡CANADIAN AUTHOR & BOOKMAN CREATIVE WRITING CONTEST, CA&B/Canadian Authors Association, Suite 500, 275 Slater St., Ottawa, Ontario K1P 5H9 Canada. (613)238-2296. FAX: (613)235-8237. Contest/Award Director: Editor. Publisher: Diane Kerner. Annual contest/award. Estab. 1983. Categories: fiction, nonfiction, poetry. Unpublished submissions only (except in school paper). Deadlines posted on entry forms. Entry form carried in fall and winter issues of *Canadian Author & Bookman*. Form must come from magazine. "Teacher nominates and may only nominate ONE student." Entries not returned. No entry fee. Awards $100 for each fiction, poetry and nonfiction — teachers get matching award. Judging by CA&B staff-selected judges. Contest open to high school, private school, college and university students. Works published in summer issue of magazine.

CHILDREN'S BOOK AWARD, Sponsored by Federation of Children's Book Groups. 30 Senneleys Park Rd., Northfield Birmingham B31 1AL England. (021)427-4860. Coordinator: Jenny Blanch. Annual contest/award. Estab. 1980. Purpose of the contest/award: "The C.B.A. is an annual prize for the best children's book of the year judged by the children themselves." Previously unpublished submissions only. Deadline for entries: December 31. Entries not returned. Awards "a magnificent silver and oak trophy worth over $6,000 and a portfolio of children's work." Judging by children. Requirements for entrants: Work must be fiction and published during the current year (poetry is ineligible). Work will be published in our current "Pick of the Year" publication.

*THE CHILDREN'S BOOK AWARD, Child Study Children's Book Committee, Bank Street College, 610 W. 112th St., New York NY 10025. (212)222-6700 ext. 503. Award Director: Anita W. Dore. Annual award. Estab. 1942. Purpose of the award: to honor books for children and young people which deal realistically and positively with problems in their world. Previously published submissions only. Deadline for entries: Dec. 31. SASE for award rules and entry forms. No entry fee. Awards a $500 plus citation. Judging by committee. Material chosen from books submitted by publishers and review for possible listing in our publications. Works published in our annual booklet, *Children's Books of the Year*.

CHILDREN'S CHOICE AWARD, Harris County Public Library, Suite 200, 49 San Jacinto, Houston TX 77002. (713)221-5350. Director: Elizabeth J. Ozbun, Children's Specialist. Annual contest/award. Estab. 1978. Purpose of the contest/award: "The objective of the program is for children to select their favorite author, to read and to use the public library. Children are free to select any published author." Deadline for entries: "Election is held in March. Children are given a blank ballot and are invited to fill in the name of their favorite author. The winning author receives a framed certificate. The author with the most votes wins." No entries from authors are accepted.

CHILDREN'S READING ROUND TABLE AWARD, Children's Reading Roundtable of Chicago, 3930 North Pine Grove, #1507, Chicago IL 60613. (312)477-2271. Annual award. Estab. 1953. "Annual award to individual who has made outstanding contributions to children's books. Individual is nominated by membership, and selected by a committee from the membership, and finalized by a special committee of members, as well as nonmembers of CRRT." Awards a recognition certificate and stipend of $250. Award recipients have been authors, editors, educators and illustrators. "Note that our award recognizes *contributions* to children's literature. This includes people who are neither writers nor illustrators."

THE CHRISTOPHER AWARD, The Christophers, 12 E. 48 St., New York NY 10017. (212)759-4050. Christopher Awards Coordinator: Peggy Flanagan. Annual contest/ award. Estab. 1969 (for young people; books for adults honored since 1949). Previously published submissions only; must be published between January 1 and December 31. Deadline for entries: "books should be submitted all year." Entries not returned. No entry fee. Awards a bronze medallion. Books are judged by both reading specialists and young people. Requirements for entrants: "only published works are eligible and must be submitted during the calendar year in which they are first published."
Tips: "The award is given to works, published in the calendar year for which the award is given, that 'have achieved artistic excellence, affirming the highest values of the human spirit.' They must also enjoy a reasonable degree of popular acceptance."

*THE COMMONWEALTH CLUB'S BOOK AWARDS CONTEST, The Commonwealth Club of California, 595 Market St., San Francisco CA 94105. (415)597-6700. Executive Director: James D. Rosenthal. Annual contest. Estab. 1932. Purpose of the contest is the encouragement and production of literature in California. Previously published submission; must be published from January 1 to December 31. Deadline for entries: January 31. SASE for contest rules and entry forms. No entry fee. Awards gold and silver medals. Judging by the Book Awards juries. The contest is only open to California writers/illustrators. "The award winners will be honored at the Annual Book Awards Luncheon."

‡CRICKET LEAGUE, *Cricket,* the Magazine for Children, 315 5th Street, Peru IL 61354. (815)224-6643. Address entries to: Cricket League. Monthly. Estab. 1973. "The purpose of Cricket League contests is to encourage creativity and give children an opportunity to express themselves in writing, drawing, painting, or photography. There are two contests each month. Possible categories include story, poetry, art, or photography. Each contest relates to a *specific theme* described on each *Cricket* issue's Cricket League page. Entries which do not relate to the current month's theme cannot be considered." Unpublished submissions only. Deadline for entries: the 25th of each month. Cricket League rules, contest themes and submission deadline information can be found in the current issue of *Cricket.* "We prefer that children who enter the contests subscribe to the magazine, or that they read *Cricket* in their school or library." No entry fee. Awards children's books or art/writing supplies. Judging by *Cricket* Editors. Obtains right to print prize-winning entries in magazine. Requirements for entrants: Any child age 14 or younger can enter. Restrictions of mediums for illustrators: Usually artwork must be black and white only. Refer to contest rules in current *Cricket* issue. Winning entries are published on the Cricket League pages in the *Cricket* magazine 3 months subsequent to the issue in which the contest was announced.

DELACORTE PRESS PRIZE FOR A FIRST YOUNG ADULT NOVEL, Delacorte Press, Books for Young Readers Department, 666 Fifth Ave., Dept BFYR, New York NY 10103. (212)765-6500. Contest/Award Director: Lisa Oldenburg. Annual award. Estab. 1982. Purpose of the contest/award: To encourage the writing of contemporary young adult fiction. Previously unpublished submissions only. "Entries must be submitted between Labor Day and New Year's Day of the following year. The real deadline is a December 31 postmark. Early entries are appreciated." SASE for contest/award rules. No entry fee. Awards a $1,500 cash prize and a $6,000 advance against royalties on a hardcover and paperback book contract. Judged by the editors of the Books for Young Readers Dept. of Delacorte Press. Rights acquired "only if the entry wins or is awarded an Honorable Mention." Requirements for entrants: The writer must be American or Canadian and must *not* have previously published a YA novel. He may have published anything else.
Tips: "Books (manuscripts) should have a contemporary setting and be suitable for ages 12-18, and be between 100 and 224 pages long. *Summaries are urgently requested.*"

DREXEL CITATION, Drexel University, College of Information Studies, Philadelphia PA 19104. (215)895-2474. Director: Shelley G. McNamara. Annual award. Purpose of the award: "The Drexel citation is an award that was established in 1963 and has been given at irregular intervals since that time to honor Philadelphia authors, illustrators, publishers or others who have made outstanding contributions to literature for children in Philadelphia. The award is co-sponsored by The Free Library of Philadelphia. The recipient is selected by a committee representing both the College of Information Studies and The Free Library of Philadelphia. There is only one recipient at any given time and that recipient is recognized at an annual conference on children's literature presented each year in the spring on the Drexel campus. The recipient receives an individually designed and hand-lettered citation at a special award luncheon during the conference."

*ETHICAL CULTURE SCHOOL BOOK AWARD, Ethical Culture School, 33 Central Park West, New York, NY 10023. (212)874-5200. Resource Specialist: Nancy Bautz. Annual contest/award. Estab. 1975. Purpose of the contest/award: "The children choose the winning book." Previously published submissions only: must have been originally published in the preceding year. Deadline for entries: December 15. "Letters are sent to publishers, who submit the books." Entries not returned. No entry fee. Awards consist of "a scroll with the winner's name and the name of the book." Judging by the children. "The books are displayed in the library during the contest—January through April."

SHUBERT FENDRICH MEMORIAL PLAYWRIGHTING CONTEST, Pioneer Drama Service, Inc., P.O. Box 22555, Denver CO 80222. (303)759-4297. Director: Steven Fendrich. Annual contest/award. Estab. 1990. Purpose of the contest/award: "To encourage the development of quality theatrical material for educational and community theater." Previously unpublished submissions only. Deadline for entries: March 1st. SASE for contest/award rules and entry forms. No entry fee. Awards $1,000 royalty advance and publication. Judging by Editors. All rights acquired when work is published. Restrictions for entrants: Any writers currently published by Pioneer Drama Service are not eligible.

‡FLORIDA STATE WRITING COMPETITION, Florida Freelance Writers Assoc., P.O. Box 9844, Fort Lauderdale FL 33310. (305)485-0795. Juvenile Chairman: Jean Pollack. Annual contest/award. Estab. 1984. Picture Books/under 6 years: 400 words maximum. Short Fiction: all age groups judged together/ages 7-10—400-900 words; ages 12 and up—2,000 words maximum. Nonfiction: All age groups judged together/ages 7-10: 500 words maximum, ages 12 and up—2,000 words maximum. Book Chapter (fiction or nonfiction: ages 7-10—1,000 words maximum; ages 12 and up—3,000 words maximum.

Previously unpublished submissions only. Entry fee is $5 (members), $7 (non-members). Awards $100 first prize, certificates or second through fifth prizes. Judging by teachers, editors and published authors. Judging criteria: Interest and readability within age group, writing style and mechanics, originality, salability. Deadline: March 15. For copy of official entry form, send #10 SASE.

*‡4-H ESSAY CONTEST, American Beekeeping Federation, Inc., P.O. Box 1038, Jesup GA 31545. (912)427-8447. Contest Director: Troy H. Fore. Annual contest. Essay topic: "The Results of Honey Bee Pollination in My Community." Unpublished submissions only. Deadline for entries: before April 30. No entry fee. 1st place: $250; 2nd place: $100; 3rd place: $50. Judging by American Beekeeping Federation's Essay Committee. "All National entries become the property of the American Beekeeping Federation, Inc., and may be published or used as it sees fit. No essay will be returned." "Essayists *should not* forward essays directly to the American Beekeeping Federation office. Each state 4-H office is responsible for selecting the state's winner and should set its deadline so state judging can be completed at the state level in time for the winning state essay to be mailed to the ABF office before April 30, 1992."

DON FREEMAN MEMORIAL GRANT-IN-AID, Society of Children's Book Writers, P.O. Box 66296, Mar Vista Stn., Los Angeles CA 90066. Estab. 1974. Purpose of contest/award: to "enable picture book artists to further their understanding, training and work in the picture gook genre."Applications and prepared materials will be accepted between January 15-February 15. Grant awarded and announced on June 15. SASE for contest/award rules and entry forms. SASE for return of entries. No entry fee. Annually awards one grant of $1,000. "The Grant-In-Aid is available to both full and associate members of the SCBW who, as artists, seriously intend to make picture books their chief contribution to the field of children's literature."

GOLDEN KITE AWARDS, Society of Children's Bookwriters, Box 66296, Mar Vista Station, Los Angeles CA 90066. (818)347-2849. Coordinator: Sue Alexander. Annual contest/award. Estab. 1973. "The works chosen will be those that the judges feel exhibit excellence in writing, and in the case of the picture-illustrated books—in illustration, and genuinely appeal to the interests and concerns of children. For the fiction and nonfiction awards, original works and single-author collections of stories or poems of which at least half are new and never before published in book form are eligible— anthologies and translations are not. For the picture-illustration awards, the art or photographs must be original works (the texts—which may be fiction or nonfiction— may be original, public domain or previously published). Deadline for entries: December 15. SASE for contest/award rules. Self-addressed mailing label for return of entries. No entry fee. Awards statuettes and plaques. The panel of judges will consist of two children's book authors, a children's book artist or photographer (who may or may not be an author), a children's book editor and a librarian." Requirements for entrants: "Must be a member of SCBW." Works will be displayed "at national conference in August."
Tips: Books to be entered, as well as further inquiries, should be submitted to: The Society of Children's Book Writers, % Sue Alexander, 6846 McLaren, Canoga Park, CA 91307.

*GOLDEN PEN AWARD, Spokane Public Library Young Adult Advisory Committee, 906 W. Main, Spokane WA 99201. (509)838-4735. Youth Services Coordinator: Eva-Maria Lusk. Annual contest/award. Estab. 1980. Purpose of the contest/award: for the "author who has given us the most reading pleasure." Entry fee is a free copy of the *published book*. (No manuscripts or galley proofs). Award is a gold pen and pen holder.

HIGHLIGHTS FOR CHILDREN FICTION CONTEST, 803 Church St., Honesdale PA 18431. (717)253-1080. "Mss should be addressed to Fiction Contest. Editor: Kent L. Brown Jr." Annual contest/award. Estab. 1980. Purpose of the contest/award: to stimulate interest in writing for children and reward and recognize excellence. Unpublished submissions only. Deadline for entries: February 28; entries accepted after January 1 only. SASE for contest/award rules and entry forms. SASE for return of entries. No entry fee. Awards 3 prizes of $1,000 each in cash, (or, at the winner's election, attendance at the Highlights Foundation Writers Workshop at Chautauqua). Judging by *Highlights* editors. Winning pieces are purchased for the cash prize of $1,000. Requirements for entrants: contest open to any writer. Winners announced in June.
Tips: "This year's contest is for stories set in a country other than the United States or in an ethnic culture within the United States. Length up to 900 words. Stories should be consistent with *Highlights* editorial requirements. No violence, crime or derogatory humor."

*‡HOOT AWARDS, WRITING CONTEST, PHOTO CONTEST, POETRY CONTEST, COVER CONTEST, *Owl Magazine,* 56 The Esplanade, Toronto, ON M4V 1G2 Canada. (416)868-6001. Annual contest/award. Purpose of the annual contests/awards: "to encourage children to contribute and participate in the magazine. The Hoot Club Awards recognizes excellence in an individual or group effort to help the environment." Unpublished submissions only. Deadlines change yearly. Prizes/awards "change every year. Often we give books as prizes." Winning entries published in the magazine. Judging by art and editorial staff. Entries become the property of the Young Naturalist Foundation (*Owl Magazine*). "The contests and awards are open to children up to 14 years of age."

AMELIA FRANCES HOWARD-GIBBON MEDAL, Canadian Library Association, Ste. 602, 200 Elgin St., Ottawa ON K2P 1L5 Canada. (613)232-9625. Chairperson, Canadian Association of Children's Librarians. Annual contest/award. Estab. 1971. Purpose of the contest/award: "the main purpose of the award is to honor excellence in the illustration of children's book(s) in Canada. To merit consideration the book must have been published in Canada and its illustrator must be a Canadian citizen or a permanent resident of Canada." Previously published submissions only; must be published between January 1 and December 31. Deadline for entries: February 1. SASE for contest/award rules and entry forms. Entries not returned. No entry fee. Awards a medal. Judging by selection committee of members of Canadian Association of Children's Librarians. Requirements for entrants: illustrator must be Canadian or Canadian resident. Winning books on display at CLA Headquarters.

L. RON HUBBARD'S ILLUSTRATORS OF THE FUTURE CONTEST, L. Ron Hubbard Library, P.O. Box 3190, Los Angeles CA 90078. (213)466-3310. Director: Frank Kelly-Freas. Annual contest. Estab. 1988. Purpose of the contest: "To find, reward and publicize new speculative fiction illustrators, so that they may more easily attain to professional illustrating careers." Unpublished submissions only. Deadlines: December 31, March 31, June 30, September 30. SASE for contest rules and entry forms. No entry fee. Awards quarterly: $500 to each of three winners; awards annual grand prize: $4,000. Requirements for entrants: "The Contest is open to those who have not previously published more than three black-and-white story illustrations, or more than one process-color painting, in media distributed to the public. Open to works of science fiction and fantasy." Black and white mediums only. "Winners receive offers of publication of their story illustration in the 'L. Ron Hubbard Presents Writers of The Future' series of annual anthologies from Bridge Publications. Quarterly co-winners enter a second competition for the annual Grand Prize of $4,000 illustrating assigned stories. All quarterly winners are brought to the annual Hubbard Awards event, where the Grand Prize winner is announced."

L. RON HUBBARD'S WRITERS OF THE FUTURE CONTEST, L. Ron Hubbard Library, P.O. Box 1630, Los Angeles CA 90078. (213)466-3310. Director: Algis Budrys. Annual contest. Estab. 1984. Purpose of the contest: "To find, reward and publicize new speculative fiction writers, so that they may more easily attain to professional writing careers." Unpublished submissions only. Quarterly Deadlines: December 31, March 31, June 30, September 30. SASE for contest rules and entry forms. No entry fee. Awards Quarterly: 1st Place $1,000; 2nd Place $750; 3rd Place $500. Annual Grand Prize: $4,000. Requirements for entrants: "Contest is open to any new or amateur writer—must not have professionally published a novel or novella, or more than three short stories. Contest is for short stories or novelettes of science fiction or fantasy. Winners and some finalists receive offers of publication in the 'L. Ron Hubbard Presents Writers of the Future' series of annual anthologies from Bridge Publications, Inc. WOTF Anthology authors are invited to a special writing-career management workshop, with travel, tuition and lodging paid by the contest."

INTERNATIONAL READING ASSOCIATION CHILDREN'S BOOK AWARD, Sponsored by the Institute for Reading Research-International Reading Association, 800 Barksdale Rd., P.O. Box 8139, Newark DE 19714-8139. (302)731-1600. FAX: (302)731-1057. Public Information Associate: Wendy L. Russ. Annual contest/award. To submit a book for consideration, send 10 copies to: Eileen M. Burke, 48 Bayberry Rd., Trenton NJ 08618. Categories: young readers—4-10, older readers—10-16. Must be published between January 1990 and December 1990. Deadline for entries: December 1 of each year. SASE for contest/award rules and entry forms. Awards a $1,000 stipend and medal. Requirements for entrants: Must be a writer's first or second book. Award is presented each year at annual convention.

*IOWA CHILDREN'S CHOICE AWARD, Iowa Educational Media Association, 9 Coventry Lane #3, Muscatine IA 52761. (319)262-8218. Director: Beth Elshoff. Annual contest/award. Estab. 1979. Purpose of the contest/award: to encourage children to read more and better books; to provide an avenue for positive dialogue between teacher, parent and children about books and authors; to give recognition to those who write books for children. The award is unique in that it gives children an opportunity to choose the book to receive the award and to suggest books for the yearly reading list. Deadline for entries: February 15. "Students in grades 3-6 throughout Iowa nominate." Awards a brass-plated school bell. Judging by "students in grades 3-6 throughout Iowa."

IUPUI YOUTH THEATRE PLAYWRITING COMPETITION AND SYMPOSIUM, Indiana University-Purdue University at Indianapolis, 525 North Blackford Street, Indianapolis IN 46202. (317)274-2095. Director: Dorothy Webb. Entries should be submitted to W. Mark McCreary, Literary Manager. Contest/award every two years. Purpose of the contest/award: "To improve both the artistic quality and quantity of dramatic literature for young audiences and to explore literary and artistic standards of dramatic literature intended for young people." Unpublished submissions only. Deadline for entries: September 1, 1992. SASE for contest/award rules and entry forms. No entry fee. "Awards will be presented to the top ten finalists. Four cash awards of $1,000 each will be received by the top four playwrights of whose scripts will be given developmental work culminating in polished readings showcased at the Symposium held on the IUPUI campus. Major publishers of scripts for young audiences, directors, producers, critics and teachers attend this Symposium and provide useful reactions to the plays. If a winner is unable to be involved in preparation of the reading and to attend the showcase of his/her work, the prize will not be awarded. Remaining finalists will receive certificates." Judging by professional directors, dramaturgs, publishers, university professors. **Tips:** "Write for guidelines and entry form."

THE EZRA JACK KEATS NEW WRITER AWARD, Writing Contact: Hannah Nuba, Director, %The New York Public Library Early Childhood Resource and Information Center, 66 Leroy St., New York NY 10014. (212)929-0815. Biennial contest/award. Estab. 1986. Purpose of the contest/award: "Award to writers of books done in the tradition of Ezra Jack Keats that appeal to very young children, capture universal qualities of childhood in a multicultural world and portray strong family relationships." Previously published submissions only: Must be published the year of contest or the year before. Deadline for entries: December. SASE for contest/award rules and entry form. Entries not returned. No entry fee. Awards silver Ezra Jack Keats Medal and $500. "Books that reflect the tradition of Ezra Jack Keats: represent the multicultural nature of the world and extend the child's awareness and understanding of other cultural/ethnic groups; capture the universal qualities of childhood; portray strong family relationships; appeal to children ages 9 and under. The author should have published no more than six books. Picture books are judged on the outstanding features of the the the text. Candidates need not be both author and illustrator."

*‡KENTUCKY STATE POETRY SOCIETY ANNUAL CONTEST, Kentucky State Poetry Society, 5018 Wabash Place, Louisville KY 40214. (502)366-8900. Contest Director: R. Franklin Pate. Annual contest. Estab. 1966. Unpublished submissions only. Deadline for entries: July 10. SASE for contest rules and entry forms. Categories 2-6 are free, all others $1. $5 for grand prix. Awards certificates of merit and cash prizes from $1 to $100. Sponsors pick judges. "One-time printing rights acquired for publication of 1st prizes in *Pegasus*, our annual journal." Contest open to all. "No illustrations, please." "First place winners will be published in *Pegasus* and all other winners will be displayed at our annual awards banquet."

KERLAN AWARD, Kerlan Collection, 109 Walter Library, 117 Pleasant St. SE, University of Minnesota, Minneapolis MN 55455. (612)624-4576. Curator: Karen Nelson Hoyle. Annual award. Estab. 1975. "Given in recognition of singular attainments in the creation of children's literature and in appreciation for generous donation of unique resources to the Kerlan Collection." Previously published submissions only. Deadline for entries: November 1. Anyone can send nominations for the award, directed to the Kerlan Collection. No materials are submitted other than the person's name. No entry fee. Award is a laminated plaque. Judging by the Kerlan Award Committee—three representatives from the University of Minnesota faculty (from the College of Education, the College of Human Ecology, and the College of Liberal Arts); one representative from the Kerlan Collection (ex officio); one representative from the Kerlan Friends; one representative from the Minnesota Library Association. Requirements for entrants: open to all who are nominated. Anyone can submit names. "For serious consideration, entrant must be a published author and/or illustrator of children's books (including young adult fiction) and have donated original materials to the Kerlan Collection."

‡ELIAS LIEBERMAN STUDENT POETRY AWARD, Poetry Society of America, 15 Gramercy Park, New York NY 10003. (212)254-9628. Contest/Award Director: Elise Paschen. Annual contest/award. Purpose of the contest/award: Award is for the best unpublished poem by a high or preparatory school student (grades 9-12) from the U.S. and its territories. Unpublished submissions only. Deadline for entries: December 31. SASE for contest/award rules and entry forms. Entries not returned. No entry fee. Award: $100. Judging by a professional poet. Requirements for entrants: Contest open to all high school and preparatory students from the U.S. and its territories. School attended, as well as name and address, should be noted. Line limit: none. "The award-winning poem will be included in a sheaf of poems that will be part of the program at the award ceremony, and sent to all PSA members."

*MAGAZINE MERIT AWARDS, Society of Children's Book Writers, Suite 718, 7095 Hollywood Blvd., Hollywood CA 90028. Award Director: Dorothy Leon. Annual award. Estab. 1988. "For outstanding original magazine work for young people published during that year and having been written or illustrated by members of SCBW." Previously published submissions only. Entries must be submitted between January 31 and December 15 of the year of publication. SASE for award rules and entry forms. No entry fee. Must be a SCBW member. Awards 3 plaques—1 for fiction, 1 for nonfiction and 1 for illustration. Judging by a magazine editor and two "full" SCBW members. "Every magazine work for young people by an SCBW member—writer, artist or photographer—is eligible during the year of original publication. In the case of co-authored work, both authors must be SCBW members. Members must submit their own work. Required are: 4 copies each of the published work and proof of publication (may be contents page) showing the name of the magazine and the date of issue."

1992 MANNINGHAM POETRY TRUST STUDENT CONTESTS, National Federation of State Poetry Societies, Inc., Box 607, Green Cove Springs FL 32043. (904)284-0505. Chairman: Robert E. Dewitt. Estab. 1980. Purpose of the contest/award: "two separate contests: grades 6-8; grades 9-12. Poems can have been printed and can have won previous awards. Deadline for entries: April 15, 1992. "Submit one poem neatly typed on standard typewriter paper. Submit one original and one copy. On copy only, type: (1) name (2) complete home mailing address (3) school (4) grade. Student's teacher must certify originality. Awards $50 first; $30 second; $20 third; and five honorable mentions of $5 each.
Tips: Winners will be announced at the 1992 NFSPS convention, and checks will be mailed shortly beforehand. Send SASE if you wish to receive a winner's list.

*‡THE MENTOR ESSAY CONTEST FOR HIGH SCHOOL SENIORS, "Mentor" Newsletter, P.O. Box 4382, Overland Park KS 66204. (913)362-7889. Contest Director: Maureen Waters. Annual contest. Estab. 1989. Purpose of the contest/award: "to encourage and support the art and practice of mentoring." Unpublished submissions only. Deadline for entries: March 31. SASE for contest rules and entry forms. Entry fee is $2. Awards $100, plus essay is published in "Mentor." Judging by editor of "Mentor." Acquires or purchases 1st NA serial rights for submitted and winning material. Writers must be high school seniors, or home-school equivalent. Works published in a future issue of "Mentor." "Writer should thoroughly understand the concept of mentoring."

VICKY METCALF BODY OF WORK AWARDS, Canadian Authors Association, Suite 500, 275 Slater St., Ottawa, ON K1P 5H9 Canada. (613)238-2296. FAX: (613)235-8237. Attn: Awards Chairman. Annual contest/award. Estab. 1963. Purpose of the contest/award: to honor a body of work inspirational to Canadian youth. Deadline for entries: December 31. SASE for contest/award rules and entry forms. Entries not returned. No entry fee. Awards $10,000 and framed certificate. Judging by panel of CAA-appointed judges including past winners.
Tips: "The prizes are given solely to stimulate writing for children by Canadian writers," said Mrs. Metcalf when she established the award. "We must encourage the writing of

✱ ***The asterisk before a listing indicates the listing is new in this edition.***

material for Canadian children without setting any restricting formulas."

VICKY METCALF SHORT STORY AWARD, Canadian Authors Association, Suite 500, 275 Slater St., Ottawa, ON K1P 5H9 Canada. (613)238-2296. FAX: (613)235-8237. Attn: Awards Chairman. Annual contest/award. Estab. 1979. Purpose of the award: to honor writing by a Canadian inspirational to Canadian youth. Previously published submissions only; must be published between January 1 and December 31. Deadline for entries: December 31. SASE for contest/award rules and entry forms. Entries not returned. No entry fee. Awards $3,000 to Canadian author and $1,000 to editor of winning story if published in a Canadian periodical or anthology. Judging by CAA-selected panel including past winners.

THE MILNER AWARD, Atlanta-Fulton Public Library/Friends of the Atlanta Fulton Public Library, One Margaret Mitchell Square, Atlanta GA 30303. (404)730-1710. Exec. Director: Rennie Jones Davant. Annual contest/award. Estab. 1983. Purpose of the contest/award: "The Milner Award is an annual award to a living American author of children's books. Selection is made by the children of Atlanta voting for their favorite author during Children's Book Week." Previous winners not eligible. "The winning author is awarded a specially commissioned work of the internationally famous glass sculptor, Hans Frabel, and a $1,000 honorarium." Requirements for entrants: "Winner must be an American author, able to appear personally in Atlanta to receive the award at a formal program."

‡MISSISSIPPI VALLEY POETRY CONTEST, North American Literary Escadrille, P.O. Box 3188, Rock Island IL 61204. Director: Sue Katz. Annual contest. Estab. 1971. Categories for high school, junior high and elementary students. Unpublished submissions only. Deadline for entries: September 15. SASE for contest rules and entry forms. Entry fee of $3 will cover up to 5 poems submitted. Awards cash from $35-125. Requirements for entrants: Open to any student or adult poet, writer or teacher.

NATIONAL JEWISH BOOK AWARD FOR CHILDREN'S LITERATURE, JCCA Jewish Book Council, 15 E. 26th St., New York NY 10010. (212)532-4949. Awards Coordinator: Dr. Marcia W. Posner. Annual contest/award. Estab. 1950. Previously published submissions only; must be published in 1991 for 1992 award. Deadline for entries: November 19. SASE for contest/award rules and entry forms. Entries not returned. No entry fee. Awards $750. Judging by 3 authorities in the field. Requirements for entrants: contest for best Jewish children's books, published only for ages 8-14. Books will be displayed at the awards ceremony in NYC in June.

*NATIONAL JEWISH BOOK AWARD–PICTURE BOOKS, (Marcia & Louis Posner Award), Jewish Book Council, 15 E 26th St., New York NY 10010. (212)532-4949. Awards Coordinator: Dr. Marcia W. Posner. Annual contest/award. Estab. 1980. Previously published submissions only; must be published the year prior to the awards ceremony–1991 for 1992 award. Deadline for entries: November 19. SASE for contest/ award rules and entry forms. Entries not returned. No entry fee. Awards $750. Judging by 3 authorities in the field. Requirements for entrants: subject must be of Jewish content, published. Works displayed at the awards ceremony.

*‡NATIONAL PEACE ESSAY CONTEST, for high school students, United States Institute of Peace, P.O. Box 27720, Central Station, Washington DC 20038-7720. (202)429-3846. Contest Director: Hrach Gregorian. Annual contest. Estab. 1987. "The writing competition gives students the opportunity to do valuable research and writing on a topic of importance to the future of peace with freedom and justice." "Submissions, instead of being published, can be a classroom assignment;" previously published entries must have appeared between September 1, 1991 and February 14, 1992. Deadline for entries: February 14, 1992 (postmark deadline) ("The opening and closing dates vary only slightly.") "Interested students, teachers and others may write or call to receive free contest kits. Please do not include SASE." No entry fee. State Level Awards are college scholarships in the following amounts: 1st place $500; 2nd place $250; 3rd place $100. National winners are selected from among the 1st place state winners. National winners receive 1st place $10,000, 2nd $5,000 and 3rd $3,500 in college scholarships. Judging is conducted by volunteer education professionals from across the country and by the Board of Directors of the United States Institute of Peace. "All submissions become property of the U.S. Institute of Peace to use at its discretion. The U.S. Institute of Peace may use, at its discretion and without royalty or any limitation, any winning essay." "Students grades 9-12 in the U.S., its territories and overseas schools may submit essays for review by completing the application process. Please—no illustrations." "National winning essays for each competition will be published by the U.S. Institute of Peace for public consumption."

‡THE 1992 NATIONAL WRITTEN & ILLUSTRATED BY . . . AWARDS CONTEST FOR STUDENTS, Landmark Editions, Inc., Box 4469, Kansas City MO 64127. (816)241-4919. Contest/Award Director: Teresa Melton. Annual awards contest with 3 published winners. Estab. 1986. Purpose of the contest/award: to encourage and celebrate the creative efforts of students. There are three age categories (6-9 years of age; 10-13; and 14-19). Unpublished submissions only. Deadline for entries: May 1, 1992. Contest rules available for self-addressed, business-sized envelope, stamped with 58¢ postage."Need to send a self-addressed, sufficiently stamped book mailer with book entry" for its return. Entry fee of $1. Prize: "Book is published." Judging by national panel of educators, editors, illustrators and authors. "Each student winner receives a publishing contract allowing Landmark to publish the book. Copyright is in student's name and student receives royalties on sale of book. Books must be in proper contest format and submitted with entry form signed by a teacher or librarian. Students may develop their illustrations in any medium of their choice, as long as the illustrations remain two-dimensional and flat to the surface of the paper." Works will be published in 1993 in Kansas City MO for distribution nationally and internationally. Winner and runners-up in each age category will receive college scholarships from the R.D. and Joan Dale Hubbard Foundation: winner, $5,000; second place, $2,000; third, fourth, and fifth places, $1,000 each.

*THE NENE AWARD, Hawaii Association of School Librarians and Hawaii Library Association, Children and Youth Section, Haleiwa Elementary School, 66-505 Haleiwa Rd., Haleiwa HI 96712. (808)637-4995. Award Director: Reva Dacanay. Estab. 1964. "The Nene Award was designed to help the children of Hawaii become acquainted with the best contemporary writers of fiction, become aware of the qualities that make a good book and choose the best rather than the mediocre." Previously published submissions only. Books must have been copyrighted not more than six years prior to presentation of award. Work is nominated. Awards Koa plaque. Judging by the children of Hawaii. Books must be fiction, written by a living author, copyrighted not more than six years ago and suitable for children in grades 4, 5 and 6.

NEWBERY MEDAL AWARD, Association for Library Service to Children—division of the American Library Association, 50 E Huron, Chicago IL 60611. (312)280-2163. Executive Director, ALSC: Susan Roman. Annual contest/award. Estab. 1922. Purpose of the contest/award: for the most distinguished contribution to American children's literature published in the U.S. Previously published submissions only; must be published prior to year award is given. Deadline for entries: December. SASE for contest/award rules and entry forms. Entries not returned. No entry fee. Medal awarded at banquet during annual conference. Judging by Newbery Committee.

THE SCOTT O'DELL AWARD FOR HISTORICAL FICTION, 1100 E. 57th St., Chicago IL 60037. Award Director: Mrs. Zena Sutherland. Annual contest/award. Estab. 1981. Purpose of the contest/award: "To promote the writing of historical fiction of good quality." Previously published submissions only; must be published between January 1 and December 31 of each year. Deadline for entries: December 31. "Publishers send books, although occasionally a writer sends a note or a book." SASE for contest/award rules and entry forms. No entry fee. Award $5,000. Judging by the advisory committee of *The Bulletin of the Center for Children's Books* at the University of Chicago." Requirements for entrants: "Must be published by a U.S. publisher in the preceding year; must be by an American citizen; must be set in the North or South American continent; must be historical fiction."

OHIOANA BOOK AWARDS, Ohioana Library Association, 1105 State Departments Bldg., 65 S. Front St., Columbus OH 43215. (614)466-3831. Director: Linda R. Hengst. Annual contest/award. "The Ohioana Book Awards are given to books of outstanding literary quality. Up to 6 Book Awards are given each year. Awards may be given in the categories of: fiction, nonfiction, children's literature, poetry and books about Ohio or an Ohioan. Books must be received by the Ohioana Library during the calendar year prior to the year the Award is given and must have a copyright date within the last two calendar years." Deadline for entries: December 31. SASE for contest/award rules and entry forms. No entry fee. "Any book that has been written or edited by a person born in Ohio or who has lived in Ohio for at least five years" is eligible.

HELEN KEATING OTT AWARD FOR OUTSTANDING CONTRIBUTION TO CHILDREN'S LITERATURE, Church and Synagogue Library Association, Box 19357, Portland OR 97280. (503)244-6919. Chair of Committee: Lottie Kula. Annual contest/award. Estab. 1980. "This award is given to a person or organization that has made a significant contribution to promoting high moral and ethical values through children's literature." Deadline for entries: February 1. "Recipient is honored in July during the conference." Awards certificate of recognition and a conference package consisting of registration, meals and housing and a complementary 1 year membership. "A nomination for an award may be made by anyone. It should include the name, address and telephone number of the nominee plus the church or synagogue relationship where appropriate. Nominations of an organization should include the name of a contact person. A detailed description of the reasons for the nomination should be given, accompanied by documentary evidence of accomplishment. The person(s) making the nomination should give his/her name, address and telephone number and a brief explanation of his/her knowledge of the nominee's accomplishments. Elements of creativity and innovation will be given high priority by the judges.

*OUTSTANDING PENNSYLVANIA AUTHOR AND/OR ILLUSTRATOR, Pennsylvania School Librarians Association, 1201 Yuerdon Dr., Camp Hill PA 17011. Chair: Susan Wolfe. Annual contest/award. Estab. 1975. Purpose of the contest: "to recognize an author and/or illustrator who is a present or former Pennsylvania resident or whose work represents or reflects Pennsylvania and who has made a notable contribution to the field of literature for youth." Previously published submissions only. Deadline for entries: October 1. Work must be nominated. No entry fee. Awards a certificate. Judging by awards committee.

PLEASE TOUCH MUSEUM BOOK AWARD, Please Touch Museum, 210 N. 21st St., Philadelphia PA 19103. (215)963-0667. Education Manager: Angela Cooper. Annual award. Estab. 1985. Purpose of the award: "Award is given to an outstanding concept book for children three and younger." Previously published submissions only. Deadline for entries: December 15. SASE for award rules and entry forms. No entry fee. Includes

Book Award Celebration Day, hologram winner and citation from Mayor. Judging by selected jury of children's literature experts, librarians, literacy officials and child development specialists. Education store purchases books for selling at Book Award Celebration Day and throughout the year.

‡**PUBLISH-A-BOOK CONTEST**, Raintree Publishers, 310 W. Wisconsin Ave., Milwaukee WI 53203. (414)273-0873. FAX: (414)273-0877. Editor-in-Chief: Walter Kossman. Send written entries: PAB Contest, 11 Prospect St., Madison NJ 07940. Annual contest/award. Estab. 1984. Purpose of the contest/award: to stimulate 4th, 5th and 6th graders to write outstanding stories for children. Unpublished submissions only. Deadline for entries: January 31. SASE for contest/award rules and entry forms. "Entries must be sponsored by a teacher or librarian." Entries not returned. No entry fee. Grand prizes: Raintree will publish four winning entries in the fall of 1990. Each winner will receive a $500 advance against an author royalty contract and ten free copies of the published book. The sponsor named on each of these entries will receive 20 free books from the Raintree catalog. Honorable mentions: each of the twenty honorable mention writers will receive $25. The sponsor named on each of these entries will receive ten free books from the Raintree catalog. Judging by an editorial team. Contract issued for Grand Prize winners. Payment and royalties paid. Requirements for entrants: contest is open only to 4th, 5th and 6th graders enrolled in a school program in the United States or other countries. Books will be displayed and sold in the United States and foreign markets. Displays at educational association meetings, book fairs. "We also have a separate contest for children in grades 2 and 3, established in 1989. All of the above is the same with the exception of the grades, deadline of March 1 and number of winners will be one."

*‡**THE AYN RAND INSTITUTE'S FOUNTAINHEAD ESSAY CONTEST**, The Ayn Rand Institute, P.O. Box 6004, Inglewood CA 90312. (213)306-9232. Contest Director: Dr. Michael S. Berliner. Annual contest. Estab. 1986. "To introduce high school juniors and seniors to the fiction and nonfiction writings, as well as the ideas, of Ayn Rand, novelist and philosopher. To encourage well-organized, analytic writing; to place issues important to young people, such as independence and integrity, before them." Unpublished submissions only. Deadline for entries: April 15. Contest rules and entry forms available to high school juniors and seniors for SASE. No entry fee. Awards one first prize $5,000 cash; 5 second prizes $1,000 each; 10 third prizes $500 each. Judging by 1) Educational Testing Service, 2) a panel of writers, professors and professional people, 3) winner is selected from top entries by a university professor. Essay becomes property of the Ayn Rand Institute. Entrant must be in last two years of secondary school. The Institute publishes the winning essay in its newsletter.

‡**ANNA DAVIDSON ROSENBERG AWARD FOR POEMS ON THE JEWISH EXPERIENCE**, Judah L. Magnes Museum, 2911 Russell St., Berkeley CA 94705. (510)849-2710. Poetry Award Coordinator: P. Friedman. Annual award. Estab. 1986-87. Purpose of the contest/award: to encourage poetry in English on the Jewish experience. Previously unpublished submissions only. Deadline for entries: August 31. SASE for contest/award rules and entry forms by July 31. SASE for list of winners. Awards $100-1st Prize, $50-2nd Prize, $25-3rd Prize; honorable mention certificates; *$25 Youth Commendation (poets under 19)*. Judging by committee of 3. There will be a reading of winners in December at Museum. Prospective anthology of winning entries.

✝ *The double dagger before a listing indicates the contest is for students.*

Tips: Write for entry form and guidelines *first*; entries must follow guidelines and be accompanied by entry form.

CARL SANDBURG LITERARY ARTS AWARDS, Friends of the Chicago Public Library, Harold Washington Library Center, 400 S. State St., Chicago IL 60605. (312)269-2922. Annual contest/award. Categories: fiction, nonfiction, poetry, children's literature. Published submissions only; must be published between June 1 and May 31 (the following year). Deadline for entries: September 1. SASE for contest/award rules and entry forms. Entries not returned. No entry fee. Awards trophy and $1,000. Judging by authors, reviewers, book buyers, librarians. Requirements for entrants: native born Chicagoan or presently residing in the six county metropolitan area. Two copies must be submitted by September 1. All entries become the property of the Friends.

*‡SCHOLASTIC ART AWARDS, Scholastic, Inc. 730 Broadway, New York NY 10003. (212)505-3566. Program Manager: Diane McNutt. Annual award. Estab. 1927. Purpose: encouragement and recognition of student achievement in the visual arts."There are 15 categories: oil, acrylic, watercolor, pencil drawing, ink drawing, pastel, crayon, charcoal, mixed media, printmaking, graphic design, fiber arts and textile design, sculpture, ceramics, jewelry and metalsmithing, photography, portfolio. Awards consist of cash awards, scholarships and prizes. Unpublished submissions only. Some areas have sponsors who conduct a regional preliminary judging and exhibition." SASE for award rules and entry forms. Entry fees vary depending on which region a student lives and deadline. Judging by art educators, artists, photographers and art administrators. All rights are given to Scholastic Inc. Requirements for entrants: students in grades 7-12. National winners exhibited in different city each year. "Write to Scholastic Art Awards, 730 Broadway, New York NY 10003 for information."

*‡SCHOLASTIC WRITING AWARDS, Scholastic, Inc., 730 Broadway, New York NY 10003. (212)505-3566. Awards Coordinator: Lori Maccione. Annual award. Estab. 1923. Purpose of award: "Encouragement and recognition of student achievement in creative writing." Group I (Grades 7, 8, 9): 1. short story (600-1,800 words), 2. essay (500-1,500 words), 3. poetry (35-100 lines), 4. dramatic script (approx. 30 pgs.) TV, film, radio, stage. Group II (Grades 10, 11, 12) 5. short story (1,300-3,000 words), 6. short short story (600-1,300 words), 7. essay (600-1,500 words), 8. poetry (50-200 lines), 8. poetry (50-200 lines), 9. humor (600-1,500 words), 10. dramatic script (approx. 30 pgs.) TV, film, radio, stage. Unpublished submissions only. Deadline for entries: January 17 (postmark), except in central Pennsylvania. SASE for contest/award rules and entry forms. No entry fee. Cash awards, prizes and scholarships. Judging by English teachers, professional writers and editors. Scholastic owns publishing rights. Open to students in grades 7-12 only. Some works published in Scholastic magazines. Please contact: Scholastic Writing Awards, 730 Broadway, New York NY 10003.

SCIENCE WRITING AWARD IN PHYSICS AND ASTRONOMY, The American Institute of Physics, 335 E. 45th St., New York NY 10017. (212)661-9404. Contact: Manager, Public Information Division. For information contact the Public Information Division. Annual contest/award. Estab. 1987. Purpose of the contest/award: to stimulate and recognize writing that improves children's understanding and appreciation of physics and astronomy. Previously published submissions only; must be published between October 1 and September 30 (the following year). Deadline for entries: October 10. "Entries may be submitted by the publisher as well as the author." Entries not returned. No entry fee. Awards $3,000 and an engraved chair. Judging by a committee selected by the Governing Board of the AIP. Requirements for entrants: "entries must be articles or books, written in English or English translations, dealing primarily with physics, astronomy or related subjects directed at children, from preschool ages up to fifteen years old. Entries must have been available to and intended for young people. Your signature on submission will constitute your acceptance of the contest rules. Postmarked no later than January 31."

*SEQUOYAH CHILDREN'S AWARD, Oklahoma Library Association, 300 Hardy Drive, Edmond OK 73013. (405)348-0506. Annual contest/award. "To encourage the reading of books of literary quality." Nominated works are placed on a master list. Students choose winners from the list. Previously published submissions only. No entry fee. Awards a plaque. Judging by children in grades 3-6 in Oklahoma schools. Requirements for entrants: open to American authors.

‡SEVENTEEN FICTION CONTEST, 9th Fl., 850 Third Ave., New York NY 10022. Fiction Editor: Adrian Nicole LeBlanc. Annual contest/award. Estab. 1945. Unpublished submissions only. Deadline for entries: April 31. SASE for contest/award rules and entry forms. Entries not returned. No entry fee. Awards cash prize. Judging by "external readers, in-house panel of editors." If first prize, acquires first North American rights for piece to be published. Requirements for entrants: "Our annual fiction contest is open to anyone between the ages of 13 and 21 on April 31. Submit only original fiction that has never been published in any form other than in school publications. Stories should be between 1,500 and 3,000 words in length (six to twelve pages). All manuscripts must be typed double-spaced on a single side of paper. Submit as many original stories as you like, but each story must include your full name, address, birth date and signature in the top right-hand corner of the first page. Your signature on submission will constitute your acceptance of the contest rules."

SFWA NEBULA AWARDS, Science Fiction Writers of America, Inc., Box 4335, Spartanburg SC 29305. (803)578-8012. Executive Secretary: Peter Dennis Pautz. Annual contest/award. Estab. 1966. Purpose of the contest/award: to recognize meritorious achievement of short stories, novelettes, novellas and novels published the previous calendar year in the science fiction/fantasy genre. Previously published submissions only; must be published between January 1 and December 31 of the previous calendar year. "Works are nominated and selected by our active membership." Entries not returned. Awards a trophy. Judging by the active membership of the SFWA, Inc.

CHARLIE MAY SIMON BOOK AWARD, Arkansas Elementary School Council, Arkansas Dept. of Education, #4 Capitol Mall, Room 301B, Little Rock AR 72201. (501)682-4371. Award Director: James A. Hester. Annual contest/award. Estab. 1970. Purpose of contest/award: to promote reading—to encourage reading of quality literature and book discussion. Previously published submissions only; must be published between January 1 and December 31 of calendar year; all books must have recommendations from 3 published sources. No entry fee. Awards a medallion. Contest open to entry by any writer, provided book is printed in year being considered.

GEORGE G. STONE CENTER FOR CHILDREN'S BOOKS RECOGNITION OF MERIT AWARD, George G. Stone Center for Children's Books, The Claremont Graduate School, 131 E. 10th St., Claremont CA 91711-6188. (714)621-8000 ext. 3670. Contest/Award Director: Doty Hale. Annual contest/award. Estab. 1965. Purpose of the contest/award: given to an author or illustrator of a children's book or for a body of work for the "power to please and expand the awareness of children and teachers as they have shared the book in their classrooms." Previously published submissions only. SASE for contest/award rules and entry forms. Entries not returned. No entry fee. Awards a scroll by artist Richard Beasley. Judging by a committee of teachers, professors of children's literature and librarians. Requirements for entrants: "nominations are made by students, teachers, professors and librarians. Award made at annual Claremont Reading Conference in spring (March)."

SYDNEY TAYLOR MANUSCRIPT COMPETITION, Association of Jewish Libraries, 15 Goldsmith St., Providence RI 02906. (401)274-1117. Director: Lillian Schwartz. Annual contest. Estab. 1985. Purpose of the contest: "This competition is for unpublished writers of fiction. Material should be for readers aged 8 to 12 years, with universal appeal that will serve to deepen the understanding of Judaism for all children, revealing positive aspects of Jewish life." Unpublished submissions only. Deadline for entries: January 15. SASE for contest rules and entry forms. No entry fee. Awards $1,000. Judging by qualified judges from within the Association of Jewish Libraries. Requirements for entrants: Must be an unpublished author.

*THUMB AREA WRITERS CLUB SPRING WRITING CONTEST, Box 27, Sandusky MI 48471. Contact: TAWC President. Annual contest/award. Estab. 1984. Purpose of the contest: "to give beginning writers a chance to compete with other beginners." Deadline: June 15. SASE for contest/award rules and entry forms. Entry fee is $2. Awards cash and/or certificate. Judging by club members. Winning entries may be published in *Thumbprints*. "Writer must be a Michigan resident and not have sold more than three manuscripts in category entered."

*‡1992 TIME EDUCATION PROGRAM STUDENT WRITING AND ART COMPETITION, *TIME* magazine, Time Education Program, Box 1000, Mt. Kisco NY 10549-0010. (800)882-0852. Annual contest. "The aims of this competition are reflective of *TIME* Magazine's basic mission—to communicate ideas and information with intelligence, style and meaning." Previously unpublished submissions only. Deadlines for entries: February 1 of each year. . SASE for contest rules and entry forms. No entry fee. Awards for writing: Grand Prize: $5,000; 3 Second Prizes: $2,500 each; 4 Awards for Excellence: $500 each. Awards for Art: 3 First Prizes: $1,000 each; 3 Awards for Excellence $500 each. Judging by *TIME* editorial staffers and educators. Rights to submitted material acquired or purchased. Open to any high school or college student in the U.S. or Canada. "Submissions must be no larger than 11×17; original 2 dimensional pieces." Works published in May 1991 issue of *TimeLines*.

*‡VEGETARIAN ESSAY CONTEST, The Vegetarian Resource Group, P.O. Box 1463, Baltimore MD 21203. (301)366-VEGE. Address to Vegetarian Essay Contest. Annual contest. Estab. 1985. Unpublished submissions only. Deadline for entries: May 1 of each year. SASE for contest rules and entry forms. No entry fee. Awards $50 savings bond. Judging by awards committee. Acquires right for The Vegetarian Resource Group to reprint essays. Requirements for entrants: ages 19 and under. Winning works may be published in Vegetarian Journal, instructional materials for students. "Submit 2-3 page essay on any aspect of vegetarianism, which is the abstinence of meat, fish and fowl. Entrants can base paper on interviewing, research or personal opinion. Need not be vegetarian to enter."

‡VFW VOICE OF DEMOCRACY, Veterans of Foreign Wars of the U.S., 34th & Broadway, Kansas City MO 64111. (816)756-3390. Director: Gordon Thorson. Annual contest/award. Estab. 1960. Purpose of the contest/award: to give high school students the opportunity to voice their opinions about their responsibility to our country and to convey them via the broadcast media to all of America. Deadline for entries: November 15. No entry fee. Awards prizes with monetary awards ranging from $1,000-18,000. Requirements for entrants: "10th, 11th and 12th grade students in public, parochial and private schools in the United States and overseas are eligible to compete. Former national and/or 1st place state winners are not eligible to compete again. U.S. citizenship is required."

THE STELLA WADE CHILDREN'S STORY AWARD, AMELIA Magazine, 329 E St., Bakersfield CA 93304. (805)323-4064. Editor: Frederick A. Raborg, Jr. Annual contest/award. Estab. 1988. Purpose of the contest/award: "with decrease in the number of religious and secular magazines for young people, the juvenile story and poetry must be preserved and enhanced." Unpublished submissions only. Deadline for entries: August 15. SASE for contest/award rules for return of entries. Entry fee is $5 per adult entry; there is no fee for entries submitted by young people under the age of 17, but such entry must be signed by parent, guardian or teacher to verify originality. Awards $125 plus publication. Judging by editorial staff. Previous winners include Maxine Kumin and Sharon E. Martin. "We use First North American serial rights only for the winning manuscript." Contest is open to all interested. If illustrator wishes to enter only an illustration without a story, the entry fee remains the same. Illustrations will also be considered for cover publication. Restrictions of mediums for illustrators: no restrictions, though submitted photos should be no smaller than 5×7. Illustrations (drawn) may be in any medium. "Winning entry will be published in the most appropriate issue of either AMELIA, CICADA or SPSM&H—subject matter would determine such. Submit clean, accurate copy."

*WASHINGTON POST/CHILDREN'S BOOK GUILD AWARD FOR NONFICTION, % Patricia Markun, 4405 "W" St. NW, Washington DC 20007. (202)965-0403. Annual contest/award. Estab. 1977. Purpose of contest: "to encourage nonfiction writing for children of literary quality. Awarded for the body of work of a leading American nonfiction author." No entry fee. Awards $1000 and an engraved crystal cube (paperweight). Judging by a jury of Children's Book Guild librarians and authors and a *Washington Post Book World* editor. "One doesn't enter. One is selected."

‡WE ARE WRITERS, TOO!, Creative With Words Publications, Box 223226, Carmel CA 93922. (408)649-1862. Contest/Award Director: Brigitta Geltrich. Annual contest/award. Estab. 1975. Unpublished submissions only. Deadline for entries: May 31. SASE for contest/award rules and entry forms. SASE for return of entries "if not winning poem." No entry fee. Awards publication is an anthology. Judging by selected guest editors and educators. Contest open to children only (up to and including 18 years old). **Tips:** Writer must request contest rules.

WESTERN HERITAGE AWARDS, National Cowboy Hall of Fame, 1700 NE 63rd St., Oklahoma City OK 73111. (405)478-2250. Director of Public Relations: Dana Sullivant. Annual contest/award. Estab. 1961. Purpose of the contest/award: The WHA is presented annually to encourage the accurate and artistic telling of great stories of the West. Categories include fiction, nonfiction, children's books, poetry. Must have been published in previous contest year. Previously published submissions only; must be published the calendar year before the awards are presented. Deadline for entries: December 31. SASE for contest/award rules and entry forms. Entries not returned. No entry fee. Awards a Wrangler award. Judging by a panel of judges selected each year with distinction in various fields of western art and heritage. Requirements for entrants: the material must pertain to the development or preservation of the West, either from a historical or contemporary viewpoint. Historical accuracy is vital. "There is an autograph party preceding the awards. Film clips are shown during the awards presentation."

LAURA INGALLS WILDER AWARD, Association for Library Service to Children—a division of the American Library Association, 50 E. Huron, Chicago IL 60611. (312)280-2163. Executive Director, ALSC: Susan Roman. Contest/award offered every 3 years.

Purpose of the contest/award: to recognize an author or illustrator whose books, published in the U.S., have over a period of years made a substantial and lasting contribution to children's literature. Awards a medal. Judging by committee which chooses several authors—winner is chosen by vote of ALSC membership.

PAUL A. WITTY SHORT STORY AWARD, International Reading Association, 800 Barksdale Road, P.O. Box 8139, Newark DE 19714-8139. (302)731-1600. Chair of Committee: Dorothy Grant Hennings. Annual contest. Estab. 1986. Purpose of award: "The entry must be an original short story appearing in a young children's periodical that regularly publishes short stories for children. (These would be periodicals generally aimed at readers to about age twelve.) The awarded short story should serve as a reading and literary standard by which readers can measure other writing and should encourage young readers to read by providing them with enjoyable and profitable reading." Previously published submissions only. Deadline for entries: "The entry must have been published for the first time in the eligibility year; the short story must be submitted during the calendar year of publication; thus a story will be considered but one time; the story may be entered into the award competition by its publisher. A story may be entered into the competition by members of the subcommittee or other members of IRA. Anyone wishing to nominate a short story should send it to the designated Paul A. Witty Short Award Subcommittee Chair as early as possible. The chair will then request that the publisher send two copies of the story in manuscript form by the stated deadline. Both fiction and nonfiction writing are eligible; each will be rated according to characteristics that are appropriate for the genre." Interested authors should send inquiry to IRA in Newark, DE. Award is $1,000 and recognition at the annual IRA Convention.

ALICE LOUISE WOOD OHIOANA AWARD FOR CHILDREN'S LITERATURE, Ohioana Library Association, 1105 State Departments Bldg., 65 S. Front St., Columbus OH 43215. (614)466-3831. Director: Linda R. Hengst. Annual award. Estab. 1991. Purpose of the award: "Award of $1,000 to an Ohio author whose body of work has made, and continues to make, a significant contribution to literature for children or young adults." SASE for award rules and entry forms. Requirements for entrants: "Born in Ohio, or lived in Ohio for a minimum of five years; established a distinguished publishing record of books for children and young people; body of work has made, and continues to make, a significant contribution to the literature for young people; Through whose work as a writer, teacher, administrator, or through community service, interest in children's literature has been encouraged and children have become involved with reading."

WORK-IN-PROGRESS GRANTS, Society of Children's Book Writers, P.O. Box 296, Mar Vista Station, Los Angeles CA 90066. Annual contest. "The SCBW Work-In-Progress Grants have been established to assist children's book writers in the competition of a specific project." Four categories: 1. General Work-In-Progress Grant. 2. Grant for a Contemporary Novel for Young People. 3. Nonfiction Research Grant. 4. Grant for a work whose author has never had a book published. Requests for applications may be made beginning October 1. Completed applications accepted February 1-May 1 of each year. SASE for applications for grants. In any year, an applicant may apply for any of the grants except the one awarded for a work whose author has never had a book published. (The recipient of this grant will be chosen from entries in all categories.) Four grants of $1,000 will be awarded annually. Runner-up grants of $500 (one in each category) will also be awarded. "The grants are available to both full and associate members of the SCBW. They are not available for projects on which there are already contracts." Previous recipients not eligible to apply.

YOUNG ADULT CANADIAN BOOK AWARD, % Unionville Library, 15 Library Lane, Markham, Ont. L3R 5C4. (416)477-2641. Contest/Award Director: Nancy E. Black. Annual contest/award. Estab. 1981. Purpose of contest/award: "to recognize the author of an outstanding English-language Canadian book which appeals to young adults between the ages of 13 and 18 that was published the preceding calendar year. Information is available for anyone requesting. We approach publishers, also send news releases to various journals, i.e. *Quill & Quire.*" Entries are not returned. No entry fee. Awards a leather-bound book, sometimes author tour. Requirement for entrants: a work of fiction (novel or short stories), the title must be a Canadian publication in either hardcover or paperback, and the author must be a Canadian citizen or landed immigrant. Award given at the Canadian Library Association Conference.

YOUNG PEOPLE'S LITERATURE AWARDS, Friends of American Writers, 1634 N. Wood St., Chicago IL 60622. (312)235-2686. Director: Ms. Marianne Duignan. Annual award. Estab. 1960. Previously published submissions only. Deadline for entries: December 15. "At maximum, the entry must be the third published prose work by the writer. To receive an award in 1992, publication must have been in 1991." SASE for awards rules and entry forms. No entry fee. Awards cash to the writer; certificate of merit to the publisher.

YOUNG READER'S CHOICE AWARD, Pacific Northwest Library Association, 133 Suzzallo Library, FM-30, Graduate School of Library and Information Science, Seattle WA 98195. (206)543-1897. Secretary: Carol Doll. Award Director: Terry Hyer, 812 E. Clark, Pocatello ID 83201. Annual contest/award. Estab. 1940. Purpose of the contest/award: to promote reading for enjoyment. Previously published submissions only; must be published 3 years before award year. Deadline for entries: February 1. SASE for contest/award rules and entry forms. No entry fee. Awards a silver medal, struck in Idaho silver. "Children vote for their favorite (books) from a list of titles nominated by librarians, teachers, students and other interested persons."

‡YOUNG WRITER'S CONTEST, Young Writer's Contest Foundation, Box 6092, McLean VA 22106. (703)893-6097. Executive Director: Kathie Janger. Annual contest/award. Estab. 1984. Purpose of the contest/award: to challenge first through eighth graders and to give them recognition; in so doing, we aim to improve basic communication skills. Unpublished submissions only. Deadline for entries: November 30. SASE for contest/award rules and entry forms. Entries not returned. Entry fee is $15 per school (or, if school does not participate, the individual may pay the fee). "All participating students and schools receive certificates; winners' entries are published in our anthology: *Rainbow Collection*: Stories and Poetry by Young People." Judging by writers, editors, journalists, teachers, reading specialists. "All rights surrounding winners' entries are given to YWCF, via consent and release form. Participants must be currently enrolled in grades 1-8; no more than 12 entries per school may be submitted; we accept poems, stories and essays. *Rainbow Collection*: Stories and Poetry by Young People is published in May of each year, and is distributed (25,000 cc. in 1989) to libraries, school systems and charitable organizations. The YWCF complements classroom writing programs and creates a cycle of encouragement and performance; writing is critical to all fields of endeavor; we reward the students' efforts—not just the winners.' "

Clubs/Organizations

Children's writers and illustrators can benefit from contacts made through organizations such as the ones listed in this section. Professional organizations provide a writer or artist with a multitude of educational, business and legal services. Much of these services come in the form of newsletters, workshops or seminars that provide tips about how to be a better writer or artist, types of business records to keep, health and life insurance coverage you should carry or organizational competitions to be aware of.

You will notice that some of these organizations welcome anyone with an interest, while others are open to professionals only. Still, others have varying levels of membership such as the Society of Children's Book Writers. SCBW offers associate memberships to those with no publishing credits. Those who have had work for children published are full members. Feel free to write for more information regarding any group that sounds interesting. Be sure to inquire about membership qualifications as well as services offered to members.

An added benefit to being a member of an organization includes being able to network with others with similar interests, creating a support system to help you through tight creative and financial periods. Important contacts can be made through your peers, and as it is in any business, knowing the right people can definitely help your career. Membership in a writer's or artist's group also presents to a publisher an image of being serious about your craft. Of course, this provides no guarantee that your work will be published, but it offers an added dimension of credibility and professionalism.

ACTION FOR CHILDREN'S TELEVISION (ACT), 20 University Rd., Cambridge MA 02138. (617)876-6620. President: Peggy Charren. Purpose of organization: "ACT is a national nonprofit children's television advocacy organization working to encourage diversity in children's television and to eliminate commercial abuses targeted to young children." Qualifications for membership: "payment of $20 yearly membership dues." Membership cost: "Begins at $20, members may contribute more if they wish." Sponsors workshops/conferences; open to nonmembers. "ACT sponsors annual Achievement in Children's Television Awards for children's television series, home videos and public service campaigns." Awards a certificate. Contest open to nonmembers.

*ARIZONA AUTHORS ASSOCIATION, 3509 E. Shea Blvd., #117, Phoenix AZ 85028-3339. (602)996-9706. President: Cyndi Greening. Purpose of organization: Membership organization offering professional, educational and social opportunities to writers and authors. Membership cost: $40/yr. professional and associate; $50/yr. affiliate; $20/yr. student. Different levels of membership include: Professional: published writers; Associate: writers working toward publication; Affiliate: professionals in publishing industry; student: full-time students. Workshops/conferences: monthly educational workshops; contact office for current calendar. Newsletter provides information useful to writers (markets, book reviews, calendar of meetings and events) and news about members. Non-member subscription $40/yr. Sponsors Annual Literary Contest. Awards include total of $1,000 in prizes in several categories. Contest open to non-members.

THE AUTHORS GUILD, 330 W. 42nd St., 29th Floor, New York NY 10036-6902. (212)563-5904. Assistant Director: Peggy Randall. Purpose of organization: membership organization of 6,700 members that offers services and information materials intended to help authors with the business and legal aspects of their work, including contract problems, copyright matters, freedom of expression and taxation. Qualifications for membership: book author published by an established American publisher within 7 years or any author who has had three works, fiction or nonfiction, published by a magazine or magazines of general circulation in the last 18 months. Associate membership also available. Annual dues: $90. Different levels of membership include: associate membership with all rights except voting available to an author who has work in progress but who has not yet met the qualifications for active membership. This normally involves a firm contract offer from a publisher. Workshops/conferences: "The Guild and Authors League of America conduct several symposia each year at which experts provide information, offer advice, and answer questions on subjects of interest and concern to authors. Typical subjects have been the rights of privacy and publicity, libel, wills and estates, taxation, copyright, editors and editing, the art of interviewing, standards of criticism and book reviewing. Transcripts of these symposia are published and circulated to members." Symposia open to members only. "The *Author's Guild Bulletin*, a quarterly journal, contains articles on matters of interest to writers, reports of Guild activities, contract surveys, advice on problem clauses in contracts, transcripts of Guild and League symposia, and information on a variety of professional topics. Subscription included in the cost of the annual dues."

THE AUTHORS RESOURCE CENTER, Box 64785, Tucson AZ 85740-1785. (602)325-4733. Executive Director: Martha R. Gore. Purpose of organization: to help writers, graphic artists understand the business and professional realities of the publishing world—also have literary agency (opened March 1, 1987) and artists agency (opened January 1990) that markets members' books and illustrations to publishers. Qualifications for membership: serious interest in writing or cartooning. Membership cost: $60 per year for aspiring and published members. "Professional development workshops are open to members at a discount and to the general public. TARC instructors are actively publishing and often have academic credentials. The *Tarc Report* is published bimonthly and includes information about markets, resources, legal matters, writers workships, reference sources, announcement of members' new books, reviews and other news important to members. Subscription included in membership fee. *TARC* was established in 1984."

CANADIAN AUTHORS ASSOCIATION, 275 Slater St. #500, Ottawa, Ontario K1P 5H9 Canada. (613)238-2296. FAX: (613)235-8237. Contact: Executive Director. Purpose of organization: to help "emerging" writers and provide assistance to professional writers. Membership is divided into two categories for individuals: Member (voting): Persons engaged in writing in any genre who have produced a sufficient body of work; Associate (non-voting): Persons interested in writing who have not yet produced sufficient material to qualify for full membership, or those who, though not writers, have a sincere interest in Canadian literature. Persons interested in learning to write may join the Association for one year at a reduced rate. Membership cost: $90 members, $90-associates, $60-introductory rate. Workshops/conferences: 70th Annual Conference, June 20-26, 1991 in Ottawa, ON. "The conference draws writers, editors and publishers together in a congenial atmosphere providing seminars, workshops, panel discussions, readings by award-winning authors, and many social events." Open to nonmembers. Publishes a newsletter for members only. Also publishes a quarterly journal and a bienniel writer's guide available to nonmembers. "The Association created a major literary award program in 1975 to honor writing that achieves literary excellence without sacrificing popu-

Refer to the Business of Children's Writing & Illustrating
for up-to-date marketing, tax and legal information.

lar appeal. The awards are in four categories—fiction, (for a full-length novel); nonfiction (excluding works of an instructional nature); poetry (for a volume of the works of one poet); and drama (for a single play published or staged). The awards consist of a handsome silver medal and $5,000 in cash; they are funded by Harlequin Enterprises, the Toronto-based international publisher." Contest open to nonmembers. Also contests for writing by students and for young readers (see Vicky Metcalf and Canadian Author & Bookman Awards); sponsors Air Canada Awards.

*LEWIS CARROLL SOCIETY OF NORTH AMERICA, 617 Rockford Rd., Silver Spring MD 20902. (301)593-7077. Secretary: M. Schaefer. "We are an organization of Carroll admirers of all ages and interests and a center for Carroll studies." Qualifications for membership: "An interest in Lewis Carroll and a simple love for Alice (or even the Snark)." Membership cost: $20/year. There is also a contributing membership of $50. "We plan to hold a conference in 1994." Publishes a newsletter.

THE CHILDREN'S BOOK COUNCIL, INC., 568 Broadway, New York NY 10012. (212)966-1990. Purpose of organization: "A nonprofit trade association of children's and young adult publishers, CBC promotes the enjoyment of books for children and young adults, and works with national and international organizations to that end. The CBC has sponsored National Children's Book Week since 1945." Qualifications for membership: Trade publishers of children's and young adult books are eligible for membership. Membership cost: "Individuals wishing to receive mailings from the CBC (our semi-annual newsletter, CBC FEATURES, and our materials brochures) may be placed on our mailing list for a one-time-only fee of $45. Publishers wishing to join should contact the CBC for dues information." Sponsors workshops and conferences. Publishes a newsletter with articles about children's books and publishing. Listings of free or inexpensive materials from publishers. Nonmembers subscription: $45, one-time fee only.

CHILDREN'S READING ROUND TABLE OF CHICAGO, #1507, 3930 N. Pine Grove, Chicago IL 60613. (312)477-2271. Information Chairperson: Marilyn Singer. Purpose of organization: "to support activities which foster and enlarge children and young adults' interest in reading and to promote good fellowship among persons actively interested in the field of children's books." Qualifications for membership: "Membership is open to anyone interested in children's books. There are no professional qualifications; however, the majority of our members are authors, freelance writers, illustrators, librarians, educators, editors, publishers and booksellers." Membership cost: $15 for year (July 1 through June 30), applicable to members within our Chicago meeting area; Associate Membership $10, limited to persons outside the Metropolican Chicago Area or who are retired. "All members have same privileges, which include attendance at meetings; newsletter, *CRTT Bulletin;* yearbook published biennially; and access to information about CRRT special activities." Workshops/conferences: Children's Reading Round Table Summer Seminar for Writers & Illustrators, given in odd-numbered years. The 2-day seminar, at a Chicago college campus, usually in August, features guest speakers and a variety of profession-level workshops, manuscript critiquing and portfolio appraisal. Enrollment is open members and nonmembers; one fee applicable to all. Meals included, housing extra. Also, Children's Reading Round Table Children's Literature Conference, given in even-numbered years. One-day program, at a Chicago college campus, usually in early September. Program includes guest authors and educators, variety of workshops, exhibits, bookstore, lunch. Enrollment open to members and nonmembers; one fee applicable to all. *CRRT Bulletin, Children's Reading Round Table of Chicago* is published seven times a year, in advance of dinner meetings, and contains articles; book reviews; special sections of news about authors and artists; librarians and educators; publishers and booksellers. An Opportunity Column provides information about professional meetings, workshops, conferences, generally in the Midwest area. The *Bulletin* is available to members on payment of dues. Sample copies may be requested. Awards: "We do give an honorary award, the Children's Reading Round Table Annual Award, *not* for a single book or accomplishment but for long-term commitment to children's literature. Award includes check, lifetime membership, plaque. Nominations can be made *only* by CRRT members; nominees are not limited to membership."

*CHRISTIAN WRITERS GUILD, 260 Fern Lane, Hume Lake CA 93628. (209)335-2333. Director: Norman B. Rohrer. Purpose of organization: a 48-unit home study, 3-year correspondence course. Qualifications for membership: the ability to think clearly and a commitment to editorial communication. Membership cost: $495 total: $35 down, $15/month. Different levels of membership. "One can join for $45 annually to receive help on his or her editorial projects." Sponsors workshops and conferences. "Conference held at Hume Lake each year for certain in July, then elsewhere as we have invitations." Publishes a small sheet called the "Quill o' the Wisp."

*FLORIDA FREELANCE WRITERS ASSOCIATION, P.O. Box 9844, Fort Lauderdale FL 33310. (305)485-0795. Executive Director: Dana K. Cassell. Purpose of organization: to act as a link between Florida writers and buyers of the written word; to help writers run more effective communications businesses. Qualifications for membership: "None—we provide a variety of services and information, some for beginners and some for established pros." Membership cost: $90/year. Sponsors annual conference held third weekend in May. Publishes a newsletter focusing on market news, business news, how-to tips for the serious writer. Non-member subscription: $39—does not include Florida section—includes national edition only. Sponsors contest: annual deadline March 15. Guidelines available fall of year. Categories: juvenile, adult nonfiction, adult fiction, poetry. Awards include cash for top prizes, certificate for others. Contest open to nonmembers.

GRAPHIC ARTISTS GUILD, 11 West 20th St., New York NY 10011. (212)463-7730. Executive Director: Paul Basista. Purpose of organization: "To unite within its membership all professionals working in the graphic arts industry; to improve the economic and social conditions of professional artists and designers; to improve industry standards." Qualification for full membership: 51% of income derived from artwork. Associate members include those in allied fields, students and retirees. Initiation fee: $25. Full memberships $100-175/year. Associate membership $55-95/year. Sponsors "Eye to Eye," a national conference exploring the relationships between artists/artists and artists/clients. Publishes "Graphic Artists Guild Handbook, Pricing and Ethical Guidelines." "Advocates the advancement and protection of artists' rights and interests."

INTERNATIONAL BLACK WRITERS, Box 1030, Chicago IL 60690. (312)995-5195. Executive Director: Mable Terrell. Purpose of organization: to encourage, develop and display writing talent. Qualifications for membership: the desire to write and willingness to work to excel in the craft. Membership cost: $15/year. Different levels of membership include: senior citizens and youth. Workshops/conferences: 1991 conference, June 15-17, Chicago IL. Open to nonmembers. Publishes a newsletter detailing issues of importance to writers, competitions. Nonmembers subscription: $15/year. Sponsors an annual writing competition in poetry, fiction and nonfiction. Deadline: May 30th. Awards include plaque and certificates. Contest open to nonmembers.

*THE INTERNATIONAL WOMEN'S WRITING GUILD, P.O. Box 810, Gracie Station, New York NY 10028. (212)737-7536. Executive Director & Founder: Hannelore Hahn. IWWG is "a network for the personal and professional empowerment of women through writing." Qualifications: open to any woman connected to the written word regardless of professional portfolio. Membership cost: $35 annually; $45 annually for foreign members. "IWWG sponsors 13 annual conferences a year in all areas of the U.S. The major conference is held in August of each year at Skidmore College in Saratoga Springs NY. It is a week-long conference attracting more than 300 women internationally." Also publishes a 28-page magazine, *Network*, 6 times/year.

LEAGUE OF CANADIAN POETS, 24 Ryerson Ave., Toronto, Ontario M5T 2P3 Canada. (416)363-5047. FAX: (416)860-0826. Executive Director: Angela Rebeiro. President: Maria Jacobs. Inquiries to Executive Assistant: Dolores Ricketts. The L.C.P. is a national organization of published Canadian poets. Our constitutional objectives are to advance poetry in Canada and to promote the professional interests of the members. Qualifications for membership: full—publication of at least one book of poetry by a professional publisher; associate membership—an active interest in poetry, demonstrated by several magazine/periodical publication credits. Membership fees: full—$160/year, associate—$50/year. Holds an Annual General Meeting every spring; some events open to nonmembers. "We also organize reading programs in schools and public venues. We publish a newsletter which includes information on poetry/poetics in Canada and beyond. Also publish the books *Poetry Markets for Canadians*; *Who's Who in the League of Canadian Poets*; *When is a Poem* (teaching guide) and its accompanying anthology of Canadian Poetry *Here is a Poem*; plus a series of cassettes. We sponsor a National Poetry Contest, open to Canadians living here and abroad." Rules: Unpublished poems of any style/subject, under 75-lines, typed, with name/address on separate sheet. $6 entry fee (includes GST) per poem. $1,000-1st prize, $750-2nd, $500-3rd; plus best 50 published in an anthology. Inquire with SASE. Contest open to Canadian nonmembers. Organizes two annual awards: The Gerald Lampert Memorial Award for the best first book of poetry published in Canada in the preceding year and The Pat Lowther Memorial Award for the best book of poetry by a Canadian woman published in the preceding year. Deadline for both the poetry contest and award is January 31 each year. Send SASE for more details.

*NATIONAL STORY LEAGUE, 3516 Russell #6, St. Louis MO 63104. (314)773-5555. Board Member, Story Art Contributor: E.G. Stirnaman. Purpose of organization: to promote the art of storytelling. Qualifications for membership: the wish to become a good storyteller and to work at it. Annual dues: $15. Publishes a magazine of story art. Non-member subscription: $5. Sponsors storywriting contest (original). Awards include cash and publication. Contest open to non-members.

NATIONAL WRITERS CLUB, Ste. 620, 1450 S. Havana, Aurora CO 80012. (303)751-7844. Executive Director: James Lee Young. Purpose of organization: association for freelance writers. Qualifications for membership: associate membership—must be serious about writing; professional membership—published and paid (cite credentials). Membership cost: $50-associate; $60-professional; $15 setup fee for first year only. Workshops/conferences: TV/Screenwriting Workshops, NWC Annual Conferences, Literary Agency, Editing and Critiquing services, Local Chapters. National Writer's School. Open to nonmembers. Publishes industry news of interest to freelance writers; how-to articles; market information; member news and networking opportunities. Non-member subscription $18. Sponsors poetry contest; short story/article contest; novel contest; nonfiction book proposal contest. Awards cash awards for top three winners; books and/or certificates for other winners; honorable mention certificate places 11-20. Contests open to nonmembers.

NATIONAL WRITERS UNION, 13 Astor Place, 7th Floor, New York NY 10003. (212)254-0279. National Director: Anne Wyville. Purpose of organization: Advocacy for freelance writers. Qualifications for membership: "Membership in the NWU is open to all qualified writers, and no one shall be barred or in any manner prejudiced within the Union on account of race, age, sex, sexual preference, disability, national origin, religion or ideology. You are eligible for membership if you have published a book, play, three articles, five poems, one short story or an equivalent amount of newsletter, publicity, technical commercial, government or insitutional copy. You are also eligible for membership if you have written an equal amount of unpublished material and you are actively writing and attempting to publish your work." Membership Dues: Annual writing income under $5,000, $55/year; annual writing income $5,000-25,000, $95/year; annual writing income over $25,000, $135/year. National union newsletter quarterly, issues related to freelance writing and to union organization. Nonmember subscription: $15.

*THE NEBRASKA WRITERS GUILD, P.O. Box 30341, Lincoln NE 68503-0341. (402)477-3804. President: David Kubicek. Purpose of organization: to provide support and information to professional and aspiring writers. "To be an active member, you must meet at least one of these criteria: have published and placed on sale through regular channels one or more books; have received payment for 5,000 words of prose published in magazines or newspapers of 2,500 circulation or more; have written for television, radio or other media seen or heard by an authenticated audience of 2,500 or more; present evidence of a continuous body of poetry to be judged on the basis of number and quality of publications, regardless of payment or circulation. If you don't qualify as an active member but are interested in the publishing industry, you may join the NWG as an Associate Member." Membership cost: Active and Associate member, $10/year; youth member (has same benefits as Assoc. member but for people under 18), $7/year. Different levels of membership include: Active member—professional writers; Associate member—aspiring writers, editors, publishers, librarians, etc.; Youth member—18 or younger. Workshops/conferences: two conferences/year—April to October. Publishes newsletter. Provides market and how-to information and news about the Guild and its members.

PEN AMERICAN CENTER, 568 Broadway, New York NY 10012. (212)334-1660. Purpose of organization: "To foster understanding among men and women of letters in all countries. International PEN is the only worldwide organization of writers and the chief voice of the literary community. Members of PEN work for freedom of expression wherever it has been endangered." Qualifications for membership: "The standard qualification for a writer to join PEN is that he or she must have published, in the United States, two or more books of a literary character, or one book generally acclaimed to be of exceptional distinction. Editors who have demonstrated commitment to excellence in their profession (generally construed as five years' service in book editing), translators who have published at least two book-length literary translations, and playwrights whose works have been professionally produced, are eligible for membership. An application form is available upon request from PEN Headquarters in New York. Candidates for membership should be nominated by two current members of PEN. Inquiries about membership should be directed to the PEN Membership Committee. Friends of PEN is also open to writers who may not yet meet the general PEN membership requirements. PEN sponsors more than fifty public events at PEN Headquarters in New York, and at the branch offices in Boston, Chicago, Houston, San Francisco and Portland, Oregon. They include tributes by contemporary writers to classic American writers, dialogues with visiting foreign writers, symposia that bring public attention to problems of censorship and that address current issues of writing in the United States, and readings that introduce beginning writers to the public. PEN's wide variety of literary programming reflects current literary interests and provides informal occasions for writers to meet each other and to welcome those with an interest in literature. Events are all open to the public and are usually free of charge. The Children's Book Authors' Committee sponsors regular public events focusing on the art of writing for children and young adults and on the diversity of literature for juvenile readers. National union newsletter covers PEN activities, features interviews with international literary figures, transcripts of PEN literary symposia, reports on issues vital to the literary community. All PEN publications are available by mail order directly from PEN American Center. Individuals must enclose check or money order with their order. Subscription: $8 for 4 issues; sample issue $2. Pamphlets and brochures all free upon request. Sponsors several competitions per year. Monetary awards range from $700-12,750.

*PUPPETEERS OF AMERICA, INC., #5 Cricklewood Path, Pasadena CA 91107. (818)797-5748. Membership Officer: Gayle Schluter. Purpose of organization: to promote the art of Puppetry. Qualifications for membership: interest in the art form. Membership cost: single adult, $35; junior member, $20; retiree, $25; group or family, $55; couple, $45. Sponsors workshops/conferences. Publishes newsletter. *The Puppetry Journal* provides news about puppeteers, puppet theatres, exhibitions, touring companies, technical tips, new products, new books, films, television, and events sponsored by the Chartered Guilds in each of the 8 P of A regions. Subscription: $30.

*SAN DIEGO WRITERS/EDITORS GUILD, 3235 Homer Street, San Diego CA 92106. (619)223-5235. Treasurer: Peggy Lipscomb. "The Guild was formed January, 1979 to meet the local writers' needs for assignments and editors who seek writers. The use of the Guild as a power to publicize poor editorial practices has evolved. We hope to meet writers' needs as we become aware of them and as members are willing to provide services." Activities include: monthly social meetings with a speaker, monthly newsletter, membership directory, workshops and conferences, other social activities. Qualifications for membership: published book; three published, paid pieces (nonfiction, fiction, prose, poetry), paid editor, produced screenplay or play, paid and published translations, public relations, publicity or advertising. "All professional members must submit clear evidence of work and a brief résumé. After acceptance, member need not requalify unless membership lapses." Membership cost: $25 annual fees, $40 member and spouse, $12.50 full-time student and out-of-state or county member. Different levels of membership include: associate and professional. Workshops/conferences: Fiesta/Siesta Conference. Open to nonmembers. Publishes a newsletter giving notice of meetings, conferences, contests.

SCIENCE FICTION WRITERS OF AMERICA, INC., P.O. Box 4335, Spartanburg SC 29305. (803)578-8012. Executive Secretary: Peter Dennis Pautz. Purpose of organization: to encourage public interest in science fiction literature and provide organization format for writers/editors/artists within the genre. Qualifications for membership: at least one professional sale or other professional involvement within the field. Membership cost: annual active dues — $60; affiliate — $42; one-time installation fee of $10; dues year begins July 1. Different levels of membership include: affiliate requires one professional sale or professional involvement; active requires three professional short stories or one novel published. Workshops/conferences: annual awards banquet, usually in April or May. Open to nonmembers. Publishes newsletter. Nonmember subscription: $15 in U.S. Sponsors SFWA Nebula® Awards for best published SF in the categories of novel, novella, novelette, and short story. Awards trophy.

SOCIETY OF CHILDREN'S BOOK WRITERS, Box 66296, Mar Vista Station, Los Angeles CA 90066. (818)347-2849. Chairperson, Board of Directors: Sue Alexander. Purpose of organization: to assist writers and illustrators working or interested in the field. Qualifications for membership: an interest in children's literature and illustration. Membership cost: $40/year. Different levels of membership include: full membership — published authors/illustrators; associate membership — unpublished writers/illustrators. Workshops/conferences: 30-40 events around the country each year. Open to nonmembers. Publishes a newsletter focusing on writing and illustrating children's books. Sponsors Don Freeman Award for illustrators, 4 grants in aid.

SOCIETY OF ILLUSTRATORS, 128 E. 63rd St., New York NY 10021. (212)838-2860. Director: Terrence Brown. Purpose of organization: To promote interest in the art of illustration for working professional illustrators and those in associated fields. "Cost of membership: Initiation fee—$200. Annual dues for Non-Resident members (those living more than 125 air miles from SI's headquarters) are $217. Dues for Resident Artist Members are $369 per year, Resident Associate Members $430." Different levels of membership include: *Artist Members* "shall include those who make illustration their profession" and through which they earn at least 60% of their income. *Associate Members* are "Those who earn their living in the arts or who have made a substantial contribution to the art of illustration." This includes art directors, art buyers, creative supervisors, instructors, publishers and like categories. "All candidates for membership are admitted by the proposal of one active member and sponsorship of four additional members. The candidate must complete and sign the application form which requires a brief biography, a listing of schools attended, other training and a résumé of his or her professional career." Candidates for *Artist* membership, in addition to the above requirements, must submit examples of their work. Sponsors The Annual of American Illustration. Awards include gold and silver medals. Open to nonmembers. Deadline: October 1. Sponsors "The Original Art;" Deadline: July 15th.

*SOCIETY OF MIDLAND AUTHORS, % Bowman, 152 N. Scoville, Oak Park IL 60302. (708)383-7568. President: Jim Bowman. Purpose of organization: create closer association among writers of the Middle West; stimulate creative literary effort; maintain collection of members works; encourage interest in reading and literature by cooperating with other educational and cultural agencies. Qualifications for membership: to be author or co-author of a book demonstrating literary style and published by a recognized publisher or author of published or professionally produced play and be identified through birth or residence with IL, IN, IA, KS, MI, MN, MO, NE, ND, OH, SD or WI. Membership cost: $15/year dues. Different levels of membership include: regular—published book authors; associate, nonvoting—not published as above but having some connection with literature, such as librarians, teachers, publishers, and editors. Workshops/conferences: program meetings, Newberry Library, Chicago, held 5 times a year, featuring authors, publishers, editors or the like individually or on panels. Usually 2nd Tuesday of October, November, January, February and March. Also holds annual awards dinner at Drake Hotel, Chicago, in May. Publishes a newsletter focusing on news of members and of general items of interest to writers. Non-member subscription: $5. Sponsors contests. "Annual awards in 7 categories, given at annual dinner in May. $500 awards for books published or plays performed in previous calendar year. Send SASE to contact person for details." Contest open to non-members.

*SOCIETY OF SOUTHWESTERN AUTHORS, P.O. Box 35220, Tucson AZ 85740. President: J. Darrell Beach. Purpose of organization: fellowship among members of the writing profession, recognition of members' achievements, to stimulate further achievement, and to assist persons seeking to become professional writers. Qualifications for membership: proof of publication of a book, articles, TV screenplay, etc. Membership cost: $25 initiation plus $10/year dues. Workshops/conferences: The Society of Southwestern Authors annual Writers' Conference, held the last Saturday of January at the University of Arizona. Publishes a newsletter. "The Write Word is a quarterly newsletter about our members' activities and news of interest to them. Each spring we sponsor a fiction/nonfiction contest for beginning writers. Applications are available in February. Send SASE to the P.O. Box." (Contestants must have one item published, but not more

GET YOUR WORK INTO THE RIGHT BUYERS' HANDS!

You work hard... and your hard work deserves to be seen by the right buyers. But with the constant changes in the industry, it's not always easy to know who those buyers are. That's why you'll want to keep up-to-date and on top with the most current edition of this indispensable market guide.

Totally Updated Each Year

Keep ahead of the changes by ordering *1993 Children's Writer's & Illustrator's Market* today. You'll save the frustration of getting manuscripts and artwork returned in the mail, stamped MOVED: ADDRESS UNKNOWN. And of NOT submitting your work to new listings because you don't know they exist. All you have to do to order the upcoming 1993 edition is complete the attached post card and return it with your payment or charge card information. Order now, and there's one thing that won't change from your *1992 Children's Writer's & Illustrator's Market* - the price! That's right, we'll send you the 1993 edition for just $17.95. *1993 Children's Writer's & Illustrator's Market* will be published and ready for shipment in February 1993.

Don't let another opportunity slip by... get a jump on the industry with the help of *1993 Children's Writer's & Illustrator's Market*. Order today!
You deserve it!

(See other side for more helpful children's writing books)

To order, drop this postpaid card in the mail.

☐ Yes! I want the most current edition of *Children's Writer's & Illustrator's Market*. Please send me the 1993 edition at the 1992 price - $17.95.* (NOTE: *1993 Children's Writer's & Illustrator's Market* will be ready for shipment in February 1993.) #10307
Also send me these books to help me get published:
____(#10257) 1992 Guide to Literary Agents & Art/Photo Reps $~~15.95~~ $13.55* *(Available NOW)*
____(#10101) Writing for Children & Teenagers, $12.95,* paper *(Available NOW)*
____(#1121) The Children's Picture Book, $19.95,* paper *(Available NOW)*
____(#30082) How to Write & Illustrate Children's Books $22.50* *(Available NOW)*

*Plus postage and handling: $3.00 for one book, $1.00 for each additional book. Ohio residents add 5 1/2% sales tax.
Credit card orders call toll-free 1-800-289-0963
☐ Payment enclosed (Slip this card and your payment into an envelope)
☐ Please charge my: ☐ Visa ☐ MasterCard

Account # _____ Exp. Date _____

Signature _____

Name _____

Address _____ Phone (_____)

City _____ State _____ Zip _____

(This offer expires August 1, 1993)

30-Day Money Back Guarantee

Writer's Digest Books
1507 Dana Avenue
Cincinnati, OH 45207

6197

More Books to Help You Get Published!

NEW DIRECTORY SAVE 15%
1992 Guide to Literary Agents & Art/Photo Reps
This new directory lists agents and reps across North America, plus answers the
most-often asked questions in 12 articles by industry professionals. 400 listings
are organized into literary agents, script agents and art/photo reps. Save 15% on
this new directory when you use the attached order form. 240 pages/$15.95
$13.55/hardcover

Writing for Children & Teenagers
Filled with practical know-how and step-by-step instruction, including how to
hold a young reader's attention, where to find ideas, and vocabulary lists based
on age level, this third edition provides all the tips you need to flourish in today's
children's literature market.
265 pages/$12.95, paperback

The Children's Picture Book: How to Write It, How to Sell It
If you'd like to try your hand at writing children's picture books, this guide is for
you. It answers virtually every question about the writing and selling process:
how to choose a subject, plot a story, work with artists and editors, and market
your book. Includes advice from professional picture book writers and editors,
plus a list of agents who handle picture books.
189 pages/$19.95, paperback

How to Write & Illustrate Children's Books
A truly comprehensive guide that demonstrates how to bring freshness and
vitality to children's text and pictures. Numerous illustrators, writers, and
editors contribute their expert advice.
143 pages/$22.50

Use coupon on other side to order today!

than three.) Awards include cash prizes in fiction and nonfiction categories. Contest open to non-members.

*TEXAS WRITERS ASSOCIATION, Suite #3, 219 Preston Royal Shopping Center, Dallas TX 75230-3832. (214)363-9979. Executive Director: Jheri Fleet. Purpose of organization: "to promote and encourage all disciplines of writing, writers, literature and literacy in Texas; to help writers become aware of what is possible and to help them sieze the moment." Qualification for membership: interest in writing. Membership cost: $50, ages 21-60; $25, under 21, over 60, second family member. Different levels of membership include: professional (criteria) and general. Workshops/conferences: Spring and Fall Workshop Series, April-May, September-November; National Magazine Editors Conference, April 1992; Texas Film Conference, fall 1992. Publishes a newsletter. The focus is on writing: markets, news, information, new releases, classes, workshops — conferences, fellowships, scholarships, contests. Non-member subscription: $30.

*TEXTBOOK AUTHORS ASSOCIATION, Box 535, Orange Springs FL 32182. (904)546-1000. Executive Director: Mike Keedy. Purpose of organization: to address the professional concerns of text authors. Qualifications for membership: all authors and prospective authors are welcome. Membership cost: $50. Workshops/conferences: being formulated. Newsletter focuses on all areas of interest to text authors.

*WESTERN WRITERS OF AMERICA, P.O. Box 823, Sheridan WY 82801. (307)672-0889. Secretary/Treasurer: Barb Ketcham. Purpose of organization: an organization of professional writers helping to preserve the spirit and reality of the West. Qualifications of membership: must be a published writer. Membership cost: $60/year. Different levels of membership include: Associate — must be published, 5 magazine articles or 1 book; active — must be published, 30 magazine articles or 3 books. Workshops/conferences: Annual convention is held the last full week of June. Publishes a newsletter that keeps the members in touch with each other. WWA sponsors the Owen Wister Award. Contest open to non-members. "We also publish *The Roundup Quarterly*; non-members can subscribe for $30 per year."

*WRITERS CONNECTION, Suite 180, 1601 Saratoga-Sunnyvale Rd., Cupertino CA 95014. (408)973-0227. Editor: Jan Stiles; Vice President/Program Director: Meera Lester. Purpose of organization: to provide services and resources for writers. "We publish three regional market guides for writers." Qualifications for membership: interest in writing or publishing. Membership cost: $40/year. Workshops/conferences: Selling to Hollywood, August; Get That Novel Started; Writing the Children's Picture Book. Publishes a newsletter focusing on writing and publishing (all fields except poetry), how-to, markets, contests, tips, etc. Non-member subscription: $18/year.

Workshops

Whether you're a professional with a desire to fine-tune your craft, or a novice yearning to build fundamental skills, there are workshops offered for children's writers and illustrators of all levels. Conferences are great places to pick up solid information on a variety of topics, including successful techniques in writing and illustrating and trends in children's publishing. Some workshops even touch on business issues of concern to freelancers, such as changes in tax and copyright laws.

Be aware that not every workshop included here directly relates to juvenile writing or illustrating, but information acquired can be utilized in creating material for children. Illustrators may be interested in general painting and drawing workshops. Though they are not listed in this book, a plethora of them are held each year. Artists can find a detailed directory of art workshops offered nationwide each year in the March issue of *The Artist's Magazine*.

Listings in this section will provide you with information describing what courses are offered, where and when, and the costs. Some of the national writing and art organizations also offer regional workshops throughout the year. Write for information.

*ANNUAL ARIZONA CHRISTIAN WRITERS CONFERENCE, P.O. Box 5168, Phoenix AZ 85010. (602)838-4919. Director: Reg Forder. Writer and illustrator workshops geared toward beginner, intermediate and advanced levels. Classes/courses offered include: fiction, nonfiction, poetry, photography, music, etc. Workshops held October 31, November 1-2. Length of each session: 70 minutes. Maximum class size: 30 (approx.). Cost of workshop: $109.

*ANTIOCH WRITERS' WORKSHOP, P.O. Box 494, Yellow Springs OH 45387. (513)767-9112. Co-Directors: Sandra Love and Susan Carpenter. Writer and illustrator workshops geared toward all levels. Emphasizes "basic poetry, fiction, nonfiction—with some emphasis on genre and on screenwriting; little on children's, but we have one or two informal sessions." Workshops held second week of July. Cost of workshop: $425; includes tuition. Room and board extra.

*THE ART & BUSINESS OF HUMOROUS ILLUSTRATION, Cartoon Art Museum, 665 3rd St., San Francisco CA 94107. (415)546-3922. Administrator: Barry Gantt. Writer and illustrator workshops geared toward professional levels. "Class focus is on cartooning, but we do cover some marketing topics about children's books." Workshops held fall and spring. Length of each session: 10 weeks. Maximum class size: 30. Cost of workshop: $145, includes art and writing instruction. Write for more information.

* *The asterisk before a listing indicates the listing is new in this edition.*

*BIOLA UNIVERSITY WRITERS INSTITUTE, 13800 Biola Ave., LaMirada CA 90639. 1 (800)75WORDS. Associate Director: Susan Titus. Writer and illustrator workshops geared toward beginner, intermediate and advanced levels. Emphasizes nonfiction books and articles; fiction (short and long); poetry; children's books; song writing. Classes/courses offered include: basic magazine article writing, advanced fiction techniques and sell what you write. Workshops held July 26-29, 1992; 6 week classes, video correspondence course and ms critique service are held all year. Length of each session: 1-2 hours. Cost of workshop: $280; includes tuition and meals. "We take anyone with a desire to write."

CAPE LITERARY WORKSHOPS, Cape Cod Writers Conference, Route 132, West Barnstable MA 02668. (508)775-4811. Executive Director: Marion Vuilleumier. Writer and illustrator workshops geared toward intermediate, advanced levels. Summer workshops offered in children's book writing and children's book illustration. Workshops held in July and early August. Conference held third week in August. Intensive workshops meet Monday-Friday from 9-1. Afternoons and evenings are used to do assignments and enjoy Cape Cod attractions. Class sizes limited. Cost of workshop: $395; includes registration and tuition. Materials, room and board extra. "It is not necessary to have works-in-progress but those who do will find these workshops especially helpful. Participants are encouraged to send current work in advance."
Tips: Send for brochure for more information on workshops and accommodations.

*THE CARTOONIST AT WORK, P.O. Box 64785-85740, Tucson AZ 85712. (602)325-4733. Director: Martha Gore. Writer and illustrator workshops geared toward beginner, intermediate, advanced and professional levels. "The workshop is geared toward cartoonists who are already syndicated or are working toward becoming syndicated. This will be given for the first time. The instructor will be a cartoonist who is already syndicated and has had work published in book form." Workshops to be announced. Length of each session: 6 hrs. Maximum class size: 20. "We have our own facilities, which will include a gallery for work done by our members." Cost of workshop: $100; includes all materials, a brown-bag lunch, all sessions. Send SASE for details. "Cartoonists with the proper credentials will be invited to submit a portfolio of their work to our literary agency for possible representation."

*CHILDREN'S BOOK PUBLISHING: A COMPREHENSIVE BOOK ILLUSTRATION WORKSHOP, Rice University, P.O. Box 1892, Houston TX 77251-1892. (713)527-4803. Contact: Workshop Coordinator. Illustrator workshops geared toward intermediate, advanced, professional levels. "This workshop is intended for persons with a background in art who wish to begin or advance their careers in children's book illustration. Award-winning illustrator Diane Stanley will take participants through the entire process of illustrating a book for children, using both lectures and hands-on work to guide them." Workshops held late July/early August. Length of each session: 9:00 a.m.-12:00 p.m.; 1:00-4:00 p.m. Workshops held on Rice University campus. Cost of workshop: $375. Fee does not include supplies; a supply list will be provided. Write for more information.

*CHILDREN'S BOOK PUBLISHING: AN INTENSIVE WRITING & EDITING WORKSHOP, Rice University, P.O. Box 1892, Houston TX 77251-1892. (713)527-4803. Contact: Workshop Coordinator. Writer workshops geared toward beginner, intermediate, advanced, professional levels. "Lectures and laboratories designed to help writers take their writing projects from the idea stage to the publishing market." Classes/courses offered include: Picture books from the writer's point of view; Writing nonfiction books; Plotting—from idea to end. Workshops held in late July/early August. Length of each session: Morning lectures: 9:00 a.m.-11:45 a.m.; Afternoon laboratories: 1:00-4:15 p.m. Workshops held on Rice University campus. "Submission of a ms is optional, but must be submitted according to guidelines." Write for more information.

CHILDREN'S LITERATURE CONFERENCE, Hofstra University, U.C.C.E., 205 Davison Hall, Hempstead NY 11550. (516)463-5997. Writers/Illustrators Contact: Lewis Shena, director, Liberal Arts Studies. Writer and illustrator workshops geared toward beginner, intermediate, advanced, professional levels. Emphasizes: fiction, nonfiction, poetry, submission procedures, picture books. Workshops held April 11, 1992, Saturday, 9:30 a.m.-4:30 p.m. Length of each session: 2 hours. Maximum class size: 35. Cost of workshop: $50; includes 2 workshops, reception, lunch, panel discussions with guest speakers, e.g. "What An Editor Looks For." Write for more information. Co-sponsored by Society of Children's Book Writers.

DRURY COLLEGE/SCBW WRITING FOR CHILDREN WORKSHOP, Drury College, Springfield MO 65802. (417)865-8731. Assistant Director, Continuing Education: Lynn Doke. Writer and illustrator workshop geared toward beginner, intermediate, advanced, professional levels. Emphasizes all aspects of writing for children and teenagers. Classes/courses offered include: "Between Author and Editor: One Editor's View," "Marketing Yourself," "An Editor Works with Illustrators," "No Place for Cowards: Writing Tough Scenes," "Picture Books, or How to Write for Little Bitty Short People," Digging Up the Bones: Researching the Nonfiction Book," "Children's Interests: What's In It for Me? and Who's In It for You?" and "Skywalking: Poetry that Kids Love." One-day workshop held in November. Length of each session: 1 hour. Manuscript and portfolio consultations (by appointment only). Maximum class size: 25-30. $45 registration fee; individual consultations $25. Send SASE for more information.

*EDUCATION WRITERS ASSOCIATION NATIONAL SEMINAR, 1001 Connecticut Ave. NW, Washington DC 20036. (202)429-9680. Administrative Assistant: Kristina Blakey. Writer workshops geared toward beginner, intermediate, advanced and professional levels. Emphasizes topics in education, education writing, investigative reporting in education, narrative writing. Workshops held April 2-5, 1992 (annual meeting); regional conferences. Length of each session: 4 days/1 day. Cost of workshop: $195 for annual meeting; includes 4 day—¾ lunches; 1 dinner; continental breakfast. Write for more information.

*FLORIDA STATE WRITERS CONFERENCE, P.O. Box 9844, Ft. Lauderdale FL 33310. (305)485-0795. Executive Director: Dana K. Cassell. Writer workshops geared toward beginner, intermediate, advanced and professional levels. Emphasizes juvenile, novels, books, articles, business management and legal writing. Workshops held 3rd weekend in May. Length of each session: 1 hour. Maximum class size: varies according to topic. Accomodations are typical hotel facilities. Cost of workshop: varies (single-day through complete packages). Write for more information.

*FLORIDA SUNCOAST WRITERS' CONFERENCE, Dept. of English, Univ. of South Florida, Tampa FL 33620. (813)974-2421. Director: Ed Hirshberg. Writer and illustrator workshops geared toward intermediate, advanced, professional levels. Workshops held last weekend in January. 30-100 class sizes. Cost of workshop: $95; $75 students; includes all sessions, receptions, panels. Conference is held on St. Petersburg campus of U.S.F.

*GREEN LAKE CHRISTIAN WRITERS CONFERENCE, American Baptist Assembly, Green Lake WI 54941-9300. (800)558-8898. Vice President of Program: Dr. Arlo R. Reichter. Writer workshops geared toward beginner, intermediate and advanced levels. Emphasizes poetry, nonfiction, writing for children, book length manuscripts. Classes/courses offered include: same as above plus one-session or two-session presentations on marketing, church school curriculum writing, devotional writing and retelling Bible stories. Workshops held July 11-18, 1992; July 10-17, 1993. Length of each session: Saturday dinner through the following Saturday breakfast. Maximum class size: 20. Writing and/or art facilities available: housing, conference rooms, etc. "No special equipment for writing." Cost of workshop: $80; includes all instruction plus room and meals as selected. Write for more information. "The conference focuses on helping writers to refine their writing skills in a caring atmosphere utilizing competent, caring faculty. This annual conference has been held every year since 1948."

HIGHLIGHTS FOUNDATION WRITERS WORKSHOP AT CHAUTAUQUA, 711 Court St., Honesdale PA 18431. (717)253-1192. Conference Director: Jan Keen. Writer workshops geared toward beginner, intermediate and advanced levels. Classes/courses offered include: "Children's Interests," "Writing Dialogue," "Beginnings and Endings," "Rights, Contracts, Copyrights," "Science Writing." Workshops held in July 18-25, 1991, Chautauqua Institution, Chautauqua, NY. Maximum class size: 100. Write for more information.

MARITIME WRITERS' WORKSHOP, Dept. Extension & Summer School, P.O. Box 4400, University of New Brunswick, Fredericton, New Brunswick E3B 5A3 Canada. (506)453-4646. Week-long workshop geared to all levels and held in July. Length of each session: 3 hours per day. Group workshop plus individual conferences, public readings, etc. Maximum class size: 10-12. Cost of workshop: $220 tuition. Meals and accomodations extra. 10-20 ms pages due before conference (deadline announced). Scholarships available.

*MIDLAND WRITERS CONFERENCE, Grace A. Dow Memorial Library, 1710 W. St. Andrews, Midland MI 48640. (517)835-7151. Conference Co-chairs: Margaret Allen or Eileen M. Finzel. Writer and illustrator workshops geared toward beginner, intermediate, advanced and professional levels. "We always have one session each on children's, poetry and basics." Classes/courses offered include: romance writing, how to write poetry, writing for the wonder age (youth), your literary agent/what to expect, choosing a powerful setting and writing popular fiction. Workshops held June 13, 1992. Length of each session: concurrently, four one-hour and two-hour sessions. Maximum class size: 40. "We are a public library." Cost of workshop: $45; $35 seniors and students. Choice of workshops and the keynote speech given by a prominent author (last year Andrew Greeley). Write for more information.

*MOUNT HERMON CHRISTIAN WRITERS CONFERENCE, Mount Hermon Christian Conference Center, P.O. Box 413, Mount Hermon CA 95041. (408)335-4466. Director of Public Affairs: David R. Talbott. Writer workshops geared toward beginner, intermediate, advanced and professional levels. Emphasizes religious writing for children via books, articles; Sunday school curriculum; marketing. Classes/courses offered include: Suitable Style for Children; Everything You Need to Know to Write and Market Your Children's Book; Take-Home Papers for children. Workshops held annually over Palm Sunday weekend: in 1992 the dates are April 10-14, 1992. Length of each session: 5-day residential conferences held annually. Maximum class size: 45, but most are 10-15. Conference center with hotel-style accommodations. Cost of workshop: $425-525 variable; includes tuition, resource notebook, refreshment breaks, full room and board for 13 meals and 4 nights. Write for more information.

*MYSTERY WRITERS OF AMERICA, Midwest Chapter, Box 8, Techny IL 60082. (708)729-4538. Director: Betty Nicholas. "We have a broad spectrum of sessions and the level of the registrants varies from beginners to regularly selling professionals." Deals with techniques for writing mystery fiction. Faculty includes professional mystery writers as well as representatives of law enforcement and related fields whose expertise can be helpful to mystery writers. One-day workshop held in June, Northwestern University, Evanston IL. Maximum registration: 150. Cost of workshop: $60 for members, $70 for nonmembers; includes lunch. Write for specific information on the current year's program.

*OZARK CREATIVE WRITERS, INC. CONFERENCE, 6817 Gingerbread Ln., Little Rock AR 72204. (501)565-8889. President: Peggy Vining. Writer's workshops geared to all levels. "All forms of the creative process dealing with the literary arts. This year we have expanded to songwriting." Always the second weekend in October at Inn of the Ozarks in Eureka Springs, Arkansas (a resort town). Morning sessions are given to main attraction author . . . six one-hour satellite speakers during each of the two afternoons. Two banquets. "Approximately 125 to 150 attend the conference yearly . . . many others enter the creative writing competition." Cost of Workshop: $25-30. "This does not include meals or lodging. We do block off fifty rooms prior to September 1 for OCW guests." Write for contest rules for entering competition. "Reserve early."

*PORT TOWNSEND WRITER'S CONFERENCE, Centrum, Box 1158, Port Townsend WA 98368. (206)385-3102. Director: Carol Jane Bangs. Writer workshops geared toward intermediate, advanced and professional levels. Emphasizes writing for children and young adults. Classes/courses offered include: Jane Yolen master class; intermediate/advanced writing for children. Workshops held mid-July. Length of each session: 10 days. Maximum class size: 20. Writing facilities available: classrooms. Cost of workshop: $300 (approx.); includes tuition. Publication list for master class. Write for more information. $50 deposit necessary. Applications accepted after December 1 for following July; workshops fill by February.

ROBERT QUACKENBUSH'S CHILDREN'S BOOK WRITING AND ILLUSTRATING WORKSHOP, 460 East 79th St., New York NY 10021. (212)744-3822. Contact: Robert Quackenbush. Writer and illustrator workshops geared toward beginner, intermediate, advanced, professional levels. Emphasizes picture books from start to finish. Classes/courses offered include: fall and winter courses, extend 10 weeks each — 1½ hour/week; July workshop is a full five day (9 a.m.-4 p.m.) extensive course. Workshops held fall, winter and summer. Maximum class size: 8. Writing and/or art facilities available: work on the premises; art supply store nearby. Cost of workshop: $500 for instruction. Write for more information.

*RUTGERS UNIVERSITY ONE-ON-ONE PLUS, Professional Development Studies, Rutgers School of Communication Information and Library Studies, 4 Huntington St., New Brunswick NJ 08903. (908)932-7169. Director, Professional Development: Jana Varlejs. Writer and illustrator workshops geared toward beginner, intermediate and professional levels. "Writers/illustrators with work in progress are paired with published authors/illustrators, editors, etc. to discuss their work." Classes/courses offered include: submitting book ideas, tips on dummying picture books, how a publisher markets your book. Workshops held annually, usually in October. Length of each session: 1 day. Maximum class size: 50. Cost of workshop: $45; includes registration, lunch, refreshments. Submit application and sample of work. Write for more information.

*SAN DIEGO STATE UNIVERSITY WRITERS' CONFERENCE, The College of Extended Studies, San Diego CA 92182. (619)594-5152. Extension Director: Jan Wahl. Writer workshops geared toward beginner, intermediate and advanced levels. Emphasizes nonfiction, fiction, screenwriting, advanced novel writing. Classes/courses offered include: Learning to Think Like an Editor, Writing for Television and Motion Pictures, Writing Children's Nonfiction and Picture Books. Workshops held 3rd weekend in January each year. Length of each session: 50 minutes. Maximum class size: 100. Cost of workshop:

1991 fees were $177; included Saturday reception, 2 lunches and all sessions. Write for more information.

*SCBW NEW ENGLAND CONFERENCE, location varies from year to year. For information, contact Jane H. Mruczek, Regional Advisor. (203)563-7794. Writer/illustrator workshops geared toward all levels. Emphasizes writing and illustrating for the children's market. One-day workshop usually held in the Spring includes keynote speakers and many workshops. Length of each session: 8-5 p.m. Conference limit: 250. "Specific cost yet to be determined; usually includes all-day conference, lunch. Conference is open to both published and unpublished writers and illustrators of children's books (and magazines) and anyone else interested in those aspects of children's books."

*SEATTLE PACIFIC CHRISTIAN WRITERS CONFERENCE, Humanities Dept., Seattle Pacific University, Seattle WA 98119. (206)281-2109. Director: Linda Wagner. Writer workshops geared toward beginner, intermediate, advanced levels. Emphasizes "excellence in writing for the religious market. Stress on the craft of writing." Workshops held last week of June. Length of each session varies. Maximum class size: "varies—usually not more than 40." Cost of workshop: $175.

SEMINARS FOR WRITERS, % Writers Connection, Ste. 180, 1601 Saratoga-Sunnyvale Rd., Cupertino CA 95014. (408)973-0227. FAX: (408)973-1219. Program Director: Meera Lester. Writer's workshops geared toward beginner, intermediate levels. Length of each session: six-hour session usually offered on a Saturday. Maximum class size: 35-40. Occasional seminars on writing for children (approximately 2-3 per year). Bookstore of writing, reference and how-to books. Monthly newsletter by subscription. Write for more information.

*SOCIETY OF CHILDREN'S BOOK WRITERS—FLORIDA REGION, 2000 Springdale Blvd., Apt. F-103, Palm Springs FL 33461. (407)433-1727. Florida Regional Advisor: Jean Shirley. Writer and illustrator workshops geared toward beginner, intermediate, advanced and professional levels. Subjects for 1992 to be announced. Workshop held in the meeting rooms of the Palm Springs Public Library, 217 Cypress Lane, Palm Springs FL. Maximum class size: 100. Cost of workshop: $30 for members, $35 for nonmembers. Write for more information. "We plan to give one conference a year to be held on the second Saturday in September."

SOUTHERN CALIFORNIA SOCIETY OF CHILDREN'S BOOK WRITERS ILLUSTRATORS DAY, 11943 Montana Ave. #105, Los Angeles CA 90049. (213)820-5601, 457-3501. Regional Advisor: Judith Enderle. Illustrator workshops geared toward beginner, intermediate, advanced, professional levels. Emphasizes illustration and illustration markets. Conference includes: presentations by art director, children's book editor, and panel of artists/author-illustrators. Workshops held annually in November. Length of session: full day. Maximum class size: 100. "Editors and art directors will view portfolios. We want to know if each conferee is bringing a portfolio or not." Cost of 1990 workshop: $60 members, $65 students, $70 nonmembers; bring your lunch, handouts included. SCBW Membership: $40/yr.
Tips: "This is a chance for illustrators to meet editors/art directors and each other. Writers Day held in February. National conference for authors *and* illustrators held every August."

SPLIT ROCK ARTS PROGRAM, University of Minnesota, 306 Wesbrook Hall, 77 Pleasant St. SE, Minneapolis MN 55455. (612)624-6800. Registrar: Vivien Oja. Writer and illustrator workshops geared toward intermediate, advanced, professional levels.

Workshops offered in writing and illustrating books for children and young people. 1992 workshops begin July 5. Length of each session: One week intensive, Sunday night to Saturday noon. 2 college credits available. Maximum class size: 16. Workshops held on the University of Minnesota-Duluth campus. Cost of workshop: $270-300; includes tuition and fees. Amounts vary depending on course fee, determined by supply needs, etc. "Moderately priced on-campus housing available."
Tips: Complete catalogs available March 15. Call or write anytime to be put on mailing list. Some courses fill very early.

SUMMER WRITERS CONFERENCE, Hofstra U - U.C.C.E. - Davison 205, Hempstead NY 11550. (516)463-5997. Writers/Illustrators Contact: Lewis Shena, director, Liberal Arts Studies. Writer workshops geared toward beginner, intermediate, advanced, professional levels. Emphasizes fiction, nonfiction, poetry, children's literature, stage/ screen. Classes/courses offered: "Besides workshops, we arrange a series of readings and discussions." Workshops held Monday-Friday—2 weeks—July 6-17, 1992. Length of each session: daily, approximately 2½ hours of workshop plus once only 1-2 hours of one-on-one meeting time with instructor. Maximum class size: 20. Writing/art facilities available: lecture room, tables, any media required will be obtained. Cost of workshop: noncredit, approximately $525; includes 2 workshops per day—special readings—special speakers. Credit and dorm rooms available at additional cost. Write for more information.

*MARK TWAIN WRITERS CONFERENCE, 921 Center St., Hannibal MO 63401. (314)221-2462. Director: James C. Hefley. Writer workshops geared toward beginner, intermediate and advanced levels. Emphasizes fiction, nonfiction, photography. Workshops covering poetry, humor, Mark Twain, newspapers, freelancing, the autobiography and working with an agent. Workshops held June 15-19, 1991. Always in June. Length of each session: 50-90 minutes. Maximum class size: 12-20. Writing facilities available: computers. Cost of workshop: $325; includes all program fees, room, meals and group photo. Write for more information.

*UNIVERSITY OF KENTUCKY WOMEN WRITERS CONFERENCE, 106 Frazee Hall, University of Kentucky, Lexington KY 40506-0031. (606)257-3295. Conference Director: Betty Gabehart. Writer workshops geared toward beginner, intermediate, advanced, professional levels. Classes/courses offered include: annual ms workshops for poets, playwrights, children's writers, short fiction writers. Workshops held October 28-31, 1992. Length of session: 3 hours. Cost of workshop: $10/day + $10-15/day conference registration. Submit ms by deadline, 3 months before conference. 20 pages maximum; 4 poems maximum/6 pages; essays/10 pages maximum. "Write to obtain brochure, available mid-August, 1992, outlining daily events, visiting writers bio info, registration costs/ procedures."

VASSAR INSTITUTE OF PUBLISHING AND WRITING: CHILDREN'S BOOKS IN THE MARKETPLACE, Box 300, Vassar College, Poughkeepsie NY 12601. (914)437-5900. Program Coordinator: Maryann Bruno. Director: Barbara Lucas. Writer and illustrator workshops geared toward beginner, intermediate, advanced, professional levels. Emphasizes "the editorial, production, marketing and reviewing processes, on writing fiction and nonfiction for all ages, creating the picture book, understanding the markets and selling your work." Classes/courses offered include: "Writing Fiction," "The Editorial Process," "How to Write a Children's Book and Get It Published." Workshop in 1991, June 16-23. Length of each session: 3½-hour morning critique sessions, afternoon and evening lectures. Maximum class size: 55 (with three instructors). Cost of workshop: approximately $675, includes room, board and tuition for all critique sessions, lectures, and social activities. "Proposals are pre-prepared and discussed at morning critique sessions. Art portfolio review given on pre-prepared works." Write for more information.

Tips: "This conference gives a comprehensive look at the publishing industry as well as offering critiques of creative writing and portfolio review."

*WESLEYAN WRITERS CONFERENCE, Wesleyan University, Middletown CT 06459. (203)347-9411, ext. 2448. Director: Anne Greene. Writer workshops geared toward beginner, intermediate, advanced and professional levels. "This conference is useful for writers interested in how to structure a story, poem, or nonfiction piece. Although we don't always offer classes in writing for children, the advice about structuring a piece is useful for writers of any sort, no matter who their audience is." Classes in the novel, short story, fiction techniques, poetry, journalism, and literary nonfiction. Guest speakers and panels offer discussion of fiction, poetry, reviewing, editing and publishing. Individual manuscript consultations available. Workshops held annually the last week in June. Length of each session: 6 days. "Usually, there are 100 participants at the Conference." Classrooms, meals, lodging and word processing facilities available on campus. Cost of workshop (in '91): tuition—$415, room—$85, meals (required of all participants)—$165. "Anyone may register; people who want financial aid must submit their work and be selected by scholarship judges." Write for more information.

*WESTERN RESERVE WRITERS AND FREELANCE CONFERENCE, Lakeland Community College, Clocktower Dr., Mentor OH 44060. (216)943-3047. Coordinator: Lea Leever Oldham. Writer workshops geared toward beginner, intermediate, advanced, professional levels. Emphasizes fiction, photography, greeting card writing, science fiction and fantasy writing, poetry. Classes/courses offered include: Writing For Children in Whole Language & Curriculum. Workshops held in mid-September. Length of each session: 7 hrs. Cost of workshop: $39; includes sessions and lunch. Write for more information at above address or at 34200 Ridge Road #110, Willoughby OH 44094.

WILLAMETTE WRITERS ANNUAL WRITERS CONFERENCE, 9045 SW Barbur Blvd, Suite 5A, Portland OR 97219. (503)452-1542. Conference Chair: Linda Stirling Wanner. Writer workshops geared toward beginner, intermediate, advanced, professional levels. Emphasizes all areas of writing. Classes/courses offered include: romance writing; A-B-C's of writing; basic techniques; desk top publishing; how to research—step by step process; science fiction panel, dialogue, etc. Opportunities to meet one-on-one with leading literary agents and editors. Workshops held second week of August 1992. Length of each session: 1½ hours. Write for more information.

*WRITE TO SELL WRITER'S CONFERENCE, 8465 Jane St., San Diego CA 92129. (619)484-8575. Conference Director: Diane Dunaway. Writer and illustrator workshops geared toward beginner, intermediate, advanced, professional levels. Emphasizes How-to, Trends, Read and Critique; Workshops led by writers, editors and agents. Classes/courses offered include: Writing the Picture Book, Middle Grade, YA; Illustrating for Children's Books. Workshops held 2nd weekend in May. Length of each session: 50 minutes. Maximum class size: 100. Conference is held at the Irvine Marriott; workshops are held in individual classrooms. Cost of workshop: $195. Cost of conference for Friday evening through Sunday and two lunches. "Just bring chapters and/or artwork." Write for more information.

Market conditions are constantly changing! If you're still using this book and it is 1993 or later, buy the newest edition of Children's Writer's & Illustrator's Market *at your favorite bookstore or order directly from Writer's Digest Books.*

*WRITERS STUDIO SPRING WRITERS CONFERENCE, 3403 45th St., Moline IL 61265. (309)762-8985. Coordinator, Pro Tem: David R. Collins. Writer workshops geared toward intermediate level. Illustrator workshops geared toward beginner level. Emphasizes basic writing and mechanics. Classes/courses offered include: writing for children, romance writing, poetry, writing for sports and regional magazines, marketing, young adult writing. Workshops held April 11, 1992. Length of each session: 1 hour. Maximum class size: 20. Workshop is free. Write for more information.

WRITING FOR YOUNG PEOPLE, 1908 S. Goliad, Amarillo TX 79106. (806)353-4925 or 358-3717. Writer and illustrator workshops geared toward beginner, intermediate levels. Emphasizes "varying aspects of writing for the children's market, especially technique and marketing." Workshops held in October. Length of each session: one-day conference or workshop (8:30-4:00). Cost of workshop: approx. $45.
Tips: Location—Region XVI Education Service Center, Amarillo, TX. "Our event is a one-day conference with 3-4 speakers experienced in some facet of the children's market (authors, editors, librarians, booksellers, illustrators). Ms evaluations offered for additional fee." Sponsored by Society of Children's Book Writers, West Texas Chapter.

*WRITING MULTICULTURAL BOOKS FOR CHILDREN AND YOUNG ADULTS, The Authors Resource Center & The Artists Resource Center, P.O. Box 64785, Tucson AZ 85740. Director: Martha Gore. Writer workshops geared toward beginner, intermediate, advanced, professional levels. Illustrator workshops geared toward professional levels. Emphasizes children's and YA books for all multicultural children and YA. "Dates to be announced." Length of each session: 3 hrs., plus meeting time with published authors. Maximum class size: 20. Bookstore setting. Cost of workshop: $50, plus materials. No requirements prior to registration. Send SASE for details. "This is an opportunity for writers and illustrators to learn about the fastest growing segment of the children's market. Participants will be invited to submit their work for possible representation by the TARC Literary Agency."

Glossary

Advance. A sum of money that a publisher pays a writer prior to the publication of a book. It is usually paid in installments, such as one-half on signing the contract; one half on delivery of a complete and satisfactory manuscript. The advance is paid against the royalty money that will be earned by the book.

AIMP. Association of Independent Music Publishers.

All rights. The rights contracted to a publisher permitting a manuscript's use anywhere and in any form, including movie and book-club sales, without additional payment to the writer.

Anthropomorphization. To attribute human form and personality to things not human (such as animals).

ASAP. Abbreviation for as soon as possible.

ASCAP. American Society of Composers, Authors and Publishers. A performing rights organization.

B&W. Abbreviation for black and white artwork or photographs.

Backlist. A publisher's list of books not published during the current season but still in print.

Biennially. Once every two years.

Bimonthly. Once every two months.

Biweekly. Once every two weeks.

Bleed. Area of a plate or print that extends beyond the actual trimmed sheet to be printed.

BMI. Broadcast Music, Inc. A performing rights organization.

Book packager. Draws all elements of a book together, from the initial concept to writing and marketing strategies, then sells the book package to a book publisher and/or movie producer. Also known as book producer or book developer.

Business-size envelope. Also known as a #10 envelope, it is the standard size used in sending business correspondence.

Camera-ready. Art that is completely prepared for copy camera platemaking.

Caption. A description of the subject matter of an illustration or photograph; photo captions include names of people where appropriate. Also called cutline.

Clean-copy. A manuscript free of errors and needing no editing; it is ready for typesetting.

Contract. A written agreement stating the rights to be purchased by an editor or art director and the amount of payment the writer or illustrator will receive for that sale.

Contributor's copies. Copies of the issues of magazines sent to the author or illustrator in which his/her work appears.

Copy. Refers to the actual written material of a manuscript.

Copyediting. Editing a manuscript for grammar usage, spelling, punctuation, and general style.

Copyright. A means to legally protect an author's/illustrator's work. This can be shown by writing ©, your name, and year of work's creation.

Cover letter. A brief letter, accompanying a complete manuscript, especially useful if responding to an editor's request for a manuscript. A cover letter may also accompany a book proposal. A cover letter is not a query letter.

Cutline. See caption.

Disk. A round, flat magnetic plate on which computer data is stored.

Division. An unincorporated branch of a company.

Dot-matrix. Printed type in which individual characters are composed of a matrix or pattern of tiny dots.

Dummy. Hand-made mock-up of a book.

Final draft. The last version of a "polished" manuscript ready for submission to the editor.

First North American serial rights. The right to publish material in a periodical before it appears in book form, for the first time, in the United States or Canada.

Flat fee. A one-time payment.

GAG. Graphic Artists Guild.

Galleys. The first typeset version of a manuscript that has not yet been divided into pages.

Gatefold. A page larger than the trim size of a book which is folded so as not to extend beyond the edges.

Genre. A formulaic type of fiction, such as adventure, mystery, romance, science fiction or western.

Glossy. A black and white photograph with a shiny surface as opposed to one with a non-shiny matte finish.

Gouache. Opaque watercolor with an appreciable film thickness and an actual paint layer.

Halftone. Reproduction of a continuous tone illustration with the image formed by dots produced by a camera lens screen.

Hard copy. The printed copy of a computer's output.

ILAA. Independent Literary Agents Association, Inc.

Illustrations. May be artwork, photographs, old engravings. Usually paid for separately from the manuscript.

Imprint. Name applied to a publisher's specific line or lines of books.

IRC. International Reply Coupon; purchased at the post office to enclose with text or artwork sent to a foreign buyer to cover his postage cost when replying or returning work.

Keyline. Identification, through signs and symbols, of the positions of illustrations and copy for the printer.

Kill fee. Portion of the agreed-upon price the author or artist receives for a job that was assigned, worked on, but then canceled.

Layout. Arrangement of illustrations, photographs, text and headlines for printed material.

Letter-quality submission. Computer printout that looks like a typewritten manuscript.

Line drawing. Illustration done with pencil or ink using no wash or other shading.

LORT. League of Resident Theaters.

Mechanicals. Paste-up or preparation of work for printing.

Middle reader. The general classification of books written for readers 9-11 years of age.

Modem. A small electrical box that plugs into the serial card of a computer, used to transmit data from one computer to another, usually via telephone lines.

Ms, mss. Abbreviation for manuscript(s).

One-time rights. Permission to publish a story in periodical or book form one time only.

Outline. A summary of a book's contents in 5-15 double spaced pages; often in the form of chapter headings with a descriptive sentence or two under each one to show the scope of the book.

Package sale. The editor buys manuscript and illustrations/photos as a "package" and pays for them with one check.

Payment on acceptance. The writer or artist is paid for his work at the time the editor or art director decides to buy it.

Payment on publication. The writer or artist is paid for his work when it is published.

Photocopied submissions. Submitting photocopies of an original manuscript instead of sending the original. Do not assume that an editor who accepts photocopies will also accept multiple or simultaneous submissions.

Photostat. Black-and-white copies produced by an inexpensive photographic process using paper negatives; only line values are held with accuracy. Also called stat.

Picture book. A type of book aimed at the preschool to 8-year-old that tells the story primarily or entirely with artwork.

PMT. Photostat produced without a negative, somewhat like the Polaroid process.

Print. An impression pulled from an original plate, stone, block, screen or negative; also a positive made from a photographic negative.

Proofreading. Reading a manuscript to correct typographical errors.

Query. A letter to an editor designed to capture his/her interest in an article you purpose to write.

Reading fee. An arbitrary amount of money charged by some agents and publishers to read a submitted manuscript.

Reporting time. The time it takes for an editor to report to the author on his/her query or manuscript.

Reprint rights. Permission to print an already published work whose rights have been sold to another magazine or book publisher.

Response time. The average length of time it takes an editor or art director to accept or reject a manuscript or artwork and inform you of the decision.

Rights. What you offer to an editor or art director in exchange for printing your manuscripts or artwork.

Rough draft. A manuscript which has been written but not checked for errors in grammar, punctuation, spelling or content. It usually needs revision and rewriting.

Roughs. Preliminary sketches or drawings.

Royalty. An agreed percentage paid by the publisher to the writer or illustrator for each copy of his work sold.

SAR. Society of Author's Representatives.

SASE. Abbreviation for self-addressed, stamped envelope.

SCBW. Society of Children's Book Writers.

Second serial rights. Permission for the reprinting of a work in another periodical after its first publication in book or magazine form.

Semiannual. Once every six months.

Semimonthly. Twice a month.

Semiweekly. Twice a week.

Serial rights. The rights given by an author to a publisher to print a piece in one or more periodicals.

Simultaneous submissions. Sending the same article, story, poem or illustration to several publishers at the same time. Some publishers refuse to consider such submissions. No simultaneous submissions should be made without stating the fact in your letter.

Slant. The approach to a story or piece of artwork that will appeal to readers of a particular publication.

Slush pile. What editors call the collection of submitted manuscripts which have not been specifically asked for.

Software. Programs and related documentation for use with a particular computer system.

Solicited manuscript. Material which an editor has asked for or agreed to consider before being sent by the writer.

SPAR. Society of Photographers and Artists Representatives, Inc.

Speculation (Spec). Writing or drawing a piece with no assurance from the editor or art director that it will be purchased or any reimbursements for material or labor paid.

Subsidiary rights. All rights other than book publishing rights included in a book contract, such as paperback, book club and movie rights.

Subsidy publisher. A book publisher who charges the author for the cost of typesetting, printing and promoting a book. Also vanity publisher.

Synopsis. A brief summary of a story or novel. If part of a book proposal, it should be a page to a page and a half, single-spaced.

Tabloid. Publication printed on an ordinary newspaper page turned sideways.

Tear sheet. Page from a magazine or newspaper containing your printed story, article, poem or ad.

Thumbnail. A rough layout in miniature.

Transparencies. Positive color slides; not color prints.

Unsolicited manuscript. A story, article, poem, book or artwork sent without the editor's or art director's knowledge or consent.

Vanity publisher. See subsidy publisher.

Word length. The maximum number of words a manuscript should contain as determined by the editor or guidelines sheet.

Word processor. A computer that produces typewritten copy via automated typing, text-editing, and storage and transmission capabilities.

Young adult. The general classification of books written for readers ages 12-18.

Young reader. The general classification of books written for readers 5-8 years old. Here artwork supports the text as opposed to picture books.

Age-Level Index
Book Publishers

The age-level index is set up to help you more quickly locate book markets geared to the age group(s) for which you write or illustrate. Read each listing carefully and follow the publisher's specific information about the type(s) of manuscript(s) each prefers to read and the style(s) of artwork each wishes to review

Picture books (preschool-8-year-olds)

Advocacy Press
Aegina Press/University Editions
African American Images
Aladdin Books/Collier Books for Young Readers
Alyson Publications, Inc.
American Bible Society
Arcade Publishing
Atheneum Publishers
Author's Connection Press, The
Barrons Educational Series
Beacon Press
Boyds Mills Press
Bradbury Press
Bright Ring Publishing
Candlewick Press
Capstone Press Inc.
Carolina Wren Press/Lollipop Power Books
Carolrhoda Books, Inc.
Cascade Pass Inc.
Chariot Books
Charlesbridge
Child Graphics Press
China Books
Chronicle Books
Clarion Books
Clyde Press
Cobblehill Books
Concordia Publishing House
Coteau Books Ltd.
Council for Indian Education
Crocodile Books, USA
Crown Publishers (Crown Books for Children)
Davenport, Publishers, May
Davis Publications, Inc.

Dawn Publications
Delacorte Press and Doubleday Books for Young Readers
Denison Co. Inc., T.S.
Dial Books for Young Readers
Discovery Enterprises, Ltd.
Distinctive Publishing Corp.
Dutton Children's Books
Eerdmans Publishing Company, Wm. B.
Esoterica Press
Farrar, Straus & Giroux
Four Winds Press
Free Spirit Publishing
Golden Books
Gospel Light Publications
Greenwillow Books
Grosset & Dunlap
Harbinger House, Inc.
Harcourt Brace Jovanovich
HarperCollins Children's Books
Harvest House Publishers
Hendrick-Long Publishing Company
Holiday House Inc.
Holt & Co., Inc., Henry
Homestead Publishing
Houghton Mifflin Co.
Humanics Limited
Hyperion Books for Children
Ideals Publishing Corporation
Jalmar Press
Jewish Publication Society
Jones University Press/Light Line Books, Bob
Jordan Enterprises Pub. Co., Inc.
Joy Street Books
Just Us Books, Inc.
Kar-Ben Copies, Inc.
Kendall Green Publications
Kingsway Publications

Knopf Books for Young Readers
Kruza Kaleidoscopix, Inc.
Lee & Low Books, Inc.
Lester Publishing Limited
Lion Books, Publisher
Lion Publishing Corporation
Little, Brown and Company
Lodestar Books
Lothrop, Lee & Shepard Books
McElderry Books, Margaret K.
Macmillan Children's Books
Mage Publishers Inc.
Magination Press
March Media, Inc.
Metamorphous Press
Midmarch Arts Press
Morehouse Publishing Co.
Morris Publishing, Joshua
Muir Publications, Inc, John
NAR Publications
North Light Books
Oddo Publishing, Inc.
Open Hand Publishing Inc.
Orchard Books
Our Child Press
Owen Publishers, Richard
Pacific Press
Parenting Press, Inc.
Paulist Press
Pelican Publishing Co. Inc.
Perspectives Press
Philomel Books
Pippin Press
Potter Inc., Clarkson N.
Preservation Press, The
Price Stern Sloan
Prometheus Books
Quarry Press
Random House Books for Young
    Readers
Read'n Run Books
Rosebrier Publishing Co.
St. Paul Books and Media
Scholastic Hardcover
Scholastic, Inc.
Scribner's Sons, Charles
Speech Bin, Inc., The
Standard Publishing
Star Books, Inc.
Stemmer House Publishers, Inc.
Sunburst Books
TAB Books
Tambourine Books
Troll Associates

Trophy Books
Troubador Books
Tundra Books of Northern New York
Tyndale House Publishers
Victor Books
Volcano Press
W.W. Publications
Walker and Co.
Waterfront Books
Waterston Productions, Inc.
Whitman & Company, Albert
Williamson Publishing Co.
Winston-Derek Publishers, Inc.
Women's Press
Woodbine House

Young readers (5-8-year-olds)

Advocacy Press
Aegina Press/University Editions
African American Images
Aladdin Books/Collier Books for
    Young Readers
American Bible Society
Arcade Publishing
Atheneum Publishers
Author's Connection Press, The
Barrons Educational Series
Beacon Press
Behrman House Inc.
Bluestocking Press
Bold Productions
Boyds Mills Press
Bradbury Press
Bright Ring Publishing
Candlewick Press
Capstone Press Inc.
Carolina Wren Press/Lollipop Power
    Books
Carolrhoda Books, Inc.
Cascade Pass Inc.
Chariot Books
Chicago Review Press
Child Graphics Press
China Books
Chronicle Books
Clarion Books
Clyde Press
Cobblehill Books
Colormore, Inc.
Concordia Publishing House
Council for Indian Education
Crossway Books

Crown Publishers (Crown Books for Children)
Davis Publications, Inc.
Dawn Publications
Delacorte Press and Doubleday Books for Young Readers
Denison Co. Inc., T.S.
Dial Books for Young Readers
Discovery Enterprises, Ltd.
Distinctive Publishing Corp.
Dutton Children's Books
Eerdmans Publishing Company, Wm. B.
Enslow Publishers Inc.
Esoterica Press
Farrar, Straus & Giroux
Free Spirit Publishing
Friendship Press, Inc.
Golden Books
Gospel Light Publications
Greenwillow Books
Grosset & Dunlap
Harbinger House, Inc.
Harcourt Brace Jovanovich
HarperCollins Children's Books
Harvest House Publishers
Hendrick-Long Publishing Company
Herald Press
Holiday House Inc.
Holt & Co., Inc., Henry
Homestead Publishing
Houghton Mifflin Co.
Humanics Limited
Hyperion Books for Children
Ideals Publishing Corporation
Incentive Publications, Inc.
Jalmar Press
Jewish Publication Society
Jones University Press/Light Line Books, Bob
Jordan Enterprises Pub. Co., Inc.
Joy Street Books
Just Us Books, Inc.
Kar-Ben Copies, Inc.
Kendall Green Publications
Kingsway Publications
Knopf Books for Young Readers
Kruza Kaleidoscopix, Inc.
Lee & Low Books, Inc.
Lerner Publications Co.
Lester Publishing Limited
Liguori Publications
Lion Publishing Corporation
Little, Brown and Company

Lodestar Books
Lothrop, Lee & Shepard Books
Lucas/Evans Books Inc.
McElderry Books, Margaret K.
Macmillan Children's Books
Magination Press
March Media, Inc.
Meadowbrook Press
Metamorphous Press
Midmarch Arts Press
Morehouse Publishing Co.
Morris Publishing, Joshua
Mosaic Press
NAR Publications
North Light Books
Oddo Publishing, Inc.
Open Hand Publishing Inc.
Orchard Books
Our Child Press
Owen Publishers, Richard
Pacific Press
Parenting Press, Inc.
Paulist Press
Perspectives Press
Philomel Books
Pippin Press
Players Press, Inc.
Potter Inc., Clarkson N.
Preservation Press, The
Price Stern Sloan
Prometheus Books
Random House Books for Young Readers
Read'n Run Books
Review and Herald Publishing Association
Rosebrier Publishing Co.
Rosen Publishing Group, The
St. Anthony Messenger Press
St. Paul Books and Media
Scholastic Hardcover
Scholastic, Inc.
Scribner's Sons, Charles
Shoe Tree Press
Speech Bin, Inc., The
Sri Rama Publishing
Standard Publishing
Star Books, Inc.
Stemmer House Publishers, Inc.
Stepping Stone Books
Sunburst Books
TAB Books
Tambourine Books
Troll Associates

Trophy Books
Troubador Books
Tundra Books of Northern New York
Tyndale House Publishers
Victor Books
Volcano Press
W.W. Publications
Walker and Co.
Waterfront Books
Waterston Productions, Inc.
Watts, Inc., Franklin
Weigl Educational Publishers
Whitman & Company, Albert
Williamson Publishing Co.
Winston-Derek Publishers, Inc.
Women's Press
Woodbine House

Middle readers (9-11-year-olds)

Addison-Wesley Publishing Co.
Aegina Press/University Editions
African American Images
Aladdin Books/Collier Books for
    Young Readers
American Bible Society
Arcade Publishing
Archway/Minstrel Books
Atheneum Publishers
Author's Connection Press, The
Avon Books
Barrons Educational Series
Beacon Press
Behrman House Inc.
Blue Heron Publishing, Inc.
Bluestocking Press
Bold Productions
Boyds Mills Press
Bradbury Press
Bright Ring Publishing
Candlewick Press
Capstone Press Inc.
Carolrhoda Books, Inc.
Cascade Pass Inc.
Chariot Books
Chicago Review Press
Child Graphics Press
China Books
Chronicle Books
Clarion Books
Clyde Press
Cobblehill Books
Concordia Publishing House
Council for Indian Education

Crossway Books
Crown Publishers (Crown Books for
    Children)
Davis Publications, Inc.
Dawn Publications
Delacorte Press and Doubleday
    Books for Young Readers
Denison Co. Inc., T.S.
Dial Books for Young Readers
Discovery Enterprises, Ltd.
Distinctive Publishing Corp.
Dutton Children's Books
Eerdmans Publishing Company, Wm.
    B.
Enslow Publishers Inc.
Farrar, Straus & Giroux
Fiesta City Publishers
Four Winds Press
Free Spirit Publishing
Friendship Press, Inc.
Golden Books
Gospel Light Publications
Greenhaven Press
Greenwillow Books
Grosset & Dunlap
Harcourt Brace Jovanovich
HarperCollins Children's Books
Harvest House Publishers
Haypenny Press
Hendrick-Long Publishing Company
Herald Press
Holiday House Inc.
Holt & Co., Inc., Henry
Homestead Publishing
Houghton Mifflin Co.
Hyperion Books for Children
Incentive Publications, Inc.
Jewish Publication Society
Jones University Press/Light Line
    Books, Bob
Jordan Enterprises Pub. Co., Inc.
Joy Street Books
Just Us Books, Inc.
Kendall Green Publications
Kingsway Publications
Knopf Books for Young Readers
Kruza Kaleidoscopix, Inc.
Lee & Low Books, Inc.
Lerner Publications Co.
Lester Publishing Limited
Liguori Publications
Lion Books, Publisher
Lion Publishing Corporation
Little, Brown and Company

Lodestar Books
Lothrop, Lee & Shepard Books
Lucas/Evans Books Inc.
Lucent Books
McElderry Books, Margaret K.
Macmillan Children's Books
March Media, Inc.
Meadowbrook Press
Meriwether Publishing Ltd.
Metamorphous Press
Midmarch Arts Press
Morehouse Publishing Co.
Morris Publishing, Joshua
Mosaic Press
Muir Publications, Inc, John
North Light Books
Oddo Publishing, Inc.
Open Hand Publishing Inc.
Orchard Books
Our Child Press
Pacific Press
Pando Publications
Parenting Press, Inc.
Paulist Press
Pelican Publishing Co. Inc.
Perspectives Press
Philomel Books
Pippin Press
Players Press, Inc.
Potter Inc., Clarkson N.
Preservation Press, The
Press of Macdonald & Reinecke, The
Price Stern Sloan
Prometheus Books
Random House Books for Young
    Readers
Read'n Run Books
Review and Herald Publishing Asso-
    ciation
Rosebrier Publishing Co.
Rosen Publishing Group, The
St. Anthony Messenger Press
St. Paul Books and Media
Scholastic Hardcover
Scholastic, Inc.
Scientific American Books
Scribner's Sons, Charles
Shoe Tree Press
Skylark/Books for Young Readers
Speech Bin, Inc., The
Standard Publishing
Star Books, Inc.
Stemmer House Publishers, Inc.
Sterling Publishing Co., Inc.

Sunburst Books
TAB Books
Tambourine Books
Troll Associates
Trophy Books
Troubador Books
Tundra Books of Northern New York
Tyndale House Publishers
Victor Books
Volcano Press
Voyageur Publishing Co., Inc.
W.W. Publications
Walker and Co.
Waterfront Books
Watts, Inc., Franklin
Weigl Educational Publishers
Whitman & Company, Albert
Williamson Publishing Co.
Winston-Derek Publishers, Inc.
Women's Press
Woodbine House

Young adults (12 and up)

Aegina Press/University Editions
African American Images
Aladdin Books/Collier Books for
    Young Readers
Alyson Publications, Inc.
American Bible Society
Archway/Minstrel Books
Atheneum Publishers
Author's Connection Press, The
Avon Books
Back to the Bible
Barrons Educational Series
Behrman House Inc.
Blue Heron Publishing, Inc.
Bluestocking Press
Boyds Mills Press
Bradbury Press
Candlewick Press
Chariot Books
Chicago Review Press
Chronicle Books
Clarion Books
Clyde Press
Cobblehill Books
Concordia Publishing House
Council for Indian Education
Crossway Books
Davenport, Publishers, May
Davis Publications, Inc.
Dawn Publications

Delacorte Press and Doubleday Books for Young Readers
Dial Books for Young Readers
Discovery Enterprises, Ltd.
Distinctive Publishing Corp.
Dutton Children's Books
Enslow Publishers Inc.
Facts on File
Farrar, Straus & Giroux
Fiesta City Publishers
Free Spirit Publishing
Golden Books
Gospel Light Publications
Greenhaven Press
Greenwillow Books
Grosset & Dunlap
Harcourt Brace Jovanovich
HarperCollins Children's Books
Harvest House Publishers
Haypenny Press
Hendrick-Long Publishing Company
Herald Press
Holiday House Inc.
Holt & Co., Inc., Henry
Homestead Publishing
Houghton Mifflin Co.
Hunter House Publishers
Hyperion Books for Children
Incentive Publications, Inc.
Jewish Publication Society
Jones University Press/Light Line Books, Bob
Jordan Enterprises Pub. Co., Inc.
Joy Street Books
Kendall Green Publications
Kingsway Publications
Knopf Books for Young Readers
Lerner Publications Co.
Lester Publishing Limited
Liguori Publications
Lion Books, Publisher
Lion Publishing Corporation
Little, Brown and Company
Lodestar Books
Lothrop, Lee & Shepard Books
Lucas/Evans Books Inc.
Lucent Books
McElderry Books, Margaret K.
Macmillan Children's Books
Meadowbrook Press
Meriwether Publishing Ltd.
Merrill Publishing
Metamorphous Press
Midmarch Arts Press

Morehouse Publishing Co.
Naturegraph Publisher, Inc.
North Light Books
Open Hand Publishing Inc.
Orchard Books
Our Child Press
Pacific Press
Pando Publications
Paulist Press
Pelican Publishing Co. Inc.
Perspectives Press
Philomel Books
Players Press, Inc.
Preservation Press, The
Press of Macdonald & Reinecke, The
Price Stern Sloan
Prometheus Books
Read'n Run Books
Review and Herald Publishing Association
Rosen Publishing Group, The
St. Anthony Messenger Press
St. Paul Books and Media
Scholastic Hardcover
Scholastic, Inc.
Scientific American Books
Scribner's Sons, Charles
Shaw Publishers, Harold
Shoe Tree Press
Speech Bin, Inc., The
Standard Publishing
Star Books, Inc.
Stemmer House Publishers, Inc.
Sunburst Books
TAB Books
Tambourine Books
Texas Christian University Press
Troll Associates
Trophy Books
Troubador Books
Tundra Books of Northern New York
Vanitas Press, The
Voyageur Publishing Co., Inc.
W.W. Publications
Walker and Co.
Waterfront Books
Watts, Inc., Franklin
Weigl Educational Publishers
Williamson Publishing Co.
Winston-Derek Publishers, Inc.
Women's Press
Woodbine House

Age-Level Index
Magazine Publishers

The age-level index is set up to help you more quickly locate magazine markets geared to the age group(s) for which you write or illustrate. Read each listing carefully and follow the publisher's specific information about the type(s) of manuscript(s) each prefers to read and the style(s) of artwork each wishes to review.

Picture books (preschool-8-year-olds)

Chickadee
Cochran's Corner
Cricket Magazine
Day Care and Early Education
Dolphin Log
Highlights for Children
Humpty Dumpty's Magazine
Ladybug, the Magazine for Young Children
My Friend
National Geographic World
Nature Friend Magazine
Science Weekly
Scienceland
Sing Out!
Single Parent, The
Skipping Stones
Together Time
Turtle Magazine

Young readers (5-8-year-olds)

Atalantik
Chickadee
Child Life
Childrens Playmate
Cochran's Corner
Cricket Magazine
Day Care and Early Education
DynaMath
Friend Magazine, The
Highlights for Children
Home Altar, The
Hopscotch
Humpty Dumpty's Magazine
Instructor Magazine
Jack and Jill
Kid City

Ladybug, the Magazine for Young Children
Lighthouse
My Friend
Nature Friend Magazine
Noah's Ark
Pockets
School Magazine, Blast Off!, Countdown, Orbit, Touchdown
School Mates
Science Weekly
Scienceland
Sharing the Victory
Sing Out!
Single Parent, The
Skipping Stones
Spark!
Wonder Time
YABA Framework
Young Judaean

Middle readers (9-11-year-olds)

Atalantik
Boys' Life
Bradley's Fantasy Magazine, Marion Zimmer
Businesship
Cat Fancy
Child Life
Childrens Digest
Clubhouse
Cobblestone
Cochran's Corner
Cricket Magazine
Crusader
Current Health I
Discoveries
Disney Adventures
Dolphin Log

DynaMath
Faces
Faith 'N Stuff
Free Spirit
Friend Magazine, The
Goldfinch, The
Highlights for Children
Home Altar, The
Hopscotch
Instructor Magazine
Jack and Jill
Junior Trails
Kid City
Lighthouse
My Friend
National Geographic World
Nature Friend Magazine
Noah's Ark
On the Line
Owl Magazine
R-A-D-A-R
Ranger Rick
School Magazine
School Mates
Science Weekly
Shofar
Sing Out!
Single Parent, The
Skipping Stones
Spark!
Superscience Blue
Take 5
3-2-1 Contact
Touch
Venture
YABA Framework
Young Crusader, The
Young Judaean
Zillions
Choices

Young adults (12 and up)

Aim Magazine
Atalantik
Boys' Life
Bradley's Fantasy Magazine, Marion
    Zimmer
Businesship
Career World
Careers
Challenges
Clubhouse
Cobblestone

Cochran's Corner
Current Health II
DynaMath
Exploring
Faces
FFA New Horizons
Free Spirit
Guide Magazine
Hicall
High Adventure
Hobson's Choice
International Gymnast
Keynoter
Lighthouse
Listen
My Friend
National Geographic World
Nature Friend Magazine
New Era Magazine
Nickelodeon
On the Line
Owl Magazine
Pioneer
Racing for Kids
Scholastic Math Magazine
School Mates
Science Weekly
Seventeen Magazine
Sharing the Victory
Sing Out!
Single Parent, The
Skipping Stones
Sports Illustrated for Kids
Story Friends
Straight
Take 5
'Teen Magazine
Teen Power
3-2-1 Contact
TQ
Venture
Voice
With
YABA Framework
Young Salvationist
Youth Update
Zillions

Index

Other Books of Interest
for Children's Writers and Illustrators

Annual Market Books
Artist's Market, edited by Lauri Miller $21.95
Guide to Literary Agents and Art/Photo Reps, edited by Robin Gee $15.95
Humor & Cartoon Markets, edited by Bob Staake (paper) $16.95
Novel & Short Story Writer's Market, edited by Robin Gee (paper) $19.95
Photographer's Market, edited by Sam Marshall $21.95
Poet's Market, by Judson Jerome $19.95
Songwriter's Market, edited by Brian Rushing $19.95
Writer's Market, edited by Mark Kissling $25.95

Writing for Children
The Children's Picture Book: How to Write It, How to Sell It, by Ellen E. M. Roberts (paper) $19.95
Families Writing, by Peter R. Stillman (paper) $12.95
How to Write & Illustrate Children's Books, by Treld Pelkey Bicknell & Felicity Trotman $22.50
Writing for Children & Teenagers, 3rd Edition, by Lee Wyndham/Revised by Arnold Madison (paper) $12.95
Writing Young Adult Novels, by Hadley Irwin & Jeannette Eyerly $14.95

Illustration
Illustration & Drawing: Styles & Techniques, by Terry R. Presnall $16.95
Painting Watercolor Portraits that Glow, by Jan Kunz $27.95
Putting People in Your Paintings, by J. Everett Draper (paper) $19.95

Reference Books
Beginning Writer's Answer Book, edited by Kirk Polking (paper) $13.95
Business & Legal Forms for Authors & Self Publishers, by Tad Crawford (paper) $15.95
The Complete Guide to Self-Publishing, by Tom & Marilyn Ross (paper) $16.95
Getting Started as a Freelance Illustrator or Designer, by Michael Fleischman (paper) $16.95
How to Sell Your Photographs & Illustrations, by Elliott & Barbara Gordon (paper) $16.95
How to Write a Book Proposal, by Michael Larsen (paper) $10.95
How to Write with a Collaborator, by Hal Bennett with Michael Larsen $11.95
Knowing Where to Look: The Ultimate Guide to Research, by Lois Horowitz (paper) $16.95
12 Keys to Writing Books that Sell, by Kathleen Krull (paper) $12.95
The 29 Most Common Writing Mistakes & How to Avoid Them, by Judy Delton (paper) $9.95
Word Processing Secrets for Writers, by Michael A. Banks & Ansen Dibell (paper) $14.95
The Writer's Book of Checklists, by Scott Edelstein (self-cover) $16.95
The Writer's Digest Guide to Manuscript Formats, by Dian Dincin Buchman & Seli Groves $17.95

Graphics/Business of Art
Airbrushing the Human Form, by Andy Charlesworth (cloth) $19.95
Artist's Friendly Legal Guide, by Conner, Karlen, Perwin & Spatt (paper) $18.95
Basic Graphic Design & Paste-Up, by Jack Warren (paper) $13.95
Business & Legal Forms for Fine Artists, by Tad Crawford (paper) $12.95
Business & Legal Forms for Illustrators, by Tad Crawford (paper) $15.95
Color Harmony: A Guide to Creative Color Combinations, by Hideaki Chijiiwa (paper) $15.95
Complete Airbrush & Photoretouching Manual, by Peter Owen & John Sutcliffe (cloth) $24.95
The Complete Book of Caricature, by Bob Staake (cloth) $18.95
The Complete Guide to Greeting Card Design & Illustration, by Eva Szela (cloth) $27.95
Creative Ad Design & Illustration, by Dick Ward (cloth) $32.95
The Creative Artist, by Nita Leland (cloth) $27.95
Design Rendering Techniques, by Dick Powell (cloth) $29.95
Dynamic Airbrush, by David Miller & James Effler (cloth) $29.95
Getting It Printed, by Beach, Shepro & Russon (paper) $29.50
The Graphic Artist's Guide to Marketing & Self Promotion, by Sally Prince Davis (paper) $15.95
Handbook of Pricing & Ethical Guidelines—7th Edition, by Graphic Artists Guild (paper) $22.95
How to Draw & Sell Cartoons, by Ross Thomson & Bill Hewison (cloth) $18.95

How to Draw & Sell Comic Strips, by Alan McKenzie (cloth) $19.95
How to Succeed as an Artist in Your Hometown, by Stewart Biehl (paper) $24.95
How to Understand & Use Design & Layout, by Alan Swann (paper) $21.95
The Professional Designer's Guide to Marketing Your Work, by Mary Yeung (cloth) $29.95
Type: Design, Color, Character & Use, by Michael Beaumont (paper) $19.95
Typewise, by Kit Hinrichs with Delphine Hirasuna (cloth) $39.95

Watercolor

Painting Nature's Details in Watercolor, by Cathy Johnson (paper) $21.95
Tony Couch Watercolor Techniques, by Tony Couch (paper) $14.95
Watercolor Painter's Solution Book, by Angela Gair (paper) $19.95
Watercolor Tricks & Techniques, by Cathy Johnson (cloth) $24.95
Watercolor Workbook, by Bud Biggs & Lois Marshall (paper) $21.95
Watercolor: You Can Do It!, by Tony Couch (cloth) $26.95

Mixed Media

Colored Pencil Drawing Techniques, by Iain Hutton-Jamieson (cloth) $24.95
Exploring Color, by Nita Leland (paper) $24.95
Getting Started in Drawing, by Wendon Blake (cloth) $24.95
Keys to Drawing, by Bert Dodson (paper) $21.95
The North Light Illustrated Book of Painting Techniques, by Elizabeth Tate (cloth) $27.95
Oil Painting: Develop Your Natural Ability, by Charles Sovek (cloth) $27.95
Painting Seascapes in Sharp Focus, by Lin Seslar (paper) $22.95
Pastel Painting Techniques, by Guy Roddon (paper) $19.95
The Pencil, by Paul Calle (paper) $19.95
Realistic Figure Drawing, by Joseph Sheppard (paper) $19.95
Decorative Painting for Children's Rooms, by Rosie Fisher (cloth) $29.95

A complete catalog of Writer's Digest Books and North Light Books is available
FREE by writing to the address shown below. To order books directly from the
publisher, include $3.00 postage and handling for 1 book, $1.00 for each additional
book. Allow 30 days for delivery.

Writer's Digest Books/North Light Books
1507 Dana Avenue, Cincinnati, Ohio 45207
Credit card orders call TOLL-FREE
1-800-289-0963

Write to this same address for information on *Writer's Digest* magazine, Writer's
Digest Book Club, Writer's Digest School, Writer's Digest Criticism Service, North
Light Book Club, Graphic Artist's Book Club, *The Artist's Magazine*, *HOW* Magazine
and *Story* Magazine.

Prices subject to change without notice.